2020

SHANGHAIRANKING
CONSULTANCY

ShanghaiRanking
Consultancy

www.shanghairanking.com

图书在版编目(CIP)数据

上海交通前 200 名世界研究型大学概览 = Shanghai Jiao
Tong Top 200 Research Universities
encyclopedia：英文／（英）琼斯编.—上海：上海交通大学
出版社,2013
　　ISBN 978 - 7 - 313 - 09787 - 3

　　Ⅰ.①上…　Ⅱ.①琼…　Ⅲ.①高等学校 - 研究 - 世界 -
英文　Ⅳ.①G649.1

　　中国版本图书馆 CIP 数据核字(2013)第 109048 号

上海交通前 200 名世界研究型大学概览
Shanghai Jiao Tong Top 200 Research Universities
（英）琼斯　编

上海交通大学 出版社出版发行
（上海市番禺路 951 号　邮政编码 200030）
电话：64071208　出版人：韩建民
上海景条印刷有限公司印刷　全国新华书店经销
开本：890mm×1240mm　1/16　印张：20.5　字数：1028 千字
2013 年 5 月第 1 版　2013 年 5 月第 1 次印刷
ISBN 978 - 7 - 313 - 09787 - 3/G　定价：50 美元

版权所有　侵权必究
告读者：如发现本书有印装质量问题请与印刷厂质量科联系
联系电话：021 - 51002888

Contents

Foreword
Dr Ying Cheng

An Introduction to the Academic Ranking of World Universities

Building world-class universities has been the dream for generations of Chinese. At the 100th anniversary of Peking University in May 1998, the then president of China declared that the country should have several world-class universities, resulting in the "985 Project", a program specially designed for building world-class universities in China. At that time, many top Chinese universities including Shanghai Jiao Tong University set up their strategic goals to become world-class universities, most of them set up timetables. However, there was no consensus on many fundamental questions about world-class universities, such as what is the definition of and criteria for a world-class university? How many world-class universities should there be in the world? What are the positions of top Chinese universities in the world higher education system?

In order to answer many of these questions, a team led by Prof. Nian Cai Liu at the Center for World-Class Universities (formerly the Institute of Higher Education) of Shanghai Jiao Tong University had spent two years on the benchmarking of top Chinese universities with four groups of US research universities, and another two years on the creation of a global university ranking. Upon the request of many colleagues from various countries, the Center for World-Class Universities decided to publish the ranking on its website.

The Academic Ranking of World Universities (ARWU) was first published in June 2003, and then updated on an annual basis. ARWU uses six objective indicators to rank world universities, including the number of alumni winning Nobel Prizes and Fields Medals (10%), number of staff winning Nobel Prizes and Fields Medals (20%), number of highly cited researchers selected by Thomson Reuters (20%), number of articles published in journals of Nature and Science (20%), number of articles indexed in Science Citation Index – Expanded and Social Sciences Citation Index (20%), and per capita performance of a university (10%). About 1200 universities are ranked by ARWU every year and the best 500 are published.

Although the initial purpose of ARWU was to find the global standing of top Chinese universities, it has attracted a great deal of attention from all over the world. The mainstream media throughout the world regularly reports the ARWU. Hundreds of universities cite the ranking results in their campus news, annual reports and promotional brochures. A survey on higher education published by The Economist commented ARWU as "the most widely used annual ranking of the world's research universities". Burton Bollag, a reporter at Chronicle of Higher Education wrote that ARWU "is considered the most influential international ranking".

One of the factors for the significant influence of ARWU is that its methodology is globally sound and transparent. ARWU tries to rank research universities in the world by their academic or research performance based on internationally comparable third-party data that everyone could check. No subjective measures are taken. Nevertheless, there are still many methodological and technical problems. ARWU emphasizes the research function of universities. The fundamental role of universities - teaching, and their contributions to society are not well taken into account. In addition, ARWU is biased in favor of universities in English-speaking countries and universities strong in hard sciences. Technical problems include definition of higher education institutions, affiliated units of institutions, and attribution of publications to institutions. My colleagues and I have been working hard to study these problems and improve the ARWU.

Ever since the publication of ARWU, we have received numerous requests, asking for us to provide rankings of world universities by fields or by schools/departments. In response to these requests, since February 2007, the Center for World-Class Universities began to publish the Academic Ranking of World Universities by Broad Subject Fields (ARWU-FIELD). ARWU-FIELD provides the world's top universities in five broad subject fields, including Natural Sciences and Mathematics, Engineering/Technology and Computer Sciences, Life and Agriculture Sciences, Clinical Medicine and Pharmacy, and Social Sciences. In November 2009, the Academic Ranking of World Universities by Subject Fields (ARWU-SUBJECT) was published; the five ranked subjects are Mathematics, Physics, Chemistry, Computer Science and Economics/Business. Both ARWU-FIELD and ARWU-SUBJECT employ a similar methodology to that which is used in the ARWU.

Any ranking is controversial and no ranking is absolutely objective, therefore users should carefully examine the ranking methodologies before looking at the ranking results. For any kind of decision-making, rankings should be used only as a starting point and more comprehensive analysis are always necessary.

—

Dr Ying Cheng

Executive Director, Center for World-Class Universities, Shanghai Jiao Tong University, Shanghai, China

Chapter 1
Introduction

University of Waterloo

Whilst rankings in themselves act as a useful initial guide as to the relative strengths between universities in particular areas, it is quite an impossible task to portray the different character, philosophy, values and many of the strengths one can expect between universities in such a format. We are fortunate not to live in a uniform world, many structural, linguistic and cultural differences play a key role in determining the ways in which universities are represented in ranking systems.

Although rankings are an excellent initial guide, at the Shanghai Ranking Consultancy we passionately believe that every single one of the top 200 universities are excellent institutions, helping great young minds achieve their dreams and fulfil their potential through the knowledge, friendships, experience and skills one can expect to develop at university.

Perhaps equally as importantly, certainly lesser well known, is the role that leading universities play in the discovery and dissemination of new knowledge, pushing the frontiers of our understanding to meet countless challenges as in the fight against cancer, Alzheimer's disease and HIV/AIDS. The scope of university research is so enormous in its scale that quantifying it all in a single volume is an impossible task. Research universities today are working tirelessly to better understand critical

phenomena such as global climate change, the demographic shift towards an ageing society and the myriad impacts that globalization are having on the ways we can expect to lead our lives.

Undoubtedly there are universities developing ideas and technologies today, which will help meet challenges we don't even know exist yet. Some even have this at the heart of their philosophy such as President Daniel Zajfman of Israel's Weizmann Institute: "I think the role of universities is to solve problems that people don't even know exist. If we just solve the problems of today, we are basically doing the job of everyone else. But the focus and the profile of universities as has always been in the past, and I hope it will stay like this is to be able to provide knowledge for the sake of knowledge. That has always been the goal. When we look at the values of knowledge for the sake of knowledge, we realize 100 years later what we can do with this."

At the same time, our leading research universities grapple with some of the most inspirational concepts and ideas known to humankind such as trying to understand the origins of the universe, the origins of life on earth, the nature of consciousness and the depths of the ocean; as well as perhaps the most compelling of all – in the quest for extraterrestrial life. The recent Higgs Boson Particle discovery is a truly inspirational piece of science that helps

us answer questions such as who we are, and what connects the universe together. Equally one cannot forget the landing on Mars, and what the discoveries made there could herald for human perspective. Both are remarkable achievements with research universities at the helm, exemplifying the spirit of curiosity, inspiration, collaboration and discovery that such institutions bring to our world today.

When confronted with the philosophical and technological leaps mankind has made in recent centuries, one could easily be mistaken in thinking that we already have all the answers in today's era of instant communications and mass connectivity. It is quite surprising that universities are really the only institutions investigating the most fundamental questions. With their roots in the renaissance period, universities stand out today as the leaders in our ongoing quest to transform what was unknown yesterday, into what is known today.

Perhaps none of this would be possible, however, without the most basic essence of what a university is – a place where we can freely question what is around us, and what is presented to us. Whilst breakthrough discoveries in the hard sciences more often than not capture headlines, there is a fundamental concept that underpins all activity at a university; our own curiosity.

The *Shanghai Jiao Tong Top 200 Research Universities Encyclopedia* shares in this curiosity. A book of this kind has never been produced before, with direct interviews conducted the world over to bring the most important features of the world's leading universities to an international audience of those most connected to these wonderful institutions. Principally this book is for anyone that is curious, however three distinct groups arise – young aspirational people interested in attending a leading university, interested stakeholders in the global research and development community and universities themselves.

The ambition of the *Shanghai Jiao Tong Top 200 Research Universities Encyclopedia* is great, perhaps too much for a single book; but certainly acts as a very clear first step towards bringing together the core strengths, cultures, learning environments and philosophies of the world's leading research universities together in one single volume.

For young people around the world, university is an enormous opportunity. Not just as the next step in a career, but as a platform to fulfil one's curiosities about the world of ideas and natural phenomena around us. At the dawn of the 21st century, university offers you the opportunity to take the first steps as tomorrow's global citizens. Regardless of where you call home, there are incredible universities the world over eager to attract the brightest, most imaginative and hardest working. From Japan to Brazil, via Europe and the United States there are unique institutions that could be best suited to your interests and aspirations. We present the leaders to you in this book.

With the opportunities of globalization however, there are also very clear challenges. Whether that be in finding the right career or developing a way of living sustainably into the future; university offers an excellent platform to make a positive contribution both to ones own chances, as well as making a broader contribution to the incremental growth in humankind's understanding. One can now expect to get directly involved in research, develop entrepreneurial skills and have the opportunity to make contributions to both society and the economy through the options available at university. The well-trodden career path is far from the only option in today's world. Texas A&M University President R. Bowen Loftin believes young people should increasingly think about developing into "Job creators as opposed to job takers" upon their graduation from university.

On the one hand, the *Shanghai Jiao Tong Top 200 Research Universities Encyclopedia* aims to inspire young people the world over to see university not just as a traditional step towards a career. Although generations before were able to rely upon career opportunities that arose from university, today's students are increasingly focused upon making new discoveries, contributing towards society and developing into

University of Zurich

entrepreneurs. Through university, young people are increasingly able to pursue their curiosities with freedom and flexibility; contributing to the continued development of human knowledge at the global level and beyond.

Without a doubt, young people constitute the world's richest resource of imagination and curiosity. Nevertheless, they are far from the only group with interests in the world's leading research universities. The student population may be the heart and soul of any university campus, but vital sources of funding are increasingly shifting to external partners in a mutually beneficial, symbiotic relationship with knowledge and funding at its heart.

For key stakeholders in the global research and development community, whether that be in the public, private sector or donor community, universities are undoubtedly at the centre of this international network. Changing funding dynamics, a growing appetite for relevance and industry experience amongst the student community, combined with a very clear strategic focus upon translating discoveries into society have made universities increasingly open to collaborative research operations. Naturally, university approaches and successes in collaborative arrangements vary enormously across borders and between cultures. Many universities based in the same city, province or state also

have very different approaches. The *Shanghai Jiao Tong Top 200 Research Universities Encyclopedia* presents the world's leading research universities' core strengths and their different approaches to working on collaborative projects, as well as to translating new discoveries into the real economy. There remain clear differences in the ways that issues such as intellectual property rights are managed and shared that are also touched on throughout. What is clear is that whilst remaining our most profound research institutions, driven undoubtedly by human curiosity; leading research universities are becoming more open to partnerships, and are key pillars in the continued shift towards a knowledge-based economy with the development of exciting new technologies and discoveries on a weekly basis.

University of Hamburg

Universities have to continue to adapt to the changing dynamics of government policy, globalization of research, study and funding sources amongst myriad other changes in the external environment. From the approach to research and translational strategies, through to the development of multi-disciplinary learning opportunities, the strategic approach varies enormously between leading institutions around the world. By conducting direct interviews with the world's leading universities, we present the varying approaches to help continue to inform the context of your own direction.

Finally, the *Shanghai Jiao Tong Top 200 Research Universities Encyclopedia* aims to inspire. The process involved in its production has been epic, with direct interviews conducted the world over to bring the cutting edge research programs and teaching philosophies of the world's leading universities into the grasp of those most interested in their developments and distinguishing points. Our aim is to help the global community, both young and old to better understand who is actually working towards a cure for cancer and a solution to global climate change; and at the same time to demonstrate who is undertaking inspirational work in helping us better understand the origins of the universe, the nature of human consciousness and a means for us to guarantee a safe and sustainable food, energy and water supply for future generations. Without a doubt, many of the pioneering institutions in these fields are discussed in this volume.

University of Waterloo

University of Nottingham, Ningbo Campus

University of Colorado Boulder

UNIVERSITY
Search

| UCL - Université catholique de Louvain | Search |

Advanced Search

Research performance: silver medal for Belgium

Announces

UCL researchers rank high thanks to the Belgian «Interuniversity Attraction Poles» (IAP) Programme. A study describes why Belgian researchers rank among the world's highest thanks to the IAP programme.

http://www.uclouvain.be\michel.gevers\BelgianResPerf.Pdf

http: www.belspo.be\IAP

Examples of UCL's research structures that improve people's life

WELCOME: Wallonia Electronics and COmmunications MEasurements

UCL's WELCOME facility is a new characterisation platform that supports innovation in electronics and telecommunications fields.

http://www.uclouvain.be\welcome

WINFAB, UCL unveils its new micro-nanofabrication lab

WINFAB is UCL's micro-nanofabrication platform which provides researchers and students with a cleanroom environment and high-tech equipment.

http://www.uclouvain.be\en-winfab

Hoover Chair celebrates 20 years

In the last 20 years, UCL's Hoover Chair has become a major player in ethical issues related to the economic and social sphere.

http://www.uclouvain.be\en-chaire-hoover

Images for «UCL» - Report images

Announces

EURAXESS encourage researcher mobility

This UCL-European Commission initiative gives researchers the opportunity to advance their career by facilitating mobility.

http://www.uclouvain.be\en-euraxess

UCL contributes to 6 million euro fund to host foreign post-docs

UCL on behalf of Académi universitaire Louvain has joined forces with the European Commission in the first large-scale fundin of foreign post-docs.

http://ec.europa.eu/euraxess/index.cfm/jobs/fgDetails/33321

Louvain International Desk (LID)

The LID helps foreign researchers and their families at each step of their international mobility. This personalised service aims to provide up-to-date information as well as individualised assistance in all areas, whether administrative or legal, or concerning everyday life in the new host community.

http://www.uclouvain.be\en-lid

Welcome & WinFab
10 min. walking

Chaire Hoover
10 min. walking

TECLIM
10 min. walking

de Duve Insitute
30 min. by bus

Paris
2 hours by train

London
3 hours by train

UCL
Université catholique de Louvain

There's one solution for all your research and personal needs: UCL

Researchers head toward the heart of Europe to benefit from a privileged environment. Renowned for its continuous pursuit of quality, innovation and scientific research, UCL has earned a reputation as a world-class institution that pampers researchers and caters to all their needs. Share knowledge and understanding in an inviting and inclusive environment with the best minds of Belgium and beyond.

www.uclouvain.be

In 1964,

we put our stake in the ground.

Today,

we're making our mark

in the world.

First in the U.S. among universities under 50. Fourth in the world.

The first shovel broke ground for the University of California, Irvine just 49 years ago. Today, UC Irvine is ranked first in the U.S. and fourth in the world among universities under 50 years old by *Times Higher Education.* Their analysis examined our learning environment, research discoveries and industry innovations. Now, UC Irvine is a progressive powerhouse challenging the ivy-covered legacies. Our world-class ranking is a direct result of faculty and student contributions that impact the world. **Turning research into reality.**

UNIVERSITY OF CALIFORNIA
SANTA CRUZ
Creative Rigor

Chapter 2
Research Universities
International Importance

From Ancient Greece through the Renaissance and into the 21st Century, humankind has forever been linked by the intangible driving force that is our own curiosity. Once described as the "lust of the mind", and considered by Einstein as our most important virtue; the awe inspiring research conducted at leading research universities is perhaps the greatest manifestation of curiosity's power in our world today.

Democritus (460BC), often considered to be the father of science was Ancient Greece's pioneering investigator into the sub-atomic nature of matter, hypothesizing about an atomic structure of the universe. Equally, the nature of the stars and planets around us have been, and still are of enormous influence on our perceptions and way of life stretching back to Ancient Egyptian civilization. Today's discoveries of the Higgs Boson Particle and our continuing quest to see further out into the universe, as well as to understand its nature and composition link together curiosity's reign over the human imagination, throughout our consciousness and its ongoing evolution.

Whilst universities are best known for their leadership in formal education, they are sometimes considered to dampen one's curiosity in favour of ambition. It could perhaps be considered ironic that our leading universities today are undoubtedly curiosity's cornerstones, expressed in the myriad research programs and growing web of collaborative inter-linkages they are active in today. The solutions for countless international challenges from a cure for cancer and HIV/AIDS through to a sustainable energy, food and water future for us all will most likely be found at leading research universities.

As today's world is increasingly characterized by global challenges, it is tempting for universities to simply direct all of their efforts into areas such as these. The problem with this approach is that many of the solutions to complex challenges were found unintentionally. The driver was curiosity. The key to solving a problem or challenge is understanding it first, the foundation of understanding is curiosity; research universities are humankind's only remaining institutions whose fundamental driving force is curiosity.

President Daniel Zajfman of the Weizmann Institute offers an Israeli perspective. "We are all running after making new discoveries and it seems that sometimes, we spend a lot of money in trying to solve the problem. But if you look at the history of science, you will find that most of the discoveries were never made by trying to solve a problem, rather by trying to understand how nature works, so our focus is on understanding."

Pro-Vice Chancellor for Research of the University of Sheffield Professor Richard Jones shares a similar focus. "Answering many of today's complex questions involves us knowing a great deal more about the most fundamental basic systems in the natural world; and then using this knowledge to re-design the technologies we are interested in."

Weizmann Institute

Monash University

Curiosity Killed the Cat?

Nevertheless, the debate throughout our leading universities continues about how research interests are defined, and how to balance curiosity with practical problem solving, and today's more pragmatic reality of having to attract vital research funds and partners. This conundrum is well summarized by Monash University's Vice Chancellor Ed Byrne.

"The starting point for any leading university has to be academic freedom, and the ability to go wherever your research and teaching interests take you. Academics therefore choose their own research interests at the end of the day. However, for those research programs to be successful they have to be sustained in terms of funding and grants that support such interests, as well as quality of outputs in terms of papers and discoveries produced."

The world's best-funded and most confident research universities such as the University of Cambridge tend to allow academic curiosity to reign supreme, Vice-Chancellor Sir Leszek Borysiewicz believes that: "The University of Cambridge's approach to research is reflected by the fact that it is not possible to pick out specific core strengths or foci; our approach as an institution is very much bottom up. Our ambition is to provide an environment whereby those that come to study and research here are able to freely follow their interests; Cambridge does not stipulate the direction of the research that is undertaken here. The University of Cambridge is fortunate to be broad enough to sustain excellence across a very diverse range of disciplines."

Others however, prefer to approach major global challenges as a critical part of their strategy. According to Professor Deborah Terry, the University of Queensland's strategy "places a strong priority on what I would call problem oriented research. That is research that is geared towards addressing and solving those key challenges that are by definition global."

According to President Feridun Hamdullahpur, the University of Waterloo uses a similar approach by "developing its core strengths very strategically by looking at what the main challenges and unanswered questions are in the world today; and then leveraging core strengths to approach some of these issues in a multi-disciplinary way through the University of Waterloo's research centres."

Increasingly the perspective is that the dichotomy between how research interests are defined simply doesn't exist; that in essence all research is driven by fundamental curiosities. But simply, the way that discoveries are managed into the market place or society has an impact on perceptions within the context of the debate. President David Naylor of the University of Toronto explains. "Our view is that it's very important that a large amount of curiosity driven research is underway, but in a climate that encourages and supports those investigators who want to move it from the fundamental towards the applied.

The reason we see this as a false dichotomy is not because we are simply prepared to see large amounts of activity turned into contract research. On the contrary, although we partner effectively with industry, our reputation rests uniquely on the work initiated by our faculty. But what we have found time after time is that if colleagues have running room and support, they will move what appeared first to be quite fundamental discoveries towards some application."

At the same time, leading institutions such as Israel's Technion balance the direction of research, according to President Peretz Lavie "developmental concepts are developed in two ways. Some are top down and some are bottom up. Top down is when the administration meets, and together with scientific leaders on campus, reaches a decision that let's say, nanotechnology would be in the future a major driving force in scientific research. So, the administration decides this is where we are going to invest development money, and then we start raising the money. On the other end, there are developments that come from the rank and file, from the bottom up."

Some institutions such as Rockefeller University, Caltech or the Weizmann Institute focus very little attention on directing anything, not even the academic discipline. The focus is simply on attracting the best people in the world, giving them the space to think and follow whatever curiosities they may have. Rockefeller University's status as the most decorated institution in the history of the Nobel Prize for Medicine and Chemistry with 24 winners in total perhaps vindicates curiosity as humankind's ultimate vehicle for discovery.

Andrew Hamilton, Vice Chancellor of the University of Oxford is a strong advocate of this approach. "Academic freedom and independence is fundamental to the University of Oxford's philosophy and is at the core of how the university operates and is governed. This means there are always protections that need to be in place to ensure that fundamental research is not distorted by partnerships whose goals may diverge away from those of our academics. We ensure that the research at the University of Oxford is curiosity-driven."

Monash University

Monash University

Our Discipline or Everyone's?

As questions become more complex, and major challenges continue to blur the boundaries between traditional academic disciplines, the time of the single lone researcher making paradigm shift discoveries at the foundation of a single academic discipline is increasingly a tradition of the past. We have reached a point on our pathway of discovery whereby academic disciplines are less and less distinct from each other, and interactions between different areas of expertise are essential for innovation and discovery to take place. At the same time, external pressures place specific demands on research institutions around complex questions and challenges, using funding to incentivize how priorities are defined. Dymph van den Boom, Rector of the University of Amsterdam summarizes the evolution of academic disciplines:

"The interdisciplinary approach has to do with the expansion in the kinds of research questions people ask, as well as from the disciplinary perspective. But also if you look at what grant organizations do, they provide money for what they call grand challenges or societal challenges, and if you want answers to those kinds of research questions, you often have to cross the boundaries of your own discipline to even be able to come up with the first steps towards an answer to those bigger questions. So, I think the focus on the different kinds of research questions, which are no longer confined to single disciplines forces researchers to cross the border of their own discipline, and cooperate with colleagues from other disciplines to be able to answer those questions. That forces people not only to co-operate with researchers from other disciplines, but also to come up with what I would call transdisciplinary concepts, and new theories that are no longer based upon one discipline."

President Michael McRobbie of Indiana University believes that a similar trend in funding has influenced strategy in the USA. "As the National Science Foundation has put a greater premium on multidisciplinary, multi-institution, multi-investigator collaborations. This means that these boundaries don't just stop in the United States as far as we're concerned, they continue around the whole world. That's one of the driving forces behind what has been seen in terms of the increased internationalization of education in the broader sense."

Sir Howard Newby, Vice Chancellor of the University of Liverpool believes this trend is being mirrored in the United Kingdom: "The University of Liverpool has recently re-organized its research strategy in order to reflect many of the major challenges we face such as sustainability and global health, with a view to making us more competitive to many of the major

research grants that are concerned with these issues. Increasingly, public research budgets in particular are being allocated to major questions where an inter-disciplinary approach that leverages critical mass between researchers is the most appropriate methodology to answer such questions. In many ways a favoured supplier or demand led approach to research is emerging as a result. This is a significant change from the past whereby individual academics would submit ideas for funding. The University of Liverpool has responded to these changes by auditing our core strengths, and encouraging a multi-disciplinary approach across such disciplines so as to ensure we are as competitive as possible."

Although statistics are relatively limited from a funding perspective, Chancellor Holden Thorp at the University of North Carolina at Chapel Hill has collated data that suggests US$240 million of the university's 2012 US$767 million research budget came directly to multi-faculty and multidisciplinary research programs.

When looking at phenomena such as the evolution of academic disciplines, it comes as little surprise that there is variation between regions and cultures. At the broadest level, the greatest disciplinary focus is found in continental Europe; whereas the inter-disciplinary approach is most espoused in North America. The differences between institutions are increasingly narrowing, however, towards one whereby the interfaces of disciplines are increasingly viewed upon as the most fertile ground for discovery and innovation; whilst disciplinary excellence remains the foundation of such interactions working.

President David Naylor of the University of Toronto is very clear on the benefits of inter-disciplinary research. "Any powerful research university with strengths across multiple disciplines has a huge comparative advantage provided it facilitates the convergence of those disciplines, and the people who are advancing them. Those huge challenges that confront humankind on this hot and crowded planet are only going to be addressed by that type of synergy between people with strikingly different disciplinary backgrounds, and often-different cultural and analytical perspectives. It's one of the tremendous advantages of diversity, breadth and depth."

Perhaps most advanced globally in terms of merging the boundaries between academic disciplines is Arizona State University. President Michael Crow has led Arizona in a strategy of differentiation, whereby the university's academic profile is focused upon intellectual fusion around major international challenges. President Crow's philosophy is for.

"ASU's research strengths and initiatives assume intellectual fusion and represent opportunities that we believe will advance discovery and innovation. We need fundamental disciplines like physics or chemistry or engineering. But that alone is insufficient so we put our emphasis on differentiation. Our approach is to identify an intellectual trajectory that addresses a range of problems, which may sound like a subtle deviation from standard practice, but it is actually quite meaningful.

The transdisciplinary research we conduct in the Biodesign Institute, for example, advances biologically inspired design to address global challenges in healthcare, sustainability, and national security. The Global Institute of Sustainability (GIOS) brings together scientists and engineers with government policymakers and industry leaders to develop solutions to critical challenges.

Sustainability represents an integrated systems level approach to such issues as rapid urbanization, water quality, habitat transformation, the loss of biodiversity, and the development of new forms of renewable energy. GIOS integrates something like 40 disciplinary areas around that theme, and the objective is to advance science as well as to position us for breakthrough impacts."

On the other hand, many European universities such as Heidelberg, although enthusiastic about the benefits of inter-disciplinary research, "want to maintain focus on supporting disciplinary strengths." Rector Bernhard Eitel cautions: "We do not want the scientist who knows everything but not anything."

Director Marc Mezard of Ecole Normale Superieure shares this perspective. "ENS has to balance the interdisciplinary approach with strong traditional disciplines, which are very important also. So, what we are doing here in Ecole Normale is that on one side we are maintaining and helping to develop our strong traditional disciplines as I told you in physics, archaeology and so on. At the same time we are developing some specific projects, which are more oriented and thought of in terms of global challenges."

Chancellor Robert Birgeneau of UC Berkeley leans slightly in the other direction in that. "Generally, UC Berkeley tries to stay at the forefront of 21st century challenges as well as, of course, protecting traditional disciplines."

As the scale, expense and complexity of today's research questions continues to grow, interdisciplinary research collaboration is increasingly being considered a necessity as traditional academic disciplines become synergized by the questions and challenges that link them.

North Carolina State University

University of Sheffield

University of Rochester

President Eric Kaler of the University of Minnesota, Twin Cities has a strategy that places "a growing emphasis on collaborative research. It is just too difficult, today's problems are too large, too complex, and sometimes cost prohibitive for any single institution. So, our strength is to act in unison as opposed to independently."

Although President Kaler's perspective links in to the growing importance of research partnerships, his perspectives are widely shared throughout the academic community, Chancellor Mark Wrighton of Washington University in St Louis believes that. "Increasingly the challenges in science, engineering and medicine are ones that need to be addressed not just by disciplinary strength, but by bringing many disciplines together."

President of Georgia Tech George Peterson agrees that. "Many of the new emerging technologies, and most of the new exciting discoveries, will occur at the boundaries of traditional disciplines." As a result the university is "identifying ways that new emerging interdisciplinary fields that span technology, science, politics, business, law, and the arts, can be organized to provide an opportunity for faculty with different backgrounds to come together to work on similar issues and problems."

This touches on a key point, in the varying strategic approaches that leading research universities are developing in order to harness the new opportunities presented at the interfaces of traditional academic disciplines. Although the vast majority of leading research universities are advocates of the interdisciplinary approach to research, one can perhaps deduce the level of institutional development from their strategies in this growing trend towards amalgamating expertise. From a general perspective, institutions that have developed specific infrastructure such as interdisciplinary research centres are the furthest advanced in this approach, whilst those with broader collaborative projects and grass roots interactions are less demonstrably engaged with interdisciplinary collaboration. Other factors come into play such as the institutional culture and proximity of departments within the overall campus layout.

President of the University of Strasbourg, Alain Beretz, for example, points out that "although the multi-disciplinary approach is of growing importance, it is not something that can be enforced at the presidential level within a university. The key point is the attitudes of academics, and the most important thing is to provide the best possible working conditions for world-class research to take place, and multi-disciplinary orientated interactions to thrive."

Peter Lennie, Provost of the University of Rochester believes that culture and the campus setup play a huge role in how successful the university has been in working collaboratively. "Our compact campus makes it easy for people to learn what others are doing, and one of my jobs is to make sure that information flows freely so that people are well informed. But we don't bang people's heads together and tell them that they have to start multidisciplinary collaborations. We offer modest help to people who want to start them, but what's key is a culture in which people are engaged and curious about what other people do, and are encouraged to seek partners when they've got a problem they can't solve on their own. That's what brings about the most fruitful multidisciplinary work."

President Barbara Snyder of Case Western Reserve University also believes that a compact campus plays an important role. "Interdisciplinary research is one of our hallmarks, one of the things I think we do particularly well, and partly I think that's a function of our relatively small size and the compactness of our campus. The ability of people to sit down together and talk about their ideas, not that it can't happen electronically; but somehow things seem to spark when people are actually able to get together on the campus."

Equally and perhaps most importantly of all, Chancellor Harvey Perlman of the University of Nebraska, Lincoln believes that leadership plays a key role. "It is relatively simple to engage a faculty from a wide variety of disciplines as long as you find the right leadership. One example is we have just created a new centre for brain biology and behaviour which resulted from hiring a pair of researchers who came in to do MRI studies of brain development, so as to understand learning and other things. We now have some 70 faculty members spread across the social sciences spectrum that are collaborating together, we are building a major research facility and installing an MRI machine."

Brown University

Many universities such as the University of California, Irvine have a rich tradition of developing interdisciplinary institutes; UC Irvine's 50 such institutes have been developed over the past 35 years. Given the significance of interdisciplinary research, increasingly institutes are reporting new findings directly to university executive leadership, such as with 17 of the University of Georgia's 80 interdisciplinary institutes.

The additional benefit for student experiences through interdisciplinary institutes is not lost on Chancellor Kumble Subbaswamy of the University of Massachusetts, Amherst. "Graduate students get trained in separate fields but are enriched by working with people from other disciplines. This model has worked so well here that we have emphasized this in our other research centers involving neural science, molecular and cellular biology, informatics, nanotechnology, and so on." The Martin School at the University of Oxford represents quite a unique approach, according to Vice Chancellor Andrew Hamilton.

"The Oxford Martin School very much underlines the interdisciplinary approach in focusing on problem-driven scholarships. It sets out to research issues that tackle the most pressing challenges of the 21st century; the School puts the structures and mechanisms in place whereby multiple disciplines come together to work on possible solutions. An example is the world's ageing populations; disciplines from genetics through to human psychology to the social sciences come together to explore how society can grapple with the issues that will need to be addressed. Other major areas of research at the School include the impact of technology, climate change, international migration and tropical disease. The School supports over 30 individual research teams from across the University of Oxford to consider some of the biggest questions that concern our future."

University of California, Irvine

Giancarlo Ruocco, Vice Rector for Research at the University of Rome acknowledges that interdisciplinary collaboration is less well developed at some European universities, although this strategic direction is increasingly taking hold. "The University of Rome has 63 different departments; almost all of them are mono-disciplinary, but we are pushing the interaction between different departments. There are different inter-departmental centres and centres devoted to interdisciplinary research. We, also, are trying to push different activity, different initiatives and to put together different disciplines to work mutually."

At the same time, Bert van der Zwaan, Rector of Utrecht University, whilst advocating the interdisciplinary approach, employs the strategy in a different way. "In contrast to the United Kingdom or United States, Utrecht never organizes within the context of new schools, even not in new institutes. We try to leave people in their place, and try to have virtual collaborations. The idea of establishing new institutes or schools is not encouraged here because it takes a lot of effort, a lot of energy and gives to some extent inflexibility."

As one would expect the approach in Europe is not uniform. Germany's second most prolific producer of patents is the University of Freiburg, which has been a strong advocate of the development of inter-disciplinary centres and institutes for the past 25 years. The university now houses 17 such institutes, the first of which, focusing on material sciences was established in 1989.

Equally, Belgium's UC Louvain has long advocated interdisciplinary institutes, with one of the most recent additions to its portfolio being in nutrition and health; drawing together expertise from medicine, agriculture, psychology, nutrition and health amongst other disciplines. The advantage of this approach is not lost on Pro Rector for Research Vincent Yzerbyt. "With this approach we can provide a wide range of solutions to a given problem. Obviously a problem is not going to be solved only by looking at it from one perspective; you need a range of expertise."

University of Rome

University of California, Irvine

Denmark's Aarhus University, although at a relatively nascent stage of developing interdisciplinary centres, is following the Anglo Saxon model with the establishment of seven institutes, two of which focus upon nanoscience and the brain. MINDLab draws together research groups from philosophy, the business school, psychology, anthropology, health sciences and natural sciences to further our understanding of how the human brain works. The long-term plan is to have over 200 researchers in the institute that stands in the global top 10 in this particular field of expertise.

The level of consensus and strategic impetus varies significantly between leading research universities on the trend towards interdisciplinary research. But it is clear that both internal trends in the complexity of research questions, combined with external demands in terms of funding and the international focus on major global challenges continue to lead university research operations in this direction. From Australasia and Asia to the Americas via Europe cultural, structural and institutional idiosyncrasies ensure diversity in how the evolution of disciplines plays out.

University College London has adopted the interdisciplinary approach at an institutional level, focusing on four global challenges that straddle the university's core strengths, explains Provost Malcolm Grant.

"The main thrust of UCL's multi-disciplinary research comes in the recently established UCL Global Challenges, of which there are four.

The first of these is Global Health, a core strength at UCL; which we are now building upon by introducing a range of other disciplines such as engineering, anthropology and economics that introduce new perspectives into the questions raised by this major international challenge.

The second major challenge is concerned with Sustainable Cities, leveraging our strengths at the Bartlett School. Given the growing proportion of the world's inhabitants living in cities, we view the ways in which cities operate as vitally important to a sustainable future. As a sub-set of this initiative we are launching a project called London 2061, a 50-year forward look at what the major drivers of change in the city will be.

The third key challenge that we are investigating is Well-Being and Healthy Ageing, working to better understand the economic, architectural, social amongst other themes' impact of the changing demography we are witnessing throughout western society in particular.

The final area we are looking at is inter-cultural interactions to better understand the great tribes of the world from a range of perspectives within the social sciences and humanities. The Global Challenges program is immensely exciting for us, we have invested a great deal in this so as to best equip the university to produce authoritative work on issues such as the impact of climate change on global health."

University of Sheffield

Research Partnerships

Interdisciplinary research has collaboration at its foundation. The natural extension of this cooperative spirit is in the progression of partnerships leading research universities are engaged in, both with each other, as well as countless other institutions in the public, private and philanthropic sectors. Although philosophies as to the purpose, cost, benefit and outcome of such relationships vary significantly between institutions, regions and cultures; the general trajectory is shifting towards more engagement with the private sector, and a greater focus upon translating research discoveries into the real economy for broader societal benefit.

Rector Antonio Loprieno of the University of Basel offers a European perspective: "There is an intense dialog between two cultures with respect to the connection between academia and business. One is the culture you encounter in the Swiss Federal Institute of Technology (ETH) and would find in some quarters of our own pharmaceutical department. That is, a culture of deep integration and partnership between the public and private sectors. However, there is still a very strong part in many continental universities that is opposed to such integration. Those of a certain tradition, including the University of Basel, still maintains a resistance of commercial interests for fear that this will introduce an element of control over purely academic research. This latter view considers the university as a structure of society that should receive money only from the state and, while it is no longer in the majority, it does contribute to our culture."

On the other hand, the cultural approach in much of the United States differs, President of Carnegie Mellon University Jared Cohon explains.

"We see inter-institutional collaboration and inter-sectorial collaboration, as in with companies to be just a natural next step up from interdisciplinary collaboration. If you are truly committed to solving the problem, as we are, and in particular problems that matter in the real world, then, you're happy to take collaborators from wherever you may find them, if they can contribute to the solution of the problem. That's the premise and motivation for all of this, which makes us, I have to say, technically a good partner whether you're another university, a company or in government. We believe strongly in partnerships because again, we can leverage that to have a greater impact."

Many others such as President Wolfgang Herrmann of the Technical University of Munich, view research partnerships not just as necessities in an environment of complexity, but also as an important part of their mission. "Partnerships are really essential; science has become so complex that as an isolated institution you never can make significant advances in these complex scientific challenges. For that reason we exploit our network in the international science community on the one hand, but also in industry, because our understanding of the university's mission includes supporting the economy of our country."

From an infrastructure and equipment perspective, according to Chancellor Tom Apple, partnerships have enabled the University of Hawaii, Manoa to develop some of the world's best infrastructure. "When we are talking about the 30-metre telescope, we have a whole bunch of partners on that, but it's located here. So, we are sort of the home team, but we do have partners on a lot of these projects, particularly astronomy as these are fantastically expensive tools, and pieces of equipment. We get enormous amounts of funding from the federal agencies, the National Science Foundation in particular.

Monash University

We are probably the top site in the world for astronomy in terms of our instrumentation here."

Vice Chancellor Andrew Hamilton of Oxford views partnerships as an opportunity to extend the impact of the university's research findings. "The University of Oxford has a long tradition of embracing the world around us. We welcome the opportunity to partner with a diverse range of both private and public sector institutions to ensure our research excellence has the greatest impact possible throughout the international community. With regards to the work we do on tropical medicine, the research centre we have in Thailand is in partnership with Mahidol University. This is of particular importance from the perspective of capacity-building in developing countries."

Partnerships are also of great importance for Chancellor Gene Block of UCLA, with the university engaged across a diverse spectrum of institutions.

"External research partnerships are important and can take many different forms. Some of the large research issues today represent global challenges and require multi-national

research efforts to find solutions. Like several other major institutions in the U.S., UCLA forms strong partnerships with other universities throughout the world.

UCLA is also working with private companies and community, state and federal agencies to help solve issues where we share a common interest. I think one example would be in Los Angeles with our effort on developing 'green industries'. Clean Tech LA is a public private partnership to help develop companies in Los Angeles focused on products that help reduce our carbon footprint."

From a strategic approach however, some are moving towards quality over quantity. Traditionally universities have been very open to a high volume of memorandums of understanding or partnership proposals. Today, however the approach is becoming far more selective, based upon specific criteria and obvious synergies and/ or benefits. Chancellor Nicholas Zeppos of Vanderbilt University is a strong advocate of this strategic approach.

"I think that when we started looking at partnerships, what we really started to think about, and I think it was different from what other universities

were doing. We were not interested in necessarily saying we've signed 500 partnership agreements with universities and colleges around the world. We really took a different approach, which is; are there university partners, are there public entities or are there private sector companies where because of our excellence, and our investments would be really good partners? We tried to leverage our areas of distinction, and look for partners in those areas, and build what I would call faculty-to-faculty relationships driven by common fundamental research in educational and training questions. I tend to emphasize that I want partnerships to be deep and meaningful, and to leverage off of our respective strengths."

Under the leadership of Vice Chancellor Leszek Borysiewicz, the University of Cambridge's approach is even more selective.

"The importance of partners is also of great importance to the University of Cambridge, what we very much emphasize though is that any partnerships have to be based upon shared goals and genuine synergies. I believe that such goals and synergies develop from the bottom up and have to be fostered at this level. As a result, the University of Cambridge works at the project level to encourage the greatest frequency of interactions between our academics and external partners. If we can find interesting synergies at a project level that is the point where we begin to look at further stages of sustainable collaboration, which could ultimately become institutional level long-term partnership agreements. It doesn't matter if such partners are private sector companies or other research universities, what matters the most is that there are synergies present, and that our partners are the best in their respective fields. The University of Cambridge will only work with partners who are considered to be the best in their respective field. We will always look at the capacity of our potential partners to engage in the very best levels of research as judged by international standards alone."

Rector Lauritz Broder Holm-Nielsen of Aarhus University is more open, however, and willing to work with a diverse array of collaborators provided that such agreements are transparent. "We have no hesitation, the more partnerships the better. However we must have upfront openness in the agreements. When something has to be kept a secret, we just have to agree on that from the beginning, so everybody who participates knows the conditions. At the moment, we probably have about 650 contracts with private companies. Altogether, Aarhus University runs about 6,000 individually financed research projects."

This touches on another interesting point as to the mechanisms and process for such partnerships to take place, and the structures that result. The approach at Cambridge, as with many other universities, is for partnerships to be fostered at the grass roots between faculty, and then perhaps to develop into institutional relationships over time. The situation in France or Germany is a little different at a domestic level given the enormous influence institutions such as CNRS or Max Planck have in the research arena. Such relationships are often an intrinsic part of the university landscape with institutions often co-located, and benefiting from joint appointments of academic staff.

Such is the case at the University of Goettingen explains President Ulrike Beisiegel. "We are not only a university, but we are embedded in a research campus. That means there are five Max Planck institutions, which are in very close collaboration, also, with joint contracts and scientific interests. So particularly our neurobiologists, they are involved, and not only Max Planck institutions, but also Leibniz Institutions."

President of the University of Strasbourg, Alain Beretz explains however, that the dynamic is rapidly changing as focus upon collaborative relationships intensifies. "The mechanisms for partnerships vary a great deal from interactions between individual scientists to the research work done by company's research and development departments as to the best universities to partner with. I think a lot of this has been traditionally based upon reputation, but this is now changing as universities and companies are becoming a lot more proactive; especially with the work now being done by universities' technology transfer offices."

The growing trend towards collaborative research partnerships carries obvious benefits. The correlation between cost and complexity in research endeavours is positive, institutions can share costs and infrastructure. Equally, one can expect economies of scale from research partnerships whereby more fieldwork, data and analysis is available at a lower overall institutional cost. Naturally, collaborative efforts are more productive as a result.

Working in partnership also ensures relevance, in that the research foci are directly related to areas of shared focus, with a broader economic and/ or societal value. In turn there are great benefits for students and researchers in their exposure and experience with industry and public institutions outside of the academic environment alone.

Multiple member strategic alliances such as the League of European Research Universities and International Association of Research Universities have grown in prominence as the international complexion of leading research universities' activities continues to become more and more pronounced.

Despite all of the positives, some concerns do linger in relation to partnerships, particularly with private sector players. The main concern is that the growing proliferation of joint funding agreements will impinge upon the basic principles of academic freedom and curiosity led research, with universities performing research on demand instead. At the same time, the rights to any intellectual property that results from collaborative research efforts has traditionally been a major stumbling block to the smooth negotiation of mutually beneficial agreements.

Seoul National University

University of Auckland

Global Challenges

As our leading universities' research strategies continue to transcend the boundaries of disciplines, and increasingly focus upon collaborative efforts to better understand and devise solutions to some of the most complex questions known to humankind; the active role they play in addressing major global challenges should come as little surprise. Without doubt, leading research universities are the key institutions in our world today pioneering knowledge based solutions to a raft of major global challenges, and complex phenomena yet to be fully, or even remotely understood.

The extent to which world-class research universities see it as their role to lead on such issues, and how their strategic approach differs therein, varies to some extent across cultural boundaries and institutional missions. One key theme unites the entire top 200 however; everyone is contributing.

President Lee Si-Chen of Taiwan University for example is a strong believer in the local approach. "By solving the problems facing our local society we contribute to the international solutions of the problems. So, we are going to solve local problems and bring our experience to the international community and say: 'See, we solved the problems in our society using this method. You can use this as a reference.' So, if everybody proposes and brings their solution to their society then they can form a general solution."

However, President Joseph Sung of the Chinese University of Hong Kong believes that a multi-lateral global approach is the way forward for major challenges that know no borders. "There are many phenomena for which we need to work with universities from other nations or other continents in order to address global issues. For example, climate is a very obvious example, climatology. We would like to have partners from Europe, from North America and even from Africa to work together with us to monitor global climate change."

The perspective of Brown University's Vice President for Research, Clyde Briant transcends the margin between the local and the global.

"We very much want our research to have an impact, and if it's going to have an impact that will almost certainly be at an international level. Probably each country will have particular factors or needs in relation to those major issues, but nevertheless, they remain international problems. Whether it's the environment, whether it's issues around poverty or homelessness, whether it's security, all of these things need to be worked on at an international level.

It is going to be important for all research universities, whether in this country or outside of the United States; or whether it's Brown or other universities, if they are going to solve these problems, they will need international collaboration with partners who can bring the perspectives of different nations together on these serious issues."

By combining a long-term perspective with the vibrancy of youth, Vice Chancellor of the University of Auckland, Stuart McCutcheon believes leading research universities have a pivotal role to play.

"I think that research universities are really critical to addressing global challenges. I think if you look at what research universities are capable of delivering in terms of knowledge to address those challenges, they are unique. They're different from government research laboratories because they have the span from very fundamental research through to the applied, whereas many government research labs are at the applied short-term fix end. But, also because we have bright young students who think about things in different ways, and change the social fabric of the institution. So I think it really is quite critical that universities operate in that space."

University of Auckland

President Patrick Deane of McMaster University considers engaging on major global challenges a prerequisite of the status afforded to leading research universities. "We have a major obligation, and if we aren't looking at those big questions we are not deserving of the big privileges we have as an institution." President Angel Cabrera of George Mason University echoes President Deane's sentiments.

"It is our responsibility to play a role and that's what our commitment is. We have a global problem-solving network that we are creating with leading institutions around the world. If universities are not constantly presenting data, analysis, insights or proposed solutions to the big challenges whether it is issues of climate change or sustainable access to energy, population growth, access to food, to clean water, issues of poverty and economic development. If we do not have answers or at least insights and value to create, then literally we are not doing our job."

President Daniel Zajfman of the Weizmann Institute is not so sure however.

"There must be, maybe not the majority, but maybe a good proportion of intellectuals and scholars being involved in issues that are way beyond the horizons we can look at. I think that is the role of universities. Now, it does not mean we cannot when called upon try to solve the problems of today. But I think the whole value and the big advantage of this freedom of thinking in what is called a university, is really in the value of the knowledge for the sake of knowledge. We do live in a world where it seems we need to solve problems. I am not saying that we should not solve them, but I'm not sure that universities are the places where these issues should be solved."

University of Cologne Rector Axel Freimuth agrees, although global challenges are of great importance they cannot occupy a university's entire mission.

"Our vision is indeed to contribute to the solution and understanding of these global challenges by different ways like basic research, education, and raising awareness of these questions.

But it does not mean that we would focus entirely on activities in these global challenges because we also strongly believe that a university must be a place where you can ask questions of any kind, and not just in some key topics."

Professor Adam Tickell, Pro Vice Chancellor for Research at the University of Birmingham believes it is important for research universities to play a role, but not to get carried away, and to stick to their institutional strengths.

"In terms of global challenges, I think it is of vital importance for universities to focus upon what they have specific strengths in, as opposed to trying to spread out and follow ideological views on what is important."

With all the talk of major global challenges it is quite easy to lose the human perspective. President Peretz Lavie of the Technion considers the most important challenges to be far closer to home.

"When I look at it as the President of the Technion, I look for challenges in my small world of the Technion. My challenge is in the last four years until the end of 2013, one in five faculty members' of the Technion will be a new faculty member recruited at some point in the last four years. This is a change of generations. My major challenge is how to ensure that the new generation is going to be better than the previous generations. How can I provide them with the means to do the research with the best students, with the environment and the government that they need in order to excel, and to lead education as the previous generations did.

University of Birmingham

University of Birmingham

This is a major challenge for me as the President. The second is how to maintain the balance between globalization, and taking care of what we need in Israel. How much should you go out, and how much you should focus on internal issues. This is the second challenge. The third challenge is how you will continue your everyday life, and still maintain the spirit of achievement and excellence after such a peak."

Georgia Tech President George P. Peterson subscribes to the grass roots perspective, in that inspiring the great young minds that attend universities is the best hope for the future.

"Our goal is to train and educate our students so that they're well positioned to address these global problems. The biggest challenge we have is this idea that we are trying to move from an industrial economy to an information economy."

Given the ability of universities to spend many years on the most fundamental questions, UCLA Chancellor Gene Block considers it hard to perceive solutions to major global challenges without their involvement.

"I think universities are essential because global challenges are inherently complex problems that take time to solve. Industry-centred research necessarily focuses more on the not-too-distant future. We tend to provide the fundamental discoveries that will be essential to address the most challenging issues of our day. If you think about health challenges, such as the costs associated with Alzheimer's disease or diabetes, we are going to require major breakthroughs in our understanding of the human brain and endocrine system in order to find cures. This is work that can probably only be undertaken in labs at our research universities. I think the same is true for our most pressing environ-mental challenges, which will require sophisticated models and perhaps technology development. Industry will play a role here, but universities will almost certainly provide the fundamental discoveries and 'know how' to help us address our most pressing environmental issues."

According to Chancellor Robert Birgeneau of UC Berkeley, the shift away from research as a priority in broader society leaves research universities as essential institutions in pushing human understanding and capacity forwards in overcoming major global challenges.

"I think that universities broadly have major roles to play, as corporations have remarkably short-term time horizons. When I was young I worked at Bell Laboratories. At that time at Bell Labs, we had more freedom to do undirected basic research than virtually anybody in any U.S. university. This is because Bell Labs had extraordinarily enlightened management whose time horizon was decades rather than months. An important part of the US economy still rests on inventions made at Bell Laboratories. Bell Laboratories still exists but it bears little relation to the wondrous institution that existed in the 60's and 70's when I worked there.

"Similarly, IBM had great research laboratories along with Xerox, RCA, General Electric, etc ... In Europe there was Philips, Siemens, Brown-Boveri, etc ... These are all gone at least as places where creative basic research is done. One might have expected that government laboratories would have been able to step in to fill the void but they are very constrained by politics. This means that for society to achieve significant scientific, technological and ultimately economic progress, the responsibility now rests almost entirely with major research universities both nationally and internationally. In my view, this has not been fully understood by industry or governments whether in the U.S., Europe or Asia.

"It is a challenge but that is what we do. If universities do not look to the long term, then no other institution in society is going to. Corporations typically look at time scales of three months, which is the frequency of their quarterly reports. Governments are always looking at the next election. This leaves it to us to deal with the long term. I have been working on high temperature superconductivity for 25 years, and we still do not seem any closer to a solution."

President Bernie Machen of the University of Florida finds it hard for universities to get away from their role in contributing knowledge based solutions to major challenges; they are the first places that everyone else comes to for answers.

"Major research universities are the first places that governments go. Industry, and maybe even world health organisations come to us to help solve problems and challenges that are not solvable right now; so there is no shortage of people seeking us out and, for the most part, providing funds to help us seek them."

As changes in technology continue to change our perceptions, and daily interactions worldwide, whilst global challenges reverberate as a result; Iowa State President Steven Leath believes there is no geographical constraint upon where challenges begin or end anymore. It is simply the right thing to do for research universities to get involved and contribute.

"I think it's critical. We are in a smaller and smaller world. Many of the problems that affect one part of the world, will eventually affect another part, or are repeated somewhere else. So the sooner we can get on solving these big problems whether it is global climate change or food, the better. We have to look at them from a global perspective." A brief history of some of the humankind's most pressing challenges and unanswered questions within the context of leading research universities is perhaps the best means of elucidating their influence.

What are we? Where did we come from? What is out there?

Perhaps the most basic questions of all, these three simple queries have occupied human consciousness for many millennia, and continue to divide opinion today along themes of logic, science, philosophy and faith. Perhaps July 2012 marked the unification of science and faith in the discovery of the Higgs Boson, often referred to as the God Particle. Following years of collaboration between leading theoretical physicists from the world's leading research universities, their congregation in July at the European Organisation for Nuclear Research (CERN) in Switzerland, confirmed the existence of the Higgs Boson.

The Higgs Boson first predicted to exist some 50 years ago by Peter Higgs et alia at the University of Edinburgh is widely acknowledged to confirm much of the Standard Model. Our most agreed upon theoretical framework to describe the mechanisms of the universe, what it contains and what links everything together that is part of it. The standard model was finalised in the 1970's following many years of international collaboration between physicists from amongst other institutions, the world's leading research universities.

There is general consensus on everything being made up of mass, the combination of matter and energy ($E=MC^2$) first postulated by Albert Einstein (ETH Zurich, University of Zurich, University of Bern, Caltech & Princeton). But the nature and origins of such mass remains somewhat an unresolved predicament. The Big Bang theory pervades our understanding of the origins of the known universe. The answers to the question of mass, and therein what we are made from, and what links us all together are to be found in the first second or so following the big bang. Energy and matter need something to draw them together and create mass; that glue is now widely acknowledged to be the Higgs Boson particle.

Needless to say, the interaction between curiosity, universities and the universe did not begin with Albert Einstein. One would perhaps have to go back to the Universities of Krakow, Bologna and Padua in the late 15th and early 16th centuries where Nicolaus Copernicus' study of anatomy, philosophy and astronomy were to help inform his great theoretical works on the Heliocentric Model, whereby the sun was at the centre of the Earth's orbit; not the other way around.

Some 50 years after Copernicus finished his groundbreaking works in his native Poland, Galileo Galilei continued the University of Padua's rich tradition of academic inquiry into the nature of the Universe and its structure with his defence of Copernicus' Heliocentric theory, and improvements made to the telescope that later facilitated his discovery of Jupiter's 4 Galilean moons.

Following a journey through Austria (University of Graz), Czech Republic (University of Prague) and Germany (University of Tuebingen) and a full grasp of Johannes Kepler's laws of planetary motion. One would have to move onto the University of Cambridge in the late 17th Century, and rendezvous with Sir Isaac Newton's Principia Mathematica and mathematical descriptions of gravity based upon Kepler's laws, before the final doubts about the heliocentric model were removed. Newton went on to build the first reflecting telescope, the practical basis for most research grade telescopes that are in use today.

Into the 19th Century, again at the University of Cambridge, Charles Darwin's curiosity in natural philosophy and classifying wildlife was first stimulated before his influential voyage aboard the HMS Beagle to the Galapagos Islands. A journey that laid the foundation for his theory about the evolution of humankind, culminating in his seminal works on natural selection and the origin of our species.

University of Edinburgh

University of Iowa

University of Iowa

ANNOUNCING INCREDIBLY SMALL NEWS IN THE FIGHT AGAINST CANCER.

One of the biggest developments in cancer treatment could soon come from an extremely small source. Using nano-engineered carriers, we may be able to release chemotherapy drugs inside tumors — with no damage to the rest of the body's cells. And tumors simply will never see what hit them. Continuously exploring ways to combine disciplines like engineering and medicine is another reason why Boston University has become one of today's great research institutions. And why thinking differently about our world begins with BU. Find out more at **bu.edu/discover/cancer**

The world needs to know.

Johns Hopkins University

It was the partly the incomplete nature of Sir Isaac Newton's work that inspired Albert Einstein's general theory of relativity and Max Planck's (Universities of Kiel, Berlin & Goettingen) origination of Quantum Theory. Widely acknowledged to be the two foundation stones of modern physics today, the origins of the standard model and ultimately the quest for the Higgs Boson particle. A discovery that has the potential to unite all mass in the universe, according to its most basic structural feature of form.

The quest for the Higgs Boson at CERN is the grandest science experiment of all time, it gives an indication of the lengths curiosity will take us in the pursuit of a greater understanding of what we are, and where we came from; and the influence that leading research universities have on such endeavours.

This work is by no means over, as theoretical physicists, mathematicians, evolutionary biologists and a host of complimentary expertise continue to grapple with cryptic phenomena such as string theory, quarks, dark matter, gluons and leptons to find the definitive answer to these most fundamental of questions.

Professor Steven Hawking at the University of Cambridge was the first to try and unite Einstein's theory of general relativity with Max Planck's quantum theory in a theoretical description of the cosmos, a challenge that remains unresolved today in the realms of theoretical physics.

In trying to better understand where we came from, both Uppsala University and Stony Brook University are conducting studies in Africa analysing DNA data to find the exact origins of where humankind actually began. Stony Brook's Turkana Basin Institute is examining fossils up to 4.5 million years old to help map precisely the trajectory of humankind's development. A theme of examination whose origins are in Charles Darwin's pioneering journey to the Galapagos Islands on the HMS Beagle.

Under the leadership of Professor Kei Hirose, Director of Tokyo Tech's Earth-Life Science Institute (ELSI); researchers in Japan are investigating fundamental questions as to the origins of planet Earth, and the life our planet supports today.

From world-class physics departments such as at the University of Colorado Boulder to the University of Tokyo's Kavli Institute; our continued explorations into the fundamental nature of all natural phenomena, and a single theory that unites it all continues in earnest at the world's leading research universities.

Questions relating to what is out there, as in what is there beyond planet Earth in the vast expanse of the universe, have captured our imaginations throughout the annals of history. It is with little doubt that our exploration of space continues to capture our shared imaginations most vividly. Leading research universities play a pivotal role in the missions and projects that serve to answer our questions, and further our curiosity as to what we will find in the cosmic expanse beyond our home planet.

One such project at the forefront of headlines today, has its namesake at the driving force behind its mission. On August 6th 2012 at 8:25pm GMT, the Curiosity Rover safely landed on the surface of Mars; not the first time this has happened, but a remarkable achievement nevertheless. What we discover on Mars has the potential to change so much about human perception. What if irrefutable evidence of life is found there? What does that mean for the thousands of years of philosophy that we have been accustomed to? What does it mean for the identity of humankind and planet Earth? How will we cope with the transition from being alone in a vast expanse to one of many? What does it mean for the potential of the rest of the Solar System, let alone the Universe, and the Multiverses potentially beyond that?

Leading research universities have been pondering such questions for many years, and it was their expertise that was of fundamental importance in landing Curiosity on Mars. Without a doubt Caltech's management of NASA's Jet Propulsion Laboratory has been unequivocal in its importance to missions such as Curiosity.

Today, at least eight other NASA probes are travelling through the solar system to explore other planets such as the Moon, Jupiter, Saturn, Mercury and Pluto, as well as the dark void beyond the end of our Solar System. All such probes count on the contributions of leading research universities. The University of Maryland – College Park, UC Boulder, the University of Iowa, the University of Cambridge, Johns Hopkins University and the University of Washington in St Louis are just a handful of the leading research universities that are making enormous contributions to our growing capacity to physically explore the Solar System and Universe beyond our home planet.

As it stands, our exploration of the deep universe physically is beyond our technical capacity; thus the responsibility presently rests with institutions such as the University of Hawaii, Manoa and University of California, Santa Cruz with their world leading observational infrastructure. Many of their telescopes' basic designs are based upon Sir Isaac Newton's reflective technology first introduced to astronomy some 300 years ago. Less related Renaissance technology is the Space Telescope Science Institute housed at Johns Hopkins University, the ground station for the Hubble Telescope. A pioneering space telescope, whose observations have led to a number of new discoveries in astrophysics.

One such discovery was the 2011 Nobel Prize winning work of UC Berkeley's Professor Saul Perlmutter, Australian National University's Professor Brian Schmidt and Johns Hopkins' Professor Adam Reiss for their observations of supernovae in determining the increasing speed in the rate of expansion of the universe. Dark matter is one of the real mysteries of the cosmos, which, whilst appearing to be fundamental to the mechanics of the universe, remains a phenomenon that we know very little about. Astronomers at New York University have created the largest ever three-dimensional maps of massive galaxies and dark matter to help provide additional understanding. Equally, researchers at UC Santa Cruz are taking a lead on furthering our understanding of what dark matter is, and how it affects the behaviour of the universe.

Astrophysicist Karl Gerbhardt at the University of Texas, Austin has recently revealed a little more about Black Holes, another enigmatic phenomena found throughout the universe. Using the world's third largest telescope Professor Gerbhardt identified the largest known black hole in the universe, thought to weigh some 17 billion times more than our sun.

Research universities in their on going hunt for exoplanets although at a nascent stage are leading the search for life beyond Earth. France's Joseph Fourier University has discovered 100 since 1998, with Planet Gl667CC most resembling Earth.

HOW CAN DISCARDED CELL PHONE BATTERIES LEAD TO A DRAMATIC REDUCTION IN CHILD MORTALITY?

FUNNY, WE ASKED OURSELVES THE SAME QUESTION.

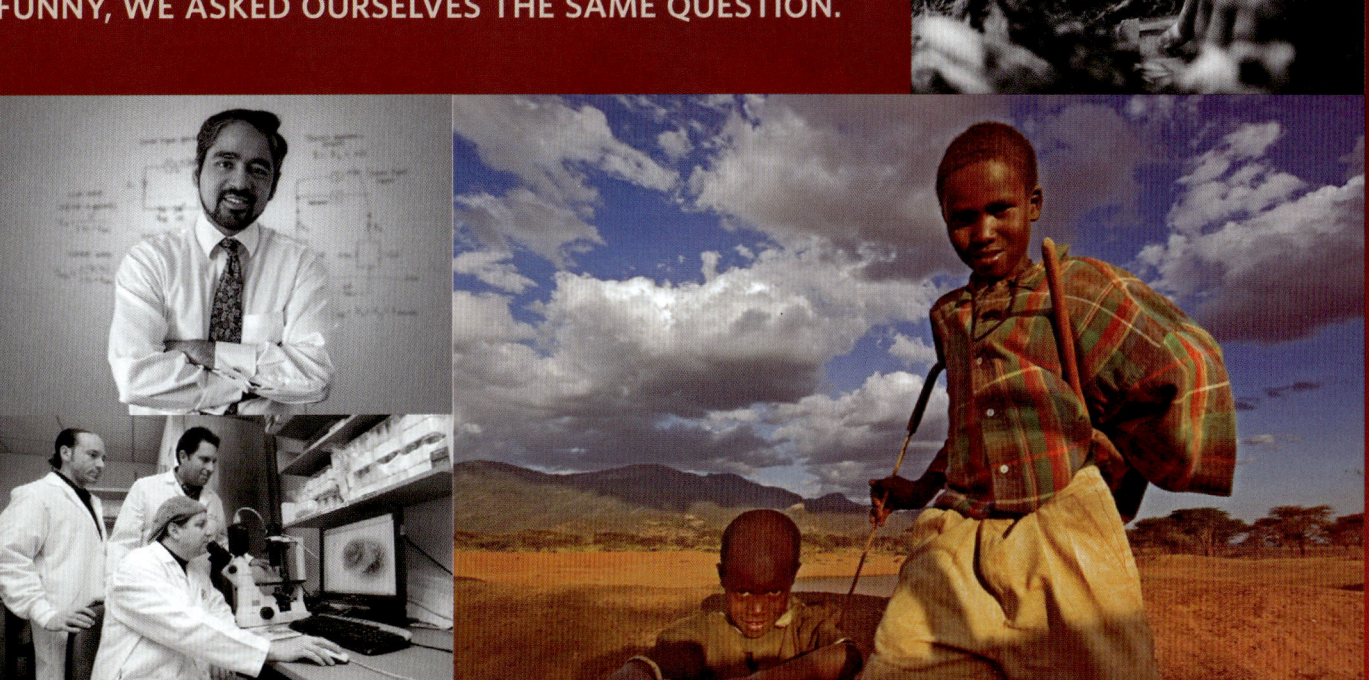

There are places where thousands of children won't live to the age of five. There are places where thousands of cell phone batteries are thrown away every day. And there are scientists who, by asking the right questions, found a life-saving link between the two. Reusing discarded cell phone batteries, we created affordable and effective solar-powered pulse oximeters for early detection of pneumonia. It's looking at challenges in new ways like this that has made Boston University one of today's leading centers of knowledge. And why thinking differently about our world begins with BU. Find out more at **bu.edu/discover/batteries**

The world needs to know.

Stockholm University

University of Hamburg

What are we doing about Global Climate Change?

Global climate change by its very nature is a complex phenomenon, incorporating inputs from volcanic emissions, plate tectonics and solar radiation through to oceanic processes and human activities such as industrial development, fossil fuel based energy and deforestation.

The collaborative work of hundreds of research universities in partnership over several decades in collecting data, developing climate models and testing trends against them has resulted in global climate change based upon human activity as an established science today. Culminating in the 2007 Nobel Peace Prize being awarded to the IPCC, as well as the countless research universities that have contributed to our understanding of the reasons underlying global climate change.

Professor Paul Crutzen, an atmospheric chemist first demonstrated man-made impacts on climate whilst at the University of Stockholm, with his seminal work demonstrating depletion of the ozone layer as a result of man-made emissions. Professor Crutzen's Nobel Prize in Chemistry was shared with his research collaborators – Dr Mario Molina and Professor Frank Sherwood Rowland, both of whom conducted their research at the University of California, Irvine.

Germany's University of Hamburg is another one of Europe's leading research universities with a strong commitment to better understanding and devising solutions to global climate change through its Integrated Climate System Analysis and Prediction cluster of excellence.

Researchers at the Technical University of Munich, through an international satellite mission of the European Space Agency are measuring ocean currents from space; again contributing to our understanding of climate change and its impacts upon ocean levels and patterns.

Australian National University with the largest cluster in Australasia engaged with climate related research has employed an interdisciplinary approach, with foci ranging from the basic science of climate change through to devising better public policy approaches designed to help society adapt to its impacts.

The question of climate change is never too far from modern discourse as a myriad of institutions and political leaders lay claim to being staunch advocates of combatting some of its underlying causes. Nevertheless, the question still remains – what are we doing?

Professor Nicholas Stern of the London School of Economics through the 700-page Stern Review of the Economics of Climate Change has urged for a lot more to be done, with very clear conclusions that the costs of acting now will be far lower than in the future, if we do not begin to invest.

Although the challenge spans a myriad of issues and human interactions with the environment, the question of long-term sustainable energy is increasingly intertwined with our successful management of CO_2 emissions, and subsequent global climate change. At the same time, introducing non-carbon based fuels is a vital way to ensure sustainable energy security. The sorts of revolutionary technologies developed at research universities are a vital part of the mix.

Professor Stephen Salter first developed the technology for the generation of renewable electricity derived from wave energy at the University of Edinburgh.

Increasingly researchers are looking towards organic solutions too as part of our future energy mix. Researchers at Uppsala University are investigating means of developing algae based fuels using photosynthesis as a catalyst. Japan's University of Tsukuba has also put faith in the potential of algae as a means of producing a sustainable source of fuel. This theme is continued at Caltech, with researchers investigating a methodology to produce fuels by simply combining water, CO_2 and sunlight. UCLA researchers also see potential in this approach, investigating new energy sources, including converting electricity and CO_2 to liquid fuel, and using proteins as raw material for biofuels.

Universities with clear expertise throughout the biological sciences such as the University of Ghent are also contributing towards a diversified energy future, with the development of new bio-fuel based technologies.

Wind technologies' efficiency and commercial viability continue to be improved at leading research universities such as the Technical University of Denmark and Kyushu University in Japan. Researchers at Kyushu have recently developed a new form of turbine called the Wind Lens, heralding energy output some threefold more efficient than conventional wind turbines. The quest for a safe, sustainable and commercially viable means of introducing hydrogen based fuels into the energy mix continues to be pioneered at leading research universities. Again, Kyushu and the Technical University of Denmark as well as Princeton are all leaders in this potentially game changing field of energy generation.

Similarly to hydrogen, nuclear fusion is considered to be a game changing technology that could herald an almost unlimited amount of renewable energy at a low, sustainable cost with negligible impact upon the broader environment. The University of Padua, in partnership with Euratom is committed to fully investigating the potential of nuclear fusion. Similarly, the University of Rochester, through the Laboratory for Laser Energetics is investigating means of translating fusion's theoretical possibilities into a practical reality for energy generation.

The sun's pre-eminence as the Earth's source of energy places solar power at the forefront of any realistic efforts to re-balance our energy supply towards one that is more stable and sustainable. The University of Toronto has pioneered the development of new technologies that will enable solar cells to be painted onto surfaces, and begin converting solar energy into electricity immediately. Meanwhile, researchers at the University of New South Wales set a world record in 2011 for the most efficient mass-produced crystal silicon solar cell at 19.4%.

As well as a means of generating more sustainable forms of energy, the infrastructure as it stands for storage and transmission requires significant upgrades if it is to operate well alongside new technologies. As it stands, the key challenge with introducing renewable technologies to the mainstream electricity grid is the issue of storing the energy. Unfortunately the sun doesn't shine 24 hours a day, and the wind doesn't blow all year round; thus it is vitally important to be able to store renewable sources to enable them to provide base load power.

Stony Brook University has recently recruited one of the world's leading battery researchers in Professor Esther Takeuchi to lead on developing knowledge and technology based solutions to the storage challenge, without a doubt the key factor preventing the widespread roll out of renewable energy sources. UCLA is also tackling the question of storage with the help of graphene, one of the world's most recently discovered materials. Thus far, UCLA researchers have used graphene to begin the development of super-capacitors – electronic instruments that can charge and discharge hundreds of times faster than conventional batteries.

Again at UCLA researchers are forging ahead with the development of smart grid technologies that will facilitate far more flexible and efficient transmission of electricity between energy source and point of use. This avenue of research is perhaps led by researchers at North Carolina State University where smart solid-state transformers under development will have a revolutionary impact on the efficiency of the electricity grid. Many universities such as Kyushu University, for example, are examining means of mitigating the impact of carbon-based energy sources. Researchers at Kyushu are widely acknowledged to be some of the world's leaders in the development of reliable

and commercially viable means of carbon sequestration and storage.

Beyond energy production, next generation transportation technologies are of vital importance in ensuring our sustainable future. ETH Zurich was one of the first research universities to innovate in this way with the development of catalytic converters – key instruments in use to reduce the harmful emissions generated by cars. The University of Auckland has continued the automotive theme, with the development of induction power for electric cars, whereby cars can be electronically charged without being plugged in. In case you were wondering where the electric cars would come from, the Technical University of Munich is a global leader in the development of highly efficient electric cars. The University of Waterloo is also a key contributor to the development of sustainable automobiles, with countless next-generation components in development to help improve the performance of electric cars.

The University of Waterloo is also working to devise strategies for our adaptation to the changing environments we are witnessing in the face of climate change. Cities such as Dhaka in Bangladesh and Lagos in Nigeria will endure the brunt of sea level rise. The University of Waterloo's interdisciplinary approach aims to help communities adapt to their changing land and cityscapes, as the impact of climate change on our environment becomes ever more pronounced.

As well as focusing on the development of new technologies, the University of Delaware's Energy Institute is focusing upon encouraging a change in behaviours at the grass roots level. An approach many believe will have an enormous impact on our collective environmental footprint, and the rate of environmental change as a result.

University of Hamburg

21st Century Physics

Few could have conceived the impact that Friedrich Miescher's discovery of nucleic acid at the University of Tuebingen in 1869 would have on the course of scientific enquiry into the early 21st century. Such is the nature of curiosity-driven research, that Professor Miescher's discovery of the substance that carries our DNA set off a chain of investigation that led to the enormous excitement surrounding contemporary biology in the early 21st century.

President Marc Tessier-Lavigne of Rockefeller University explains: "I think that the 20th century was a century of physics, and the 21st century is the century of biology. There has been a revolution in our understanding of biological mechanisms over the past 20 years, the sequencing of the human genome, the development of powerful technologies to interrogate normal physiology as well as pathology, and the rise of human genetics."

President Daniel Zajfman of the Weizmann Institute shares a similar perspective. "There is a huge evolution that is taking place in our understanding of biology, it might not be exactly the same type of evolution that happened a hundred years ago in physics. But it's clearly a new paradigm shift. If you ask yourself what is happening, interestingly in this case, it is really the technology, which is driving the field. The ability to sequence whole genomes, the huge capacity of looking at proteins and understanding of structures and so forth that allows us to look at, I would say, very complex systems. Of course added to it, is the idea that maybe after all, biology cannot be reduced."

From Tuebingen, one would have to leapfrog forward to the University of Cambridge in 1953 where Professors Francis Crick and James D. Watson first suggested the correct double helix structure of DNA to find the beginnings of the paradigm shift in our understandings of biology, genetics and all its complexity; that has culminated in the widespread excitement that engulfs this field today.

In another epic round of international multiple university collaboration between the United States, UK, Japan, Germany, France and Spain amongst others. The mapping of the human genome was completed in 2001; with approximately 23,000 different genes identified and ordered in their relative positions within the overall structure of DNA. These 23,000 genes make up only 2% of our genome, but at the time were thought to be the only active parts of it.

The growing availability of data and exponential upgrades in computing power, however, continue to de-bunk this initial hypothesis in that the 4 million gene switches in the remaining 98% of our genome are indeed active, and greatly influence our susceptibility to disease and ill-health, amongst countless other characteristics.

Researchers at Yale for example, have identified the genes that are responsible for high blood pressure,

osteoporosis, dyslexia and Tourette's Syndrome. University of Massachusetts Medical School Professor Craig Mello won the 2006 Nobel Prize in Medicine for his discoveries relating to RNA interference with the structure of genes. This has helped researchers around the world better understand various diseases, as well as develop innovative treatments to severe illnesses such as cancer.

These advancements in our depth of understanding of the human genome, coupled with the enormous computing power able to analyse the "big data" sets now ubiquitous throughout leading research universities has galvanised the beginnings of a revolution in predictive and personalised medicine; predicted to run its course throughout the 21st century. Medical practice at the end of this century, as a result, will look very much different to what it is today.

As part of this revolution, leading research universities the world over have invested heavily in their existing infrastructure to further our understanding and capabilities in foci such as genetics, bio-informatics, and personalised medicine. Both UC Santa Cruz and Washington University in St Louis took leading roles in the initial mapping of the human genome, and now have world leading facilities in genetics and genomics. UC Santa Cruz has one of the world's foremost cancer related genome research programs; acting as the user portal for the United States' National Cancer Institute's cancer genome research program. An initiative set to significantly expand our understanding of how individual genetic make ups relate to our susceptibility to various cancers.

University College London, Imperial College London and King's College London are investing £650 million in the development of the Francis Crick Institute, forecast to be Europe's foremost biomedical facility. Furthermore, institutions such as Rice University and the University of Washington continue to invest a great deal in their I.T. infrastructure, so as to be able to manage the enormous data sets that are now being generated by the on going revolution in genetics, genomics and bio-informatics. The Weizmann Institute is also investing heavily in this field with a US$100 million investment in Israel's National Centre for Personalised Medicine. New York's Mount Sinai School of Medicine is also investing US$100 million with a view to developing one of the best genomics programs and research infrastructures in the world.

Rutgers University is home to the world's largest university bio-repository of genetic data in the Rutgers University Cell & DNA Repository. Researchers at Vanderbilt have also developed one of the world's largest DNA data banks in BioVU.

Following the discovery of stem cells by University of Toronto professors Ernest McCulloch and James Till in the early 1960's, another wave of new innovation has taken hold within the biomedical sciences. The potential of stem cells in treating countless ailments

from blindness to Alzheimer's disease are enormous. As a result the wave of investment and discovery in the area of stem cell research coming from leading research universities comes as little surprise.

The University of Toronto has capitalised upon McCulloch and Till's initial discovery with the development of one of the world's leading centres for stem cell research. Professor James Thomson at the University of Wisconsin, Madison further added to our growing understanding of stem cells with his discovery of human embryonic stem cells in 1998. Researchers at Osaka University have been some of the first in the world to develop successful treatments and clinical applications with the use of somatic stem cells. Kyoto University's Dr Shinya Yamanaka won the 2012 Nobel Prize in medicine for discovering that mature cells can be converted to stem cells.

On the 5th July 1996, Dolly the Sheep, the first mammal ever to be cloned using an adult somatic stem cell was born. Researchers at University College London are currently making great strides in curing blindness with the use of stem cells, whilst researchers at the University of Sheffield are making similar progress in restoring hearing with the use of stem cells. Two of many applications for what is widely expected to develop into a revolutionary form of medical treatment as the 21st Century moves forward.

In an era of continuing global population growth and resultant food insecurity, one should look no further than Nobel Peace Prize Laureate, Dr Norman Borlaug for the influence revolutionary biology and modern agricultural techniques can have in helping to overcome the growing challenge of food security. Dr Borlaug, often nicknamed "the father of the Green Revolution" developed high yield, disease resistant strains of wheat and exported them to countries such as Mexico, India and Pakistan. Dr Borlaug is often credited with saving 1 billion lives; by averting starvation. The university where he conducted much of his research, Texas A & M retains its institutional focus on agriculture and helping to ensure that food security concerns decline, as opposed to increase over the course of the 21st century.

Iowa State University is another such institution committed to the use of advanced biology to ensure a sustainable and secure future food supply. The university has developed more plant genoplans and plant gene varieties than just about any other university in the world. Iowa State is pioneering techniques such as the use of nanotechnology to deliver proteins and DNA into plant cells, a completely new approach to genetic engineering. In a world where much of our most fertile agricultural land is consumed by swelling urban sprawls, and the rise of global population and collective food expectations grow in line with increasing overall wealth, innovative new agricultural techniques such as these are vital to ensure a secure food security for all communities throughout the world.

University of Massachusetts – Amherst

Weizmann Institute

University College London

Medicine

Although the history of medicine stretches all the way back to our earliest knowledge of antiquity, one would have to again re-visit Italy's University of Padua in the early 13th century to first encounter a research university's engagement with the medical sciences. First established in 1595, Padua's renowned anatomical theatre was the world's first; having to operate in secrecy for much of its existence because of papal rules outlawing medical research on deceased human subjects.

Today, the breadth of influence that leading research universities have on developments in the medical sciences is breath-taking. The scale and scope of ongoing medical research at leading research universities makes it almost impossible to quantify; certainly within the context of this volume. Needless to say, there are an array of specific medical challenges today such as cancer, avian flu, obesity or HIV/AIDS that occupy our consciousness to a greater extent than others such as the common cold. Leading research universities are at the forefront of these challenges.

University of Queensland

Cancer

Although Hippocrates (460BC – 370 BC) first identified cancer in Ancient Greece; the increasing number of cases linked to a growing and ageing population has seen cancer as an ailment evolve into a very modern phenomenon within our collective consciousness. Research universities the world over have responded to the challenge of cancer by extending our understanding of the basic mechanisms that underlie its development, and continuing to pioneer new treatments from vaccines through to genetic treatments that mitigate cancer's spread and mortal impact.

Professor Theodor Boveri first identified the genetic basis for cancer at the University of Munich in 1902. Marie and Pierre Curie won the 1903 Nobel Prize in physics for their discovery of radiation – the first non-surgical cancer treatment. Whilst in 1965 McGill University Professors Sam Freedman and Phil Gold first discovered carcinogenic-embryonic antigen (CEA), the leading diagnostic method for cancer. It wasn't until 1968 at the University of Bristol that Professor Anthony Epstein and his team identified the first human cancer virus; now their namesake as the Epstein-Barr Virus.

LMU Munich

Landmark discoveries such as these don't happen every day. Nevertheless, leading research universities continue to surprise us with the basic understanding they develop, and innovative treatments that result on a bewilderingly regular basis.

Professor Olivera Finn at the University of Pittsburgh has developed a vaccine that triggers immunity to colon cancer. At the University of Queensland, Professor Ian Frazer's work led to the development of the cervical cancer vaccine Gardasil, resulting in significantly lower rates of the Human Papillomavirus (HPV); that causes cervical cancer. Professor Harald zur Hausen at the University of Heidelberg first identified HPV in 1983, winning him the Nobel Prize for Medicine in 2008.

Professor of Oncology Brian Druker at the Oregon Health & Science University played a key role in the discovery of Gleevec. A revolutionary cancer drug that whilst heralding a revolution in personalized cancer treatment, continues to save tens of thousands of lives. Researchers at Yale University were the first to treat cancer with chemotherapy.

Developing a better understanding of the genetic basis of cancer has been pioneered by researchers at the Johns Hopkins University, 90% of all sequenced cancers have been completed by Johns Hopkins Researchers. UC Santa Cruz, whilst not having a medical school is a leader in furthering our understanding of the genetics of cancer with its responsibility for all of the US National Cancer Institute's genomic data.

A spin-out company established by researchers at the University of Nottingham has developed a simple blood test to detect lung cancer at a very early stage. Lung cancer is the most significant killer of all cancers with late prognosis playing a significant part of that. This new prognostic methodology has immense life saving potential around the world. In a similar vein, researchers at UCLA have developed a saliva test that is able to detect cancer.

Medicines such as Cisplatin and Carboplatin were discovered at Michigan State University; combined they have been responsible for saving millions of lives worldwide. Professor Kazunori Kataoka at the University of Tokyo has developed nanocapsules capable of identifying and delivering treatment directly to cancerous cells. Similarly researchers at Boston University have designed nano-engineered carriers that deliver chemotherapy drugs directly to tumours avoiding any damage to healthy tissue in close proximity.

Heidelberg University

Obesity

The growing burden of obesity upon individuals, health care systems and societies worldwide is very much a modern phenomenon. Closely linked to the development of cancer, diabetes and cardiovascular disease, obesity is increasingly being recognised as one of the world's most deadly health afflictions. Researchers such as at the University of North Carolina, Chapel Hill's Gillings Institute are pioneering our understanding of obesity and means of trying to stem its prevalence throughout the world.

Equally, researchers at the University of Sydney are investing some AU$385 million in the Charles Perkin Centre. An interdisciplinary institute that will house 1000 researchers investigating the causes of obesity, diabetes and cardiovascular disease; and the means to combat their continued growth.

At Cornell University, Professor Brian Wansink's work on mindless eating is helping better understand the neurological processes, external factors and reward systems that drive eating habits. Often nicknamed "The Sherlock Holmes of food", Professor Wansink's work is of great importance in improving our understanding of eating habits and cultural factors that cause obesity.

On more of a cerebral level, Vanderbilt's Professor Roger Cone has identified the receptors in our brain that regulate metabolism and appetite. Whilst one could be mistaken for considering this discovery academic, it provides us the opportunity to start developing new treatments that could modify eating habits.

Brown University

HIV/AIDS

Ever since it was first discovered as the cause of AIDS by Professor Robert Gallo and his team in 1983, the spread of HIV/AIDS has been the source of tragic epidemics throughout many of the most vulnerable communities in the world today. Whilst universities such as the University of California, San Francisco played a leading role in the discovery of HIV; the real challenge today is to cure or vaccinate against it once and for all. The the search for the silver bullet treatment to HIV/AIDS goes on and leading research universities continue to develop some of the most important treatments to mitigate its effect; as well as leading many of the projects to mitigate its spread.

Emory University in the United States has been one of the world's leading contributors to the fight against HIV/AIDS. Lifesaving drugs such as 3TC and Emtriva were developed at Emory; as it stands 90% of United States' citizens receiving treatment for HIV/AIDS are using drugs that were developed at Emory.

Professor Julio Montaner of the University of British Columbia has recently found that treatment with established anti-retroviral drugs serves as a means of significantly reducing transmission rates of HIV. Whereas Professor Robert Bailey at the University of Illinois, Chicago has found that male circumcision dramatically reduces the rate at which HIV is spread. Both are vitally important in reducing the spread of the virus.

Professor David Baltimore at Caltech is investigating ways in which gene therapy can be used to help treat HIV/AIDS. Researchers from Monash University's Burnett Institute have identified the specific cells where the HIV virus lies hidden when patients undergo anti-retroviral treatments. This is a vital piece of the puzzle in pinning the HIV virus down and eradicating it from patients' immune systems.

In remote parts of the developing world, reliable testing for the HIV virus has traditionally acted as a major stumbling block to helping halt the disease's spread. Researchers at Northwestern University have developed a low cost, high accuracy, portable testing device to help overcome this critical challenge.

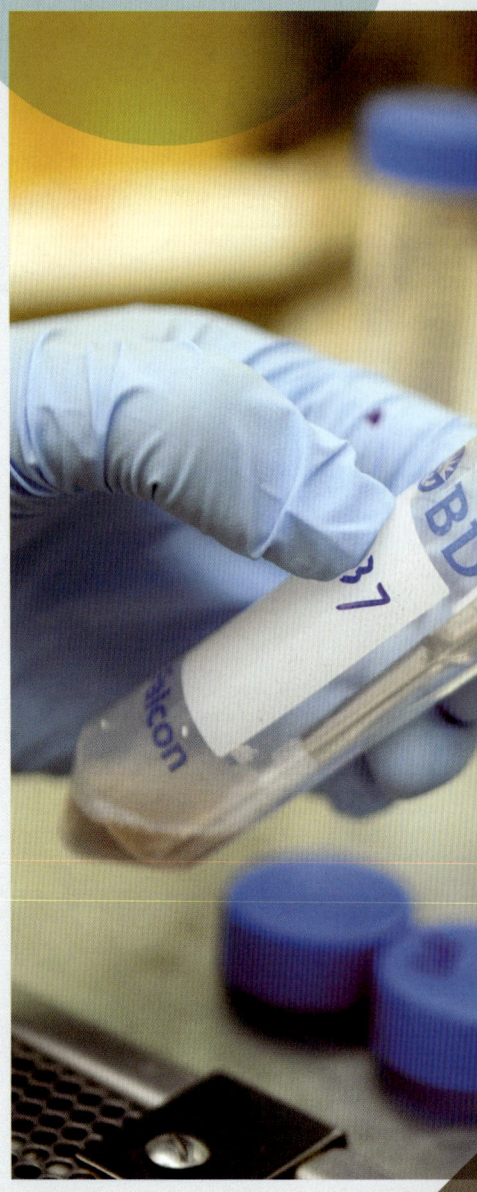

University of North Carolina at Chapel Hill

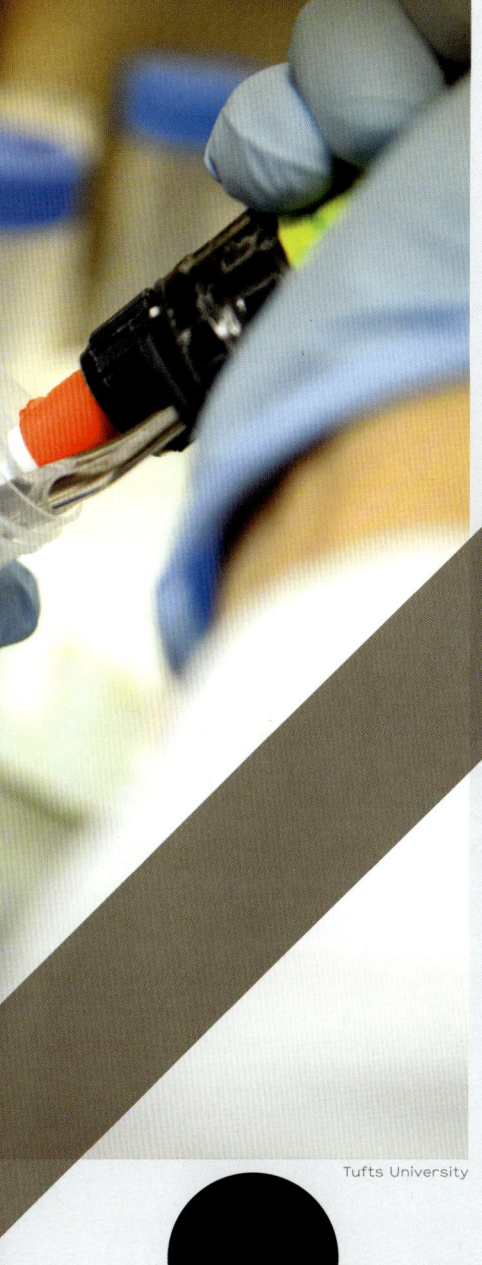

Brain, Mind & Consciousness

Another one the world's great mysteries is the nature of human consciousness. Rene Descartes' maxim, "I think therefore I am", still reverberates around philosophy departments and debates today. In one of life's great ironies, we still don't actually know exactly what thinking is. In order for us to be able to get a grasp of this, we need to know a lot more about the most complex and mysterious machine in the known universe — the human brain.

Led by EPF Lausanne in coordination with 80 partner institutions throughout Europe, the 1 billion euro Human Brain Project (HBP) is the most ambitious neuroscience project ever. The brain consists of some 100 billion neurons, connected by some 100,000 billion synapses; the HBP aims to map and then simulate the entire human brain using supercomputing power as yet unparalleled in its capacity. When one considers that each simulated neuron requires the equivalent computing power of a standard laptop; the processing power involved becomes almost philosophical.

The HBP aims to create the most accurate model of the human brain ever produced, enabling us to understand, treat and exploit it. Brain diseases are an enormous challenge the world over, in Europe neurological disorders cost health services more than heart disease, cancer and diabetes all combined. By developing the most accurate simulation of the brain we will not only get closer to answering philosophical questions such as, what is consciousness? We will also be able to develop highly effective treatments to some of the most challenging brain diseases such as Alzheimer's and Parkinson's. Marking drastic improvements in life quality and life style for our oldest generations.

The EU initiative, widely expected to be subject of a rival US led project called the Brain Activity Map. Unannounced as we go to press, the Brain Activity Map is expected to draw together expertise from universities throughout North America mapping the human brain in a project that is expected to cost some US$3 billion over the course of the next 10 years; with broadly similar objectives to the Human Brain Project.

Tufts University

Although countless universities such as in Princeton's Neurosciences Institute conduct pioneering research on the human brain and neurological disorders. Huge collaborative efforts such as the HBP are necessary to make real paradigm shift discoveries in our understanding of the human brain, and ways in which to treat the disorders that affect it.

Our better understanding of how the brain works, and thus who we are carries with it enormous philosophical importance. At the same time, there is immense value in improving our understanding from a medical perspective. Neuro-degenerative disorders are perhaps the most silent of epidemics creeping up on our progressively ageing societies. The costs financially, but more importantly in quality of life are enormous — and growing.

Universities the world over from Tuebingen in Germany, Rutgers in the United States, UCL in the UK and Tel Aviv in Israel are working tirelessly in world class neurosciences departments. It is widely agreed that a fundamental, and detailed understanding of how the brain works is vital for us to be able to begin to roll back the growing tide of neurodegenerative disorders effecting our ageing populations.

Individual institutions are, however, making progress. Researchers at the University of Minnesota, Twin Cities for example have successfully reversed the effects of memory loss in laboratory animals, even after neurons have died; an unprecedented achievement.

As the importance of interdisciplinary research grows throughout the international research scene, it should come as no surprise that the neurosciences are not the only discipline investigating means of coping with the general trend of ageing societies in the world today.

Researchers at the University of Groningen for example, are focusing on healthy ageing, as in developing lifestyle changes and dietary habits that will enable us to stay active for longer as we grow into old age. The Jean Mayer Human Nutrition Research Center at Tufts University follows a similar philosophy in working to better understand the role of nutrition in the prevention of age-related chronic and infectious diseases.

Researchers at the University of Tokyo's Institute of Gerontology have gone so far as to begin work on developing a model for what a future aged society will look like, and how it will function.

University of Göttingen

Rich Medical Traditions

One would not be doing the role leading research universities play in the medical sciences justice by exclusively covering some of the most pertinent medical challenges we encounter today. There is a rich and diverse tradition of translating discoveries made in the lab through to the benefit of society. Without a doubt the medical sciences best exemplify this tradition of leading research universities.

In 1902, for example Sir Ronald Ross of the University of Liverpool was awarded the Nobel Prize for his discovery that mosquitos carried the malaria virus. Today, as malaria remains a major threat to global health a means of prevention is edging closer. Researchers at Vanderbilt University for example, have developed compounds that disrupt mosquitoes' sense of smell; a key milestone in the fight against the transmission of insect-borne diseases.

Following Sir Alexander Fleming's accidental discovery of penicillin in 1928, Professors Ernest Chain and Edward Abraham successfully isolated and concentrated it at the University of Oxford in 1940. Undoubtedly one of history's most important medical discoveries, for which all three received the Nobel Prize for medicine in 1945. Professors Richard Peto and Richard Doll have continued Oxford's tradition of leadership in matters relating to global health with their conclusive studies linking smoking and chronic disease.

Northwestern University

One of modern medicine's key challenges is undoubtedly the onset of anti-biotic resistant superbugs such as methicillin-resistant staphylococcus aureus (MRSA). Researchers at the University of Waterloo are making exciting discoveries in the quest for drugs that these viruses are less resistant to. At the same time, researchers at the University of Southampton are in the process of developing cleaning equipment based upon the ways in which whales communicate (microscopic bubbles). This new equipment will act as highly effective cleaning apparatus in hospitals with very little requirement for so many of the chemical cleaning substances used today.

Northwestern University's legendary Professor Rick Silverman invented Lyrica. Not only the most valuable invention ever produced at a university in dollar terms (tens of billions); also a vital drug for ailments such as epilepsy, Parkinson's disease and anxiety.

Perhaps even more interesting, but of less value from a monetary perspective was Professor Louis Lasagna's discovery that taking a pill, even one that had no medicine can have a "placebo effect". Also known as the "father of clinical pharmacology", Professor Lasagna's discovery during research trials at Johns Hopkins University is considered one of the most influential discoveries in the medical sciences going all the way back to the time of Hippocrates. In another one of the most important medical discoveries of all time, Professor Jonas Salk led the discovery of the Polio Vaccine at the University of Pittsburgh in 1952.

Researchers at the University of California, Davis immunology department have a vaccine for salmonella currently in development, another milestone discovery in the medical sciences that could have a positive impact on peoples' lives throughout the world.

Contemporary computing power combined with the volume of data available is opening up an entirely new avenue of research in the medical sciences. The University of Washington is one of the leading institutions in this field, currently producing some of the most profound data sets on global health and the prevalence of disease worldwide.

Transplant surgery is a last resort, reserved for only the most desperate medical scenarios; nevertheless it is often taken for granted as a standard medical procedure today. Without the work of Paris Diderot's Nobel Prize winning Professor Jean Dausset in his characterization of the genes that contribute to the histocompatibility complex; our ability to transplant organs between donor and recipient would be significantly reduced. Institutions such as the University of Pittsburgh have carried Professor Dausset's contribution forward. The 17,000 organ transplants conducted at Pittsburgh have established the university as the world's transplantation capital.

University of Waterloo

Bioengineering

The interdisciplinary research focus at leading universities has started to throw up some very intriguing new innovations. Perhaps the heartland of interdisciplinary research, the interface between medicine and engineering has the potential to bring the prospect of cyborgs, a hybrid of human and machine out from the imagination of science fiction, and into the reality of our daily lives. The enormous potential for commercialisation within this sphere of medical research adds further incentive for researchers. Perhaps the birthplace of the integration of engineering and medical sciences was the University of Minnesota, Twin Cities with Professor Earl Bakken's invention of the pacemaker.

Today, researchers at EPF Lausanne and Harvard University are working in collaboration to develop bionic eyes; electronic devices that could replace dysfunctional or damaged organic eyes. Researchers at the University of Melbourne have followed suit, and gone one step further, with the development of both bionic eyes, as well as bionic ears that could replace ears for those hard of hearing.

Far from having an exclusive concern with the senses, researchers at the University of Lund developed the first artificial kidney, whilst researchers at Rice University and UCLA are leading on the development of an artificial heart; and researchers at the University of Virginia have an artificial pancreas in development.

One of the additional objectives of the Human Brain Project (discussed above) is the development of next generation computers. Neuromorphic computers are forecast to significantly outperform the machines we use today by combining the processing power of micro-electronics with the flexibility of human intelligence; both an incredibly exciting and starkly worrying prospect.

Researchers at Brown's Institute for Brain Sciences have opted to compliment the brain with technological innovation, as opposed to using the blue print of the brain to enhance the capacity of existing technologies. Electrodes have been successfully fitted to the brain, enabling us to control everything from a computer mouse to a moving vehicle; a remarkable achievement with life changing potential for many sections of society.

Researchers at the University of Tsukuba have perhaps advanced our path towards integrating electronics and organics the furthest. The development of Hybrid Assistive Limb (HAL) is the world's first cyborg type robot. It works by detecting a weak muscle electric current that precedes actual muscle movement, and has been heralded for the impact it could have on the lives of the disabled.

Brown University

EPF Lausanne

Technology

The illustrious history of humankind's development of, and relationship with new technologies would be far starker if one tried to recount it without the influence of leading research universities. One could be forgiven for believing that we have somehow reached the apex of technological sophistication manifested in ubiquitous technology, instant telecommunications and Internet access culture and the ability to land robots on Mars. Reading over this chapter however, it is clear we are a relatively far distance from the apex wherever that may be. And if history is a guide, significant strides towards that place will benefit greatly from contributions of the world's leading research universities.

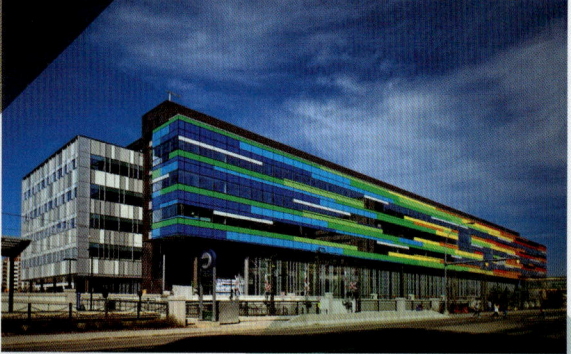

University of Alberta

Much of the work by solid state physicists such as Sir Neville Francis Mott at the University of Bristol and Julius Edgar Lilienfeld of the University of Leipzig contributed to the development of the transistor; perhaps the most important invention of the 20th century. Certainly, considered to be the foundation stone of the modern electronics and communications revolution. Of course, the invention of the transistor would have been impossible without the development of a thermionic or vacuum tube; discovered by Sir John Ambrose Fleming in 1904.

Throughout the middle of the 20th century, much of the core work relating to microelectronics was conducted in institutions such as Bell Labs; however as the 20th century grew older and the relative influence of research universities surged; pioneering work in microelectronics is in the main, conducted by researchers at leading universities. Taiwan University for instance, is widely recognised at the beginning of the 21st century as one of the most advanced institutions in the world in the development of microchips, circuits and semi-conductors.

Professor Hideo Hosono at Japan's Tokyo Institute of Technology has led the discovery of a number of superconductors and related materials. Anyone using an iPad should save a thought for Professor Hosono. His team is responsible for the high performance oxide transistor IGZO-TFT whose most common application is in the iPad. Virginia Tech's Professor Fred Lee is another engineer leading the ongoing revolution in microelectronics. As Director of Virgina Tech's Center for Power Electronics Systems, Professor Lee helped develop the multi-phased voltage regulator module; a vital piece of equipment contained in every single Intel processor since the year 2000.

Mathematics Professors John Kemeny and Thomas Kurtz helped facilitate an explosion in computer and software development with their co-development of BASIC, one of the most popular programming languages in the history of computing, that still exists in various different forms today.

Perhaps equally as important from a programming perspective is the development of the Lempel-Ziv data compression algorithm, first created

University of New South Wales

by Abraham Limpel and Jacob Ziv at the Technion in 1978. The Lempel-Ziv algorithm's influence has not diminished, as it remains in use in the vast majority of smart phones today.

The development of the World Wide Web, the basis of the modern Internet really needs no introduction. Few though are aware that Sir Tim Berners Lee, a leading professor of computer science developed the World Wide Web in partnership with colleagues at CERN. Now the director of the World Wide Web Consortium, and senior researcher with the Massachusetts Institute of Technology, Sir Tim Berners Lee is working to further the evolution of the Internet by encouraging government and major institutions to release their data for free re-uses. It is hoped that a revolution such as this will lay the foundation for an enormous wave of innovation and development of new applications for the Internet.

Phenomena such as quantum entanglement and quantum discord, first investigated by Albert Einstein in the 1930's have grown into foundation blocks of one of the most exciting areas of technological development, in that of quantum computing. The National University of Singapore, University of Sydney, University of California – Santa Barbara, Virginia Tech and the University of New South Wales are just a handful of the institutions racing towards the development of this new technology. In an almost mind-boggling effort of accuracy, researchers at the University of New South Wales developed the world's smallest working transistor. A single atom placed precisely in a silicon crystal, perhaps the basic building block for tomorrow's computers.

The computing revolution has not come without challenges, security being undoubtedly the concern most alive in the mind's eye. Cryptographers throughout the international research community appear to be in a perpetual state of competition, challenging themselves to crack ever more complex passwords and cryptographic protection systems. The world record currently belongs to researchers at Kyushu University who recently set a new record with the successful cryptanalysis of a 278-digit (923-bit)-long pairing-based cryptography. Although 142.8 days to crack a code does not sound too impressive, considering it was predicted to take several hundred thousand years; little over 4 months is quite an extraordinary achievement.

The pantheon of technologies that have been developed at research universities, brought into society and then disappeared as something better or more efficient replaces it is extensive and continues to grow. Equally, the exciting new technologies under development at leading research universities such as quantum computing, and the revolution in nanotechnology currently underway at pioneering institutions such as Northwestern University are set to keep this cycle in motion for centuries to come.

University of New South Wales

DISCOVERY OF STEM CELLS

JAMES TILL & ERNEST MCCULLOCH '48

IDEAS

DISCOVERY OF INSULIN

FREDERICK BANTING '16, '22
CHARLES BEST '21, '22, '25
J.J.R. MACLEOD
J.B. COLLIP '12, '13

TONY PAWSON

10 NOBEL PRIZE LAUREATES

82 RHODES SCHOLARS

FIRST SUCCESSFUL SINGLE AND DOUBLE LUNG TRANSPLANTS

JOEL COOPER
GRIFFITH PEARSON '49, '52

PAINTABLE SOLAR CELLS

TED SARGENT '98

RESEARCH

KYOTO PRIZE FOR STUDIES IN CELL COMMUNICATIONS

FREE THE CHILDREN

CRAIG KIELBURGER '07

MORE THAN 200 START-UP COMPANIES

ISOLATION OF GENES CAUSING EARLY-ONSET ALZHEIMER'S

PETER ST GEORGE-HYSLOP

OPPORTUNITIES

DISCOVERY OF COSMIC RAYS

JOHN CUNNINGHAM MCLENNAN '92, '00

RAY JAYAWARDHANA

EXOPLANET BREAKTHROUGHS

THE SPEECH-AID APP "MYVOICE"

ALEXANDER LEVY '10
AAKASH SAHNEY '12

THE FIGHT TO ERASE INTERNET CENSORSHIP

RON DEIBERT

238 CANADA RESEARCH CHAIRS

BOUNDLESS

IMPACT

500,000 ALUMNI IN 174 COUNTRIES

INNOVATION

14 SUPREME COURT JUSTICES

34 INTERDISCIPLINARY GRADUATE PROGRAMS

63 PROFESSIONAL PROGRAMS

STUDENTS FROM 175 COUNTRIES

4 CANADIAN PRIME MINISTERS

1,000 STUDENT CLUBS & TEAMS

800 UNDERGRADUATE &150 GRADUATE PROGRAMS

RAYMOND PARKER (CONTRIBUTOR)

POLIO VACCINE

FIRST SKIN-GENERATING DEVICE

AXEL GUENTHER
MILICA RADISIC

INVENTION OF PABLUM

FREDERICK TISDALL '16
THEODORE DRAKE '14
ALAN BROWN

Our international peers recognize the University of Toronto for our expansive range of disciplines, our depth of academic excellence and our life-changing contributions reaching across the globe. This remarkable breadth is preparing our students for the challenges of an increasingly borderless world.

Visit **UTORONTO.CA**

UNIVERSITY OF TORONTO

50 years of evolution in 10

intellectual fusion

excellence

access

impact

"One of the most radical redesigns in higher learning."
– Newsweek

Ten years ago, Arizona State University embarked on a mission to create a new model of higher education – a New American University – to simultaneously increase enrollment and performance. We have torn down academic walls and forged new disciplines, tripled research volume, created new campuses, and awarded 146,000 degrees while improving academic performance and impact across the board. And we did it with speed and scale that has garnered worldwide attention.

Watch what we do in the next decade.   **about.asu.edu**

ASU ARIZONA STATE UNIVERSITY

Chapter 3
Research & Development

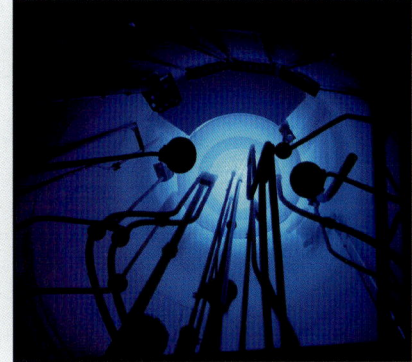

Mainz University

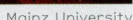
Mainz University

As the availability of public funding for research universities continues to shrink, and the level of priority placed upon basic research by the private sector wanes; the dynamics of international research and development activity are changing. Once the foundation of growth in the US economy, private-sector research laboratories, such as Bell, are increasingly becoming a thing of the past. Equally, policy shifts such as the introduction of the 1980 Bayh-Dole Act in the United States has made direct involvement in development of new discoveries a far more interesting proposition for leading universities.

Stony Brook University's President, Dr Samuel Stanley sees an opportunity for universities in the rolling back of corporate R&D funding.

"I think we're trying to expand that world now to have more innovative partnerships with industry, again we think that's very important as we look at research in the US, and I would suspect the trend is the same globally because all these corporations are multinational. There's a pullback of R&D, and particularly R at many of the major companies. You don't have a Bell Labs essentially anymore, and so innovation is naturally finding a home in the research universities, and the start-up companies that often emerge from those universities; or that are guided by faculty from those universities."

Rector Ursula Nelles of the University of Münster believes that Europe is following a similar path to the United States in this trend.

"As public funding is reduced more and more because of the financial crisis in Europe, funding has to be replaced somehow. We are under pressure, and in need of additional financial sources. You can compare it a bit to the situation in the United States during the early 70s, when 70-90% of the universities

were publicly funded; and during the last 40 years the relation between public and private funding has changed in favour of private funding. One can say we are 35 to 40 years behind, and now we are following those developments to a lesser extent."

Aside from the financial incentives at the heart of this shift; some of the basic drivers behind the evolution of collaborative research partnerships also come into play as the trajectory of some research universities' role as the source of new ideas, also moves to incorporate a role as the engines of economic growth.

In particular, the increasing cost and complexity of today's research questions make partnerships an obvious strategic direction so as to minimize risk. Furthermore, research relevance is increasingly important. By connecting with external partners, particularly in the private sector, research universities can ensure that what their staff and students are curious about has broader relevance. Perhaps of greatest importance of all is the sense of duty universities feel to the taxpayers that fund their research, to translate new findings out for the benefit of society and the economy as a whole.

Chancellor Mark Wrighton of Washington University in St Louis certainly feels this sense of responsibility. "We feel that with the great investment being made in us, largely by the public through federal sponsorship, we have a responsibility to move what we do to benefit society as rapidly as possible."

Dr Patrick Aebischer, President of EPF Lausanne couldn't agree more. "The transfer of technology is much more local and regional, and that brings taxes, and through the taxpayer, our institutions are financed, so if we do not take this very seriously, we would never get the taxpayer to invest in our institutions. I think we have a fiduciary responsibility to do that.

So I say we have three missions; education, education to research and transfer of technology to create wealth and a strong economy in the region where you are."

Vice President for Research Jim Hughes of the University of Maryland, Baltimore focuses on the extended capacity such partnerships bring in terms of translating discoveries. "In addition to being a good revenue source, what excites us about industry collaboration is that it also can help lead more quickly to new products being brought to the market, and ultimately that's how we're best going to impact areas such as health care; by collaborating with companies to get new products to the market."

Vice Chancellor of the University of Auckland, Stuart McCutcheon agrees. "Developing ongoing partnerships with the industrial sector is very important, not only because it provides support for our researchers and students; and potentially job opportunities to the students; but also because we want to take our research out into the community. If you take something like induction power, if you can find an international partner to take that technology up, to do the work needed to establish this as the standard by which other manufacturers will operate, then your technology has a much wider impact than if you are trying to do it yourself. So those partnerships are very important."

President Eric Kaler of the University of Minnesota, Twin Cities values industrial partnerships from more of an academic perspective. "I think it's maybe 10% financial and 90% recognition that the problems that our industrial partners can bring to us are deep, are intellectually challenging, and are fundamental enough to be appropriate for a university environment. It also is a real manifestation of our land grant charter."

R, D or R&D?

Whilst one would be hard pressed to find an academic that did not want to see their discoveries translated outside of the laboratory for the benefit of society, there are quite clear and obvious differences between how universities perceive their roles. Some are exclusively interested in fundamental research, where others are more concerned with linking together research discoveries through a technology transfer office; and many others that have established entire science parks containing corporate research arms, and a healthy spawn of spin-out companies whose roots reside in the ideas of faculty and students.

One would struggle to draw distinctions across geographical boundaries about the approach between different research universities. The 1980 Bayh-Dole Act was a real stimulus for research universities in the United States to focus on the development side of their research function. However, the nature and mission of individual universities is generally more important when considering their interest in developing discoveries into products and services. Engineering and technical universities such as Imperial College London, MIT, Technion and ETH Zurich are in general far more open to the development side of research. The key cultural difference between research universities and the external market however is timescale.

President Ralph Eichler explains ETH Zurich's perspective: "Our expertise is not in product development however, where industry can begin selling within the next half year. This is not our aim; we have more of a long-term perspective. Our PhD programs are for three years, so the problem that can be solved over the course of three years, that's the time scale that we try to help industry see the next step. We can afford to have failures in research, but industry not so much. We work with young people that don't know yet what doesn't work, so they have innovative ideas. The mix of young people with experienced scientists; this is what gives universities such strength."

University of Washington President Michael Young sees a balance emerging between how universities maintain a focus on basic research, whilst also contributing to the research and development priorities of their corporate partners. "In America, for example, four of the five big pharmaceutical firms have largely abandoned research. They do virtually no research anymore; they sort of buy it up. That's not in the long run a sustainable model for them, and the question is can we do development as we have with Boeing and other companies' research agendas that don't short change basic research; but do satisfy the needs for companies to do the translational and developmental work as well? I think that's very possible. I think we are absolutely going to have to move in that direction."

Caltech President Jean Lou-Chameau doesn't see why such relationships cannot be win-win. "Basically, our effort is to view the faculty as a partner, to view the investors, venture capitalists and corporations as partners. We want everybody to succeed, and we want everybody to feel good about the agreement that we put in place. There is no deal breaker in any discussions that we have, and we are not greedy; we understand that to bring an idea to the market takes much more than the idea. We work with our faculty to make them understand that, and also make the investor and the corporate understand the needs of the faculty. It has proven to be a very open transparent relationship that I think has served very well for Caltech and for our partners."

Bernhard Eitel, Rector of Heidelberg University although supportive of the trend towards translation, remains committed to basic research as the university's central mission. "We do not do industrial research, we do fundamental research but we prepare a little bit of the interface to application. So, I think the gap of translating basic fundamental research results must be bridged, and from our side we support building this bridge for translating fundamental research results into application, but we do not do application."

According to President Daniel Zajfman of the Weizmann Institute, basic research is the university's exclusive mission; there is very little direct interaction with external industrial partners. "We believe that our role is to provide knowledge. We believe that the role of the industry is to take that knowledge and to make a product out of it. We don't know how to make products. We have no idea. So there are two roles, and one must be very clear with whom does what because usually, there's a mixture of things and sometimes it can go in the wrong direction. So the way we work is we never set up our own companies. We own no start ups. We own no companies; our scientists are not working in any companies. We don't sit on the board of any of the companies and we don't invest our money in any start up, even if we believe it is the best possible product in the world. We don't, that's a very different scheme that many other places follow."

President Wallace Loh of the University of Maryland, College Park has a very different perspective. "I believe that as the 21st century progresses, the top universities will no longer be just research universities. They will be innovation and entrepreneurship universities. My slogan is I to I – Ideas to Impact. If we think of the research university as an ivory tower, and on the top of the tower, we are discovering new knowledge or creating new knowledge, at the base of that Ivory tower, we are building innovation incubators to translate those ideas to have practical impacts both in terms of creating business ventures that create jobs and to make an economic impact; as well as ventures that improve the human condition, but don't necessarily have an economic impact."

University of Texas MD Anderson Cancer Center

Structures & Approaches

The divergence of opinion and strategic approach between various research universities makes it quite a challenge for external collaborators to understand the approach looking from the outside in. Whilst relationships are of huge importance in understanding the entrepreneurial culture of respective universities, the infrastructure in place at different institutions is also a good indication of their respective approaches to industrial partnerships and technology transfer.

Belgium's KU Leuven for example is a prolific European university in the sphere of industry partnerships and translational research. The university first established a technology transfer office in the early 1970's — the first in continental Europe, and now has a well-developed infrastructure consisting of two science parks with a third under construction, and a number of business centres and incubators to support its industrial relationships and technology transfer operations.

The University of Hong Kong, and the University of Oslo on the other hand, place less of a priority upon industry collaboration and translational research; thus the infrastructure in place to accommodate these activities is less obvious.

The University of Utrecht has developed an entire innovation eco-system connecting laboratories and faculty with business centres and incubators so as to give high potential discoveries a good chance of making it to the marketplace. The University of Maryland and the University of Southampton have innovated with the introduction of site miners; business minded PhD's that are able to visit laboratories and make commercial assessments on the new discoveries made.

The University of Amsterdam has taken a more high level, collaborative approach through the Amsterdam Economic Board. Representatives from academia, the government and industry gather at regular meetings to establish priorities for the region; and then direct research collaboration accordingly.

Canada's McGill University has taken a novel approach to developing its commercial infrastructure, by integrating its research and innovation apparatus with the local community in Montreal. The Quartier de l'innovation is a collaborative effort between McGill and one of the city's engineering schools to attract investment into, and gentrify one of the old industrial areas of the city that has suffered throughout the broad wave of industrial decline that has been felt throughout the region in recent decades.

Others such as Johns Hopkins University believe that although infrastructure is important, it is really about the culture of their faculty to be driven to take their research findings through the commercialisation process that underpins their success. With that in mind, efforts are underway to strengthen the entrepreneurial spirit amongst faculty at institutions such as Washington University in St Louis. President Robert Brown of Boston University is unequivocal in his belief in the importance of culture and the sorts of people that create the right environment.

"I think it's mainly to do with the people you hire. You hire people who are never going to give up, they are always going to be inquisitive, they are going to garner the support, they are going to interact with people within the institution and outside to understand how to work on the most important problems. Working on problems that

University of Edinburgh

really matter, not problems that are only important to a small group of people; and then you judge them harshly through the promotion and tenure system so that you make sure that the ones you decide to keep are the very best."

Fortunately for Northwestern University, Professor Rick Silverman's multi-billion dollar discovery of Lyrica serves as motivation enough for faculty to think about research discoveries entrepreneurially. Vanderbilt University has successfully fostered the university's entrepreneurial culture, and is now looking to expand its physical infrastructure so as to accommodate the new waves of activity that have followed from institutes such as their drug discovery center.

President Michael Rao of Virginia Commonwealth University believes that entrepreneurialism will become an important factor in university recruitment policy. "Innovation and entrepreneurialism is fundamental to how higher education looks forward. So, realistically whom you hire is going to be important. So, when you are hiring faculty it's really important to hire with some knowledge of the extent to which a faculty member, regardless of discipline, is really committed to ultimately taking their ideas and commercializing them in the marketplace.

Although culture is of great importance, Principal of the University of Edinburgh Sir Timothy O'Shea is quick to caution against commercial concerns dominating the institutional environment. From a commercial perspective Edinburgh is one of the most successful research universities in the world, but has never lost a sense of its core academic values.

"I think that this issue is often looked at the wrong way around. The research focus at the University of Edinburgh is clearly defined by academic curiosity, however we are very good at taking ideas and basic discoveries through the innovative process until they realize commercial value. So far this year the University of Edinburgh has produced 35 spinout companies; last year the number was 42. The infrastructure for realizing economic value at the University of Edinburgh is excellent; however the research agenda here is not defined by any commercial concern.

Although the University of Edinburgh's philosophy is clearly to allow academics and researchers to follow their own interests and curiosities, the university is statistically comparable with MIT or Stanford in terms of releasing intellectual property and the production of spin out companies."

Intellectual Property Ownership

Intellectual Property (IP) rights are without doubt the most contentious issue that arises in negotiations between research universities and their external partners. The issue is particularly complex, transcending the fundamental principles of research universities in their right to publish research findings and pursue their own curiosities; as well as encroaching on the fundamental ethos of commercial enterprise in the right to own and control one's investments. Effectively a clash of cultures, that has up until now necessitated careful negotiations and compromise in order to work.

Chancellor of the University of Massachusetts, Amherst Kumble Subbaswamy summarizes the complexity surrounding IP rights and collaborative research.

"Traditionally, the attitude at universities has been to say we will only collaborate with industry if we can keep intellectual property or have co-ownership. The private sector of course lives and dies by taking risks, and therefore having access to any patents that might emerge from the money they've spent on collaborative research is often a critical issue in their business plans and operations.

Universities also live in a world of publications. We often care more about getting the news out about the knowledge created in our research than making money out of it, because that's the culture in universities. But of course industry wants to hold on to it even if they think it may be of a general interest, or even if they think it's not of much value, they don't want somebody else to find value in it.

So there are two different cultures in these collaborations and some obvious areas where they can clash because of our very different missions. So when the two come together we have to find compromises, and that requires wise people who have been on both sides in both sectors, and it requires give and take, and that's why it's so hard I think."

Increasingly however, there is a growing view that following the euphoria of the Bayh-Dole Act, expectations of huge growth in patent related revenues led universities towards a policy of vigorously protecting their IP; and limiting its ability to reach the broader community. University of Delaware President Pat Harker advocates this perspective.

"My personal view on this is that universities tend to hold too tightly to their intellectual property, as a result they sometimes strangle it. I want to ensure that the university's interests are protected, but I'd rather loosen up a little bit our hold on the IP so that we can get it out into the world to make a difference."

The University of Glasgow has responded to the risks associated with over-protection of IP with a pioneering approach - Easy Access IP. Principal Anton Muscatelli explains the approach.

"The essence of Easy Access IP is that for the vast majority of research and development innovations produced at the university that have no immediately obvious commercial value; a one page licensing agreement is made available to the general public and private sectors to explore ways in which such innovations could be made commercially viable, or used to benefit society. There are a few simple conditions to this approach such as; acknowledgment must be made to the University of Glasgow when technologies we have developed are put into use, and that the IP must be used for the benefit of the economy and society within three years of the licensing agreement being signed, or the IP is returned to our institution. The core reasons for us implementing this model are both to assist with the continued benefit of the economy and society, as well as to continue to raise the profile of the University of Glasgow within the context of our research capacity and the discoveries we continue to make."

The rationale behind Glasgow's pioneering approach has not been lost on fellow institutions throughout the international community. The University of New South Wales has followed suit with a very similar approach, with IP available on a use it or lose it basis for industry. The University of Minnesota, Twin Cities has employed a similarly liberal approach to intellectual property. According to President Eric Kaler, the underlying philosophy behind the Minnesota Innovation Partnerships program is that the partnerships in themselves are more valuable than the royalty streams that may or may not result from them.

"The premise of the Minnesota Innovation Partnerships program is a company can come here, if they accept the option of working with the university for a very small upfront fee, we basically say: 'We will extend you an exclusive license to any technology that comes out of the partnership.' We aren't going to quibble over ownership and what the university shares or anything else. We are favouring the partnership and the other benefits of the partnership more than what we might get in a royalty stream."

University of Würzburg

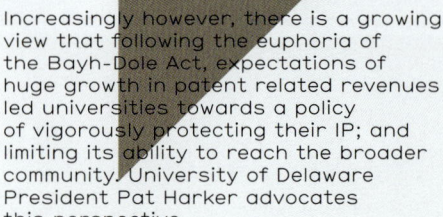

VU University Amsterdam

On the other hand, many universities consider the protection of IP as an important responsibility. It is indeed questionable according to President Michael Young of the University of Washington whether or not the easy access approach is effective in creating the right incentive structures to bring new discoveries to the external market.

"I think (Easy Access IP) is misguided because, at the end of the day my experience has been to really get the technology out the door, you need some serious infrastructure that links the business community, and the university much more closely. Simply opening the doors and saying, 'Come and take whatever you want', I think experience has proved that not a terribly effective approach...

In the initial period following the passing of the Bayh-Dole Act in cases when there was no intellectual property interest, the technology and the ideas were exploited less than 15% of the time. When you could take intellectual property interest in it, it was exploited 65% of the time. So, there have been attempts at the open door policy that have not really worked, and my experience has been that in order to justify creating the infrastructure that really does get the stuff out the door, you have to create incentive structures."

Cornell University

Dr Tony Frank, President of Colorado State University agrees with President Young's sentiments.

"I think the idea that we shouldn't protect the intellectual property of universities; the discovery should just be out there. I think some of that actually misses the point; that if an idea or discovery is not protected, it's hard to get a commercial sector partner to pick it up and invest in it. Then sometimes it sits on the shelf and it doesn't really go anywhere. I think you can actually go the reverse direction and too much open exchange of intellectual property can actually hurt the commercialization of IP."

Reconciling public and private sector cultures presents a considerable challenge to President of Texas A&M Dr. Bowen Loftin; particularly when focused upon the issue of IP.

"IP ownership is always a big challenge. Many universities like ours, especially public universities, assert ownership of the IP of their faculty, even though they may be paid to do the work by a private sector organization. So, that's sort of a difficult bridge for a company to overcome is, 'Why am I paying you and then you own the property you have created with my money?' We work through that pretty hard, and we provide licensing approaches for companies who have invested in research here that are attractive to them. So, we have been able to bridge that gap a bit, but it is still a struggle to explain to a company why we own the IP they paid us to develop. That's one point that just has to be worked on continuously."

One thing is clear, that the IP debate has some distance to run given the divergence in views between leading universities. With this in mind, Vice-Chancellor Ian Young of Australian National University stresses the importance of understanding and compromise.

"It's a matter of having an open mind and coming to every negotiation with an understanding that in any partnership, a successful partnership is about all the parties actually prospering from it. So in commercialising intellectual property, there's got to be something in it for the university, but there's also got to be something in it for your commercial partner there as well."

Chapter 4
Teaching, Learning & Beyond...

Georgia Institute of Technology

The rigours of the global economy continue to place ever-greater demands on today's graduates. Increasingly the requirements of the world's leading employers range from a combination of arts and sciences skills, international awareness, multi-cultural confidence and language ability. Universities' pedagogical approach has had to adapt with a diverse array of options from interdisciplinary and problem based learning options, through to study abroad programs designed to help equip graduates for the growing sets of requirements expected for success in today's globalized economy.

Equally, and perhaps of more importance to our economies and way of life has been the growing emphasis from universities in helping students become directly involved in research, and foster their own entrepreneurial spirit. Success stories such as those of Mark Zuckerberg, Chris Klaus and Steve Jobs have started to serve as a great inspiration to young people. The traditional approach to university, whereby an undergraduate degree was enough proof of ability to then step into a corporate career have passed. Increasingly our destiny is in our own hands.

Universities are now preparing young people to create companies, jobs and even industries themselves using the skills they learn combined with their own sense of youthful imagination and creativity. Equally, developing potential solutions to major global challenges are not the exclusive domain of politicians and leading academics; young people are just as capable provided they develop the right level of understanding. Universities today are the perfect platform to develop that level of knowledge and understanding, and then let the path of curiosity, creativity and imagination take its own direction.

President of Virginia Commonwealth University Michael Rao passionately believes that the university experience serves as the first step for today's younger generation to really make a difference in the world.

The University of Glasgow

"Getting a degree at VCU, we tell students over and over, is not just taking 40 courses; it is not just accepting transmitted knowledge. It's about critical thinking. It's about problem solving. It's about developing, in the course of your four years here, a passion to lead in an area, to solve a problem, to create something that's never been created. Ultimately, that's my dream for this institution. I want to see that all of our students ultimately have the ability to create value and to really develop a budding sense of what their contribution would be in the world."

Something about Everything
or Everything about Nothing?

One of the most pronounced pedagogical innovations in ensuring young graduates are equipped with the necessary skills to work at the highest level in today's globalized economy is the shift towards interdisciplinary teaching and learning. Universities are increasingly developing dual degree programs, introducing new options for students to combine their areas of interest, as opposed to the more rigid traditional degree program. Some are even giving students the complete freedom to develop their own degrees. As one would expect however, the approach to this is very mixed; whereas some universities perceive interdisciplinary learning to be one of the most important tenets of a modern university education, others fear that this approach will ultimately dilute the disciplinary expertise one could expect to achieve from traditional pedagogies.

Students at Brown University for example, are simply admitted to the university as a whole. There are no pre-defined degree programs or schools and faculties that students are assigned to. This "Open Curriculum" approach was pioneered back in 1969 at Brown; whereby students select a major area of study and then compliment with their own interests, however eclectic they may be.

The approach at Georgia Tech is similar with the introduction of the X-Degree. Students effectively have the freedom to integrate their own curiosities into their study program. Engineering degrees in particular have traditionally been quite rigid, pre-defined affairs. The introduction of programs like the X-Degree has brought far more flexibility and creativity.

The interdisciplinary model is increasingly being adopted in Asia as well. The National University of Singapore has introduced a broad based curriculum, whereby students will spend approximately 60% of their study time on their core degree subject, and the rest a combination of complimentary programs defined by individual student curiosity.

The "Melbourne Way", recently introduced at the University of Melbourne has interdisciplinary learning as one of the foundation components. For Professor James McCluskey, Vice-Chancellor for Research, the benefits are clear. "Breadth means that students have to be taken outside of the disciplinary area that the primary degree was in. So we find a lot of running off and sampling business, or sampling law, or sampling languages. Some of the students do further studies in musical areas in which they have skills, as well as many of the scientists doing humanities and arts subjects to broaden their thinking, and

ending up being much better at writing things than they would have been if they had just studied science. So the breadth component has been a really important innovation in the Melbourne Way because it has meant the students that emerge are just that little bit broader, and just that little bit more exposed, and no longer narrowly defined by core subjects."

The University of Western Australia (UWA) has also followed this approach. 2012 was the first year that the institution's new undergraduate curriculum was rolled out. UWA has condensed 70 different undergraduate courses into five broad programs – science, arts, commerce, design, and an elite B.Phil. program for the most gifted students.

Given the administrative challenges surrounding organising interdisciplinary learning, Chancellor Randy Woodson of North Carolina State has encouraged its development with a focus upon specific problems or competitions.

"Interdisciplinary research is easy to envision because scientists, engineers and others tend to come together to address big problems and bring their science to the table. Interdisciplinary education is more of a challenge because curricula are designed to be deep in a field of study, and it's a little harder to take students out of that box and give them the exposure to broader disciplines. So, what we're trying to do here is to create opportunities for students to come together across colleges in majors to address, whether it is a design problem, or some emerging technology issue. We are trying to create this environment through various kinds of contests and various kinds of disciplines. We're trying to give students a way to come together across the university to work in teams to address important research questions."

ETH Zurich's unique approach involves rigorous first year training in the basic natural sciences such as physics, chemistry and maths before being able to broaden one's disciplinary horizons in subsequent academic years.

Whilst interdisciplinary learning sounds great, there are also some cautionary perspectives, in that the growing enthusiasm for the trend could overshadow the importance of a good foundation of understanding in particular disciplinary areas. President Joseph Sung of the Chinese University of Hong Kong certainly subscribes to this perspective.

"We do have some multidisciplinary courses but we have to a strike a balance. If it is a double degree with a shorter time and cannot really go into providing the proper education of either of the disciplines, then we will not do it. We do have, for example,

University of Frankfurt

California Institute of Technology

National University of Singapore

joint programs between law and business and also medical and business school joint programs and so on but we have not been creating a lot of double degrees. If it is a double degree, we have to make sure that it is actually adding value to the student's learning progress and not just because they can get an additional degree because of that."

Rector Axel Freimuth of the University of Cologne also considers the disciplinary approach to still be of greatest importance.

"We have a strong tradition in the disciplinary approach, and of course the faculty strongly want to preserve that because somehow the professors are convinced that this subject is very important, and they are always convinced that you have to go into detail. In fact, they are right. You have to go into detail at some points definitely so that you know how you do that. I mean, not going into detail is the biggest mistake you can make from my point of view in academic education because you want to have people with degrees that are able to solve problems and have in-depth knowledge."

Rector of the University of Tübingen Bernd Engler's perspective takes both sides of the debate into account, placing particular emphasis upon awareness of where useful synergies are.

"The University of Tübingen supports the idea that excellence is primarily disciplinary excellence, and you have to know the basics of your discipline. However what we want our students to be much more aware of is the methods that other disciplines apply, which could easily be applied to the discipline that you are majoring within. I think it is the awareness building that is more important."

The philosophy at the University of Bern takes on more of a progressive approach. Undergraduate studies are firmly rooted in the disciplines, however a more interdisciplinary twist comes into play as students reach masters and PhD level.

The debate goes on, and will continue as the external environment influences how universities are organized, and what students expect. Increasingly however, young people are being given the freedom to follow their heart and intuition in what really interests them; having faith they will find what they love to do on that path. Similarly to research, our own curiosity is perhaps the best guide for us to define how we find our path in life. Increasingly universities the world-over are helping to facilitate our pursuance of such curiosities through their study programs.

Mainz University

University of Rochester

Innovation in Teaching

The shortcomings of the traditional university teaching model, whereby students are lectured to in an illustrious grand hall by a single professor have long been recognised as insufficient in developing the necessary skills to ensure success for graduates in the broader global economy today. On top of that, countless technological innovations have expanded the capacity of universities to be able to offer additional teaching platforms, and resources to students that further enhance their learning experiences.

Problem-based learning is one of the most prominent of pedagogical innovations. First developed at Canada's McMaster University, President Patrick Deane provides an insight into how the practical approach works.

"Students learn through basically a problem-based approach. If you think of an educational method based on the analysis of, and response to practical problems in the field. This is the discovery, and it characterizes much of what is done across campus in many, many disciplines."

Another key challenge for universities is to ensure that students are actively engaged in course materials, and important skills such as the ability to formulate arguments and debate them confidently are well developed in graduates. The collegiate structure synonymous with the Universities of Oxford and Cambridge is perhaps the best example of an intimate teaching and learning approach working well in the world's leading research universities.

Vice Chancellor of Oxford, Professor Andrew Hamilton is a strong believer in the multiple merits of the collegiate approach.

"The collegiate structure is deliberately designed as an incubator for interdisciplinary learning and development. We don't have a specific college for economists or medics, but each of the 38 colleges contains a mixture of students and faculty from a range of different departments. Students will be surrounded by chemists or historians, depending upon their degree choice. But when they return to college they have the opportunity to converse with philosophers or languages students. This fosters the open-minded, interdisciplinary approach that we treasure so much at Oxford, and the same time applies for graduate students also.

The tutorial teaching method is at the heart of the Oxford experience for undergraduates, and is unique to Oxford and Cambridge. It fosters very close, direct engagement between students and academics. This involves weekly or twice weekly meetings between students and their teachers; and there is no place to hide. The tutor, a leader in their field, will discuss the subject for an hour with usually no more than two students. Students must be on top of their material: they will need

Pierre and Marie Curie University

Aarhus University

University of Auckland

to be able to present their ideas and arguments in a structured and ordered way. This is an excellent system in that it enables our graduates to marshal their thoughts and arguments in a clear and logical way. It is a system that builds intellectual confidence because the students are engaging with leading academics.

By the time our students graduate they have learnt debating skills that allow them to challenge their tutors and the received wisdoms of their respective fields. In my view, this is exactly what higher education is all about, developing critical and analytical thinking as opposed to simply absorbing information. This approach is the foundation to Oxford's long-held tradition of fostering innovation."

Unsurprisingly, new communications technologies are playing an ever more important role in how leading research universities deliver course materials to students, and expand upon the availability of their own teachers and lecturers. Innovations such as Coursera now make it possible for students in Australia, Germany or Brazil to virtually attend lectures in the United States.

Monash University's Vice Chancellor Ed Byrne is a firm believer in this sort of innovation and open-minded teaching approach.

"Monash University is very much committed to the concept of a blended education, whereby students are exposed to a variety of pedagogies and innovative approaches to teaching environments and technologies; so as to give them the best possible learning experience. We are very much on a journey, as knowledge becomes increasingly globalised we are on a path towards always applying the most appropriate technologies and techniques to ensure that our teaching is easily available in the most appropriate and effective formats.

We will often suggest for our students to watch an outstanding lecture from, for example, a Nobel laureate at Stanford or MIT covering quantum mechanics as a means of preparation for one of our own course series. It makes a great deal of sense to make use of these new formats and opportunities as they become available."

Many universities also emphasize more abstract skills through their teaching and learning approach. Caltech, for example has an honour code whereby students take exams in their own time and space; simply being trusted not to cheat. Caltech President Jean-Lou Chameau considers this aspect of institutional culture vital to learning outcomes.

"I think that in the university the most important thing we can teach our students is integrity and to have a good sense of ethics. Caltech is committed to the honour code; it is something that's been in place for a long, long time going back 60-70 years. It is important to the culture that the students are extremely committed to it. There is a strong culture to behave in the right way. Basically we are

asking people to be good citizens and to respect each other, and that I believe is very important and it is clearly part of the Caltech culture."

Leadership is also a critical skill that the world's leading universities are working ever harder to develop in their graduates. Universities such as Texas A&M, the University of Illinois, Chicago, Oregon State University and the University of Minnesota, Twin Cities have some of the most active programs; encouraging students to actively work on community projects and contribute to the communities that form an important component of the university's eco-system.

Whilst a university education is an important component, it is far from being the only ingredient in young people's aspirations to enter the professions. Practical industry experience is an area of growing import both in the eyes of employers as well as developing the right skills and confidence levels in fresh graduates. Universities have responded to this challenge through the introduction of a raft of industry placement options whereby students can get hands on work experience either in a commercial or research capacity whilst studying for their degrees.

The University of Waterloo has the world's largest co-operative study program, placing thousands of students each year with an array of public and private sector partners throughout the international community. According to President Feridun Hamdullahpur the co-operative program is at the heart of the university's mission, and of great significance for graduates' career aspirations.

"The University of Waterloo has always had a solid foundation in experiential learning, and the cooperation and collaboration between business and academia. Our co-operative program is world class. We have always wanted our students and researchers to have frequent exposure to real world problems and real world applications; but to always think about these entrepreneurially. The best way to grow the university in this way has been to collaborate very closely with the private sector and external partners.

As its stands, approximately 60% of our students participate in our co-operative education programs, where students alternate academic study terms with experiential work terms, gaining hands-on experience in business and public sector organizations. There is an increasingly diverse array of international locations for our students to choose from.

The co-operative education opportunities experienced by Waterloo students are a great deal more than a route to graduate employment. They provide an excellent platform for University of Waterloo students to learn valuable skills in business and management that can be developed in almost any sphere of life whether that be academia, research, business or all three."

Tomorrow's Leaders

The general retrenchment in OECD economies in recent years, home to the vast majority of the world's leading research universities, combined with a broad aspirational shift in many young people away from working in blue chip corporations has stimulated most leading universities now to encourage their students to become directly involved in research and development.

The pioneering examples set by industry leaders such as Mark Zuckerberg, Sergey Brin and Steve Jobs have re-calibrated what leading young minds want to achieve with their lives. It almost seems as though the graduate career path is no longer fulfilling or worthwhile enough, and that the challenge of entrepreneurialism; although more daunting is far more rewarding financially, philosophically and spiritually. The entrenchment of today's economic malaise has only served to amplify young people's aspirations to express themselves and their ideas through companies of their own.

At the same time, many of the world's major challenges and unanswered questions crave innovative new ideas from those with no fear of failure; that have not yet been drawn into the dogma of established knowledge surrounding them. Perhaps the most competitive environment in global higher education today, is amongst universities trying to attract the best post-graduate students.

Universities are re-organising structurally and philosophically in response to these trends. There are now far more opportunities than before for young people to get directly involved in research and start to test some of their own ideas. On top of that, universities are developing a wealth of new infrastructure from advanced technology transfer offices and new business incubators through to innovation competitions so as to stimulate and facilitate as much creative entrepreneurial activity from the student body as possible. As many university missions expand to take on the role of innovator into the economy, students are increasingly being looked upon as the largest untapped resource of innovation in the world economy.

The idea of going into business independently is tremendously daunting. The risk and responsibility involved is enormous, universities are now positioning themselves as a cushion for much of that weight. Helping to develop the necessary skills in their students so as they can guide their ideas and inventions through the commercialisation process and into the real economy for sustained, long-term success.

Israel is perhaps the most successful country in the world with regards to university innovation and student entrepreneurialism. At the heart of this success are institutions such as the Technion. President Peretz Lavie is passionate about the university's economic impact.

University of Alberta

Cornell University

"The reason Israel is a start-up nation is because of Technion graduates. 85% of our engineering students are involved in the high-tech sector in Israel, 42% were involved in starting a new company, and one in four has at least one patent after graduating from the Technion. Most of them are in managerial and leading positions, and if you take the number of Israeli companies registered on the NASDAQ, which is close to 120, we are second or the third after the US. I think China now has about the same number. Half of them are either funded or run by Technion graduates. So, there is something in the education of the Technion that instils in the students the spirit of pioneering, innovation, entrepreneurship and leadership."

Remarkable successes such as these have brought about great change amongst universities in recent years. Encouraging innovation and entrepreneurialism amongst students are some of the most pertinent priorities for university leaders and their administration. The ways in which this is approached however, are subject to significant variation.

The University of Washington for example has a very strong focus on engaging students in hands on research; thus creating the right atmosphere and knowledge set for entrepreneurial ambitions to be realised. President Michael Young is particularly proud of the sheer volume of research hours conducted by students.

"What we are trying to do is create an environment in which students can be the next generation of knowledge creators. So, getting students into the laboratories and giving them opportunities to take what they learn in class and find a concrete way to try to develop that in a practical way is very important. We have about 6000 undergraduates involved in a significant way in research. By significant, we counted that as ten hours a week or more. About a million hours worth of research is done by our undergraduates on an annual basis."

Indiana University sponsors undergraduate research through specific programs such as the Jesse Cox Scholars Program. Funding is provided through faculty to encourage and support undergraduate research programs. Given the enormous success of this approach, the university is investing additional funds directly into its expansion.

The University of Maryland, College Park is going a step further by integrating entrepreneurial studies into the core curriculum with a new academy. President Wallace Loh is a passionate believer in the potential of entrepreneurially minded students to rapidly develop into engines of innovation and economic growth.

"We have just created an academy for innovation and entrepreneurship. We are saying every single graduate of this university will be exposed to innovation and entrepreneurship by the time they graduate regardless of your discipline. You can be major in economics, English literature, business or engineering, and you will be exposed to innovation and entrepreneurship just like every student has to take basic English or basic math and so on. This will be part of the core curriculum."

Complementary courses in entrepreneurialism are a common approach. The University of Toronto, and the Technical University of Munich have both linked entrepreneurship together from both a teaching and research perspective. With infrastructure in place such as Toronto's MaRS Innovation site where students can develop their new found knowledge in practice. UC Santa Cruz's computer games design undergraduate degree enables students to work directly with faculty on ideas for computer game development, integrating their entrepreneurial ideas directly into the core curriculum.

National University of Singapore students have some of the best opportunities of all. Students are able to spend a year abroad in one of the world's leading entrepreneurial hubs such as Silicon Valley, studying at a partner university and working as an intern in one of the many institution's start up companies.

Competition as the source of innovation has emerged as another key strategy for universities in helping encourage their students to develop their entrepreneurial and creative skills. 40% of Georgia Tech's students are directly involved with research. To help stimulate business ideas the InVenture Prize has been introduced. Carrying a first prize of US$15,000 and a firm commitment from the university's technology licensing office to help commercialize winning ideas, InVenture offers an excellent incentive for students to develop their ideas more concretely.

Although not traditionally associated with university education, the focus upon entrepreneurialism has grown in accordance with young people's aspirations. Research, long held as one of the core missions of leading universities is now being extended out to the real economy on multiple levels. Although the translational potential of faculty level research is a more familiar route, student level research and development is an exciting and growing platform; widely considered to herald vast potential for future innovation and economic development.

The Path to Global Citizenship

In today's international conversation, the idea of global citizenship within the context of globalization seems almost dogmatic. It is not until you think about what it really means and the opportunities that it presents; that the concept starts to seem daunting and difficult to achieve. One could naturally be forgiven for believing the very notion of being a global citizen the reserve of jet setter businessmen, politicians or the rich and famous.

Whilst the discourse of our interconnectedness has become all too familiar, and discoveries such as the Higgs Boson continue to prove it on all manner of levels. The key challenge that we are presented with as young people is how to make an abstract theme such as this, become a concrete reality in our every day lives.

Internationalization is a very broad concept, globalization for universities in a sense. We are not yet fully certain about what it means in its entirety. One thing is certain in that it translates into opportunity. The world's leading 200 research universities are all working to extend themselves at an international level. This means global research collaboration, furthering our understanding of global phenomena and developing solutions to global challenges.

It also means educating global citizens. Every top 200 university is eager to attract curious, hard-working young people regardless of where they call home. The obstacles to studying what interests us the most, at the places that offer the greatest value continue to disintegrate. University is the platform for young people to begin their path towards global citizenship. Traditional notions of the past, in that one's choices are limited by national boundaries are less and less relevant. The differences in approach, structure and value one can expect from universities around the world vary enormously. The opportunities available continue to defy traditional limitations; the world is increasingly ours.

My Life at Rochester

"I've loved every moment of being a Rochester student."
—Karen Farbman '14

TODAY AT ROCHESTER

7:30 am:	Head to the gym, get breakfast on the way back to the dorm
10 am:	Take test in math class on complex variables
11 am:	Head to Hebrew class (stay for office hours with Professor Andreatta)
12:15 pm:	Study for quantum physics class, grab lunch
2:15 pm:	Take shuttle over to Eastman School of Music for flute lesson
3:50 pm:	Shuttle back and grab a chai tea at Starbucks
4 pm:	Chamber orchestra: rehearsal (practice that Dvorak piece beforehand!)
6:15 pm:	Make dinner in my room, email my sister favorite photos from my internship in Germany last summer
7 pm:	Ballet Performance Group: rehearse for upcoming cancer fundraiser
9 pm:	Go to resident advisor meeting
10 pm:	Start paper on Jewish mysticism
11:30 pm:	Lights out!

About me

- Was raised in Connecticut
- Chose Rochester for its science and music programs, research opportunities, and academic freedom
- Am a physics and music major, math minor
- Am also a Take Five Scholar, which gives me a tuition-free fifth year on campus to explore Jewish studies
- Play the flute in University's Wind Symphony, Symphony Orchestra, and Chamber Orchestra
- Dance in the on-campus Ballet Performance Group
- Serve as a resident advisor and math teaching assistant

The University of Rochester's unique open curriculum allows for both focus and flexibility at one of the world's top research universities. Maybe you'll complete a double major, study abroad, intern at a local or international company, conduct individualized research, or take lessons at our Eastman School of Music. Or maybe you'll do it all. If you want to study what you love, collaborate with faculty, do real research, and shape your own education, Rochester might be the place for you. **Discover your academic path at Rochester.**

UNIVERSITY *of* ROCHESTER

Rochester, New York, USA
www.rochester.edu/mylife

Research Excellence

Globally renowned award-winning faculty, including a Nobel Laureate and winners of the Fields Medal, the King Faisal International Prize, and other awards.

Recipient of one of 9 World Premier International Center Initiative (WPI) grants allocated by the Japanese Government.

Active in research collaboration, especially with other Asian countries.

High-Quality Education

9 schools and 14 graduate schools covering a wide range of disciplines, such as medicine, natural sciences, liberal arts, social sciences and engineering.

Recipient of major Government grants for international education activities, including the Global 30 Project, the Re-Inventing Japan Project, and the Leading Graduate Education Program.

One of 13 universities entrusted with Global 30, a Government project to promote the internationalization of education. Offers a wide range of specialized fields taught in English, from natural sciences to humanities and social sciences.

NAGOYA UNIVERSITY

http://www.nagoya-u.ac.jp/en/

Internationalization

10,000 undergraduates and 6,000 graduate students, 10% of whom are international students.

Over 300 different lectures offered in English, from natural sciences to humanities and social sciences.

More than 200 international partners.

Sufficient support and services provided for international students and scholars.

Over 600 dormitory rooms provided for newly-arrived international students.

A leading national university

located in the heart of Japan

Rank › 151 – 200

Name › Zhejiang University
Region › Asia/Pacific
Country › China
Founded › 1897

www.zju.edu.cn

Core Research Strengths

First established in 1897, Zhejiang University's long history of academic enquiry has culminated today in the university pioneering an interdisciplinary research approach to the research enterprise. Although broad based with approximately 44,000 students, 8000 academic staff and in excess of US$450 million in research funding, Zhejiang University is very much synonymous with core research strengths in chemistry, engineering and the computer sciences.

Zhejiang University's extensive network of government sponsored research laboratories specialise in its core base of chemistry, engineering and computer science, as well as being complemented by strengths in agriculture, biotechnology and microbiology.

The National Laboratory of Silicon Materials is one such institute at ZU, combining the university's strengths in multiple disciplines as well as the basic and applied facets of research to better understand the basic behaviours and qualities of silicon; then to apply this knowledge towards the development of cutting edge semi-conductors. Over the course of the past 10 years, this multiple award-winning lab has developed 10 patents, and published over 300 academic papers covering continued developments in our understanding of, and applications for silicon based semi-conductors.

Established in 2002, the Centre for Engineering and Scientific Computation (CESC) is one of ZU's leading interdisciplinary research facilities. Further underscoring the university's strengths in engineering and computer science, this institute works to expand ZU's research capacity throughout the disciplines with the assistance of high performance computing. The CESC draws in expertise from a variety of disciplines such as physics, energy engineering, civil engineering and engineering mechanics to work on complex research questions associated with areas such as computational algorithms and software, high energy physics and the physics of new materials and computational structure technologies.

Major Discoveries

Zhejiang University retains a leading position with respect to Mainland China's universities in terms of journal publications and patent awards. Once referred to as the Cambridge of the East by renowned historian and biochemist Joseph Needham, ZU's rich tradition of innovation and discovery has seen countless developments throughout the engineering, chemical and computer sciences.

Researchers at ZU are at the cutting edge in the development of solid oxide fuel cells (SOFC's), developing new materials combinations that will maintain high energy conversion, low noise, low pollutant emission, and low processing cost; however bring down the high operational temperatures that have been the fundamental challenge associated with SOFC's up until today.

Partnerships, Innovation & Translational Research

Zhejiang University National Science Park, with a total area of 113 hectares has been established specifically to further expand ZU's group of research collaborators, and stimulate transfer of the technologies and innovations made at the institution into the real economy. Presently the Zhejiang Science Park has over 100 enterprises established, as well as 10 agencies providing potential entrepreneurs and established businesses with service and consultation regarding law, finance, investment, patent applications and technology transfer.

Through the International Relations Office, Zhejiang University continues to expand upon its portfolio of universities, government institutes and private sector companies working alongside the university in collaborative research. Similarly to most leading Chinese universities, a fundamental part of ZU's mission concerns fostering the linkages between research, education and the economy. International partnerships are welcomed enthusiastically; given the opportunity they provide to expose China's leading industries and research universities to the forefront of innovation at the international level.

Teaching, Learning & Student Life

Since its first enrolment of international students in 1979, Zhejiang University has since welcomed over 25,000 students from approximately 150 different countries. Students are encouraged to participate with research at as early a stage as possible in their career, with numerous opportunities for student entrepreneurialism also available through the ZU National Science Park.

ZU's long tradition of multiculturalism on campus has set the foundation for a vibrant and diverse student life, with numerous opportunities for extra-curricular activities in sporting, social, media and other such associations to complement one's academic endeavours.

Located approximately 180km southwest of Shanghai, a relatively small distance on the Chinese scale, students at Zhejiang University have good opportunities to branch out in their spare time and visit some of China's better known urban centres, whilst at the same time enjoying the relative calm and tranquillity at ZU's campus setting.

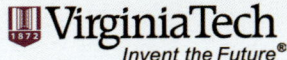

Rank › 151 – 200

Name › Virginia Tech
Region › Americas
Country › United States
Founded › 1872

www.vt.edu

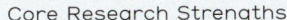

Core Research Strengths

Research at Virginia Tech is broad-based, but has world-class programs in applied sciences, engineering, and technology. These strengths are channelled to answer priorities across three broad themes: Energy, Materials and Environment; Innovative Technologies and Complex Systems, Health Sciences. The university is currently engaged in a number of exciting projects across these areas, says university President, Charles Steger.

"We are developing powerful, new computational tools to extract knowledge from formerly incomprehensible datasets. Our HokieSpeed supercomputer debuted in November 2011. It is among the fastest supercomputers in the world and is exceedingly practical. Supercomputing requires vast amounts of energy, but HokieSpeed is among the most energy-efficient. Virginia Tech also produced it at a fraction of the cost of supercomputers with similar capabilities. With it, our faculty and students tackle problems in science, engineering, and medical research that were once considered intractable."

An additional area of growing importance involves wireless communications and security, Wireless@Virginia Tech is an established initiative that focuses on the challenges of mobile devices, wireless networking, antenna advancements, and the creation of communications systems that are adaptive, yet secure. Virginia Tech has built a research environment that accelerates wireless innovation by crossing disciplines such as electrical engineering, computer science, mathematics, economics, and business. Our students go on to become leaders in academia, industry, and government. Given its location in 'coal country', it is understandable that the university has a significant energy focus too.

"We are responsible for research in sustainable energy sources for the state, nation, and world, as well as for exploring the socioeconomic and environmental implications of energy and coal use", says the President. "We have led the way in coal-mining reclamation research and are creating and refining the world's options for capturing and storing carbon dioxide, which contributes to global climate change."

Major Discoveries

Any recent device that contains an Intel processor — and that can be anything from a laptop to a smartphone — has a little bit of Virginia Tech inside. Intel, a multibillion-dollar global company that introduced the world's first micro-processor, built its new generation of computer processors with the help of Fred Lee, a Tech electrical engineering professor and director of the Center for Power Electronics Systems, a National Science Foundation Engineering Research Center. By 2000, every Intel processor used a revolutionary power supply source, known technically as a multi-phased voltage regulator module, which Virginia Tech helped to develop.

Partnerships, Innovation & Translational Research

One way that Virginia Tech seeks to boost the amount of research becoming commercially successful is through an innovative IP and royalty scheme. Any royalties or fees that come from a piece of research are evenly split between the university and the authors. The university also has strategic research alliances with major corporations, explains President Steger.

"We have one-off relationships with various corporations that fund research; sometimes we get a tiny part of it, sometimes a much larger part of it. For example we have a major advanced manufacturing research centre that we operate jointly with Rolls Royce to develop next generation jet engines. We also work, for example, with General Motors Corporation in our transportation research area." As a rule Virginia tends to form these alliances with larger organisations and has research relationships with many of the Fortune 200 companies. The key to this success, says the President, is a combination of consistency and flexibility. "Each major project has a separate agreement but we also have established a protocol, which enables the IP negotiations to go very smoothly."

Teaching, Learning & Student Life

One of the most positive elements of the learning experience at Virginia Tech is the effort that the university makes to ensure that the student learning experience is shaped by the multidisciplinary nature of its research. To that end Virginia has established

The Research Institutes of Virginia Tech to manage interdisciplinary study. This collaboration between disciplines isn't confined to campus either, says President Steger. "We have put together some joint course offerings with several institutions around the world, and we have actually designed a lab with our students and engineering students at Technical University of Darmstadt and Shanghai Jiao Tong in China and they are all working on the same project. We connect through the Telepresence that Cisco provided us; it's really quite high quality television communications. They meet on a regular basis, they are all working on the same project, and I think the learning experience has been really fantastic for them."

Indeed, internationalism is a strong part of a student's life at Virginia Tech. While other institutions are only now trying to attract international students, Virginia has been doing so since the 1940s and currently has the largest international student population in Virginia. It's also keen to send its students in the other direction, says the President. "We are strongly encouraging our students to spend time studying abroad to learn about other cultures."

For those students who stay on campus Virginia has plenty to offer. One of the first things that a keen architectural lover may notice is that most of the university's gothic buildings are made from "Hokie Stone," actually local limestone, which is cut from the university's own quarries and has distinct brown and pink hues. The university is located in the small town of Blacksburg, which has a population of less than 40,000 and located about 250 miles from Washington D.C. The town's laidback charm and well-planned amenities have seen it win several lifestyle awards. For example in 2011 American magazine Business Week named it the "Best place in the US to raise kids". Seated in the northern Blue Ridge Highlands region of Virginia there is plenty of nature for students to explore. The area is also filled with history and students can tour the 18th century Smithfield Plantation and countless 19th century churches.

Rank › 151 – 200

Name › Virginia Commonwealth University
Region › Americas
Country › United States
Founded › 1837

www.vcu.edu

Core Research Strengths

One of the nation's top research universities, Virginia Commonwealth University spends more than $260million in sponsored research, bringing together faculty experts and student scholars to collaborate across multiple disciplines. The university is very comprehensive in terms of education, and a large component of its research has been focused on the area of medicine and applied medicine.

The university's research is shaped by its strategic plan, known as 'Quest for Distinction', says President Michael Rao. "Whatever you are working on in a scientific context, it's probably going to take some time. So, along the way you have to have the ability to understand the social, behavioural or even historical aspects of what you are doing. Cancer and diabetes are perfect examples. So, we know that it's unlikely that in our lifetime we will completely cure cancer and diabetes altogether. But we do know that there are some behaviours, there are some things that we as humans do that are causing us to be more predisposed to having cancerous growths, and to diabetes and related illnesses. So, it's important for us to research these social and behavioural areas, because knowing what you can do to avoid some of those things can save lives. That means you can't really just have the scientists work on cancer, you have to have the social scientists as well."

Part of the thinking behind this reasoning is a desire to see that research results in life-changing improvements. "Our commitment has been to the kind of research that has a short timeframe to the marketplace in terms of its value. We are interested specifically in research that cuts across the entire institution and all of its disciplines."

Major Discoveries

In keeping with Virginia's emphasis on bringing research to markets, some of its best discoveries are applications that are already improving lives around the world. For example Hemospray is an endoscopic haemostatic device that stops bleeding. Another similar product is Animalclot, which was introduced in the veterinary medicine market. It's an electrospun haemostatic bandage that aids veterinarians who are conducting surgery.

Partnerships, Innovation & Translational Research

Virginia welcomes partnerships with private-sector firms, but only if they benefit the university, says President Rao. "Partnerships are absolutely encouraged, but they also need to be well-defined. You have to have good policy that gives you an opportunity to set parameters around what constitutes our role in a partnership. We are not for sale, so, we cannot sell our souls as an institution. One of the ways you avoid that is by having a good strong policy that gets tested through a centralized research office that helps folks decide what can be an engagement or contractual agreement with an external party or not."

The university follows a similar approach with IP. "Many of the IP decisions are done on a case-by-case basis and with good rationale for why what we are doing will add real value. If it's something that we don't believe will have real value or could compromise our integrity as an institution then we won't pursue it." The university is more active when it comes to academic partnerships and has agreements with 15 different institutions throughout the world. One of the prominent examples is VCU campus in Qatar.

Teaching, Learning & Student Life

VCU is situated in the heart of Richmond, the capital of Virginia. It is a diverse cultural city, surrounded by historic neighbourhoods, parks and the James River. The river offers many opportunities for a day out. Its banks are ideal for picnics or pleasant walks, while Richmond's location at the fall line means that it also has many rapids, which are great for white water rafting.

With more than 1 million people living in the greater metropolitan area there are also plenty of restaurants and shops throughout the city. The spread of attractions across the city is one of the great charms of Richmond – which is often called 'a city of neighbourhoods'. Each neighbourhood has its own distinct character and identity, and all are recognised by Richmonders as zones, almost as though the city were a collection of several small towns.

The university's 31,000 students are split between two Richmond campuses – Monroe Park and MCV – and satellites in Northern Virginia, Qatar and Charles City County. One of the special features of life on campus is the close interaction between students and faculty, says President Rao. "There is a climate at VCU in which students and faculty tend to learn together. Part of our definition of a research university is that research is a part of everyone's learning. It's not segmented. It's not separated from teaching. So, when we have faculty members who do research, we really expect them to engage students in that research."

To further that goal the university has created the Center for Teaching Excellence at VCU. "It's a very strong dedication of resources with teaching experts who faculty can go to, to help establish presentations, use technology and engage students in ways that they haven't been able to engage before."

Rank › 151 – 200

Name › University of Wuerzburg
Region › Europe
Country › Germany
Founded › 1402

www.uni-wuerzburg.de

Core Research Strengths

Julius-Maximilians-Universität Würzburg (or "Julius-Maximilian's University of Würzburg"), takes its official name from two prominent figures in its history. However, nowadays it is more commonly known as the University of Würzburg. The institution has roots going back to the 15th century and in that time has established itself as one of the world's leading research universities. Some of its discoveries, like the first observation of the X-rays by W.C. Röntgen, have changed the world.

Historically the university has focussed its research efforts in accordance with 'The Four Pillars'. They are: humanities, law and economics, life sciences, natural science and technology.

But despite its illustrious history the university is not hidebound by tradition. Indeed in the last twenty years it has reorganised its research departments to improve capacity for interdisciplinary research. The first multidisciplinary steps were taken in the fields of medicine, science, and humanities. These interdisciplinary centres have by now become an internationally prominent trademark of the University of Würzburg. The funding for many of these research centres comes from the German Research Foundation (DFG). Winning funding from the DFG is a highly competitive process and serves as recognition of the university's success.

One of the university's main strengths is in medicine. Würzburg uses an array of specialised institutes, such as the Rudolf Virchow Centre for Experimental Biomedicine, to focus its medical research. The university hospital is another important part of research infrastructure for this field. It allows researchers to study and understand conditions and it's also good for the patients. After all, they receive excellent medical care and benefit from the latest standards in medical therapy.

Würzburg's recent push to create all these research centres has pushed the University into the top-level of German academic institutions. It also does well on the international level, rating highly in many disciplines of science, especially biology, medicine, physics, and psychology.

Major Discoveries

Over the years the university's researchers and scholars have won 14 Nobel prizes. The most recent came in 2008 when Haral zur Hausen won the Nobel Prize in Medicine for his discovery of human papilloma viruses causing cervical cancer. Not only is it a prestigious award but it's also a discovery that could save many lives.

Partnerships, Innovation & Translational Research

The restructuring of the university's research infrastructure has helped to attract increasing amounts of private funds. The university takes many innovative approaches to helping its research attract commercial interest. One example of its unconventional approach is that it enters teams of students and researchers into the Business Plan Competition of North Bavaria (BPWN). Each team has to come up with a business plan or technology application with commercial potential. The top ten ideas receive €500 – it might not seem much but it's enough to motivate students and junior academics – and attract attention from potential business partners. In the 2012 competition three of the university's team finished in the top ten.

Another, more conventional, way that the university interacts with the outside world is with academic alliances. It has 54 university partnerships in more than 35 countries across the world. It also has 56 agreements on a faculty/institute level and more than 300 Erasmus partners. Having so many Erasmus partners has led to an influx of international students. At present around 1,700 international students attend the university from more than 100 source countries. There are also scores of international professors or researchers visiting the university at any one time. They're served by The International Office, which acts as the central reference point for any of the university's international endeavours.

Teaching, Learning & Student Life

One of the best things about studying at Würzburg is getting to know the city. It's known locally as "a young old city", because on one hand it has more than 1,400 years of history, while on the other it's got one of the youngest populations in Germany. That creates a wonderful mix of old architecture and traditions with a vibrant, dynamic culture. Traditional wine festivals and taverns do a bustling trade next to clubs and cellar parties. And for students looking to get away from the stresses of work there are a variety of parks and gardens to relax in. If that's not enough, the city is surrounded by wonderful countryside. The university itself is located in the spacious Hubland Campus, which sits on a hill at the eastern edge of the city. In 2011 the university decided to open Campus Nord, to accommodate extra students.

Despite its illustrious history Würzburg's university is still a relatively average size with just 24,000 students and 400 professors. Yet the university's age is clearly reflected in the course catalogue available to students. Classic subjects that have been taught there for hundreds of years sit alongside new additions. For example students can now choose to study in emerging fields such as Nanostructure Technology or Technology of Functional Materials.

UNIVERSITY OF WATERLOO

Rank › 151 – 200

Name › University of Waterloo
Region › Americas
Country › Canada
Founded › 1957

www.uwaterloo.ca

Core Research Strengths

The University of Waterloo (UW) has strategically developed its core research strengths over several years, focusing resources and investment on areas that present major challenges for people and our planet over the course of the coming century. The University of Waterloo also has a thriving entrepreneurial culture, with researchers working closely alongside industry, enabling discoveries made at the university to reach broader society as quickly and efficiently as possible.

The University of Waterloo's external research funding is close to US$200 million each year, with core specializations in hi-tech engineering fields including nano-technology, automotive manufacturing, quantum computing and quantum cryptography. On top of these core strengths, UW's strategic focus has evolved into international leadership positions in areas of critical societal importance, including: ageing, energy security, biotechnology, sustainable energy technologies, and water security.

Given the complexity of these issues, the University of Waterloo has for many years pioneered a multidisciplinary approach to research and discovery, developing broad-based research programs to serve society's pressing needs. President Feridun Hamdullahpur elucidates further on the importance of interdisciplinary research to UW: "These are global issues that require a great deal of imagination throughout a range of disciplines to really get to their essence and understand them in all of their complexity. This approach is very much encouraged at the University of Waterloo throughout our portfolio of strategic research strengths and beyond."

Rooted in its commitment to societal relevance and high-impact research, the University of Waterloo is a leader in several key fields. Most recently, UW cemented its leadership role in quantum and nano research, opening the Mike & Ophelia Quantum-Nano Centre on campus in the fall of 2012.

Major Discoveries

UW researchers are at the forefront of developing new technologies for tomorrow's automobiles, with numerous breakthroughs having been made in nanotechnology and material sciences for the development of next generation components such as batteries for electrical vehicles now undergoing the transition into commercialisation.

Researchers in the university's chemistry department have made some very exciting discoveries in the field of antibiotics, and in particular developing drugs that are less susceptible to resistance from viruses such as methicillin-resistant staphylococcus aureus (MRSA).

Researchers from the International Research Initiative on Adaptation to Climate Change (IRIACC) are working to devise strategies to combat the impacts of climate change of coastal megacities such as Lagos in Nigeria.

Partnerships, Innovation & Translational Research

Rooted in the industrial heartland of Ontario, UW's tradition of collaborative research continues today with the largest co-operative education program of its kind in the world. Researchers and student entrepreneurs work alongside hundreds of industrial partners and spin off companies in collaborative research operations and student internship programs.

President Hamdullahpur believes that innovation, collaboration, and partnership are key to UW's future, just as those values have shaped its rich and unique heritage "The University of Waterloo's origins are rooted in the legacy of industrial development in this region. The University of Waterloo was founded, in part, to provide the engineering and scientific skill that Canada's rapidly industrializing economy needed. As a result, the philosophy of the university has always had a solid foundation in experiential learning, as well as the cooperation and collaboration between business and academia.

Our co-op program is world class. We have always wanted our students and researchers to have frequent exposure to real world problems and real world applications; but to always think about these entrepreneurially. The best way to grow the University in this way has been to collaborate very closely with the private sector and external partners."

UW's tradition of collaboration and partnership with private enterprise has led to the development of an exceptionally entrepreneurial student body and faculty. Many market-leading innovations, in sectors including technology and telecommunications, trace their origins to the university. Research in Motion, the manufacturers and operators of BlackBerry, are perhaps the best-known example of a growing portfolio of companies founded by UW faculty, students and alumni.

Teaching, Learning & Student Life

Approximately 60% of UW students participate in co-operative education programs, gaining valuable experience working alongside leading companies in either a research or internship capacity. External collaboration both in terms of research and working experience is without a doubt the most distinctive aspect of the University of Waterloo experience. Throughout their experiences at UW, co-op students can expect to engage with real world challenges, working with companies and organizations across a broad range of fields and industries.

There are a number of additional support programs such as VeloCity; where student entrepreneurs are constantly exposed to business leaders, mentorship and coaching. They subsequently come out of this residence with a very entrepreneurial spirit, developing start-ups of their own and developing into business leaders of the future.

Students graduating from UW can expect to be very well prepared for enterprise and industry. President Hamdullahpur highlights the institutional philosophy: "The University of Waterloo is a place that guarantees academic excellence, research excellence and a very integrated approach to learning, whereby experience forms a foundational element. Our research cuts across barriers and is very much strategically relevant to many of the major issues and challenges that we face today."

University of Waterloo
Canada

THE UNIVERSITY OF WARWICK

Rank › 151 – 200

Name › University of Warwick
Region › Europe
Country › United Kingdom
Founded › 1965

www2.warwick.ac.uk

Core Research Strengths

The University of Warwick is a public research university located in Coventry, United Kingdom. It was founded in 1964 as part of a government initiative to expand the number of universities in the UK. It took its first intake of 450 undergraduates in 1965 and now has in excess of 24,000 students. It is ranked in the top 10 of all UK university league tables.

In 2000 the University opened its new Medical School. Warwick now commands an annual research budget of £86.3million. Interestingly Warwick is one of the few universities in the UK which generates more of its income through its own earned income activities than it receives in Government grants, which has allowed it to invest generously in research facilities and undergo rapid growth.

Warwick is one of the UK's leading research universities and the quality and impact of its research is demonstrated by its excellent research rankings. The last Research Assessment Exercise (RAE) was conducted in 2008 with Warwick ranked at 7th overall in the UK (based on multi-faculty institutions) and the top University in the Midlands region.

In order to respond effectively to global challenges, Warwick has now reconfigured its research around the Global Research Priorities programme (GRPs). This focuses the University's multidisciplinary research on key areas of international significance, bringing together expertise from across faculties and departments. Current themes for the GRPs are: connecting cultures; energy; food security; global governance; individual behaviour; innovative manufacturing; international development; science and technology for health.

Major Discoveries

Professor Christopher Zeeman is one of the founders of engulfing theory in piecewise-linear topology and is credited with working out the engulfing theorem (independently also worked out by John Stallings) which can be used to prove the piece-wise linear version of the Poincaré conjecture for all dimensions above four. Warwick astrophysicists have also discovered a number of exoplanets.

Partnerships, Innovation & Translational Research

Warwick pursues a policy of internationalisation through collaborations with other institutions. In particular its alliance with Monash University in Australia and it is the only European university to join a partnership with New York University (as part of a consortium to establish a Center for Urban Science and Progress (CUSP) in New York City.

Another part of the strategy is the Warwick in Africa Teaching Project. An educational programme, funded philanthropically. Warwick students spend part of their summer vacations teaching Mathematics and English in Johannesburg, Dar Es Salaam and Accra; a parallel scheme enables African teachers to enhance their classroom skills

Warwick undergraduates and postgraduates experience a unique programme of in-situ study in Venice, using the University's full-time base in Venice, the Palazzo Pesaro Papafava. This offers a unique European location, encouraging collaborative projects with international partners. The success of the programme was recognised in 2010 when Warwick won the Venice Prize for Cultural Communication.

One of the main points of liaison with external partners from the private sector is Warwick Ventures Ltd. It creates and nurtures spin-off companies based on University research. 60 companies have been created since 2000, with a combined annual turnover of around £10 million.

Teaching, Learning & Student Life

The University of Warwick covers 400 hectares on the borders of Coventry and Warwickshire. Through careful design, landscaping and stewardship, the University campus has become increasingly attractive even as it has grown steadily in size. There has been extensive tree planting and the creation of eight lakes and ponds, which have provided a haven for wildlife as well as a very pleasant location for the local community.

Like many leading universities, Warwick has a very international feel with students and staff from over 120 different countries representing a diversity of backgrounds. But where perhaps Warwick stands out is the community feel on campus. It provides a great resource for the local community, with excellent facilities open to the public such as Warwick Arts Centre and the University Sports Centre.

This university campus is constantly evolving and developing. In the last five years students have benefitted from the Warwick Digital Laboratory, which was opened in 2008, while Warwick Arts Centre, including Butterworth Hall, underwent a £6.9 million redevelopment that was completed in Spring 2009. In January 2010 the newly rebuilt Students' Union building was re-opened. A new hall of residence, Bluebell View, opened in 2011 and a further new 527-bed hall, Sherbourne, opened in 2012. The University's Sports Centre completed a £1.5 million pound refit in 2013.

A £92 million National Automotive Innovation Campus (NAIC) is to be established alongside Warwick's WMG depart (Warwick Manufacturing Group). NAIC is funded through the UK Government and WMG's industrial partners Jaguar Land Rover (JLR) and Tata Motors European Technical Centre (TMETC).

A new International Institute for Product and Service Innovation at WMG, was completed in 2012. The idea is to provide Midlands SMEs with access to leading product and service design technology, while it should also give students cutting edge experience.

universität
wien

Rank › 151 – 200

Name › University of Vienna
Region › Europe
Country › Austria
Founded › 1365

www.univie.ac.at

Core Research Strengths

The University of Vienna was founded in 1365, making it the oldest university in the German-speaking world. Vienna is organised into 15 faculties and four centres, which research a wide array of disciplines ranging from Catholic theology to computer science. Currently there are 6,700 researchers at the university, around 1,000 of whom are in projects financed with the aid of third-party funds.

In order to foster particularly innovative fields of research that have not yet been established at the University of Vienna, inter-faculty research platforms have been provided to act as organisational units.

The fact that Vienna is so comprehensive and works hard to link subjects is one of its biggest strengths, says Rector Heinz Engel. "We have so many people and so many disciplines here that there is a lot of room for cooperation and for trans-disciplinary research, and we are one of the few universities that can even do trans-disciplinary research between humanities and natural sciences."

One good example of that is Vienna's Institute for Archaeological Science, says the Rector. "It is quite unique, at least in Europe, in that archaeology is practised using methods from physics or chemistry, such as geo-prospecting. So they have ground-penetrating radars, not looking for mines but looking for archaeological things. They use airplanes and mathematical computer science methods to analyse the ground, looking for hidden objects, and that is a thing which can only be done at such a large university."

Not all multidisciplinary projects involve fields that contrast so dramatically, concedes Rector Engel. "For example molecular biology is a field that is hard to combine with humanities. Instead we can cooperate very well with all the different life sciences in our university and then the other disciplines at the Medical University."

Major Discoveries

The university has been making important discoveries for centuries, however, one year in particular is deserving of a mention. In 1936 the university had the proud distinction of two members of staff winning a Nobel Prize. Victor Frank Hess won the Nobel Prize in Physics for his discovery of cosmic radiation. At the same time Otto Loewi won the Nobel Prize in Medicine for discoveries relating to chemical transmission of nerve impulses.

Partnerships, Innovation & Translational Research

The University of Vienna Technology Transfer Office is tasked with promoting the transfer of technology to industry. Meanwhile a separate body, the Technology Transfer Group, manages the patents and other intellectual property of the University of Vienna. It does through licensing and by assisting University start-up companies. It also supports researchers in establishing research collaborations with industry.

Any leading university must have an international outlook, says Rector Engel. "We achieve this through our students, 20% of whom are international. It is also evident in our research output. We don't just publish in English or German but in all kinds of different languages. This means that our research can be of importance in Eastern Europe, it can be of importance in Southern Europe, it is read by people in France because it is written in French, it is read in China because it is written in Chinese, and things like this; this is also part of our strength that we have all different kinds of people who come from all over the world and speak different languages."

Teaching, Learning & Student Life

Vienna has many claims to fame: classical music, many sites of historical interest and a vibrant theatre and restaurant scene – it is one of the world's great cultural capitals. Indeed any international student will love the 'inner city'; three-square kilometres of stunning architecture, highlighted by palaces and churches. But Vienna isn't just a place for the highbrow visitor. Most students also enjoy exploring the outer districts, where the bulk of Vienna's 1.7 million inhabitants live. There's the Naschmarkt (snack market) where Viennese go to eat, the 7th District with its huge shopping street and Bohemian flair; and the 19th District which has vineyards inside the city limits. Yet often what impresses foreigners most is far more prosaic, with many visitors being struck by the city's clean functionality.

The university also has plenty to offer. With 91,000 students it is one of the biggest in Europe while its 188 study programmes, offers the widest range of study programmes available in Austria. The university places a particular emphasis on research-led teaching and undergraduates are given ample opportunity to involve themselves in projects with faculty members.

This commitment to producing young researchers continues throughout the study programme. For example, the University of Vienna has set up new, structured Doctoral Programmes, the so-called Initiativkollegs (Initiative Groups) to complement the previous doctoral studies with individual supervision. Thus, the University of Vienna supports young scientists and academics in shaping their careers according to international standards.

Another noticeable feature of student life in Vienna is that classes are a melting pot of people from around the world. Thanks to its membership of the ERASMUS-Partnership students from approximately 130 countries attend more than 10,000 lectures at the University of Vienna every year.

EBERHARD KARLS
UNIVERSITÄT
TÜBINGEN

Rank › 151 – 200

Name › University of Tuebingen
Region › Europe
Country › Germany
Founded › 1477

www.uni-tuebingen.de

Core Research Strengths

The Eberhard Karls Universität Tübingen is one of Europe's oldest universities and a major research force throughout a diverse range of academic disciplines with the exception of engineering. Without a doubt Tübingen's main strengths are in the medical sciences for which its research capabilities have been recognised and awarded by the German government's Excellence Initiative. The "University of Excellence" title reflects Tübingen's farsighted institutional strategy, quality teaching, and above all, ground-breaking research strengths across a number of disciplines.

Under the excellence initiative, the University of Tübingen is home to an excellence cluster, the Center for Integrative Neuroscience (CIN), and the Graduate School for Learning, Educational Achievement and Life Course Development (LEAD). The work carried out at CIN helps improve diagnostics and treatment for impairments of movement, memory and perception, as well as providing impetus for technological innovations. The LEAD Graduate School examines how to provide greater access to high-quality education and improve the broad base of education in today's information-based society.

The university also has an impressive network of infrastructure to support research, says Rector Bernd Engler. "For example, we have the first GMT laboratory for the university production of peptides, which will be able to help vaccinate against various cancers. We have even been granted permission to patent our own medical production."

Major Discoveries

One of Tübingen's greatest discoveries came in 1869 when Friedrich Miescher discovered nucleic acid, the substance that carries DNA. He has since been dubbed the "Grandfather of DNA"

Partnerships, Innovation & Translational Research

Rector Engler knows universities are keen to attract funding to improve research capabilities but he thinks it's important for institutions to be realistic. "You don't get an external partner for

nothing. They only come if you already have your strengths." Indeed it was Tübingen's strengths in medicine that led to a partnership with the Hertie Foundation. "They have built a huge research building with hundreds of researchers here in Tübingen. Meanwhile the neuroscience faculty is now partnering the National Health Initiative for neurodegenerative diseases."

Tübingen also has four collaborative research centers, is involved in three trans-regional collaborative research centers, and hosts a number of research training units – all sponsored by the German Research Foundation. Tübingen's core research strengths have also led to the establishment in Tübingen of three Max Planck Institutes and four Helmholtz Association medical research centers.
When it comes to private-sector partnerships, things are more complicated, concedes Rector Engler. "We have moved towards big company cooperation in recent years but we still have a long way to go. We have cooperation with BASF – a large chemical firm – with some important medical companies and with Siemens. These alliances are primarily in the field of health science and health technology."

When it comes to academic partnerships, the university sets a wider net. It has partnerships with more than 150 educational institutions in 45 countries, particularly in North America, Asia and Latin America, as well as with all the countries in Europe. This academic internationalisation also extends to the student body, with some 12% of students in Tübingen coming from abroad, and many of the University's German students pursuing part of their studies in another country. The university has also established three external branches – in China, Japan and South Korea.

Teaching, Learning & Student Life

The town of Tübingen is a beautiful, historic university town. The first thing a visitor will notice is the picturesque rivers, that go right through the centre of Tübingen. Stay a little longer and they may start to realise why it has often been voted as having the best quality of life in Germany. Without doubt one of the main reasons for Tübingen's

special atmosphere is the university. With 28,000 students living among the nearly 90,000 inhabitants, the university completely dominates the town. The student effect is even more noticeable because it is not a campus university, but is spread across 175 buildings throughout the town. There are four areas with a major concentration of university institutions. The university uses a number of buildings in the old town of Tübingen, some of which date back to the foundation of the university.

For Rector Engler this unique setup has many advantages. "Everything is shorter because you spend less time travelling. We've also noticed that it improves interaction between disciplines, because you can just walk down the road and you are in different academic environments, all of which are approachable and close."

Given the university's strong medical focus, one of the most important areas in the town is a spot known as the Klinikum. That's where the university's 17 university hospitals and 12 specialist medical centres are. It is said that medical students need exposure to a variety of patients, well the Klinikum certainly has that, with a total of 1,500 beds, more than 67,000 patients and 330,000 outpatients, per year.

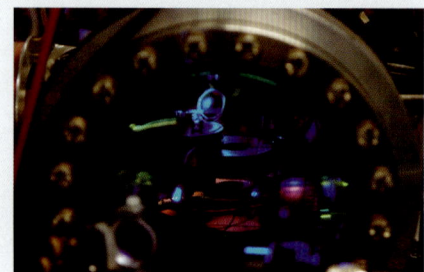

筑波大学
University of Tsukuba

Rank › 151 – 200

Name › University of Tsukuba
Region › Asia/Pacific
Country › Japan
Founded › 1949

www.tsukuba.ac.jp

Core Research Strengths

"Imagine the future" is the slogan for the University of Tsukuba; rooted in the university's emphasis on research as a means of having a direct impact on the future. Vice President Akira Ukawa defines Tsukuba's institutional philosophy "For the University of Tsukuba it means we can define our own future, as people we can understand the challenges that we face and the opportunities that there are in the world. We can imagine the future ourselves. That's what it means to me. Our philosophy is that knowledge-based and research-based solutions are available. We just need to put in the time and the effort, then we can do whatever we want."

There is a strong tradition in fundamental sciences such as in physics and chemistry, but concurrently there is a push for innovation through cross-disciplinary research and collaboration.

The university is also involved in the creation of new academic fields of enquiry. Tsukuba has been at the forefront of the research and development of supercomputing, in science and technology since the 1980s. Cybernics is an entirely new field that blends together robotics, neuroscience and information technology.

Researchers are innovating in the area of biological energy research, pioneering the development of oil from algae. Whilst in the life sciences researchers in the Centre for Behavioural Molecular Genetics are working to better understand the fundamental basis of our sleeping and waking cycle, heralding great potential for help with countless sleeping disorders.

There is also a significant amount of research undertaken in sports science. The Sport Performance and Clinic Laboratory (SPEC) looks at improving athletic performance through motion analysis, and was involved in preparing athletes for the London Olympics.

Major Discoveries

Tsukuba boasts three Nobel Laureates as past faculty members. Twice in physics, and most recently the 2000 chemistry prize for the discovery and development of conductive polymers.

Two scholars have recently received outstanding contribution medals from the Japanese government: Dr Yoshiyuki Sankaifor pioneering the field of Cybernics, and Dr Makoto Watanabe for his research on producing fuel from algae.

HAL (Hybrid Assistive Limb) was developed at the university, winning numerous awards. It is the world's first cyborg-type robot, which integrates a human body with a robot. It works by detecting a weak muscle electric current that precedes actual muscle movement and has been heralded for the impact it could have on the lives of the disabled.

Partnerships, Innovation & Translational Research

One of the university's key partnerships is the cooperation within Tsukuba Science City. There are 16 government and over 300 public and private research laboratories, many of which are in collaboration with Tsukuba. This cooperative research generates about $60 million dollars in funding.

There are two organizations for managing innovation and technology transfer. The Industry Relations and Technology Transfer Office (IRTT) was established to strengthen relations among university, industry and governmental institutions. Its mission is to contribute to the progress of industry and society by transferring research findings to the public. Knowledge transfer and industrial liaison is promoted through the Tsukuba Industrial Liaison and Cooperative Research Centre (ILC). Its mission is to support university-industry cooperative research, and facilitate the translation of technologies to industry. Both organisations are involved in the development and support of spin-off companies such as Cyberdine Inc and SoftEther Inc.

Teaching, Learning & Student Life

One of the largest campuses in Japan and set in the heart of the Tsukuba Science City, a location centred around 60 educational and research organizations with state-of-the-art-facilities, students benefit from a forward-thinking approach to teaching and learning. Tsukuba has a broad

spectrum of academic fields. There are nine undergraduate schools and seven graduate schools that incorporate disciplines such as sciences, humanities to sports science and art. The university emphasises interdisciplinary learning to promote a more rounded education so students are able to take courses across departments and count credits from other schools and colleges.

Tsukuba has a celebrated sporting tradition, with a top athlete-training centre that offers comprehensive support for the physical, mental and emotional aspects of competing in world-class sporting events. Sports departments across the board turn out high performing athletes that excel in national and international competitions, including the Olympic games.

Internationalization is a top priority and the university has set an ambitious goal of increasing the foreign student ratio to 1 in 4 by 2020. Tsukuba is one of the Global 30 Project universities – a specific infrastructure for establishing a university network of internationalization. This involves creating new English-based degree programmes at both graduate and undergraduate level in all disciplines and aggressively recruiting foreign faculty members.

For Japanese students there are efforts to improve language skills, and promote and expand dual-degree programmes with leading overseas universities. There is planned collaboration with other Science City based institutions and a thoroughly integrated community-based experience for international students on campus. Tsukuba currently has offices in China, Vietnam, Uzbekistan, Germany and Tunisia, which are strategic international frontiers for Japan; and partner universities in 57 countries and regions.

Rank › 151 – 200

Name › University of Tennessee — Knoxville
Region › Americas
Country › United States
Founded › 1794

www.utk.edu

Core Research Strengths

Established in 1794, the University of Tennessee – Knoxville is one of the United States' oldest universities, and the flagship university of the state of Tennessee. With annual research funding averaging out at approximately US$170 million annually, and 28,000 students spread throughout approximately 300 degree programs the institution is diverse in its expertise. Within this portfolio of diversity, there are however some specific fields that UT – Knoxville can claim to have world-class expertise in; namely agriculture, energy and engineering.

In partnership with the Oak Ridge National Laboratory, a US$1.6 billion facility at the forefront of United States' energy research; UT Knoxville researchers are working on the development of next generation technologies to ensure a sustainable and secure energy future. In quite a unique arrangement, there are nine governor's chairs shared between Oak Ridge and UT – Knoxville designed to attract some of the world's most talented energy related researchers to work at both institutions with salary responsibilities shared between the two. Smart grid and nuclear engineering technologies are particular areas where UT Knoxville and Oak Ridge are at the forefront of our international understanding today.

Material science is an area within engineering where UT – Knoxville is distinguished internationally. New facilities are presently under construction that will combine expertise from the university's engineering, physics and chemistry departments along with research expertise from Oak Ridge National Laboratory.

Partnerships, Innovation & Translational Research

UT – Knoxville's collaborative research efforts are not confined to Oak Ridge National Laboratory. The university is an active partner with both federal agencies, industry partners and counterpart universities at the international level. Industry partners include leading corporations such as Boeing and Eastman Chemical. Perhaps of greatest interest is the partnership alongside the National Science Foundation, whereby the world's fastest supercomputer housed at an academic institution – Kraken has been developed.

UT – Knoxville is currently in the process of developing incentive schemes for academic and research staff to transfer discoveries made at the university into the external marketplace.

Teaching, Learning & Student Life

With around 25 clubs, sporting life is an integral part of the culture at UT Knoxville. The football and basketball teams unify all students as well as the local community in their support; home fixtures are often carnival like events bringing together all aspects of the community involved with the university to cheer on the "Volunteers". The Anderson Entrepreneurial Center is at the forefront of UT – Knoxville's efforts to stimulate entrepreneurialism amongst the student community, providing additional support both in teaching and advice, as well as providing financial incentives through a variety of competitive processes for students to succeed in taking their ideas and innovations to the external market.

Back in the lecture hall, students can expect to be involved in research at an early stage, with the undergraduate office for research encouraging participation so as to ensure that students realise their maximum potential and get the best they possibly can from their degree. As well as the opportunity to get involved in research, students are increasingly able to follow the trajectory of research activities in their study programs – that is studying throughout different disciplines. The best example of that today is the interdisciplinary PhD in partnership with Oak Ridge Laboratory

for some of the world's brightest young minds to try to tackle the most complex questions surrounding our energy future.

With over 450 clubs and associations, the social life at UT Knoxville is open and vibrant. Students can engage in a myriad of activities from sporting challenges and recreation at the world-class facilities to preparing for a career in the media writing in one of the university magazines or blogs.

Looking forwards, the Top 25 Strategy is the flagship plan led by Chancellor Jimmy Cheek to improve the standing of UT – Knoxville in rankings and to raise the institutional profile at the global level. Raising the profile of diversity as well as recognition amongst international students is an important element within this overall strategy.

UNIVERSITY OF
Southampton

Rank › 151 – 200

Name › University of Southampton
Region › Europe
Country › United Kingdom
Founded › 1902

www.southampton.ac.uk

Core Research Strengths

Established in 1952, today the University of Southampton is a forward-thinking institution with a global reputation for engineering, computer science, optoelectronics, nanotechnology and medicine. The University of Southampton's coastal location also plays a significant influence on the University's research interests, with international expertise in numerous marine and maritime related fields.

As a hosting partner to the UK's world-class National Oceanography Centre, the University of Southampton is widely acknowledged as being an international leader in furthering our understanding of oceans and maritime environments. On top of this, the University has great expertise in maritime engineering, ranging from the construction of offshore drilling platforms to the design of cruise liners. The University of Southampton's maritime expertise also extends to less obvious, however equally interesting areas such as marine archaeology and maritime law. Expertise throughout the marine and maritime fields has culminated in the recent launch of the Southampton Marine and Maritime Institute (SMMI); set to be the world's leading institute for marine and maritime innovation, education and expertise.

Through the pioneering work of Professor Sir David Payne, the University of Southampton has led internationally for a generation now in the field of optoelectronics. Drawing upon the University's rich traditions in computer and web science, the University now leads in the development of our understanding and use of the Internet. This has culminated in the work of Professors Sir Tim Berners-Lee and Nigel Shadbolt pioneering the "Open Data Revolution" in the UK; whereby government institutions and corporations alike are being encouraged to release the enormous records of raw data they have stored so as to facilitate the development of new digital applications and innovations.

Major Discoveries

A new transistor made from graphene – the world's thinnest material – has been developed by a research team in Electronics and Computer Science. This could result in even smarter computerised communication and electronic devices in the future.

David Barker, Professor of Clinical Epidemiology at the University of Southampton discovered the relationship between low birth weight and the lifetime risk of chronic adult diseases, including ageing, heart disease, diabetes, osteoporosis, obesity and lung problems. This links the risk of developing illnesses in adult life to poor nutrition in the womb.

Partnerships, Innovation & Translational Research

The University of Southampton's traditions provides the University with an excellent basis for external collaboration, Vice-Chancellor Professor Don Nutbeam elaborates further: "The University of Southampton's history has always been that of a technical university, this focus was the forerunner of the institution ever since its creation 60 years ago. My sense is that this technical focus has always placed a natural emphasis upon working alongside business, for the ultimate mutual benefit of students, the University and our partners."

The University of Southampton today, is one of Europe's leading research universities with regards to external collaborative agreements alongside private sector partners. The University's collaborative agreements take place throughout a myriad of disciplines and companies. The newly established SMMI, developed in collaboration with Lloyd's Register, is the UK's largest private sector collaborative investment.

The University of Southampton also works very closely with Rolls Royce in computational engineering and vibration research, as well as long-standing partnerships with IBM, Microsoft and British Aerospace. In the field of high performance sports engineering, the University of Southampton is a centre of international excellence, contributing to significant UK sporting successes, including gold medals in the Beijing and London Olympics.

In technology transfer the University of Southampton is also world-class, with an impressive track record as a partner to business and the public sector and as a source of invention and innovation. The University of Southampton has an impressive record of commercialising its research by 'spinning out' companies. Since 2000, the University has spun out 13 successful companies in fields ranging from respiratory medicine to the discovery of new materials.

Teaching, Learning & Student Life

In distinction from most UK-based universities, the University of Southampton has pioneered the interdisciplinary approach to learning, with students able to modify their education's direction by mixing their course schedule with countless options available from the University's newly implemented standardised timetable. Vice-Chancellor Professor Don Nutbeam elaborates further on taking the benefit of this approach: "If a student were studying mechanical engineering they would be able to take complimentary courses, such as modules in business or a second language, so as to give them the range of skills to make the most of their core degree subject. The key objective driving these changes is to add breadth to depth. The way that I view this change is that we are giving students the opportunity to fully take advantage of their attendance at a broad-based research university."

The University of Southampton is well-known for its welcoming and vibrant Students' Union, with new arrivals at the University able to take part in numerous activities from sports to media broadcasting; as well as make new friends quickly both through the Union and the system of residence halls whereby by all first year arrivals are provided with accommodation alongside their newly arrived colleagues.

UNIVERSITÉ
PARIS DESCARTES

Rank › 151 – 200

Name › University of Paris Descartes
Region › Europe
Country › France
Founded › 1971

www.univ-paris5.fr

Core Research Strengths

The University of Paris Descartes began life as medical institution, but as time went by, more specialities were added. It still has a strong medical emphasis, with a health department that is known throughout Europe, but it has also expanded to cover humanities.
The university now has 17 disciplinary groups, each defining its own teaching and research theme.

Vice President Professor Arnaud Ducruix, believes that the core research strengths of the University Paris Descartes are in biology and clinical medicine. "These areas are where we have all of our excellent papers in major journals such as Nature & Science. We are also very strong at the interface between neuroscience and psychology and we have very good interaction between our clinical psychologists and neuro-biologists."

Another good partnership is between the chemistry and biology departments, says Vice President Ducruix "Given the rising importance of biotechnology to the pharmaceutical industry the combination of chemistry and biology has lots of commercial potential" notes the Vice President.

Paris Descartes University has also developed well-respected faculties in other areas. Indeed it is the only university in Paris to provide research in four wide disciplinary fields — science and technology, human and social sciences, law and economics and management.

In order to get the best of its strength across disciplines the university has restructured its research efforts. It has created new centres, known as the Paris Descartes University Institutes (IUPDs), while research focus is now organised in priority thematic axes (ATPs)

Major Discoveries

Alain Marty made recent discoveries in neurobiology for which he was awarded a medal from France's National Scientific Research Center (CNRS).

Partnerships, Innovation & Translational Research

The university's international academic alliance strategy is focused on Germany, Brazil, Canada, China and Russia, says Vice President Ducruix. In order to attract the very best students the university has developed a number of English-language courses in strategic fields, such as biotechnology, to make it easier for international students.

Unsurprisingly for a university with such medical expertise its main external partners are pharmaceutical companies and government health agencies. Both provide a steady stream of funding, says the Vice President.

Of course, the other way to interact with the private sector is through technology transfer. And when it comes to this theme Vice President Ducruix believes the university is one of the best in the country.

"We have an excellent approach to intellectual property that is very conducive to partnerships. French universities are often thought of as not being open to industry partnerships; however, I think our approach proves that to be wrong. One area of concern in France is a lack of industrial research and partnerships are an excellent way to fill this gap in a collaborative way."

To this end the university has developed a special service to help its academics develop IP, protect patents and establish private-sector partners. This project received a massive boost recently in the form of a €200million grant from the Society for the Acceleration of Technology Transfer (SATT).

Teaching, Learning & Student Life

Paris is one of the most visited destinations in the world, and being located in such a beautiful, historic capital is clearly a plus for students. Moreover, the university itself owns 50 acres of developed property including prestigious buildings such as la Sorbonne. Indeed any student who likes art, architecture or history would greatly appreciate the university's rich cultural assets. Paris Descartes University has many museums, including the 'Museum of

Medicine History'. Meanwhile the university's headquarters is also a cultural delight. It contains works of outstanding quality, such as a set of Gobelins tapestries, numerous pictures by Van Clève, Philippe de Champaigne, Rigaud, Nattier, and Girodet, and some marble statues by J.B. Lemoyne and Houdon.

Paris is one of the few cities in the world that can offer such cultural riches. However, the Vice President is refreshingly honest about the city's drawbacks. "What is unfortunate are the costs of living in Paris, and the distance that students have to travel to get to university. Transportation is very difficult; we still have the same infrastructure that we had in the 1960's. We have many students that spend more than three hours on a train each day."

Of course there is nothing the university can do to fix Paris's transportation infrastructure. But it can compensate by rewarding students when they arrive for their studies. "I think in teaching and learning we do very well", says Vice President Ducruix. "Our standards of teaching are very high and we continue to invest several hundred thousand Euros each year into pedagogical innovation. We are very open to new ideas and will always try to invest in those that we find interesting."

UNIVERSITÀ
DEGLI STUDI
DI PADOVA

Rank › 151 – 200

Name › University of Padua
Region › Europe
Country › Italy
Founded › 1222

www.unipd.it

Core Research Strengths

Founded in 1222, the University of Padua's research traditions stretch back centuries before the European renaissance in the sciences and arts; steeping the institution in an ancient tradition of research and innovation back to some of the most basic questions concerning the human anatomy and our place in the universe. Indeed, the University of Padua has one of the richest traditions of academic inquiry, counting pioneering researchers such as Galileo Galilei, William Harvey and Nicolaus Copernicus amongst its former faculty.

Less known today within the context of leading international research universities, the University of Padua remains a major contributor to the continuing evolution of human understanding in a number of academic disciplines such as information technology, green and sustainable energies, medicine, psychology, biology, archaeology, philosophy and physics. The university is a significant player in these areas throughout the European and international research environment.

Increasingly autonomous as an institution from government direction, the University of Padua has opted for a direction of more flexibility in recent years; concentrating increased attention and resources towards the multidisciplinary research approach so as to tackle complex research questions and major global challenges as efficiently as possible.

Major Discoveries

The University of Padua was the pioneering institution investigating the human anatomy. The world-renowned anatomical theatre first began conducting human dissections in the early 16th Century, and stands today as a testament to the university's rich traditions in the biological and medical sciences.

With both Nicholas Copernicus and Galileo Galilei amongst the University of Padua's former faculty; the institutional influence on our understanding of the solar system and universe around us developed at the University of Padua is almost unprecedented in its legacy. In a more contemporary sense, the University of Padua through the Euratom international research program is one of the pioneering international collaborators further developing our understanding of the potential for nuclear fusion as a means of generating energy. Widely regarded as the paradigm shift technology to guarantee sustainable, clean energy for many generations into the future.

Partnerships, Innovation & Translational Research

The University of Padua's traditions with international research collaborations stretch centuries back to the institution's pioneering development of our understanding of human anatomy in the late 16th century. Today the University of Padua works throughout both the private and public sectors, as well as with counterpart institutions from around the world to collaborate on critical research questions.

Padua's geographical location in the highly productive North/North-Eastern area of Italy has enabled the university to develop a number of key strategic partnerships with leading firms based in the area such as Electrolux, Fiat, Infineon, Novartis as well as a number of mutually beneficial collaborative partnerships with small and medium size enterprises in the region. Nevertheless, the University's appetite for industry partnerships continues to grow and diversify beyond the scope of opportunities in Italy, with the strategy increasingly focusing upon building strategic relationships with industry partners whose interests bring about obvious synergies with the University of Padua's research strengths.

Through the Coimbra Group the University of Padua is an active collaborator with leading European research universities. A number of partnerships with leading US universities such as Boston University, and growing expansion into Latin America (Argentina, Mexico and Brazil) and Asia (Korea, China and India) see the University of Padua actively expanding its global network following a recent 50% increase in the university's budget available for international engagement. From a technology transfer perspective, the University of Padua has taken great steps in recent years to modernise this feature of the research enterprise; having produced an average of 5 spin out companies over the course of the past 10 years; a number significantly higher than average when compared with counterpart institutions throughout the region.

Teaching, Learning & Student Life

From a teaching and learning perspective, the University of Padua provides excellent opportunities for its students to engage in industry work experience and internships through the institution's network of partners throughout Italy, significantly enhancing research experiences and graduates' competitive advantages in the employment market. Furthermore, the university continues to advance international opportunities in its curriculum as is the case with the new masters in Neuroscience, which is completely offered in English; inviting visiting professors from around the world to enrich existing course programs, expanding the proportion of English language instructed courses for potential international students.

Students in attendance at the University of Padua's first impressions will be dominated by the university's almost unparalleled history of scientific discovery, manifested in the institution's splendid renaissance architecture and rich assortment of galleries and collections relating back to the illustrious alumni and faculty once in attendance. Quality of life for students in Padua is excellent with accommodation at a very high standard for excellent value, and living expenses relatively inexpensive when compared with institutions' in Italy's better-known urban centres.

University of Padua
Italy

Rank › 151 – 200

Name › University of Nebraska – Lincoln
Region › Americas
Country › United States
Founded › 1869

www.unl.edu

Core Research Strengths

The University of Nebraska — Lincoln (UNL) is a research leader in areas spanning the sciences and humanities. Research expenditures, one indicator of institutional quality, exceeded $253 million at UNL in 2012. During a recent 10-year span, UNL ranked seventh of major U.S. research institutions in the percentage growth in total National Science Foundation (NSF) R&D federal research expenditures.

Research related to food, fuel and water are key areas of strength at UNL. "Our faculty are improving crop yields, creating energy-efficient technologies and developing plant materials for use as biofuels," said Prem Paul, UNL's vice chancellor for research and economic development.

The university recently established the Robert B. Daugherty Water for Food Institute, a global center for research, education and policy analysis relating to use of water for agriculture. The world's population is expected to increase by 40 per cent, and worldwide demand for food will double by 2050. "Nebraska will provide the knowledge base on how to grow more food with less water," says Paul.

UNL also leads in other areas like materials and nano science research. "About 10 years ago, UNL faculty were awarded a prestigious NSF-funded Materials Research Science and Engineering Center. On the back of that success, we secured federal and private support to construct a new nano science research facility," Paul said.

UNL Chancellor Harvey Perlman said establishment of multi-disciplinary centers is vital to the university's research success. "We generate research momentum by finding ways to get faculty from various disciplines to collaborate. UNL recently created a new Center for Brain, Biology and Behavior, a unique partnership between athletics and academics. It will enable investigations related to behavior and performance, including study of concussions."

Major Discoveries

The genetic trait used to develop soybeans resistant to the herbicide dicamba was discovered by a UNL biochemist. A team of UNL chemists discovered "nano ice" – double helixes of ice molecules that resemble the structure of DNA and self-assemble under high pressure inside carbon nanotubes. Three UNL alumni received the Nobel Prize in recognition of their contributions to chemistry and genetics.

Partnerships, Innovation & Translational Research

One of UNL's historic roles has been to develop research that helps drive Nebraska's economy, and that tradition continues, Perlman said. "We have a very significant partnership with Bayer CropScience, a German-based company. Because of our faculty members' research expertise, they designated Lincoln as the North American headquarters of their global wheat initiative. We also have a major collaboration with Monsanto, which is broader than just crop genetics."

To encourage additional private-public partnerships, UNL is developing the 250-acre Nebraska Innovation Campus (NIC) to connect industry partners with university talent and facilities. ConAgra Foods is NIC's first tenant and will lead programs related to food science. In addition to NIC, NUtech Ventures and the Office of Industry Relations serve as liaisons that connect the talent and abilities of individuals, companies and the university.

UNL also has formed alliances with global organizations, including China's State Administration of Grain and India's Ministry of Food Processing Industries. The university is home to the scientific management office for the Antarctic Geological Drilling Program (ANDRILL). Funded by NSF, ANDRILL is a multi-national collaboration led by UNL and partners from six other countries: the U.K., Germany, New Zealand, Italy, Brazil and the Republic of Korea.

Teaching, Learning & Student Life

UNL is located in Lincoln, a city of 250,000 people that has many of the cultural and entertainment benefits of a much larger city, but which retains the feel of a friendly Midwestern community. Home to the most parkland per capita in the U.S., an extensive bike trail network, diverse employment opportunities and a low cost of living, Lincoln is one of the fastest growing metro areas in the Midwest.

This setting is a definite advantage, said Paul. "UNL is adjacent to Lincoln's downtown, which is convenient for students. Lincoln is a place where all students, especially those from abroad, feel safe and welcome. Athletics plays a big role here, and the fine and performing arts also have a major presence in our community."

UNL was the first U.S. university west of the Mississippi River to award a doctoral degree. Today, UNL offers more than 100 graduate degree programs and more than 150 undergraduate degree programs. During the fall of 2012, for the ninth straight year, UNL was among the top 50 public universities listed in U.S. News and World Report's annual evaluation of America's Best Colleges.

UNL is a research-extensive institution with a strong emphasis on undergraduate education. "We encourage undergraduates to participate in research," said Perlman, "and our signature programs exemplify this commitment to undergraduate success." For example, the university's UCARE program connects faculty and students to work on joint research projects. More than 3,000 undergraduates and 280 faculty mentors have participated in the program since its creation.

University of Nebraska – Lincoln
United States

UNIVERSITÀ
DEGLI STUDI
DI MILANO

Rank › 151 – 200

Name › University of Milan
Region › Europe
Country › Italy
Founded › 1924

www.unimi.it

Core Research Strengths

With around 65,000 students, the University of Milan is a giant and easily one of the largest in Europe. In Milan it's often known just as Statale (state) to distinguish it from the private universities in the city. It has a strong research emphasis and is the only Italian member of the 21-strong League of European Research Universities (LERU).

The university's research programme is organised into 31 Departments. Despite the broad focus there are certain core areas that stand out as particularly strong, says former vice-rector for Research Alberto Mantovani. "We think we are very strong in the general field of life sciences, in bio-medical. We also have great expertise in physics."

As is common with its international peers the university has restructured its research programmes to encourage multidisciplinary projects. For example, its life science and bio-medical expertise is arranged according to certain key themes, such as 'Healthy food for Healthy Life', and fighting cancer. Another theme-based research unit is called Unistem – a stem cell research group led by Elena Cattaneo, a prominent scientist in the field.

Not all research projects have such global aims. For example, one recent research programme used the university's leading position in digital sound to work with La Scala the city's famous opera house.

"We think that synergetic interactions are key in both developments of basic science as well as to translation into society", says the Research Director. To prove his point he cites nanotechnology as another example. "We have a strong tradition in the general field of nanotechnology, and this is also related to one of the initiatives that we have in terms of data transfer. We are making an effort to combine people who are very strong in nanotechnology per se, with the people in the life sciences, bridging and putting together these competences both in terms of basic science and in terms of industrial application."

Major Discoveries

Many physicists of the University, where the great scientist Joseph Goggles created a school of study at the highest level, have participated in what was undoubtedly the scientific news of 2012: the discovery of the Higgs Boson Particle. Moreover, Fabiola Gianotti studied at the University of Milan and took her first steps as a scientist; she currently leads the ATLAS Project at CERN.

Partnerships, Innovation & Translational Research

Located deep in Italy's industrial heartland means the university is spoilt for choice when it comes to finding good private-sector partners, says former vice-rector for Research Mantovani. Indeed the university often contacts local companies to find ways they can work together. "The structure of the industrial system in Italy is based on small and medium-size enterprises. Often these companies are a natural partner because they lack full research facilities themselves."

The university has also created an incubator, which is a joint venture between itself, a local bank and a bank foundation to help commercialise the university's best work. The Filarete Foundation has a series of technological platforms to help start-ups mature enough to become commercial successes. Another initiative is that the university and private sector combine to pay for the cost of post-doctoral research in certain fields.

The final part of the university's commercialisation strategy is its new technology transfer office UNIMTT. The office handles the patenting of research that originates at the university. To date the office has established around 200 patents in different fields.

Teaching, Learning & Student Life

Milan may be Italy's second-largest city but it is the main commercial and trading centre of the country. It is home to many of Italy's leading firms and also hosts the Italian Stock Exchange. Aside from business, Milan has many cultural attractions to offer students. It is one of the world's leading fashion and design centres, has scores of museums, theatres, churches and its Cathedral has even been named a UNESCO World Heritage site. Furthermore, if any prospective student likes football they can choose between the two teams of the city, AC Milan and Inter. The rich array of cultural and commercial attractions explains why The New York Times ranked the city as one of the best places to live in the world.

Milan is also very well located as a travel hub. Depending on the direction you travel you can be at the mountains, coast or lakes within just a few hours.

One of the aspects of the student experience that distinguishes Milan from its international peers is the relatively low numbers of international students. However, former vice-rector for Research Mantovani says the university is working hard to rectify that. "We launched an international course in medicine, and this has been very successful because the tuition fee is ridiculously low, and I think that the quality of the teaching is also very good. It would compare favourably with any medical high-ranking course in the world."

At present the university offers 136 undergraduate and postgraduate courses across eight faculties. However, that number is likely to increase as the university adds to its course portfolio in a bid to bolster its international appeal.

UNIVERSITY OF MIAMI

Rank › 151 – 200

Name › University of Miami
Region › Americas
Country › United States
Founded › 1925

www.miami.edu

Core Research Strengths

With more than US $350 million in annual sponsored research funding distributed among 12 colleges and schools, as well as a number of multidisciplinary institutes and centres; the research portfolio at the University of Miami is diverse, spanning a myriad of disciplines from architecture to marine biology.

Receiving approximately 65% of the University of Miami's total research funding, the Leonard M. Miller School of Medicine's US $200 million annual research budget places the medical and life sciences at the very forefront of the University's research portfolio. Multidisciplinary research centres addressing major public health challenges such as ageing, cancer, HIV/AIDS and diabetes—combined with institutes that unite a variety of disciplines to push the boundaries on new scientific frontiers in stem cell research, genomics and genetics – very much define UM's research strategy in the life and medical sciences. The Miller School is located in the Miami Health District, one of the largest medical science districts in the United States, thus facilitating the development of expertise in a variety of inter-related medical disciplines on a single site.

Aside from the life and medical sciences, the University of Miami is distinguished by expertise in oceanography and the marine sciences. Established in the 1940s, the Rosenstiel School of Marine and Atmospheric Science has grown from relatively humble beginnings into what today is recognised as one of the preeminent international research centres investigating the entire spectrum of marine and ocean sciences. Rosenstiel School facilities include a salt-water wave tank, a five-tank Conditioning and Spawning System, multi-tank Aplysia Culture Laboratory, Controlled Corals Climate Tanks, DNA analysis equipment and an invertebrate museum with 400,000 specimens.

In the humanities and social sciences, UM has achieved significant strides. It is home to a new Center for the Humanities, and with its Center for Latin American Studies, the institution is a leader in research focused on that region of the world. UM's Institute for Cuban and Cuban-American Studies and its Cuban Heritage Collection with particular expertise on Cuba given the Miami region's socio-cultural historical ties with the region.

Major Discoveries

The University of Miami's Rosenstiel School is the lead institution of a research consortium funded with $112 million to study the environmental and ecological impact of the Deepwater Horizon explosion and oil spill in the Gulf of Mexico.

Researchers at the Miller School's Interdisciplinary Stem Cell Institute engage in largest-scale clinical trials that investigate the ability of stem cells to repair damaged organs.

Researchers led by Margaret Pericak-Vance, director of the John P. Hussman Institute for Human Genomics at the Miller School of Medicine, have discovered four new genes linked to the development of Alzheimer's Disease.

Partnerships, Innovation & Translational Research

Having received billions of dollars in research funding throughout its history, the University of Miami is an experienced collaborator in the public, private and third sectors. Similar to the vast majority of leading research universities, the institution's approach to external partnerships is guided by academic principles of transparency and curiosity-driven research.

UM Innovation is the home of technology advancement at the University of Miami and serves to nurture and integrate vibrant and comprehensive research initiatives.

An immensely exciting development at the University of Miami from a collaborative and translational research perspective is the ongoing development of the UM Life Science & Technology Park—an enormous facility set to position the University as a global leader in biomedical research. The first phase of the UM Life Science & Technology Park was completed in 2011, with the grand opening of the 252,000-square-foot R&D Building 1. The park will provide world-class infrastructure, equipment and interdisciplinary research opportunities to the 1700 or so biomedical companies currently located in Miami, as well as open the door to international collaboration with the world's leading companies in this immensely exciting sector of economic development and academic discovery.

Teaching, Learning & Student Life

Learning by doing very much defines the pedagogical philosophy at UM, with students encouraged to get involved directly with research projects and the creation of new knowledge upon arrival at the University. Faculty mentors support undergraduate research efforts, helping students to devise interesting questions to answer, structure research methodologies and present results.

The development of leadership and communication skills combined with local social development activities makes UM a leader in community outreach programs. Students are encouraged to develop an understanding of the local community, build a social network, and develop valuable skills above and beyond a typical undergraduate degree program.

The skills one can expect to develop in UM's research intensive curriculum and leadership-focused community outreach programs are complemented by a myriad of international opportunities, including a study abroad program and an organizational arrangement for student internships that places thousands of students each year with prospective employers and local industries.

UNIVERSITY of MARYLAND
THE FOUNDING CAMPUS

Rank › 151 – 200

Name › University of Maryland Baltimore
Region › Americas
Country › United States
Founded › 1807

www.umaryland.edu

Core Research Strengths

The University of Maryland is recognized as one of America's preeminent public research universities and specializes in medicine, pharmacy, dentistry, nursing, public health, law and human services. It spent $530 million on research in 2012.

Vice President of Research, Jim Hughes, notes within the university's health focus there are a number of important research strands. "The broad area of infectious disease is a major research strength at UMB, representing nearly one quarter of our total research funding. We have a very strong centre for vaccine development, doing work on a variety of diseases impacting the developing world such as malaria and cholera. We also have a very large institute addressing HIV/AIDS. Both programs are very engaged in conducting clinical trials and helping to build the healthcare infrastructure in sub-Saharan Africa.

Those areas are natural funding candidates because of the massive impact successful research can have on saving lives. Another well-funded area is cancer, says Vice President Hughes. "Our Greenebaum Cancer Center is ranked #11 out of 900 cancer programs in the United States. The Center offers patients access to the newest therapies currently available through 200 clinical trials each year. Our Department of Radiation Oncology is one of the top ten departments for research in the United States and has made major contributions to patient care by more precisely delivering radiation treatment to tumours. Clinical care will be further advanced with the opening of the Maryland Proton Treatment Center in 2014."

The final strand of health care research is neurosciences, says the Vice President. "We have one of a small number of programs nationally that offer advanced management and treatment modalities to patients with Parkinson's disease and movement disorders, multiple sclerosis, stroke, epilepsy, Alzheimer's disease, spasticity and neuromuscular disease. Our pharmacy school is particularly strong in drug development, computer aided drug design and drug delivery."

Major Discoveries

Given the university's strong health focus it is little surprise that this discipline has brought some of its most notable successes. Perhaps the most striking is that when he was at the National Institutes of Health, Maryland's Prof. Robert Gallo, MD, co-discovered the HIV virus as the cause of AIDS, arguably one of the most important medical discoveries of the last half-century. Angela Brodie, Ph.D., has won the prestigious Charles F. Kettering Prize for her pioneering work in developing aromatase inhibitors, a new class of drugs widely used today to treat breast cancer. A live oral cholera vaccine developed by Myron Levine, MD, DTPH, is currently under-going Phase 3 clinical trials.

Partnerships, Innovation & Translational Research

As is common with American medical research universities, Maryland has close and productive ties with commercial partners. "Last year we worked with 200 biotech and pharmaceutical companies around the world", says Vice President Hughes. "They sponsored over $40 million worth of research here and a variety of projects. Some of it was translational research to develop new drugs and diagnostics others were clinical trials. We have a big focus on increasing that and this work with corporations has actually been the fastest-growing part of our portfolio. In addition to being a good revenue source, what excites us about that is that it also can help lead more quickly to new products that can come to the market."

To fuel further translation of research and the commercialisation of new drugs, diagnostics and devices, the University of Maryland established a 12-acre Bio-Park bringing much-needed laboratory and office space to the area and encouraging collaboration among biotechnology companies and the university.

When it comes to the great IP debate Hughes says that Maryland believes in tight control. "If we invent it, we own it. If it is invented jointly with the company we jointly own it, and we would give the company an option to license the rights to that intellectual property."

Teaching, Learning & Student Life

The university's strong research focus is reflected in student and staff numbers. There are just 6,349 students against 6,717 faculty members and staff. That offers students unparalleled opportunities to marry their studies with research. Indeed scientists and students work side by side in state-of-the-art facilities. Students also benefit from the Bio Park, the community of life science companies and academic research centers.

Students can also have the opportunity to benefit from the university's alliances, says Vice President Hughes. "Increasingly, our students and faculty are benefitting from the complementary programs of our sister institution, the University Maryland College Park. They have top-ranked programs in engineering, computer sciences, natural sciences, and business. Likewise, their students are benefitting from our strengths in the health sciences, law, and social work. Expanding these collaborations is a top priority of both universities, particularly in areas of convergence such as health informatics, bioengineering, and public health."

Likewise there are opportunities for students to become involved in the university's African work.

Another element of the learning experience that students should be aware of is Maryland's ethos of helping the community. In total the university gives more than 2 million hours a year in service to the public.

The campus itself is located on the west side of downtown Baltimore, within walking distance from M&T Bank Stadium and Camden Yards, homes of local sports teams the Baltimore Ravens and Baltimore Orioles. Known as 'Charm City' for its friendly locals, the bustling city of Baltimore is ideal for students looking for active diversions outside of study time. The Inner Harbour has been one of America's major seaports since the 1700s and offers a wonderful place for students to explore, shop, eat and party. Another attraction is the National Aquarium where more than 16,000 undersea and land creatures are on display.

JOHANNES GUTENBERG
UNIVERSITÄT MAINZ

Rank › 151 – 200

Name › University of Mainz
Region › Europe
Country › Germany
Founded › 1477

www.uni-mainz.de

Core Research Strengths

Johannes Gutenberg University Mainz (JGU) is a globally renowned research institution of national and international recognition. This reputation comes thanks to its outstanding individual researchers as well as extraordinary research achievements in the field of particle and hadron physics, materials sciences, earth system sciences, translational medicine, life sciences and media studies. JGU has almost 4,000 scientists and more than 150 specialised institutes and clinics. A sign of the university's success is the recognition it received in Germany's excellence initiatives. The Cluster of Excellence on "Precision Physics, Fundamental Interactions and Structure of Matter," which is primarily a collaboration between particle and hadron physicists, and the Graduate School of Excellence "MAterials Science IN MainZ" are considered among the elite research groups worldwide.

In addition, Mainz University runs sophisticated, large-scale facilities used intensively by international researchers, such as the TRIGA nuclear reactor and the electron accelerator MAMI. "Our main campus, located near the city center, hosts almost all academic disciplines as well as the Mainz University of Applied Sciences and four leading research institutes, namely the Max Planck Institute for Chemistry, the Max Planck Institute for Polymer Research, the Helmholtz Institute Mainz, and the Institute of Molecular Biology. The integration of a University Medical Center and two Art Schools is unique within the German academic landscape", says President Georg Krausch. "Interdisciplinary discourse is therefore a hallmark of our university."

Major Discoveries

Research teams of Mainz University have developed analytical instruments for the Mars rovers Spirit and Opportunity.

Mainz physicists are involved in the Large Hadron Collider project at CERN in Geneva. They are also contributing to the XENON Dark Matter Project at the Gran Sasso underground laboratory (Italy) and the international IceCube research project (Antarctica).

Partnerships, Innovation & Translational Research

Research at JGU is linked to a highly dynamic environment of non-university research institutes. Close cooperation with partners in industry and public administration is already a well-established practice. Furthermore, close strategic cooperation with research institutes of the Max Planck Society, the Helmholtz Association and the Leibniz Association plays a central role. Thus JGU has built a global network in the areas of science and research. The international work of its scientists is supported by a network of 145 alliances with partner universities on all continents.

Indeed if you include the ERASMUS program, it has a further 700 international alliances. One of the most powerful results of that international strategy is student and researcher exchange. Moreover, unlike many of its peers international travel isn't just an option at Master's level but a requirement throughout the learning process. As a result Mainz exchanges a high proportion of its student body and research staff with core exchange partner countries being France, Poland, Spain, China, South Korea and the US. Moreover, its location in the Rhine-Main area, one of Europe's leading industrial centres, gives it good access to private business.

Teaching, Learning & Student Life

With about 37,000 students from about 130 nations, JGU is one of the ten largest universities in Germany, as well as one of the oldest. "At Mainz University, we give excellent young researchers the space they need to design and run path-breaking research projects and develop long-term career perspectives", says President Georg Krausch. "Our campus is an intellectually stimulating and vibrant international environment. Life at JGU is enriched by the presence of some 4,500 foreign students. Living and working together, our students are encouraged to engage in a dialog that crosses cultural boundaries, enhancing understanding and helping to overcome international barriers."

Thanks to closely harmonized curricula, students can earn university degrees by studying in two or even three different countries, among them France, Italy and Canada. Characterized by its large emphasis on research-oriented teaching, JGU offers a total of 147 subjects, with 127 Bachelor's and 105 Master's degree programmes.

Mainz stands for conviviality and cosmopolitanism. An ancient city, that 2,000 years ago formed an outpost of the Roman Empire, Mainz is full of culture. In addition to the historic attractions there is a lively cultural scene. Personalities such as Barbarossa and Gutenberg have left their mark on the metropolis on the Rhine, which is today a picturesque home for people and business.

JGU owes much to the man whose name it bares and his achievements. President Georg Krausch sums up: "Our university is devoted to the spirit of its namesake: fostering innovative ideas, moving people's minds, and employing knowledge in order to transcend borders. This is the mission that JGU has set itself."

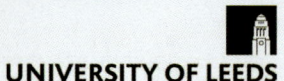

UNIVERSITY OF LEEDS

Rank › 151 – 200

Name › University of Leeds
Region › Europe
Country › United Kingdom
Founded › 1884

www.leeds.ac.uk

Core Research Strengths

The University of Leeds is one of Britain's leading public research universities with an annual research budget in excess of £120 million. According to Pro-Vice Chancellor (Research and Innovation) Professor David Hogg, those funds are used to drive research across a number of academic areas.

"For example, we have a major research theme in sustainability, part of which is a focus on the subject of water and its future security. The group that co-ordinates this work, Water@Leeds involves 200 researchers from a wide range of departments right across the University. This multidisciplinary approach has worked extremely well."

The University collaborates on major global challenges through its membership of the World Universities Network (WUN), explains Professor Hogg. "The World Universities Network has identified three major global challenges, which we are working towards. The idea is that research projects will be spawned between member institutions, with funding following from international institutions, companies and governments."

Closer to home the University is using its local assets to research healthcare delivery and related policies. "The city of Leeds is home to the largest teaching hospital in Europe, and perhaps unsurprisingly, we are doing great things in the area of medical research. There are close, positive partnerships with the Leeds Teaching Hospitals NHS Trust and many of our departments, ranging from medicine and healthcare to engineering and social sciences. This collaborative approach has resulted in considerable expertise being developed throughout this discipline."

In 2011 world-leading medical engineering research at Leeds led by Professors John Fisher and Eileen Ingham was rewarded with the Queen's Anniversary Prize, the country's highest accolade for an academic institution.

Major Discoveries

From 1912 to 1913, William Henry Bragg, Cavendish Professor of Physics, and his son William Lawrence Bragg developed X-ray spectrometry in the University's laboratories. More than 20 Nobel prizes in physics, chemistry and medicine, including Watson and Crick's momentous work on the structure of DNA, have since relied on the technique they pioneered. Both Braggs were awarded Nobel prizes for their work in 1915.

Leeds chemist Professor Stephen Burkinshaw has created 'virtually waterless washing', a patented, polymer-based cleaning system that promises to transform the cost and environmental impact of aqueous cleaning by using tiny reusable beads that suck up stains.

Partnerships, Innovation & Translational Research

The University of Leeds is very keen to partner with government and private industry, says Professor Hogg. Understandably the government is a natural partner when it comes to the University's work in healthcare. However, the Pro-Vice Chancellor notes that there is an increasing demand from an array of private-sector firms to work with the University across a range of disciplines.

"We have partnerships with globally-recognised private sector-groups including Arup and Marks & Spencer. In fact the entire M&S Corporate archive is based on our campus", says Professor Hogg. "The University engages across the board in private sector partnerships and we are seeing that more and more, private sector companies are looking to universities to help add value to their ongoing research operations. Companies are narrowing down their focus to particular institutions that they work well with, both in terms of their operational synergies, and the chemistry of relationships between individuals."

The University has set up an office to facilitate relations with external partners. Indeed, the Pro-Vice Chancellor proudly notes: "The University of Leeds was one of the first UK institutions to develop a technology transfer office and begin spinning out successful companies."

Since 1995, the University of Leeds has produced 101 'spinout' companies, the second largest number in the higher education sector in the UK, and it currently has 44 active spinout companies.

Teaching, Learning & Student Life

With 33,000 students from 145 countries Leeds is one of Britain's biggest universities and part of the prestigious Russell Group — the 24 leading research universities in the UK. The University runs more than 560 undergraduate and 300 postgraduate courses, one of the widest ranges in the UK. Leeds has also been awarded 17 National Teaching Fellowships — more than any other UK university — reflecting the excellence of its teaching.

"The University is one of the giants of the UK system, and our size means we can facilitate an enormous amount of the cross disciplinary work that results in both very interesting breakthroughs from a research perspective, but also a vast range of opportunities for students to expand upon their initial focus whilst studying here," says Professor Hogg.

But life at Leeds isn't all work and no play, stresses the Pro-Vice Chancellor. "Our university has an enormous student population and a tremendous student union with a raft of activities and societies. We offer a huge amount of support for our students. For example, Leeds for Life is an exciting initiative which provides students with an excellent platform to define and hone how their learning and extracurricular activities lead into career opportunities for them. This contributed to a huge spike in Leeds' scores in the annual survey of student satisfaction, the National Student Survey (NSS)."

University of Cologne

Rank › 151 – 200

Name › University of Koeln
Region › Europe
Country › Germany
Founded › 1388

www.uni-koeln.de

Core Research Strengths

The University of Cologne is one of the oldest and largest universities in Germany. True to its motto 'Good ideas. Since 1388', the University continues to successfully combine novelty with tradition in its research and teaching.

In 2012, the University of Cologne was awarded the status of an 'excellence university' following its success in a nationwide competition initiated by the German federal and state governments to promote top-level research and enhance quality education.

Like many modern institutions the University of Cologne now organises its research according to issue-based topics. "One of the main topics is the study of ageing associated diseases", says Rector Axel Freimuth. "In this area 50 participating scientists and their scientific groups at the level of professors investigate various issues in genetics, medicine and biochemistry."

Another important topic is behavioural economic engineering and social cognition, says the Rector. This involves the social sciences, economics and psychology departments.

The third topic is quantum matter and materials. "We cover the full spectrum from very basic mathematical-oriented research to applications, for example, in organic electronics. We are also doing a lot of work on so-called highly correlated electron systems."

The fourth issue-based topic is socioeconomic, cultural and political transformations in the Global South, which is based on numerous cooperative research structures and – as all the other topics – has a very strong societal relevance.

The fifth area is intercultural education. At present this research programme is not as advanced as the others. However, it's an area that the Rector expects to grow significantly over the next five years. "Intercultural education is an important topic in itself but especially so for the University of Cologne as we are one of Europe's biggest institutions for teachers' education. We offer teacher training at all levels with all types of subjects. Moreover, our University is located in

a very internationally oriented city as Cologne has a large Turkish community, for instance."

Major Discoveries

In 1950 Kurt Alder won the Nobel Prize in Chemistry for the discovery and development of the diene synthesis. In the early 1960s, Nobel Prize laureate, Max Dellbrück, founded the first Institute for Genetics in Germany at the University of Cologne. More recently, in 2007, Peter Grünberg won the Nobel Prize in Physics for the discovery of giant magnetoresistance.

Furthermore, within the last twenty years, ten professors of the University of Cologne were awarded the Gottfried Wilhelm Leibniz-Prize, which is the highest remunerated research prize awarded in Germany.

Partnerships, Innovation & Translational Research

The University of Cologne maintains very effective partnerships with other German institutions. It works particularly closely with Max Planck and Helmholtz Institutes.

"They are excellent", enthuses Rector Freimuth. "We have a real day-by-day collaboration with these partners, and all the Max Planck directors are part of our faculty."

The international segment of Cologne's partnership policy is often led by individual professors, says the Rector. "We have a pretty large and growing international network of approximately 250 cooperation agreements that are often the work of small groups of scientists."

However, the Rector is keen to expand such international alliances into more expansive, formal agreements. One example of such a partnership is the new collaborative research unit with Pennsylvania State University and others funded by the German Research Foundation.

Teaching, Learning & Student Life

The University of Cologne is a so-called city university, as it was founded in 1388 by Cologne citizens and established in the city centre.

Therefore, campus and city life are closely interlinked to the mutual benefits of both members of the University and the citizens of Cologne. Another distinctive element of the 'Cologne experience' is that the University is located in the Rhineland – a mega-urban region that opens up great post-graduate employment opportunities for the University's students especially in the media, cultural, business and industry sectors.

About half of the 42,000 students study in just four profession-oriented areas: business administration, law, medicine, and teacher education. The University has made significant investments in order to better prepare its students for the professional market. For example, in 2008 the University launched the Professional Center providing profession-oriented teaching programmes and career-related training and networking.

The student body at Cologne already feels very international, says Rector Freimuth. "At the moment we have around 11% international students but we would like to increase this share." To that end the University's international office together with the centres for international relations in each of the Faculties and the satellite offices in Beijing, Delhi and New York have set up various programmes to support highly qualified international students and to expand the international exchange programme.

Christian-Albrechts-Universität zu Kiel

Rank › 151 – 200

Name › University of Kiel
Region › Europe
Country › Germany
Founded › 1665

www.uni-kiel.de

Core Research Strengths

Kiel University was originally founded in 1665, and today is home to three of Germany's top research areas – known as clusters of excellence. With Kiel situated on the coast of the Baltic Sea, it is perhaps little surprise, that one of the clusters is focused on marine sciences. It is the centre of Germany's marine science industry and has a leading world position. In accordance with the increasingly multidisciplinary approach now taken by universities, the Kiel Marine Science cluster utilises different disciplines, such as biology, chemistry, geology and physics.

The second research focus is life sciences. Here the university specialises in inflammation and has invested heavily in a DNA sequencing centre. The third research area is nanotechnology, this centre draws heavily on the university's strengths in material sciences.

The final cluster looks at how humans interact with physical landscapes. It includes palaeontology and but also examines global changes in landscapes – i.e. climate change. Indeed the university hosts its own supercomputer for numerical modelling of global climate change and bio-geochemical cycles.

Obviously these clusters of excellence dominate the university's research efforts. However, University Vice President, Professor Thomas Bosch, is keen to highlight that the university also makes important contributions in other academic fields. "There are many research programs that are not included in the clusters of excellence. The university funds individual research efforts and provides about 30% of a project's cost. This type of independent research is important because it gives an innovative impulse and provides a necessary amount of flexibility and adjustment that keeps the academic research area at its excellent level. To keep the basis for individual research programs it is not only essential for academic freedom, but also the essence for continuous innovations within the exploratory focus."

Major Discoveries

Otto Fritz Meyerhof, who was awarded the 1922 Nobel Prize in Medicine for his discovery of the fixed relationship between the consumption of oxygen and the metabolism of lactic acid in the muscle. Other famous scientists are Hans Gerhard Creutzfeld, Otto Diehls (Nobel Prize in Chemistry, 1950) Hans Geiger, Heinrich Rudolf Hertz, and Max Planck.

Partnerships, Innovation & Translational Research

As the home to so many clusters of excellence it is inevitable that the university receives strong public sector funding. However, Vice President Bosch acknowledges that "success in scientific research requires strong partnerships with non-university institutions." To that end the university has established the Kiel Alliance for Research and Education (KARE) – a strong regional network, which is based on partnerships with members of scientific institutions, politics, the private sector, and society in order to promote science at Kiel University.

Unlike some academics, who seem to mistrust private sector partners, the Vice President says he "is proud to call numerous national and international institutions, scientific centres, corporations, foundations, and a vast circle of sponsors our partners." After all, he points out, "They foster pioneering research and help our University become one of the leading universities in northern Europe."

Historically Kiel's international academic links have been governed by its geographical location. It has long had special links with the neighbouring countries of Scandinavia and the Baltic Sea region. More recently it has striven to develop strong ties with countries all over the world, from Canada to China. At university level, about 50 partnership agreements have been established in Europe, the Americas and Asia.

Teaching, Learning & Student Life

Kiel is a middle-size university with around 25,000 students and about 400 professors. For students, one of the most overriding parts of their experience will be the proximity to the sea. Kiel remains an important port, and it is ideally located for students who want to explore Scandinavia. From the lecture hall to the beach in twenty minutes, It is only a stone's throw to the seaside resorts that line up along the coast outside the city. Proving that relaxation and study are not mutually exclusive, students seeking tranquillity and fresh sea breezes simply pack a few books and go down to the Baltic.

Another huge advantage for students is that they can benefit from the impressive research facilities at the various clusters of excellence. Germany is one of the world's most advanced industrial economies and students at Kiel will have a front row seat on the research powerhouses that give Germany its competitive advantage.

And, unlike other universities, where undergraduates are kept at arm's-length from leading professors, here an expert in the field supervises every student. This interaction is enhanced through weekend seminars and field trips.

Students also benefit from the university's partnerships. Kiel has more than 200 partner universities within the framework of the European Erasmus programme. This leads to a robust exchange programme, which exposes the students to new cultures and experiences.

UIC UNIVERSITY OF ILLINOIS AT CHICAGO

Rank › 151 – 200

Name › University of Illinois at Chicago
Region › Americas
Country › United States
Founded › 1982

www.uic.edu

Core Research Strengths

The University of Illinois at Chicago (UIC) is a relatively young institution, formed 30 years ago when the University of Illinois Medical Center merged with the University of Illinois at Chicago Circle. With research expenditures of $381 million, UIC is the largest public research institution in the Chicago metropolitan region, with a full complement of fifteen academic colleges in the arts, sciences, and the humanities and a full range of medical and health sciences programmes.

Chancellor Paula Allen-Meares explains the university's research strategy in the health sciences: "Much of our research focuses on health disparities, health care, and innovations in the delivery of health care services, as well as technological advances such as robotic surgery. We have a focus on biomedical innovations. We have a focus on global health innovations – technology, health informatics, sustainability and engineering."

UIC's College of Medicine is the largest in the U.S. One example of an innovative project in the university's medical programme is the violence reduction scheme CureViolence, says the Chancellor. "Violence is treated as a medical epidemic. This was started here at UIC, tested in violent, high crime locations in the city of Chicago, and has its findings and practices spread throughout the world." It's a good example, says the Chancellor, of how the university's research tries to address the issues and challenges of urban communities.

Like all leading universities UIC takes a multidisciplinary approach to research. Recently, the Chancellor launched the Interdisciplinary Research Initiative to seek innovative proposals that integrate different disciplines around urgent matters. "For example, the Humanities and Food Science Initiative will focus on food as it relates to food distribution and food production, which is a global problem just like energy and water that are becoming more and more significant," she said.

Major Discoveries

Despite its short history the university has made some very significant scientific breakthroughs. One area where it has particularly shone is the treatment of AIDS. UIC epidemiologist Robert Bailey discovered that male circumcision dramatically decreases the chances of contracting HIV AIDS. This amazing find, which could save millions of lives, was cited by "Time" magazine as one of the top medical advances in the world in 2007. That success came on the back of the AIDS drug Prezista, which was developed by a UIC chemistry professor.

Partnerships, Innovation & Translational Research

The university's impressive research budget is the result of a number of valuable partnerships with various private and public organisations. Principal public partners include The National Institutes of Health (NIH), The National Science Foundation and the U.S. Department of Defence. Key private partners include Baxter International, among others.

The university also has a deliberately translational approach, says the Chancellor. "Right now, there are over 1200 partnerships, locally and globally, as we work to create synergy with different corporate, community, and government institutions. So I think it's a part of our DNA. We are an engaged university. We are deeply committed to partnerships and interdisciplinary research that will make a difference in terms of the quality of life of the people, the state, the nation, and the world."

Students are another great way for the university to expand its reach, says Vice Chancellor for Research, Mitra Dutta. "We have exchanges with institutes in Milan and Turin and there have been agreements with Sweden, as well as with Brazil for exchange students and dual degree programs." However, despite the array of programmes, Vice Chancellor Dutta thinks more should be done. "We are looking to exploit more of these. China is very interested in partnerships with us as are Iraq and other middle-eastern countries."

Teaching, Learning & Student Life

For international students one of the great attractions of UIC is its location in Chicago, one of America's most iconic cities. The city has everything, from a bustling downtown to a scenic shoreline alongside Lake Michigan. There's no doubt it's a big plus, admits Chancellor Allen-Meares. Moreover, it can also be used to enhance students' education. "We use this great American and global city as a venue, as an opportunity for students to become engaged in art, architecture, non-profits and businesses. We have a variety of internships and research projects involving students in the field… in neighbourhoods, with community groups, businesses, the arts, and theatre, to name a few. I think that these aspects of the metropolitan area contribute handsomely to the educational preparation of our students."

Being located in such a large city makes it possible to give students valuable commercial experience, says Vice Chancellor Dutta. One of many examples is UIC's Innovation Center. "This center is supported by three colleges," says Dutta, "Engineering, Business Administration, and Architecture and the Arts. Students from these three colleges work together on projects that are brought to the Center by local companies. Students love it and the companies love it."

Surprisingly, for such a well-funded, comprehensive institution, there are only around 27,500 students at the university. That means there is a very low student to faculty member ratio – around 17:1 – which allows for a more personal learning experience. Moreover, the teaching staff are highly qualified with 83% of full-time instructional faculty holding a PhD or equivalent.

Universität Hamburg
DER FORSCHUNG | DER LEHRE | DER BILDUNG

Rank › 151 – 200

Name › University of Hamburg
Region › Europe
Country › Germany
Founded › 1919

www.uni-hamburg.de

Core Research Strengths

Universität Hamburg is the major research and educational institution in northern Germany. Home to about 41,000 students, the University's academic staff comprises 6,500 employees, as well as 700 full professors. In accordance with its Structure and Development Plan (STEP) Universität Hamburg has become a research university with clearly-defined research areas and a broad spectrum of subjects offered in six schools.

The University has established numerous research foci as well as an extensive partner network with leading institutions on a regional, national and international scale. Universität Hamburg sees itself as a university for a sustainable future and is committed to sustainable research. All of Hamburg's schools have taken great strides towards sustainability.

The Centre for a Sustainable University (KNU) was founded as an academic platform at Universität Hamburg in the winter semester of 2011/2012. It acts as both a laboratory and think-tank for new ideas, approaches, procedures and methods pertaining to the questions, problems and prospects facing a forward-looking university. Within the context of the discourse on sustainability, it pools the following interdisciplinary tasks: initiating and promoting academic projects on sustainability, strengthening cooperation and networking efforts both internally and externally, monitoring, evaluating and assuring quality of sustainable teaching and long-lasting education The Centre for a Sustainable University bases its work on the sustainability principles formulated by the Brundtland Report.

In 2007 Universität Hamburg implemented its cluster of excellence in climate research as part of Germany's Excellence Initiative. KlimaCampus Hamburg provides a competence and training center for climate research and earth system sciences. Universität Hamburg's CLISAP cluster of excellence Integrated Climate System Analysis and Prediction receives funding from The German Research Foundation (DFG).

In 2012 Universität Hamburg received federal funding for an additional cluster of excellence: the Hamburg Centre for Ultrafast Imaging (CUI): Structure, Dynamics and Control of Matter at the Atomic Scale. The CUI focuses on the real-time observation of atomic motions. In addition to climate, earth, and environment Hamburg's key research foci comprise: matter and the universe, neurosciences, multilingualism, governance, heterogeneity and education, health economics, manuscript research, law, economics, infection research and structural biology.

The Schools of Psychology and Medicine established the neuroscience focus in close cooperation with the University Medical Centre Hamburg-Eppendorf (UKE).

There is a further key research area in the Department of Humanities. Hamburg's Centre for the Study of Manuscript Cultures at the Africa-Asia Institute houses the Collaborative Research Centre "Manuscript Cultures in Asia, Africa and Europe." This is a broad field of research that receives funding from the DFG. The main focus is on the very first manuscripts from China and Africa. Hamburg's researchers specialize in detecting ancient manuscripts, even in remote areas of Africa. They dig up precious treasures, read and analyse them, partly thanks to generous funding from the DFG.

Campus Life

Universität Hamburg has 150 different buildings located throughout the city. Its main campus, however, is located at Von-Melle-Park and in the neighbouring Eimsbüttel district. Universität Hamburg has six schools, each home to several departments of related subjects. The scientific staff is supported by approximately 6,600 staff members in technical support, libraries, laboratories, health care and administration. Approximately 4,600 people work at the UKE and 2,000 in the other schools and the University Administration.

President Lenzen stresses: "Our academic program is based on the close interaction of students, professors and research assistants. We have implemented junior research groups to provide excellent young scholars and scientists with an opportunity to assume full-scale leadership responsibilities. Young researchers with outstanding academic achievements receive financial support, and are able to create and lead their own research groups. They select their own doctoral students and postdocs, thus becoming independent and gaining the experience needed in pursuing professorial careers."

The University has implemented an internationalization strategy and established a Department of International Affairs. Hamburg's approach focuses on attracting an increasing number of excellent international scholars and scientists. Currently, about 10 per cent of the staff are comprised of international academics, but is forecasted to increase to 25 per cent due to recent appointments.

UNIVERSITY OF GOTHENBURG

Rank › 151 – 200

Name › University of Gothenburg
Region › Europe
Country › Sweden
Founded › 1891

www.gu.se

Core Research Strengths

With 2700 researchers in 38 departments throughout 8 faculties and one of the largest student populations in Scandinavia, the University of Gothenburg's (UGOT) research portfolio is broad and diverse. Although UGOT is particularly well-known for its expertise throughout the medical sciences, the university is also strategically focusing on five broad areas of societal importance that draw various areas of expertise together in collaboration: Health, Culture, Environment, Democracy & Social Development and Knowledge Formation & Learning.

One of the largest hospitals in Northern Europe, the Sahlgrenska University Hospital is at the heart of UGOT's Health related research enterprise, combining basic research with clinical treatment facilitating new findings throughout the spectrum of the medical sciences.

Home to Northern Europe's largest faculty of performing arts, culturally orientated research is a key feature at UGOT. The scope of culturally orientated research activities at UGOT crosses the boundaries between the natural sciences, social sciences and humanities.

Of enormous cultural importance throughout Scandinavia is the environment, and environmental sustainability. Few other institutes reflect this as much as the Centre for Environment and Sustainability (GMV); a joint initiative between UGOT and the Chalmers University of Technology. The GMV works both domestically and at the international level to further our understanding of the myriad of environmental impacts societal change are having on the environment as well as devising potential solutions to these challenges.

Through the profile area of Democracy & Social Development, the UGOT is able to build upon existing strengths in areas such as gender studies, development economics, statistics and transportation studies, as well as help better understand the impacts of broader economic and societal change upon areas such as infrastructure and the economy.

Perhaps of greatest importance for a return to strong global economic growth and sustainability is the foundation of knowledge. UGOT's research area examining questions surrounding Knowledge Formation & Learning is particularly strong in developing innovative new pedagogies that will be effective utilising 21st century technologies to communicate 21st century phenomena.

Major Discoveries

The University of Gothenburg's great strength in the medical sciences is reflected in its Nobel Prize – awarded to Professor Arvid Carlsson for his work on dopamine and its effects on Parkinson's Disease.

Partnerships, Innovation & Translational Research

UGOT prides itself as an open university, welcoming an array of collaborative research partners from the public, private and third sectors. UGOT's Research and Innovation Service is the most important interface for external partners to navigate to the areas of expertise that most interest them. The Research and Innovation Service has streamlined the process for external collaborators by facilitating tailor-made solutions based upon respective requests.

The Research and Innovation Service also facilitates the translation of new discoveries and innovations onto the external market; guiding researchers through the necessary steps for patent, financing and licensing; as well as helping with the establishment of spin out companies. As an added bonus, students are also welcomed into the Research and Innovation Service to learn more about entrepreneurialism and gain the important set of business skills that will enable them to take their own discoveries from the university laboratory to the broader market.

International cooperation is also an integral part of UGOT's culture, the university is currently participating extensively in research projects at the international level; and has 900 exchange agreements that facilitate the 1700 international students currently studying at the university.

Teaching, Learning & Student Life

Experiential learning is a hallmark of the UGOT experience, with students working on real-world issues from the very beginning of their career, collaborating with professors, fellow-students and industry in order to ensure they are as best prepared as possible for future careers either in a research, academic or business capacity.

Sweden is particularly attractive as an international study destination given the exceptionally high value derived from how cheap tuition is, combined with the high quality study environment and safety throughout society. Similarly to the majority of Scandinavian universities, the proportion of English language programs at UGOT continues to grow as internationalisation phenomena has an ever more important impact upon institutional strategy.

Nicknamed the Event City, there are always countless events in Gothenburg. As Sweden's second largest city and a renowned student centre home to many universities; UGOT is the most oversubscribed university in Sweden partly due to the excellent social and nightlife opportunities one can find outside of study time in the surrounding city.

Rank › 151 – 200

Name › University of Buenos Aires
Region › Americas
Country › Argentina
Founded › 1821

www.uba.ar

Core Research Strengths

Founded in 1821, and now having grown to educate approximately 320,000 students the University of Buenos Aires (UBA) is Latin America's largest university by enrolment. The research offering is extensive; UBA's some 28,000 staff has expertise throughout the entire spectrum of academic disciplines. The research enterprise is organised into a series of institutes that manage the various fields of expertise such as in the Institute of Astronomy and Spatial Physics or the Institute of Biomedical Engineering. UBA's various research institute's come under the management of their respective faculties, in accordance with international norms, inter-disciplinary research is of growing importance, as well as the linkages between basic research and application.

The Institute of Urbanism, Territory and Environment is particularly distinguished in its understanding of urbanization processes in the Latin American context; an area of growing importance given the continued expansion of cities globally and the trend's implications looking forwards.

The Institute of Biomedical Engineering is a good example of UBA's growing focus upon interdisciplinary research, bringing expertise together from the medical and engineering sciences for the development of innovative new technologies to help overcome illness and disability.

Major Discoveries

With four Nobel prizes, UBA has produced more winners than any other Spanish-speaking research university. Professor Luis Leloir was the first Spanish-speaking winner of the Nobel Prize in chemistry for his discoveries relating to the primary mechanisms of galactose metabolism; significantly furthering our understanding of conditions such as lactose intolerance.

Partnerships, Innovation & Translational Research

Community outreach and extension are a fundamental tenet of UBA's mission. The university is an active participant in Argentine society contributing through community projects in areas such as medicine, the environment, human rights and education.

UBA engages in numerous collaborative research projects with an international portfolio of universities, as well as national research institutions in Argentina. Collaborative research with industry partners is relatively underdeveloped.

Teaching, Learning & Student Life

The University of Buenos Aires is one of the few remaining universities where tuition is free for both domestic and international students; although diversity at the institution is presently limited this could change, as students from many OECD countries look further afield in the face of growing tuition fees.

UBA's various facilities are located throughout the city of Buenos Aires. Often referred to as the "Paris of Latin America", students can expect beautiful surroundings in Latin America's most attractive capital city. With over 300,000 students in attendance one can expect to meet friends from all walks of life, as well as their share of future leaders with most of Argentina's political leaders educated at UBA. UBA has a strong tradition of political activism and involvement; perhaps the most renowned political activist amongst UBA's alumni is Ernesto "Che" Guevara.

UNIVERSITÄT BERN

Rank › 151 – 200

Name › University of Bern
Region › Europe
Country › Switzerland
Founded › 1528

www.unibe.ch

Core Research Strengths

The University of Bern, which dates back to the 16th century, has a comprehensive offering including 8 faculties and some 160 institutes. Since 2000 the university has restructured its research programmes, explains Rector, Professor Martin Täuber.

"The way we have been working for the last several years is that we have a general strategy for the university that involves having a few internationally highly visible areas in research, which are organised through specific centres. One of the prominent fields is in climate research which has been a traditional strength for many years, including as leaders in some of the international organisations related to climate research and policies. Secondly we have been traditionally strong in physics, particularly in high-energy physics. We are strongly involved with this type of high-tech research, particularly as it is ongoing at CERN. Also, space sciences are very strong, with a highly successful collaboration with partners at the University of Geneva."

The university also uses a multidisciplinary approach to focus its research, says Professor Täuber. "The real big issues of science that affect the world can only be solved by collaborative and interdisciplinary efforts, with different teams involved, with different techniques and approaches. Science today is about bringing together different groups of people on issues and problems that are important."

One example of the university's multidisciplinary approach can be found in humanities and social sciences. For example there is a centre working on sustainable development of North – South interrelationships and globalisation. This looks at scientific issues – for example the southern hemisphere's need for sufficient and clean water, food, health and technology. While a second, complementary centre deals with international trade regulations.

Major Discoveries

Ex alumni Kurt Wüthrich won the Nobel Prize in Chemistry for his development of the nuclear magnetic resonance spectroscopy to study the hydration of metal complexes.

Partnerships, Innovation & Translational Research

The university's first network of partnerships is, naturally enough, other institutions from Switzerland. Its international academic alliances tend to be focussed on its research strengths. For example, its climate centre and the sustainability centre are internationally prominent and are both connected extensively, including to the UN, the WHO, and governmental agencies supporting international sustainability work. Meanwhile, being based in the same country as CERN means that Bern's high-energy physics team comes into contact with scientists from around the world.

Unlike some of its peers, which seem to be desperate to spread a wide net internationally, Bern has been much more circumspect in allying with foreign universities. "We have some international relationships, we have one with Wuhan University for instance, but we are carefully selecting a few partners who bring something to us, and where we can bring something to them", explains the Rector.

The private sector partnerships are generally much more local, says Rector Täuber. "We try to keep within the region of Bern, which has a lot of smaller companies, and many companies in biomedical sectors, bio-tech companies etc." To facilitate these external relations the university has established a technology transfer office, which has since won awards for its innovative approach. "It's a growth area and we have rising numbers of contracts and collaborations with companies in the private sector, as well as an increasing number of spin offs."

Teaching, Learning & Student Life

With around 16,000 students Bern is a relatively small university. That small size means that, unlike other universities, which have moved out to the outskirts, it has stayed in the centre. Most institutes and clinics are still in the Länggasse, the traditional university district adjoining the city centre, and within walking distance of one another. That creates a pleasant atmosphere for students and makes it easy to get around.

For Rector Täuber the university's location is a definite plus. "It's a very pleasant city, it's beautiful, it's easy to live in, in the summer you can swim in the river and in the winter you can go skiing in the great mountains close by. That is part of studying also, it should be fun, if you go to college or university, you should enjoy your life there as well, and of course work hard. I think these aspects make Bern rather distinctive compared to other universities."

When it comes to the learning approach, undergraduates should be aware that most courses are not multidisciplinary. However, later on, at the Masters level and particularly at the Doctoral level, studies become a lot more interdisciplinary. The reason for this, says the Rector, is to make sure students can walk before they run. "Our philosophy is still that you have to have a solid disciplinary basis in a scientific field, at least have a bachelor degree in the field then you can open your spectrum for collaborations that start working across the fields. If you don't bring your own solid craftsmanship, so to speak, it's not going to be as effective as if you had a solid base."

Rank › 151 – 200

Name › University Libre Bruxelles
Region › Europe
Country › Belgium
Founded › 1834

www.ulbruxelles.be

Core Research Strengths

The Université libre de Bruxelles' academic tradition has long been committed to curiosity-led research, addressing fundamental questions at the heart of core sciences such as physics, mathematics, chemistry, molecular biology, physiology and also of the human and social sciences. ULB is an institution distinguished in Belgium for its strong tradition of winning Nobel Prizes, a hallmark of the institutional commitment to basic research.

Investment of ULB's US$200 million research budget is defined at the grass roots, with academic curiosity being the defining tenet in the institutional research direction. This high level of academic freedom, combined with ULB's geographical location at the heart of Europe, has made the university particularly successful in establishing international partnerships and in attracting external funding for collaborative research efforts.

In line with broader trends amongst leading research universities, ULB's boundaries between faculties and specialized departments are reducing in favour of a broader strategy of interdisciplinary research, whereby collaborative teams partner across disciplines with perceived synergies, such as medicine and engineering. ULB's inter-disciplinary approach is cautious however, given the overall institutional strategy of ensuring strength in core disciplines as a precursor to any such collaborative efforts.

Major Discoveries

3 Nobel Prizes, 24 Francqui Prizes, 1 Fields Medal, 3 Wolf Prizes and 1 Abel Prize are testament to ULB's success in pursuing curiosity-led research and investigating fundamental questions that have the potential to open up entirely new paths or research enquiry.

Today ULB researchers are at the forefront of a number of fundamental questions relating to the basic molecular processes that underlie the development of cancer, have contributed to the discovery of the Higgs Boson and influence international understanding of arctic marine biology and the geology of meteorites.

Partnerships, Innovation & Translational Research

ULB is an active international research collaborator alongside leading universities such as the University of Cambridge, the University of Oxford, and UC Berkeley. The university is a leading contributor to multi-lateral university associations such as the Network of Universities from the Capitals of Europe (UNICA). ULB's active collaboration with leading research universities is indicative of the institutional commitment to both basic and applied research, addressing fundamental questions that progress human understanding of our environment and surroundings.

From the applied research and private sector perspective, ULB has traditionally had strong relationships with industry in Belgium. The university is now increasingly focused on expanding its research portfolio into deeper and more mutually beneficial industrial collaboration, providing that principles of academic curiosity are kept intact, and clear synergies exist between ULB and external collaborators.

The Technology Transfer Office (TTO) acts as ULB's interface between discoveries made in the university's laboratories and market potential in the external economy. The TTO currently has a portfolio under management of 168 patents, 37 spin-off companies, 3 incubators, an investment fund and a biotechnology business park — Biopark Charleroi Brussels South. Whilst additional revenue streams are of interest through the commercialisation of research, the TTO's core mandate is to bring benefit into society and the broader economy through the discoveries made in ULB's laboratories and departments.

Teaching, Learning & Student Life

ULB's 40 undergraduate and 235 graduate programmes integrate traditional academic instruction with the growing trend towards direct involvement in research and problem-based learning. Students are able to "learn through doing" in an applied setting, whilst exploring the theoretical content of their respective programmes. As one progresses from undergraduate towards PhD level, the approach becomes increasingly multidisciplinary, with students able to diversify according to their own curiosities, aspirations and interests. ULB's tradition of grass roots directed research has successfully percolated through to the university's pedagogical philosophy.

Feeding through from ULB's increasing emphasis on bringing research discoveries from the university's laboratories to the open market, the university places great emphasis upon encouraging entrepreneurial skills development throughout the student community. ULB is focusing on becoming one of the pre-eminent PhD hubs in the European Union, with entrepre-neurialism and technology transfer being a key pillar of this ambition. ULB's excellence in basic research has set an excellent foundation for this strategic ambition; the key challenge now is to foster an entrepreneurial culture to match recent investments in infrastructure, so as to facilitate more of a translational philosophy amongst the student community.

ULB's location at the heart of Europe brings with it countless advantages in terms of study, culture, sports and leisure activities, quality of life and the availability of internship and career opportunities. Students can expect to enjoy a vibrant social life at the heart of the European Union. ULB provides a unique opportunity for great young minds the world over to enjoy the cosmopolitan culture found in Europe's most influential city.

Rank › 151 – 200

Name › Tsinghua University
Region › Asia/Pacific
Country › China
Founded › 1911

www.tsinghua.edu.cn

Core Research Strengths

Often referred to as the MIT of China, Tsinghua University has a very strong tradition in the engineering and computer sciences; and continues to lead China's strides towards development in these ever more competitive fields of engineering and academic endeavour. Tsinghua's pivotal strengths in advanced computer sciences and electronic engineering have attracted significant research funding; with the university receiving some US$250 million annually in sponsored research from the Chinese National Science & Technology Programs. As host institution to the Tsinghua National Laboratory for Information Science and Technology, the university's national leadership in these fields is without doubt.

Tsinghua's excellence in the computer sciences has its foundation in the university's world-class Department of Mathematical Sciences. First established in 1927, the department has paved the way for the university's leadership by developing institutes such as the Institute of Computational Mathematics and Operations Research.

Far from being confined to expertise in just one or two disciplines, Tsinghua has undertaken a significant program of expansion in recent years, with the establishment of numerous research programs and institutes in a diverse array of fields from renewable energies to Nano technology and materials science, through to bio-informatics and stem cell research.

Major Discoveries

Having developed over 11,000 patents between 1985 and 2010, Tsinghua University's reputation is one increasingly associated with cutting edge innovation. One such example of this is award winning Professor Yong Qiu, whose pioneering work on organic opto-electronics culminated in the development of an Organic Light-Emitting Device in 2010.

Partnerships, Innovation & Translational Research

A key part of Tsinghua's mission is the transfer of technology for the benefit of both society and the economy. First established in 1983, Tsinghua's Science and Technology Development Department has led nationally in developing the most effective model for Chinese universities to link industry, economic development and education through research.

Tsinghua University has extensive relationships throughout China, partnering with universities, regions, local municipalities, cities and leading industrial companies. Today, Tsinghua has over 1500 separate collaborative relationships with signed funding agreements in excess of US$100 million.

Established in 2001, Tsinghua's Centre for International Technology Transfer (TCIT) acts on behalf of the university and its industrial partners in developing collaborative research agreements internationally with leading counterpart universities, as well as private sector enterprises. The principal objective of the TCIT is to promote international technology transfer, bringing resources from abroad to benefit Chinese industry, as well as extending Chinese innovation out to the international market place.

Established in 1995, the Tsinghua University-Industry Cooperation Committee (UICC) acts as the main interface between Tsinghua University and its private sector partners. The UICC has an extensive membership of major multinational companies and Chinese industrial leaders; an interface of particular interest for institutions and enterprises interested in developing closer collaboration with such partners. The UICC provides a suite of services to its membership ranging from information and technology services to invites to specific "hot spot" conferences; all with a view to furthering Tsinghua University's capacity to develop China's innovative capacity. Tsinghua's portfolio of industry partners now spans the globe with companies such as Huawei, China Telecom, Bao Steel, Sony, Siemens and Toyota all well established partners of the university.

Collaborative efforts alongside world-class universities are also a critical component of Tsinghua's research strategy. The university's partners extend to some of the world's most prestigious and well-respected institutions such as with the Tsinghua – Cambridge – Massachusetts Low-Carbon Energy Union working alongside MIT and the University of Cambridge to develop low carbon energy solutions to today's challenges associated with energy security and global climate change.

Teaching, Learning & Student Life

Academic reform at Tsinghua University in recent years has been characterized by a growing emphasis on the development of innovative skills, creativity and practical problem solving amongst students. Programs such as the Tsinghua Xuetang Talent Program and Outstanding Engineering Education Plan are placing far greater emphasis on the individual talents of students through greater investment in teaching and learning capacity. The primary strategic objective ofPresident Chen Jining is greater investment of personnel and faculty, with a view to continued improvements in the calibre of Tsinghua graduates. Tsinghua University's culture is one of an actions speak louder than words approach, with students and faculty alike encouraged to focus their attention on practical problem solving and the rigours of research.

Tsinghua's doors are firmly open for international students the world over to benefit from the university's work ethic, as well as the beautiful Qing dynasty landscaped grounds the institution is located on. With downtown Beijing on Tsinghua's doorstep, as well as over 100 student associations and clubs to choose activities from, those in attendance at Tsinghua can expect to work hard, whilst at the same time significantly improving their understanding of Chinese culture and language, as well as developing a new network of friends in the country.

THE UNIVERSITY OF TEXAS
MD Anderson
~~Cancer~~ Center
Proton Therapy

Making Cancer History®

Rank › 151 – 200

Name › M. D. Anderson Cancer Center
Region › Americas
Country › United States
Founded › 1941

www.mdanderson.org

Core Research Strengths

Considered the preeminent cancer institute in the US, University of Texas MD Anderson Cancer Center invested approximately US$647 million in research through 2012. MD Anderson's research programme is considered one of the most productive in the world relating to our understanding of and means of combatting numerous forms of cancer. The clinical facility is also considered one of the best in the world, with cancer patients travelling from around the world to receive treatment at MD Anderson.

It holds 12 Specialized Programs of Research Excellence (SPORE) grants from the National Cancer Institute (NCI). These indicate their expertise in cancers such as bladder, brain, breast, head and neck, leukaemia, lung, lymphoma, melanoma, ovarian, pancreatic, prostate and uterine.

There are five general areas of research for all stages of cancer and clinical trials that act as research studies for new drugs, diagnostic procedures and therapy, which is conducted through seven research institutes. MD Anderson has expertise throughout the entire spectrum of our understanding of, and responses to cancer from the basic biological processes that underpin its development, to innovative new treatments and means of adjusting one's lifestyle to mitigate the development of cancer in the first place.

Multidisciplinary research has been launched in the Moon Shoots Program that uses researchers and clinicians from different fields to find ways to accelerate the pace of converting scientific discoveries into clinical advances. The Institute for Applied Cancer Science facilitates collaboration between academic medicine and biotechnology.

Major Discoveries

MD Anderson has achieved much in its commitment to "Making Cancer History" from basic research to detections, prevention, management and therapy. Some of these include:

› Developed mammography technology, showing that mammography can detect breast cancer at early, highly curable stages, leading to the adoption of standardized screening mammography.

› Pioneered ambulatory care of patients undergoing chemotherapy in cost-effective outpatient settings, now a standard practice worldwide.

› Demonstrated that chemotherapy can safely be given after the first trimester to pregnant women with breast cancer.

› Discovered the first successful chemotherapy (vincristine) for children with inoperable Wilms' tumor, a kidney cancer.

› Pioneered limb-sparing surgery for bone tumours and other sarcomas by implanting donor bones, and then using expandable metal prosthesis.

Partnerships, Innovation & Translational Research

The Office of Technology Commercialization (OTC) is responsible for the assessment, patenting and licensing of innovations and new technologies developed at MD Anderson. Its four point operational vision involves investing capital in a patent portfolio, seeking investment partners, managing operations to maximize returns, and seeking long term growth in license income and equity portfolio value. The technologies commercialised include new drugs, diagnostics, devices, and therapies used in cancer diagnosis and treatment. The OTC is also active in forming start-up companies around the innovations developed by researchers and faculty. However collaboration and material transfers are handled through the Office of Sponsored Programs (OSP).

MD Anderson is located at the heart of the Texas Medical Center, the largest single medical complex in the world. This platform facilitates collaborative efforts between MD Anderson and its various sister institutions, in what is without doubt one of the most active hubs of medical research in the world.

Teaching, Learning & Student Life

The main campus is located in the Texas Medical Center in Houston. Students at various levels are educated at the School of Health Professions, which offers bachelor's degrees in eight health disciplines; and the Graduate School of Biomedical Sciences that covers fields such as cancer and stem cell biology, cancer immunology, cancer genetics and systems biology of cancer. There are also numerous residency and fellowship programmes for physician and non-physician positions.

The MD Anderson Summer Experience offers paid research programs to high school, college; graduate and medical school students interested in careers in cancer research. There is also a non-competitive track that runs more as an unpaid internship.

The Global Academic Programs (GAP) facilitates educational exchange and collaboration with MD Anderson's sister institutes around the world.

UTHealth
The University of Texas
Health Science Center at Houston

Rank › 151 – 200

Name › UT Health — Texas
Region › Americas
Country › United States
Founded › 1972

www.uthouston.edu

Core Research Strengths

The University of Texas Health Science Center at Houston, founded in 1972, has become recognised internationally as one of the world's great research universities. Its $240 million research budget helps fund nearly 1,000 research projects.

The university is comprised of six separate schools, explains Executive Vice President of Academic and Research Affairs George Stancel, Ph.D. "There is a medical school, dental school, school of public health, school of nursing, graduate school of biomedical sciences and a school of biomedical informatics. That last school is unique and to our knowledge, it's the only one of its kind in America. It focuses exclusively on the information sciences as they are applied to biology and medicine."

One of the advantages of having these six schools is that it allows for a wide range of interdisciplinary work, says Stancel. "We can do collaborative research across the six different schools that is simply not possible at other universities."

The institution's research approach is affected by its location in the Texas Medical Center (TMC), says Stancel. "There are more than 50 other institutions in the TMC and more than 5 million patients every year. That matters because if one wants to do translational research that involves human subjects, the sheer numbers are available. One of our tremendous strengths is the ability to do translational research where we can look at the whole spectrum of research activities."

UTHealth also specialises in public health and policy. "One can make all the wonderful discoveries in a laboratory or the clinical trial, but if you can't really get that treatment out to people, you really haven't achieved what you want to do," Stancel says.

Major Discoveries

UTHealth faculty members have made many critical discoveries during their careers, both at UTHealth and through other appointments. They include Stanley Schultz, M.D., whose work formed the basis for oral rehydration therapy for people suffering from diarrheal diseases; R. Palmer Beasley, Ph.D., who established the link between hepatitis B transmission from mothers to newborns and subsequent liver cancer; Dianna Milewicz, M.D., Ph.D., whose team has discovered multiple genes that predispose people to aortic aneurysms; and Barry Davis, M.D., Ph.D., who led a landmark study revealing that diuretics were superior to newer, far more expensive medications in treating hypertension.

Other important discoveries have come from Eric Boerwinkle, Ph.D., whose research has uncovered genes related to common chronic diseases in humans; Craig Hanis, Ph.D., who found genetic markers linked to an increased risk of diabetes in Mexican Americans; and Ernst Knobil, Ph.D., whose discoveries led to understanding how human fertility is regulated and enabled the treatment of infertility.

Partnerships, Innovation & Translational Research

As with many leading universities, UTHealth is keen to develop international academic alliances. "We are very strategic about the international affiliations that we develop," says Stancel. "We identify institutions that share our interests in research so we may work together on common problems that can benefit both institutions' faculty and students. We have close to 100 formal affiliation agreements with universities around the world."

The university is just as keen to expand the international horizons of its students because it improves their medical capabilities, says the Executive Vice President. "We need to have opportunities for our U.S. students to get involved in either research or education in different communities because the virus or the bacteria doesn't stop at the Rio Grande River. It comes across."

Teaching, Learning & Student Life

UTHealth's location comes with many benefits, says Stancel. "Houston is incredibly diverse. We have wonderful ethnic communities. Houston sits on the Gulf of Mexico, so we are one of the largest ports in America. You have international large banking firms, big shipping companies and you have embassies and consulates that add to the international flavour of the city." The mix of people means that the city is home to a variety of great restaurants with diverse cuisines. Another benefit for students is that Houston is inexpensive, with a much lower cost of living than other American cities.

Another facet of UTHealth's appeal is the "outstanding education in the biomedical sciences." The university educates more healthcare professionals than any health-related institution in the State of Texas and features the nation's seventh-largest medical school. It also includes a psychiatric hospital and a growing network of clinics throughout the region. This expansive network of education infrastructure means that students can gain valuable medical experience. The university's primary teaching hospitals include Memorial Hermann-Texas Medical Center, Children's Memorial Hermann Hospital and Harris Health System's Lyndon B. Johnson Hospital.

The city's diversity is also helpful from a learning perspective, says Stancel. "It is critical for our clinical and translational research programs that we be able to study populations with different genetic backgrounds and different dietary habits. That variety is available right here in Houston."

香 港 大 學
THE UNIVERSITY OF HONG KONG

Rank › 151 – 200

Name › The University of Hong Kong
Region › Asia/Pacific
Country › Hong Kong, China
Founded › 1911

www.hku.hk

Core Research Strengths

The University of Hong Kong (HKU) is well known for being a comprehensive university with research excellence spanning ten faculties. However, its Vice-Chancellor and President, Professor Lap-Chee Tsui, believes that the university's Li Ka Shing Faculty of Medicine stands out.

"The Faculty of Medicine has really made significant research contributions, particularly in the areas of infectious diseases, liver disease and cancer. Other research areas, such as Chemistry, are also performing strongly, with our chemists very well cited internationally and winning international awards," says Professor Tsui.

In other disciplines, such as Social Sciences and Law, the impact is very strong regionally, especially in Mainland China. But overall, the university strategically identifies research areas and themes that reflect issues of local, regional and global concern, thus maximising the strength and scope of its academic endeavours.

Like many world-class universities, HKU follows an interdisciplinary approach that encourages interaction between different areas of expertise. What, however, is different about HKU are the ways it achieves that goal. For example, Professor Tsui takes the novel step of hosting luncheons with colleagues from various faculties.

"I have luncheons with them to bring the different disciplines in the same room, and I would make sure that they talk to each other, because just over lunch sometimes they have ideas that other people have never heard of. So many things happen over lunch."

Major Discoveries

Given the university's expertise with infectious diseases it is perhaps little surprise that it has the largest collection of flu strains. For example, it played an important role in battling Severe Acute Respiratory Syndrome – more commonly known as SARS – which affected the whole region in 2003. The excellence of its research is reflected in the fact that the virus that causes the syndrome – the coronavirus – was first identified at HKU.

Partnerships, Innovation & Translational Research

In recent years, the university has recognised that it needs to change how it manages technology transfer with the private sector. For example it recently established a dedicated office to act as the interface with external partners. But the change is much more profound than simply opening an office, says President Tsui, it is a "total transformation".

"In the old days, the university encouraged the teachers to start companies, but clearly that is not a model that a publicly funded institution should pursue. Instead, we now encourage knowledge transfer or the intellectual property to be utilised, but without necessarily owning companies. In effect, we encourage our teachers to partner with people who understand how to run companies and commercial ventures."

Prof. Tsui also sees the process differently from other universities. "Instead of 'knowledge transfer', we call it 'knowledge exchange' because I understand we can also learn a lot from the community. Therefore, the teachers have to learn and have more interaction with the community. This is how we build excellence."

Teaching, Learning & Student Life

Having a university situated in the heart of one of the world's major business and finance centres is a massive help for engendering a sense of entrepreneurialism amongst students. Indeed HKU runs lots of field programmes that allow students to work with, and learn from, local businesses.

When it comes to academic work inside the classroom, the university has a very student-focused approach, says Professor Tsui. "Study has to be student-centred. It is about 'teaching', obviously, but we also emphasise 'learning' as the unit of discussion, which is how much a student will learn. Therefore, learning outcomes and learning objectives have to be clearly articulated for every course." Like many of his counterparts, Professor Tsui recognises that a leading university must be international in its outlook. However, he feels that this

internationalisation cannot be measured through exchange programmes or student numbers alone.

"Internationalisation is a mind-set. It's not just saying how many percentages of faculties or students have come from different countries. We are not talking about numbers. In fact, we are talking about the mind-set that is in our teaching; internationalisation is part of the curriculum. Of course, science and technology, as I have said earlier, perhaps is always very international, at least at a basic level, but there may also be some international elements in terms of application and so on."

"In the Humanities and areas such as Law, we definitely want to bring in different perspectives in a discussion – in terms of an issue like human rights, for example, which our University is quite well known for – and that means having different opinions and a diversity of ideas. I think this is definitely going to create a very dynamic learning environment for students. So, therefore it is not just about numbers, but we are talking about the content, the quality of the thinking. Of course, internationalisation also means sharing with others." Sharing with others, partnership, engagement, diversity, quality and excellence – these are the themes that Professor Tsui keeps returning to. And ultimately, these are exactly the qualities that make HKU what it is today.

University of Glasgow

Rank › 151 – 200

Name › The University of Glasgow
Region › Europe
Country › United Kingdom
Founded › 1451

www.gla.ac.uk

Core Research Strengths

With an annual research budget of approximately £130million the University of Glasgow is regarded as one of the UK's top-tier research institutions. Principal of the University of Glasgow, Professor Anton Muscatelli says the money is used to fund research across a wide number of disciplines.

"The University of Glasgow employs a broad based approach ranging from disciplines such as medicine all the way through to the social sciences; within this range though it is important to understand that there are approximately a dozen or so core priority areas of research. For example, within the medical sciences there is a clear emphasis on cancer research."

The University of Glasgow is widely regarded as one of the leading cancer research universities in Europe. A position it has cemented with the recent opening of a £30million Translational Research Centre for Cancer. The University of Glasgow also has very strong research capacity in science and engineering. Again the approach is centre-led, this time through the university's leading nano-fabrication research facility. Another leading centre is the Polyomics Facility, which was funded by the Wellcome Trust.

But Principal Muscatelli is also keen to stress the university's strengths in other areas. "With regards to the Social Sciences, the University of Glasgow has some of the strongest UK departments in areas such as economics and finance, as well as in fields such as public policy and criminal justice. With regards to the arts, Glasgow is the leading global university in the field of Scottish Studies focusing on areas such as Celtic and Gaelic History and Literature, as well as Art History, Cultural Policy and Film and the Cultural and Creative Arts."

Major Discoveries

Unsurprisingly for a university that's existed for more than half a millennia the University of Glasgow has a rich history of discovery.

At present the University of Glasgow is one of the largest participants at CERN in Geneva on the Large Hadron Collider.

Partnerships, Innovation & Translational Research

One way that the university engages with international partnerships is through collaborations with other universities. For example it currently has research partnerships with Columbia University in the US and the Confucius Institute in Tianjin. Principal Muscatelli believes these "partnerships are of immense importance for the international evolution of Glasgow's research priorities and the experiences we can expose our people to."

When it comes to its relationships with the private-sector, Glasgow has one of the most unique approaches in the world. A major challenge for leading universities is how to collaborate with corporations and use intellectual property. And, as the Principal explains, Glasgow has come up with a radical solution to the problem. "For the majority of our IP The University of Glasgow has recently rolled out a free licensing scheme called Easy Access IP whereby the vast majority of the intellectual property developed at Glasgow is made available to the public and businesses at no cost. The University of Glasgow has pioneered this approach, and is the world's first major university to adopt this methodology; we have now been approached by several universities throughout the UK that are interested in adopting this approach as the way forward."

Teaching, Learning & Student Life

With approximately 23,000 students and more than 6,000 staff Glasgow is one of the UK's bigger universities. But recently the university's structure has been changed, says Principal Muscatelli.

"The University had 9 faculties and approximately 50 departments that moved into 4 colleges and 19 schools respectively, plus 7 cross-cutting research institutes. The whole idea and drive behind this was to try to maximize opportunities for collaboration whilst maintaining a strong set of researchers that had the freedom to focus on their respective specialisms. This has been a very interesting period, over the past two years since these changes were completed we have started to see a range of benefits emerge in the

breakthroughs being made by our researchers."

Another big change taking place is the makeup of the student body. "The University of Glasgow is placing a huge focus on further increasing the international profile of our student population", says the Principal. "Glasgow currently has 15% international students; this will soon increase to 20% of the student population. Internationalization is at the core of The University of Glasgow's 2020 strategic plan, our engagement with China forms one of the key tenets to this strategy. We value the levels of diversity we have at the University of Glasgow, from both international and rest of UK students, and very much believe that our student population values this diversity also."

THE UNIVERSITY
OF AUCKLAND
NEW ZEALAND
Te Whare Wānanga o Tāmaki Makaurau

Rank › 151 – 200

Name › The University of Auckland
Region › Asia/Pacific
Country › New Zealand
Founded › 1883

www.auckland.ac.nz

Core Research Strengths

Founded in 1883, Auckland is now the country's largest university with 38,500 students, producing nearly 10,000 graduates each year. It's also a strong research university and has been rated as having a third of New Zealand's top researchers.

Vice Chancellor Stuart McCutcheon believes that biological sciences are one of the university's main strengths. "A large part of the country's industry is related to the biological sciences, and areas like food production. We also have a very strong drug discovery capability it's the largest drug discovery team in New Zealand, with particular capabilities in areas such as cancer, diabetes and, neurological diseases. We also have a major cancer research centre, brain research centre and we host the National Centre of Research Excellence for drug discovery."

Another of the university's leading centres is the Auckland Bioengineering Institute. The institute is ranked as one of the best in the world for its field, and the Vice Chancellor thinks that its success is down to its interdisciplinary approach. "It brings together capability in the university from the Faculty of Medical and Health Sciences, from the Faculty of Engineering and from the Faculty of Science in terms of computer science and mathematical modelling capabilities; and that operates really across all of the human physiological systems, modelling from the Nano scale right up to the whole body scale."

That same multi-disciplinary research is found across the university, says Vice Chancellor McCutcheon. Another example, he notes, is the Centre for Brain Research.

"This centre looks at everything to do with the brain and neurological disease. By linking together our researchers across the university we are able to create very large teams that can address some of these challenges and opportunities that might otherwise be difficult to address."

Major Discoveries

In the 1960s Professor Sir Graham Liggins found that treating pregnant women with steroids could prevent premature babies dying from inadequate lung function. This discovery has saved thousands of lives worldwide.

In this century one of the most important discoveries has been induction power – a technique to charge electric vehicles without plugging them in. With commercial agreements recently signed this invention could soon start changing the world around us.

Partnerships, Innovation & Translational Research

International partnerships are very important, says the Vice Chancellor. "We have focused on a limited number of high value partnerships rather than trying to have vast numbers of MOU's." The University of Auckland is the only university to be a member of both the Association of Pacific Rim Universities, the Worldwide Universities Network and Universitas 21.

In order to facilitate relations with its many external private sector partners, the University has set up a research commercialisation company called Auckland UniServices. It has been "very successful", says the Vice Chancellor, with about two and a half thousand live contracts with commercial companies both in New Zealand and overseas at any one time.

The IP policy is a very important part of the strategy, says the Vice Chancellor. "IP created by our staff as staff members is owned by the university. The university delivers all of that intellectual property to UniServices, which goes through the patenting, protection and commercialization process. If we are successful in commercializing, then the university's profits from the commer-cialization will be split one third to the inventors, one third to the inventors' department or school, and one third to the university. We generally don't sell IP. We generally license that because if you license IP to a spin out, which then fails you have the opportunity if you construct things the right way to repatriate the IP, and to look at other ways of commercializing it."

Teaching, Learning & Student Life

With its spectacular landscapes and famous extreme sports, New Zealand has plenty to offer students. The Vice Chancellor, acknowledges that it's a big plus. "People who come here call it paradise. Students can get connected to New Zealand quite quickly, and there is within a short distance of central Auckland a wide range of sporting and recreational pursuits. Our students drive to the mountains to go skiing. Equally, they can be at the beach in less than a half an hour, they can be in forests within an hour if they head west, or a little further to the north. There is a raft of possibilities within a very short distance of the campus."

When it comes to the learning experience, students will receive ample research opportunities. "Quite a lot of our students will do a period of study offshore during their degree. It might be a semester abroad, it might be an overseas research project, and we encourage them to get research and learning experiences offshore as well as at home."

Given that the makeup of the student body is very international, it helps that Auckland is cosmopolitan, says Vice Chancellor McCutcheon. "It is the most multi-cultural city in New Zealand, which means that students coming here to study have inbuilt support mechanisms because there are local communities relevant to most of those international students."

香港中文大學
The Chinese University of Hong Kong

Rank › 151 – 200

Name › The Chinese University of Hong Kong
Region › Asia/Pacific
Country › Hong Kong, China
Founded › 1963

www.cuhk.edu.hk

Core Research Strengths

Given the university's name, it's little wonder that one of its main areas of expertise is Chinese studies. Indeed the study of Asian cultures is the flagship of CUHK's research. But, as President Joseph Sung explains, that's not the university's only speciality.

"We also have a very strong faculty of engineering which was started by Professor Charles Kao, the Noble Laureate in Physics of 2009. We also excel at agriculture and biotechnology. For example, we have a State Key Laboratory in Agricultural Biotechnology that works closely with China first to study the genomics of different crops, which can grow in more extreme environments such as higher salinity of the water or drought, and also then to produce higher protein content in those crops."

With the world's population expected to increase by 30% by 2050 this is a very exciting area, facing one of humanities most serious problems – how to feed itself.

As a professor of Medicine himself, Sung has an understandable affection for the Medical Faculty. "The biomedical studies in this university is also one of our flagships. Professor Dennis Lo is a world leader in using plasma DNA to detect fetal DNA from pregnant women, a ground-breaking method in antenatal diagnosis. Because of the special environment in the healthcare system in Hong Kong, in which the majority of patients are actually being served in the public hospitals, we have the capability of doing some carefully-designed clinical trials. As a result, there are quite a few important clinical papers published in top-notch journals such as the New England Journal of Medicine and the Lancet that changed medical practice around the world, which come from this university."

Inter-disciplinary research teams have been established in the following areas;

1 › Neural and Cognitive Science – To study the normal development of language ability and disorders such as dyslexia, autism and post-stroke speech disorder.

2 › Big Data Decision Analytic – By setting up a platform using a data-intensive research methodology so as to aid the analysis of information from healthcare, climate, social media and logistics database;

3 › "Smart City" Research and Development – To explore how future cities should be developed in order to maintain sustainability and efficiency in energy consumption, whilst preserving cultures and traditions.

In all these research themes, national and international networks and partnerships have been built.

Major Discoveries

The CUHK has several world medical firsts. In 1992 it established the world's first comprehensive and multi-functional Skin Bank. Their surgeons here performed the first laparoscopic gall-bladder surgery in Asia. In the past two decades, researchers in CUHK have pioneered several innovative therapies for peptic ulcer bleeding, including the use of endoscopic hemostasis and treatment of Helicobacter pylori, a bacteria discovered in human stomach.

Partnerships, Innovation & Translational Research

Like many of his counterparts around the world, President Sung sees the potential in partnerships with industry. However, he admits that while some progress has been made, there is more work to be done.

"Partnering industry is very important for certain specialities or disciplines such as engineering, medical science as well as environmental science. However, since there are not that many industries in Hong Kong, and also the funding in research in Hong Kong comes from the UGC which is University Grant Committee, it's inclined to fund more upstream research – basic research. Therefore, in the past two decades more emphasis has been put on basic research instead of very downstream applied research."

Partnerships have been more successful in the medical field. As one of the leading medical research centres in Asia, CUHK has a wealth of specialised knowledge and technology to share with the public.

Teaching, Learning & Student Life

Hong Kong may be thousands of miles away from Oxford and Cambridge, but thanks to CUHK's founders, the institutions share some similar traditions. CUHK has a collegial system, with nine separate colleges, each are responsible for personal and social development, as well as general education. It may seem a cosmetic difference but it has a big impact on the student experience, says Prof Sung. "College is different from student hostels because it is not just providing accommodation but it has its own academic and teaching campus. We provide colleges with tutors and professors so that they would offer courses which we call College General Education, and also choose activities such as doing community service as experiential learning."

The other factor that makes CUHK stand out among Asian universities is the strong focus it puts on the liberal arts studies. There are many interdisciplinary courses available at CUHK such as urban studies, earth system science and environmental studies. One very popular course in CUHK is called Global Business Studies, which is a joint program between CUHK, University of Copenhagen and University of North Carolina. Students from HK, Denmark and the United States will form a class and spend one semester in each country to enrich their international exposure.

Technical University of Denmark

DTU

Rank › 151 – 200

Name › Technical University of Denmark
Region › Europe
Country › Denmark
Founded › 1829

www.dtu.dk

Core Research Strengths

Thanks to its origins as an early 19th century polytechnic, the Technical University of Denmark has always had a strong emphasis on creating value and promoting welfare by exploiting the interaction between the technical sciences and the natural sciences. The university received a big boost in 2007 when five National Research Institutions merged with DTU. That expanded the university's research capabilities and brought extra funding contracts with the Danish government. Nowadays it has a meaty €246.5 million research budget to carry its 19th century aim into the 21st century.

The university does not follow a broad-based approach, says university President Anders Bjarklev. "We keep the focus on what we are good at – i.e. the engineering disciplines – and collaborate closely with national and international universities, researchers, industry and authorities. A key element of engineering is to work together with other people who have complementary expertise." One of DTU's chief goals, says President Bjarklev, is to be among the 10 leading technical universities in Europe. To that end the university has implemented a detailed research strategy, he explains. One part of the plan is investment.

"We have – and are continuously – investing heavily in infrastructure. We operate and maintain state-of-the-art processing equipment and cleanroom facilities, which allow us to employ nanotechnology in small-scale production/fabrication within broad technology areas. We have fused departments and created interdisciplinary networks, which strengthens our international impact, and enhances our ability to collaborate with academic and industrial partners throughout the world." Indeed, as a result of this investment biotechnology is now one of the fastest-growing fields in DTU. Mechanical and electrical engineering are other core research strengths.

Much of DTU's research capabilities are aimed at humanity's key problems. One such area is society's transition from fossil fuels to other sources of energy, says Bjarklev. "Our chemical engineering experts have been working on various technologies where you could store fresh hydrogen more compactly and

more safely. So, I would say DTU has been quite successful in enhancing the technology and finding alternative ways to store chemical components and energy."

Major Discoveries

Denmark is home to one of the world's leading wind turbine manufacturers, Vestas, and DTU is working hard to make sure that the country keeps its edge in that competitive field. It has some unique full-scale research facilities – including a test centre for large wind turbines up to 250 metres in height. Those research facilities are thrown open to national and international companies in a bid to attract private-sector collaboration. The university's science and technology parks also help companies build on DTU's research.

The university also has an impressive track record of bringing ideas to market. Last year, DTU made more than 100 new inventions, was awarded some 60 patents and founded 3 new companies on IP from the university. The DTU also has a strong programme of international academic partnerships, says President Bjarklev. "These alliances cover not only research, but also educational programmes, innovation and collaboration with industries. Our main partner universities are in Europe and in Asia.

Partnerships, Innovation & Translational Research

Denmark is home to one of the world's leading wind turbine manufacturers, Vestas, and DTU is working hard to make sure that the country keeps its edge in that competitive field. It has some unique full-scale research facilities – including a test centre for large wind turbines up to 250 metres in height. Those research facilities are thrown open to national and international companies in a bid to attract private-sector collaboration. The university's science and technology parks also help companies build on DTU's research.

The university also has an impressive track record of bringing ideas to market. Last year, DTU made more than 100 new inventions, was awarded some 60 patents and founded 3 new companies on IP from the university. The DTU also has a strong programme

of international academic partnerships, says President Bjarklev. "These alliances cover not only research, but also educational programmes, innovation and collaboration with industries. Our main partner universities are in Europe and in Asia.

Teaching, Learning & Student Life

Officially the university is headquartered just to the north of Copenhagen, but has facilities in practically every region of Denmark. However, one thing all of the campuses have in common is a "special Scandinavian atmosphere", says the President.

It's not a category that shows up in university rankings or league tables but he feels it is one of DTU's strongest assets. "At DTU students and teachers work more informally than at most other universities. Classes are never cancelled and serious study takes place in a relaxed and social atmosphere. Education is largely based on the students' active participation and taking independent responsibility. Students learn to work individually and in groups. They also learn to ask questions, be innovative and to find and explore interrelationships. There is a refreshing lack of hierarchy at DTU. Professors go by their first name and are easily accessible to students. DTU has an open door policy, so if you need to talk to your professor, you just knock on their door, or send them an e-mail."

This filters down to the organisation of the university. Student representatives and the management of the university work closely together, with regular three-monthly meetings. "Another unique feature is that our students have access to all our amazing facilities as a matter of course", says the President. "They have hands-on access because teamwork, networking, and entrepreneurship are essential qualifications for a modern engineer." Moreover those facilities are in the process of being upgraded. Four new teaching and research buildings are being built during the next three years. The idea behind the new buildings is to put students in close contact with researchers and increase the opportunities for students to understand how research works.

Rank › 151 – 200

Name › Stony Brook University
Region › Americas
Country › United States
Founded › 1957

www.stonybrook.edu

Core Research Strengths

A member of the prestigious Association of American Universities (AAU), Stony Brook University is a leading public research university in the Northeast United States. With an annual research budget of more than $182 million, Stony Brook funds more than 1,800 active sponsored projects. The university's key research strengths are in science, engineering and applied sciences, basic medical sciences and applied medical science.

Within those areas there are three research programmes that particularly stand out because they are trying to "answer the big questions," says President Samuel L. Stanley Jr., MD. "The first is a programme in nuclear physics that is investigating the origins of the universe."

Another major line of research is the university's efforts to uncover clues about the roots of humankind. "We carry out research at the Turkana Basin Institute in Kenya, where we're discovering some of the best fossils known to exist. We're looking at human origins from as far back as 4.5 million years to as recently as 10,000 years ago," says President Stanley.

The other key area is energy, says President Stanley. "Like everyone else, we're interested in alternative forms of energy, but many of them are dependent on having better storage systems. So we have hired a leading scientist, Esther Takeuchi, to develop a center that will really focus on improving batteries and storage." One of the university's advantages in this field is that it manages Brookhaven National Laboratory, the only Department of Energy National Laboratory in the Northeast of the United States. "In terms of managing laboratories, it puts us in the same league as Berkeley, Stanford and University of Chicago," says the President.

Major Discoveries

It is a testament to the depth of research prowess at Stony Brook that some of its finest discoveries have come in fields not even discussed above. For example, Professor Paul Lauterbur first constructed a Nuclear Magnetic Resonance image in Stony Brook's Department of Chemistry in the 1970s. This pioneering work revolutionised medicine and led to Lauterbur's 2003 Nobel Prize in Medicine.

Partnerships, Innovation & Translational Research

The university's steady track record of bringing research to the market is reflected in the $10 million in license revenues it earns each year. Meanwhile, every year researchers at the university apply for a combined total of around 80 patents. But success has not made the university complacent.

"We're trying to find unique ways to partner with industry," says President Stanley. "So we've set up a building called the Center of Excellence in Wireless and Information Technology (CEWIT) where faculty and researchers work on ideas with market potential." The university has also established a CEWIT in Korea where researchers work with leading firms such as Samsung.

While these partnerships have obvious benefits for the university, the President believes that they're increasingly popular with corporations too. "There's a pullback of research and development – particularly research – at many of the major companies, so innovation is naturally finding a home in the research universities and the start-up companies that often emerge from those universities or that are guided by faculty from those universities."

Teaching, Learning & Student Life

Now is certainly a good time to join Stony Brook as a student as the university is in the midst of an exciting new programme called Project 50 Forward. It's a cross-university initiative that aims to improve academic and operational excellence. One tenet of this plan, for example, is that the university is hiring 250 additional faculty over the next five years to improve the faculty/student ratio.

In many ways Project 50 Forward is just carrying on Stony Brook's long-established tradition of delivering the best education possible, says the President. "It's much easier to make a small university seem large than it is to make a large university seem small, and we work to do that through our undergraduate colleges, education courses and through our small honours courses. We find ways to give students an individual experience."

Another significant Stony Brook advantage is its location. It is less than an hour's drive from New York City, meaning that students can enjoy all the cultural benefits of one of the world's most lively cities. Whether a student likes art, theatre, world cuisine or history, New York has it all. Being so close to such a major transport hub also makes Stony Brook very convenient for international students. Life on campus couldn't be more different from the hustle and bustle of New York.

Stony Brook is a peaceful place with a calming atmosphere that is ideal for serious study. Its 1,039-acre campus on Long Island's North Shore encompasses the main academic areas, a premier academic medical center and hospital, a new 85,000 square-foot campus recreation center, an 8,300-seat stadium and sports complex, and the Research and Development Park. Active students can take advantage of a wide range of sports programmes, while surfers, swimmers and beach lovers in general will be pleased to know that it's only a short trip to the Atlantic coast.

Rank › 151 – 200

Name › Shanghai Jiao Tong University
Region › Asia/Pacific
Country › China
Founded › 1896

www.sjtu.edu.cn

Core Research Strengths

Founded in 1896, Shanghai Jiao Tong University (SJTU) is one of the oldest institutions of higher learning in China. As early as the 1930's, SJTU has gained a reputation of nurturing top engineers. In 2005, a leading medical university – Shanghai Second Medical University was merged into SJTU. Today SJTU is among the best research universities in China and it is widely recognized for its strong research capacity in Engineering and Medicine, SJTU's Mechanical Engineering, Naval Engineering and Clinical Medicine are ranked top in China according to the national subject ranking done by the China Academic Degrees & Graduate Education Development Center.

SJTU has 31 academic schools, offering 203 Ph.D. programs and 28 post-doctorate programs; it also has 11 key state laboratories and state engineering research centers. The annual research income of SJTU is among the highest in China, SJTU's number of research grants received from the National Natural Science Foundation has been ranked first in China for many years. Its number of research papers, number of patents, and number of State Science & Technology Awards are all ranked at the very top among Chinese universities.

Major Discoveries

SJTU's professors and researchers have been performing cutting edge research and many of their research findings were recognized as internationally advanced, these include: identifying new mechanisms for differentiation and apoptosis of leukemic cells, controllable synthesis and self-assembly of hyper branched polymers, fluid flow, heat and mass transfer at the Nano-scale, as well as research in antibiotic metabolic engineering.

As a university with a very strong tradition in engineering, SJTU has made significant contributions to the development of various industries in China. Examples include: perfluoro-iono-mer exchange materials, the application of solar energy air conditioning and high efficiency heating, non-silicon MEMS technology, miniaturized high-performance microwave antennas, and the development of tissue engineering.

Partnerships, Innovation & Translational Research

Aiming to be at the forefront of modern technology, and to meet the strategic requirements of economic development, SJTU keeps enhancing cooperation between industry, academia, and research institutions by establishing partnerships with dozens of large enterprises. SJTU set up Shanghai Zizhu Science-based Industrial Park, together with Zijiang Holdings and the Minhang District Government, which has attracted over 100 enterprise research centers over 10 years. Household names such as Microsoft and Intel are all active investors. The establishment of Zizhu University Students & Teachers Entrepreneurship Center provides significant support for SJTU's Tech Innovation Programs and Innovative Talent Development.

Shanghai Zizhu Advanced Industrial Technology Research Institute (AITRI) is an independent institutional corporate co-founded by Minhang District Government and SJTU. Located in the Greater Zizhu Area including Minhang campus and in Zizhu Science and Technology Park, AITRI, when fully completed, will cover an area of about 600 acres. AITRI focuses on four areas: new energy, advanced manufacturing and new materials, digital information technology and health care. There are several public service platforms within AITRI, including Intelligence of Economic Knowledge (IEK), the Intellectual Property Office, the Investment Fund Club and Projects Clustering Division. The first batch of research institutes that AITRI housed include the National Engineering Research Center of Digital Television, the National Energy Smart Grid (Shanghai) R & D Centers, the Wind Power Research Center, the National Engineering Laboratory for Automotive Electronic Control Technology, The National Engineering Laboratory of Information Analysis and many others.

The first round of projects settled in AITRI include the Cross-Strait Broadband Wireless Communications Test Network R&D Center, the Forging Engineering Technology Center, the Nano Thin Film Solar Cell R & D Center and the Xin'ao Clean Energy (Shanghai) Joint R & D Center. Serving as a bridge linking industries and technologies,

AITRI aims to form a new pattern that allows industry to promote and initiate technological breakthroughs and allow these technologies to trigger further knowledge based industrial development. AITRI is committed to promoting high-tech pioneer studies, thereby tapping potential market demand, and leading the development of new industries.

Teaching, Learning & Student Life

From the early stage of its development, SJTU took a first-class education as its principal mission. This philosophy has evolved today treating education as an idea of knowledge exploration, capacity development and personal growth. Students from SJTU have won top international prizes in various competitions, including the ACM (Association for Computing Machinery) International Collegiate Programming Contest, the International Mathematical Contest in Modelling and the Electronics Design Contests.

The university has established experimental programs and courses for undergraduate education and professional education with high-quality resources and facilities. Additionally, research has been integrated into teaching and learning. The university developed 400 comprehensive and innovative courses, accounting for 85 percent of the total number of the experimental courses. It has also increased its investment in the teaching of experimental programs and continues to encourage participation in research projects and questions at all levels.

PEKING UNIVERSITY

Rank › 151 – 200

Name › Peking University
Region › Asia/Pacific
Country › China
Founded › 1898

www.pku.edu.cn

Core Research Strengths

Founded in 1898 as China's first comprehensive university, Peking University has continued this tradition into the 21st Century with its research expertise spread throughout a diverse array of fields. Nevertheless, Peking University is held in particularly high esteem for its research strengths throughout the arts and humanities with a particular emphasis on Chinese literature, poetry and art; as well as national leadership in the natural sciences.

Peking University is home to 20 schools and departments in the humanities and social sciences, demonstrating excellence throughout a breadth of research interests from the School of Marxism through to the Guanghua School of Management. Peking University is widely considered to be the pre-eminent global research institution in areas connected to China, Chinese history, anthropology, politics, culture, philosophy and art though the institution's 232 research centres covering these topic areas.

Peking University's strengths throughout the natural sciences have traditionally been exclusive to single discipline basic research; however vsimilarly to most other leading international research universities, Peking 's research strategy is increasingly evolving towards the interface of disciplines with expertise brought together from both the basic sciences, applied sciences and business in order to fulfil the university's mission of helping contribute to the continued development of the Chinese economy and society.

Major Discoveries

Peking University has traditionally been the founding place of the most influential socio-political and cultural movements in China; and has served the country's most prominent political leaders. The Communist, Nationalist and Liberal schools of thought were founded at Peking University. Peking University is also very well known for its contribution to Chinese literature, poetry and art with the publication of groundbreaking books such as Hong Zicheng's A History of Contemporary Chinese Literature.

Partnerships, Innovation & Translational Research

Peking University, similarly to China's leading research universities has in recent years significantly stepped up activity with regards to developing its international network of both research collaborators and affiliates for faculty and student exchange. Peking University now has well-established relationships with some of the world's leading research universities such as Stanford, Cornell, Yale and the University of Chicago.

Peking University's research enterprise is managed through the Office of Scientific Research, the interface through which potential collaborators should commence discussions. Whilst the university has not traditionally focused upon conducting collaborative research with industry, this is an increasing priority as PU's traditional mission of leading the cultural and social development of China is increasingly intertwined with national economic development.

Teaching, Learning & Student Life

Having had the original campus located in the Forbidden City, Peking University's tradition of architectural splendour is unprecedented amongst Chinese universities. Located today in Beijing's western suburb of Haidian, a hotbed of academic endeavour; Peking University's campus is located amongst former Qing Dynasty royal gardens; retaining many traditional structures and historical buildings.

Peking University's several thousand international students not only benefit from a wonderfully pleasing aesthetic environment, but also an institution located at the centre of Chinese culture and political power; offering perhaps the best window of understanding into the world's emerging new power than any other university in the world.

Peking University's traditions at the heart of China's socio-political development runs closely throughout the university's culture, with countless global leaders and statesmen regularly in attendance at the university giving speeches and seminars. Notable recent speakers such as Bill Clinton, Tony Blair and Henry Kissinger only serve to further enhance the atmosphere of leadership that Peking University displays.

Leadership forms an important part of student development at Peking University, with student associations and extra-curricular activities very much geared up towards stimulating and honing one's leadership skills. Peking University's more than 200 student clubs facilitate a range of interests such as sports, community service, media and the creative arts.

OSU
Oregon State
UNIVERSITY

Rank › 151 – 200

Name › Oregon State University
Region › Americas
Country › United States
Founded › 1858

www.oregonstate.edu

Core Research Strengths

Oregon State University's (OSU) US$281 million research expenditures in 2012 were spread throughout the university's diverse array of internationally leading research departments, ranging from the agricultural sciences and oceanography through to nuclear engineering and microbiology. OSU's diversity is very much underscored by its status as a land, sea, sun and space grant university; one of only two such institutions in the United States.

OSU's diversity and flagship status has a significant influence over its research strategy. Vice President of University Relations Steve Clark explains: "We take the mission of education and research very seriously, and we believe there's a connection between our research mission, the economy, academic advancement of our communities, of our state, of our nation and world. So, we tie those together. We do research. Yes, we teach. But we link them together. And the university has a strategic plan that is focused on three predominant areas that are founded upon a very strong liberal arts education." Advancing the science of sustainable earth systems is one of OSU's strategic focuses within the university's strategic plan. Harnessing its world-class disciplinary strengths as in agriculture, marine sciences and forestry, Oregon State is working to better understand how our eco-systems will respond to massive population growth, and the most effective means of adapting to the challenges posed by phenomena such as food an energy security.

Under the banner of improving human health and wellness, Oregon State promotes a concept called "One Health." This second core research area considers all factors relating to health and human wellness. One Health looks throughout a diverse array of disciplines at preventive means of maintaining optimal human health and wellness through the university's colleges of Public Health and Human Sciences, Pharmacy and Veterinary Medicine, and the OSU Extension Service. OSU's veterinary school is closely involved with this program, treating animals as not external to human health, but animal well-being as something that is integral to maintaining human health.

Promoting Economic Growth and Social Progress forms the final strand of OSU's three-pronged university-wide strategy. Drawing together disciplinary expertise from throughout the humanities and social sciences, combined with technological excellence in areas such as energy and Nano-technology, OSU is working to develop the technologies and skilled workforce required for a 21st century global economy and international society.

Major Discoveries

Undergraduate Chemistry senior Sam Bartlett, with guidance from assistant professor Chris Beaudry developed the most efficient and productive method yet reported for a fundamental step commonly used to synthesize new molecules. A revolutionary piece of science especially for an undergraduate student, and the work done by Bartlett and Beaudry has potential applications for industries and researchers the world over. OSU also is presently participating in one of the world's largest ever oceanography research projects: the Ocean Observatories Initiative (OOI). Through its network of sensor systems, the OOI will measure an array of geological, biological, chemical and physical variables in the ocean enabling better monitoring and understanding of the on-going changes that occur within our marine environments.

Partnerships, Innovation & Translational Research

Oregon State's 42 percent increase in industry-sponsored research over the past two years is indicative of the university's growing focus on collaborative partnerships with the private sector. OSU's Office for Commercialization and Corporate Development (OCCD) supports both the translation of research findings into the real economy, as well as acting as the interface between Oregon State researchers and corporate entities interested in leveraging benefits from their expertise. Thus far in the 2013 financial year, the OCCD has agreed 30 collaborative research contracts with industry and submitted the disclosure of 30 different inventions, a remarkably high frequency of activity when compared both nationally and internationally.

Teaching, Learning & Student Life

Oregon State's philosophy rests upon close collaborative relationships between faculty and students, with a strong emphasis upon fulfilling potential. Vice President Clark highlights that: "The ethos at Oregon State is to invest in individuals, to invest in students individually and to help them learn, mature in some cases, and achieve outstanding things." International enrolment at OSU has doubled in recent years as an institutional focus grows Oregon State University's commitments to the state of Oregon, but also its capacity to have an impact globally; and benefit from the university's strategic location on the U.S. West Coast facing the rapidly emerging East Asian region.

OSU's international focus is far from limited to attracting students to its campus. The university has a well-established global network of partner institutions to facilitate OSU students' ambitions to experience study abroad. OSU students from around the world can expect a very warm welcome from people throughout the state of Oregon given the mutually beneficial relationship that has developed at the university. An Oregonian himself, Vice President Clark explains the importance of this symbiotic relationship.

"Oregon has a population of approximately 3.5 million people. It's not dense except in a few places, Portland for example. OSU has a physical presence in all 36 counties. We have offices, experiment stations, forest research labs, and OSU Extension Offices everywhere, and we literally have employees including researchers working throughout the state of Oregon. We did an economic impact study called Impact 2012, and we learned that our overall economic impact internationally is $2.06 billion. In the state of Oregon, it's just under that – about $1.93 billion. $950 million dollars of our economic impact is within our local Corvallis campus community, but another $983 million is throughout the state of Oregon. That means that our faculty, our researchers, our extension agents and our students are actually involved in economic change, and in significant activities relating to lifestyle, health and community that are not only delivering on the economy, but that are making cultural and social improvements."

OREGON
HEALTH
&SCIENCE
UNIVERSITY

Rank › 151 – 200

Name › Oregon Health & Science University
Region › Americas
Country › United States
Founded › 1974

www.ohsu.edu

Core Research Strengths

As one of the nation's top biomedical research institutions, Oregon Health & Science University has an annual research budget over $350 million to fund more than 3,000 research projects ranging from studies in the basic sciences to studies on prevention, detection and the treatment of disease.

Neuroscience is one of the strongest research areas at OHSU, says Vice President of Research Dr. Daniel Dorsa. "We are routinely ranked in the top five institutions in the country when it comes to neuroscience funding from the National Institutes of Health. Meanwhile with the formation of the OHSU Knight Cancer Institute, oncology studies are very robust and a growing part of our research portfolio. I would also include immunology and biomedical informatics as additional strengths."

OHSU's researchers adopt an array of multidisciplinary and collaborative approaches to solving the most intractable problems in human health – including diseases of the central nervous system, cardiovascular-related research, cancer, rare genetic disorders, and infectious disease.

"As for collaborations, the future of healthcare depends on inter-professional partnerships between nursing, medicine, dentistry, and pharmacy in a way that has never been done before. We have a strong commitment to interdisciplinary and inter-professional education. In fact, our commitment is so strong; we are in the midst of building a collaborative education and research building on the Willamette River called the OHSU/OUS Collaborative Life Sciences Building. At that location, we will be training dentists, physicians, nurses and pharmacists in the same setting so that they will learn to work as medical teams."

Major Discoveries

OHSU's Dr. Brian Druker played a key role in the discovery of Gleevec, a drug marketed by Novartis, which was initially used to treat a form of leukaemia but now is being used to treat many different cancers. Since receiving FDA approval in 2001 it is estimated that the drug has saved more than 100,000

lives. Its discovery signalled the dawn of the era of personalized medicine.

Many future advancements are expected to come out of the OHSU Advanced Imaging Center. The center specializes in the advancement of MRI technology for various uses including the diagnosis of breast cancer and functional MRI studies geared towards understanding the worldwide obesity epidemic.

Partnerships, Innovation & Translational Research

The university serves as a catalyst for the region's bioscience industry and is an incubator of discovery. It has a long track record of translating its research into commercial success stories that improve the lives of millions. Since 1970 OHSU research has generated 74 start-up companies. This trend is accelerating as 43 companies have been created since 2000. In the past five years, an average of nearly four start-up companies per year developed out of OHSU research, while the university has disclosed 135 inventions in 2012 alone.

As a general rule, the new companies have specialized in pharmaceutical development, medical devices, computer technology and environmental health.

The Technology Transfer and Business Development Office manage the start-up process. This office licenses OHSU's intellectual property; links business with OHSU technologies and expertise; negotiates industry research collaborations; and launches companies based on OHSU technologies.

Teaching, Learning & Student Life

As Oregon's only public academic health center, OHSU takes its commitment to the state very seriously. The university's medical facilities care for more than 235,000 patients each year from around the region. In addition, OHSU plays a leadership role in coming up with solutions to longstanding health problems faced throughout the state and the nation. OHSU has worked to improve health care access, increase transparency, take part in the evolution of medical ethics and address America's health workforce shortages.

OHSU's dedication to patient care is not just good for the state, it also mattersto students. After all, caring for so many patients provides students with a chance to learn first-hand how research can deliver tangible improvements. OHSU emphasizes patient-centred care, with students learning not only in classrooms but also at patients' bedsides, physician's offices and community settings, such as homeless shelters, juvenile detention centres, elementary schools and child care centres throughout Oregon.

Dr Dorsa has no doubt that this approach is one of the things students really like about the university. "Students appreciate the very collaborative environment which has been established here. We try to keep the doors open in the laboratories and research rooms so that the students can learn a lot more than they would have if they were just embedded in one laboratory."

Another big plus for students, says Dr. Dorsa, is the surrounding campus. "Oregon is really quite spectacular and unique. Two hours from OHSU in one direction is the Oregon coast, two hours away in the other direction are the mountains, where you can hike, camp and ski. So, if you are a student at OHSU it is still possible to get away and enjoy that part of life. That's a very attractive thing for current and future students. We call it the Mount Hood effect. When you look out and you see a beautiful view of the mountain, it's hard to leave this place."

NC STATE UNIVERSITY

Rank › 151 – 200

Name › North Carolina State University
Region › Americas
Country › United States
Founded › 1887

www.ncsu.edu

Core Research Strengths

With more than 34,000 students and more than 8,000 faculty and staff, North Carolina State University is a comprehensive university known for its leadership in education and research, and globally recognized for its science, technology, engineering and mathematics leadership. The university commands a $325 million annual research budget.

"We are a very technical based university," explains Chancellor Randy Woodson, "and we're particularly strong in quantitative sciences, statistics and applied mathematics."

A core research strength is engineering. The university has the third largest college of engineering in the United States. Within engineering, nuclear, industrial, chemical, and the traditional disciplines of mechanical and aeronautical stand out in particular.

The life sciences are also an important part of NC State's research portfolio. Traditionally, because of the state's agricultural base, the university's life science efforts have focused on species that have agricultural relevance such as plants and microbes.

"Within that context you'll find a lot of strength in genetics," says Woodson. "We have a member of the National Academy of Sciences who is a fruit fly geneticist and another member of the academy that specialises in insect genetics."

Interdisciplinary research is a key part of the university's approach. Interestingly Woodson thinks that it is a natural process.

"Interdisciplinary work is easy to encourage because scientists and engineers and others tend to come together to address big problems and bring their science to the table."

He also highlights the key role that research grants play.

"I think that the extent to which the funding agencies are pushing us to be interdisciplinary creates more opportunities for researchers to work in teams where you bring people together across the university."

Major Discoveries

The smart solid-state transformers developed by researchers at the FREEDM Systems Center have been ranked as one of the 10 most important emerging technologies by MIT's Technology Review. Smart transformers will have a revolutionary impact on the electrical grid, making power supplies more efficient and reliable, as well as enabling renewable technologies to be more easily integrated into the power system.

Partnerships, Innovation & Translational Research

North Carolina's success at working with commercial partners is reflected in the fact that it's ranked third among all public universities (without medical schools) in industry-sponsored research expenditures.

One reason for that is location, says the chancellor. "We are right in the middle of the very innovative part of the country in what's called Research Triangle Park. Most of our research partnerships are built around our connections to industry. Because of our strength in programs like agriculture, textiles and engineering, our work tends to be very relevant to emerging industries. We pride ourselves on having a very low bureaucratic threshold for engaging with private research enterprises." Another important partnership is with the National Science Foundation, says Woodson.

"Every year the NSF funds two or three new engineering research centers. These are very large collaborative partnerships across multiple universities. We are the only university in America now to have two active engineering research centers, and we just had a new one funded in electrical engineering related to wearable biomedical devices that monitor health parameters and physiological parameters. So I think we do an excellent job of partnering with other universities as well."

That success is carried abroad too, through agreements with universities in China, Chile and the Czech Republic.

Teaching, Learning & Student Life

About a quarter of NC State students live on campus and that creates a lively atmosphere. Student traditions, such as the Krispy Kreme Challenge – where students have to eat doughnuts in the middle of a long-distance race – and the Shack-A-Thon – where they live in temporary shacks on campus – make service a core part of the NC State experience.

Life inside the classroom is pretty special too, says Woodson. "It's a real combination of a research park and a university. Our students can go to class in the morning, work in a faculty member's lab in the afternoon, and do an internship with a company without ever leaving campus."

Centennial Campus is a unique community of collaboration. Industry and government partners work alongside faculty, staff, post-docs and students conducting cutting-edge research in state-of-the-art facilities. Home to more than 130 corporate and government research partners, as well as incubator companies and NC State research units, Centennial Campus is the premier university research campus in the country.

It's not just a case of having lots of companies in a research park. The university has designed its courses to give students a combination of instruction, research opportunities and on-the-job experience. After a classroom-based course element students will either work in laboratories – where they work side-by-side with leading researchers in their fields – or at off-campus internships and co-ops that expose them to real-world challenges and experiences. The idea is that by the time NC State students graduate, they have not only mastered their area of expertise, they have gained valuable job experience.

Rank › 151 – 200

Name › UNAM
Region › Americas
Country › Mexico
Founded › 1910

www.unam.mx

Core Research Strengths

Home to over 320,000 students and approximately 35,000 staff at anyone time, the National Autonomous University of Mexico (UNAM) is one of the world's largest universities encompassing a diverse array of research expertise. In recent years UNAM's stature has grown significantly, with the university home to many of Mexico's premier national research institutes. UNAM's research institutes increasingly look towards interdisciplinary challenges that are relevant to Mexico and the developing world. UNAM dominates the Mexican research landscape with approximately 60% of all published research produced in Mexico originating from UNAM researchers and departments.

Today UNAM's research eco-system consists of 28 institutes, 17 centres, 3 programs and 1 unit spread throughout Mexico from the central campus in Mexico City to sites as far away as the Yucatan. UNAM's research infrastructure averages approximately 6000 research projects annually resulting in approximately 3500 academic articles and 600 books published each year. The research infrastructure is organised into 2 main coordinating offices – the Humanities Coordinating Office and the Scientific Research Coordinating Office.

The Scientific Research sub-system is organised into 19 institutes and 10 centres grouped within 3 broad areas of knowledge; biological sciences and health, physics and mathematics and earth sciences and engineering. Similarly the Humanities research sub-system is organised into a collection of institutes and centres. Some of UNAM's best-known research institutes are the Institutes of Astronomy, Biotechnology and Nuclear Sciences.

Major Discoveries

Without a doubt the most important and internationally renowned research discovery made at UNAM was by Professor Mario Molina who won the 1995 Nobel Prize in Chemistry for his work alongside Paul Crutzen and Sherwood Rowland on the threat of CFC's to the Earth's ozone layer.

Partnerships, Innovation & Translational Research

Through UNAM's array of outreach programs, the university works closely with corporate partners, leveraging research infrastructure to assist with services such as product design and testing, process development, applied research, competitive intelligence, specialized information services and training programs. Equally UNAM works in partnership with government agencies and NGO's providing a similar set of services on offer to the private sector.

Teaching, Learning & Student Life

Students in attendance at UNAM can expect to be in very good company with many of Mexico's most influential personalities from business, academia and politics having studied at the university. Carlos Slim, the world's wealthiest man studied at UNAM, as well as many of the country's presidents. UNAM's influence is not constrained to Mexico nevertheless, with several Latin American leaders also counted amongst the alumni.

Listed as a World Heritage Site by UNESCO in 2007, UNAM's main campus is an extensive site housing teaching and learning facilities, museums, various cultural and sporting facilities and even the Olympic stadium from the 1968 games.

UNAM is quite distinctly partitioned between baccalaureate, undergraduate and postgraduate teaching. The baccalaureate programs are relatively unique for a university; however today UNAM currently has approximately 110,000 students in this school's various sites throughout Mexico City. Undergraduates have a selection of 85 undergraduate degrees to choose from under the management of 18 different faculties.

Icahn School of Medicine at Mount Sinai

Rank › 151 – 200

Name › Mount Sinai School of Medicine
Region › Americas
Country › United States
Founded › 1963

icahn.mssm.edu

Core Research Strengths

Icahn School of Medicine at Mount Sinai is a premiere medical school in the United States. With an annual budget exceeding $1.5 Billion, Mount Sinai is a leader in biomedical education and research, and provides top quality patient care. Over 1,100 outstanding students are enrolled in six highly competitive programs that lead to M.D, Ph.D. or masters degrees. The annual research budget alone is $375M, and Mount Sinai ranks among the top twenty schools throughout the United States in NIH funding. State-of-the-art laboratories support cutting-edge research, and abundant clinical venues offer superb patient care and clinical training opportunities.

In partnership with the venerable Mount Sinai Hospital, the School serves one of the most diverse and complex patient populations in the world. "We are a medical school that has a seamless relationship with its hospital and a very large health care system", explains Dean Dennis Charney, M.D. "We have a great hospital with strong diagnostic and treatment programs, and a school with outstanding research programs, combining the best of both," says Dean Charney.

Driven by a culture of innovation and discovery, Icahn School of Medicine at Mount Sinai is in the midst of implementing a $2.25 billion strategic plan that emphasizes translational science. "Our basic science, translational and clinical research are very much geared towards discoveries that change the way medicine is practiced. We are structured to be a leader in developing new medicines, new ways of diagnosing and preventing human disease," explains the Dean.

Sixteen multidisciplinary institutes have been established to foster intensive collaboration along a continuum running from the laboratory to patient care. Disease-focused institutes focus on cancer, heart disease, the brain, immunology, viruses, diabetes, obesity and childhood-onset diseases. Core technology institutes specializing in genomics, translational and molecular imaging, stem cell research, experimental therapeutics, personalized medicine and translational epidemiology complement these institutes. According to Dean Charney, "We are spending well over $100M to build one of the best genomics programs in the United States, if not the world. Our technology provides an infrastructure for our scientists to move their discoveries towards new medicines and new devices."

Major Discoveries

Mount Sinai's intensive research and clinical programs have led to many groundbreaking advances in medicine. Building on a history replete with "firsts," recent contributions include creation of the first genetically engineered influenza vaccine, new treatments for ovarian and prostate cancer and therapies for inherited metabolic diseases. "We have a very strong cardiovascular research group which uses stem cell techniques, molecular biology and genetics to discover new approaches to treating the diseased heart and reversing heart failure," notes Dean Charney.

The late Dr. Rosalyn Yalow, a member of the Mount Sinai faculty, was the second woman ever to win the Nobel Prize in Medicine, for her work with insulin binding antibodies.

Partnerships, Innovation & Translational Research

Icahn School of Medicine at Mount Sinai encourages faculty, students and trainees to be attuned into opportunities to transfer their discoveries from the laboratory to the marketplace. Through its Office of Technology and Business Development, which has more than doubled in size this past year, Mount Sinai facilitates patent applications, research collaborations with industry and entrepreneurial partnerships that can translate research to commercial applications.

"Major pharmaceutical companies have had challenges in developing drugs of global impact, so increasingly they are looking for win-win partnerships with academic medical centers," explains the Dean. "Mount Sinai has taken a Silicon Valley approach that it is all about making discoveries, and then turning them into something that really makes a difference in the lives of our patients, our community and our society.

Teaching, Learning & Student Life

Icahn School of Medicine at Mount Sinai is located in the heart of New York City, one of the world's most international cities and a hub for academics, theatre, the arts, food, sports – whether students come from the United States or abroad, there is something for everyone. Mount Sinai's Manhattan campus is across the street from Central Park, offering open spaces, greenery and fresh air.

The New York location also forms a large part of students' learning experiences, explains Dean Charney. "To the north of our campus are East and Central Harlem, which are among the poorest communities in the United States, while just to the south are some of the richest people in the world. Patients from both of those groups come to Mount Sinai each week, giving us exposure to a range of medical needs and issues."

"Virtually all of our medical students are involved in research, a full spectrum ranging from understanding the impact of poverty on disease to the most basic science. Indeed, many of our medical students take a year off to gain additional research experience."

The Dean places enormous importance on the quality of Mount Sinai's educational programs. "I tell our faculty that if you want to be successful at Mount Sinai you must be not only an outstanding clinician or scientist, but also a great teacher. The future of our medical school, and medicine in general, are all about training the best and the brightest for the future."

KYUSHU UNIVERSITY

Rank › 151 – 200

Name › Kyushu University
Region › Asia/Pacific
Country › Japan
Founded › 1903

www.kyushu-u.ac.jp

Core Research Strengths

First established as Japan's fourth Imperial University in 1911, Kyushu University has since evolved and expanded into one of Japan's leading research universities, whose expertise spans a multitude of research interests and disciplines. With total funded research in the region of US$250 million annually, Kyushu University has been able to develop an extensive enterprise encompassing synergies between disciplines, and a myriad of external partners such as government agencies, industrial corporations and counterpart universities.

President Setsuo Arikawa highlights Kyushu's leadership role today: "Kyushu University is Japan's gateway to the broader Asian region. We are in closer proximity to Korea than to Tokyo, this has enabled us to take leadership in many greatly interesting and exciting research projects, whilst at the same time developing great connections inside and outside of Japan."

Kyushu's leadership role is manifested today in a myriad of enormously exciting research projects. Perhaps the most distinctive is the International Institute for Carbon-Neutral Energy Research (I2CNER). With a newly constructed facility just completed, this ground-breaking institute will draw expertise together to investigate cutting edge new technologies such as hydrogen based energy generation and carbon sequestration / storage with a view to developing a more sustainable global energy future. Led by Professor Petros Sofronis, the I2CNER demonstrates the growing international profile of research at Kyushu University.

Major Discoveries

Led by internationally acclaimed researcher Professor Chihaya Adachi, researchers at the Center for Organic Photonics and Electronics Research (OPERA) have pioneered the development of organic electronics with the discovery of metal-free electroluminescent molecules. These designs have huge potential for the development of organic light-emitting diodes (OLED); paving the way for the development of organic based electronic lighting and displays.

Teaching, Learning & Student Life

Kyushu' University's 11 undergraduate and 18 graduate schools present those in attendance at the university with an enormous range of diversity in their study programs. Increasingly students are able to take advantage of the scale and scope throughout Kyushu, by combining their interests through interdisciplinary study programs. This has been pioneered through the development of the Graduate School and Graduate Faculty structure.

President Arikawa explains in more detail the diversity of opportunity one can expect whilst studying at Kyushu University: "Research, teaching and fostering innovation are so intertwined that they cannot be separated. In 2000, Kyushu University launched its Graduate School – Graduate Faculty System, this was the first attempt of its kind. Unlike conventional faculty structures, our unique organizational structure enables a diverse range of flexible participation by our faculty staff in undergraduate education, postgraduate education and research."

Kyushu University's new Ito Campus adds considerably to the already well-established array of world-class facilities on offer for students. Established in 2005, the Ito Campus' world class setting, combining ancient heritage structures with 21st century postmodern architecture in a natural, harmonious environment, comprised of woodlands and nature is one of Asia's most breath-taking campus sites.

The international community has not missed such developments, with Kyushu's "Gateway to Asia" status reinforced by the university having one of the most diverse student populations in Japan. Presently 10% of Kyushu's 19,000 students originate from international destinations. This number is set to grow as the institutional strategy is for a significant increase in the proportion of English language instruction courses up to approximately 25% of total instruction. Kyushu University's world-class excellence in teaching, learning and research combined with the growing support for international students through facilities such as the International Student and Researcher Support Center, and highly cost-effective nature of tuition makes the university a serious competitor on the international stage.

Kyushu University is also blessed with an excellent location. In close proximity to East Asian neighbours China and Korea; students at Kyushu have the opportunity to investigate the Asian region in their spare time, as well as develop a network of contacts in some of the world's most important emerging economies. Kyushu's southern climate is significantly milder than the rest of Japan, with far more benign winters than further North, and the added benefit of numerous beach locations to cool off during the humid summer months. Fukuoka City's cost of living is significantly lower than counterpart Japanese cities, adding significantly to the value proposition presented by the city with living expenses a critical aspect of planning for life in Japan.

Most of President Arikawa's academic career has been at Kyushu University, few are better placed to provide an overview of the benefits of being located there than he. "Fukuoka is an attractive and compact city to live in for many reasons. For example, these include the low cost of living, mild weather, kind, warm-hearted people, beautiful natural surroundings and well-developed transportation. Fukuoka is historically renowned as Japan's gateway to Asia due to its geographical proximity and diplomatic relations. Such historical and cultural ties with international society have made Fukuoka grow into a friendly, open-minded, cosmopolitan city, which welcomes international residents and visitors from overseas with warm hospitality. Our university has a strong network and partnership with the local and government community in terms of welcoming students, researchers and academics from around the world."

九州大学

Our centennial motto is

「九大百年，躍進百大」

"Leading the field in the next 100 years, leaping into the World Top 100"

九州大学
KYUSHU UNIVERSITY

Research at Kyushu

Both broad-based and of exceptional quality, Kyushu University's research portfolio continues to expand the frontiers of our understanding of some of the international community's most critical challenges today. Despite the broad base of expertise, Kyushu is increasingly becoming synonymous with energy, as the university leads some of the international community's most exciting projects in this field.

Energy & Environment

Without a doubt the most exciting focus within Kyushu's energy portfolio today is the International Institute for Carbon-Neutral Energy Research (I2CNER), the newest program of the World Premier International Research Center Initiative (WPI). I2CNER's core objectives are incredibly exciting; to expand the scientific base that will facilitate the development of a hydrogen-based economy, and the breakthroughs required for CO_2 capture and storage; two of the world's most exciting and prospective technologies in today's fight against global climate change.

I2CNER is investigating numerous innovative approaches to the development of these exciting new technologies, ranging from the development of low-cost means of hydrogen production to highly efficient fuel cells through to means of storing hydrogen.

The Wind-Lens turbine, a new apparatus for the development of wind power thought to be as much as 300% more efficient than conventional means is another exciting energy related innovation under development at Kyushu's Research Institute for Advanced Mechanics. Wind-Lens turbines have already been located on the seashore of Fukuoka City and on a floating structure at the ocean surface of Hakata Bay. The improved safety and efficiency of Wind-Lens technologies makes them a serious contender as an alternative means for existing wind turbines.

The energy and environment theme continues with the Global Centers of Excellence program of Novel Carbon Resources Sciences, investigating both means of producing energy in an efficient and environmentally friendly manner; whilst at the same time promoting the development of technologies that will maximise the value of Earth's finite carbon based resources.

The Center of Excellence for Asian Conservation Ecology as a Basis of Symbiotic Society is working to develop conservation science whereby the dynamic interactions between humans and ecosystems are quantified, analysed and modelled. This analysis is taking place within the context of Asia where enormous environmental change is taking place. Researchers hope to develop a methodology whereby bio-diversity and habitat loss can be minimised in the face of rapid economic and lifestyle changes.

Mathematical Excellence

Another remarkable technology under development at Kyushu is next-generation cryptography. In partnership with the National Institute of Information and Communications Technology (NICT) and Fujitsu Laboratories, researchers at Kyushu recently broke the world cryptography record with the successful cryptanalysis of a 278-digit (923-bit)-long pairing-based cryptography. Until now the cryptanalysis of pairing-based cryptography of this length was thought to take several hundred thousand years, having been able to break this in 142.8 days using a new approach this research has set the technical foundation for a whole new way of thinking about this essential technical element of the 21st century's digital age.

A continuation of the mathematical theme is the establishment of the Institute of Mathematics for Industry (IMI). The first of its kind in Asia, under the leadership of Professor Wakayama the IMI brings together pure mathematicians to work in collaboration for the development of industry relevant applications that have arisen from the continued progress made in theoretical mathematics. The ambition of the IMI is to reorganize pure and applied mathematics into a fluid and versatile form capable of responding to the needs of industrial technologies. This pioneering approach will lead to unprecedented collaborations between mathematics and industry with the expectation that highly competitive and exciting technologies will follow thereafter.

Stem Cell Research & Biological Sciences

Through the Global Center of Excellence (COE) Program; Cell-fate Decision: Function and Dysfunction in Homeostasis, Kyushu is one of the leading nodes in an international network of research universities investigating the most basic of cell behaviours. It is expected that our understanding of such functions will herald the development of new medical treatments.

Kyushu's expertise in the biological sciences is not limited to stem cell research however. Japan's Centre of Excellence (COE) program has also supported broader growth in the university's traditional expertise in this hugely exciting field. Major research projects focus on modern aspects of molecular, cellular and population biology. The interdisciplinary approach defines the university's strategy with participating academic staff coming from 6 different faculties and one research institute at the university.

Partnerships, Innovation & Translational Research

Research partnerships with counterpart universities run into the hundreds throughout the international community from Africa and Latin America to Australia, the United States and Europe. Increasingly however, Kyushu is building upon its traditional status as Japan's gateway to East Asia by developing closer links with leading research institutions and research led companies in China and South Korea. The Research Institute for East Asia Environments (RIEAE) is an excellent example of this evolution, with Kyushu's closest collaborators found in Korea and China. As one looks forwards into a future increasingly defined by challenges associated with environmental sustainability and energy security, pioneering universities such as Kyushu are set to grow in importance for the diverse array of corporations and research institutions with an interest in developing expertise in related technologies.

IOWA STATE UNIVERSITY

Rank › 151 – 200

Name › Iowa State University
Region › Americas
Country › United States
Founded › 1858

www.iastate.edu

Core Research Strengths

Iowa State University of Science and Technology, more commonly known as Iowa State University(ISU), is a research-intensive institute. During its proud history it's produced a distinguished list of alumni and staff including, senators, a US Vice President, astronauts, scientists, Nobel and Pulitzer Prize winners, along with a host of other notable individuals in their respective fields.

Being located in the heart of America's Corn Belt means few will be surprised to learn that ISU has a strong agricultural focus. "We work in basic and applied fields in agriculture as well as across both the plant and livestock industries", explains ISU President Steven Leath. "We are constantly tweaking our research strategy to make use of new technologies, new science and new partnerships. We're drawing heavily on our strong biology, agricultural base. We are also trying to couple that with the fact that as a state, we probably have more capacity for food production and biomass production than any other state in the United States."

The result is high-tech expertise across a range of agricultural issues. "We probably have developed more plant genoplans and plant gene varieties than just about any other university in the world. We have a huge plant-breeding program here. We developed some techniques to use nanotechnology to deliver proteins and DNA into plant cells, which is a whole new way to do genetic engineering."

But just because ISU has a strong agriculture focus, doesn't mean it isn't interested in other areas. "In more general terms, any of the biological sciences including bio-fuels and bio-energy in particular are strengths at Iowa State University. We are also strong in material sciences and benefit greatly from the presence on our campus of the U.S. Department of Energy's Ames Laboratory. The final area I'd like to highlight, which may seem very different from the rest, is virtual reality and the technologies associated with this."

Major Discoveries

The most recent recognition of the university's research success came just last year when Danny Shechtman, a member of Iowa State faculty and a researcher for the Ames Laboratory, won the Nobel Prize in Chemistry for his discovery of Quasicrystals.

Partnerships, Innovation & Translational Research

The university is keen to work with private-sector partners. To that end it has reorganised the board that oversees its technology transfer processes. "One of the major steps we have taken is to get members of the business community on the board", explains the President. "They probably value IP differently than does a typical faculty member, and they really guide us as to the best way to transfer the science out to the public. We have completely changed our partnership model, so we're very flexible. Companies can own IP, we don't have to retain ownership, so, you'll see a very relationship oriented partnership and it's far less focused on IP than ever before."

The university has also taken steps to revamp its internationalisation strategy. One part of the plan has been to attract more international students, says President Leath. "Historically, Iowa State has not been a very diverse place. We hit an all time record this year of 11.5% of the student body being international. Although it's not a huge percentage, it's a great stride. So the strategy seems to be working to make our university better known, and to recruit students from outside the US."

Teaching, Learning & Student Life

Iowa State University is located in Ames, a typically friendly Midwestern town of 60,000 people. Only 30 minutes away is the state capital, Des Moines, a metropolitan area of more than 500,000. Because of the variety of activities and events, ISU students spend much of their time on campus. One of the most charming features of the 2,000-acre campus is the array of historic buildings, many of which are listed in America's National Register of Historic Places.

"It is a very beautiful and spacious campus", says President Leath. "We are fortunate that it has not become overcrowded with new buildings and lost that special 'campus feel'. In fact the essential part of the campus has remained largely the same for over a hundred years."

Even more encouraging for future students is that the university is investing in a major campus beautification program with the goal of making it one of America's most beautiful university campuses.

"The beautiful atmosphere also helps to create a good atmosphere that's conducive to learning", says the President. "It's a very collegial place, very friendly place and a very helpful place; many people who come here say it's not an exciting place to visit, but it's a great place to live and they find everyone here is very welcoming."

Another distinct element of student life on campus is entrepreneurship. Thanks to generous donations the university has been able to build dedicated centres to help students realise commercial plans and launch start-ups. "I think we have taken a more aggressive approach in this area than any other university", says President Leath.

Students going to ISU should also be prepared for a multidisciplinary learning approach as the majority of students take courses that cut across departmental lines.

GEORGE MASON UNIVERSITY

Rank › 151 – 200

Name › George Mason University
Region › Americas
Country › United States
Founded › 1957

www.gmu.edu

Core Research Strengths

Named after a key figure in America's founding as an independent nation, George Mason University gained its status as an independent institution in 1972. Today it's a powerful research force with more than 1,400 full-time instructional and research faculty members covering a broad range of fields. Those research personnel and accompanying infrastructure are organized in accordance with Mason's mission. As a result it has created multidisciplinary centers to address key themes.

One theme is "Global". Here faculty address issues of human rights and social justice to direct involvement in conflict resolution; from understanding human behaviour in developing countries to understanding the impact of weather changes on those peoples. The next theme is "Life Quality". Investigators explore learning and behaviour. Staff members range from experts on aging and disability to neuroscientists. There are also scientists who focus on developing new and innovative treatments for infectious disease and cancer.

George Mason's location in the greater Washington, D.C. metropolitan region lends itself to involvement in and analysis of the activities of local, state and the federal government. This it is natural that another of its main themes is "Policy and Governance". Another theme is one that can be found in various forms at most leading universities – "Sustainability". Investigators working on this broad topic cover everything from understanding and predicting climate change to conserving endangered species; and from developing a better understanding of human interaction with our environment to developing energy alternatives.

The fifth theme is called "Science Frontiers and Complex Systems" and involves mixing together a number of distinct scientific disciplines. The final research theme is "Security". Here Mason researchers explore the myriad ways security is addressed in our contemporary society. Research strengths range from cyber security to national security.

Major Discoveries

One area in which Mason particularly stands out is economics. Over the years various faculty members have completed groundbreaking research that has revolutionized the field. This has been duly recognized by the research community. For example, in 2002 Vernon L. Smith won the Nobel Prize for having established laboratory experiments as a tool in empirical economic analysis, especially in the study of alternative market mechanisms.

Partnerships, Innovation & Translational Research

Mason has a very outward perspective, and is keen to establish research alliances with a range of different organisations. One key group of partners are government bodies, such as the National Institutes of Health, NASA, the National Science Foundation and the Defense Advanced Research Projects Agency. Likewise, Mason's Center for Secure Information Systems is designated as a Center of Academic Excellence (CAE) as well as a Center of Academic Excellence in Research (CAE-R) in Information Assurance Education by the National Security Agency.

Meanwhile private sector companies can partner with Mason's leading research teams. And the Mason Enterprise Center provides resources to help small businesses expand, improve their organizations and strengthen the regional economy.

Teaching, Learning & Student Life

Mason's main campus is situated on 677 acres just south of the City of Fairfax, Virginia, and just 15 miles outside of Washington, D.C., giving students the best of both worlds. On one hand they'll enjoy being close to one of the world's biggest cities, while on the other they have the quality of life that comes with one of the largest and most beautiful residential campuses in Virginia.

There's no shortage of things for students to do. They can intern with the Justice Department, visit museum exhibits, explore historic Georgetown, catch a Nationals baseball game, or even attend congressional hearings. Moreover, Mason provides a free shuttle service to connect students to all of the fun events and activities in its lively neighbourhood of greater D.C.

Fairfax has a lot to offer too. It is a historic gem, which provides a traditional residential college experience. Fairfax and the surrounding area have many activities for outdoor enthusiasts. Mason has many athletic facilities on campus and even a zip line and a 50-foot vertical ropes challenge course at its Prince William Campus, a brief shuttle ride away. This campus recently opened housing for graduate students, and along with Mason's Arlington Campus and Loudoun County site, offers a curriculum to meet its region's educational needs.

Mason's emphasis on multidisciplinary research carries over to the learning courses. Indeed, it provides innovative and interdisciplinary undergraduate, graduate and professional courses of study that enable students to exercise analytical and imaginative thinking, and make well-founded ethical decisions. Another benefit for students is the quality of staff. Mason works hard to ensure its faculty are highly qualified and entrepreneurial, excellent at teaching, active in pure and applied research, capable of providing a broad range of intellectual and cultural insights and responsive to the needs of students.

Mason is keen to establish itself as a truly international institution with partner institutions around the world. One way it does this is through the Center for Global Education. Its study abroad program has been rated highly, offering dozens of options ranging from one-week spring break courses to a full year.

ERASMUS UNIVERSITEIT ROTTERDAM

Rank › 151 – 200

Name › Erasmus University
Region › Europe
Country › Netherlands
Founded › 1973

www.eur.nl

Core Research Strengths

Erasmus University has bundled its education and research into four areas of expertise: Health – Faculty of Medicine and Health Sciences/Erasmus MC and institute of Health Policy & Management (iBMG); Wealth – Erasmus School of Economics and Rotterdam School of Management, Erasmus University; Governance – Erasmus School of Law and Faculty of Social Sciences; Culture – Erasmus School of History, Culture and Communication, Faculty of Social Sciences and Faculty of Philosophy.

These focus areas are then organised into 20 research schools that have been accredited by the Accreditation Committee (ECOS) of the Royal Netherlands Academy of Arts and Sciences (KNAW). However, these schools can't afford to rest on their laurels as the KNAW reviews accreditation every six years.

As a result Erasmus' schools are striving to ensure that they remain elite institutes. Erasmus School of Economics and Rotterdam School of Management are among the leading economic and business schools in Europe, the same goes for Erasmus Medical Centre in the medical sciences.

The biomedical cluster plays a leading role in the field of genomics and bioinformatics. The Forensic Molecular Biology department works together with the Netherlands Forensic Institute (NFI). Erasmus Rotterdam Health conducts major long-term genetic epidemiological studies among the elderly and children. Meanwhile the Institute of Health Policy and Management (iBMG) forms a multi-disciplinary bridge between medicine and the health sciences on the one hand, and social sciences on the other.

The Tinbergen Institute (TI) is one of the top research institutes and graduate schools in economics and finance in the world. It uniquely combines the best of three leading Dutch Universities, of which Erasmus University Rotterdam is one.

Major Discoveries

One of the university's most famous academics is Jan Tinbergen. He won the Nobel Prize for Economics in 1969.

In 1956 he founded the university's Econometrics Institute.

More recently, virologists of Erasmus MC performed breakthrough research on diseases like SARS and H5N1 – Avian flu.

Partnerships, Innovation & Translational Research

Erasmus is keen to work with the private sector and has established a technology transfer office to act as a liaison with external partners. The TTO employs several experts in different fields, that all have experience in technology transfer. Some specialise in helping academics protect their ideas, sign deals with commercial partners and set up new companies. The office also helps with licensing technology.

When it comes to academic interaction, the research schools Erasmus Institute for Management (ERIM) and the Tinbergen Institute lead the way by attracting PhD students, research fellows and visiting professors of repute from all corners of the world. The university also has several exciting academic joint ventures, such as the English-language programme International Business Administration, the Erasmus Executive Development programme (EED) and the Erasmus University Centre for Contract Research and Business Support (ERBS).

Another key element of the university's internationalisation strategy is student exchange. Erasmus has agreements in place with some 240 universities in nearly 50 countries worldwide. One of the distinct aspects of the programme is that Erasmus offers international students in their 3rd year of study the possibility to participate in specialised non-degree courses, either as an exchange student or as a 'freemover'. This opens up the Erasmus experience to students from countries or universities that may not be part of its network of exchange programmes.

Teaching, Learning & Student Life

Rotterdam's role as a strategic port means that much of the city was destroyed by aerial bombardment in the Second World War. But out of that tragedy has sprung a new city with some of the most innovative architecture in Europe. Moreover

Rotterdam has retained its position as a vital port. Indeed it was the busiest port in the world until being superseded by Shanghai in 2004. As a result it is a lively multicultural city, with a very international outlook.

Erasmus University Rotterdam has two campuses, Woudestein and Erasmus MC. Both are located near the centre of Rotterdam and are easy to reach using public transport. Woudestein campus houses the majority of Erasmus University's faculties and research schools. There are also excellent study facilities such as the auditorium and the university library, as well as catering facilities, the sports complex and the Erasmus Expo & Congress Centre.

Erasmus MC houses the Erasmus University Medical Centre. Erasmus MC, situated in the heart of Rotterdam, is the Netherlands' largest and most multi-faceted academic medical centre. Because of its height and remarkable design it is a genuine Rotterdam landmark.

In September 2013, a third campus will be opened, also in the centre of Rotterdam: the new Erasmus University College. A broad interdisciplinary bachelors programme, a top education for top students from all over the world. A distinguishing feature of the education provided by Erasmus University Rotterdam is the combination of academic training, international orientation and social relevance – education that is closely interwoven with excellent scientific research, in which the spotlight is on the student and the integration of novel approaches utilising new ICT remains a key strategic focus.

Rank › 151 – 200

Name › Dartmouth College
Region › Americas
Country › United States
Founded › 1769

www.dartmouth.edu

Core Research Strengths

Dartmouth is a broad based research university with expertise throughout an array of academic disciplines from engineering to the medical sciences, arts and humanities. Dartmouth's expertise in the social sciences is particularly renowned, The university's graduate schools in business, medicine, and engineering, its graduate programs in the arts and sciences, and its distinctive interdisciplinary undergraduate curriculum, distinguishes it among its peers.

The Tuck School of Business leads internationally with expertise in a range of topic areas of growing importance to today's globalized economy; with world-class capabilities in corporate governance, digital strategies and the impact of new technologies on business, leadership, international business, capital markets, and entrepreneurship.

Comprised of more than 40 multidisciplinary institutes and centers, the Geisel School of Medicine offers a diverse array of exciting new areas of medical research, such as the neurosciences, advanced imaging, quantitative biology, healthcare policy science and scholarship. Through its relationship with the Dartmouth-Hitchcock Medical Center, Dartmouth is working to expand cancer detection and treatment options, and is recognized as a world leader in oncology research.

The Thayer School of Engineering is known for the innovative ways in which it incorporates the liberal arts into a broad-based and innovative curriculum focusing on cutting edge technology that blends engineering with medicine, business, and the social sciences. Dartmouth also is home to more than 50 centers and institutes, where ground-breaking scholarship takes place in a broad spectrum of areas, including, to name just a few, cyber security, Native American Studies, Arctic Studies, and public policy.

Major Discoveries

Dartmouth researchers are presently pioneering the development of a new, more effective vaccine for tuberculosis as this deadly disease displays signs of resurgence in the developing world. Dartmouth researchers Professors

Charles Sullivan & Jason Stauth are pioneering the continued growth in efficiency of solar technologies towards a viable alternative to fossil fuels. The Masters in Healthcare Delivery Science is a ground breaking new degree program conducted through the Tuck School of Business and the Geisel School of Medicine.

Dartmouth is home to the United States National Center on Post-Traumatic Stress Disorder.

Through the Dartmouth Atlas Project and the Wennberg International Collaborative, Dartmouth conducts leading policy research on healthcare delivery and effectiveness around the world.

The computer language, BASIC was co-developed at Dartmouth by mathematicians John Kemony and Walter Kurtz, and Dartmouth was home to the first national conference on Artificial Intelligence.

Partnerships, Innovation & Translational Research

Dartmouth's long held culture of entrepreneurialism and innovation is equalled by the tradition of external collaboration throughout the public, private and third sectors. Strategic partnerships are an ever-present priority for Dartmouth, with the Technology Transfer Office acting as the key conduit between Dartmouth researchers and external partners. Whilst Dartmouth is an experienced research collaborator, the university's core principles of curiosity led research and academic freedom remain at the heart of the research enterprise. The effects of Dartmouth's multidisciplinary and collaborative approaches resonate far beyond the confines of the institution, creating jobs, new opportunities and bringing essential new innovations into society.

Innovation and entrepreneurship are core values at Dartmouth, with innovators throughout the university's schools encouraged to take new ideas to the market. The Thayer School in particular is a close collaborator with the Tuck School of Business and Dartmouth's Technology Transfer Office (TTO) working to translate patents and discoveries into license revenues and

start up companies. Dartmouth has one of the highest patent issuance rates of the Ivy League and is a vital driver of knowledge based economic development in New England, as well as more broadly throughout the United States.

Teaching, Learning & Student Life

Dartmouth students at both the graduate and undergraduate levels enjoy unparalleled access to world-class researchers and scholars. Inspired teaching is expected at Dartmouth and results in Dartmouth being consistently recognized as exemplary in U.S. rankings. The size and scope of the campus facilitate an unusual degree of collaboration across disciplines, making the educational experience at Dartmouth one that fosters collaboration at all levels.

Dartmouth also offers superb graduate education opportunities. The School of Arts and Sciences offers opportunities to earn doctoral degrees in a variety of programs. Senior executives are trained at the Tuck School of Business, leading clinicians and researchers at the Geisel School of Medicine, and an exciting array of innovative start-ups have been developed by graduates of the Thayer School of Engineering.

At all levels, Dartmouth's collaborative spirit contributes to a unique and seamless intellectual experience, where entrepreneurs inform medical practitioners, engineers promote new areas of study in management, and scientists work with colleagues in the humanities to apply their collective expertise to the world's most complex challenges.

Rank › 151 – 200

Name › Colorado State University
Region › Americas
Country › United States
Founded › 1870

www.colostate.edu

Core Research Strengths

Founded in 1870 as the Colorado Agricultural College, Colorado State University is now among the nation's leading research universities and commands an annual research budget of $330million. Of that, around $236million comes from federal sources, $48.2million from local funds and the remainder from private contracts. Its research is centred on infectious disease, atmospheric science, clean energy technologies, environmental science and biomedical technology.

President Tony Frank believes that one of the university's strengths is that it has long seen research as a multidisciplinary activity. "Our focus, both historically and currently, has been generally around the interface of areas. It wouldn't necessarily be a specific discipline perhaps, but the strength has been bringing together what I would call an academic cluster, where you'll bring in not just engineers and physical scientists, but also everything from economists, social scientists that sort of phenomenon. The themes that we've historically been very strong in are water, environmental impacts, veterinary medicine. In that particularly, we're probably one of, if not the world leader or one of the top two in comparative oncology. I think pretty much without much of argument the top zoonotic infectious disease veterinary medical center."

"Also, I would argue more recently, the interface around clean and renewable energy and all the pieces that go with that, including, as you know, water use, which plays back to our historic strengths. Also writ large food production, around the theme of not only having a strong, historically strong agricultural college that focused on beef and wheat production as you'd expect given the industry around our area, but also now this issue of what are the challenges we need to meet to feed nine billion people; understanding that we need to do so with more sensitivity to the sustainability of soils, the environmental impacts of large scale agriculture and certainly for many areas, the low Colorado included water usage."

Major Discoveries

Many of Colorado State's alumni and professors have made discoveries of significant importance. It's a testament to the university that many of these are not Americans, but international professors who have worked at the university at some point in their distinguished careers. For example, former Colorado State professor, Paul Crutzen, won the Nobel Prize in Chemistry in 1995 for his work on the ozone layer.

Partnerships, Innovation & Translational Research

When it comes to interacting with the private sector, President Frank believes it is important to change the traditional academic mindset. "If we can get researchers and post-Docs starting to think about the commercial application of protecting their IP it will encourage more translational success." Key to translating academic research into useful commercial products and services is CSU Ventures. With specialized expertise in patenting, licensing, and entrepreneurship, CSU Ventures works with faculty, industry, and investors to commercialize innovative CSU research. The program was enhanced in 2007, to include support for each of CSU's Superclusters in Cancer, Clean Energy, and Infectious Disease.

CSU Ventures manages IP on behalf of the university; however, it does not undertake to manage the entire commercialization process. Instead, it works to engage private companies, which are better suited to downstream research and product development, to rapidly bring new ideas to market.

"What we do best is do research. We want the intellectual property to be in someone else's hands to manage. We don't particularly want to own or control the commercialization process, that's not what we're best at. If a company wants to work with us, we're more interested in having funding for our scientists."

Teaching, Learning & Student Life

Colorado State is situated on nearly 5,000 acres of land, including the main campus, a foothills campus, an agricultural campus, and a mountain campus. This natural setting is definitely a big part of its appeal for students, says President Frank. "The physical nature of the campus is kind of an open campus, obviously in the Rocky Mountains region, there's a lot of natural beauty and from our campus you can see the mountains. There are a lot of green spaces that I think fits with a lot of the environmental and ecosystem research at the campus."

Inside the classroom students can choose from more than 150 programmes. But while there is a great variation in the disciplines on offer, they all share a common thread. The learning approach – based on the land-grant philosophy – combines intellectual classroom pursuits with hands-on experience in the field and laboratory. Moreover, faculty staff work side-by-side with students and encourage participation both in and outside the classroom. It's a welcome change from some leading research universities where 'super star' academics don't like to teach undergraduates.

Students should also be aware that they will be given the opportunity to study abroad in nearly any country of the world. CSU-sponsored and affiliated programs are offered in Africa and the Middle East, Asia, Europe/Eurasia, Latin America and the Caribbean, and Oceania.

Rank › 151 – 200

Name › Cardiff University
Region › Europe
Country › United Kingdom
Founded › 1883

www.cardiff.ac.uk

Core Research Strengths

One of Britain's best public research institutions, Cardiff University is the only Welsh member of the Russell Group. The university is recognised in independent government assessments as one of Britain's leading research universities and the University's breadth of expertise encompasses the humanities; the natural, physical, health, life and social sciences; engineering and technology.

The university is a keen advocate of the interdisciplinary approach, which is led through its three major new Research Institutes: neurosciences and mental health, cancer stem cells and sustainable places.

The Neuroscience and Mental Health Institute has cemented Cardiff's place as an acknowledged world leader in neuroscientific genetics. Meanwhile the European Cancer Stem Cell Research Institute takes a pioneering approach to an emerging science, and will draw on Cardiff's clinical trial strength for both haematological and solid cancers.

The other new Institute, the University's Sustainable Places Research Institute, combines strengths in planning, architecture, social science, law, business and many scientific, technological, engineering, mathematical and biomedical disciplines to take a unique multidisciplinary approach to the creation of sustainable city-regions around the world.

While the new Institutes have attracted lots of attention it would be unfair to overlook Cardiff's other strongly performing disciplines. For example, the university's biodiversity research aims to understand the ecological, health and genetic consequences of environmental change on biological diversity.

Major Discoveries

Unsurprisingly some of the university's most noticeable discoveries have come in the field of medicine. The most recent discovery took place in 2012 when Professor Andy Sewell made a breakthrough in understanding diabetes. He and his team isolated a T-cell from a patient with type 1 diabetes, and in a world first, witnessed it attacking insulin.

Partnerships, Innovation & Translational Research

Given the university's focus on medical issues it is little surprise that it has a close partnership with NHS Wales. The Welsh Government and the City and County of Cardiff are other notable public sector partners for research-led policy making. But Cardiff University's influence is not restricted to the UK. It also has links with international governments, their agencies and related bodies worldwide, including with the United Nations, the World Health Organisation and NATO.

Similarly the university's partnerships with business and commerce are both local and global. The Innovation Network is particularly notable in supporting small and medium sized enterprises. Internationally Cardiff works with multinational corporations such as Sony and IBM. One reason for the host of commercial tie-ups is the university's eagerness to 'do business with business'.

Cardiff University goes out of its way to make itself available to meet potential and existing research sponsors. And businesses know that academic staff and researchers can provide input at a variety of levels from advising on approaches to collaboration and funding mechanisms, making formal presentations to sponsors and providing legal/contractual support to formalise links.

When it comes to academic partnerships Cardiff is a truly global institution. It has formal links with more than 35 countries including 38 partnerships with China, 16 in the US and 12 with Malaysia. It partners with 'Santander Universities' and the Fulbright and Marshall Commissions, allowing for teaching and other collaborations to flourish with North and South America.

Teaching, Learning & Student Life

The University is located in the heart of Wales' capital. In recent years, substantial investment has been made in the University estate, including the expansion of life sciences facilities and recent developments such as the University's new flagship health education centre, the Cochrane Building, offering students the latest teaching, library and state-of-the-art simulation facilities.

Whilst Cardiff is not a campus university, many students say that it 'feels like one'. That's probably because, unlike most civic universities, most of the University's student residential accommodation is within easy walking distance of lecture theatres, libraries and the students' union.

When it comes to accommodation a place in one of the university's 5,300 study bedrooms is guaranteed to all first-year undergraduates entering through the normal admissions cycle. The vast majority of student residences are single en-suite study bedrooms in self-catered flats — and students enjoy some of the lowest rents in the UK, according to a survey by the National Union of Students.

As for life inside the classroom, students can expect to participate in, and benefit from, the university's interdisciplinary research focus.

Another important element of the courses is that they are designed to help students find employment after graduation. Many of the University's degree schemes provide partial or complete exemption from relevant professional examinations and more than forty schemes of study benefit from accreditation and input from professional bodies.

Professor Colin Riordan was appointed President and Vice-Chancellor of the University in 2012 with the clear ambition for the University to be consistently ranked among the top 100 in the world and the top 20 in Britain. To help achieve this aim, he is focusing the University's energy on four key areas: research, education, internationalisation and engagement with Cardiff and Wales.

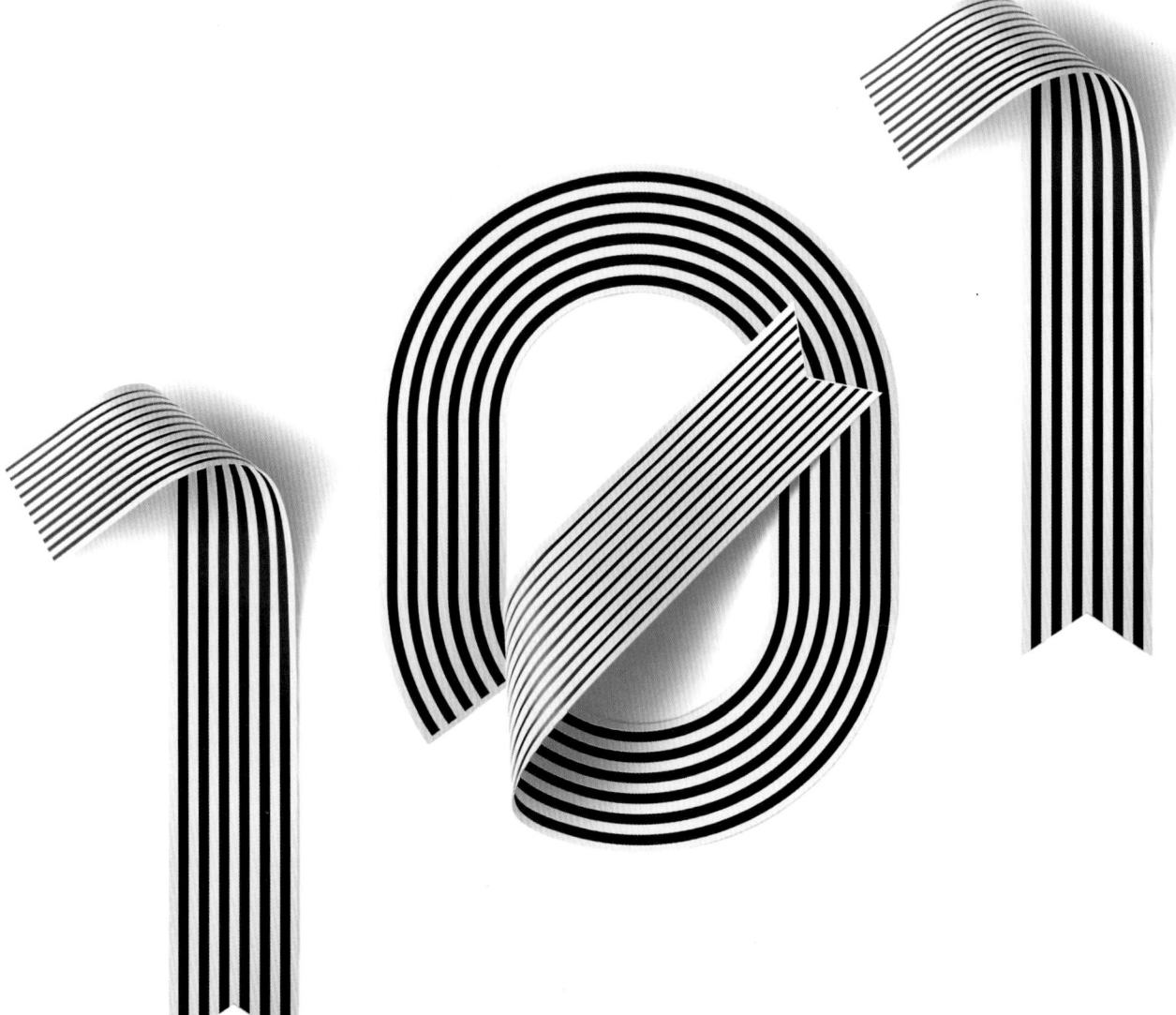

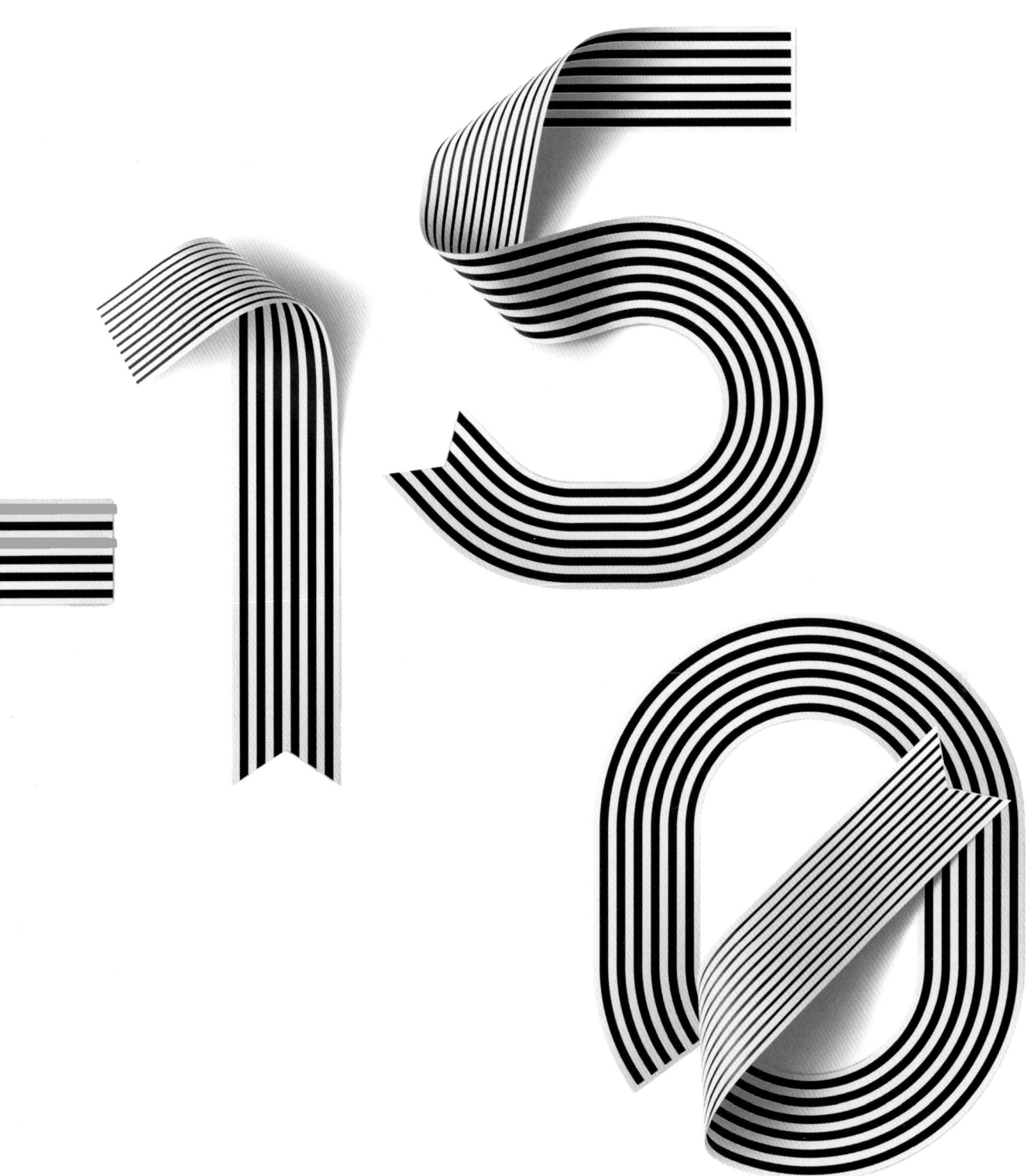

Rank › 101 – 150

Name › VU University Amsterdam
Region › Europe
Country › Netherlands
Founded › 1880

www.vu.nl

Core Research Strengths

VU University's research policy is based on the belief that outstanding research can only be achieved through outstanding researchers. That is why VU University Amsterdam invests in talent. It helps explain how VU University has grown from its humble beginnings to become a modern research university specialising in a limited number of interdisciplinary research areas.

These research foci are organized through interdisciplinary research institutes, with faculty members and students from multiple faculties working together to forge new breakthroughs. These interdisciplinary research institutes work along four main themes, which are intended to respond to European societal challenges – Human Health & Life Sciences, Science for Sustainability, Connected World and Professional Services.

Human Health and Life Sciences (H2LS) - With increased prosperity, people live not only longer, but also want to stay in good health for longer. H2LS organizes education and research in medical and human-related health and life sciences to make this possible.

Science for Sustainability (S4S) – The sustainable use of limited natural resources is essential for human life on earth. S4S connects fundamental knowledge about these resources to knowledge about changes in society: the effects of human activities on the condition of the earth, climate change and society's response to this.

Connected World – Technology has made the world more connected than ever. This theme investigates the technology that enables changes, such as the development of e-Science, the associated structural, societal and cultural changes and the consequences for our world.

Professional Services - In recent years, the business services sector, particularly the financial sector, has been under societal and moral pressure. In this theme VU University works to develop mechanisms for corporate social responsibility, behaviour enforcement and integrity.

Major Discoveries

Perhaps one of the most interesting pieces of research to come from VU University in recent years was Prof. Dorret Boomsma's work on human behavioural genetics. Her department has built up the Netherlands Twins Register into one of the largest and most representative twins database in the world. It comprises information on almost 30,000 identical and non-identical twins; Prof. Boomsma was awarded with the 2001 NWO Spinoza Prize (the highest scientific award in the Netherlands) for this work.

Partnerships, Innovation & Translational Research

VU University understands that to find answers to scientific and societal questions it must look beyond the boundaries of scientific disciplines and seek collaboration with partners in society, the government and the business sector.

One of the most striking aspects of VU University's relationship with the outside world is its Open Access research policy. It actively encourages researchers to publish articles that can be read, downloaded, copied, printed and distributed by anyone who is interested. University leadership feel that research funded by public money should be freely available to the public.

This generosity extends beyond the shores of the Netherlands. The Renewable Energy in Africa (RENEW) research programme by the Amsterdam Global Change Institute (AGCI) is a prime example. Projects like this allow developing countries to reap the benefits of scientific knowledge and experience of VU University.

In the same vein VU University has developed the Globe Programme. It subsidises study or placement periods between three and ten months in non-European countries. As a result VU University has contracts with over 70 universities in 25 countries outside of Europe.

Teaching, Learning & Student Life

For most students Amsterdam needs little introduction. Its liberal drug policy and thriving nightlife have made it one of the most popular European destinations for young people. But there's a lot more to the city than a hedonistic weekend break. As a student of VU University, you stand to benefit from all the advantages offered by the capital. The VU University campus is just a fifteen-minute bike ride from the lively centre of Amsterdam, where there are numerous shops, places of entertainment, parks, and pavement cafes.

Amsterdam is virtually unique in having all the advantages of a big city – culture, history, good food, entertainment and extensive public transport – but with relatively few of the drawbacks. The city is small, there are plenty of quiet spots where you can kick back and relax and, thanks to its canals, its centre has relatively little traffic.

The university also has a lot to offer. With more than 24,000 students you won't be short of classmates and new friends. And with almost 60 Bachelor's degree programmes and more than 100 Master's degree programmes, VU University offers a wide choice of study options. The programmes are of a high quality, the atmosphere is very conducive to study and the teaching staff are easily accessible.

In part that's because of the layout of the university. Almost all of VU University's students, staff and programmes are located in a campus in the business district of Amsterdam. Accordingly, in the course of your studies, it is very easy to familiarise yourself with other scientific disciplines. The university's learning style also plays a role. Indeed VU University devotes considerable attention to personal study advice. For example, right at the start of your course of study, you will be introduced to your programme's study advisor.

WAGENINGEN UNIVERSITY
WAGENINGEN[UR]

Rank › 101 – 150

Name › University of Wageningen
Region › Europe
Country › Netherlands
Founded › 1876

www.wageningenur.nl

Core Research Strengths

Founded in 1876 as an agricultural research institution Wageningen University has since developed expertise in climate change, lifestyles, natural environment and animal welfare. Indeed the University Rector, Professor Martin Kropff, feels that the best way to class the university's strengths is along certain key themes: "food and food production, the living environment, people, health, lifestyle and livelihood."

One reason that the university has expanded its remit is that to fully understand many agricultural problems it also needed expertise in other disciplines. Rector Kropff explains: "If you know everything about viruses but you have no clue how this interacts with plants, animals or people, then it's useless. So you need T-shaped skills, and also to engage throughout all of the disciplines. It is something we really pay attention to in our programmes."

One of the university's key strengths is its network of dedicated research institutes. It has acquired many over the years and received a massive boost when it inherited the former research institutes of the Dutch Ministry of Agriculture. These specialised research institutes earn €333million in research contracts alone. Meanwhile the general university itself earned €96million from research contracts. Thanks to its dedicated focus and strong funding channels WU belongs to the top six of the most cited research institutes in the domains of ecology/environment, plant production, and agriculture.

The university's strong emphasis on research is reflected in the fact that while it is only a small university – with about 12,000 students – 1,500 of them are PhD level.

Partnerships, Innovation & Translational Research

Although Wageningen is a small university it has a very extensive international reach. One way this manifests itself is in the student body. For example, 35% of masters students and 65% of PhD students come from abroad.

Another way that the university expands internationally is through international partnerships, says Rector Kropff. "We have links with the CGIR, and we also have all kinds of global alliances; recently for example we started the global alliance of food security with major players like Davies and INRA in France. So we participate in many international networks."

Because, by their very nature, agricultural themes tend to cross borders WU has a longstanding record of successfully conducting and coordinating large European projects within the current and past EU Framework Programmes. As a result research is not carried out in isolation but implemented in close collaboration with stakeholders and partners in the public and private sectors.

While most of those Europe-wide projects tend to be funded by public agencies the university also has an 'open door' policy with industry. Wageningen UR offers a large number of facilities such as test locations, laboratories and offers many products and services such as knowledge databases, computational models and area maps. These facilities and services attract a steady stream of agribusiness firms.

Teaching, Learning & Student Life

Very few universities can offer the 'hands-on' experience available at Wageningen. Because of its history of growing through the acquisition of various research centers, students have access to some of Europe's leading agricultural and biological facilities. Moreover the research buildings have been adapted to contain classrooms.

While proud of the university's physical infrastructure Rector Kropff also wants to highlight the standard of teaching. "For six years now we have ranked, in terms of teaching, as the best university in the Netherlands and that is because we have a pretty special approach to education, which is basically, relatively small scale with a low student-to-teacher ratio."

The university has also developed a novel way to ensure that its top staff members are dedicated to teaching.

"We have a funding mechanism in which we fund research activities. So if they do more teaching they get more funds – that's very important as well. Teaching is not the last thing to do, but teaching is really rewarded also in terms of time. It's in our genes, our staff, and our students to really make something out of it."

The university follows a blended learning approach which means it uses many different ways to teach the materials; working in groups, applied groups, good lectures by top scientists, e-learning. This whole combination enables the students to learn very effectively.

Wageningen is a very small town, yet within an hour's train journey of Amsterdam, the Netherland's lively capital city. Moreover, situated in densely populated northwest Europe it is also a great launch pad for journeys to neighbouring countries. For those who stay in the town life in Wageningen is generally peaceful and laid back. Students there live by the motto "no bike, no life" – basically the local transport system is not great so any incoming student should be prepared to cycle. However, if you like sports you will love the university. It's comprehensive De Bongerd sports centre has everything from swimming to squash.

UNIVERSITY
of VIRGINIA

Rank › 101 – 150

Name › University of Virginia
Region › Americas
Country › United States
Founded › 1819

www.virginia.edu

Core Research Strengths

The University of Virginia (UVa) has a research budget of more than $338 million per year. This money is used to fund many areas of research, but the main areas of focus are bioengineering, nanotechnology, information science & technology, big data, and energy and the environment.

To address these themes, UVa encourages collaboration between scientists and scholars from across various disciplines. This multidisciplinary approach has proven successful in creating new applications for today's urgent and significant social issues.

About 40% of funding is spent on health-related research, which is one of the university's main foci, says President Teresa Sullivan. "Our largest research operation is in medicine, and in medicine it is common to have people from many different fields collaborating. For example, we have a large program to develop an artificial pancreas, and this work requires people with many different kinds of backgrounds. Because of this program, we are one of the leading centers for the treatment of pancreatic cancer and diabetes."

The university is also very strong in the humanities. The College and Graduate School of Arts and Sciences receives around 25% of UVa's total funding, making UVa a leading institution in humanities, social sciences, and arts scholarship.

"In the United States, UVa is widely regarded as a leader in humanities," says President Sullivan. "For example, recently one of our faculty received the $150,000 dollar Bollinger Prize for Poetry. We also have a former Poet Laureate of the United States as a member of our faculty. We are also one of the leaders in digital humanities. This is a very interdisciplinary field which requires people with traditional training in language and literature but also with skills in statistics, methodology, digitization, and so on."

Major Discoveries

The university's faculty were instrumental in the evolution of internet networking and connectivity, perhaps the most significant invention in the last half century. Physics professor James McCarthy was the lead academic liaison to the government in the establishment of SURANET, and the university has also participated in ARPANET, Abilene, Internet2, and Lambda Rail.

Partnerships, Innovation & Translational Research

Like many leading American universities, Virginia is keen to work with the private sector, says President Sullivan. "We are quite open to partnerships. For example we have strong important corporate partnerships with Rolls Royce and AstraZeneca."

The university is also keen to encourage its faculty to commercialise its research. Indeed it has recently revamped its technology transfer procedures to encourage more spin offs. "We realised that we have to support faculty members in terms of disclosing an invention and in terms of obtaining a patent. We also bring venture capitalists to the university a couple of times a year and train faculty to make pitches so that we can move ideas more quickly from the lab bench to the market."

Another important change has been with IP policy. "We have become much friendlier in the last three years towards the inventor," notes the President. Under the new approach the university will still expect some return, either through royalties or an equity share, but it also gives considerable scope for the inventor to profit too.

Teaching, Learning & Student Life

The university is set in the charming town of Charlottesville, the cultural and commercial capital of Central Virginia. The city has earned a reputation as a writers' and readers' paradise, with more newspaper readers per capita than anywhere else in America. Every spring it hosts the annual Virginia Festival of the Book that attracts thousands of avid readers from across the country. Other cultural highlights include Monticello, the home of Thomas Jefferson, Ash Lawn-Highland, the home of James Monroe, and Montpelier, the home of James and Dolly Madison, recently reopened to the public for tours, tastings, and horseracing.

The beautiful Virginia countryside is also a big draw for international students. Sitting at the foothills of the Blue Ridge Mountains and at the headwaters of the Rivanna River, Charlottesville's close proximity to the Blue Ridge Mountains and the Atlantic Ocean allows residents to enjoy a mild climate with four distinct seasons.

The university also has a lot to offer students, says President Sullivan. "Many of our students collaborate in research projects with faculty members, often as early as their first year, and we are trying to build a culture in which students who have a good research idea can apply for internal research funds. We have an annual research competition among our students, which is really extraordinary in quality. In fact, we have begun inviting venture capitalists when they come to the university to hear pitches from our students; last year, three of our students attracted venture money for their projects."

"At UVa, the close interaction of students and faculty occurs both in the classroom and beyond the classroom in informal settings. This close interaction is a hallmark of the student life here."

US

University of Sussex

Rank › 101 – 150

Name › The University of Sussex
Region › Europe
Country › United Kingdom
Founded › 1961

www.sussex.ac.uk

Core Research Strengths

As a founding member of the 1994 Group of Research Intensive Universities, the University of Sussex has long been a vocal player in the British public research scene. One of the key features of the university is that its structure provides a multidisciplinary approach to both research and teaching, says Vice Chancellor Professor Michael Farthing.

To make his case he points to the School of Global Studies; which encompasses Anthropology, Geography, International Relations and Development Studies.

"All these are quite disparate disciplines but very much inter-related in terms of the core research questions that they are concerned with. The foundation of this approach is to have practical, functioning research programs and taught courses across a diverse range of disciplines very much encouraging our students to move throughout the campus within the context of a variety of elective; as well as to have our researchers and academics collaborating throughout the university's range of expertise. This approach is very much in line with the fundamental ethos of the University of Sussex, that of multi-disciplinary teaching and collaborative researching."

"Another core ethos of the University of Sussex is to have a broad based research agenda throughout a comprehensive range of disciplines within the core areas of the sciences, social sciences and the arts; within this spectrum there are a number of core areas of expertise one could pick out."

Perhaps the most striking area of excellence, says Vice Chancellor Farthing, is in the sciences. "The University of Sussex has core expertise in the field of DNA stability and repair. Work is already under way in this area with the Medical Research Council (MRC) and the programme is one of the leading research programs of its kind in the UK, (within the top 3); and renowned globally by leading researchers and experts in these particular fields of medical science."

Major Discoveries

Despite its being barely 50 years the university has distinguished itself in the fields of science and medicine with several Nobel Prize winners and groundbreaking discoveries.

In 2001 Professor Paul Nurse was awarded the Nobel Prize in Physiology for his discovery of protein molecules that control the division of cells in the cell cycle.

Partnerships, Innovation & Translational Research

The University of Sussex's research programme is funded by a wide range of public and private sources. However, traditionally most of the funding has come from major research institutes in the public sector and charitable organisations.

Surprisingly, given its world-leading science and medical departments, the university has been slow to tap private sources of funding. Vice Chancellor Farthing is both candid about the past and is confident of securing more private partnerships in the future. "In terms of private sector funding, the University of Sussex has lagged behind some of our counterpart universities in terms of the research work we have undertaken in collaboration with private companies, however this has been improving with some spectacular recent successes"

"Our research departments have close relationships with a range of government bodies and research institutes in this way, and regular collaboration takes place as a result. Equally, the University of Sussex also has frequent conversations amongst industry with a view to developing solutions for issues faced in the private sector"

Teaching, Learning & Student Life

Set up as the first wave of 'glass plate' universities in post-war Britain, Sussex has always had clear founding ideals. One of the primary aims was that it would bring higher-education to a previously underserved area, and that close relationship with the surrounding community remains today.

Starting from afresh also meant that the university could adopt a pioneering approach to learning, says the Vice Chancellor.

"A good example is the Arts – Sciences Program whereby students studying arts related subjects are encouraged to take a science related electives each year, and vice-versa for sciences students with the arts. The University of Sussex was one of the first British universities to really focus upon fostering and developing the multi-disciplinary approach to research, teaching and learning that is now increasingly advocated and encouraged throughout the UK system."

The Vice Chancellor thinks another factor is the school system.

"The sustained and rapid rise of Sussex has its roots in the very close links that have always been fostered between the students and our respective schools. There is a very strong focus on seminars and student interactions very much based upon the Oxbridge model. On top of this, the University of Sussex has clearly identified that increasingly students demand more than just their course with the introduction of Sussex Plus aimed at providing a far more rounded experience encouraging activities such as entrepreneurship and volunteering. University is not just about learning in our view, personal and professional development is increasingly looked upon by both employers and students as equally important."

Rank › 101 – 150

Name › University of Strasbourg
Region › Europe
Country › France
Founded › 1537

www.unistra.fr

Core Research Strengths

Thanks to the worldwide reputation of its teams, research is a major asset for the University's development. The scale of research activity at Strasbourg is substantial, involving a European Doctoral College, 10 doctoral schools and 77 research units. The university's impressive funding infrastructure received a massive boost recently when it was awarded an endowment of approximately €1billion from the French Excellence Initiative. It's a huge boost, says University President Professor Alain Beretz. "This funding will help us devise a whole suite of tools such as research grants and postgraduate grants that will enable us to encourage world-class research to take place in a free and autonomous way."

Until now, says Professor Beretz, the university has sought "to maintain strengths across a broad spectrum of academic disciplines, and to ensure that as a whole we work in a multi-disciplinary manner leveraging all of these strengths to answer the most challenging fundamental questions."

However, within this broad-based approach there are certain areas that stand out. Life science, chemistry, material science and mathematics are all particularly strong, says the President. The multidisciplinary approach that Strasbourg is adopting is common across leading universities. However, what stands out is its model for enacting it. "Although the multi-disciplinary approach is of growing importance, it is not something that can be enforced at the presidential level within a university", admits the President.

"The key point is the attitudes of our academics, and the most important thing for us is to provide the best possible working conditions for world-class research to take place and multi-disciplinary orientated interactions to take place."

Given the university's success so far, the extra €1billion will surely help create even more ideal conditions for world-class research.

Major Discoveries

In 1987 Jean-Marie Lehn, who has since had a centre named after him, won the Nobel Prize in Chemistry for his development and use of molecules with structure-specific interactions of high selectivity. Much more recently Jules Hoffmann won the 2011 Nobel Prize Medicine for discoveries concerning the activation of innate immunity.

Partnerships, Innovation & Translational Research

Surprisingly, for a university that has benefited so greatly from public-sector funding, Strasbourg is very keen to develop partnerships with business. It was one of the first French universities to establish a technology transfer office, notes President Beretz. Moreover the university has received a €37million grant to develop the office further.

"This funding will not only be used for conventional technology transfer related activities such as contract research and intellectual property valorisation that we already do well at Strasbourg, but also for new strategies such as proof of concept research.

"Proof of concept is one of the key missing links between the fundamental research our academics undertake and the stages of innovation required at an industry level, to make new concepts economically viable from a commercial perspective. The University of Strasbourg does not always have the capacity to take new ideas to the prototype or proof of concept stage; this is an area that we are very interested in developing partnership arrangements. We will be investing in developing capacity to take ideas that emerge from our academic research into a prototype stage. This will enable us to take them directly to the market."

If successful it should open up another lucrative funding stream for the university.

Teaching, Learning & Student Life

The city of Strasbourg is a very international city with a rich cultural setting that offers an extremely enjoyable life style. Strasbourg frequently hosts concerts, festivals and live entertainment, which students are ideally located to enjoy. The university campus covers a vast area near the centre of the city, located between the "Cité Administrative", "Esplanade" and "Gallia" bus-tram stations. Strasbourg is also well-located in the international context. On the border with Germany and relatively close to Switzerland it offers students an incredible opportunity to know three countries and cultures.

Like its home city the university is also very international, says the President. "We are one of the most international French universities, and more than 20% of our student population comes from international locations. This proportion continues to increase and is over 40% at the postgraduate level."

Because the university has such a broad-based approach, it offers a particularly wide range of areas for study, covering all major disciplines: arts, literature and languages, law, economics, management and the social sciences.

Another attractive feature is that courses are designed to help students gain employment after graduation, says the President. "Because the University of Strasbourg has very strong traditional links in terms of undertaking collaborative research with private sector partners, we work alongside private companies in both research partnerships and bi-lateral arrangements for graduate employment. This creates excellent opportunities for students to impress future employers."

Rank › 101 – 150

Name › University of Sao Paulo
Region › Americas
Country › Brazil
Founded › 1934

www5.usp.br

Core Research Strengths

Established in 1934 to further the development of Brazil's military, educational and administrative institutions; as well as to help as a departure from previous periods of relative instability towards one of more scientific and intellectual progress. The University of Sao Paulo (USP) has since grown into Latin America's largest and most influential university. Home to approximately 90,000 students and 6,000 academic staff at any single point in time, USP is responsible for 25% of Brazil's total academic publications in major journals. Although the medical sciences are perhaps USP's greatest area of relative strength, it comes as little surprise that the university enjoys an extensive range of research strength given the size and scale of the institution overall.

Bridging the divides between academic disciplines has been the strategic focus of the administration in recent years, culminating in an array of Research Support Centers (NAP's) collaborating across the disciplines on complex challenges. Without a doubt, this strategy makes USP more attractive to international funding bodies, but also helps focus capacity on issues of relevance, whilst at the same time helping to develop human resources both at the academic and student level. Approximately 2000 USP researchers have since been involved in the submission of 122 research proposals resulting in 43 on-going collaborative research projects.

USP's 43 Research Support Centers cover a myriad of research fields from Nanotechnology and robotics through to bioinformatics and conservation in the Antarctic. Bioenergy and sustainability, robotics, marine biodiversity, technology for hybrid materials, cell therapy, medical imaging, cardiovascular disease and hypertension are some of the leading research foci under management in the NAP's.

Research is an essential part of the University of Sao Paulo's mission since its foundation, with a tradition to value all areas of knowledge. Thus, as much emphasis is put into hard science and technology as is devoted to the social sciences and humanities. Moreover, the USP has always promoted the interaction between hard sciences and humanities.

Major Discoveries

As Latin America's most intensive research university, USP is responsible for breakthroughs throughout a range of academic disciplines.

USP researchers recently discovered the amplified influence of Amazon Rainforest fires on the intensity of storms through their work on Smoking Rain Clouds.

Partnerships, Innovation & Translational Research

USP's portfolio of international research collaborations has begun to grow significantly in accordance with the growing impact of the university's research portfolio. Established in December 2010, the European Studies Institute of Brazil (IBE) is one such example of the growing interlinkages between USP and the international research community. With the philosophy of multidisciplinary research as its foundation, the IBE works to invigorate the exchange of knowledge between Brazil and the European Union.

From a domestic perspective, USP remains a close partner of some of Brazil's most important research funding institutions, working in partnership alongside institutions such as FAPESP and CAPES. USP Inovacao acts as the key interface between USP and external partners, bridging expertise with funding and potential partners. On top of this USP Inovacao acts as the conduit for discoveries and research breakthroughs made at USP to reach the broader market through licensing agreements and spin out companies.

Teaching, Learning & Student Life

Since its foundation in 1934, cultural leaders of São Paulo society invited some of the most prestigious scientists from Europe to come to the new university to settle the roots of a research Institution in the state that was, and still is, the richest in Brazil. Names like Luigi Fantappié, Claude Levi-Strauss, André Weil, Gleb Wataghin, Fernand Braudel, Pierre Monbeig, Emilio Willems, Herbert Baldus, among many others, are in the list of scholars from those initial days.

USP's spirit of knowledge generation and innovation attracts the best students in the country; as a result entry is particularly competitive. Many of Brazil's industrial and political leaders are among USP's former alumni, and make an important contribution to the progress of the state and the country.

More recently, USP has broadened its vision including social and cultural projects among its activities, giving the members of its community exceptional opportunities to link research, teaching and extension activities.

USP offers 247 undergraduate programs, 239 graduate programs, and more than 950 extracurricular programs. All degrees are classified into three major areas, those being the humanities, exact sciences and biological sciences.

Furthermore, the university houses four important museums, which receive over half a million visitors per year. Over 85% of the academic staff members are full time employees. This reinforces the university's commitment to achieving excellence in terms of its personnel and in the generation of knowledge.

SAPIENZA
UNIVERSITÀ DI ROMA

Rank › 101 – 150

Name › University of Roma - La Sapienza
Region › Europe
Country › Italy
Founded › 1303

www.uniroma1.it

Core Research Strengths

Since its founding over 700 years ago, Sapienza has played an important role in Italian history, and has been directly involved in key changes and developments in society, economics and politics. It has contributed to the development of Italian and European science and culture in many areas of knowledge.

Internationally renowned scientists work in many disciplines ranging from arts and humanities to physics and engineering. The university promotes research activities through individual grants funded by community bodies such as Marie Curie Fellowships, ERC grants and/or other international public or private organisations.

Given its location at the head of one of the ancient world's great empires it is perhaps little surprise that one of the University of Rome's best disciplines is archaeology. "We have an archaeology department which is very strong", says Deputy Rector Giancarlo Ruocco. "But our researchers do not stay in Italy. Right now we have different researchers involved in discovery in the South Arctic and North Arctic area."

Another important field for the university is mathematics, says the Deputy Rector. "Italy is more or less leading the study of mathematics in Europe and our department is one of the best in the country." Being a broad-based university it researches a wide range of subjects, but of those physics, computer sciences and the life sciences are also core strengths.

Like many of its peers, the University of Rome seeks to combine these strengths in various dedicated, multidisciplinary research groups, says the Deputy Rector. "There are different inter-departmental centres, centres devoted to interdisciplinary research. Also, we are trying to push different activities and initiatives to put together different disciplines to work together. For example, we have recently created, in collaboration with the Italian Institute of Technology, a research centre dedicated to nanotechnology in medicine, a centre in which researchers from the medical and biological fields are working with engineers and physicists as well."

Major Discoveries

Like any top university Rome has its fair share of Nobel Prize winners. But perhaps more interesting are some of its less traditional achievements. For example, the discovery of Byzantine coins helped a team of Sapienza archaeologists identify the lost city of Meteleis west of the Nile Delta.

Partnerships, Innovation & Translational Research

When it comes to technology transfer Sapienza has established the Office for Research Enhancement and Innovation (UVRSI), which works in synergy with the Vice-Rector and with the Commission for Research and Technology Innovation. UVRSI coordinates processes related to the connection between the university and public or private external individuals from Italy or abroad.

The office doesn't just process patents but actively tries to improve ties with the private sector by organising meetings with academics. It also tries to foster an entrepreneurial culture among young researchers to improve their ability to transform innovative ideas into commercial realities. So far the approach is yielding results, and the office has supported the creation of 22 spin-off companies since 2002.

Sapienza has also worked hard to build international academic relationships. For example, it runs a special programme for visiting professors and researchers to boost the quality of education and research programmes. It has a similar approach with international students, around 8,000 of whom are currently enrolled at Sapienza.

Teaching, Learning & Student Life

Sapienza is the largest university in Italy and one of the biggest in Europe with an incredible 130,000 enrolled students. For newcomers one of the most striking things about the university – apart from its size – is its location. Rome is one of the world's most popular tourist destinations and understandably it has come to be seen as something of a perk for those studying at the university. With a history spanning back to 753BC Rome is viewed by many as one of the birthplaces of Western civilisation. Fortunately for students today, many remains of that illustrious past still remain. It is listed as a UNESCO heritage site and some of its most iconic places, such as the Vatican and the Colosseum, are among the most visited spots on earth.

The main campus is close to the city centre, though many students joke that due to its enormous size – it is the biggest university campus in Europe – it feels like a city itself. Rome's inordinate amount of history, art and culture make it an inspirational place to learn. It's also well situated in Italy, offering easy access to the Mediterranean coast in one direction and ideal mountains for skiing in the other. Students should note that some campuses are in the wide Lazio region.

Life inside the classroom has plenty of variety. As befitting its huge size Sapienza offers a vast array of courses including degree programmes, PhD courses, one to two year professional courses and specialization schools in many disciplines. A recent development is the School for Advanced Studies, which aims to deliver a multidisciplinary learning experience. It provides students with courses and activities aimed at encouraging and developing their capabilities through scientific and cultural experiences.

Rank › 101 – 150

Name › University of Pisa
Region › Europe
Country › Italy
Founded › 1343

www.unipi.it

Core Research Strengths

The University of Pisa was officially established in 1343, when it was proclaimed a 'Studium Generale'. Nowadays the university is part of the Pisa University System, which includes the Scuola Normale Superiore and the Sant'Anna School of Advanced Studies.

In its long, prestigious history the university includes many famous names among its ex-alumni and faculty. Perhaps the most influential was Galileo Galilei, who was born and studied in Pisa, and became professor of mathematics in 1589.

Of course no research institute can afford to stay rooted in the past, and the University of Pisa has recently restructured its organisations and human resources to meet the new challenges of international research. Thanks to these efforts it has built an excellent reputation both in its traditional strengths of natural sciences and mathematics and also in newer areas such as social sciences, medicine, engineering, agricultural and other applied sciences.

Research in these fields is organised into 20 departments and many high-level research institutes. These centers are a combination of historic institutes, for example it has the oldest academic botanical gardens in Europe, with newer ones. Like many of its peers the university is also placing an increased emphasis on multidisciplinary research. For example its school of medicine is collaborating with the computer sciences department to study innovative approaches in computer-aided surgery. Likewise its pharmacy school is now working closely with the biology department and the agriculture department to work on innovative synthetic methodologies to obtain bioactive compounds.

As is perhaps fitting of a university seated in one of the cradles of Western civilisation, Pisa excels in the study of the Ancient World. It leads the world not just in the understanding of Greater Greece and the Roman Provinces, but also of ancient Arabia and Egypt. Indeed Pisa was the first European university to have a course in Egyptology.

Major Discoveries

Given the university's long history and broad base of disciplines it is hard to single out one discovery in particular. However, Pisa's work in modern physics deserves a mention. In 1938 Enrico Fermi, won the Nobel Prize in Physics for his demonstrations of the existence of new radioactive elements produced by neutron irradiation. That success was followed up in 1984 when Carlo Rubbia won the same award.

Partnerships, Innovation & Translational Research

Internationalisation is considered as a key priority for the University of Pisa. It implements this goal through a multi-pronged strategy.

One element of the strategy is alliances with other universities. For example it's also the only university in Italy, which has become a member of the Universities Research Association. Another is through student exchanges. This is managed by the international relations office ("Ufficio Relazioni Internazionali), which encourages student mobility within the Socrates-Erasmus Programme, and the Erasmus Mundus Programme. The final part of the strategy is international research. For example, thanks to a framework agreement presented on 28 January 2013, the University of Pisa and the Massachusetts Institute of Technology of Boston join forces and competences to give impulse to joint research projects.

The university is also keen to interact with the private sector, which it does through the Research Office. The office has a mandate to promote university research, augment technological innovation in the industrial sector, and attract funding. It does this in two ways. One is internally, within the university. It offers entrepreneurial training and funding, helps manage IP and promotes research results. The other way is externally. This is through direct collaboration with companies – ie contracts, collaboration projects and specific training.

Teaching, Learning & Student Life

Famous for its 'leaning tower' Pisa is one of the most popular tourist destinations in Italy. The tower itself is a UNESCO World Heritage site but there are also many other medieval and Renaissance monuments of interest. Another benefit for students is that it is a small town making it easy to travel around by bicycle. It is also well connected with Italy's other major cities. The countryside surrounding the city also has plenty to offer. It is close to both the beaches and the mountains, creating excellent opportunities for day trips and excursions.

As for the university, it has grown to become a "city within a city" as its enormous campus caters for around 50,000 students per day. Almost all departments of the University of Pisa are located in the core of the city, either in prestigious buildings of the old city, or in an ever-growing number of modern structures, some of which are located in the centre and some at its outskirts. Most facilities are within 20 minutes walking distance from the centre of the city.

Thanks to its size and illustrious history the university is able to offer great choice to students. Indeed, one can chose from 60 undergraduate and 74 postgraduate degree programmes in all the main areas of knowledge and advanced professional education. The University has 19 research doctoral programmes; it also offers 68 third cycle specialisation programmes and 88 special shorter professional programmes of further education at the first and second cycle levels, including an MBA. Students will also benefit from the fact that research and teaching are combined in all fields and levels.

Rank › 101 – 150

Name › University of Paris Diderot
Region › Europe
Country › France
Founded › 1970

www.univ-paris-diderot.fr

Core Research Strengths

Traditionally recognised for strengths in mathematics and physics, Université Paris Diderot is increasingly shifting its focus towards more of an interdisciplinary profile searching out innovations at the interfaces of its three areas of activity: medicine and life sciences, basic and experimental science, humanities and social sciences. Indeed, President Vincent Berger considers this to be one of the most important points about the university:

"The most important point about Paris Diderot is that we are the only fully comprehensive university in central Paris, and one of the leading comprehensive institutions in France. Our overall strategy is to foster cutting edge research and innovation at the frontiers of all disciplines. Interdisciplinary research is now extremely important for us."

Recently set up within its walls, the Paris Humanities Institute is an excellent example of this interdisciplinary culture in action, with social and STEM scientists collaborating closely to build greater understanding of theoretical and intellectual questions. Equally, the Energies of the Future Institute draws upon expertise not just in physics; but also in chemistry, biology, psychology, computer science, geography and sociology to help develop next generation energy solutions for a more sustainable future.

Some of the most exciting interdisciplinary collaborations are resolutely international, and Paris Diderot is presently engaged in the Planck Mission to observe and better understand the cosmological background. In a first, the university has recruited Nobel Laureate George Smoot from the University of California, Berkeley to lead this effort in furthering our basic understanding of the universe around us.

Major Discoveries

Nobel Laureate in Medicine Jean Dausset was awarded the prize in 1980 for his discovery and characterisation of the genes that contribute to the major histocompatibility complex, significantly contributing to our ability to transplant organs between donor

and recipient. In the humanities and social sciences, Julia Kristeva was the first ever recipient of the Holberg Prize in 2004.

Partnerships, Innovation & Translational Research

In a frank admission President Berger concedes "Significant private sector partnerships have never been part of the French academic culture or history." However in a dynamic environment for universities he believes the benefits are significant enough to bring about change: "I think that things are changing today. We see possibilities such as securing international research funding, identifying new research topics, access to data and instruments that would not otherwise be available, and opportunities for research commercialisation." A clear indication of the changing attitude towards private sector collaboration is President Berger's own recruitment from the private sector. Paris Diderot has also recently opened a fundraising foundation.

Although the university's attitude towards external collaboration is changing, basic research will always be the priority; with researchers given the freedom to follow their own curiosities. Where change is expected however, is the approach towards promoting research discoveries at Paris Diderot. According to President Berger "The best way of promoting our research is by always pursuing new commercialisations and promoting our work through research and development alongside industry. Activities in these areas are very much growing now at the University of Paris – Diderot."

Whilst still retaining very strong domestic relationships with major institutes such as CNRS and INSERM, at the international level Paris Diderot is developing strategic partnerships with selected major institutions in Brazil (University of Sao Paulo), Argentina (Buenos Aires), South Korea (SNU), China (Wuhan University), the Middle East (University of Sharjah) and North America (University of Chicago, University of Illinois at Urbana Champaign).

Teaching, Learning & Student Life

With the vast majority of facilities located along the banks of the Iconic River Seine, students at Paris Diderot are offered a cosmopolitan experience at the heart of one of the world's great capital cities. For those that enjoy haute cuisine, fine arts and fashion there are few better destinations worldwide. At the same time, Paris is diverse with an array of sporting opportunities and internationally renowned nightlife. For those that are interested in European travel, the city acts as one of the major transport hubs for all major destinations throughout the continent, especially with the widely acclaimed highspeed train network. As a result, Paris is considered one of the most attractive places for international students; ranking highly throughout a plethora of rankings and surveys.

Paris Diderot has a good balance between postgraduate, graduate and undergraduate students, President Berger is particularly proud of the approach to teaching throughout these tiers of academic achievement: "Although over half of our students are at graduate and postgraduate level, we pay great attention to the undergraduate experience in making sure that the students have exposure to our whole scope of activities throughout the disciplines, as well as early exposure to research and clinical training."

Rank › 101 – 150

Name › University of New South Wales
Region › Asia/Pacific
Country › Australia
Founded › 1949

www.unsw.edu.au

Core Research Strengths

The University of New South Wales (UNSW) is a member of the Group of Eight, a coalition of Australia's leading research universities. Located in Sydney, it is the only Australian research-intensive university established with a unique scientific, technological and professional focus.

The University's research effort is focused on issues judged to be critical to the future, from climate change and renewable energies to life saving medical treatments and breakthrough technologies. Key areas of strength are biomedical sciences; water, environment and sustainability; next generation materials and technologies; social policy, government and health policy; information and communications technology, robotics and devices; and business, law and economics. Underpinning and emerging areas of strength are fundamental and enabling sciences; contemporary humanities and creative arts; and defence and security.

UNSW is an acknowledged world leader in photovoltaics, HIV/AIDS research and quantum computing. In a recent evaluation of national research activity and quality, it was one of only four Australian universities to receive an average rating of "above world standard" in the 88 research fields assessed.

The University is home to a number of national centres for research excellence and is affiliated with many of Australia's outstanding research institutes.

Vice-Chancellor and President Professor Fred Hilmer is proud of the University's focus on some of the most difficult challenges facing society, noting that the University's interdisciplinary research centres are specially designed for that purpose.

"Probably the most tangible example is our Energy Technology Building, opened in 2012," Prof Hilmer says. "This is the centre of cross-faculty research into a wide range of energy technologies as well as energy economics and policy analysis."

Major Discoveries

In 2012, in a remarkable feat of micro-engineering, UNSW physicists working in the ARC Centre for Quantum Computation and Communication technology developed the world's smallest working transistor - consisting of a single atom placed precisely in a silicon crystal. This unprecedented atomic accuracy may yield the elementary building block for a future quantum computer with unparalleled computational efficiency. Also in 2012 a team of UNSW engineers from the same Centre created the first working quantum bit based on a single atom in silicon, opening the way to ultra-powerful quantum computers of the future.

In 2011 UNSW solar cell researchers scored a world record double, achieving a new world benchmark of 19.3 percent efficiency for a mass-produced, crystalline silicon solar cell. They then improved that result a month later to advance the record to 19.4 per cent. The previous record for cells created with this process was 18.9 per cent.

Partnerships, Innovation & Translational Research

UNSW has strong collaborative links with industry and business, regularly topping national industry linkage grants. One of its most successful partnerships has been with a major international steel company to produce so called "green steel" using a world-first, environmentally friendly process for recycling end-of-life plastics/rubber.

In 2011, UNSW became the first university in Australia, and one of the first in the world, to offer the majority of its intellectual property to companies for free. The aim of Easy Access IP is to spark greater collaboration between universities and industry and put more university-generated research into real world applications.

Teaching, Learning & Student Life

UNSW is recognized as one of Australia's leading research and teaching universities, attracting a significant proportion of high achieving and talented students from around Australia and internationally. With eight faculties in Sydney and the UNSW

Canberra campus, it has one of Australia's most diverse student populations, welcoming international students from more than 120 countries. This diversity makes for a vibrant, cosmopolitan student experience, while internationally focused curricula and extensive exchange programs ensure a global education.

Innovative research and teaching, together with strong international and industry links, give UNSW graduates a competitive edge, with starting salaries and employment rates among the highest in Australia.

Students can choose from more than 500 co-curricular activities to gain extra skills. A green and contemporary campus provides one of the highest levels of on-site accommodation of any Australian university as well as top quality sporting and recreational activities.

When it comes to understanding student life at UNSW it helps to remember the University's motto hand and mind. The motto is imbued in the University's courses, says Prof. Hilmer. "Almost every program is informed by world-class research while offering real life practical exposure."

WESTFÄLISCHE WILHELMS-UNIVERSITÄT MÜNSTER

Rank › 101 – 150

Name › University of Münster
Region › Europe
Country › Germany
Founded › 1780

www.uni-muenster.de

Core Research Strengths

When it was founded in 1780 the Westfälische Wilhelms-Universität (WWU) Münster had four core faculties: theology, philosophy, law and medicine. However, since then it has grown to become a comprehensive university, covering everything apart from engineering.

Despite its broad research base, some core disciplines stand out in particular, says University of Münster Rector, Professor Ursula Nelles. Indeed she proudly notes that the university's mathematics, chemistry and geoscience departments are all ranked in the top 5 of the whole country. Another core area is humanities, which she describes as "the base of the university".

Like many of her international peers, the Rector is convinced that the best way for the university to leverage its varied research strength is to create multidisciplinary groups.

"In the humanities numerous representatives from historical and cultural disciplines have come together to deal with themes relating to politics, cultures and religions of the pre-modern age", says the Rector. "There is also a proven tradition of cooperation in the field of research between disciplines which embrace not only history, but also medieval philology, ancient history, law, Islamic studies and the two theological faculties."

In recent years the university has set up a host of dedicated centres to make the best use of its interdisciplinary strength, says Rector Nelles. "For example the Battery Research Centre MEET, the Centre of Molecular Imaging or the Centre for Nonlinear Science live on the variety of the research carried out at WWU."

The University's research success has been rewarded by the government and it is now home to two of Germany's national Clusters of Excellence: "Religion and Politics" and "Cells in Motion". As is common in Germany each cluster receives around € 5 million per year from the German Research Foundation.

Major Discoveries

Students and professors from the university have won great acclaim for their research, including ten Leibniz Prizes, four European Advanced Investigators Grants and three European Starting Grants. However, one of the most significant discoveries came from Johannes Georg Bednorz: He studied chemistry and mineralogy from 1968 on at the WWU and discovered high-temperature superconductivity in ceramics, for which he won the 1987 Nobel Prize in Physics.

Partnerships, Innovation & Translational Research

Like many German research-intensive universities, some of Münster's most important partners are local research institutes. Various faculties work closely with Max Planck Institutes, the Fraunhofer-Gesellschaft and Leibniz Institutes.

"Cooperating in research with these institutes plays an important role in WWU's profile", explains Rector Ursula Nelles. "There is strong co-operation between the German Aerospace Centre in Berlin and WWU's Institute of Planetology, to give you one example only." The university also has international academic alliances. Indeed it has signed more than 550 academic and educational partnerships around the world and is member of the "International Research Universities Network" (IRUN) Besides that the University of Münster is a member of the group of the 15 biggest German research-oriented universities with medical faculties ("German U 15") who will jointly promote their strategic interests.

When it comes to partnerships with the private sector, Münster's approach is shaped by the structure of German industry. Considering Germany's famous backbone of small and medium-sized companies, known as Mittelstand, it is little surprise that Münster helps smaller companies with research projects. "Our research facilities and expertise make us a very attractive partner for these smaller companies", says Rector Nelles. "Especially when it comes to basic research for practical applications." The university also works with large multinationals. For example, it cooperates closely with German engineering conglomerate Siemens in the field of molecular imaging.

To help with technology transfer the WWU has established the "Arbeitsstelle Forschungstransfer", an innovation office. It acts as an interface between science, business and the public, promoting the transfer of research, knowledge and technology to industry and business.

Teaching, Learning & Student Life

When it comes to studying students have many options, with more than 250 courses. One of the distinguishing features of undergraduate life at WWU is its new initiative for teaching and studying – know.teach.learn. This scheme aims to improve the quality of teaching and give struggling students advice.

Münster also has a big impact at doctoral level. For example it confers almost 700 doctoral degrees a year, making it one of the five most important institutions in Germany for producing junior research staff. At present these programmes are currently run in three formats: Postgraduate Groups sponsored by the DFG (German Research Foundation), Graduate Schools and Junior Staff Groups.

The other important part of the student body is the international element, says Rector Nelles. "We are very strong in the ERASMUS programme; compared with the other German universities we have the largest number of incomings and outgoings. Nearly eight per cent of our students are international, so around 3000 students overall. Generally they are from Latin America, South-East Asia and the Baltic States. This internationalisation is important because it gives students an exposure to working with people from other countries that will prove helpful in their careers."

Université de Montréal

Rank › 101 – 150

Name › University of Montreal
Region › Americas
Country › Canada
Founded › 1878

www.umontreal.ca

Core Research Strengths

With a total of approximately 65,000 students in attendance and as the largest fully comprehensive Francophone university in the world, Université de Montréal has strengths throughout a diverse array of academic disciplines. Approximately US$530 million in annual research funding positions the University of Montreal as the fourth most active research university in Canada.

Université de Montréal's expertise throughout the arts, humanities and social sciences perhaps represents the university's greatest areas of capability, with specific strengths in topic areas such as philosophy, theoretical and applied ethics, ethnic, multicultural and linguistic studies, as well as international studies.

Research in the medical and life sciences also stand out as some of the institution's core research strengths, with internationally renowned expertise in infection and immunovirology, the heart, blood and vascular system, functional genomics and integrative genetics, cancer studies and the neurosciences. Université de Montréal is the only Canadian university active in every field of health teaching and research, from veterinary medicine to optometry, audiology and nursing.

The natural sciences and mathematics round off Université de Montréal's third broad area of comprehensive excellence, home to cutting-edge research programs in astrophysics and astronomy, basic and applied materials science, medicinal chemistry and pharmacology, agri-food biotechnology, simulation and modelling.

The university's excellence across such a diverse range of academic disciplines has laid the foundation for the development of linkages throughout its diverse portfolio. Université de Montréal is increasingly working at the interdisciplinary level to satisfy the growing demands of competitive international funding grants, and more importantly to support the dynamism of researchers; to integrate their ideas and areas of interest within diverse teams of expertise.

Major Discoveries

In 1956, Hans Selye of the university's Institute of Experimental Medicine and Surgery coined the term "stress." He used the word in the title of his seminal work on what was then a new concept in diagnostics: "adaptation syndrome," or the pathological response of the body to natural or inflicted trauma.

Half a century later, stress remains an important area of research for the university. For example, scientists at the Centre for Studies on Human Stress have recently found that childhood bullying changes the structure surrounding a gene involved in regulating mood, thus making victims more susceptible to mental health difficulties as they mature.

Partnerships, Innovation & Translational Research

With some 600 agreements with partner universities throughout the international community, Université de Montréal is a very well experienced collaborator: 50% of the institution's published papers are completed in partnership with academics based outside of Canada. For linguistic reasons, the vast majority of the university's partners are in Europe; the G3 partnership between the University of Geneva, Université Libre de Bruxelles and Université de Montréal is it's most in-depth platform for collaborative efforts and student exchange. Increasingly, however, Université de Montréal is branching its partnership base out to amplify strong traditional links with the Americas and Africa.

Established in 2001, Univalor acts as the Université de Montréal's technology transfer office. There is growing enthusiasm for translational research as not simply an act of business enterprise, but as a duty to the local communities that support the Université de Montréal's research operations.

Université de Montréal Rector Guy Breton elaborates further on the changing dynamic in how technology transfer is perceived: "Our communities strive to produce wealth that is economically efficient, but we have also to produce wealth that is socially inclusive. If we are creating knowledge that creates wealth, it should be good for everybody, and everybody should be involved in these innovation transfers."

Teaching, Learning & Student Life

Teaching and learning at the Université de Montréal takes place collaboratively, with students very much encouraged to work in groups solving specific problems through the highly effective "Case Solutions" approach. On top of this, entrepreneurialism plays an increasingly important role at Université de Montréal as highlighted in the case of the medical sciences by Rector Breton "We have an entrepreneurship centre where the students of all programs may go to learn about how to become an entrepreneur and how to foster the ideas that fit with good technology transfer. We also want to add a special certificate for all graduated health professionals so they are able to develop into entrepreneurs. Dentists, physiotherapists, physicians, optometrists, vets, and doctors are aspiring entrepreneurs but they don't have entrepreneurship training in their curriculum. It's about offering training in entrepreneurship to health professionals so they'll have good entrepreneurship skills."

The Université de Montréal is very much the heartbeat of Montreal's thriving social and cultural scene. The vast majority of Université de Montréal's 65,000 students live off campus, sharing accommodation throughout the city and further adding to the plethora of services and cultural opportunities on offer to students throughout the city.

UMASS — WORCESTER

Rank › 101 – 150

Name › UMASS – Worcester
Region › Americas
Country › United States
Founded › 1962

www.umassmed.edu

Core Research Strengths

As a medical school and graduate school of biological sciences, the research mission at the University of Massachusetts Medical School – Worcester (UMMS) is confined to the life and medical sciences with leading research programs investigating treatments for a diverse range of diseases and medical conditions. With funded research totalling approximately US$300 million each year, UMMS' 270 researchers are very well equipped to develop solutions to some of the most pressing challenges in global health today.

Under the leadership of world renowned Professor Shan LU, UMMS is particularly renowned for the institution's work on vaccines with major contributions to the development of vaccines for global health threats such as avian flu and HIV.

UMMS is also a pre-eminent leader in genetics and biotechnology. The university has capitalised upon major breakthroughs made in our understanding of RNA; to now building a collection of expertise and infrastructure around the recently established Advanced Therapeutics Cluster that will house cutting edge expertise in RNA biology, stem cell biology and gene therapy.

UMMS is increasingly employing an interdisciplinary strategy to further our understanding of the basic mechanisms underlying and investigate effective treatments for some of the most devastating illnesses affecting mankind today. The Cancer Center of Excellence, Heart and Vascular Center of Excellence, Diabetes Center of Excellence and Musculoskeletal Center of Excellence are at the forefront of international research concerning these health care challenges.

Major Discoveries

UMMS researcher Craig Mello discovered RNA interference in the structure of genes, resulting in the 2006 Nobel Prize. This discovery has since helped researchers develop technologies and techniques to better understand various diseases. Since this discovery UMMS has pioneered a range of RNA therapies, and innovative gene based therapies to a variety of cancer and other sever illnesses such as amyotrophic lateral sclerosis (ALS).

Partnerships, Innovation & Translational Research

UMMS' strong commitment to its research mission branches out well beyond the confines of the institution with the institution being one of the National Institutes of Health key partners, a major player in the healthcare innovation ecosystem in the North Eastern United Stated alongside UMASS system partners and a number of industry partners. UMMS remains very much open to working alongside a growing portfolio of industry partners in collaborative research, and contract research arrangements on the understanding that academic principles are at the heart of the institution and the foundation of partnerships. The Office of Technology Management (OTM) within the office of the Vice Provost for Research should be the first point of call for interested industry and external partners.

The Office of Technology Management also manages the translational research operations at UMMS, taking initial innovations and discoveries through the patent process and then transferring into the market through start up companies or licensing agreements. UMMS' track record in developing innovative new technologies is very strong for an institution of its relatively small size, generating licensing and technology transfer revenues in excess of US$50 million each year, complemented by a consistent pipeline of start up companies coming to the market place each year.

UMMS' collaborative efforts are embedded in the public service mantra of the USA's leading public universities. Through the Commonwealth Medicine Initiative, UMMS provide opportunities for local healthcare agencies to maximise their resources through best sharing practices with an internationally leading institution, as well as providing health care services to some of the most vulnerable sections of local society in Massachusetts.

Teaching, Learning & Student Life

UMMS is divided into three separate schools, that of the Graduate School of Medicine, the Graduate School of Biomedical Sciences and the Graduate School of Nursing.

The School of Medicine has approximately 125 newly enrolled students each year, and is consistently ranked as one of the best professional schools in the United States. Students can expect to be trained intensively in all aspects of primary care, with first year students working in community practice shortly after induction. Graduates of the School of Medicine are thoroughly prepared in all areas of primary care from communication skills through to scientific and patient advocacy skills; resulting in very high success rates for UMMS School of Medicine Graduates in the National Resident Matching Program.

The Graduate School of Biomedical Sciences prepares students with scientific backgrounds relevant broadly to medical sciences for research directly relating to human disease. Students can expect a research-intensive curriculum, with a myriad of multidisciplinary opportunities facilitating the combination of study areas based upon individual curiosities, interests and aspirations. Since first being established in 1979 with 7 students, the Biomedical Sciences PhD program continues to gain national and international recognition for excellence.

UMASS
AMHERST

Rank › 101 – 150

Name › University of Massachusetts
Region › Americas
Country › United States
Founded › 1863

www.umass.edu

Core Research Strengths

Since being established as a land-grant university in 1863, the University of Massachusetts has grown to command an annual research budget of $194million.

The university was originally set up to provide instruction and research for the state's important agricultural sector. It has long moved past that narrow remit and now specialises in energy, social sciences, life sciences, chemistry and the liberal arts; yet some traces of that historical mission still remain, explains Chancellor Kumble Subbaswamy. "The work of our food science department is very important for the local economy. For example it has conducted research for products such as cranberries, which are an important crop here in Massachusetts. Our researchers look for alternative uses for food products and processing and that helps industry in the region and beyond."

Another interesting historical quirk of the university is that it was one of the early pioneers of multidisciplinary research, says Chancellor Subbaswamy. "It started down this path of facilitating interdisciplinary research long before people recognised that that was an essential direction for today's complex problems. The Polymer Science and Engineering Centre that we have had here for 40 years shows how chemistry, physics and engineering can come together to create collaborations that flourish."

"That model has worked so well here that we have emphasised this in our other research centres involving neural science, molecular and cellular biology, informatics, nanotechnology, and so on. All of these are highly interdisciplinary programs where in some instances they've been spun off as autonomous units, which make it much easier to collaborate across disciplines. Without doubt this campus has been enriched by having had that foresight in a field like polymer science and engineering for a long time. So that's a model that is very heavily used here."

Major Discoveries

Perhaps the most striking evidence of how far the university has expanded from its traditional agricultural research base are the ground-breaking discoveries it has made in other fields. For example the 1993 Nobel Prize in Physics was awarded jointly to Russell Hulse and Joseph H. Taylor, Jr. for the discovery of a new type of pulsar, a discovery that has opened up new possibilities for the study of gravitation.

Partnerships, Innovation & Translational Research

In recent years the university has redoubled its efforts to improve technology transfer, says the Chancellor. "The University of Massachusetts Innovation Institute works to reduce the barriers for industrial collaboration by using more sophisticated approaches to IP negotiations. We have also recently formulated some new procedures and created new model master agreements that seem to have broken through some barriers for us."

So far the approach appears to be working. IP disclosures, patent applications, patents issued and licenses issued have all increased steadily since 2007. As a result the university now earns more than $2million a year through licensing revenues.

The university has also extended its academic alliances. For example it is part of the Massachusetts Green High Performance Computing Consortium, which involves Harvard, MIT, Boston University and Northeastern University.

Another move has been to expand relationships with international universities, explains the Chancellor. "The aim is for more internationalisation and international activities on campus. We want to see students from abroad come here and attend at undergraduate level. We've always had graduate students, in fact in some instances they've dominated, but that's not been the case at undergraduate level."

Teaching, Learning & Student Life

UMass Amherst, the flagship campus of the University of Massachusetts system, which is a member of the Five College Consortium consisting of Amherst, Hampshire, Mount Holyoke and Smith colleges, is located on nearly 1,450-acres in the scenic Pioneer Valley of Western Massachusetts. The valley sits right in the centre of much of New England's most fertile farmland.

The nearest city is Springfield, nicknamed "The City in a Forest", because more than 12% of the city is parkland. Meanwhile, students who like hiking and nature will love exploring the unspoilt forests, the Connecticut River, the Holyoke and Mount Tom mountain ranges and rolling meadows that make Pioneer Valley such a popular tourist destination. Needless to say there are an abundance of outdoor activities, covering everything from fishing to golf. If students want a more urban setting, the large city of Boston is just 90 miles away.

The campus setup helps to create a positive learning environment, says Chancellor Subbaswamy. "Because it is a college town with five prominent institutions within a very close proximity of one another, it provides a climate in which the students learn as much if not more outside of a classroom than they do inside the classroom."

It also helps that the town and campus both share a rich history of activism. "The students and local townspeople get involved in important issues of the day. One example would be sustainability and this campus is considered to be one of the most sustainable campuses in the country. For instance, our power plant is one of the most advanced on any university campus in terms of having reduced the carbon footprint."

UNIVERSITY OF LIVERPOOL

Rank › 101 – 150

Name › University of Liverpool
Region › Europe
Country › United Kingdom
Founded › 1881

www.liv.ac.uk

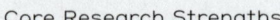

Core Research Strengths

A member of the Russell Group of leading UK research universities, the University of Liverpool is a world-leader in innovation, attracting more than £150M in research income every year.

Moreover, that research excellence is very focused, explains Vice Chancellor Professor Sir Howard Newby. "The University of Liverpool has traditional strengths in the sciences with approximately 70% of the student population studying STEM subjects. In addition, there have been eight Nobel Prize winners at the University of Liverpool. Today, from a medical sciences perspective the University has very clear strengths in immunology, infectious disease and personalized medicines designed to suit the metabolisms of patients."

Despite the focus on science, the university also excels in other areas, says the Vice Chancellor. "Liverpool is ranked in the UK top five for both History and English. Our school of architecture is the oldest in the UK, ranked second in the country by the last RAE; this school has particular expertise in the use of digital technologies for design. The University of Liverpool also has major strengths in engineering with a particular edge in aeronautical engineering."

Like many institutions the university has had to reorganise its research strategy recently to become more competitive in winning grants. "Increasingly, public research budgets in particular are being allocated to major questions where an inter-disciplinary approach that leverages critical mass between researchers is the most appropriate methodology to answer such questions. In many ways a favoured supplier or demand led approach to research is emerging as a result. This is a significant change from the past whereby individual academics would submit ideas for funding."

The University of Liverpool has responded to these changes by encouraging a multi-disciplinary approach to ensure the university remains as competitive as possible.

Major Discoveries

Professor Oliver Lodge, the University's first Professor of Physics, made the world's first public radio transmission in 1894 and demonstrated the first use of the X-ray for surgical purposes two years later.

Allan Downie, Professor of Bacteriology from 1943 to 1966 was instrumental in the eradication of smallpox.

The University has a total of eight Nobel Laureates to its name including: Sir Ronald Ross (1902) for his discovery relating to the means of the spread of malaria.

Partnerships, Innovation & Translational Research

The University of Liverpool has long led the UK in terms of international academic partnerships. For example, in 2006 it became the first British university to establish an independent university in China – Xi'an Jiaotong-Liverpool University (XJTLU).

The University has launched a network of collaborations with universities in Chile, Mexico and Spain in order to allow Liverpool students to complete part of their degree at one or more of these institutions via a range of options such as projects or placements.

These international academic partnerships can also improve links with the private sector, explains the Vice Chancellor. "Our Chinese campus is located in very close proximity to one of the Shanghai region's largest industrial parks, containing 86 of the Forbes 500 leading companies. We are now starting to see research based links beginning to develop between ourselves and these companies."

Those new links come on the back of established links with Unilever, AstraZeneca and NNL, in the fields of materials, pharmaceuticals and nuclear energy respectively.

Getting the balance right between academic and commercial interests is a challenge, concedes Vice Chancellor Newby. "The basis for research is always going to be the academic curiosity of outstanding researchers, although further down the track of research and innovation private or commercial partners do get involved when progress starts to take off in an interesting way for them. There certainly is no conflict in these types of relationships; much of their functionality really depends upon the flexibility and approach of both parties."

Teaching, Learning & Student Life

The University is mainly based around a single, 100 acre, urban campus approximately five minutes-walk from Liverpool City Centre. It contains 192 non-residential buildings that house 69 lecture theatres, 114 teaching areas and state-of-the-art research facilities. Moreover, the student facilities are set to improve further. In 2011 the University made a commitment to invest £600M into its campus to benefit both research and the student experience.

The city itself is another plus, says the Vice Chancellor. "Following a recent branding exercise, we have learnt that Liverpool is also an excellent international brand. It is an amazingly funky and edgy city that has fostered an unrivalled affection amongst its student population."

When it comes to life in the classroom, the university is focused on making sure courses lead to jobs after graduation. "The University of Liverpool is one of only two UK universities alongside Bristol that teaches all three clinical sciences in medicine, dentistry and veterinary science. On top of this, a very high proportion of Liverpool's degrees are licensed such as law, architecture and engineering. As a result, the University of Liverpool has a very strong vocational focus upon employability. This is a clear distinguishing point for us. In coming to Liverpool, you will not only get a first class education, but also into a degree scheme that provides an entry route into the professions."

THE UNIVERSITY
OF IOWA

Rank › 101 – 150

Name › University of Iowa
Region › Americas
Country › United States
Founded › 1847

www.uiowa.edu

Core Research Strengths

The University of Iowa is a major national research university located on a 1,900-acre campus in Iowa City. It has world-renowned research programmes in genetics, hydraulics, biomedical discovery, communication sciences, developmental and aging studies, global health, sustainability, and humanities scholarship. The UI has also enjoyed a long history of leadership in the visual and performing arts and in creative writing.

Like many of its peers, its research is organised according to an interdisciplinary strategy, says university Provost Barry Butler. "We recently established cross-disciplinary clusters focused on five "grand challenges." The aging brain and mind cluster, for example, includes faculty from medicine, engineering, law, education, psychology and several other units."

Another good example of the university's work is in water sustainability, says Vice President for Research and Economic Development, Dan Reed. "We have a large centre that looks at environmental, water and air quality worldwide. The Iowa Flood Center is working to provide communities accurate, scientific information to help them better understand their flood risk. We also have an Iowa Initiative for Sustainable Communities, through which graduate students work in various Iowa communities directly with developers, planners, and city leaders to address pressing sustainability concerns. We have a large IISC program underway in Iowa city where students have been researching and mapping renewable energy sources for every parcel of land in the community."

Major Discoveries

Iowa scientists, including the late James Van Allen, have been pioneers in space research, designing and building research instruments for more than 50 successful U.S. satellites and space probes.

Partnerships, Innovation & Translational Research

The university has a rich history of successfully turning research into successful products in the market place. In recent years Iowa has revamped its organisation to encourage more commercial links between its faculty and the outside world, says Vice President Reed. "We have gone out of our way to focus our efforts and we've put external people who really understand technology transfer on our research foundation board. We have hired people within departments, particularly medicine, to help faculty figure out exactly what should be commercialised."

The university is also very keen to expand its international presence, says Provost Butler. "We want to bring the world to Iowa and we want to take Iowa to the world."

International students from 100 countries make up 11% of the university's enrolment while Iowa also sends many students abroad.

The university also runs special international courses, says the Provost. "We have some digital telemedicine programmes in Eastern Europe. It's a good example of how we rely on our strengths to take us around the world. Another is the International Writing Program, where we bring in around 30 international writers every year. They return home and they are ambassadors for us and help spread the good reputation of our university.

Teaching, Learning & Student Life

The university is located in Iowa City, an urban area that includes a collection of small towns with a total population of around 100,000. While Iowa City is a small town, the presence of the university leads to a wide variety of cultural opportunities, such as large athletic events. During summer, students can enjoy weekly downtown jazz and pop concerts, while all through the year they can see major poets, writers, artists, historians, scientists, and others speak or perform in university venues or read at local bookstores. Excellent public schools, close, safe, and comfortable neighbour-hoods, and a highly educated population mean that Iowa City frequently appears high on 'best-place-to-live' listings in national magazines. The nearby countryside, good state parks, and the Iowa River provide many opportunities for walking, biking, and boating.

President Mason believes that this special setting holds much charm for students. "Iowa City is a very unique place to live. It's small, with a very easy lifestyle because the university is such an important part of it. We're the centre of the universe for writing programs through a variety of renowned courses. In fact our Writers' Workshop was the first creative writing degree program in the United States and the model for contemporary writing programs.

Workshop alumni have won seventeen Pulitzer Prizes, as well as numerous National Book Awards and other major literary honours. Three recent U.S. Poet Laureates have been graduates of the Workshop. In 2003, the Workshop received a National Humanities Medal from the National Endowment for the Humanities. Ironically while Iowa City is quite small, the university itself is large with more than 30,000 students. Their learning is split between 11 different colleges and students can expect to visit quite a few of these, regardless of their chosen major, says Provost Butler.

"When it comes to their academic programmes, they're encouraged to go beyond their major. Our general feeling is that your degree is one thing of value, but educational pursuits beyond degree requirements are of significant importance when you are out in the world. Students enlarge their educational experience through minors, certificate programs and extracurricular activities.

UNIVERSITY
of HAWAI'I
MĀNOA

Rank › 101 – 150

Name › University of Hawaii at Manoa
Region › Americas
Country › United States
Founded › 1907

www.hawaii.edu

Core Research Strengths

The University of Hawai'i at Mānoa is among the top 50 research universities in the United States, and in many research areas, it is among the very best in the world. The largest and oldest of the UH campuses, UH Mānoa offers a diverse array of undergraduate and graduate degrees, including more than 50 distinct PhD programs. With extramural funding of $489 million in 2011, it is one of only 16 US land-, sea-, and space-grant universities. The university houses some of the world's most distinctive research infrastructure, harnessing its unique position at the center of the Pacific Ocean to excel internationally in fields such as oceanography and astronomy.

Centers of ocean research excellence include the Daniel K. Inouye Center for Microbial Oceanography: Research and Education (C-MORE) and the coupled ocean-atmosphere climate studies at the International Pacific Research Center. The Departments of Oceanography and Ocean Resources Engineering maintain at Station ALOHA, 60 miles north of Oahu, the 25-year Hawaii Ocean Time series and the Aloha Cabled Observatory, the deepest on the planet. Tropical marine science research at the Hawaii Institute of Marine Biology includes coral reef ecology, biogeochemistry, evolutionary genetics and marine mammal sensory perception. Also at UH Mānoa, the Hawaii Natural Energy Institute runs one of only three national centers for offshore renewable energy, focusing on ocean thermal energy conversion and wave energy.

Astronomy is another field where the University of Hawai'i at Mānoa is leading the world with its research and facilities. With 16 different telescopes available for the university and its partners to observe the universe, the Institute for Astronomy conducts research into galaxies, cosmology, stars, planets, and the sun. The university continues to make ground-breaking additions to its space sciences infrastructure, including partnership in the new Advanced Technology Solar Telescope, currently under construction and capable of viewing objects on the sun's surface as small as 30km across. The university will also host the world's first-ever 30 meter telescope, part of a US$1.4 billion project.

As part of an emerging area of excellence in health sciences and social welfare, the UH Cancer Center focuses research on epidemiology, molecular carcinogenesis, prevention, quality of life in cancer survivors, and new therapeutic approaches.

The University of Hawai'i at Mānoa is also home to one of the most extensive Asian and Pacific studies programs in the world, and teaches as many as 28 different Asian-Pacific languages.

Major Discoveries

Extra-solar planets (exoplanets) the size of Earth are common. UH Mānoa researchers captured the first direct images of an exoplanet in the process of forming around its star.

Pioneering our understanding of nutrient cycling and oxygen generation by microbes in the ocean.

The only university with dedicated rocket-launch capability for its own satellites, the Hawai'i Space Flight Laboratory will support the 2013 launch of a Super Strypi rocket carrying a UH-developed Earth-observing satellite called HiakaSat.

Partnerships, Innovation & Translational Research

The immense portfolio of research infrastructure managed by the University of Hawaii at Mānoa brings with it an extensive network of partners that help fund, manage, maintain and use its facilities. For example, the University of Hawai'i manages the world's largest observatory for optical, infrared, and sub-millimeter astronomy at the 4,200-meter-high summit of Mauna Kea. Here, the university acts as the "home team" working in partnership with federal agencies, research institutes and universities from around the world to keep the world's foremost collection of telescopes in operation.

Despite Hawai'i's relative geographic isolation from the world's major commercial or industrial centers, the University of Hawai'i at Mānoa has an active strategy to develop additional collaborative partnerships with private sector firms, and to increase the role of venture capital in its translational research operations.

Teaching, Learning & Student Life

The University of Hawai'i at Mānoa is located in a rainbow-filled residential neighborhood just minutes from Waikīkī and other O'ahu attractions, but students should not expect to study in paradise for their entire experience. There are many opportunities to spend time either on the mainland United States or at one of the university's many partner institutions worldwide.

New technologies have been embraced to enable problem-based and interactive learning. This "hybrid learning" approach incorporates online learning platforms to add value to classroom activities, enable discussion, and help students develop collaboration skills. Chancellor Tom Apple details the objectives of this approach. "We are trying to develop higher order thinking skills that we feel our students need, and are trying to incorporate a lot of experiential learning. So, we are moving towards making sure students do research and internships. We put a big emphasis on getting students engaged in research--and I don't just mean science or engineering, I mean in all of our disciplines.

"Encouraging students to be entrepreneurial is really important," Chancellor Apple continues. "It is a very rare case where the student comes right out of college and can jump in and start their own business. But I think you plant the seed in college, so they learn some of the issues of how to lead and how to be entrepreneurial."

University of Hawaii at Manoa
United States

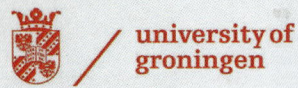
university of groningen

Rank › 101 – 150

Name › University of Groningen
Region › Europe
Country › Netherlands
Founded › 1614

www.rug.nl

Core Research Strengths

The University of Groningen was founded in 1614. It is one of the oldest universities in the Netherlands and, with around 30,000 students, is also one of its largest.

University President, Professor Sibrand Poppema says that although Groningen is a comprehensive research university, there are some areas in particular that stand out: "We are world-class in material science, chemistry, organic solar cells and nano-science." Those research strengths are being directed towards three thematic challenges: healthy ageing, energy and sustainable society. And, because these themes don't nicely respect academic boundaries, most of the research groups at the University of Groningen are multidisciplinary.

"Healthy ageing is not about getting older, but about staying healthy longer, and it is probably the most important subject because what we really want is people to stay healthy for a longer period so they can work longer," says Professor Poppema. To solve the problem the university is conducting research across many disciplines to improve existing methods of prevention, care and treatment. "This challenge has so many different aspects that we have people in science, geography and demography, psychology, sociology and even economists working on this."

The Groningen Energy and Sustainability Programme (GESP) are handling the other two themes. However, the President says that will change soon. "We want to establish an Energy Academy, called Energy Academy Europe, EAE."

However, that's not to undermine the importance of sustainability, says President Poppema. "One of today's major challenges is to keep our world in balance in the midst of a potpourri of far-reaching globalization, migration, increasing information availability, interwoven economic systems and legislative territories that sometimes overlap. These issues are summed up in the sustainable society focus area."

Major Discoveries

Groningen has had a number of extremely successful alumni and professors. One of the most notable is Heike Kammerlingh Onnes, who won the Nobel Prize in Physics in 1913 for his work liquefying helium and discovering superconductivity.

Partnerships, Innovation & Translational Research

One of the chief ways that the university engages the wider world is through strategic academic alliances. The university participates in national and international research programmes, and many Groningen-based researchers collaborate with colleagues from all over the world on a daily basis.

Generally these research-led interactions take place under the auspices of international groupings. For example the university is part of the U4 network with fellow lowland universities Uppsala, Göttingen and Ghent; the Coimbra network; Tsinghua, Fudan and Peking Universities in China; Osaka in Japan; IT Bandung and Gadja Madah in Indonesia; Sao Paulo and UNAM in Latin America; UBC and Maryland in North America.

The university sees also students as having a key role to play in its internationalisation strategy, says President Poppema. "We want our students to go out, so we are very active in Erasmus Mundus programmes, I think we are in eight different Erasmus Mundus programmes and have applied for a few more."

When it comes to the private sector the university works hard to leverage the country's long association with natural gas. To that end it has created the Energy Delta Institute with two local gas companies – Gasunie and GasTerra. Large multinationals, such as Shell, RWE and Gazprom, are also involved in the project.

Teaching, Learning & Student Life

As the economic and cultural capital of the region, the city enjoys a bustling reputation, while retaining a safe community character. One of the most striking features about Groningen is its youthful population. Roughly a quarter of the city's 193.000 inhabitants are students. Unsurprisingly the concentration of young people has led to a proliferation of busy bars, restaurants, theatres, museums and sports facilities. The city is also home to a variety of architecture. Some parts retain a medieval feel while others are home to post-modern blocks. If you feel like a break from city life, Groningen is surrounded by picturesque countryside. A short bike ride will take you to the famous flat landscape and 'Wadden Sea'.

The university also has a lot to offer. Like the city it is a mix of historic buildings in the inner-city quarters and brand new academic centres. In total it has nine faculties, 27 research centres and institutes, and more than 175 degree programmes. Each faculty offers Bachelor's, Master's, PhD, and Exchange programmes, while some also offer short certificate courses. The quality of its teaching course was confirmed when the EU awarded it the Diploma Supplement and the ECTS label.

And if you are a foreign student, you won't be short of friends in the same situation, says the President. "The University of Groningen already has 4000 international students with over 120 different nationalities – we hope to reach 5000 international students in 2015. Indeed 20% of the staff and 60% of all PhD students are already from abroad."

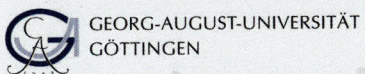

GEORG-AUGUST-UNIVERSITÄT GÖTTINGEN

Rank › 101 – 150

Name › University of Goettingen
Region › Europe
Country › Germany
Founded › 1737

www.uni-goettingen.de

Core Research Strengths

Founded in 1737, Georg-August-Universität Göttingen is a research university of international renown with a strong focus in research-led teaching. One of the most distinctive aspects of the university is that it is embedded in the Göttingen Research Campus. Indeed to fully understand the university's research capabilities, it must be looked at as part of a network of first-class research establishments that also include the Göttingen Academy of Sciences, the German Primate Centre, the German Aerospace Centre, and five nearby Max Planck Institutes.

"Together", says University President Ulrike Beisigel, "these local partners form an alliance for collaboration in research and teaching arguably unique in Germany in terms of its depth and breadth. Successful elements of which include jointly run collaborative research centres, junior research groups and infrastructure facilities, as well as combined professorial appointments."

Being part of the research campus means that the university has the infrastructure to support high-level research capabilities across a number of key areas. One of the most important is neurobiology, says President Beisigel. While another of the main fields is materials research. Both of these areas are investigated through a multidisciplinary approach with support from several scientific disciplines.

Several new centres have been established to support new multidisciplinary themes. CeMIS handles the emerging subject of modern Indian studies, while CeMEAS tackles modern East-Asian Studies. Given the rapid economic growth expected in these parts of the world, these are research areas that will have increasing economic and political significance. Another interesting research initiative lies in the humanities, where the university has a focus on religious science.

In addition, the University of Göttingen has set up several Courant Research Centres within the framework of its Institutional Strategy, funded in the first program phase of the German Excellence Initiative. The centres take an interdisciplinary approach to address innovative research topics, and each one offers excellent working conditions for up to three junior research groups. This novel concept has proven successful in attracting excellent scientists and scholars from all over the world to Göttingen.

Major Discoveries

When it comes to breakthroughs, Göttingen University has one of the best records in Germany. It is associated with more than 40 Nobel Prize winners. One of the most famous is Max Planck, whose work on quantum theory won him the Nobel Prize in Physics in 1918.

Partnerships, Innovation & Translational Research

Of course the university's most important partnerships are with its network of allied research institutes. However, it is also starting to develop more alliances with the private sector, says the President. "The Göttingen Research Campus now has several associate partners, some of them regional companies that are among the world's leading companies in their respective fields."

The other way the university works with the private sector is through its technology transfer office, MBM Science Bridge.

When it comes to public sector international alliances, co-operation in science and research are still very much led by individual scientists and research teams, says President Beisigel. "There is a kind of science-driven international exchange where we have to give support to the researchers."

Students are also a way for the university to form international alliances. "At the moment, 11% of our students are international. Our strategy is to have a good exchange of students incoming and outgoing, and to give them all the necessary support", says the President.

Teaching, Learning & Student Life

There is an old Latin saying about life in Göttingen, "Extra Gottingam non est vita, si est vita, non est ita" (There is no life outside Göttingen. Even if it is life, it is no life like here). Given the City's small size and provincial feel that quote sometimes feels tongue-in-cheek, but it is certainly true that Göttingen has a unique atmosphere. Many of the university's old customs still continue to this day. For example, any potential student thinking of studying for a PhD at the university should remember that every PhD student who has just passed their oral doctoral test usually sits in a wagon decorated with flowers and balloons. They are then driven around the city, accompanied by relatives and friends, and taken to the central square where the old town hall. The "newly born doctor" shall climb up to the statue of Gänseliesel (a poor princess in an old fairy tale), kiss Gänseliesel and give bouquets to her.

The university is spread out in several locations around the city, drawing the President to make comparisons with Oxbridge. "Göttingen University is a big campus altogether while Göttingen is a small city, so the atmosphere is like Oxford, Cambridge and so on. There is not much of the city that is not connected to the university. Here it's just a five-minute stroll for everything, and that is an advantage for the students as well."

At present there are around 25,000 students studying a range of nearly all the academic disciplines across 13 faculties. The variety of subjects is a big advantage for students, says President Beisigel. As "such a spectrum of subjects enables overarching issues to be tackled with an interdisciplinary perspective, even at undergraduate level."

**GOETHE
UNIVERSITÄT**
FRANKFURT AM MAIN

Rank › 101 – 150

Name › University of Frankfurt
Region › Europe
Country › Germany
Founded › 1914

www2.uni-frankfurt.de

Core Research Strengths

Goethe University Frankfurt is a leading research university in Germany that takes pride in its tradition as a civic institution. Founded in 1914 by wealthy local citizens, Goethe University regained its autonomy as an endowed institution in 2008.

Last year the University received €136 million in external research funding. Among them were three national clusters of excellence, awarded as part of the German federal excellence initiative competition, as well as several research clusters funded competitively by the Hesse state government and other sponsors.

The areas of research excellence span the full spectrum of disciplines. One cluster of excellence, Macromolecular Complexes, draws in scholars from biochemistry, chemistry and biosciences, whereas the Cluster of Cardiopulmonary Systems combines cutting edge basic sciences with preclinical and clinical studies in the field of heart and lung diseases. "We are particularly proud to have a world-class Cluster that involves the social sciences and humanities and deals with the Formation of Normative Orders", says Prof. Rainer Klump, Goethe University's Vice-President.

The university utilises its location in Germany's financial hub, with a centre called the House of Finance. This centre has received substantial funding from the financial industry and co-operates closely with the German and European banks and regulatory agencies. Another important institute outside of the cluster of excellence structure is the Centre for Biodiversity and Climate Change. It is run in cooperation with Frankfurt's Senckenberg Institute. The University also has an important centre for nuclear physics and another for educational science.

Major Discoveries

The University has produced 15 Leibniz Prize winners - the most prestigious academic honour in Germany - and 19 Nobel Prize winners. The most recent of the latter came in 1998 when Horst Ludwig Störmer won the Nobel Prize in Physics for the discovery of a new form of quantum fluid with fractionally charged excitations.

Partnerships, Innovation & Translational Research

The University's origins are key to understanding its attitude to interaction with the private sector, says Vice President Klump. "We were not founded by state institutions but by the interested citizenry of Frankfurt. As a result we have always had strong links with the local business community."

Today Frankfurt is probably the German research university that is most engaged with business, says the Vice President. "For example, we have almost 40 funded chairs. This concept is not very widespread in Germany, but we get a lot of money from private-sector businesses such as banks and chemical firms that sponsor chairs here in the various departments."

Another innovative step is the lecture series that is designed to attract citizens and business people from Frankfurt and the Rhein-Main region to come to the university.

Goethe University has also developed a global network of strategic partnerships with top higher education institutions such as the universities of Toronto, Tel Aviv and Pennsylvania. The DAAD, Germany's national agency for the promotion of international mobility in higher education, has recently awarded close to one million Euros to Goethe University for the further development of this network of partnerships that revolves around innovative teaching methods such as research internships and joint PhD programmes. The benefits of strong international engagement are tangible to students and scholars alike. One of the University's many initiatives is the fully funded International Campus programme, which invites visiting professors from partner institutions abroad to teach at Goethe for a period of time.

Teaching, Learning & Student Life

Without a doubt the University's location is a big part of the student experience, says Vice President Klump. "I think students value that we bring them into contact with the commercial community around us. We feel that the students see studying in Frankfurt as a chance to live in a multicultural, dynamic, modern area. There is a strong linkage between university, city and region. Combine that with all the intellectual capacity that we have, and that makes it a fascinating place to study." The strong university-employer links were confirmed in late 2012 when the International Herald Tribune ranked Goethe University as a global top ten institution for graduate employability.

Goethe University's more than 43,000 students benefit from studying and living in Frankfurt, the largest financial and trading centre in mainland Europe. Despite being a major financial centre Frankfurt is also surrounded by natural beauty. It is located on both sides of the Main River southeast of the Taunus mountain range. The southern part of the city contains the Frankfurt City Forest, Germany's largest forest within a city. The combination of commerce and nature probably explains why Frankfurt is rated among the top 10 most liveable cities in the world.

Another big plus is the research-based learning approach, says the Vice President. The University is in the process of transforming its study programmes to give all students a chance to gain first-hand research experience, even at the Bachelor's level. "Our top scholars that work in our world class research clusters do not hide in their labs", says the Vice President. "Instead, they make their research accessible to wet the students' appetite for independent research."

Rank › 101 – 150

Name › University of Delaware
Region › Americas
Country › United States
Founded › 1833

www.udel.edu

Core Research Strengths

The University of Delaware traces its origins to a small private academy in 1743 but has since grown into a research-intensive, technologically advanced institution.

In the early 20th century, the university benefited from generous support from members of the du Pont family and associated company and, as a result, developed research expertise in chemistry. "That strength is still with us today", says President Pat Harker. "We're strong across the board with sciences but chemistry and chemical engineering particularly stand out."

Another, less predictable, legacy of the university's relationship with du Pont is art. "We have one of the top art conservation programs in the world because of the interest of the du Pont family and their family estate", explains President Harker. "We also have strong programs in plant and soil science, and in other areas of horticulture because of our relationship with Longwood Gardens, once the gardens of the du Pont family."

Another interesting aspect of the university's research strategy is the focus on multidisciplinary centers. In recent years it has built several multi-disciplinary research centers like the Delaware Biotechnology Institute, the Delaware Environmental Institute and The Interdisciplinary Science and Engineering Laboratory opening later this year.

A good example, says President Harker, is energy. "When we look at an area like our energy future, we don't just look at the technical aspects of it. It's useless unless we figure out how people would use it and how it impacts society more broadly. So when we tried to create an institute like the University of Delaware Energy Institute, it is really focused on the comprehensive view of energy that we, as a society, need. So we've been hiring people in the technology fields plus in the humanities, and in the policy arena."

Major Discoveries

The du Pont influence continues to be felt in the university's proudest moments. For example its most recent

Nobel Prize came in chemistry in 2010 when Professor Richard F. Heck made progress in with palladium-catalysed cross couplings in organic synthesis.

Partnerships, Innovation & Translational Research

The long history with Du Pont shows that Delaware is open to working with private-sector partners. That ethos has stayed with the university until today, says the President. "We have deep partnerships with a variety of companies. For example, we have a deep and growing partnership with JP Morgan Chase. In fact they have facilities right in our business school focused on the broad area of financial analytics."

The university has also established the Office of Economic Innovation & Partnerships to attract more work with the private sector. "Its focus is to be a one-stop-shop for potential partners to streamline the way we do business with them. That also includes the way we share intellectual property."

Indeed Delaware is taking a very innovative approach to sharing intellectual property with private firms, says President Harker. "My personal view on this is that universities tend to hold too tightly to their intellectual property; as a result they sometimes strangle it. Of course I want to ensure that the university's interests are protected, but I'd rather loosen up our hold on the IP so that we can get this out into the world to make a difference." The President's strategy is already yielding results, with a 60% increase in patent disclosures under the new IP policy.

Teaching, Learning & Student Life

The university's mainstay is its Georgian-style campus in the small town of Newark, although it also has other facilities spread throughout the state. Newark may be small, but it's actually part of the built-up and densely populated northeast U.S. The town itself has a pleasant, relaxed atmosphere with plenty of parks for students to relax in. Moreover it is steeped in history. It is one of the oldest settlements in America and was founded by European settlers in 1694. For those who want a more lively experience, the

large cities of Baltimore and Philadelphia are less than an hour away by car.

At a lot of leading universities there are clashes between those who want to focus on research and those who want to deliver education. President Harker is keen to emphasise that this type of conflict isn't present at UD. "We try not to just say there's research versus teaching: It's all one and the same. It's about getting students engaged in creating new knowledge and learning that knowledge. So the interdisciplinary research is immediately interspersed into interdisciplinary teaching. Another important element of our course is 'problem-based learning'. Instead of teaching students by lecturing to them, we immerse students in real problems – it's a successful approach and one that we pioneered."

Also, while UD may be based in a small town in Delaware its students are expected to have a very international attitude. "We were the first university in the United States to do study abroad. Colonel Kirkbride came back from the First World War and decided that students needed to understand what was happening in Europe. So he took the first class of US students to France in the 20's, and it's something that's continued to the present day."

UNIVERSITY OF CALIFORNIA
SANTA CRUZ

Rank › 101 – 150

Name › University of California, Santa Cruz
Region › Americas
Country › United States
Founded › 1962

www.ucsc.edu

Core Research Strengths

UC Santa Cruz is a Californian public university that combines the depth and rigor of a major research university with the personalized, interactive experiences of a small, liberal arts college. It commands an annual research budget of $165 million, which is invested in UCSC's main research strengths of bioinformatics, astronomy and marine sciences.

The university has a world-leading position in the field of genomics and bioinformatics, says Chancellor George Blumenthal. "The international collaboration that led to the mapping of the human genome was actually completed at UC Santa Cruz. Computer scientists working with biologists figured out how to put the little pieces of the genome together into a searchable database. So you could say the human genome was released here."

The university is building on that success. It has continued to lead the field and has developed a genome browser that is used by researchers all over the world. Indeed UCSC's strong position was recognised by the US National Cancer Institute, which recently handed over the responsibility for its repository of all the cancer genomic data it collects. "It is impressive," proclaims the Chancellor, "that a campus that does not even have a medical school is at the forefront of medical science."

The university also has a proud history in astronomy and astrophysics. "It was at Santa Cruz that the concept of the 10-meter telescope was first envisioned. And now, UC is part of an international collaboration to build the 30-meter telescope." Astronomers at UCSC are discovering new planets and are pioneers in understanding dark matter and the structure and formation of the universe.

UC Santa Cruz is also exceptionally strong in marine sciences. "We sit on the shore of Monterey Bay and have built a dynamic hub of expertise in coastal biology and marine ecology. We also focus on ocean energy policy, conservation, restoration, and large initiatives relating to coastal ecology."

Major Discoveries

Unsurprisingly, some of the university's best discoveries have come in astronomy. For example, in 1977 Jerry Nelson designed the twin 36-mirror Keck telescopes, the world's largest optical and infrared telescopes. It was a design that revolutionized astronomy.

Partnerships, Innovation & Translational Research

UC Santa Cruz serves the innovation center of Silicon Valley and is creating a campus ecosystem and IP policies that are resulting in a number of start-up companies and technology transfers, says Chancellor George Blumenthal. "I think the main motivating factor on intellectual property is to make sure that the ideas get out there. It means that discoveries are finding their way into the marketplace."

The university believes knowledge creation and technological innovations should be shared broadly, says the Chancellor. "An example of that is Jacob Rosen, who led a team that developed technology to conduct robotic surgery. He developed seven robotic surgery systems, which he decided to give away to competing labs. He gave away that technology because he realised that establishing common research platforms worldwide will lead to far greater advances."

The university also has a number of key alliances with fellow research institutions. It is involved in various projects with the Large Hadron Collider, NASA Research Center and the California Institutes for Science and Innovation.

Teaching, Learning & Student Life

UCSC is located in the Ben Lomond Mountain ridge of the Santa Cruz Mountains, with a 2,000-acre campus set in rolling, forested hills overlooking the Pacific Ocean and Monterey Bay. The natural beauty creates an inspiring learning environment. There are a number of natural points of interest throughout the UCSC grounds, including vast meadows, thick groves of towering redwood trees, and underground caves. Another popular destination for students is Tree Nine, a large Douglas Fir tree that is more than 100 feet tall.

If students are looking for more diversion, beaches are just minutes away, and San Francisco is only 75 miles away.

"The undergraduate student experience at the University of California Santa Cruz is outstanding", says Chancellor Blumenthal. "One of the things we've really been proud of over the years, and one of our real areas of strength is when students come here as freshman students, instead of just entering at the university, they actually affiliate with a college within the university."

"It was an idea we borrowed from Cambridge University", explains the Chancellor. "And that was the original model for the campus that we've evolved since then. We have ten colleges and the idea is to give freshmen or sophomores the feeling of a small college, even though they're inside of a major research university. So the fact is, they can get the best of both worlds. They can enjoy the small college setting, and also take advantage of the research opportunities and the outstanding world-class faculty found only at a major research university."

UC RIVERSIDE

UNIVERSITY OF CALIFORNIA

Rank › 101 – 150

Name › University of California, Riverside
Region › Americas
Country › United States
Founded › 1954

www.ucr.edu

Core Research Strengths

The University of California, Riverside is one of ten universities within the prestigious University of California system. UCR spends more than $100million in research funding each year, with the majority of finance provided by federal agencies such as the National Science Foundation and the National Institutes of Health.

The university's core research strengths are health, technology, sustainability and policy. Collaborative and interdisciplinary research in these areas is conducted through dedicated centers that bring together like-minded faculty and students to tackle large scientific and social issues.

For example, in the Bourns College of Engineering, the Center for Environmental Research and Technology leads a broad programme of research and technology development on the relationship between transportation and air quality. Researchers at the center have developed engine technology that allows cars to run on a mix of hydrogen and natural gas. Another exciting invention involves an efficient and clean method of turning waste materials into a sulphur-free diesel fuel.

On the policy side, the SEARCH Family Autism Resource Center is the first center in the UC system to focus on education and advocacy for parents who are trying to navigate the maze of autism services, with a particular emphasis on low-income and Spanish speaking families. Another leading policy hub is the Edward J. Blakely Center for Sustainable Suburban Development, which helps regional leaders and policy makers design and plan for greener communities as suburbs mature.

The university's research heritage, its resources and its inland Californian location make it an ideal place for exploring air, water, energy, biodiversity, sustainability and land use issues. Riverside-based scientists working in the Citrus Variety Collection have developed more than 40 new citrus varieties, helping growers to fight pests and diseases and remain competitive in the $1.2billion-a-year California citrus industry.

Major Discoveries

It is fitting that some of the university's finest discoveries have had a big impact in the surrounding area. For example in 1963 plant physiologist Charles Coggins registered gibberellic acid for use in California citrus groves to delay fruit maturation. The ultimate result of his work was the extension of the citrus-growing season in California from four months to nine.

Partnerships, Innovation & Translational Research

International students and scholars have played an important role at UCR for many years. Indeed today there are more than 1000 international students and 350 visiting professors and researchers engaged in study, teaching and research at the university.

Many of the university's most important research partnerships are with federal agencies. As a result a dedicated office for Governmental Relations acts as the primary link between the campus and local, regional, state and federal elected officials.

UCR is also keen to develop relationships with private-sector partners. One way it does this is through the University Research Park. This is a partnership between UCR, the City and County of Riverside to create a campus for new-technology businesses. It houses companies such as Surado Solutions, Ambryx Biotechnology and Microbac Laboratories.

The other way that UCR interacts with the private sector is through technology transfer. UC Riverside maintains an active patenting and patent licensing program through Research and Economic Development's Technology Commercialisation program, ensuring that the results of research are made available for the public's use and benefit. In addition many schools and colleges also have their own corporate partnership programmes.

Teaching, Learning & Student Life

UCR is located in the vibrant inland region of Southern California on the eastern edge of Riverside, a city of nearly 300,000 that offers entertainment, arts, recreation and quality living. Riverside campus also has a lot going for it. Located on nearly 1,200 acres near Box Springs Mountain in Southern California, the park-like campus provides convenient access to the inland region. Students will enjoy the thriving arts community, the concerts, film festivals, dance performances and theatre. Meanwhile nature lovers can go for a relaxing walk in the botanic gardens or the 22-acre citrus variety collection.

Students who like outdoors activities will love the fact that the desert, beach or mountains are only ever a short distance away. For those who prefer a more urban city, UCR is only 50 miles from downtown Los Angeles, one of the world's great cities. And international students shouldn't worry about the inland location. Riverside is served by LA/Ontario International Airport – a major transport hub that makes UCR particularly convenient for international students.

With 21,000 students the University of California, Riverside is a mid-sized university. However, it offers students a wide academic choice, with 80 bachelor degree programs, 46 master's degree programs, 38 Ph.D. programs and 17 California teaching and administrative credential programmes.

Another advantage is the high quality staff. UCR faculty are national and international leaders in their fields and the 1,000-strong instructional team range from senior-level innovators to emerging young stars. This mix helps to create a dynamic and collaborative intellectual environment. Interaction between students and faculty is encouraged and there are often opportunities for joint research projects.

universität**bonn**

Rank › 101 – 150
_____

Name › University of Bonn
Region › Europe
Country › Germany
Founded › 1777

www3.uni-bonn.de
_____

Core Research Strengths

The Rheinische Friedrich-Wilhelms-Universität Bonn is rooted in a long tradition going back almost 200 years. Friedrich-Wilhelm III, the Prussian king whose name it bares, founded the university in 1818. Today, the University of Bonn is one of the largest universities in Germany, with around 31,000 students, 500 professors, 3,800 other academic staff and 1,800 technical and administrative staff. It offers a wide disciplinary spectrum comprising some ninety different degree programmes, from Agricultural Science to Tibetan Studies.

This diversity is what characterizes Bonn as a full-range university with a strong international orientation. Its academic and research profile features internationally renowned specializations in the fields of Mathematics, Physics, Astronomy, Economics, Chemistry, Pharmacology, Biosciences, Genetic Medicine, Neurosciences, Philosophy and Ethics. Other disciplines, such as Geography and Law, are of outstanding importance within the overall German research environment.

Bonn's legacy of famous professors is long and ranges from the astronomer Friedrich Wilhelm Argelander (1799-1875), through the chemist August Kekulé von Stradonitz (1829–1896) and political economist Josef Schumpeter (1883–1950) to the philologist Ernst Robert Curtius (1886–1956) and the theologists Karl Barth (1886–1968) and Joseph Ratzinger (Pope Benedict XVI). Bonn's best-known students include Heinrich Heine, Karl Marx, Friedrich Nietzsche, and Konrad Adenauer.

Major Discoveries

Bonn has numerous award-winning scientists and scholars, with two recent Nobel laureate and one Field's Medal winner among its faculty as well as more than a dozen Leibniz Prize winners. Bonn is the only German university that more than one Nobel laureate has emerged from within the last 25 years: Wolfgang Paul (Physics, 1989) and Reinhard Selten (Economics, 1994).

Partnerships, Innovation & Translational Research

The University of Bonn currently runs a number of collaborative research projects, including 14 Sonderforschungsbereiche [collaborative research centres], 15 Forschergruppen [research units], 4 Graduiertenkollegs [research training groups] funded by the German Research Foundation (DFG), and two Forschungsschwerpunkte [research focus programs funded by the Federal Ministry of Education and Research].

Under the government's Excellence Initiative the University of Bonn has been granted two Clusters of Excellence (Mathematics, Economics and Immunology) and two Graduate Schools (Economics and Physics & Astronomy in collaboration with the University of Cologne).

As a research-oriented university, Bonn builds alliances with partners at all levels. Thus, it has developed close relations with the major research institutions in the region such as the Forschungszentrum Jülich, the Deutsche Zentrum für Luft und Raumfahrt (DLR), the Center for Advanced Studies and Research (CAESAR), the recently founded Deutsche Zentrum zur Erforschung neurodegenerativer Erkrankungen (DZNE) and the local institutes of the Fraunhofer Society and Max Planck Society.

Cooperation agreements in both research and teaching also exist with approximately 60 partner universities across five continents and other partners worldwide.

Teaching, Learning & Student Life

The fact that the University sees itself as a research-led university also influences the level and orientation of teaching and studying. Students are given the opportunity of taking part actively in research projects. This thorough, research-based approach to studying represents a clear advantage for Bonn graduates on the labour market, which correlates with the high academic standing of those teaching at the University. Learning via research is the ideal way for academic and social élites to gain their qualifications.

In Bonn, the university and the city are tightly intertwined. The university and the university hospitals are two of the region's biggest employers. The alma mater owns or uses more than 350 university buildings throughout the Bonn area. The most impressive building, located in the heart of the city, is undoubtedly the historic Main Building, which was originally the palatial residence of the prince elector and is now home to the Humanities and Theologies as well as the administration. Together with the adjacent Hofgarten park, this architectural landmark is an important ingredient of Bonn University's unmistakable charm. Other important university sites include the nearby Juridicum (for Law and Economics) and the grand buildings in the Poppelsdorf district, housing Pre-clinical Medicine, Agriculture and Natural Sciences. The teaching hospitals are located above the city on Bonn's Venusberg.

Newcomers to Bonn soon grow very fond of the city – a fact confirmed by the many students and academics, from Germany and abroad, who learn, teach or research here. It wins people's hearts with its charm and sophistication, and not least because its people are welcoming and open-minded. The city, whose best known son was Ludwig van Beethoven, became famous all over the world when it was made the seat of the West German parliament and government after 1949. When Parliament and part of the government moved to Berlin, their place was taken by a large number of international organisations and important companies. Today, for example, Deutsche Telekom and Deutsche Post have their headquarters in Bonn, and several UN institutions are represented in the city.

UNIVERSITY OF BIRMINGHAM

Rank › 101 – 150

Name › University of Birmingham
Region › Europe
Country › United Kingdom
Founded › 1900

www.birmingham.ac.uk

Core Research Strengths

With a research budget of £125million the university is one of the UK's leading research-intensive universities. The research focus is spread wide. Indeed in the most recent Research Assessment Exercise Birmingham was ranked as having the most diverse range of research interests in the UK.

Nonetheless Pro-Vice Chancellor, Professor Adam Tickell, highlights medical sciences as one area where the university really excels.

"Birmingham is particularly strong in cancer treatment, housing the first Cancer Research UK Centre in the UK. The University of Birmingham also has key research strengths in immunology, stem cell research, microbiology and the treatment of infectious disease. In life and biological sciences our capacity in psychology is outstanding, with a particular focus on cognitive neuroscience. Our capacity in sports sciences is also excellent, with one of the leading departments in the UK, working alongside top sports teams such as cycling to develop the most cutting edge practices and processes designed to achieve world-class results. From an engineering perspective, we have several excellent areas, particularly in chemical engineering, formulation engineering and fluid dynamics and a team working on hydrogen powered cars. The University has recently announced a £60m investment from Rolls Royce and the UK Government in high temperature casting technologies.

The university's physics department has also been very successful, says the Pro-Vice Chancellor. "We are also very strong in cold atom physics, this works at ultra low temperatures analysing the varying behaviours between particles in these conditions as opposed to what one would typically find at sea level on Earth."

Away from the sciences, the University of Birmingham is also very strong in music and the history of art, as well as in social policy and security studies.

Like many other leading universities, Birmingham often adopts a multi-disciplinary approach to research. "Increasingly major research questions are very complicated, and the basic science root questions cannot be addressed without them being approached from a number of different disciplines and perspectives."

Major Discoveries

The university has been at the forefront of major discoveries since its establishment and has eight Noble Prize winners amongst its former staff and alumni; their work includes revealing the structure of DNA, pioneering transplant research, synthesizing Vitamin C and enabling the development of new treatments and medicines for cancer. Other research breakthroughs at the university include enabling the development of radar and the microwave oven and developing and implanting the first patient-controlled variable rate pacemaker. More recently, researchers at the university have discovered a new particle (the Chi-B) at CERN and created an 'invisibility cloak' that works by coating objects with a specific formula that works to refract light around it, thus giving the object an invisible quality.

Partnerships, Innovation & Translational Research

The University of Birmingham funds its research in a number of different ways. One option, explains the Pro-Vice Chancellor, is to pool resources with other universities. The university recently joined forces with the University of Nottingham to collaborate on a number of research programs.

"Another key reason for the multi-disciplinary and collaborative approaches to research now found throughout the UK is that universities have to provide value for money to the government and taxpayer that funds the majority of our research portfolio", says Prof. Tickell. "Consequently, the five stages of research and innovation are becoming more and more integrated, universities are increasingly able to transfer basic research conducted at their respective institutions into applicable use through links with business either via spin outs, technology transfer or longer term partnership arrangements."

The key, says the Pro-Vice Chancellor, is to work with private industry.

"I think the universities that believe they can conduct commercial research and development are a little bit deluded, institutions such as ours are simply not geared up for commercial R & D in the same way that listed private sector companies are; we do basic research which is of a completely different kind to commercial R & D. Whilst I am very keen for the University of Birmingham to continue to engage with the private sector, I think it is important for us to direct this engagement within the parameters of our core strengths in conducting basic research."

Teaching, Learning & Student Life

With 18,000 undergraduates and 8,000 postgrad students Birmingham is the largest university in the West Midlands and the 11th largest in the UK. It also ranks highly in popularity, receiving the seventh-most applications in the UK in 2011.

Being situated in the UK's second-city is a massive advantage for the university. Not only does it give a massive pool of local students – the population of Birmingham is approximately 2 million – but it also makes it easier to attract those who want to live in a big city. Birmingham's other advantage is it's huge campus, says Pro-Vice Chancellor Tickell. "The University estate occupies over 276 acres of land on two different sites and has facilities that include modern laboratories, shops, performance venues, libraries, museums, sporting facilities and art galleries."

The main campus is in Edgbaston, home to the famous cricket ground. The campus is close to the city centre but has all the amenities of a small town, as well as its own rail station. Fans of art will also like the university, says the Pro-Vice Chancellor. "The University is home to the Barber Institute of Fine Arts, housing works by Van Gogh, Picasso and Monet, the Lapworth Museum of Geology, and the Joseph Chamberlain Memorial Clock Tower, which is a prominent landmark visible from many parts of the city, and the tallest free-standing clock tower in the world. Birmingham's sporting activities have been consistently ranked within the top three in British Universities' competitions for the past 15 years."

UNIVERSITY OF AMSTERDAM

Rank › 101 – 150

Name › University of Amsterdam
Region › Europe
Country › Netherlands
Founded › 1632

www.uva.nl

Core Research Strengths

The University of Amsterdam is the largest university in the Netherlands with 32,000 students spread across seven major faculties. With 5.000 staff members, 4 open campuses within the city and collaboration with several hundred national and international institutions, it has grown into the intellectual hub of the Netherlands – inextricably linked with the city of Amsterdam, its cultural and educational centres and business community.

Five years ago the university's research efforts were completely reorganised. Disciplines were split and mixed among 15 interdisciplinary 'research priority areas'. Of these; humanities, social sciences and astrophysics are some of the best performing internationally. The massive change to the university's research structure is similar to approaches adopted in other leading universities. Indeed University of Amsterdam Rector, Dymph van den Boom, believes one reason for the transition is funding.

But while funding may seem quite a prosaic motive, this is only the beginning of a greater transition taking place in research, says van den Boom. "The focus on the different kinds of research questions which are no longer confined to one discipline forces researchers to cross the border of their own discipline and cooperate with colleagues from other disciplines to be able to answer those questions, and that forces people not only to co-operate with research from other disciplines but also to come up with what I would call transdisciplinary concepts, and new theories that are no longer based upon one discipline." Ultimately this will lead to a very different style of academia in the future, says van den Boom.

Major Discoveries

One of the leading scientists at the Clinical Psychology Department, professor Merel Kindt, succeeded in reducing fear by the administration of the beta-blocker propranolol.

The Center for research on Children, Adolescents and the Media conducts groundbreaking research bordering pedagogy, psychology and communication science.

Partnerships, Innovation & Translational Research

Like many other leading institutions the University of Amsterdam has to balance the benefits of commercial partnerships with the need for academic independence, says Rector van den Boom.

One of the steps the university has taken to increase private sector funding is the Amsterdam Economic Board. "It is a combination of representatives from government, industry and the higher education sector, and they try to define research questions that are of interest within the Amsterdam region and the companies we have here. Then we try to set up cooperative endeavours between those three parties. So, we create larger public-private partnerships within the region." A similar approach is adopted, with the help of the Ministry of Economics, to try and achieve the same goal with international companies.

The university is also trying to encourage more technology transfer. This can happen through the Amsterdam Economic board, says van den Boom. Or, another approach she is vigorously pursuing is to persuade local businesses to establish offices in the university's science park. "I think universities are interesting places to have your company so you can share the knowledge you create." So far, over one hundred companies, primarily in information technology and life sciences, have established their offices at the science park.

Teaching, Learning & Student Life

Amsterdam is one of Europe's most lively capital cities and consistently ranked in the top 10 of best places to live around the world. On one hand its libertarian attitude has attracted partygoers from around the world and helped to create a vibrant social scene. On the other it has beautiful canals, renaissance architecture and a host of museums. Another of the big attractions of Amsterdam is that it retains a 'small city feel' while being cosmopolitan and international. The Universities' campuses are dotted around the city, and for most students bicycles are the preferred mode of transport. Indeed it's possible to cycle from the north end of the city to the south in half an hour.

When it comes to life inside the classroom students will benefit from the research-led teaching programme, says Rector van den Boom. "Our educational programs are connected to our research priority areas and that gives students a great chance to experience working on important projects." Another 'hands-on' opportunity for students is the Amsterdam Centre of Entrepreneurship, which gives students commercial training and insight while still following their course.

Another feature of student life, which seems very popular, is the international element, says the Rector. "We have some programs for international students that are typically Dutch but could also be very attractive for international students. We have summer programs to present to international students the things we do, and to get the feel of what it is to study in Amsterdam. We also have connections to a number of universities in China. They provide large scholarships and have students coming over here to do Masters programs, then do a Ph.D. here, then do a post-doc here and then go back to their own university where they get a position and research money to set up their own research program within their university."

UNIVERSITY OF ALBERTA

Rank › 101 – 150

Name › University of Alberta
Region › Americas
Country › Canada
Founded › 1908

www.ualberta.ca

Core Research Strengths

With approximately US$500 million in external funding distributed throughout 400 research laboratories each year, the University of Alberta is one of Canada's leading research institutions specialising in a broad range of fields. Undoubtedly, though, there are some specific core strengths that distinguish the university internationally. It is home to one of the world's top five research laboratories focusing on machine intelligence, is an international leader in the broad areas of water research and virology, and is considered a leading institution in palaeontology. The University of Alberta's impact on the regional economy is extensive, with an estimated US$13 billion annually generated locally.

Through the Alberta Innovates Centre for Machine Learning researchers are developing intelligent technologies able to adapt to the dynamics of human behaviour throughout a wide variety of interest areas. The development of intelligent artificial prosthetics able to learn about patterns of human movement, and analytical technologies able to discern patterns and opportunities from large data sets, are two of the most exciting examples emerging from the centre. Computing science professor Jonathan Schaeffer solved the game of checkers and led development of a program able to beat the world's best poker players.

At the most basic molecular level, carbohydrate chemistry through the Alberta Glycomics Centre is a specific area of leading research in the biological sciences. Carbohydrates play a vital role in basic biological processes such as cell-to-cell responses, immune responses, infection and biological recognition. The Centre is at the forefront of this emerging field widely anticipated to have strong potential in the development of new drugs, vaccines and diagnostics.

Major Discoveries

Professor Raymond Lemieux pioneered a series of discoveries in organic chemistry, paving the way for Alberta's leadership in the field of carbohydrate chemistry through the Alberta Glycomics Centre. Lemieux's most remarkable discoveries were the synthesis of sucrose and the anomeric effect, both important findings in the contemporary field of carbohydrate chemistry.

Biochemistry professor James Collip was instrumental in the discovery of insulin. More recently, an islet cell transplantation technique pioneered at the University of Alberta has significantly improved the lives of people with Type 1 diabetes.

A hepatitis C vaccine in development at the university by Michael Houghton has been shown to be effective against all strains of the virus, a remarkable discovery that will have a positive impact on millions of lives.

Researchers at the University of Alberta first discovered the Western Canada Sedimentary Basin, underpinning the majority of the country's modern oil and gas industries. The basin contains one of the world's largest reserves of oil and natural gas, supplying much of the North American market.

Partnerships, Innovation & Translational Research

"Universities identify strategic partners and then develop meaningful long-term relationships based upon mutual benefit" is the philosophy that guides President Indira Samarasekera's approach to the growing focus on collaborative research, whether through partnerships with fellow universities, research institutes or industrial enterprises. The university has a growing partnership with the Helmholtz Institutes in Germany in health, and energy and the environment, as well as with major universities around the world such as Tsinghua University and the leading Indian Institutes of Technology in the areas of energy, water, sustainability and public health.

Located in the centre of a region widely regarded as one of the most entrepreneurial in the world, the University of Alberta is at the forefront of driving the province of Alberta's continued strength in both reputation and delivery in translating new discoveries to the real economy. President Samarasekera is keen to emphasize, however, that this is a team effort. "The Canadian government has been tremendously supportive of the national research and development scene in recent years, making a wide range of investments in projects and infrastructure; local industry has always been very active in supporting research activities, which has been hugely beneficial. On top of this support, we have been able to develop a real culture of innovation at the university, whereby there is now an expectation for new discoveries to be taken to market."

Enterprise Square is home to the university's technology transfer facility. Great success has been had in licensing technologies to existing industries and companies, although room for improvement remains in developing spinoff companies. The University of Alberta's focus is not limited to innovation at the university alone; the approach is unique in that it extends to a philosophy of technology and innovation enhancement for companies located throughout the region.

Teaching, Learning & Student Life

New facilities such as the Centennial Centre for Interdisciplinary Science and Edmonton Clinic Health Academy foster collaboration between researchers, creating a problem-based approach to learning wherein students are encouraged to work in teams across their respective disciplines to develop research-based solutions to course-related questions. University of Alberta professors have won more national awards for excellence in teaching than any other university in Canada, a resounding endorsement of the quality that students can expect to find at the institution.

Experiential learning extends into the community with a number of programs designed to enhance students' leadership skills. Furthermore, with nearly 450 student groups and associations, students can expect vibrant social and cultural experiences. The university's elite athletic programs are supported by excellent sporting facilities for the benefit of all students and staff.

Rank › 101 – 150

Name › Tufts University
Region › Americas
Country › United States
Founded › 1852

www.tufts.edu

Core Research Strengths

Tufts' 10 schools cover a diverse range of disciplines from arts and international affairs, to engineering and medicine; however the core strengths from a research perspective are in the life and medical sciences with half of the schools focused on interest areas within this classification, and the others having strong commitments in these areas.

The guiding principle for all research activities at Tufts is collaboration, with the university continuing to strive for interdisciplinary excellence across both its range of core strengths; as well as with counterpart institutions and external partners such as the Tufts Medical Center.

Given Tufts' formidable international distinction in these areas, the life and medical sciences offer the best arena to demonstrate Tufts' commitment to interdisciplinary research. Tufts works at the interface of established academic disciplines in order to address key international healthcare challenges through human collaboration and interaction. This work supports cutting-edge research at institutes specializing in cancer, molecular oncology and molecular cardiology amongst numerous other areas.

Needless to say, Tufts' research strength is not confined to the life and medical sciences. The university has a long held tradition in international relations with the Fletcher School of Law and Diplomacy, and is increasingly prominent in technical areas of engineering such as with robotics, bioengineering and telecommunications.

Major Discoveries

Louis Lasagna, former dean of Tufts' Sackler School of Graduate Biomedical Sciences, was known as the "father of clinical pharmacology" for his study that showed that taking a pill, even one that contained no medication, can have a "placebo effect." The journal Lancet has called that research one of the world's 27 most notable achievements in a medical canon dating back to Hippocrates.

Stuart B. Levy, M.D., Professor of Molecular Biology & Microbiology and Director of the Center for Adaptation Genetics and Drug Resistance at Tufts University School of Medicine, is a leader in the field of antibiotic use and resistance. He led the discovery of the spread of resistant bacteria among animals and people on a farm.

The Jean Mayer USDA Human Nutrition Research Center on Aging at Tufts University is the largest research center in the world devoted to studying the role of nutrition in the prevention of age-related chronic and infectious diseases.

Scientific advances are not limited to the above-mentioned schools and centers. Psychology faculty at the School of Arts and Sciences have recently co-authored a research paper proving scientifically that coffee improves mind-processing skills following a number of tests comparing proofreading skills depending upon the levels of coffee consumed beforehand.

Partnerships, Innovation & Translational Research

The Office for Technology Licensing and Industry Collaboration (OTL&IC) takes overall responsibility for developing Tufts' external collaborative agreements. The guiding missions held by the OTL&IC is for inventions and discoveries made at Tufts to be brought to market and society for their broader benefit, to promote research collaboration between the university and a diverse range of partners, as well as to raise funding for the university's research activities.

The university has a long-held tradition of external collaboration with industry, with the OTL&IC taking the lead in ensuring that the different cultural and operational environments one can find between private enterprises and research universities are brought together in a mutually beneficial synergy. The most common form of industry partnership at Tufts is for sponsored research. The university's policy is to take ownership of all resultant intellectual property, with flexible licensing agreements on offer for research partners and sponsors.

Teaching, Learning & Student Life

With 70 undergraduate degree programs encompassing thousands of courses within Arts and Science and Engineering to choose from, students at Tufts can expect to benefit from an interdisciplinary approach to teaching and learning, facilitating the development of a broad range of skills and knowledge based upon individual curiosities and aspirations. The teaching approach is problem based, with students very much encouraged to get directly involved in research and take their discoveries as far as possible in line with the entrepreneurial culture that buzzes around the institution.

A number of special initiatives such as the Summer Scholars, which enables undergraduates to do hands-on research with Tufts faculty, and the Institute for Global Leadership provide extra resources for young people interested in further developing their research and leadership abilities respectively. As part of the programs offered by the Institute for Global Leadership, students learn how to think critically about major global challenges and to develop leadership skills in helping overcome these challenges.

Tufts has a very strong international focus, with approximately 50% of undergraduate students spending at least one semester on a study abroad program in one of many highly sought after international destinations such as London, Madrid, Oxford, Hong Kong, Japan and Mainland China. Tufts' study abroad program is consistently ranked as one of the top 5 in North America by respected institutions such as The Princeton Review.

Impact on society is another key characteristic of the university. Tufts Tisch College of Citizenship and Public Service is unique in seeking to serve as a catalyst for active community engagement among faculty and students alike across the entire university.

東京工業大学
Tokyo Institute of Technology

Rank › 101 – 150

Name › Tokyo Institute of Technology
Region › Asia/Pacific
Country › Japan
Founded › 1881

www.titech.ac.jp

Core Research Strengths

With external research funding totalling approximately US$170 million, Tokyo Institute of Technology's research, whilst firmly rooted in the STEM subjects remains diverse; with investigations looking into an array of fundamental and applied research questions from the origins of life on planet Earth, through to the development of advanced energy-generating systems and super-conductors.

Recognised as the best science and technology university in Japan, Tokyo Tech remains focused upon its strength in the STEM disciplines, but increasingly is encouraging an interdisciplinary approach. Tokyo Tech is currently Japan's largest producer of patents, nevertheless President Yoshinao Mishima is very much committed to this strategic direction:

"Our ambition at Tokyo Tech is to be clearly recognised as a world-class science and technology university, we want to be in the top 10 research universities in the world by 2030. In order for us to achieve that, we have to be at the cutting edge with our research. Today's questions are too complex and require too many resources for single departments, or even single institutions to be at the forefront by themselves. Collaboration between departments and institutions is thus an essential strategic direction; Tokyo Tech is fully committed to partnering with other universities, government institutes and private enterprise."

Tokyo Tech's excellence in the computer sciences is centred upon one of the world's fastest supercomputers in TSUBAME 2.0; housed in the Global Scientific Information and Computing Center. TSUBAME 2.0 enables Tokyo Tech researchers to harness incredible processing power for advanced research investigations throughout the Institute's range of interests.

Professor Kei Hirose, Director of Tokyo Tech's Earth-Life Science Institute (ELSI) is leading investigations into the most fundamental questions that face humankind – What are the origins of Earth? What are the origins of Life? Under Professor Hirose's leadership, a strong interdisciplinary program will

be built-up in order to investigate the early Earth environments and the origin of living systems through cutting-edge lab experiments, computer simulations, and field observations.

Major Discoveries

Professor Hirose, Director of the ELSI has been the first researcher ever to re-create the conditions at the centre of the Earth under laboratory conditions; discovering Post-Perovskite in the process – a principal mineral in the Earth's lowermost mantle believed to have a key influence on the formation of life on Earth.

World leading materials scientist Professor Hideo Hosono has led the discoveries of a number of superconductors and related materials at Tokyo Tech. His team is responsible for the high performance oxide transistor IGZO-TFT whose most common application is in the iPad.

Partnerships, Innovation & Translational Research

As Japan's leading science and technology university, industry partnerships are almost second nature for Tokyo Tech. Private sector collaboration is closely linked to Tokyo Tech's missionin contributing to the betterment of society through the application of research discoveries to industry.

Tokyo Tech works alongside some of the world's best-known technology companies such as Samsung, Microsoft and Sharp. Since the Institute began promoting research collaboration with industry in 2004, its network of contacts and volume of research agreements has doubled. President Mishima's motivations for this progression are clear: "Tokyo Tech is taking responsibility for creating and making things, through our collaborations with private enterprise we are even better able to bring new technologies and innovations to the market for the broader benefit of society and the economy." In Japan this philosophy is known as Monotsukuri.

Tokyo Tech's Office of Industry Liaison acts as the interface between the university and its ever-expanding portfolio of industry partners. Potential

research collaborators should initiate inquiries with the university through this office.

Teaching, Learning & Student Life

Under the leadership of President Mishima, Tokyo Tech is pioneering reform in Japanese higher education, moving the approach from one that would be perceived as passive; more towards an active learning style based upon discussion and debate – very much focused on harnessing the creativity, productivity and activity of students with the research strengths of the Institute. Students get involved with research at the beginning of their studies as a basic standard, with a growing number of undergraduates and graduates taking short - and long-term internships with industry, helping to motivate them toward future commercialisation of their work.

With 12.4% of the student population originating from outside of Japan, Tokyo Tech's student body is one of the most diverse in Japan. Presently, the vast majority of students are from Asia, however with a growing number of English-taught graduate and under-graduate courses the focus is shifting towards Europe and North America. Tokyo Tech now has collaborative agreements with some of the most outstanding universities in the world, counting Imperial College London, ETH Zurich, UC Berkeley and Caltech amongst its partners for student exchange and the promotion of global human resource development.

Tokyo Tech students have access to an array of extra-curricular activities and student associations, ranging from sports clubs and orchestral ensembles through to collaborative clubs focused on overcoming manufacturing and engineering challenges such as the club, Meister which has regularly won top awards at the Japan International Birdman Rally.

TOHOKU
UNIVERSITY

Rank › 101 – 150

Name › Tohoku University
Region › Asia/Pacific
Country › Japan
Founded › 1907

www.tohoku.ac.jp

Core Research Strengths

As one of Japan's national universities, with a total budget of approximately US$1,600 million annually and in excess of 18,000 students and 6,000 staff, Tohoku University's research strengths are extensive throughout the various fields of research. Tohoku University has a rich tradition of over 100 years guided by three clear principles – Research First, Open Door and Practice Orientated Research and Education.

Since its foundation, Tohoku University has nurtured a lot of innovative research. For instance, materials scientist Kotaro Honda invented the KS and NKS types of magnetic resistant steel paving the ways for an industrial revolution in how steel was used. Hidetsugu Yagi invented the Yagi Antenna, used all over the world to receive television signals. Carrying on these traditions, the university has been conducting world-class research in various fields, including materials sciences, information and communications technology, and life sciences, as one of the leading universities in Japan.

Following the Great East Japan Earthquake, Tohoku University has undergone something of a revolution in its approach to research. With many facilities damaged by the March 2011 disaster; President Susumu Satomi has led the university towards more of an integrated approach addressing critical global challenges such as low-frequency mega disasters: "In the wake of the disaster we established a new organization, the Tohoku University Institute for Disaster Reconstruction and Regeneration Research. This organization has been focusing upon collaboration, managing reconstruction actions that have been conducted individually by our faculty members and using our expertise to its fullest extent in a strategic and organized way to overcome major challenges such as disasters." After that, Tohoku University has launched its mission of restoring Tohoku and Japan from various aspects through Eight Projects.

Partnerships, Innovation & Translational Research

Overcoming social issues that occur worldwide is not something that can be achieved by one research facility or one discipline alone. In addition, the background of technological development and diversification of industrial societies, the tasks of achieving innovation are getting more complicated and elaborate. Therefore, Tohoku University collaborates with numerous research institutes and private companies in Japan and overseas, focusing on open innovation schemes based on the collaboration of multiple entities. Such thinking led to the conclusion of university-level agreements with 176 institutions, 348 agreements on faculty-level worldwide and the participation in influential university consortia such as Association of Pacific Rim Universities (APRU), Association of East Asian Research Universities (AEARU) and Top Industrial Managers for Europe (T.I.M.E).

Further, unique in its status as Japan's only leading national university to be selected as both, Global 30 Project for the promotion of incoming students to Japan, and Project for Promotion of Global Human Resource Development for the promotion of Japanese students travelling abroad; the opportunities presented by internationalization are excellent. President Satomi believes that "It is very important for our students to acquire an international view because it enables them to get a better understanding of others and themselves. This is a huge opportunity that we fully embrace. Traditionally Japanese society has not been this way inclined, but this is now changing very quickly. We want to play a leading a role."

Teaching, Learning & Student Life

Following a visit in 1922, Albert Einstein commented that Tohoku University, located in Sendai City "Was the best place in Japan to learn and conduct research". Despite 2011's tragedy, many believe this status has not changed. Known as the "City of Trees", Sendai City is a lush city, surrounded by many cultural sites and areas for recreation. The city's surrounding Onsen (hot springs) are famous throughout Japan and excellent places to relax after a hard day's research and study.

Despite the March 2011 earthquake, Tohoku University has welcomed new students and started classes from May 2011 with just one month delay. President Satomi takes pride in this quick recovery. "A lot of students from abroad have temporarily evacuated immediately after the earthquake, but most of them have returned by May 2011 with high motivation for the new mission of the restoration from the disaster. A rise in the levels of radiation in Sendai City and its surroundings could not be detected, showing that the area was unaffected after the nuclear power plant disaster. Damaged facilities were renewed and our focus has dramatically changed. We are now looking at next generation research topics that bring together all fields of science. Tohoku is probably the best place in Japan for this kind of research; this creates an enormous opportunity for people from all over the world."

Back in the classroom, Tohoku University's century old traditions of Research First, Open Door and Practice Orientated Research & Education dominate with students encouraged to work together, ask questions and most importantly get involved with research at every opportunity. President Satomi considers research first as Tohoku University's critical value: "The essence of Tohoku is that research orientated education is the most effective means of fostering human resources. This is the basis of our university, research in education is extremely important."

Tohoku University
Japan

Research Profile

Since the devastating Great East Japan Earthquake on March 11th 2011, Tohoku University has focused its research on the new mission of leading the restoration of the Tohoku region and Japan. The university has launched eight pioneering projects designed to make major contributions to solve critical global issues including low-frequency mega disasters, with a view to designing means of overcoming major challenges such as community health care, environmental energy, information communication, marine sustainability and in particular; disaster management, recovery and restoration. Tohoku University's renewal in times of great difficulty towards global leadership is truly an inspirational story.

Disaster Science

Taking the lead on these efforts is the newly established International Research Institute of Disaster Science (IRIDeS). Established in April 2012, IRIDeS aims to become a global cornerstone of disaster mitigation, management and sciences. Using lessons learned and data gathered from the disaster that struck in March 2011, the IRIDeS is bringing together expertise from research fields as diverse as medicine, engineering and history to develop best practices throughout the five stages of the disaster management cycle. IRIDeS is pioneering a whole new academic approach to disaster mitigation bringing together research and data from around the world with the aim of developing social systems and physical infrastructure that will respond effectively to disasters. IRIDeS' six research divisions work in collaboration with a myriad of international institutions with relevant expertise such as Harvard University, and those based in particularly disaster prone locations such as the Istanbul Technical University.

Community Healthcare and New Biobank

The Project for the Reconstruction of Community Health Care epitomises Tohoku University's approach to achieve innovation through recovery and reconstruction activities. Following the destruction of numerous medical facilities in 2011, medical records were destroyed and medical staff were left without places to work. Tohoku University's approach to contributing to the recovery from this issue has been to develop a comprehensive training program for community medicine with the Tohoku University Hospital at its core, whilst at the same time developing a comprehensive bio-bank of medical information under the auspices of the Tohoku Medical Megabank project. The information captured through the Biobank Project will be shared with counterpart institutions to form a global centre of excellence for genomic medical care, genomic preventative medicine, drug development and translational research at the very forefront of the medical sciences today.

Renewable Energy and Smart City

The meltdown of reactors at the Fukushima nuclear facility caused by the disaster has forced us to reconsider the electric power supply system. Tohoku University has taken the lead on the development of more sustainable approaches through the Project for Environmental Energy. In consortia with other leading Japanese universities and businesses, the Project for Environmental Energy is piloting the development and integration of next generation energy technologies into the grid. Solar power, algae based bio-fuels and smart grid technologies are some of the most interesting technologies under investigation at the pilot site of Ishinomaki City that is located in the disaster affected coastal area of Miyagi prefecture.

Disaster-Resistant ICT

Concerns pertaining to the reliability and resilience of ICT infrastructure are an ever-present feature of the contemporary disaster discourse. The ICT Reconstruction Project aims to make such concerns a thing of the past with a comprehensive review of existing capacity, and how it has reacted to major disasters and disruptions in the past with a view to developing disaster-resistant information communications infrastructure. Established in October 2011, the Research Organization of Electrical Communication (ROEC) is at the helm of these efforts.

Marine Science

The sustainability of Marine ecosystems is an ever present concern to coastal regions the world over as we look forwards into the 21st Century. The Tsunami that struck in March 2011 and the devastation that followed was a stark reminder of these concerns. The Tohoku Ecosystem Associated Marine Sciences (TEAMS) has been launched to work collaboratively with countless universities and government agencies in order to make a full impact assessment with a view to figuring out how we can ensure the sustainability of our marine eco-systems moving forwards.

Environmental Protection

Established in April 2012, the Research Center for Remediation Engineering of Living Environments Contaminated with Radioisotopes is taking a lead globally on overcoming one of our greatest fears – that of radioactive contamination. By developing technologies that enhance our capacity to detect and remove dangerous radioactive substances; as well as the development of cultivation methods to free agricultural products of contamination the Radioactive Decontamination Project is of critical importance to man's ability to overcome the dangers of radioactive substances and environments.

Local Economy Challenges

Of huge interest to communities the world over is the Regional Industries Restoration Project. Recognising that the long-held decline in industrial communities in the Tohoku region is one that must be reversed, the project is taking more of a holistic view – recognising the importance of offering incentives to create new job opportunities. But also, equally if not more importantly re-invigorating the entrepreneurial culture and attracting investment with innovative programs. The Regional Innovative Producer School provides training programs for businesses, executives and young entrepreneurs alike to help stimulate the local economy and contribute towards industrial restoration.

Industry-University Collaboration

Local industry has been facing various difficulties since the disaster. Through the Industry-University Collaboration Development Project for Reconstruction Tohoku University tries to achieve practical application of science and technology innovations developed in the Tohoku region with the final goal to commercialize innovative technological IP in companies located in the disaster affected areas to promote the revitalization of these.

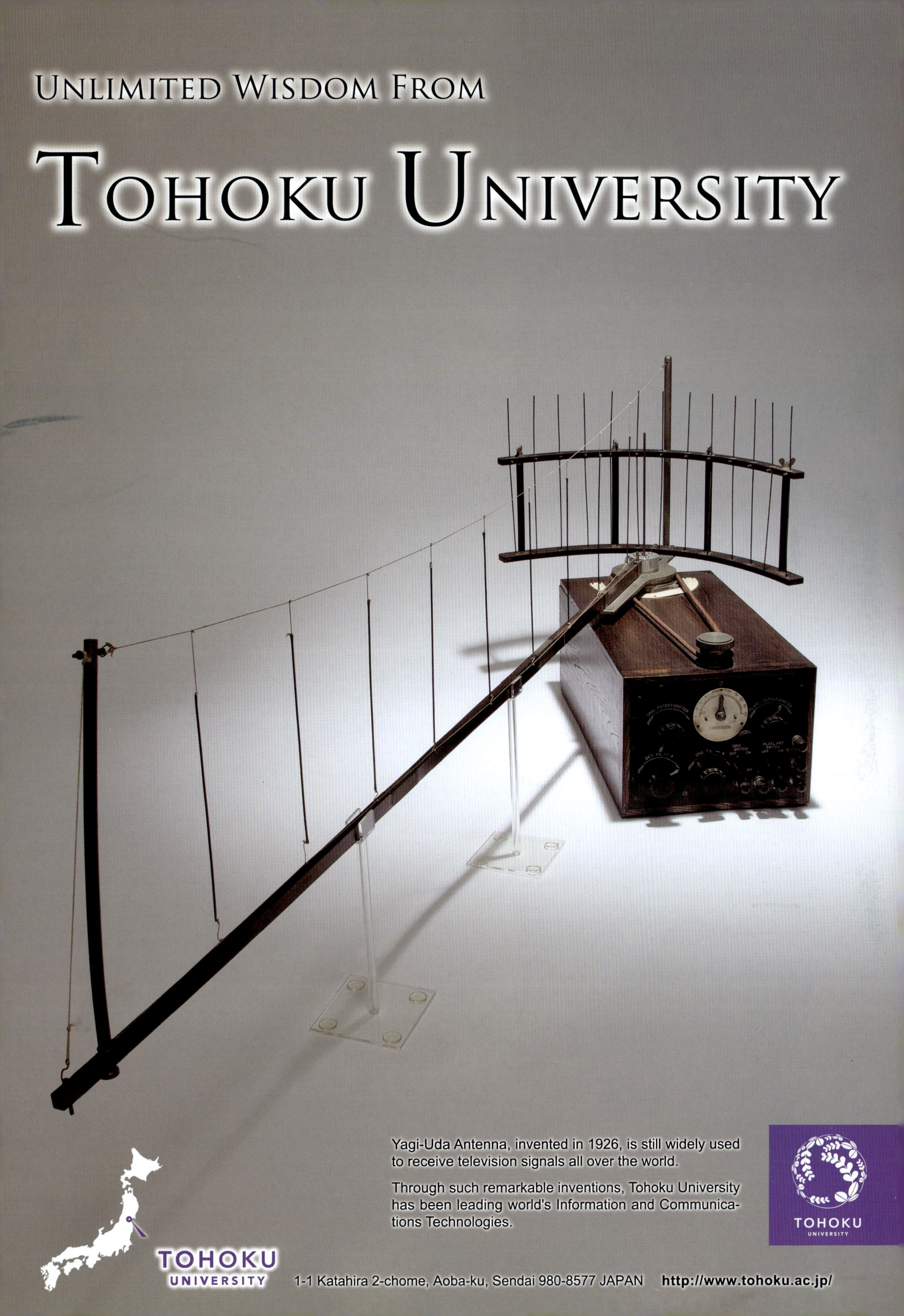

UNLIMITED WISDOM FROM
TOHOKU UNIVERSITY

Yagi-Uda Antenna, invented in 1926, is still widely used to receive television signals all over the world.

Through such remarkable inventions, Tohoku University has been leading world's Information and Communications Technologies.

1-1 Katahira 2-chome, Aoba-ku, Sendai 980-8577 JAPAN   http://www.tohoku.ac.jp/

TOHOKU
UNIVERSITY

The University Of Sheffield.

Rank › 101 – 150

Name › The University of Sheffield
Region › Europe
Country › United Kingdom
Founded › 1897

www.sheffield.ac.uk

Core Research Strengths

As one of the original 'red brick universities' the University of Sheffield has come to excel in research with five Nobel Prize winners among its alumni since it received a royal charter in 1905. Given the city's industrial heritage (in Britain, Sheffield is synonymous with the steel industry – the local football team is even nicknamed 'the blades'), it is little surprise that the university is strongly associated with engineering.

"We would certainly consider manufacturing one of the university's core strengths", says Pro-Vice Chancellor - Research & Innovation, Professor Richard Jones. "More than 67% of our Faculty of Engineering's research is independently rated as 'world-leading' or 'internationally excellent' and our vision is to compete to be the best engineering faculty in the UK."

But while Pro-Vice Chancellor Jones is proud of the university's engineering expertise, he is keen to stress that it excels in a diverse range of disciplines.

"We are home to cutting-edge research institutes such as the Sheffield Institute for Translational Neuroscience (SITraN) which is leading the fight against motor neuron disease and SPERI, the Sheffield Political Economic Research Institute, tackling big political and economic challenges. Our School of Health and Related Research (ScHARR) has had a huge impact on UK public policy through its alcohol pricing research and we also have one of the UK's leading philosophy departments. Our Department of Animal and Plant Sciences is also strong in real-world ecology research, such as how basic organisms and eco-systems respond to climate change; we are also looking at the influence of Arctic eco-systems in relation to these questions."

Partnerships, Innovation & Translational Research

Ensuring that academic research leads to 'real world' benefits is one of the great challenges for all universities. Fortunately for Sheffield, core strengths like engineering, are in great demand meaning there is no shortage of potential private-sector partners, explains the Pro-Vice Chancellor.

"The Advanced Manufacturing Research Centre (AMRC) is a unique example of transformational engineering research between our university, and leading UK manufacturers such as Rolls-Royce, international companies like Boeing as well as smaller companies in the supply chain. It has become a model for research centres worldwide."

Developing long-term strategic partnerships with industry to enrich research is key for Sheffield. For example; the university is one of Siemens' four UK 'Principal Partners' and home to the UK's first Siemens Wind Power Research Centre. "Our approach to commercial partnerships focuses upon expanding mutual research capacities. We see huge benefit from this not just in a boost to respective research budgets, but in learning more about the challenges that businesses face throughout the R&D process, as well as learning to manage commercial relationships over the long-term," says Pro-Vice Chancellor Jones.

The university is committed to maximising the impact of our ideas through the development of protectable IP; working with Fusion IP, its commercialisation partner. "Fusion IP's role is to develop the commercial viability of the innovations developed", says Pro-Vice Chancellor Jones. "This helps us understand exactly what innovations will be most interesting commercially, as well as reaching out to partners that would be interested in such ventures."

Teaching, Learning & Student Life

One of the first things that any student new to Sheffield will notice is that the City is undergoing something of a revival. After struggling to deal with the collapse of the traditional heavy industries in the 70s and 80s, Sheffield is now emerging as a regenerated city. Fortunately the city planners have plenty of natural resources to work with. Situated in the valleys of the River Don and its tributaries, it is an incredibly 'green city'. It's estimated that around two-thirds of Sheffield's entire area is green space, while a third of the city lies within the beautiful Peak District National Park. With more than 200 parks, woodlands and gardens in the city and an estimated 2.5 million

trees, Sheffield has the highest ratio of trees to people of any city in Europe.

This natural beauty is an important factor for students as Sheffield is not a campus university but instead has departments dotted around the city. The student amenities have also improved of late with a multi-million pound refurbishment of the Student's Union.

As for a student's learning experience, the university passed a recent audit by the Quality Assurance Agency for Higher Education with flying colours. In particular inspectors noted that: "The University has a structured and strategic approach to the enhancement of learning opportunities that operates across the institution. The University is effective in taking deliberate steps both to enhance the learning experience of its students, and also to identify and reward staff who demonstrate excellence in teaching, or take on national or international responsibilities in teaching policy and innovation."

The University of Georgia

Rank › 101 – 150

Name › The University of Georgia
Region › Americas
Country › United States
Founded › 1785

www.uga.edu

Core Research Strengths

With a research budget of almost $430 million in 2012, the University of Georgia made a serious impact in a number of key areas.

One of the most important themes is healthy communities, says UGA President Michael F. Adams. "We have a very strong College of Public Health; we have a strong cadre of people doing research on infectious diseases around the world. We have endowed positions in that area that have attracted some of the leading people from around the world. We are doing much research in the areas of cancer, obesity, food safety and regenerative medicine. On how we create healthy communities, not just in the States but around the world."

"Another area where we have great strengths is in the sustainability area. I'll probably start with Ecology. We have one of the top four or five colleges of agriculture in the country. We have a long-term established interest in a school of forest resources. Some of the largest pulp and paper companies in the nation have their origins here in the state, like Georgia Pacific. We do a great deal of research down at the coast on some of the barrier islands, river health and water conservation."

Of course tackling these types of themes means that the university has to encourage researchers to work with colleagues from other disciplines, says the President. "We have a number of teams that are working across departmental barriers. It's hard to do biomedical or biotechnology research, for instance, without a College of Engineering, which we established just this year. The growth in nanotechnology through the years, and the research and development in areas that have almost nothing to do with core engineering issues, are the kinds of research we are now conducting."

Major Discoveries

Researchers at the University of Georgia are constantly making new discoveries and providing insight into how the world around us works. For example at the start of 2013 a team from the Regenerative Bioscience Center made important steps in developing a putty that could help fractured bones heal much more quickly.

Partnerships, Innovation & Translational Research

Technology transfer at the university is handled by the University of Georgia Research Foundation. It has a board comprised of academics and business people, which meets quarterly. The foundation has been very successful and, as a result, UGA scores in the top 20 in the United States both on patent and royalty income, as well as the number of patents and licenses. More than 100 companies have been spun off by scientists who began their work in a lab at UGA.

In recent years the university has made a concerted effort to improve its international standing. There are several elements to the new strategy, explains the President. "Internationalisation means, first of all, being open to recruiting leading researchers from around the world. It also means sending University of Georgia students abroad for study and for research. In addition to that we own campuses in Oxford, England; in Costa Rica; in Italy, and then we have bilateral arrangements in more than 40 places around the world where our students matriculate and do research. I think a well-educated international faculty today is essential in creating the kind of climate that's going to be necessary for success in the 21st century."

Teaching, Learning & Student Life

The University has three main campuses. The main campus is based in Athens, Georgia and has almost 400 buildings spread over 759 acres. There are also two smaller campuses in nearby Tifton and Griffin and, in addition to that, there are two more satellite campuses located further afield in Atlanta and Lawrenceville.

Nestled amongst the rolling hills of northeast Georgia, Athens is a vibrant college town of more than 110,000 residents. Over the years, Athens has become a cultural hotspot, a mecca for music and the arts. It has become commonplace to see Athens highly ranked in any variety of polls, ranging from 'Best College Towns' to 'Best Places for Retirement'. The centrepiece of Athens is its downtown area, which is full of life from morning to night. More than 65 specialty shops, 55 restaurants and cafes, and 40 taverns and nightspots fill downtown and maintain a constant buzz of action.

The local area certainly enhances the UGA's appeal, says President Adams. "Athens is easily the most progressive community in the state of Georgia. It's welcoming to people from all backgrounds and ethnicities. We have everything here from international music festivals, to weekly international coffee hours."

As the most comprehensive university in the state, the UGA offers students a wide range of 140 degree programmes across many disciplines, which are organized into eighteen schools and colleges. "I have focused on the sciences because that is where a lot of the funding comes from," says the President. "But we also have a fantastic law school, a great business school and leading history and English departments. That creates a unique atmosphere on campus because we have a very diverse mix of students."

Rank › 101 – 150

Name › Tel Aviv University
Region › Asia/Pacific
Country › Israel
Founded › 1953

new.tau.ac.il

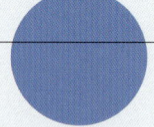

Core Research Strengths

Ranked 16th in the world in terms of scientific citations, and among the top 100 universities internationally, Tel Aviv University is also Israel's largest university with around 30,000 students. Half of these are master's and Ph.D. students, making Tel Aviv University the largest research university in Israel.

One of the distinctive features of Tel Aviv University is its comprehensiveness, says President Joseph Klafter. "We have more areas of research and teaching than any other university in Israel. We cover almost any area of knowledge which you can think of."

As a result of this broad base of research strengths the university is keen to promote interdisciplinary research collaborations. One of the best examples of this approach, says the President, is the university's leading neuroscience research programme. "It contains seven out of our nine faculties because of the breadth and complexity of brain research. We emphasize not only the computational side, but we go into the direction of more collaboration between biochemistry, psychology and the clinical aspects."

Another powerful example is renewable energy, says President Klafter. "This includes engineering, biology, chemistry, green architecture and many more disciplines."

The fact is, while these examples stand out, the possibility for cross-disciplinary collaboration is infinite. At Tel Aviv Biblical archaeologists are working with nanomaterial scientists; neurologists with management researchers; and East Asian philosophy experts with scholars of Jewish studies. Altogether, researchers advance some 3,500 projects annually across TAU's nine faculties and 125 institutes. Research teams publish rigorous, widely-cited studies that redefine and expand classic areas such as law, economics, and management, as well as drive forward interdisciplinary fields such as bioinformatics, nanotechnology, neuroscience, environmental studies, Jewish and Israel studies, and cyber-security.

Major Discoveries

Tel Aviv University has a proud history of ground-breaking discoveries. Currently, 23 drugs and medical therapies based on university technologies are in the development pipeline. Other recent achievements include the world's first "atlas" for white matter in the brain; biosensors for sniffing out cancer, pollution, and explosives; tiny nano-antennas for boosting solar energy capture; and improved flash memory.

Partnerships, Innovation & Translational Research

Unlike some universities, which are only now starting to build links with the private sector, Tel Aviv University has long looked to commercialise its research. One of its key assets in this regard is RAMOT, a university company that is responsible for the technology transfer process. "We really encourage researchers to apply for patents", says President Klafter. Indeed the results speak for themselves. Tel Aviv has registered around 2400 patents and produced 65 spin-off companies. This isn't just about making money, it has a very beneficial impact. For example, at present more than 20 drugs and medical therapies are being developed on the back of Tel Aviv research.

Another positive impact is TAU's network of bio-medical research centers and hospitals. In total it has 1,400 scientist-clinicians working at 17 affiliated hospitals serving over two million people.

And of course there are plenty of partnerships with large organisations, says the President. "Our scientists are teaming up with pharmaceutical companies like Johnson & Johnson to develop new drugs and medical technologies."

Teaching, Learning & Student Life

Situated in Israel's cultural, financial and technological capital, the university echoes many of the dynamic, pluralistic elements of Tel Aviv itself. It's an interesting place and the perfect location for a university, says the President. "Tel Aviv-Jaffa is a mix of antiquity and innovation, and the center of Israel's high-tech industry and youth culture. Israel's only stock exchange as well as nearly 40% of the country's finance and banking industry is located in Tel Aviv. There are also some beautiful beaches and some of the best art galleries, restaurants and nightclubs in the Middle East."

Indeed Tel Aviv is located on the Mediterranean coast and enjoys, on average, 318 sunny days a year. The city's public beaches are meticulously maintained and are open to visitors year-round, encouraging everything from laid back sunbathing on the sand to sporting activities such as wind surfing. Tel Aviv also has the highest percentage of young people of any city in Israel, which adds to the dynamic feel. Indeed the city's infrastructure (with green, eco-friendly bikes available for rent across the city), culture and atmosphere reflect this.

The university has plenty to offer students, says President Klafter. One of the chief benefits is its emphasis on interdisciplinary teaching. All students are exposed to this, and there is also a special interdisciplinary program for outstanding students. "Very few students are accepted, and they can choose any combination of disciplines. They combine undergraduate with graduate studies and earn a master's degree after four years. They are also exposed to research already from their second year." Another, more widely accessible academic perk, are courses on innovation and entrepreneurship

Tel Aviv University
Israel

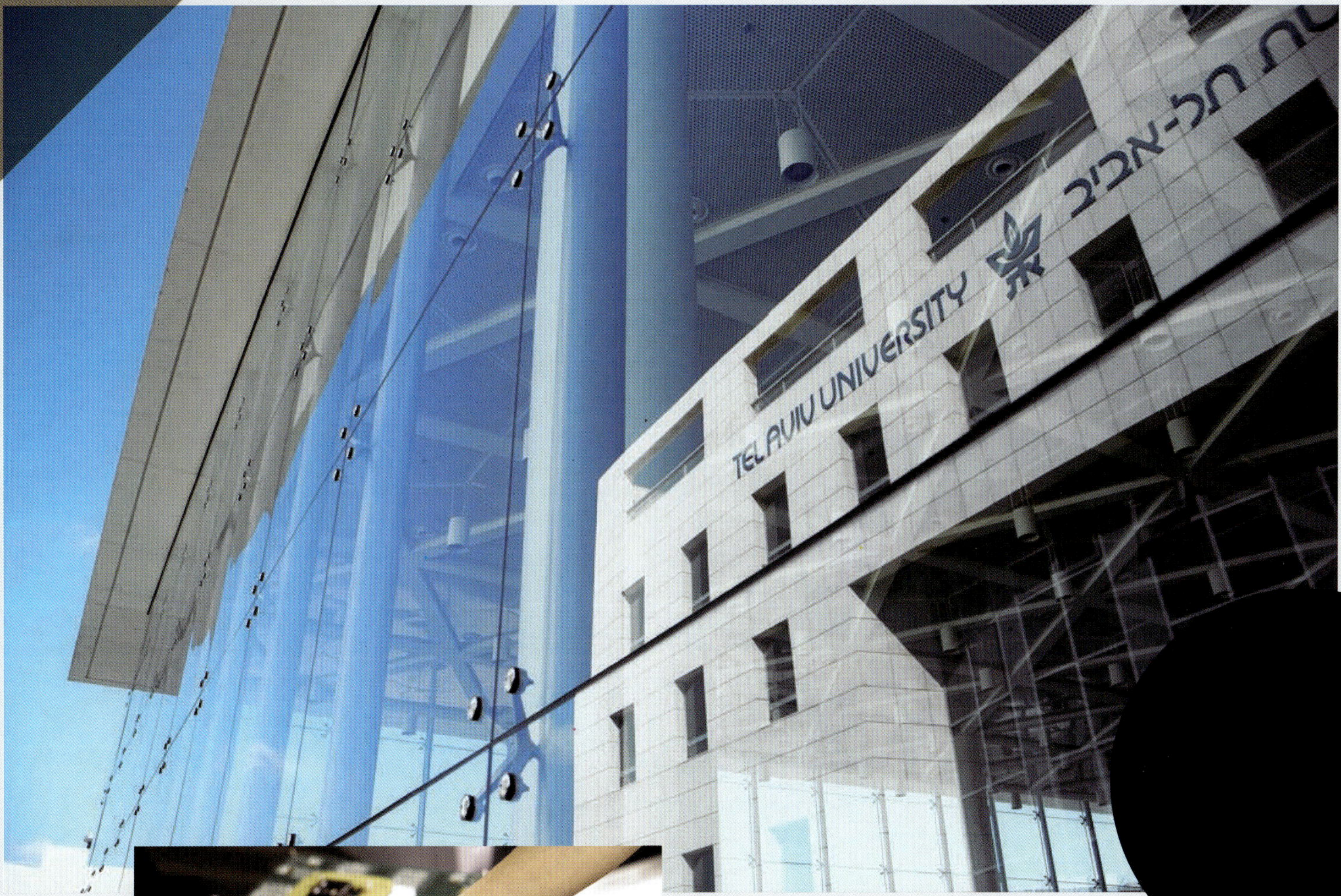

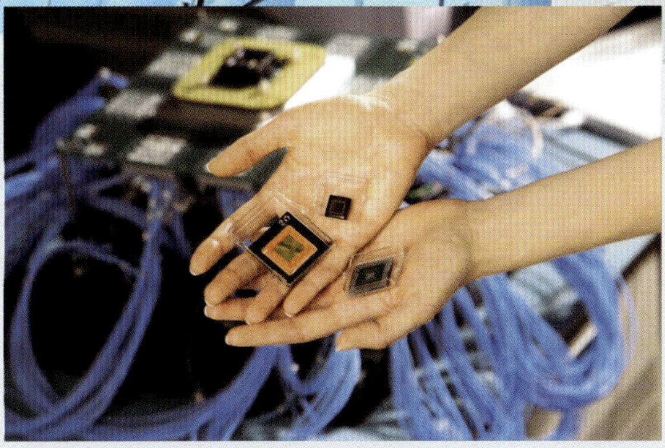

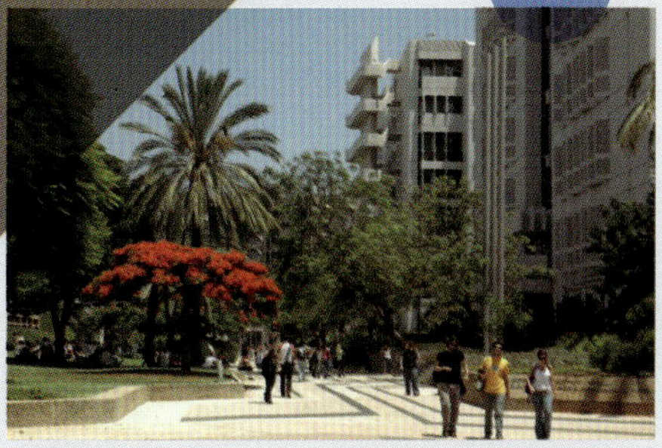

ÉCOLE POLYTECHNIQUE
FÉDÉRALE DE LAUSANNE

Rank › 101 – 150

Name › EPFL
Region › Europe
Country › Switzerland
Founded › 1853

www.epfl.ch

Core Research Strengths

The École Polytechnique Fédérale de Lausanne (EPFL) is one of the two Swiss Federal Institutes of Technology. Originally it was set up to educate engineers and scientists, be a national centre of excellence for technology, and act as a hub between academics and companies. Since Professor Patrick Aebischer became President in 2000, the university has also begun to expand into life sciences.

The institute's main research focus remains technology, says the President. "As such we are trying to look at cutting-edge engineering development and how it links with other fields, such as life science, management, finance, basic sciences and so on."

This convergence opens up exciting opportunities for a young institute like EPFL that doesn't have as much history as some of its competitors, says President Aebischer. "We are promoting a lot of the trans-disciplinary work, a lot in what we call the info-bio-nano-cogno-convergence. We are trying to sync information technology, nanotechnology, life science and cognitive science, that is maybe one of the special things of the school, and at the same time also developing high interactions with companies and promoting start-ups and innovation."

The President thinks that being a young institution even gives EPFL some advantages. "Because we are a young school, we do not have too many disciplines that have developed to the point that those fields cannot talk to each other." Moreover, in areas where EPFL lacks expertise it is free to partner the best in the world, unlike other institutes that have to work with their own departments, says the President. To prove his point he cites the example of the university's new Centre of Neural Prosthesis, which is developing bionic eyes. "We do not have a medical school, so we did this with Harvard Medical School, so we have now a very unique programme where research programmes are done together."

Major Discoveries

The university is associated with various Nobel Prizes but the discovery that most impacted the world was the development of the computer mouse by a former student called Daniel Borel, the founder of Logitech.

Partnerships, Innovation & Translational Research

Interacting with private-sector companies is written into the university's mandate, and EPFL is very successful at doing so. One way it achieves this is through the 'Innovation Quarter', which houses start-ups. Another way is by hosting private-sector research facilities on campus. For example Logitech occupies a full building to do research. Nestle is also a good example, says the President. "We've convinced them to create a new field on functional food, personalised prevention based on genomics, proteomics data, metabolomics, and so on. We are now able to personalise the profile of the patient, and to adapt the nutrition. They are now taking those two buildings to create a new Nestlé Institute of Health Science on our campus to develop this new field of functional food."

In total there are 2,000 private sector employees working on the campus innovation park and around 33% of revenues come from private sources.

Of course the other way to interact with the private sector is to spin out companies into the competitive environment. The university throws up around 20 per year and recent hits include Siri, the company behind the voice recognition system on the new iPhone.

EPFL's high-tech leadership has also drawn attention from European research funds. For example its Blue Brain project, which involves using a supercomputer to simulate the human brain, has been awarded €1billion of EU funding over a ten-year period.

Teaching, Learning & Student Life

Situated on a sole campus on the shores of Lake Geneva, EPFL offers one of the most beautiful learning environments in the world. Moreover, Switzerland has particular appeal for foreign students as its location makes it a great launch pad for further travel around Europe.

Another plus for students is that the university is busy upgrading its amenities. "We are putting a lot of effort in this", says the President. "We have built a 1000-student housing complex on campus, a conference centre and a shopping centre. When you start to go up in the rankings, students come from all over the world, you have to provide for them."

Indeed the university has become a magnet for foreign students and academics. As a result it is now Europe's most cosmopolitan technical university and receives students, professors and staff from more than 120 nationalities. "70% of our faculty is foreign, four of our five deans were recruited abroad, and we have lots of different nationalities on campus, so this is a little global world", says President Aebischer.

Another of the quirks of student life at EPFL is that, despite being a technology focused institution, all students must study 10% of their course in social sciences or humanities. That might seem counterintuitive, concedes President Aebischer, but there is a good reason behind it. "I'm a strong believer that you need social skills. They are going to be engineers and scientists, but what we want from them is to see beyond that, so we want to give them management and social skills." EPFL doesn't actually have the faculties to offer these courses but, as ever; it is willing to partner with other universities to deliver.

SEOUL
NATIONAL
UNIVERSITY

Rank › 101 – 150

Name › Seoul National University
Region › Asia/Pacific
Country › South Korea
Founded › 1946

www.snu.ac.kr

Core Research Strengths

It's estimated that every year Seoul National University receives US$60 million from the private sector to fund research. That figure received a boost recently with Samsung's decision to create a research center at the university. According to SNU President OH Yeon Cheon "This will be one breakthrough for encouraging our research efforts."

Another boost came when SNU was selected to run the three of the ten new research centers funded by the Korean Institute for Basic Sciences.

President Oh says the "remarkable" development will reshape research at the university.

"The first field is the Center for Functional Interfaces Correlated with Electronic Systems, the second one is the Center for Nano Particle Research, and the third one is the Center for RNA Research in the biosciences area. These three research centres will receive research funds of US$30 million per year over the next 10 years."

Away from the centers, another exciting development is SNU's programme for interdisciplinary research. "Seoul National University has a future programme. It's one of the interdisciplinary projects that supports so called interdisciplinary convergence studies. We are concentrating on this future program to bring natural science, social sciences and humanities together."

Another exciting development is the creative leading research program. The idea, says Oh, is to encourage faculty members who demonstrate outstanding research achievements. Under the programme, SNU provides substantial financial and administrative support for their on-going research. "We are expecting them to deliver world-class research, that's our hope."

Major Discoveries

Many of SNU's finest achievements have come in the medical field.

Professor PARK Seong Hoe, from SNU's college of medicine, has developed selective immuno suppressants for the treatment of diabetes. In another world first development, Professor HYEON Taeg Hwan and LEE Seung Hoon developed a stroke drug using Ceria nano-particles. Professor KIM VIC NARRY identified the mechanism that generates microRNA, which controls the growth and aging of cells.

Partnerships, Innovation & Translational Research

Most leading universities are keen to expand their international reach but President Oh feels that SNU has a special reason to do so.

"Korea has experienced the under developing stage, and now we are trying to escape from the developing stage and, so we are in the twenty year bridge, bridging developing countries and developed countries such as Asian countries through Central Asia, South Eastern Asian countries and Africa." Korea's unique history, says President Oh, is one reason why SNU has so much to give partners.

To achieve this international aim the university has developed a global academic system. At present it has almost 200 international faculty members, and includes special recruiting packages for high quality international students in Asia and other countries. There are also housing and other benefits for foreign students.

Fortunately for President Oh, who sees internationalisation as a key part of his role, many international students are keen to come to the university. "We have some advantages in terms of the characteristics of Korea. Many global faculty members and students are anxious to know what's going on in Korea. This is why they try to apply to SNU." But SNU isn't just waiting for students to come to Korea – it is also branching out abroad.

"This year we have established SNU in Beijing and SNU in Tokyo, even SNU in Kenya. We have sent students there, to learn and to have really good relationships with the students and faculty members in Beijing, Tokyo and Kenya. "Of course none of this comes cheap, admits President Oh. "It takes a lot of money, so I work hard for funding from the government, as well as corporations."

Teaching, Learning & Student Life

When it comes to student life at SNU, ethos is very important says President Oh. "A university is a university and our role is to create universal values. So my position is to start with the basic background of each science. That is for human beings, for other people. I think regardless of the differences in major sciences and technology, the most important thing is to care about the nature of human beings. This is love for others, to share with others the research we develop and to work with the intellectual people. According to Confucius in Asian society this is the solution and humankind should be together, not a single unit, not a single nation, not a single university. That's my philosophy; we need to establish this kind of basic value system for each university. That should be the goals of a leading university."

Another big part of SNU's appeal for students is its location in Seoul. The capital is home to one of the most vibrant, cutting-edge youth cultures in the world. And, as the success of pop video Gangnam Style demonstrates, Korean pop music – or K-pop as it's known – has never been so popular. For international students, staying in Seoul is a chance to live in one of Asia's most technologically advanced cities and gain valuable cultural understanding at the dawn of what most predict will be the 'Asian century'.

Radboud University Nijmegen

Rank › 101 – 150

Name › Radboud University Nijmegen
Region › Europe
Country › Netherlands
Founded › 1923

www.ru.nl

Core Research Strengths

Radboud University Nijmegen was founded in 1923 in the oldest city in the Netherlands. It is a student-oriented research university that facilitates ground-breaking, probing research in four primary areas of science: humanities, human & social sciences, life sciences and natural sciences.

Under the motto "not necessarily bigger, but better" the quality of the university has improved substantially over the past few years. This is particularly true of the nine leading fields of research at Radboud University, all of which are among the best in the world. These are: organic chemistry, solid state physics, microbiology, cognitive neurosciences, infectious diseases and immunology, human genetics, linguistics, entrepreneurial-based law and astrophysics.

Major Discoveries

Last year scientists from Radboud University secured no less than two of the four highly prestigious Spinoza awards (often referred to as the Dutch Nobel Prize). Professor Mike Jetten, Professor of Ecological Microbiology, for research into anaerobic bacteria, which now fulfill an important role in water purification plants.

The other winner is Professor Ieke Moerdijk, Professor of Algebra and Topology and one of the first mathematicians in the world to explore the boundaries and connections between these two seemingly very different sub-fields of mathematics.

But Radboud University is also making the headlines in the field of humanities. In 2009, Professor Ellen van Wolde, Professor of Old Testament Exegesis and Source Texts of Judaism at Radboud University Nijmegen, shocked the world with her assertion that God had not created heaven and earth, but separated them.

Partnerships, Innovation & Translational Research

In a bid to stay abreast at the global forefront of fundamental scientific research, the university is consciously expanding and intensifying collaboration with national and international scientific partners. The German partnerships stand out particularly, such as those with the Max Planck Institutes, Frauenhofer Institute and Helmholtz Institutes. Nijmegen also works alongside Dresden, Grenoble and Toulouse in the European Magnet Field Laboratory.

In 2012, the Ministry of Education, Culture & Science announced that Radboud University was to take part in two of the six selected Gravitation programmes. The allocation of these Gravitation programmes led to intensified working relationships with several strong Dutch scientific partners.

€27.6 million was assigned to language and brain research and ties were forged with the University of Amsterdam. A further € 26.9 million was made available for chemical research into dynamic materials, an area in which Radboud University is working closely with Eindhoven University of Technology and the University of Groningen.

Radboud University is committed to promoting the application of knowledge in society. The university provides a substantial package of post-initial programmes, boasting firm links with the professional field. Research is carried out in collaboration with private and public partners. The university enables new companies to be established and stimulates start-up companies that have just got off the ground. In addition, the university makes an intellectual and creative contribution to numerous cultural products, including debates, exhibitions and catalogues.

Teaching, Learning & Student Life

Education and research are closely intertwined at Nijmegen. Students are taught by lecturers who are themselves actively involved in scientific research. A mentoring system has been set up in all programmes to ensure that students are given personal supervision. The needs of excellent, well-motivated students looking for an extra challenge are satisfied at the Radboud Honours Academy, which offers extra disciplinary and interdisciplinary programmes.

Last year, the Keuzegids Universiteiten (an independent Dutch university guide) named Radboud University Nijmegen as the 'best general university' in the Netherlands. This accolade is based on the high student satisfaction scores given for the programmes, facilities and the university as a whole. Consistently high scores of 7.8 and 7.7 (on a scale of 0 to 10) for a number of years are a good measure of student satisfaction.

The green campus at Radboud University provides an inspiring environment conducive to studying, working and social interaction. Radboud University has excellent facilities for education and research. The outstanding amenities were recently expanded with a free electron infrared laser, which can produce 'tailor-made laser light', with adjustable wavelength, energy and pulse duration. The combination of FLARE laser and High Field Magnet Laboratory (HFML) has resulted in a unique user facility that attracts researchers from all around the world.

The university has an outstanding international climate. More than 22% of the academic staff are international, as are 10% of the students enrolled at Radboud University. Furthermore, every year more than 450 exchange students come to the university to take courses. An estimated 150 student associations ensure a lively social life for students attending the university.

NUS
National University
of Singapore

Rank › 101 – 150

Name › National University of Singapore
Region › Asia/Pacific
Country › Singapore
Founded › 1905

www.nus.edu.sg

Core Research Strengths

Established in 1905, the National University of Singapore (NUS) has grown rapidly over the course of the past 10 years from what was widely considered to be a teaching institution into one of East Asia's most prominent research universities. NUS' Deputy President for Research and Technology Professor Barry Halliwell, who is responsible for driving the university's research agenda, explains, "Our strategy is to have a broad range of high quality research. Within that there are a certain number of peaks of excellence, areas we are very well known in the world as being very strong in."

The university has been placed among the world's best in several areas, for example in material science and cancer research. Given the breadth and complexity of Cancer research, it is a tremendous task for any single institution to specialise across the whole area. NUS has responded to this challenge by focusing on particularly under-researched but important cancers that are more prevalent in Asia such as gastric cancer.

Following on from the Asian theme in medical research, NUS also specialises in an emerging research area broadly categorised as the Asian phenotype; relating to the different metabolisms between Asians and Caucasians and how drugs and treatments largely developed in the western world require modification to be more suitable for Asian communities.

In response to the growing complexity of major research questions, NUS is building its capacity by undertaking multidisciplinary research. Professor Halliwell noted that disciplinary strength and a collaborative culture are the foundations for this transition: "Interdisciplinary research is something we encourage, and to do interdisciplinary research you need a very strong research reputation in your own area." NUS has introduced five research clusters to lead its interdisciplinary ambitions. The clusters focus on the ageing society, finance & risk management, integrative sustainability solutions, biomedical science & translational medicine and a final one taking a holistic approach to the study of Asia.

Major Discoveries

NUS researchers have found a compound that is undergoing preclinical trials as a potential drug that can "starve" cancer cells of energy, thus preventing them from developing into a tumour.

A cross-disciplinary team at NUS has conceptualised and built a graphene device, which can be potentially used to study any kind of diseased cell, and applied it to malaria detection.

An international team, including researchers from the Centre for Quantum Technologies at NUS, have demonstrated that quantum discord, which is more robust and easier to access than the phenomenon of entanglement, can be used to enhance technology with a quantum advantage.

Researchers from the Lee Kuan Yew School of Public Policy at NUS conducted a comparative study of water governance in the Asia-Pacific region, finding that developed and developing economies have significant variations in their water governance arrangements.

Partnerships, Innovation & Translational Research

NUS' research portfolio grows in tandem with its international network of collaborative partners. Many leading companies have established research partnerships with NUS including Siemens, GE, Zeiss and Agilent. NUS is also actively involved in international academic and research networks. For instance, NUS is a member of the prominent International Association of Research Universities (IARU), alongside some of the world's highest ranked institutions such as Oxford, Yale and the University of Tokyo.

Similarly to the majority of world-class research universities, NUS has an increasing focus on translational research. Its technology transfer office is quite unique in that it manages institutional relationships with external partners and the processes associated with tech transfer, and also provides a range of courses and programs to better equip students for business and entrepreneurial activities.

Teaching, Learning & Student Life

Consistently ranked among the world's top universities, NUS adopts a global approach to transformative education. A substantial portion of its faculty members are from overseas and there is also a vibrant community of international students. Nearly 70 per cent of NUS undergraduates go overseas, and about three in 10 undergraduates go for six months or longer. NUS' comprehensive curriculum offers students multiple pathways, including over 70 joint, concurrent and double degree programmes with prestigious universities around the world.

As Singapore's flagship university, more than 80% of NUS' 27,000 undergraduates are leading young minds from Singapore. The rest are made up of international students who are mostly from Asia, although this base is taking on an increasingly cosmopolitan complexion as interest in Asia from regions such as Europe and the Americas increases.

At NUS, students enjoy a broad-based curriculum where they acquire both breadth and depth of knowledge. The NUS Graduate School for Integrative Sciences and Engineering, for instance, takes a pioneering approach by customising the curriculum for each graduate student to facilitate their transition from recognised disciplines to new areas of interest.

Students at NUS can expect to benefit from the economic and business opportunities that have become synonymous with the Asian century, whilst at the same time enjoying surroundings in a sophisticated and efficient location equipped with excellent facilities. For those that enjoy travel, Singapore is ideal, with a world-class airport enjoying close links to destinations such as Australia, India and Thailand.

**TAIWAN
UNIVERSITY**

Rank › 101 – 150

Name › Taiwan University
Region › Asia/Pacific
Founded › 1928

www.ntu.edu.tw

Core Research Strengths

Taiwan University is a very broad institute with core strengths in seven key areas. Unsurprisingly for a leading university in such a technologically advanced economy, computers and electronics feature heavily. For example the Connected Context Computing Center is working on the development of machine-to-machine technologies. TU President Si-Chen Lee feels it's an exciting new development: "In the future, machine will talk to machine. So this emerging technology is being defined and developed by our research team."

Within that field there is also another international research center working on intelligent robotics. The other key areas are cancer research, genomic medicine, system biology, theoretical science, biomedical imaging and emerging materials.

But the university's research isn't just restricted to those seven key areas, says Lee. TU also takes on specific challenges for business sectors that may involve several of those areas. "We also focus on Information and Electronics Technology. Taiwan is very strong in the ICT business. So, in this area, especially like in System on Chips (SOC) or Electronic Design Automation (EDA), we are very good. We have been recognised in the world's top international conference, ISSCC, (International Solid-State Circuit Conference) for many years, five to six years, we are no. 1 in quality and quantity of the published papers. This is a very big area of our research."

Major Discoveries

In the area of molecular imaging, TU developed the so-called Wide Band FMRI. This new technology meant that the time for a whole body MRI scan was cut from one hour to ten minutes. The university was also heavily involved in the discovery of the Higgs Boson – or 'god particle' – in the Large Hadron Collider in Switzerland. TU contributed by developing a deflector screen that was used in the discovery.

Partnerships, Innovation & Translational Research

International partnership is a massive part of TU's strategy, says President Lee. To that end the university has established scores of international centers. Some of the centers work with other leading universities while others are collaborations with international corporations.

It's a new approach, admits Lee. "We used to employ a bottom-up approach to organising partnerships. It worked through personal collaboration between faculties for international collaboration, but now our strategy is to adopt a top-down approach, that is organisation-to-organisation collaboration. That's the reason we created so many international research centers."

So far it seems to be working. For example TU's scores of alliances and joint ventures with multinationals must be the envy of many of its peers. It has jointly-owned research centers with Intel and IBM. It's also lined up with some big names on the academic side – Harvard and the University of Paris are just two recent examples.

However, despite all this success with international partnerships, President Lee feels that TU must do a better job of commercialising its know-how. "Over the years we have had many new ideas but no realisation because our infrastructure is not strong enough to support us going to business, to spin off new companies." To make his point President Lee cites the example of Google, which was spun off from a Stanford University project in 1996. "Actually, in 1996 Taiwan University started a digital library programme and we also developed a very efficient search engine but we never commercialised this. That's the drawback of our university."

It's a frank admission of failure, but now President Lee is determined to put things right. "We created a new Center for Idea Realisation, and we formed our entrepreneurial alumni association to help the university to achieve this purpose. So we are trying to bridge the gap between the idea and markets and their realisation."

Teaching, Learning & Student Life

Every leading university, says President Lee, is in a race to attract the best students. To that end TU has developed its own strategy to create a unique learning experience.

"Every university wants to go to all-English courses trying to attract international students but we put more emphasis on Chinese language, Chinese culture, Chinese traditions, literature and philosophy. Of course we provide enough English courses for international students, but our focus is on teaching the Mandarin language."

The idea, says President Lee, is that students emerge with a basic knowledge of Mandarin and a deep understanding of China and the Chinese economy – a certain advantage in the 'Asian Century'.

Away from the classroom President Lee also believes that the charms of Taiwan itself will act as an extra lure for students. "It is a very friendly place and very safe. You can walk down the street in the middle of the night, you don't worry about anything. The subway system is very efficient and clean. The living is so friendly. Also the food is excellent. Sixty years ago when over a million mainland Chinese moved here they brought different tastes from all over China."

MONASH University

Rank › 101 – 150

Name › Monash University
Region › Asia/Pacific
Country › Australia
Founded › 1958

www.monash.edu.au

Core Research Strengths

Established in Melbourne, Australia in 1958 Monash University is home to major research facilities, more than 100 research centres and 10 co-operative research centres. In 2011, its external research income was around AU$285 million.

"Monash University is a comprehensive institution", says Vice-Chancellor Professor Ed Byrne. "Our researchers have expertise throughout a wide range of disciplines from engineering and the exact sciences through to the social sciences, humanities and performing arts. Monash University has a verystrong focus on sustainability, with one of the largest sustainability institutes in the Southern Hemisphere. Water research is a major part of that; in recent years we have received over AU$130 million from the Australian Government and other partners to establish focused water research programs."

Tackling sustainable living from another perspective, researchers at Monash University's multi-disciplinary Green Chemical Futures centre aim to reduce the impact of industry and manufacturing on the environment through the design of new chemical products and processes that are non-toxic, energy efficient and waste-free.

Vice-Chancellor Byrne notes that engineering research, from nanotechnology and materials innovation to civil engineering, is a long-standing strength at Monash.

"Emerging research groups in medical bioengineering and aerospace materials and manufacture continue this tradition. We are also strong in the medical sciences, from epidemiology to structural biology and drug discovery. We probably have the strongest pharmacy and pharmacology science faculty in this part of the world."

Monash research infrastructure includes state-of-the-art imaging at the Monash Biomedical Imaging laboratory, Monash Centre for Electron Microscopy (MCEM), and the Multi-modal Australian ScienceS Imaging and Visualisation Environment (MASSIVE), along with access to the co-located Australian Synchrotron.

The Monash Biosciences Precinct comprises $100 million in state-of-the-art biomedical research facilities, housing around 500 research and support staff. The precinct includes the Australian Regenerative Medicine Institute (ARMI) which hosts the first non-European associate of the European Molecular Biology Laboratory (EMBL). In 2013, Monash will launch the New Horizons future manufacturing initiative, a $175 million centre that will co-locate around 400 researchers from Monash and the Commonwealth Scientific and Industrial Research Organisation (CSIRO), Australia's national science agency and a longstanding Monash partner. New Horizons will house research groups in sustainable energy, novel materials, and other fields where engineering design and synthesis can provide new solutions in biology and medical contexts.

Major Discoveries

1973 › Monash Institute of Reproduction and Development (MIRD) researchers Professors Alan Trounson and Carl Wood achieved the world's first IVF pregnancy.

1989 › Discovery of the anti-influenza drug Relenza (Zanamivir) by scientists led by Mark von Itzstein at the Victorian College of Pharmacy in collaboration with the CSIRO and scientists at Glaxo, UK.

Partnerships, Innovation & Translational Research

Monash is committed to international engagement across and beyond our region, with campuses in South Africa and Malaysia and affiliate arrangements with Indian and Chinese institutions for Masters and PhD level only. Another element of the university's internationalisation strategy is a formal partnership agreement with the University of Warwick,announced in 2012. As part of the alliance, the two institutions will co develop courses, co-invest in technologies and aim to attract the best researchers and students.

Many universities have partnerships, says Vice-Chancellor Byrne, but the Monash Warwick Alliance is genuinely unique. "This is perhaps the first occasion in the world of universities that an attempt has been made to create an equivalent to the alliances one finds in the world of airlines."

The university is committed to ensuring that its research makes a difference in society. Long-term relationships with industry, government, and non-governmental organisations mean that academic innovation can be translated into impact, for example through Monash's teaching and clinical research partnership with Southern Health (the major public health service in southeast Melbourne) and the Alfred Hospital (housing Australia's largest intensive care unit). Longstanding collaborators include the state's transport accident prevention agency, AusAID and the World Bank, and global companies such as GlaxoSmithKline, Airbus and Bombardier.

Teaching, Learning & Student Life

Monash University has six Australian campuses, campuses in Malaysia and South Africa, and centres in China, India and Italy.

"We have a very strong commitment to teaching our students using the very latest technologies and teaching philosophies so as to ensure they have a state-of-the art experience," says the Vice-Chancellor.

Monash's education model - the Monash Passport - is designed to ensure that students benefit from a high-quality, research-driven academic training which doesn't neglect personal development and pragmatic career prospects.

"We encourage our students to get closely involved with voluntary organisations such as international NGOs," says Vice-Chancellor Byrne.

"One of the founding mottos of Monash University is to prepare yourself not only for your own career, but also to be of use to broader society as a whole. This is certainly a philosophy we carry on and try to inculcate throughout our undergraduate community; whilst at the same time exposing our graduate population to a range of challenges that confront and develop their analytical skills."

MAYO MEDICAL SCHOOL

Rank › 101 – 150

Name › Mayo Medical School
Region › Americas
Country › United States
Founded › 1971

www.mayo.edu

Core Research Strengths

Mayo Clinic conducts basic, translational, clinical and epidemiological research at its campuses in Arizona, Florida and Minnesota and throughout the Mayo Clinic Health System. Mayo recently refocused its approach and chose to concentrate on three areas it feels will have the greatest medical impact. Research in these areas is conducted through collaborative centers that cross many disciplines and work to turn research discoveries into new therapies.

The newest is the Center for the Science of Health Care Delivery, which aims to use scientific methods to add value and efficiency to medicine. The second is the Center for Individualized Medicine, which conducts genomic research. It has existed for a couple of years but now has a new focus under new director, Gianrico Farrugia. The idea is for the Center to build upon Mayo's long history of leveraging genetic knowledge to find treatments, identify risks, or determine the right drug or dosage for patients. That effort will further expand with technological advancements.

Finally there is the Center for Regenerative Medicine, also new this year, and headed by Andre Terzic, M.D., Ph.D., known for his research on regenerative heart repair. The center will explore regenerating the body's own cells and tissue to repair injuries, improve quality of life, and perhaps even prevent some ailments by strengthening organs at risk.

Of course many of Mayo's peers also have new centers, staffed by excellent personnel. However, what makes Mayo's centers different is that all three directors report to both the leader of research and the leader of medical practice at Mayo. This will ensure that new discoveries rapidly reach patients.

As an institution Mayo never stands still and early in 2013 it announced the $5 billion 'Destination Medical Center' plan. Financing details are still being arranged with local legislators, but the plan would lead to much enlarged research facilities and double the total number of staff to more than 60,000.

Major Discoveries

Mayo has more than its fair share of distinguished academics and impressive research prizes. However, arguably its finest discovery involves something much more prosaic. In 1907 Dr. Henry Plummer invented the modern patient medical record – a simple administrative step that revolutionised medicine and is still with us today.

Partnerships, Innovation & Translational Research

Mayo has many different types of relationships with private industry. One is industry-sponsored research, which is handled through the CTSA Office of Industry Alliances. This office works closely with Mayo Clinic Health Solutions to explore commercialisation of Mayo Clinic's intellectual property and provide a liaison for private sector firms.

Mayo's desire to ensure that its research improves lives is put into effect by the Knowledge Translation Research Unit. This team focuses on translating the best available research findings into clinical practice through evidence synthesis, investigation of the patient-clinician encounter, and quality-of-care research.

In addition to these industry alliances Mayo also partners with many higher education institutions for research or education purposes. For example, while Mayo oversees some programs in their entirety, others are jointly sponsored and taught in partnership with a college or university. In addition, some programs are internships, externships and preceptorships, wherein students come to Mayo to complete the clinical training portion of their education.

Teaching, Learning & Student Life

Mayo Clinic's campus in Rochester has been the centre of Mayo Clinic operations since the 1880s and is home to Mayo Medical School. The campus is full of state-of-the-art buildings all within easy, safe and pleasant walking distance from one another. Indeed Rochester, which is Minnesota's 3rd-biggest city, is a quiet, peaceful place with around 100,000 inhabitants, a significant amount of whom work for the university. Prospective students should note that one of the key elements of Mayo's expansion plan, is to improve the amenities available to staff and students.

When it comes to the academic environment there is little room for improvement. Mayo Clinic is the largest multidisciplinary, multispecialty, integrated medical group practice in the world, seeing over 1 million patients each year. That's great for students as they're placed in meaningful contact with patients nearly every day from their first week. This incredible opportunity to gain real experience is made possible by two non-profit hospitals - Saint Marys Hospital, which has 1,157 licensed beds and 53 operating rooms, and Rochester Methodist Hospital with 794 beds and 36 operating rooms.

In addition to offering valuable patient experience the clinic also has an unrivalled array of facilities. There are numerous centers devoted to patient examinations, testing and care needs, extensive advanced research facilities and laboratory complexes, core technical facilities, a new genomics and bioinformatics center, a new advanced imaging center, and comprehensive educational facilities. Students have access to an integrated physical and digital library system, with more than 92,000 book titles, 5,000 electronic journals and 600 print journal subscriptions; in addition to online resources available. In short medical students have everything they need to develop their skills and understanding at Mayo.

Another advantage is that the clinic has 3,700 physicians and scientists on staff, the majority of whom have appointments in the College of Medicine. This creates one of the highest faculty-to-student ratios in the country.

LUND
UNIVERSITY

Rank › 101 – 150

Name › Lund University
Region › Europe
Country › Sweden
Founded › 1666

www.lunduniversity.lu.se

Core Research Strengths

Lund University has a long and vibrant history covering almost 350 years of research and teaching. It has evolved from just a few hundred students and professors being paid with meat and grain into its present form, with around 47,000 students and a position of excellence in international research.

Of course the days of paying professors in meat and grain are long gone and Lund now has one of Europe's biggest academic research budgets. More than SEK 4 billion is awarded annually to research at eight faculties, giving Lund University one of the strongest and broadest ranges of research in Sweden. It was also the only full-scale Swedish university to make the list of the 50 organisations that received funding from the European Commission's EU Seventh Framework Programme for research and development.

Vice Chancellor Per Eriksson says one reason the university receives so much funding is the way that research is organised, noting that it has a very thematic, multidisciplinary approach. "We tackle complex problems and global challenges and work to ensure that knowledge and innovations benefit society. We provide education and research in engineering, science, law, social sciences, economics and management, medicine, humanities, theology, fine art, music and drama."

Some of the university's strongest research fields are nanotechnology, climate change, stem cell biology, diabetes, neurodegenerative diseases such as Parkinson's disease, and music education.

Two major facilities for materials research are currently under construction in Lund: the MAX IV Laboratory, which will be a world-leading synchrotron radiation laboratory and ESS, a European facility that will be home to the world's most powerful neutron source. These will be of decisive importance for materials and life sciences and for industrial development.

Another exciting area, says the Vice Chancellor, is the interface between medicine and technology. "There are a number of research breakthroughs and many private-sector companies are also contributing. We have a group working using sensors and injections on the brain, and it's quite fantastic what's happening."

Major Discoveries

Lund has lent its name to many notable discoveries, such as the Bluetooth technology and the artificial kidney, but perhaps the most important – especially in terms of lives saved – was the development of the world's first nicotine medication in 1967.

Partnerships, Innovation & Translational Research

The interplay between innovation and industry is very important for universities nowadays, says Vice Chancellor Eriksson. To facilitate relations with external private-sector partners Lund has created the role of innovation officer. These innovation officers have strong academic backgrounds, and often hold PhDs themselves, but also have commercial experience. They are placed with research groups to make projects aware of how theoretical work could interact with wider society and the market.

So far the strategy has paid off. More than 22% of the Europe-wide patents awarded to Swedish individuals or organisations have come from Lund University.

Another important point of interaction is the science park, says Vice Chancellor Eriksson. "We value our science park – it is home to many industries and companies. Procter & Gamble, Ericsson and TetraPak all have very strong connections with the university."

Another way that Lund interacts with the outside world is through alliances with top class universities. Lund University cooperates with universities all over the world through bilateral agreements, educational and research programmes, networks and partnerships as well as research collaboration. It has 680 partner universities in more than 50 countries. It is also part of the League of European Research Universities (LERU), and Universitas 21.

Teaching, Learning & Student Life

Lund University is based in the Skåne region of southern Sweden and campus locations include Lund, Helsingborg, Malmö and Ljungbyhed. Lund itself was voted the best place to live in Sweden; Lund is a safe city with the healthiest and youngest population in the country. As one of the oldest cities in Sweden dating back to 990, Lund is a city of contrasts where 1000 years of history blend with modern knowledge and ideas. It combines small picturesque, cobble-stoned streets with big city attractions such as services, shopping, restaurants and cultural events.

It's also very well located. It is just 15 minutes by train from Malmö (the third largest city in Sweden) and less than an hour from Copenhagen (Scandinavia's largest city and the capital of Denmark).

"The student life is very attractive", says Vice Chancellor Eriksson. "We have something called the Lund Experience which is a unique tradition at the university. It basically means that you are encouraged to meet and mix with students from different disciplines."

Another important element of the student experience is that it feels very international, says the Vice Chancellor. "We welcome over 3000 international Master's and exchange students to Lund University every year." This internationalisation works both ways as Lund University also sends the largest number of exchange students of all higher education institutions in Sweden.

THE LONDON SCHOOL
OF ECONOMICS AND
POLITICAL SCIENCE ■

Rank › 101 – 150

Name › London School of Economics
Region › Europe
Country › United Kingdom
Founded › 1895

www2.lse.ac.uk

Core Research Strengths

Founded in 1895 by Beatrice and Sidney Webb, LSE has an outstanding reputation for academic excellence with 16 Nobel Prize winners from the ranks of LSE staff or alumni. In 2011/12 annual research income was approximately 39 million.

The reason that the research budget is lower than some of its peers is because of the areas that the LSE specialises in, explains Professor Stuart Corbridge, the Pro Director for Research & External Relations. "The university generally doesn't cover the hard sciences or languages. The LSE's core research strengths are in areas such as economics, government, social policy and law."

This focus is owing to the LSE's unique history, says the Pro Director. "LSE is a world-leading pioneer of the social sciences, having played a unique role in defining and developing key academic subjects. International relations, social policy, sociology, social anthropology, social psychology and criminology all have their origins as subjects of university study in the innovative work carried out by LSE academics."

Moreover, having a much more focused remit than some of its more comprehensive peers can be an advantage.

"LSE is ranked as the only European university with an economics department in the global top 15. Overall, the 2008 UK Research Assessment Exercise (RAE) placed LSE second equal with Oxford, behind only Cambridge in the UK; this demonstrates the quality of research at LSE."

In total there are 18 Research Centres, all managed by academic communities. LSE has one of the largest concentrations of applied economic, financial and social researchers anywhere in the world. Centres include the Centre for Analysis of Social Exclusion, the Centre for Economic Performance, the Financial Markets Group and the Suntory and Toyota International Centres for Economics and Related Disciplines.

Major Discoveries

During the 1970s Richard Morris Titmuss at the London School of Economics and Political Science found that poverty, not family circumstances, were behind the behavioural problems and learning difficulties in children from one-parent families.

Arthur Lewis led a ground-breaking study into the causes of developing world poverty.

Partnerships, Innovation & Translational Research

With a leading position in its core subjects the LSE is considered a key partner for many in the field, says Professor Corbridge.

"LSE works closely with other universities, with government, research councils and foundations, as well as with some private-sector actors to produce first-class academic work that we hope will have significant societal benefits: this is true, for example, of work conducted by LSE academics in fields such as minimum wage policies, climate change economics and the financing of long-term care."

It also has international academic partnerships, says Professor Corbridge. "LSE has established links with a relatively small number of high-quality universities across the world."

The university's advanced climate change economics research has led to lucrative partnerships with the private sector. For example it has worked with Deutsche Bank and the Alfred Herrhausen Society. "However, while there are private sector links to the LSE, these are not to the same extent that you would find at more broad based universities such as Oxford, Cambridge or Southampton," explains the Pro Director.

LSE is investing heavily in new research capacity, with a special recruitment drive in 2013 attracting hundreds of applications, many from world leading academics in their fields.

Teaching, Learning & Student Life

Research-led teaching is a big part of an LSE student's experience, says Prof. Corbridge. "LSE has taken steps in the past few years to ensure that students at the school are taught by some of LSE's best-known professors. All undergraduates coming to LSE now have to take and pass a course called LSE 100, which is aimed at familiarising students with methodological questions and public policy issues across a wide range of disciplines.

The LSE 100 course is based around a series of 'big policy' questions – can we make poverty history? Who is to blame for the global financial crisis? Is the Cold War really over? And so on – that in turn leads on to seminars that are focused on methodological questions such as: How do we begin to answer such large questions? What techniques and theories are available to social scientists and others? What are the strengths and weaknesses of such approaches? We believe this flagship course will soon attract the attention of other universities."

Of course another big part of student life at LSE is living in London. The Pro-Director believes it is a big plus for most students. "As a student at LSE, you will be based in an exciting, vibrant and colourful city. Whatever your interests or appetite you will find something to suit your palate and pocket in this truly international capital. International in flavour, London is an unparalleled environment in which to live and study. It is a centre for government and law, Europe's leading financial market and a style setting centre of cultural life. Educational benefits include libraries, professional institutes and all the resources of the University of London."

Rank › 101 – 150

Name › Joseph Fourier University (Grenoble 1)
Region › Europe
Country › France
Founded › 1339

www.ujf-grenoble.fr

Core Research Strengths

The Joseph Fourier University (UJF) organises its research enterprise into four broad areas, with the university strategically focusing on developing existing areas of expertise forecast to have the most significant economic and social benefits looking forward. This spectrum covers clusters in chemistry, biology & healthcare, computing & communication, climate change & energy sustainability; and nano science & physics. Each cluster develops its own research projects known as 'Laboratories of Excellence' or 'LabEx' that benefit from the participation of more than 50 laboratories and 2,000 PhD students. Many of the labs are run in association with the National Centre for Scientific Research (CNRS).

The Centre for Chemistry, Life & Healthcare Sciences & Bioengineering (CSVSB) is a joint effort between UJF, Grenoble University Hospital, CNRS and INSERM. CSVSB conducts a variety of research programmes ranging from basic research to clinical application. CSVSB has recently developed 6 LabEx including bio-driven chemistry, cancer treatment and therapy, parasitic pathogens and age-related diseases.

Research undertaken at the MSTIC Centre for Mathematics, Information and Communication Sciences and Technologies covers three main areas: Information and software technology; systems, signal processing and automation; mathematics, modelling and numerical simulation. As examples of success stories, one could mention the great impact of what is called model checking that has been developed at Grenoble; this is now widely used by the semi-conductor industry.

The SMINGUE Centre tackles current issues in the fields of nanotechnology and nanosciences, energy, advanced materials and design.

Major Discoveries

Medical advancements at UJF include the discovery of Taxol, an anti-cancer agent.

Recent awards to faculty and researchers include the 2007 ACM Turing Award to Joseph Sifakis, along with others, for the roles played in developing model checking into a highly effective verification technology, widely adopted in the hardware and software industries.

The planetology and astrophysical institute of Grenoble (IPAG) has discovered approximately 100 new extra solar planets since 1998. Among them is GI667Cc, the planet that looks the most like Earth.

Partnerships, Innovation & Translational Research

UJF has a long-standing tradition of international collaboration and a well-established system to set up partnerships. The aim of these partnerships is to both find financial backing for projects, as well as to make the university's work more accessible.

Since 1990, the UJF European Office has aided and supported collaborative programmes between its own and European researchers. Systems dedicated to this include International Associated Laboratories (LIA), which combines teams from laboratories affiliated with CNRS and laboratories from around the world. The 2002 International Joint Units (UMI) brings together CNRS staff within the same laboratory alongside staff from other countries, and the International Research Group (GDRI) network, which unites countries for scientific coordination on specific topics.

UJF is highly attuned to the commercial value of its research interests, and is involved in many start-up companies. Technology transfer is maintained through the university's subsidiary Floralis, which works in three ways: by supporting collaborative research, by initiating partnerships with public laboratories and private companies and supervising the technical and marketing development of new technologies before they are commercialised. In the past 15 years, 32 spin-offs have been created creating 300 jobs. UJF currently has 170 active patents.

Teaching, Learning & Student Life

As well as the allure of low tuition fees in a time when the cost of education is rocketing, UJF is the leading French university for top-level sport. Students benefit from the University of Grenoble's shared campus and facilities, as well as its state-of-the-art teaching methods that include a strong tutoring system and internship opportunities.

UJF is an international institution with more than 2,000 foreign students received each year, and over 600 participating in international exchanges. More than a third of its PhD students come from abroad. There are several international research institutes in close proximity, and every year UJF organises five international science schools for young researchers from around the world. Each school selects between 50 and 80 scientists from 20 different countries to participate. UJF also runs three Erasmus Mundus Master's programmes providing scholarships for students to study abroad.

President Patrick Lévy believes the university's location also plays a critical role in the value students can expect. "Well, it's a very nice place. Grenoble is located in a valley flanked by three mountain ranges: Vercors, Chartreuse and Belledonne, and you can even see Mont-Blanc when it's sunny. Our campus is very attractive with its 180 hectares and 30000 trees. What is interesting is the fact that we have something like 60,000 students living in town. We also have many scientific and technological facilities that attract many engineers and researchers.

The population in Grenoble is very active, very international, very interested in culture and of course very fond of sports. The natural environment is just perfect for those who like climbing, skiing or walking in the mountains."

Joseph Fourier University
France

Rank › 101 – 150

Name › Hokkaido University
Region › Asia/Pacific
Country › Japan
Founded › 1876

www.hokudai.ac.jp

Core Research Strengths

First established in 1876 as Sapporo Agricultural College, Hokkaido University (Hokudai) has since grown into a comprehensive higher education institution, and a member of the 11 top research universities of Japan collectively known as RU11. Although the research portfolio is broad, there are specific areas of expertise that distinguish Hokudai internationally.

In the medical sciences, Hokudai has world leading expertise in the study of influenza, particularly the transmission of the virus between humans and animals. Professor Hiroshi Kida, a world-renowned expert is the Head of the Research Center for Zoonosis Control. Professor Kida has tracked the precise spread from source to human of some of the world's most devastating pandemics such as the four main occurrences of influenza over the past 100 years. Professor Kida is considered to be one of the most important sources of information and guidance for multilateral organisations such as the WHO in cases of pandemic flu outbreak.

Drawing upon the research seeds in the agricultural sciences of Hokudai and the technology of the National Institute of Advanced Industrial Science & Technology for genetic modifications of plants, the Northern Advancement Center for Science & Technology has established the Green Chemical Center. Together with 5 private enterprises, this globally unique 985 square metre facility is ready to translate practical research on hydroponic cultivation of plants into food materials and feedstock for the pharmaceutical industry.

Professor Hiroki Shirato from the Department of Radiation Medicine is in the process of developing the world's first real-time tumour tracking Proton Beam Therapy (PBM). PBM is a well-established technology, but it has only been suitable up until now for cancers that can be immobilized; rendering it of little value for mobile tumours such as those in the lung. Professor Shirato's breakthrough will have a revolutionary impact upon the way such tumours are treated and their success rates.

Major Discoveries

Professor Hiroshi Kida's research has shown that migratory ducks and pigs have been the key carriers of influenza transmitted from animals to humans over the course of the past century. He has identified this trend in some of the most devastating pandemics including the Spanish influenza of 1918.

Professor Akira Suzuki was awarded the Nobel Prize in Chemistry, Hokkaido University's first, in 2010 for his pioneering work in the development of palladium cross-coupling reactions.

Partnerships, Innovation & Translational Research

Hokudai's increasing shift towards internationalisation is manifested in the university's research operation; with a diverse array of partners developing according to Vice President Takeo Hondoh's vision for a research university that thinks outside of the box "It is vital for a university such as ours to have a rich and diverse international network. We actively encourage our researchers and faculty to build research partnerships on the global scale. An excellent example of this is the partnership we have with the University of Zambia in veterinary medicine."

Hokkaido University's partnerships are not limited to other universities, with the universities' collection of industry and government partners growing significantly in recent years as the university's network of research partners grows in strategic importance.

Teaching, Learning & Student Life

With a university motto of "Be Ambitious", it is no surprise that Hokudai students are educated in an environment of no limits. One will find a frontier spirit at the heart of Hokkaido University's culture, whereby students are encouraged to take responsibility for answering the questions, and overcoming challenges at hand for their generation. Hokudai has developed a problem based teaching philosophy with respect to this, encouraging students to learn through doing.

This taps into another institutional philosophy at Hokudai, that of all around education. Students not only take on the theoretical rigours of their study programmes, the interspersing of a liberal arts tradition within each Hokudai degree encourages the development of a strong ethical identity amongst the university's graduates. This combined with an emphasis on practical learning lays down an interesting foundation for the development of graduates who are able to overcome research questions independently in a creative and innovative way.

Despite being located in the relative remoteness of Northern Japan, Hokkaido University's international ambitions are strong and continue to grow. The Office of International Affairs under the leadership of Vice President Hondoh is determined for Hokudai to be an active player on the international stage "We now have offices in China, Korea, Finland and Zambia to help facilitate partnerships in research and student exchange. We have about 300 partner universities and departments around the world, and continue to make reforms so our campus will be more attractive for international students. We are introducing more English language programs, and are fully committed to developing our concept of a bi-lingual campus where faculty and students alike can communicate in both Japanese and English."

Hokkaido University
Japan

Rank › 101 – 150

Name › Georgia Institute of Technology
Region › Americas
Country › United States
Founded › 1885

www.gatech.edu

Core Research Strengths

The Georgia Institute of Technology is one of the nation's top research universities, distinguished by its commitment to improving the human condition through advanced science and technology since its founding in 1885.

Groundbreaking research is underway in hundreds of research centers and laboratories across campus, inspiring game-changing ideas and new technologies that will help drive economic growth, while improving human life on a global scale.

The university's main research strengths are in bioengineering, bioscience, electronics and nanotechnology and, manufacturing and supply chain logistics. However, the university recently reorganised its research efforts with a new strategic plan that involves more multidisciplinary centers, explains President, G.P. "Bud" Peterson.

"We've started a new area called the Institute for People and Technology (IPaT), and it's looking at how people and technology interact, and how this impacts and affects people's lives. This draws faculty from across many disciplines but is an area that varies from assisted living to things like technology and policy. What we believe is that many of the new emerging technologies, and most of the new exciting discoveries, will occur at the boundaries of these traditional disciplines. So what we've tried to do is to identify ways that new emerging interdisciplinary fields that span technology, science, policies, business, law, and the arts, can be organized to provide an opportunity for faculty with different backgrounds to come together to work on similar issues and problems."

Another multidisciplinary theme that the university is focussing on is energy and sustainable infrastructure, says the President. "If you think about energy and sustainable infrastructure, there is expertise ranging from biology - when you think about algae as a potential energy source - to petroleum engineering and drilling. And then there are all the renewable energy formats, so it is a real multidisciplinary challenge." Perhaps the most telling sign that the university's strategic plan is working is that research funding has increased by about 50% over the last five years – hitting US $650 million in 2012.

Major Discoveries

Despite the improvements since the new strategic plan, the university has plenty of proud achievements that predate it. For example in 1980 Georgia Tech launched the Advanced Technology Development Center (ATDC), a technology business university-based incubator, that has launched more than 140 companies that, together, have created thousands of jobs and attracted more than $1 billion in investment.

Partnerships, Innovation & Translational Research

Georgia Tech was founded as an institution to try to help industrialize the state of Georgia and, as a result, has always been very open to working with the private sector. To that end it has created the Georgia Tech Enterprise Innovation Institute to liaise with business.

"Our approach is to do everything possible to help move technologies to the marketplace", says President Peterson, "once a product is in the market the commercial aspects take care of themselves." One of the best examples of that is a former student, Chris Klaus, who developed a new company called Internet Security Systems, ISS, when he was 21 years old. He later sold the firm to IBM for $1 billion.

The university isn't all about making money. It recently formed a partnership with Children's Healthcare of Atlanta, the largest children's hospital in the United States. It involves a $20 million partnership to work on paediatric health care. It also forms alliances with other research institutions, says the President. "We have a great partnership with Emory University in the biomedical area. I think that our combined expertise with Emory also makes collaborations very desirable."

Teaching, Learning & Student Life

Georgia Tech is located in midtown Atlanta, in one of the city's most energetic and vibrant neighbourhoods for business, culture, education, and entertainment. Atlanta itself is also a hot spot for music venues, theatres, shops, art galleries, museums, clubs, parks and hundreds of restaurants. Students will relish the many weekend festivals held to commemorate the city's history, cuisine, or diverse backgrounds. Meanwhile those who like fresh air and activity will love Piedmont Park. Only a few blocks from campus it is a great place to take a run or clear your head. The more adventurous can take advantage of the mountains, lakes, campsites, and hiking trails that are within an hour drive of the city.

When it comes to life inside the classroom prospective students will be pleased to know that Georgia Tech is constantly trying to improve standards. One of the best examples of this is a new pilot problem called 'the X-degree', says President Peterson. "This program allows students a tremendous amount of freedom to design their own curriculum. They can determine what courses to take, and maybe get a degree in physics or engineering or chemistry. We believe that this will allow our students to identify new interdisciplinary areas of great importance."

Another important part of the learning experience is research-led teaching. "We have approximately 40% of our students involved in our undergraduate research programs. So as undergraduate students, they can work with faculty and graduate students on research. We've got a program called the InVenture Prize, which is a competition for students who have ideas for new businesses. We will typically get 400 students or student teams that compete and the first prize is $15,000."

EMORY
UNIVERSITY

Rank › 101 – 150

Name › Emory University
Region › Americas
Country › United States
Founded › 1836

www.emory.edu

Core Research Strengths

With a mission "to create, preserve, teach, and apply knowledge in the service of humanity" Emory University is one of the United States' leading research universities, building on a unique combination of campus-based resources and global partnerships. For each of the past three years Emory has received more than $500 million in external research funding, with more than 90% of funding allocated to the health sciences.

Emory is recognised as a leader in immunology and pharmacology, having been ranked as the fourth highest contributor to the development of new drugs and vaccines for a public sector institution in the United States.

Emory is a global leader in the development of treatments for HIV/AIDS; 90% of United States citizens currently undergoing lifesaving treatment for HIV are using drugs developed at Emory. The University is also leading the development of vaccines for HIV and for numerous other major public health related challenges such as influenza, malaria, and hepatitis C.

Emory is widely regarded as a leading international institution in the neurosciences, with a particular focus on better understanding and developing treatments for Parkinson's disease, Alzheimer's disease, and autism. The university is also at the forefront in cardiology research, and it is the only cancer center in the State of Georgia designated by the National Cancer Institute. Its numerous global health partnerships include reducing smoking and smoking related illnesses and improving maternal and newborn survival rates.

Major Discoveries

Emtriva (emtricitabine) and 3TC (lamivudine), both lifesaving HIV treatments, were developed by researchers at Emory.

Emory researchers and cardiologists contributed to the development of lifesaving procedures including angioplasty and drug-eluting stents, and newer technologies such as off-pump surgery.

Belatacept, an improved immunosuppressant drug for organ transplantation, was co-developed by researchers at Emory.

Partnerships, Innovation & Translational Research

Emory engages in a number of collaborative research efforts based on its strengths in the life sciences, with a focus on developing life changing treatments and therapies for some of the most pressing international health challenges today. One such example is the strategic partnership between Emory and the Georgia Institute of Technology, whereby these two leading interdisciplinary research centres are advancing innovative fields of investigation such as biomedical engineering, regenerative medicine and nano-medicine.

Emory's Office of Technology Transfer (OTT) is one of the United States' leading offices for the management of research discoveries and innovations from the laboratory to the marketplace. Since 1992, Emory has spun out a total of 57 start up companies based on discoveries made at the university, as well as generated revenues of more than US$800 million from the commercialisation of technologies developed at the university. Life and medical sciences related innovations dominate the technology transfer operations at Emory, reflecting the university's exceptional strengths in these disciplines. The OTT currently manages more than 1,000 technologies invented by Emory scientists and physicians.

Teaching, Learning & Student Life

Emory is recognized internationally for its outstanding liberal arts colleges, graduate and professional schools as well as one of the Southeast's leading health care systems, and is located on a beautiful, leafy campus in suburban Atlanta. Admission to Emory is highly competitive.

Emory enrolls approximately 14,200 students, of whom 6,600 are undergraduate and 7,600 are graduate and professional students.

Emory offers highly-ranked liberal arts programs in Emory College of Arts and Sciences, as well as undergraduate

programs in business and nursing. Twenty percent of Emory undergraduates choose to begin their education at Oxford College, Emory's historic 1836 campus located 38 miles from Atlanta.

Emory students can expect an intimate academic experience with an exceptionally low student to faculty ratio of 7 to 1 enabling undergraduates the opportunity to develop presentation skills and research experience.

The university also offers professional programs in business, law, medicine, nursing, public health, and theology, as well as graduate studies. Emory's Laney Graduate School enrols PhD students in a wide range of approximately 40 programs, including a large Graduate Division of Biological and Biomedical Sciences; a Graduate Division of Religion; and a leading program in women's, gender and sexuality studies.

Cultural, religious, and personal diversity has grown to be synonymous with the Emory experience, with the university widely recognised as one of the leading participants of study abroad programs of United States universities, with some 40% of Emory undergraduates spending at least a semester studying abroad. Furthermore, Emory welcomes over 3600 international students and faculty from more than 125 countries to the university each year.

Boasting one of the world's busiest airport, Atlanta is one of the United States' foremost commercial hubs, home to US companies such as Coca Cola, Delta Air Lines, Home Depot, and UPS. The city provides an excellent stepping stone for aspirational students interested in gaining valuable work experience through corporate internships.

UCL
Université
catholique
de Louvain

Rank › 101 – 150

Name › Catholic University of Louvain
Region › Europe
Country › Belgium
Founded › 1425

www.uclouvain.be

Core Research Strengths

Located at the heart of Europe, at the crossroads of the Latin, German, and Anglo-Saxon worlds, the Université Catholique de Louvain (UCL) is a comprehensive university, fostering high level research in all areas: health sciences, science and technology, humanities and social sciences. Thanks to an excellent research environment (high performing international teams, technological platforms, and top-class equipment), UCL has managed to stay at the cutting edge in Europe. UCL is proud of its numerous top quality papers, research collaborations with top-notch universities and international companies. Earlier this year, UCL was delighted to being chosen as a partner in a 1-billion Euro graphene project funded by the European Research Council.

Major Discoveries

Several researchers of UCL play high-profile roles in the public debate on key issues. Jean-Pascal van Ypersele, vice-president of the Intergovernmental Panel on Climate Change (IPCC) which received a Nobel Prize in 2007, is one of the most involved Professors in the public debate about sustainable development.

Up to now, some twenty UCL researchers received the Francqui Prize, the most prestigious national scientific prize in Belgium. UCL also takes pride in having one of the largest number of ERC starting and senior grants in Belgium.

Partnerships, Innovation & Translational Research

Among the highlights, UCL has had a direct partnership with MIT ever since 1923; when Professor Georges Lemaitre (the father of the Big Bang theory) initiated the collaboration. Today, numerous other fields, like cryptology,are part of an intense exchange program.

The de Duve institute (in reference to Christian de Duve who received a Nobel Prize in 1974) is highly and directly connected with the American Ludwig Cancer Institute.

The internationally respected Hoover Chair in ethics, social, and political economy promotes a thorough interdisciplinary approach on a wide variety of issues and gathers researchers from the social sciences and humanities, medicine, science and technology.

Turning to the private sector, UCL has a fruitful collaboration with Glaxo SmithKline (GSK) regarding vaccines against cancer. That kind of collaboration has the financial support of European institutions, national and regional authorities. By the way, UCL has a whole department helping researchers find the most appropriate funding for their needs (Research Administration) and the Foundation Louvain, which is specialized in fundraising.

Vincent Yzerbyt, vice-rector for research, "Today, some 41% of our PhDs students and no less than 48% of our post-docs and researchers come from abroad. On top of an ideal location and a longstanding conviviality, what these people appreciate most is the high quality of the supervision and the state-of-the-art facilities (e.g. technology platforms), and help in identifying the most appropriate funding sources that best match their needs."

Bruno Delvaux, rector, "UCL strongly supports researchers in the promotion of their results through the Louvain Technology Transfer Office (LTTO). The LTTO helps bridge the gap between research laboratories and industry. The goal is to facilitate the flow from idea to market so as to contribute to regional economic development."

V.Y.: "Two major success stories of UCL spin-offs are IBA (Ion Beam Application) and IRIS. Both now are listed on the stock exchange. In 2012, UCL launched 6 spin-offs and sold 3. Needless to say, these revenues are reinvested in a series of new promising initiatives."

B.D.: "Another distinctive feature of UCL is its decision to anticipate our society's needs by means of the creation of multidisciplinary research centers. As a case in point, Louvain4Nutrition is an ambitious multidisciplinary center bringing together researchers from all corners

of science (bio-engineers, nutritionists, engineers, chemists, physicians, psychologists and economists...)"

In the "science & technology sector": Graphene — This year, UCL was chosen as a partner in a 1-billion Euro graphene project funded by the European Research Council. The goal of the Future Emerging Technology flagship "Graphene" is to take this revolutionary new material from academic laboratories to society, to revolutionize industries, to create economic growth and jobs. At the beginning, this consortium will coordinate 126 academics and industrial companies in 17 EU countries. The UCL team is involved in the spintronics work package.

In the field of "health science": MammoNote — One of the most recent successful spin-off companies to use technology developed at UCL is MammoNote. This uses a proprietary platform to identify, analyze and present signs of breast cancer. The Europe-based project has attracted interest from other parts of the world, including China.

In the field of "social science and humanities": Diabetes literacy — One of UCL's researchers coordinates an important EU project in order to enhance the effectiveness of diabetes self-management education of patients and to contribute to a comprehensive diabetes strategy at EU level. Its results will also be applicable to other chronic diseases where self-management plays a relevant role.

Teaching, Learning & Student Life

In terms of teaching, UCL is a trend setter using new pedagogical approaches and technologies: e-learning, learning's outcomes and other new concepts are applied every day like the "MOC" which allows teaching to 200,000 people. B.D.: "as you can see, UCL offers to researchers one of the best environments for doing research".

KU LEUVEN

Rank › 101 – 150

Name › Catholic University of Leuven
Region › Europe
Country › Belgium
Founded › 1425

www.kuleuven.be

Core Research Strengths

KU Leuven is a leading European research university dedicated to excellent research, high-quality education and service to society. Its sizeable academic staff conducts basic and applied research in a comprehensive range of disciplines. Its research activities are organised into three 'groups': Biomedical Sciences, Science, Engineering & Technology, and Humanities & Social Sciences.

All of the university's research activities have a strong European and international orientation, as evidenced by KU Leuven's role as a founding member of the League of European Research Universities (LERU). KU Leuven has been particularly successful in securing ERC grants (European Research Council) and projects in European Framework programs. KU Leuven is ranked among the top 10 European universities in European Framework funding. In terms of research output, KU Leuven consistently ranks among Europe's top 20 institutions.

The Biomedical Sciences Group conducts research at every link in the knowledge chain, from fundamental to clinical research, which allows discoveries made in the lab to be quickly developed into clinical treatments. This translational focus has produced excellent results: KU Leuven has discipline-leading research teams working in such areas as gastroenterology, immunology, transplant immunology and autoimmune disease. Its pioneering research approaches interact in multidisciplinary research collaborations such as the Leuven Medical Technology Centre (LMTC) and the Leuven Institute for Neurological diseases (LIND, with partnerships form IMEC and the Flemish Institute for Biotechnology).

The Science, Engineering & Technology Group conducts internationally renowned research in production engineering, material and nano sciences, computer science and microelectronics. Its researchers participate in some of Europe's most exciting research programs, including projects at CERN and ESRF. KU Leuven researchers play a leading role in investigating basic questions about the nature of matter and our universe. Accordingly, KU Leuven benefits from the generous support of both Flemish (FWO-Flanders, the Hercules Foundation and the Agency for Innovation IWT) and European research agencies.

Research within the Humanities & Social Sciences Group is characterised by its depth, diversity and multidisciplinary approach. Particular areas of focus are global governance, transition and market economics, and brain and cognitive sciences. The latter spans the multifaceted intersection between the humanities and neurosciences.

Major Discoveries

Major discoveries include the Tissue Plasminogen Activator (TPA), well known for its use in treating ailments such as blood clots, strokes and pulmonary embolisms, and pharmaceutical breakthroughs in the global fight against HIV/AIDS. Most recently, in an ophthalmology breakthrough, researchers developed an ocriplasmine enzyme to treat vitreomacular adhesion, a serious eye disease. The discovery was the result of years of research conducted together with the KU Leuven spin-off company Thrombogenics.

Partnerships, Innovation & Translational Research

KU Leuven established mainland Europe's first technology transfer office in the early 1970's, and has since strengthened its pioneering role as a world leader in this aspect of university research strategy. Multidisciplinary centres such as the Material Research Centre, the Centre for Drug Design and Discovery, the Genomics Core and many others are fertile platforms for further innovations.

Major discoveries in science and technology have been made in collaboration with the university's industry partners, both at the regional and international levels. KU Leuven has developed a dedicated valorisation strategy aimed at providing basic research for advanced industrial needs, and developing sustainable collaborations with industry partners. Leuven Measurement Systems (LMS) – one of the first KU Leuven spin-offs (founded 1980) and a world-leading provider of test and mechatronic simulation software and engineering services – epitomises the added value of university-industry partnerships. 100 spin-offs mainly in micro-electronics, bioengineering, biotechnology, software, data mining and management have been created in the past decades, currently employing more than 5,000 people. The university, with its portfolio of more than 400 patents, was recently ranked in the top 10 internationally in terms of license fees.

In addition, particular attention is paid to reciprocal knowledge transfer with developing countries. The university's Research for Development concept engages university partners worldwide and is particularly dedicated to creating sustainable solutions for local development in the South.

Teaching, Learning & Student Life

KU Leuven, including the academic degree programmes of 9 partner institutions, welcomes approximately 53,000 students – 15% of which are international from 140 countries to the picturesque, historical university town of Leuven. Students make up nearly half of the town's total population, creating a youthful, international and decidedly academic environment.

KU Leuven's centuries-strong position as a leading knowledge and training centre has its foundation in celebrated alumni such as Vesalius, Triverius, Rega and Erasmus. The direct and strong interface between research and teaching is central to the more than 235 degree programmes offered at the undergraduate, graduate and doctoral levels. Over 75 of these programmes are taught in English.

KU Leuven's doctoral schools organise internationally oriented PhD programmes for over 4,000 doctoral students. Both its international orientation and regional/local engagement are integral to KU Leuven's efforts to being a leading knowledge centre in Flanders, Europe and the wider world.

BCM
Baylor College of Medicine

Rank › 101 – 150

Name › Baylor College of Medicine
Region › Americas
Country › United States
Founded › 1900

www.bcm.edu

Core Research Strengths

Located in the Texas Medical Center, the world's largest medical research complex with more than US$14 billion in annual budget for all 54 member institutions, Baylor College of Medicine (BCM) is one of the world's foremost medical research institutions specialising in a diverse array of fields relating to the medical and life sciences.

BCM is ranked number three of all universities in the United States for national research funding in the biological sciences. It has more than US$363 million in total research support. BCM's position at the heart of the Texas Medical Center facilitates a thriving interdisciplinary research approach, whereby research discoveries are made at a high rate of frequency and the chance of them reaching the bedside for the benefit of society are far greater. The Baylor College of Medicine has more than 1 million square feet of laboratory space committed to full time research activity. The university works in partnership with 9 different affiliate hospitals developing clinical solutions to a diverse array of today's health challenges.

Particular areas of exceptional research excellence at BCM are molecular & cellular biology, genetics, genomics and bioinformatics with institutes such as; the Human Genome Sequencing Center, the Center for Cell and Gene Therapy at BCM, Texas Children's and The Methodist Hospital, and the National Center for Macromoelcular Imaging.

BCM also excels in cancer research with the National Cancer Institute-designated Dan L Duncan Cancer Center, and over US$87 million in funding from the Cancer Prevention and Research Institute of Texas (CPRIT). Established in 1996, the Baylor International Pediatric AIDS Initiative (BIPAI) positions BCM at the international forefront in working alongside children and families suffering the devastating effects of HIV / AIDS.

Through outreach centres in countries such as Botswana, Romania, Uganda, Lesotho, Swaziland, Malawi, and Tanzania, BIPAI has revolutionised the treatment of paediatric HIV / AIDS.

Major Discoveries

Baylor College of Medicine's leadership in biomedical research began with Dr. Michael E. DeBakey, who, in the 1950s, 1960s and 1970s, pioneered new surgical techniques in vascular repair and development of heart assisting devices. Dr. Roger Guillemin won the 1977 Nobel Prize in Medicine for his work on neuro-hormones whilst a faculty member at BCM.

Baylor College of Medicine's leadership in genome sequencing led to its designation as a major focus in completing the sequencing of the human genome and in later years, understanding of human variation and the microbiome.

Baylor genetics research, ranked number 1 in federal funding nationally, has led the way in development of mouse models of diseases and identification of important disease genes such as that for fragile X and Rett syndrome as well as understanding of the copy number variations that represent structural differences in human DNA.

Partnerships, Innovation & Translational Research

Baylor College of Medicine, since its birth in 1900, has a long and rich tradition of research collaboration within and outside its walls.

The Dan L. Duncan Institute for Clinical and Translational Research (ICTR) is a unique organisational arrangement, facilitating on-going collaborative, interdisciplinary and translational research amongst BCM and its Texas Medical Center partners.

The Baylor Licensing Group's (BLG) mission is to: "Maximize the impact of research at Baylor College of Medicine through commercial relationships that lead to the development of new products and services that benefit patients and the public." The BLG is the first point of contact for investors, businesses and service providers with an interest in licensing or investing in technology developed at BCM. Since 2007, BCM has averaged 82 new patent disclosures each year, 49 new licensing agreements, and US$10 million in licensing revenues annually.

Teaching, Learning & Student Life

The Baylor School of Medicine's location at the heart of the world's largest medical research complex, and affiliate agreements with nine partner hospitals facilitates a vast array of research exposure for medical students, as well as a myriad of choice in terms direct patient contact. Flexibility is one of the hallmarks of the BCM experience, with students given the option to combine a diverse array of specific disciplines depending upon their interests and long-term career aspirations.

The BCM Graduate School of Biomedical Sciences is among the top 10 per cent of U.S. graduate schools, according to U.S. News & World Report with degree programs in 12 different fields – from biochemistry and molecular biology to translational biology and molecular medicine.

The BCM School of Allied health Sciences is home to one of the oldest physician assistant training programs in the nation as well as one in nurse anaesthesia and the newly established master's degree program in orthotics and prosthetics.

The BCM National School of Tropical Medicine is the first such school in the U.S. solely committed to addressing the world's most pressing tropical disease issues.

Rank › 101 – 150

Name › Aix Marseille University
Region › Europe
Country › France
Founded › 2012 (historic 1409)

www.univ-amu.fr

Core Research Strengths

Following a major merger between the three campuses of Aix-Marseille on the 1st January 2012, Aix-Marseille University has now established itself as the largest university in France with over 70,000 students and approximately 7,500 personnel. Given the size and scale of the institution today, it is no surprise that Aix-Marseille has expertise throughout the entire spectrum of academic disciplines from arts, literature and social sciences, through to engineering and medicine.

Through the university's some 132 collaborative research structures, Aix-Marseille has adopted a targeted strategy addressing five major fields throughout the overall research enterprise. These focal points cover energy; environmental sciences, earth sciences and astronomy; life and health sciences, advanced sciences and technology; the humanities and social sciences. Akin to many other leading universities around the world, Aix-Marseille is now encouraging inter-disciplinary collaboration to drive knowledge growth in these areas.

The university's increasing emphasis on this approach has been rewarded significantly by the French government's "Investments for the Future" program with Aix-Marseille being awarded funding for a large number of major research projects.

Besides Aix-Marseille's growing inter-disciplinary aspirations, the university also is particularly renowned for its excellence in law. Originally founded in 1409, the law school is considered one of France's most influential institutions, with a long tradition of major contributions towards the evolution of France's legal framework.

Aix-Marseille has a particularly strong tradition in our understanding of, and ability to fight against infectious tropical diseases. Legendary French researcher Didier Raoult has been a pioneer in this field at the university. Raoult has been ranked as one of France's top ten most important researchers, producing approximately 1,000 academic papers throughout his career.

Partnerships, Innovation & Translational Research

Whilst industry collaboration remains at a relatively nascent stage in French academic institutions, Aix-Marseille collaborates closely with leading national research institutions such as CNRS and INSERM through the university's 14 collaborative institutes. Following the university's recent award of excellence as part of the French Excellence Initiative, Aix-Marseille's attractiveness and ambitions for international research partnerships have grown significantly. Aix-Marseille contributes to the broader economy in the region through its translational research operations and the university's overall ethos has become less averse to risk in recent years placing greater emphasis on the development of successful spin-out companies.

Some departments are more active in international student exchanges than others. For example, the Department of International Relations is particularly active on the European stage, proactively developing partnerships and exchange agreements throughout Europe so as to enhance the scope and effectiveness of the course program by developing students' international perspectives.

Teaching, Learning & Student Life

Considered to be France's oldest city with its origins in Ancient Greek civilization, as a bustling port and the country's second largest city, Marseille has a long tradition of international exchange and interaction. Whilst much of the charming old town remains to this day, students can also expect a bustling city with all manner of cultural, sporting and social opportunities.

With approximately 10,000 international students from 128 different countries in attendance at Aix-Marseille, the city's diversity is very much reflected in the cosmopolitan composition of the student body. With approximately 400 Erasmus partners, Aix Marseille's international mix does not end at home; students are encouraged to travel throughout Europe to further enhance their perspectives, and benefit from the different teaching and learning approaches one can expect throughout the continent.

Spread across five major campuses, with approximately 600 courses on offer for undergraduates, Aix-Marseille, as the world's largest Francophone university, offers a wealth of choice and variety in beautiful Mediterranean surroundings ideal for nourishing and nurturing bright young minds the world over.

OSAKA UNIVERSITY

Shining forth even into the 22ⁿᵈ century

Japan

KYOTO

KOBE

OSAKA

3 campuses

Suita

Toyonaka

Minoh

Students: Undergraduate: 15,541
Graduate: 6,469
International: 1,924 from 100 countries
http://www.osaka-u.ac.jp

To learn more, go to page 218

Why not choose OSAKA UNIVERSITY?

With roots stretching back to 1838, Osaka University was formally established as Japan's 6th imperial university in 1931 with two schools, Medicine and Science. Growing rapidly, Osaka University now boasts 11 undergraduate and 16 graduate schools as well as numerous outstanding research institutes and centers. What's more, graduate students pursuing master's and doctoral degrees can choose from among 49 majors.

With its three beautiful main campuses situated approximately halfway between Osaka and Kyoto cities, students can easily enjoy both the modern world and the classical, the latest and the timeless.

Whether it's biosciences, medicine, cognitive neuroscience, nanophotonics, areas in which Osaka University is a world leader or one of the 45 other majors, Osaka University is your door to the future!

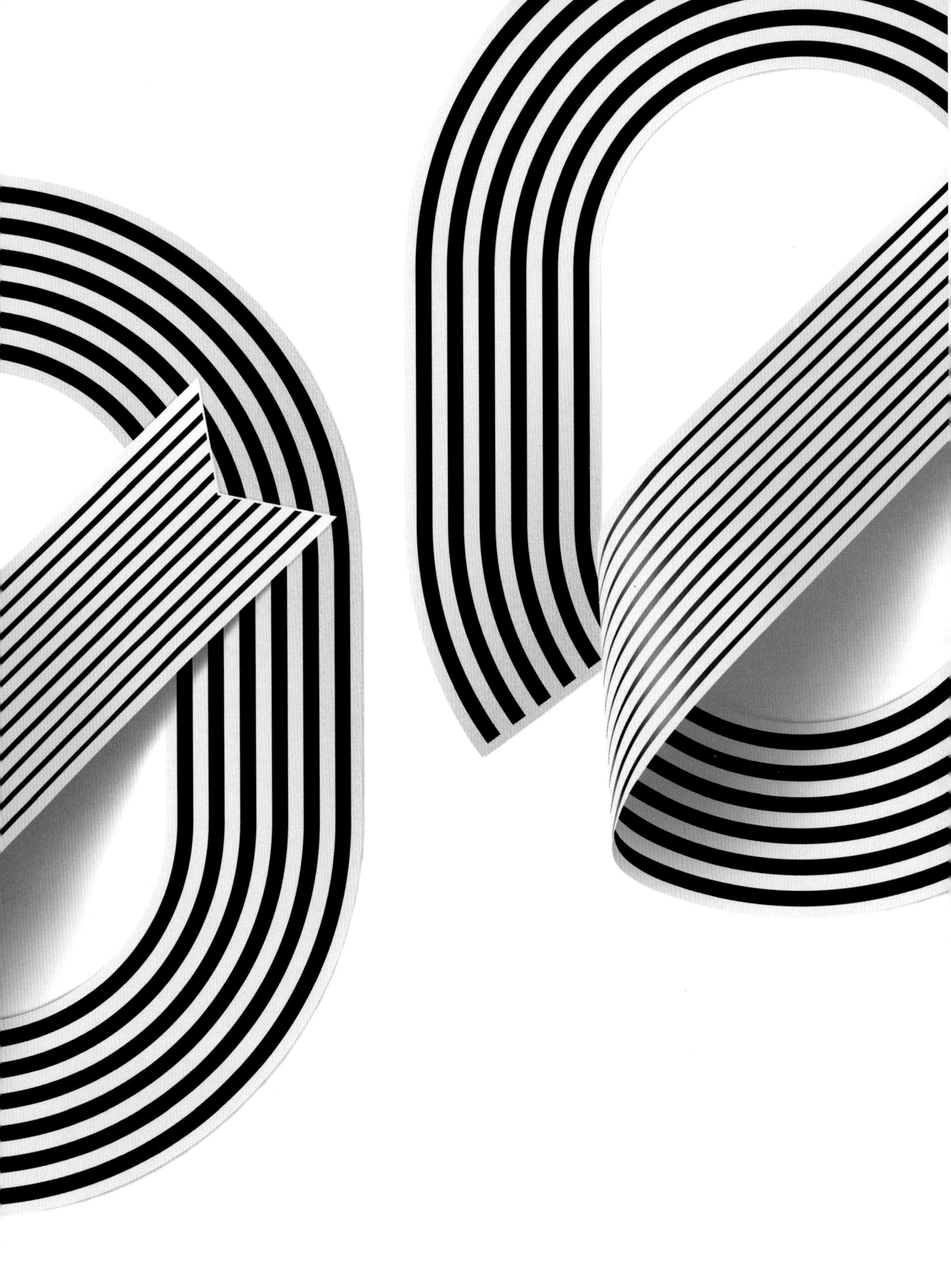

Name › University of Freiburg
Region › Europe
Country › Germany
Founded › 1457

www.uni-freiburg.de

Core Research Strengths

The University of Freiburg is one of Germany's oldest universities and has a tradition of research in the humanities, social sciences and natural sciences. Though these disciplines are still quite important to the university, it has also created a new 'triangle of research' between medicine, biology and engineering, explains Rector Hans-Jochen Schiewer.

"Since the mid-1990s, when the faculty of engineering was established, the university has worked to enhance its spectrum of applied research and find common avenues for joint work with the life sciences. One of today's challenges, which this triumvirate has been summoned to deal with, is brain disease. Our cluster of excellence 'Brain Links-Brain Tools' was designed, for example, to allow for complex studies that may bring relief for patients with Parkinson's."

This comprehensive character, which allows the university to pool disciplinary expertise to address key challenges, is also evident regarding the issue of 'security and society'. "Our departments of social and behavioural sciences, law and computer sciences work together to find solutions for critical problems such as data protection and data sharing, video surveillance and other security and resilience problems requiring technical and legal innovations that are in the interests of society. These solutions require a transdisciplinary approach. So, you see," explains Rector Schiewer, "this is a clear advantage of our institutional structure. We have excellent conditions for conducting broad-based, problem-oriented research for complex societal issues".

The university also has an interdisciplinary program in the area of "sustainability science". Research on environmental and sustainability issues are at the core of current strategic endeavours to strengthen the scientific profile of the university. "Since the University of Freiburg has long been active in the area of forestry sciences, there was a good working basis, upon which we were able to develop the new approach of sustainability science."

Major Discoveries

Throughout its illustrious history the University of Freiburg has been home to 10 Nobel laureates, while 13 of its academics have been honoured with the Gottfried Wilhelm Leibniz Prize – Germany's most distinguished research award. Two of the most influential philosophers of the 20th century, Edmund Husserl and Martin Heidegger, were also among the many bright minds at Freiburg.

Partnerships, Innovation & Translational Research

In recent years Freiburg has worked to increase the commercialisation of its research, says Rector Schiewer. "We support technology transfer into new and established companies. In Germany, we belong to the top group of universities for their high number of patents. With X-ray imaging and magnetic resonance imaging we have had some real success."

The university's commercialisation strategy is also shaped by regional policies. It is involved in several region-wide clusters combining research institutions, universities and industries. "Together with roughly 150 companies, we're trying to re-create the Upper Rhine Valley as the prime address for microsystems technologies", says the Rector.

The university also works with third-party organisations, in particular the Fraunhofer Society. It's a partnership that brings many benefits, explains Rector Schiewer. "We have a joint professorship and a joint program for continuing education called FAST –Freiburg Academy of Science and Technology – where we invite people from companies in the industrial sector and R&D departments to work with our scientists, explore new methods, and transport their ideas back into the industrial chain."

Teaching, Learning & Student Life

The curricular profile at the University of Freiburg is very attractive for students, says the Rector. "Our high quality of teaching is a prerequisite for the students' decision to study here. Our teachers and teaching programs win prizes regularly in national and international competitions." Here, too, Freiburg has a strong interdisciplinary focus. "We're convinced that problem-oriented teaching requires not only a clear concentration on a specific course of study, but should also allow flexibility to include other academic perspectives." That's why Freiburg also offers a variety of programs – 180+ courses of study – including a Bachelor of Liberal Arts and Sciences.

Furthermore, since Freiburg is very close to the French and Swiss border, the university has established partnerships with universities in Strasbourg and in Basel. This tri-national partnership allows students to take seminars and attend lectures at all three institutions, for which they receive credit points at their home universities. They can even combine programs of study. "This has proven quite attractive for many of our students", explains the Rector.

Freiburg has many extra-curricular advantages, as well. Located amidst the Rhine River valley and the mountains of the Black Forest, it has stunning landscapes. The great natural diversity and good, sunny weather makes it a perfect place to enjoy outdoor activities like hiking, mountain biking and skiing. The city has plenty of merit, too. It has a high standard of living and its inhabitants are friendly and environmentally conscious. Indeed, Freiburg is known nationwide as ' the green city', which is also reflected in the fact that the two most common forms of transportation here are bicycles and trams.

Name › Case Western Reserve University
Region › Americas
Country › United States
Founded › 1826

www.case.edu

Core Research Strengths

Thanks to an annual research budget of almost $400 million per year, Case Western Reserve University (CWRU) can support an extensive network of academic infrastructure. Occupying approximately 80% of the research budget, the medical sciences are the dominant field followed by engineering. CWRU's comprehensive portfolio however, enables the university to develop excellence in interdisciplinary fields such as health law. CWRU has more than 2,600 full-time faculty members, and hundreds more postdoctoral fellows that conduct research. This 'know how' is backed up by around 100 dedicated research institutes and an array of world-class libraries.

So far the university's heavy investment in research appears to be paying off, says President Barbara R. Snyder. Indeed, success is breeding success, and the university is now becoming a magnet for funding. "We recently won our second Clinical and Translational Sciences Award. This is an award from the National Institutes of Health, and equates to $64 million of funding for five years. We won this five years ago too, so, this is a renewal. That reflects our commitment to bring our research discoveries; we like to say, from lab to life."

One of the best things about this "lab to life" philosophy, says President Snyder, is that researchers know that their work has the potential to end up improving lives. "Those discoveries actually inform patient care in hospitals and doctors' offices all over the world. One of the best examples involved one of our neuroscience professors, Dr. Gary Landreth. He discovered that an already existing FDA-approved drug that is currently used for cancer treatment had dramatic results in reversing the symptoms of cognitive decline in mice that were genetically engineered to have Alzheimer's disease, and they have showed these improvements within quite a short time after receiving the drug."

The university's engineering department's research is also yielding results that could transform society, says the President. "Our school of engineering was part of the consortium that won a $30 million federal grant to service a national model for the development of more efficient and innovative manufacturing processes, which we think will help this part of our country recover some of its manufacturing expertise."

Major Discoveries

The President's point about discoveries leading to societal good is supported by the university's list of Nobel Prize winners. CWRU has 15 Nobel Laureates to its name, with one of the most recent coming in 2003 when alumni Paul C. Lauterbur won the Nobel Prize in Medicine for discoveries concerning magnetic resonance imaging.

Partnerships, Innovation & Translational Research

Whereas some universities are only beginning to work with the private sector, for Case Western Reserve it has long been part of its raison d'être. After all, it's hard for a discovery to benefit society if it remains in the laboratory. In general, CWRU has a two-pronged approach to its interaction with the private sector. With some discoveries it licences the technology to an established player in the market. That allows Case Western Reserve to receive a royalty stream without taking commercial risk. Another option is for the university to create a start-up. "About once every five years we spin out a company that's based on technology developed by our faculty members", says President Snyder. "For example, we have a great young company called Thermalin that is based on the research of one of our physician scientists in biochemistry, who has developed a number of analogues for insulin, some of which are stable at room temperature and stable at body temperature.

Teaching, Learning & Student Life

Situated on the shores of the massive Lake Erie, Cleveland is sometimes known by locals as the North Coast. The waterfront makes for a picturesque setting and students who need a break from work can wander along the lake's edge and take in attractions such as Cleveland's famous Rock and Roll Hall of Fame. One of the best things about studying at CWRU is that students don't have to travel far to experience some of the best that Cleveland has to offer. That's because the campus is situated in a part of town known as University Circle.

Back in class, students will benefit from the university's determination to involve everyone from undergraduates up in research. In most cases students will conduct multidisciplinary research, mixing with peers from other disciplines, says President Snyder.

"In addition to courses that are co-taught or cross-listed across disciplinary boundaries, we also have numerous other opportunities for students to observe faculty working together in labs. They get to see these faculty members collaborating and what that really means."

"We find that it influences our students. At the undergraduate level, our students often pursue multiple majors or multiple majors and minors with very interesting combinations, and at the graduate level, many of the programmes are interdisciplinary by design, and even those that aren't involved a lot of cross boundary, taking up courses in interaction as dissertations are being prepared"

Another plus are the intimate classes. Right across the board, from engineering courses to dance workshops, there is a 9:1 student-to-faculty ratio, ensuring one-on-one attention from professors, as well as vigorous class discussions that challenge perspectives and nurture new understandings.

THE UNIVERSITY OF WESTERN AUSTRALIA
Achieve International Excellence

Name › The University of Western Australia
Region › Asia/Pacific
Country › Australia
Founded › 1911

www.uwa.edu.au

Core Research Strengths

The University of Western Australia has a long and notable reputation for research and is known as the second-most research-intensive university in the country on a per capita basis. This focus is spread across nine faculties, however, Vice Chancellor Paul Johnson believes that agriculture, life sciences, biomedical science and medicine are particularly strong.

But the Vice Chancellor also acknowledges that it is difficult to fairly compare the performance of science-based subjects with those that are rooted in the arts. "We have an excellent school of music. We also have Australia's largest centre of excellence, I think probably the biggest centre of excellence ever, and that is funded to research the history of emotions. It focuses on medieval and early modern history, art, literature, music, and performance. It's a world-class research centre but humanities research isn't measured in the same way as the sciences, with the various metrics used there. So, it's always difficult to say how to rank them."

Major Discoveries

One of the most notable discoveries emerging from UWA was when Barry Marshall and Robin Warren, discovered that the Helicobacter Pylori bacterium was responsible for stomach ulcers. It was truly ground-breaking because pharmaceutical companies had been unsuccessfully searching for a cure for years. The discovery led to the development of an effective treatment and the pair were awarded the Nobel Prize for Physiology in 2005 in recognition of the fact that they had eased suffering for millions of people.

Partnerships, Innovation & Translational Research

Thanks to the China-led commodity boom, Western Australia's economy has grown at a rapid rate. Total state product in Western Australia grew by 14.2% in 2012, fuelling a huge investment boom. Indeed Perth has now joined Aberdeen and Houston as one of the three global hubs for the offshore gas and petroleum industry. Perth is also the global hub for the minerals

industry with the a significant proportion of both BHP Billiton and Rio Tinto's staff located there.

All that growth, says Vice Chancellor Johnson, has had a profound effect on the University: "We work closely with industry, particularly in energy and minerals. We were recently the first of 10 universities worldwide to sign agreements with Rio Tinto as a global education partner. We work closely with all the big players. We run research programs with Shell, Chevron, Rio, BHP and many other companies too. We do some research with some of these companies, which is very much at the forefront of what they can do in their businesses."

Another key interaction between the University and private-sector partners is through technology transfer. UWA has established the Office of Industry and Innovation as the interface for external partners. In addition to a dedicated office, the Vice Chancellor says that technology transfer happens in a lot of different ways.

"We do it by talking to people. By that I mean we do some of it through either a joint venture or a shareholding in start-up companies. We also have a number of start-up companies in which we have equity shares. But in the main, technology transfer is done through existing companies rather than start-ups. A lot of it is done in a semi or actually in a completely informal way. That is, it's done through the personal links and connections that individuals have rather than almost on a cross-institutional basis."

Teaching, Learning & Student Life

Situated on Western Australia's Swan River, five kilometres from the centre of Perth, UWA is widely acclaimed for its national-heritage listed grounds. The University's population comprises more than 24,000 students drawn from 80 countries. These students enjoy some of the best student facilities in Australia, on a campus renowned for its vibrant social, cultural and sporting life as well as its environmental beauty.

When it comes to studies UWA has, like leading international universities, completely remodelled its degree courses. The new model is similar to

what you find in many North American universities, says Vice Chancellor Johnson. "We have revised 70 or so different undergraduate degree programs and we have replaced them with 5 programs; science, arts, design, commerce and an undergraduate research-intensive degree called the Bachelor of Philosophy (Honours). All professional courses, such as Medicine, Law, Teaching and Engineering are offered at the postgraduate Masters level. The courses have been reshaped to ensure our graduates continue to be equipped for success in today's rapidly changing world."

"So, while a student might enrol in a Bachelor of Science, for example, they will take a number of subjects aside of their area of concentration, from outside of their faculty. So, we build a considerable amount of diversity and cross-disciplinary work into the program," says Professor Johnson.

NAGOYA
UNIVERSITY

Name › Nagoya University
Region › Asia/Pacific
Country › Japan
Founded › 1871

www.nagoya-u.ac.jp

Core Research Strengths

First established in 1871 as a temporary medical school, Nagoya University (NU) has since undergone several transitions and is now widely regarded as one of the world's foremost research universities. Whilst staying close to NU's traditions with great strength in the medical sciences, the university has since evolved in parallel with its host city Nagoya, with great strength in depth throughout countless academic disciplines ranging from the most fundamental questions associated with the origins of the universe, to some of today's most pressing challenges associated with sustainable energy and transportation.

NU's expertise in the medical sciences is particularly extensive. Drawing upon disciplinary excellence in areas such as biology and chemistry, the recently established Graduate School of Pharmaceutical Sciences connects fundamental research with today's illnesses by pioneering the development of new medicines enshrined in an institution strongly focused on translational research. NU's leadership in translational research is further extended by the Graduate School of Medicine, bringing together 85 affiliate hospitals, the most extensive such network of a Japanese medical school.

Nagoya University's culture of collaboration and democracy facilitates their pioneering approach to interdisciplinary research; President Michinari Hamaguchi best provides an insight into the university's atmosphere: "Our principles of Openness, Transparency and Democracy have set the foundation for the culture of collaboration and partnership at Nagoya University. Our fundamental missions of encouraging and fostering great young talent, and the development of new innovations for the benefit of society benefit a great deal from our cultural environment".

NU's collaborative culture manifests itself in the myriad of interdisciplinary research institutes at the university investigating a multitude of today's most complex questions such as the Green Mobility Collaborative Research Center, the Plasma Nanotechnology Research Center, the National Composite Research Center, the Synchotron Radiation Research Center and the Research Center for Material Science. The Kobayashi-Maskawa Institute for the Origin of Particles and the Universe (KMI) typifies NU's place at the cutting edge of interdisciplinary research. Drawing upon expertise in many sub-disciplines of physics, mathematics and computer science in order to pursue the creation of new paradigms in our understanding of particle physics beyond the standard model.

Drawing together some of the most exciting young talent through the World Premium Initiative (WPI), the Institute of Transformative Bio-Molecules is another such example of world class collaborative research at Nagoya University. Led by Professor Kenichiro Itami, the institute is working toward the development of transformative bio-molecules that will help solve some of today's most urgent challenges at the interface of chemistry and biology.

Major Discoveries

2008 – Professor Osamu Shimomura in Chemistry for his work on Green Fluorescence Protein

2008 – Professors Toshihide Maskawa & Makoto Kobayashi for their work in particle physics – notably CP violation and quarks

Partnerships, Innovation & Translational Research

With over 100 multinational companies such as the automotive behemoth Toyota having their headquarters in the Greater Nagoya region, NU's collaborative culture has led to the development of long lasting research collaborations alongside some of Japan's most competitive industries. Nagoya's growing international profile inevitably opens the door for mutually collaborative efforts alongside multinationals based outside of Japan. The university's expertise in the automotive sector, material and medical sciences provide particularly excellent opportunities for external partnerships.

Far from being limited to domestic, private sector research partnerships, NU's leadership is extended to the international scale with groups such as the Academic Consortium 21; an international network of leading universities promoting in depth research collaborations. NU has also taken the lead in the internationalization of Japan's universities with its membership and pivotal role in organisations such as the G30, Campus ASEAN and Campus Asia – East Asia's equivalent to the EU's Erasmus Mundus program.

Teaching, Learning & Student Life

Nagoya University is without a doubt, Japan's foremost innovator in its approach to facilitating the attendance of international students. Traditionally dominated by international attendees from Eastern Asia, NU has now introduced 500 different courses in the English language so as to broaden the appeal for students at the global level. Universities such as NU have long been revered for their outstanding capabilities in research; however have long been considered difficult to attend because of the language barrier. This remarkable reform distinguishes Nagoya in Japan as an institution that has truly opened its doors to the international community.

Vice President for International Affairs Yoshihito Watanabe discusses NU's revolutionary approach: "Traditionally Japanese universities have had very little English Language instruction, thus their international profile has suffered. NU has a clear vision for growth as an international university, this reform is a vital component of seeing our international strategy realised. We had to convince the faculty to get behind this reform, after some discussion they saw the benefits too and are fully behind Nagoya University's international ambitions."

Nagoya is more of an intimate city environment than counterparts such as Tokyo, with students benefiting from a significant reduction in living expenses and more of a manageable size city to get to know whilst studying. Nagoya's industrial traditions present substantive benefits for students with 95% of the university's student population having received job offers before graduation. With student fees in the region of US$6000 per annum for undergraduates, Nagoya's focus on English language instruction makes it a genuine consideration for students the world over.

MICHIGAN STATE
UNIVERSITY

Name › Michigan State University
Region › Americas
Country › United States
Founded › 1855

www.msu.edu

Core Research Strengths

With external funding exceeding $500 million annually, most of which supports research, Michigan State University is among the top research universities in the world. Founded in 1855 to combine practical agricultural instruction with a liberal education, it became a prototype for publicly supported, land-grant universities in the United States.

The university's mission is closely aligned with the needs of society, says President Lou Anna K Simon. "We're a community-based institution in the largest sense and we want our work to benefit those around us." The city of Detroit proves a fertile ground for outreach and research. MSU is currently conducting a programme there investigating how to develop urban food systems to serve an increasingly metropolitan, hungry and thirsty world.

The programme is just one example of the university's expertise in "human coupled systems", says the President. "We look at how humans and the evolution of our planet come together in ways that may be positive or negative. We have scientists working in all aspects of the environment from water to air quality to the great rivers of the world. You can take any aspect of the environment and find MSU faculty working in Michigan and around the world."

Another core strength is nuclear sciences. That may seem an odd choice, concedes President Simon, but it has its roots in the 1960s. "At the time we were very strong in physics in general and we decided to develop expertise in nuclear sciences. Now our graduate nuclear physics program is number one in the country."

The university is working with the U.S. Department of Energy to develop a $680 million Facility for Rare Isotope Beams on campus. "It's an exciting frontier of work in astrophysics as well as more fundamental nuclear physics", says President Simon.

Major Discoveries

Given the university's strength in physics it is little surprise that the discipline yielded the institution's most recent Nobel Prize. In 2007, adjunct professor Albert Fert shared the Nobel Prize in Physics for his work on giant magnetoresistance. However, more important, in terms of human impact, was Michigan State's role in the development of cisplatin/carboplatin, cancer drugs that have saved millions of lives.

Partnerships, Innovation & Translational Research

Michigan State University has a strong history of successful partnerships with the business community, but to provide better service it recently consolidated its technology transfer, entrepreneurship and business liaison offices under the MSU Innovation Center umbrella. The university has long been recognized for its strength in international engagement going back to the 1950s when it was the first major U.S. university to name a dean for international programs.

Today, MSU is one of only four higher education institutions in the U.S. to rank in the top 10 both for study abroad participation and international student enrolment. Nearly 1,400 faculty members are involved in international research, teaching, and service projects.

But the most important aspect of MSU's internationalisation strategy is that it improves lives, says President Simon. "Our work with malaria comes out of our deep commitment to Africa, and we were very pleased that we were able to work with GE Healthcare to get the first MRI unit into Malawi. Now a major study on childhood malaria using that equipment has the potential to drastically change the lives of children".

Teaching, Learning & Student Life

Spread over a leafy 5,000 acre campus in East Lansing, Michigan, the university offers students the archetypal 'American university experience'. "It is one of the biggest, greenest campuses in the nation", says President Simon. "And that helps create a great atmosphere for students." Michigan State opened a stunning new art museum in 2012 designed by London-based architect Zaha Hadid.

"We're one of the few universities of our size and calibre that admits students to the university, not to a particular college. As a result we have a common liberal education labelled integrative studies. The core courses students take don't just 'check the box' for distribution requirements, they work together to provide not only discipline-specific content but also to teach how scientists approach their work, how humanists pursue truth".

And at Michigan State, with its history of research stations dotted across the state, and now research around the world, there is the will to integrate scholarship across boundaries and distance. "There's an approach that encourages joint programs across the colleges. We pride ourselves on the number of joint appointments rather than creating separate institutes, which carry a lot of overhead and are not as adaptable as they need to be. We do a lot of joint appointments with new faculty—in health, engineering and the sciences, for example—to be able to organically grow these relationships from the time people start at Michigan State. That's part of the culture."

WEIZMANN INSTITUTE OF SCIENCE

Name › Weizmann Institute of Science
Region › Asia/Pacific
Country › Israel
Founded › 1934

www.weizmann.ac.il

Core Research Strengths

The Weizmann Institute's annual budget stands at over a billion shekels. An allocation from the government of Israel covers about one third of the budget; the rest is provided by research grants, donations and an endowment fund accrued from various sources.

The Weizmann Institute of Science has a rather distinctive research approach, says President Daniel Zajfman. "We are focused in what we call basic research; because we believe that new innovations or new ideas start out from understanding underlying scientific principles. If you look at the history of science, you will find that most discoveries have not been made by trying to solve a problem, but through the attempt to understand how nature works; so our focus is on understanding."

The institute's main research strengths are in biology, says the President. "We are investing $100 million in a National Centre for Personalized Medicine – which is a major investment in biomedical research. Our goal is to establish a national platform that can be used by all researchers in the field of biomedical research, life sciences, and in general, so that everyone from physicians to academic scientists will have the best data available for their research. We have additional programs in alternative energies, interplanetary science, robotics, and more, but our core strength is in the foundation of science: mathematics and computer science, physics, chemistry, biochemistry and biology."

Another distinctive element of research at Weizmann is the strong emphasis on working across disciplines. It serves as a meeting place for scientists from different areas of science, setting the stage for multidisciplinary collaborations and the emergence of new research fields. To encourage this creative activity, the Institute has created some 50 research institutes and centres, most of which provide an intellectual rather than physical framework for joint projects.

Major Discoveries

One of the institute's most well-known discoveries was Ada E Yonath's solving of the structure and function of the ribosome. She was awarded with the 2009 Nobel Prize in Chemistry. Other Institute discoveries include Copaxone®, for multiple sclerosis, which is Israel's first ethical drug; and a method for visual data summarization that was recently licensed to Adobe Systems Inc.

Partnerships, Innovation & Translational Research

One of the institute's main interactions with the world of finance and industry comes through Yeda Research and Development Company Ltd., which promotes the industrial applications stemming from Institute research. Since being founded in 1959, it has been involved in registering some 1,400 families of patents.

"We have patents in the world of computer science, algorithms, nanotechnology and drugs, so there is a breadth of technology out there," says President Zajfman. "In 2011, $20 billion worth of products marketed had their origins in Weizmann's license."

The reasons for the success are simple says the President. "If you really focus on outstanding people, and if you support them, these people will produce ideas that can be commercialised. The idea of technology transfer is to provide knowledge to industry. It is up to industry to take that knowledge, invest in it and transform it into a product that is marketable."

The institute also works hard to expand its international academic reach. Each year, around 500 scientists from dozens of countries around the globe visit the Weizmann Institute or come to work on its campus.

Teaching, Learning & Student Life

The Weizmann Institute is located in the town of Rehovot, which is close to Jerusalem and Tel Aviv. Rehovot was one of the first communities founded in the modern State of Israel, and it has grown into a city of 114,000 people that is known for its science and culture.

Perhaps one of the most important things to stress to international students is that the city has a very friendly feel with none of the divisions found in other Israeli cities. For example, there are no areas that are completely religious or secular, although there is a small neighbourhood in which streets are closed to traffic on the Sabbath.

The campus is very close-knit, says President Zajfman. "Another unique thing at the Weizmann Institute is the fact that more than half of our faculty are actually living on the campus grounds. This is where the most important science often takes place. Weekends and nights, kids are playing in the playground while their parents talk science."

Another attractive factor for prospective students is the near-total intellectual freedom, says the President. "Here you can focus on one research topic, but you can approach that topic from many different groups and disciplines. It doesn't matter which subject you break your scientific 'teeth' on – and that's the strength of interdisciplinary research. So, for instance, we have many students in physics and mathematics doing their PhD studies with biology professors. It is up to the professor to accept that the students can make the best use of their knowledge. We have seen that they come up with amazing results. The environment is extremely comfortable, and the labs are very well equipped. We provide something really important – something that is too often missing in the world: That is the freedom to think."

THE UNIVERSITY OF SYDNEY

Name › University of Sydney
Region › Asia/Pacific
Country › Australia
Founded › 1850

www.sydney.edu.au

Core Research Strengths

The University of Sydney is a leading comprehensive research and teaching university committed to the transformative power of education and to fostering greater knowledge and understanding of the world and its people. The University is unique among Australia's leading universities in the breadth of disciplines it offers and has more than 50,000 enrolled students, around a fifth of whom originally come from more than 140 other countries.

The University's research strategy aims to deliver multidisciplinary solutions to real-world problems, by uniting the expertise of bright minds. It recognises the limitations of traditional disciplinary boundaries in combatting the problems facing 21st-century society. As a result, Sydney has committed significant support and large-scale investment to help researchers explore new frontiers of knowledge in areas of national and global importance.

One key multidisciplinary initiative is the Charles Perkins Centre, which aims to ease the burden of obesity, diabetes and cardiovascular disease – the leading causes of mortality and disease burden in the developed world and increasingly so in many developing countries. The University is creating an AU$385 million research and education hub that will house 1000 researchers and new facilities. University Provost Professor Stephen Garton believes this approach will push the frontiers of knowledge.

"This is really bringing in all of our traditional health disciplines at the clinical and translational end, along with all the basic sciences such as molecular biology, chemistry, nutrition and dietetics, as well as the social sciences such as health economics and moral philosophy … to try and tackle major world problems of enormous significance," he says.

Funding agencies recognise the success and impact of Sydney research, and the University is among the highest recipients of competitive funding in Australia. The University also has more higher degree research students than any other university in the country.

This reputation is well deserved. The 2012 Excellence in Research for Australia government benchmarking exercise found that 75 percent of almost 100 academic fields assessed at the University of Sydney performed above world standard. The University's expertise crosses areas that include agricultural sciences, medical sciences, law, engineering, mathematics, physics and computer science.

Major Discoveries

Two major recent discoveries by University researchers include firstly, Dr Mike Biercuk's findings on quantum computing that will enable the completion of enormous calculations beyond the capability of classical computers. His international team's research with a 300-atom quantum simulator was published in the prestigious journal, Nature, and was listed in 'the 10 world-changing experiments that will shape the future' in BBC Focus magazine.

Secondly, Professor Salah Sukkarieh leads a team that has used specially designed robotic devices to increase efficiency and yield in farming and agriculture. The devices can autonomously sense, analyse and respond to their own surroundings. This automated approach has the potential to help Australia boost its crop production significantly and become the 'food bowl' of Asia.

Partnerships, Innovation & Translational Research

The University of Sydney's collaborationis strengthened by its partnerships with industry, universities, international institutions and other countries. A current area of focus is developing Australia's relationships with its geographical neighbours. For example, the University's China Studies Centre works in partnership with Chinese academia and business to better understand China's impact on the world and Australia, and improve cooperation and relations. It contributes to real-world discussions about enhancing the economic relationship between the two countries at the annual Sydney China Business Forum. The University was ranked fifth best in the world for research collaborations with Chinese academics.

Even closer to Australia, the Sydney Southeast Asia Centre brings together around 190 academics, teachers and researchers from more than a dozen faculties to forge an innovative and engaged approach to that region. Centre representatives have visited Thailand and Laos to showcase Sydney research and how it can contribute to policy-making and development in the region.

At the translational end of the research spectrum, the University helps researchers capitalise on their ideas and innovations by finding the right partners and safeguarding researchers' rights. Last year, it entered into a four-year partnership with Qantas to develop a flight-planning system that will help the airline fly optimised routes, reduce fuel consumption and improve its operations.

Teaching, Learning & Student Life

The University is also reinvigorating its teaching programs. To ensure undergraduate students have an in-depth education and to prepare them for the workforce, the University offers them community-based learning and industry placement options through an extensive network of Australian and international partners. Research students are offered support in areas critical to translating their breakthroughs into real change, such as communication skills and project management.

Outside the classroom, the University offers a vibrant, active and dynamic life that reflects its diversity and high-quality experience and includes more than 200 clubs and societies. The National Union of Students rates the University's support for student life as the best in Australia.

TEXAS A&M
UNIVERSITY

Name › Texas A&M University
Region › Americas
Country › United States
Founded › 1876

www.tamu.edu

Core Research Strengths

With a massive research budget, in excess of $705 million per year, Texas A&M ranks in the top tier of global research institutes. It is one of a select few academic institutions in the United States to hold triple federal designations as a land-grant, sea-grant and space-grant university.

This special status has a significant impact on the university's research, says President R. Bowen Loftin. "We have for over 50 years operated a campus in Galveston, Texas, on the Gulf of Mexico. Here on our main campus in College Station, Texas, we are landlocked. We have a presence on the coast and that, along with a very large Oceanography Department in College Station, provides us the ability to really tackle some very difficult issues involving the world's oceans. So, we think the Sea Grant capability helps us to project ourselves in that very complex, but very important part of the research portfolio we have.

Historically Texas A&M has excelled in research focussing on engineering and agriculture, says the President.

"We have one of the largest engineering colleges in the world here with about 13,000 students and a goal to increase enrolment to 25,000 by the year 2025. So, that strength of sheer numbers, shall we say, of faculty, of graduate students, undergraduates, in engineering, for example, does strengthen that program immensely. Agriculture, of course, historically has been large. We have one of the largest agricultural colleges in the country as well. Again, size does bring some success."

But the President is also keen to highlight some of the university's emerging research strengths.
"Our business school has been climbing up the rankings recently. We also have a very highly regarded school of architecture here, and have been doing some amazing work with life sciences."

Major Discoveries

University professors, researchers and students have made many notable discoveries over the years. Yet the one that has had the most recent impact,

was Dr. Steve Holditch's pioneering work with an alternative drilling technique known as "fracking". Thanks in part to his work, American energy companies have been able to tap unconventional reserves of gas and oil, setting the country on the path to energy independence.

Partnerships, Innovation & Translational Research

Texas A&M holds great potential in working with the private sector, says the President. "We do recognize the great value of having corporations integrated with us. Working with them keeps our educational programming relevant, and keeps our research programming relevant. We believe that industry provides us with an alternative revenue source, along with government funding for research."

To that end, one of the university's chief assets is its 400-acre Research Park. This holds ten diversified facilities and more than 500,000 square feet of space for innovative companies and organizations focused on transferring new technologies into the marketplace.

Meanwhile the success of its commercialisation strategy is reflected in the fact that in 2012 the Texas A&M System's Office of Technology Commercialization formed five start-up companies and executed 68 licensing agreements, disclosed 211 new inventions, received 29 issued patents, and filed 93 new U.S. and foreign patent applications.

The university is equally active with academic partnerships and has 122 formal agreements for collaborative research and faculty or student exchanges with 39 countries and active research programmes on all seven continents.

Teaching, Learning & Student Life

The first thing people notice about Texas A&M is the size. With 50,000 students and a physical campus of more than 5,200 acres, it is also among the United State's largest universities both in terms of enrolment and facilities.

Located in College Station, which is located about 90 miles northwest

of Houston, Texas A&M is home to the George Bush Presidential Library and Museum, in addition to other museums and art galleries. More than 1,200 public events are hosted through the university each year, including Broadway shows, concerts, performances and athletic contests. Moreover the university is very inclusive with 25% of students participating in one of the nation's largest university intramural sports programs.

The town itself is small, but intimate. In fact, College Station was recently recognized as the top "college town" in the United States. But those seeking more adventure shouldn't worry as it is located within the most populated region of Texas, near three of the 10 largest cities in the United States – Houston, Dallas, and San Antonio. There are also lots of natural features to enjoy. For example, the local climate is subtropical and temperate and winters are mild with periods of low temperatures usually lasting less than two months, while the nearby area lakes cover 180,000 acres and offer many water-based activities.

Another big attraction for students is the high calibre of staff. Close to 80% of Texas A&M's 2,754 faculty members hold doctoral degrees; more than 300 hold endowed chairs or professorships, including three Nobel Prize recipients, 16 members of the National Academy of Engineering, seven members of the National Academy of Sciences and a member of the Institute of Medicine of the National Academies. Thanks to this array of research and teaching talent, Texas A&M offers more than 120 undergraduate degree programs and 240 master's and Ph.D. programs, as well as a doctorate in veterinary medicine.

McMaster University

Name › McMaster University
Region › Americas
Country › Canada
Founded › 1887

www.mcmaster.ca

Core Research Strengths

McMaster is a public, research-intensive university whose main campus is located in Hamilton, Ontario, Canada. The University is home to close to 30,000 students and operates six academic faculties: engineering, health sciences, humanities, social sciences, science, and the DeGroote School of Business. It is also a member of the U15, a group of research-intensive universities in Canada.

With a total sponsored research income of C$345 million, the federal government is the largest source of funding, providing 57% of McMaster's research budget, while industrial partnerships contribute around 12%. McMaster is a broad based research institution, known for its distinct teaching style and strengths across many disciplines. It has historic strength in health sciences with its medical school ranked first in Canada and 14th in the world. "In this area in particular we have delivered some ground breaking work in the fields of stem cells, infectious diseases and cardiovascular research," says President Patrick Deane.

True to the University's interdisciplinary philosophy, research on human health and wellness is conducted in virtually every faculty. Emerging areas of research strength centre on aging, infectious diseases, and water. The university also shows strength in engineering. "At present a lot of our research is now being directed towards sustainable automotive options, and we have had some very substantial investments from government in that area."

Other areas of significant work are: ground breaking research conducted in the faculty of science, where researchers are working to help people with spinal cord injury walk again; the continued importance and relevance of the contemporary humanities to broader society; the innovative learning that takes place at the Ron Joyce Centre, home of the University's MBA and executive education program. And he points to another important strength – the social sciences. "In social sciences some of our best researchers are concerned with the causes and alleviation of poverty, and social inequality and related areas."

Major Discoveries

It's a testament to the truly comprehensive nature of McMaster that some of its proudest moments have come in fields not even mentioned above. For example, Myron S. Scholes helped to develop the Black-Scholes model for pricing derivatives. This is now widely used across the investment world and won him the 1997 Sveriges Riksbank Prize in Economic Sciences in Memory of Alfred Nobel. Faculty member Bertram Brockhouse, was awarded the Nobel Prize in Physics in 1994 and alumnus James Orbinski, accepted the Nobel Peace Prize in 1992 on behalf of Doctors Without Borders.

Partnerships, Innovation & Translational Research

McMaster has a very open attitude to partnerships be they with the private sector, government or other institutions of higher learning. To that end it has created the McMaster Innovation Park which is home to a growing number of joint research projects . "There are a number of different centres working with various industries and types of companies at the Innovation Park", explains President Deane. "For example, the Park is home to the McMaster Automotive Resource Centre. It is the product of collaboration with a number of auto manufacturers Fiat, Ford, and Chrysler as well as the federal and the provincial governments. It is an example of very successful collaboration between the public and private sectors that is generating innovation and new jobs."

Another way that the university commercialises research is through discoveries and start-up companies formed by its faculty. To that end it created the McMaster Industry Liaison Office (MILO), which helps researchers work with industry and move their research into society. It does this by negotiating sponsored research contracts, and obtaining funding for collaborative research with industry funding, helping researchers apply for patents, trade-marks and copyrights and also commercialising work through Southwest Ontario's technology transfer community.

Teaching, Learning & Student Life

As an internationally renowned research-intensive university, McMaster is equally known as a university of great teaching. The University works hard to bring teaching innovations and research into the classroom, and to encourage students to broaden their education through experiential learning and community involvement.

Interdisciplinary learning is a hallmark of McMaster. Undergraduate and graduate students, researchers and world-class professors are encouraged to collaborate with multiple areas of the university.

The University invented problem-based learning and evidence-based medicine, which have been taken up in many universities around the world.

All this happens within a campus located at the tip of Lake Ontario nestled next to the Niagara Escarpment. Nearby attractions include Cootes Paradise, the Bruce Trail and the Royal Botanical Gardens. For those looking for a more urban thrill, the University is just minutes from downtown Hamilton, and the activities that a major city has to offer. Buses from the region's public transit system make frequent stops on campus, facilitating travel between McMaster, Hamilton and the surrounding area.

Name › Rice University
Region › Americas
Country › United States
Founded › 1891

www.rice.edu

Core Research Strengths

Rice University is a private research university located in Houston, Texas. Opened in 1912, it now commands an annual research budget of more than $100 million. Rice is noted for its cutting-edge research with world-class faculty in the humanities, social sciences, engineering and natural sciences. It also has successful, applied science programs in the fields of artificial heart research, structural chemical analysis, digital signal processing, space science and nanotechnology.

"Rice is a broad based institution," said President David Leebron. "Although we are probably best known for certain areas of science and engineering, we have one of the best architecture schools, certainly one of the best music schools, and very distinguished faculty in areas like political science and religious studies. We have a top-10 bioengineering department; we are really good in physics, in particular we have an extremely high ranking in atomic, electrical and optical physics. So there is a wide range of research strengths."

The university also has an impressive range of research facilities. "We've invested a lot in our physical infrastructure, built the BioScience Research Collaborative, as well as a new physics building." Rice has also benefited from in-kind gifts, including two super computers donated by IBM. "This has enhanced our ability to explore potential uses of such computers in areas of biomedicine."

Like other institutions, Rice has developed a multidisciplinary approach to research, says President Leebron. "Our biggest successes at Rice tend to be in areas where we gather people across different disciplines. Take material science: it's not all done in the department of mechanical engineering and material science, much is done in other departments, and the same thing with nanoscience and nanotechnology. One of our strengths is that we have an intellectual flexibility, which makes inter-disciplinary appointments rather easy."

Major Discoveries

Despite having a smaller research budget than some of its peers, Rice punches above its weight in terms of research success. Unsurprisingly some of its most notable fields have come in its traditional strengths of physics and chemistry. For example in 1996, Robert Curl and Richard Smalley won the Nobel Prize in Chemistry for their discovery of buckminsterfullerenes.

Partnerships, Innovation & Translational Research

Partnership is a must for an institution of Rice's size, said President Leebron. "I think partnerships are absolutely critical — we are too small to be arrogant. But this small size can sometimes be an advantage. For example we do not have a medical school, but are across the street from the Texas Medical Center, which is widely viewed as the world's largest medical center. So by partnering with them we have opportunities for medical collaboration that we wouldn't have if we had a medical school."

Another way that a smaller institute like Rice can make itself felt on the global stage is through its student body, said President Leebron. "Some universities have chosen to build an overseas presence. We have chosen not to do that, but concentrated instead on delivering more doable joint degree programs, how to build more student and faculty exchange programs, and how to build joint programmes in research or teaching." It's testament to the success of this policy that Rice's student body has become significantly more international with the proportion of foreign students increasing to more than 10 per cent, including students from 82 countries.

Teaching, Learning & Student Life

Rice may be small, but its home city, Houston, is certainly not. Known as the energy capital of the world, it's a truly international city with 23 Fortune 500 companies. Despite its size, Houston is one of the safest American cities. Its merits include one of the world's best medical centers, NASA, a thriving museum and arts district, and the Houston Livestock Show and Rodeo.

There's also plenty of outdoors activities for more adventurous students, like communing with wild animals at the Houston Zoo or hiking at the Armand Bayou Nature Center. And Houston also boasts more than 160 golf courses. With just 3,708 undergraduate students and 2,374 graduate students, Rice is small by American standards. But, as the President explained, that's often a positive for students. "Rice's small size allows personal interaction between students and professors, while our eminent faculty foster the intellectual excitement of a major research university. Indeed our emphasis on education is demonstrated by a small student body and 6:1 student-faculty ratio."

Indeed President Leebron isn't the only one to feel that way — the students do too. For two consecutive years, Rice has top scored for student happiness in the Princeton Review. It has also finished top in terms of quality of life for four years.

Another reason that students like Rice so much is the special atmosphere on campus, said President Leebron. "It's a four-year system and we don't have fraternities and sororities, so there's no sense of exclusion. We assign people randomly to one of the 11 undergraduate colleges and that creates a great spirit. I think a lot of it is about putting students into an environment where they have sufficient control over that environment, sufficient responsibility, that they will solve their own problems and trust and love their fellow students."

Name › The University of Queensland
Region › Asia/Pacific
Country › Australia
Founded › 1909

www.uq.edu.au

Core Research Strengths

The University of Queensland has recently established eight interdisciplinary research institutes to achieve excellence in specific fields.

Four of UQ's institutes are focused on biomedical sciences and related areas, including: nanotechnology, bioengineering and neuroscience. The other four focus on agriculture, sustainable minerals, social science and global change.

Senior Deputy Vice-Chancellor Professor Deborah Terry believes the interdisciplinary approach is key to the success of the institutes. "Each of them is interdisciplinary, they are collaborative, and they are connected to high-quality research teams internationally. But we also expect them to work closely with researchers across the University. We explicitly support and encourage linkages between the institutes and other parts of the University."

The other defining feature of the University's approach is what Professor Terry calls "problem – oriented research".

"UQ's research is geared toward addressing and helping to solve the key challenges facing us all. You cannot be playing at the level that we want to play without engaging internationally. You have to be part of those debates. The answers to those issues are so pressing that the solutions will come only through major research teams working collaboratively to address them, and they will be international teams where you pull the best researchers from wherever they are around the world."

Major Discoveries

UQ has many notable research discoveries to its credit with major impacts on society.

For decades, UQ has held a world-leading position in hypersonic technology and, in 2002, conducted the world's first successful flight test of the hypersonic combustion engine.

Another major breakthrough was the needle-free vaccine delivery technology called the Nanopatch. Its development was led by Professor Mark Kendall, a biomedical engineer. The patch may help to revolutionize health care, particularly in remote and developing areas because it requires no refrigeration.

Professor Ian Frazer's work is also exemplary. This work led to the development of the cervical cancer vaccine Gardasil. Research has revealed that the vaccine led to a drop in the prevalence of the Human Papillomavirus (HPV) that causes cervical cancer.

The Triple P parenting program has also gained international recognition for its work giving parents evidence-based tools to raise happy and resilient young adults, as well as addressing more complex childhood disorders.

Partnerships, Innovation & Translational Research

Professor Terry believes creating successful partnerships is central to the University's continued success as a university in the world's top 100. This includes three types of partnerships – with government, industry and other institutions.

UQ has long partnered with other universities. Since the inception of Universitas 21 in 1997, the University has been part of this global network of research-intensive universities, working together to foster global citizenship and institutional innovation.

"Our data indicate that we have very productive research relationships with those universities. That is not just in terms of agreements and joint meetings, but also joint research funding and joint publications, so there are genuine outputs."

Professor Terry also emphasises the importance of alliances with the private sector. "We have a long history of collaborating with industry, and I think some of the most powerful partnerships into the future will be those that involve more than one university, plus one or more industry partners.

"For example, in a ground-breaking initiative bringing together cutting-edge research expertise in energy, water and sustainability with world-class science and engineering education, The Dow Chemical Company and UQ set up a strategic partnership that has resulted in the establishment of the Dow Centre for Sustainable Engineering Innovation.

"UQ has also partnered with many resources companies, such as Vale, Codelco, BaoSteel, and aviation firms like Boeing and Virgin. Industry links and research that is jointly funded with industry are absolutely critical."

"We also have a number of joint laboratories with China, where our PhD students spend time. We want to make sure that our students are truly global citizens who can work across borders."

Teaching, Learning & Student Life

UQ's main campus is set on a magnificent 114-hectare site surrounded on all sides by the Brisbane River, seven kilometres from the Brisbane CBD. Featuring high quality social and sporting as well as learning facilities. The University's setting also has practical advantages for students, such as a relatively easy access to part-time work.

When it comes to learning, UQ's more than 45,000 students, including 11,000 international students from more than 134 countries, benefit from the University's determination to encourage undergraduate as well as postgraduate research, and engender an interdisciplinary learning approach. UQ is noted for supporting early – and mid-career researchers, and has graduated more than 10,000 PhDs.

UQ's teachers have won more Australian awards for university teaching than any other Australian university. As part of its learning and internationalisation approaches, the University puts a strong emphasis on the Asia Pacific region.

Professor Terry notes that in the Asian Century, the University is very well positioned for students to gain experiences in Asia.

"It's something we emphasise and we would like to see more of our students undertaking a semester abroad in Asian countries, as well as other parts of the world."

UNIVERSITEIT GENT

Name › Ghent University
Region › Europe
Country › Belgium
Founded › 1817

www.ugent.be

Core Research Strengths

Since being founded in 1817, Ghent University has steadily established itself as one of Belgium's leading research universities. Traditionally, Ghent has been one of the main recipients of the Flemish budget for Development Cooperation research funding, receiving around 42% of the total. However, in recent years Ghent's research successes have led to more funding from private-sector sources.

One of Ghent's main strengths is biology, says university rector, Professor Paul Van Cauwenberge. "Bio everything! As regard to bio-related disciplines, the research and education at Ghent University is generally very extensive. That includes everything from medicine to bioengineering."
Within the bio related disciplines, Ghent University has five "spearheads" - interdisciplinary scientific research platforms in which extra money is being invested. Those five key areas are bioinformatics, general biotechnology, bio-photonics, immunology and neurosciences.

"This might look like a very narrow remit", says Rector Van Cauwenberge, "but it actually affects lots of wider areas. We have a leading position in plant biology, especially the genetics of plants and the genetic modification of them. At first we just modified rice, but now the research is extending to developing species richer in calories, resistant to infections by parasites, and so on. We are pioneering in this field, which has a lot of potential in other areas. Of course there are also lots of commercial applications."

Another wider field, of which people may not realise being so closely connected with biology is energy. Rector Van Cauwenberge elaborates: "We are experts at biofuel. Originally biofuel began with materials that can also be used for food but with many problems. Now we are developing fuels from non-edible sources. Together with other alternative energy sources like solar cells, windmills and so on as the overall solution to the energy problem becomes more diversified."

Major Discoveries

The university has had lots of Nobel Prize winners, especially in the field of medicine. Arguably its most important discovery came from former professor Leo Baekeland in 1907: he created the world's first completely synthetic plastic called Bakelite, which paved the way for a revolution in manufacturing processes.

Partnerships, Innovation & Translational Research

Ghent is very open to cooperation with the private sector and has been practising a multi-faceted engagement strategy for a long time. According to Rector Paul Van Cauwenberge: "One strand of the approach is contract research, where we are asked to use our expertise to perform some analysis or research. The second element is our industrial research fund. It is made up of 25 PhDs, who no longer want to be pure academics but act as a link between fundamental research, applied research and industry. The final part of the strategy is direct partnerships with particular companies. In genetics for example, we are working with Bayer in crop science."

Ghent also has a well-developed academic partnership strategy and has cooperation agreements with more than 500 universities around the world.

Rector Van Cauwenberge is particularly proud of the recent U4 grouping, which sees Ghent University team up with Groningen in Holland, Gottingen in Germany and Uppsala in Sweden. Looking further afield, the university is set to open its first Asian campus with the launch of a Ghent University campus in South Korea. In the first phase the site will offer programmes in biotechnology and bioengineering for 1000 students.

Teaching, Learning & Student Life

The city of Ghent is small by interna-tional standards with just 250,000 inhabitants. As a result the university's 38,000 students have a large impact on city life. The Rector is convinced that the location is a plus for students. "The city of Ghent is very lively, and is a great place for students to come and have an excellent social life. On top of

this, there is a vast range of sporting events and opportunities as well as cultural activities."

One of the highlights of the Ghent social calendar is the Gentse Feesten ('Ghent Festival') in July. It is one of the biggest and most popular cultural festivals in Europe and for 10 days, you can enjoy free music, theatre, puppet shows and street artists.

Ghent is also well placed to act as a launch pad for travels around Europe. The university itself has a welcoming atmosphere. This is forged in the institution's history when it was one of the few 'pluralistic' universities in the country independent from any religious views.

Indeed the university is so welcoming that – apart from medicine – there is no entrance exam. It also offers an array of English courses to attract international students. That's great for growth, says the Rector, though he admits it is causing a strain on resources. "We are expanding our infrastructure continuously to accommodate international students both for teaching, housing and research facilities."

Name › University of Rochester
Region › Americas
Country › United States
Founded › 1850

www.rochester.edu

Core Research Strengths

The University of Rochester is one of the United States' top-tier research universities with an annual research budget of more than $400 million. The University Provost, Peter Lennie, says that within the research portfolio one of the main strengths is optics.

"We have perhaps the foremost Institute of Optics in the United States. It was the first and it's immensely distinguished. It has produced a large fraction of all the Optics PhDs in the USA. We also have a long historical distinction in imaging and in visual science — the science of seeing."

"We have great strength in cognitive science, particularly the sciences of language. We have a powerful presence in evolutionary biology. Our Laboratory for Laser Energetics, a unique facility supported by the Department of Energy, is focused on work related to nuclear fusion."

The university is comprehensive, and has strong research focus in its seven schools. In medicine there are notable strengths in areas such as vaccine biology, respiratory and cardiac disease, among others. The Simon School of business is internationally recognized for its work on finance. Provost Lennie is particularly proud of the University's Eastman School of Music – "one of the world's great music schools."

It is now in vogue for universities to claim to be as multidisciplinary as possible - often to satisfy funding obligations. But Provost Lennie believes the most important thing is the results, not the label. "Our approach is to support the people who want to come together to solve the major problems —scientific, social, cultural — of the 21st century. We're constitutionally indifferent to the disciplinary mix; the important thing is to make it easy for the right people to get together."

Major Discoveries

The university's research efforts have been recognised with various awards including several Nobel Prizes. One that stands out, both in terms of the recipient and the discovery, was the 1997 Nobel Prize in Physics that was awarded to alumnus Steven Chu for development of methods to cool and trap atoms with laser light. Chu later went on to serve as Secretary of Energy in the Obama administration.

Partnerships, Innovation & Translational Research

Many universities are trying to increase their partnerships with the private sector; however, it's an area in which Rochester has long excelled. "The university has a rich portfolio of intellectual property", says Provost Lennie. "For the past decade, we've ranked in the top 10 nationally in income from intellectual property. Much of this has come from the medical centre, for example, in vaccines. But a good amount also comes from the basic sciences and engineering. When adjusted for institutional size, our income from intellectual property places the University in the top 2 or 3 nationally."

However, the Provost is aware that past achievements don't guarantee future success and acknowledges that research is becoming more competitive. "Our success depends on engaging with the best minds wherever they are. Major new research universities are arising in the world beyond the US and Europe, and to thrive we must establish strong research links with them."

Teaching, Learning & Student Life

Thanks to its relatively small size, learning at the University of Rochester is very much on the personal scale, and it remains one of the smallest and most collegiate among top research universities, with smaller classes, a low 10:1 student to teacher ratio, and increased interactions with faculty.

The small size is a definite advantage for students, says the Provost. "The University feels compact and that creates a special atmosphere. 86 percent of our undergraduates live on campus, and they derive enormous benefit from this residential experience. We have a huge number of student clubs—far more than at many larger universities. One of the special things about being here is the richness of musical life and students' engagement with it."

The 'size factor' also has a noticeable effect on the learning experience.

"The schools are close together. It makes it easy both for faculty to collaborate with each other across disciplines, but also for undergraduates to engage deeply in research projects with faculty in all the schools."

Outside of the university, Rochester itself has plenty to offer students. It frequently ranks highly on surveys for the 'most liveable' cities, scoring well for its local economy, recreation, housing, education, health care, transportation, ambiance, safety and climate.

In winter students can try their hand at cross-country skiing, snowshoeing, downhill skiing at Bristol Mountain and even curling. If you don't feel quite so adventurous there are plenty of coffee shops, restaurants, book stores, cinemas and museums. In summer students can enjoy the historic Erie Canal and the Genesee River, and just five miles south of Lake Ontario, Rochester offers plenty of sailing, canoeing, and hiking opportunities.

The University of Nottingham

Name › University of Nottingham
Region › Europe
Country › United Kingdom
Founded › 1881

www.nottingham.ac.uk

Core Research Strengths

The University of Nottingham's research strategy has been to harness the university's broad array of disciplinary strengths into a grouping of nine strategic research foci, designed to help develop solutions to some of the world's major contemporary global challenges. These nine core research areas are complemented by five broad areas of research excellence in which the university is able to be extremely competitive in attracting external funding, partnerships and consistently make new discoveries.

Looking ahead into the 21st century, the issue of global food security grows ever more important as population growth soars and the availability of agricultural land decreases. The University of Nottingham is an international leader in developing solutions to the challenges surrounding food security, investigating a number of research strands such as waste, societal impacts, governance & policy, distribution & production, climate change & environmental impact, as well as crops for the future with a view to contributing significantly to the international community adapting to the challenges presented by continued growth in food demand. The University won a Queen's Anniversary Prize in 2011 for its work on global food security.

The impacts of globalization continue to reverberate throughout the international community in ways both pleasantly unexpected and tragically predictable, and all that one can find in between. The University of Nottingham's Integrating Global Society research cluster draws together expertise from leading disciplines such as economics to better understand the dynamics and implications of globalisation in the 21st century.

In the medical sciences, the University excels in the areas of drug discovery, as well as drawing upon the rich traditions at the university in imaging to specialise in on-going developments surrounding biomedical imaging. The university's leadership in drug discovery derives from the diversity of expertise brought together in the Drug Discovery Priority Group, using state of the art technologies, working alongside industry throughout countless academic disciplines focused upon developing treatments to some of the most pressing ailments and illnesses in society today.

Major Discoveries

2003 Nobel Prize-winning researcher Sir Peter Mansfield developed Magnetic Resonance Imaging (MRI) at the University of Nottingham.

A University of Nottingham spin-out company has developed a blood test for lung cancer that can detect the illness three years earlier than previous tests. Given the problems associated with late diagnosis of lung cancer, this innovation will have a revolutionary impact on the prognosis and treatment of lung cancer.

Partnerships, Innovation & Translational Research

Currently ranked in the UK's top 6 universities in terms of collaborative research with business, the University of Nottingham has long been comfortable and open working alongside the private sector. Vice Chancellor David Greenwaway elucidates further on this culture at the university "There is a great strength of focus in this area from the University of Nottingham. I think it is very important to regard the University as one that has always been comfortable with research partnerships; this goes back to the historical impact that Jesse Boot had in the work that he encouraged between the Boots Company and The University of Nottingham."

The University of Nottingham's collaborative strategy involved the development of mutually beneficial long-term partnerships based upon shared values, objectives, synergies and infrastructure such as with the microbrewery facility the university operates in partnership with international brewer SAB Miller.

Teaching, Learning & Student Life

The University of Nottingham's entrepreneurial traditions were well established long before the concepts surrounding research and business collaboration became fashionable. As an early advocate of integrating business skills with teaching and learning led by Business School Dean Professor Martin Binks, the University of Nottingham has pioneered the integration of teaching and learning with business collaboration as highlighted by the Vice Chancellor, Professor Greenway "The University of Nottingham has been extremely proactive in developing multi-disciplinary partnerships between various schools such as chemistry, engineering and social sciences with the aim of building capacity for Nottingham alumni to go into business. The University of Nottingham Institute for Enterprise & Innovation has been particularly active in this area, partnering students with SMEs with a view to developing creativity and confidence in business, as well as contributing to sustained growth and improvements within the operations of our private sector partners."

The university's portfolio of international campuses in Malaysia and China, as well as its extensive network of international partner universities, offers students tremendous opportunities to develop their learning experience and skills set by studying abroad. On top of this, the University's pedagogical philosophy is firmly rooted in developing the student experience with all undergraduates benefiting from small tutorial groups as a means to debate their course materials, develop their own points of view, on top of important critical thinking skills and the ability to construct coherent and relevant arguments.

The university's motto, "A city is built on wisdom", is very much indicative of the close relationship that has developed between the university and its city with student life very much intertwined with Nottingham. The presence of students throughout the city's shops, pubs, restaurants and cultural sights is an important characteristic of local community culture.

AARHUS UNIVERSITY

Name › Aarhus University
Region › Europe
Country › Denmark
Founded › 1928

www.au.dk/en

Core Research Strengths

Aarhus University is a young, modern university established in 1928. Since then it has grown to become a leading public research university with international reach covering the entire academic spectrum.

Rector of Aarhus University, Lauritz B. Holm-Nielsen, says the university recently restructured its research focus. "I believe that our recent re-organization is strengthening the university very, very much. We now have four main academic areas (three faculties and a business school) and within these main academic areas we have 26 institutes.

There is no doubt that our Faculty of Science and Technology is very powerful and economics is excellent. The integration of the Faculty of Health Sciences, and one of the most effective Scandinavian University Hospitals is also a great asset."

The university's research capabilities have been recognised and enhanced by the Danish National Research Foundation. Indeed it is the first university in Denmark with 14 basic research centres of excellence. This funding has helped the university build and maintain world class research infrastructure. For example, Aarhus has an ion storage facility that is producing synchrotron beams allowing detailed studies of micro and nanoscopic materials that are specific to certain studies. Researchers come from around the world to use it.

Another key element of the university's research strategy is to dedicate resources to encourage complex and sufficient studies within interdisciplinary centres, says Rector Holm-Nielsen.

"The interdisciplinary centres nurse outstanding researchers from two or more of the main academic areas. In addition they are all involved in at least two and preferably three of the university's four core activities: research, talent development, knowledge exchange and education. For now we have seven interdisciplinary centres up and running. The first interdisciplinary centre was established in 2002 in nanoscience. Several centres of excellence in physics, chemistry, biology, and medicine contribute to this."

As a relatively young institution Aarhus is open to change, says the Rector. "Traditionally we have had a leading position in humanities, which to some extent has been rooted in Northern European and Danish Culture. This is now undergoing profound changes in order to better integrate arts and humanities in studies with global reach."

Major Discoveries

The university has the honour of providing the last two Nobel Prize winners from a Danish university. The most recent success came in 2010 when the Prize in Economic Sciences was awarded to Professor Dale T. Mortensen for his analysis of markets with search frictions. The 1997 prize in chemistry was awarded to Professor Jens Chr. Schou for his description of the sodium-potassium pump. Another prestigious award was given to Dr. Dorte Ravnsbæk when she received the European Young Researcher Award in 2011 for her research in the development of new materials for the storage of hydrogen.

Partnerships, Innovation & Translational Research

About 25% of the university's research funding comes from private-sector projects. These are either specific research tasks or more general services such as consulting. Rector Holm-Nielsen is keen to emphasise that Aarhus University is always open to new commercial opportunities.

"We have no hesitations, the more partnerships the better. However we must have upfront openness in the agreements. At the moment, we probably have about 650 contracts with private companies."

The university also obtains funding from public bodies. For example it jointly runs the Centre for Geomicrobiology with the Danish National Research Foundation (DNRF) and the German Max Planck Society (MPS). In total the university runs about 6,000 individually-financed research projects from a variety of private and public funds, companies, industries and governments."

Another element of the university's interaction with the outside world is with other academic institutions. Like almost everything at Aarhus, it is handled through a dedicated centre. The International Centre maintains international partnerships and combines a wide range of services for international students, PhD's and visiting scholars.

"We want to internationalize everything", says the Rector. "Research, study programs, knowledge transfer and knowledge exchange."

Teaching, Learning & Student Life

Aarhus University's main campus, is located in central Aarhus. The University Park has won worldwide acclaim for it is modern architecture. The yellow brick buildings are scattered in its green park and provides modern facilities and peace to the wide range of campus activities.

One of the most striking features about learning at the university is innovation. Because it is a young institution it is not tied by precedent and is constantly looking to develop new courses. For example the university recently created the 'student greenhouse', says the Rector. "It is a nursery for young entrepreneurial students who aspire to establish their own company. We are developing hundreds of small companies every year, though this is something students do on the side. It is a facility we run on the campus and I think it helps greatly."

Another distinctive element of the learning programme is the close link between teaching and research. Recognized researchers conduct lectures and interaction between faculty and students is encouraged.

Aarhus University
Denmark

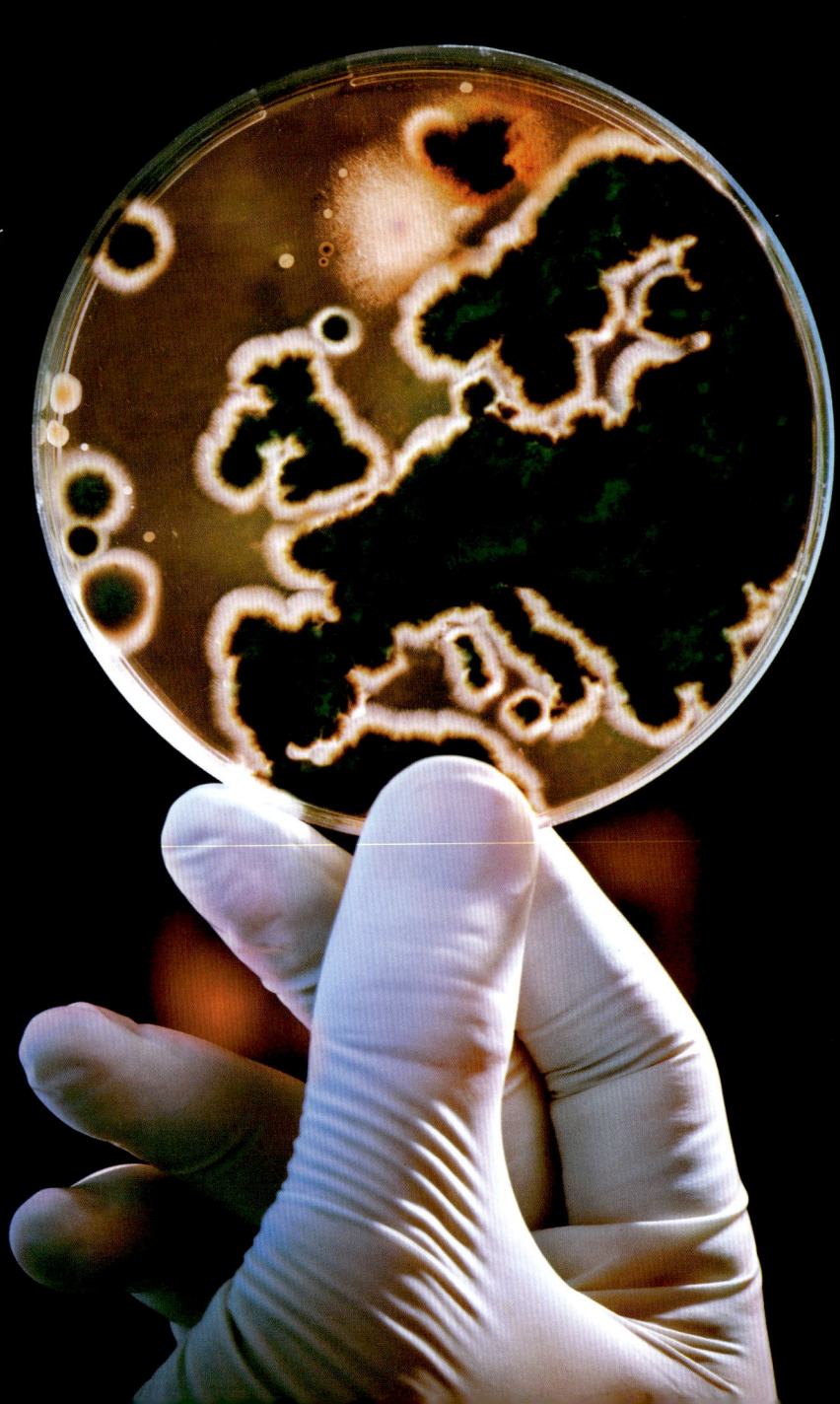

Aarhus University

Aarhus University is a modern comprehensive research university. In a short time, it has achieved a ranking among the top 100 of the nearly 20,000 universities in the world. Since 2006, the university has almost doubled its total number of students and PhD students and its research publications are among the most cited in a wide range of fields. Turnover will be approximately 1.13 billion U.S. dollars in 2013.

Research at Aarhus University is organized in four main academic areas, 26 departments and a number of interdisciplinary centres, and centres of excellence.

Arts

The Faculty of Arts serves as focal points for interdisciplinary and international collaborative research. In particular the research is excellent in anthropology, international studies, media studies, cognition, theology, philosophy, religion and pedagogical research. In addition the faculty has a strong tradition for historic and archeological research; both classical studies and up to modern Scandinavian and European Studies.

Learn more about the Faculty of Arts at arts.au.dk

Health

The Faculty of Health is engaged in basic, translational and clinical research in multiple fields in biomedicine, medicine, forensic medicine, dentistry, public health, biomedicine and related areas. Professor Jens Chr. Skou received the Nobel Prize in Chemistry in 1997 for the first discovery of an ion-transporting enzyme (Na+, K+ -ATPase).

The Faculty hosts one of the most dynamic biomedical departments in the world, and it counts some of the most unique centres and research projects in Europe. This includes the Danish Research Institute of Translational Neuroscience (DANDRITE) that performs research in brain and the nervous system, and is part of the Nordic EMBL Partnership. The Lundbeck Foundation's Initiative for Integrative Psychiatric Research (iPSYCH) that identifies biological disease mechanisms in specific mental disorders is also located at the university. The Faculty collaborates closely with Aarhus University Hospital and a range of scientific and academic institutions.

Learn more about the Faculty of Health at health.au.dk

Science and Technology

The Faculty of Science and Technology has a broad and internationally recognized range of basic and applied scientific research fields in the natural and technical sciences. Research in the fields of chemistry and materials science, biology, environmental and agricultural sciences is recognized as world class.

The faculty stands out as one of the strongest in Europe in the natural sciences. Science and Technology hosts 12 departments, a number of interdisciplinary research centres, including iNANO, and 14 centres of excellence. Researchers at the faculty have received more than 20 ERC grants over the last couple of years. As the first university outside USA, Science and Technology was named a NASA Data Hub for the Keppler Space telescope. The Faculty is furthermore the national focal point for food, agriculture, environmental research and public consultancy.

Learn more about the Faculty of Science and Technology at scitech.au.dk

Business and Social Sciences

The school has a large number of strong research environments covering the school's academic disciplines.

As an example, the school hosts a very strong labour market research environment at the Department of Economics and Business, where Professor Dale T. Mortensen was awarded the Nobel Prize in Economic Sciences in 2010. Researchers can access Danish register data that provide unique research opportunities in this field, making it possible for the research unit to develop improved models for dealing with complex economic fluctuations, and ultimately help ensure the implementation of new theories and methods in the labour market, including ways of reducing unemployment.

Learn more about the School of Business and Social Sciences at bss.au.dk

Interdisciplinary research

The major societal challenges are complex and cut across boundaries, sectors and academic disciplines. Therefore, solutions must be found through new interdisciplinary partnerships that cut across these boundaries. Consequently, Aarhus University has established seven interdisciplinary centres covering a wide range of research foci from the Arctic region to neuroscience. In addition to these centres, a large number of researchers and research groups collaborate on interdisciplinary projects across the university.

Interdisciplinary Nanoscience Center (iNANO) – inano.au.dk

MINDLab – mindlab.au.dk

Centre for iSequencing (iSEQ)

Centre for integrated Register based Research (CIRRAU) – cirrau.au.dk

Arctic Research Centre (ARC) – arctic.au.dk

Interacting Minds Centre (IMC) – interactingminds.au.dk

Participatory Information Technology Centre (PIT) – pit.au.dk

State of the art research infrastructure

Aarhus University is determined to offer a unique and modern state of the art research infrastructure. This includes for example three unique research stations in Greenland (Nuuk, Zackenberg and a station in the high Arctic), a unique radiation synchrotron source (ASTRID2), a new research vessel (AURORA), databases of environment and population data and modern laboratories.

UNI
BASEL

Name › University of Basel
Region › Europe
Country › Switzerland
Founded › 1460

www.unibas.ch

Core Research Strengths

The city of Basel is home to the oldest university in Switzerland. Founded upon the initiative of local citizens in 1460, the University of Basel is a modern and attractive centre of teaching, learning, and research situated in the heart of the historic old town.

When it comes to core research strengths Rector Antonio Loprieno identified four main areas.
"In life sciences, which is to be seen in connection with the strengths of the pharmaceutical industry here in Basel, we are strong both in fundamental and applied research. In nano-science we are the centre of the field in Switzerland and are particularly strong in fundamental research on an international level. The third area is cultural studies. In our definition cultural studies is connected with the humanist tradition at the University of Basel. Here the dialogue with society at large takes place at the level of museums; Basel has the highest concentration of museums in Switzerland and probably one of the highest in Europe. The final focus is European and global studies, which is linked to the geographical position of Basel at the border of France and Germany. This allows us a unique view of Europe, not so much from within it but from without."

The university hasn't always had so many research areas. Traditionally the University of Basel focused on humanities. But this changed in the 1930's when Adolf Portmann, a former student turned professor, encouraged the university to expand its remit and include more emphasis on life sciences.

The result, admits Rector Loprieno, is a university with almost conflicting specialties. "We try to maintain equilibrium between the historical foundation in the humanist tradition and the stronger orientation towards high-tech life sciences. While some may consider these two interests in opposition to each other the University of Basel has a tendency to superimpose them in a multidisciplinary sense."

Major Discoveries

The university has had a number of Nobel Prize winners. The most recent came in 1978 when Werner Arber won the Nobel Prize in Medicine for the discovery of restriction enzymes and their application to problems of molecular genetics

Partnerships, Innovation & Translational Research

The University of Basel is currently undergoing a great transition, says Rector Loprieno. "Traditionally the university was very much a state institution, although we are moving towards a more open culture where there is also an increased interest in partnerships, especially with private sector industry." So far the new strategy appears to be paying off with approximately 20% of the budget coming from third-party private partners. In particular the university has established links with Switzerland's powerful pharmaceutical industry and Rector Loprieno expects this trend to increase in coming years.

The university has also been very active in establishing international academic partnerships, says the Rector. Deals have been struck with German and French universities. However, Rector Loprieno is keen to stress that the university applies set criteria to such alliances. "One of the rules that we have for a partnership is that we engage in partnership only if the topic that is taught or studied in this partnership can only be studied within this partnership. We do not, in other words, offer partnership as a kind of alternative to a local existing curriculum." With that rule firmly in mind the university is now looking at possible new alliances in the Middle East and Singapore.

Teaching, Learning & Student Life

Basel University and its departments are located right in the city centre linking the picturesque medieval Old Town of Basel to the top-notch research facilities of Novartis. But with just 6,500 undergraduate and 5,800 postgraduate and doctoral students, the University of Basel is comparatively small by European standards. Another

standout feature of the student body is that it is very female – about 54% of the total and very international – approximately 23%.

There are very strong reasons for the 'international feel', explains Rector Loprieno. "The University of Basel in particular and Swiss universities more generally all have some of the highest proportions of international participation in the world. Roughly 60% of our professors are foreigners, recruited from all over the world, and roughly 23% of our students are international students. The reason for this is simple; Switzerland is a small country, the internal pool is limited and if you want to be a prestigious university you must be international. We attract a large number of students from the German-speaking world and are working on attracting students from China and India. We have recently made English, together with German, the official languages of the University of Basel."

Once students are inside the classroom they will notice that the university follows the principle of research-based teaching. It provides a broad, skills-oriented range of degree programmes closely aligned with international standards. Moreover, interdisciplinary work and the cross-faculty approach that is so central to its research efforts are also carried through to the teaching courses.

Another quirk to student life at Basel is that undergraduates benefit from expert professional advice before and during their programmes. They are also actively involved in co-determining the university's degree programmes and courses.

University of Basel
Switzerland

Research at Basel

Located in one of the global pharmaceutical and life sciences industries' epicentres, home to leading firms such as Novartis and Roche. The University of Basel's distinguished research base is in the life, medical and biological sciences and nanotechnology. Basel's strong humanist tradition, stretching back to as early as the 15th century has seen Basel develop into a cultural hub, as well as facilitating the evolution of interdisciplinary strength in emerging areas such as biomedical ethics. The university is Increasingly recognised as a global leader conducting interdisciplinary research in the molecular bio-medical sciences and at the interface of biology and physics through the Biozentrum and Swiss Nanoscience Institute respectively.

Life Sciences – The Biozentrum

First established in 1971, the Biozentrum is recognized today as one of the world's leading institutes conducting multidisciplinary research investigating the molecular basis of fundamental biological processes of life. Approximately 30 multinational research groups collaborate with each other, external institutes and industry partners to further our understanding of the most basic biological processes with a long-term strategic view towards developing new treatments for countless diseases and ailments.

Research interests at the Biozentrum cover a diverse array of interest areas at the interface of basic science such as cell growth and development, infection biology, neurobiology, structural biology and biophysics, as well as computational and systems biology. Much of the fundamental enquiry into cell division and cell growth is contributing significantly to the body of knowledge surrounding stem cells; one of the biological sciences most exciting emerging fields of study.

The Biozentrum's 550 staff publishes approximately 200 articles every year, positioning it as one of the most productive inter-disciplinary life sciences research institutes in the world. The institute's close working relationship with international pharma-

ceutical giants Roche and Novartis as well as the broader life sciences cluster in the Basel region; position Biozentrum as an experienced private sector collaborator, as well as an institute comfortable working alongside public laboratories and fellow research universities.

The excitement and demand for expertise surrounding biological sciences at the beginning of the 21st century is well understood by administrators at the University of Basel. Biozentrum's interdisciplinary PhD program is designed to prepare excellent young researchers for a career in research either in academia or the private sector. The institute's close ties to the private sector give young researchers the opportunity to experience both environments; as well as the chance for industry partners to work alongside some of the most promising young researchers at the beginning of their careers.

Biozentrum's cutting edge research foci and world-class research expertise is complimented by state of the art equipment available to the institution. Biozentrum has its very own workshop where tailored equipment is designed and manufactured on a project specific basis, as well as having access to a broad portfolio of equipment through affiliate departments and research labs at Basel.

These range from highly sophisticated light microscopes at the Imaging Core Facility, through to Titan; a very high-resolution electron microscope, standing at 4.5 metres tall, operated exclusively by remote control. The Proteomics Core Facility is equipped with a comprehensive portfolio of the latest technologies for the study of proteins. Whilst the Quantitative Genomics Facility and Biozentrum's cutting edge I.T. infrastructure enables state of the art DNA sequencing and polymerase chain reaction.

Nanotechnology – The Swiss Nanoscience Institute

Closely related to the University of Basel's expertise in molecular biology emanating from research conducted at the Biozentrum, is the university's expertise in nanotechnology. The Swiss Nanoscience Institute (SNI), is another

of Basel's priority interdisciplinary centres; capitalising upon the university's expertise at the molecular scale to draw together expertise from physics, biology and chemistry in the development of ground-breaking new technologies in areas such as quantum computing, nano biology and molecular electronics.

Although Basel is the leading coordinator of the SNI, the institute is a collaborative enterprise including input from world-class partners such as ETH Zurich, MIT, a number of IBM Research Laboratories and local firms and research institutes in Switzerland. The SNI's combination of local demand side partners and international network of expertise puts the institution in a unique position to connect international research universities and institutes with local companies in Switzerland working to expand their expertise in the growing nanotechnology space.

Industry Collaboration & Technology Transfer

The University of Basel's increasing focus upon industry collaboration and technology transfer is best embodied through institutions such as the Biozentrum and SNI. Programs such as Nano Argovia at the SNI are proactively encouraging the joint collaboration between the university's leading research institutes and innovative local enterprises. The Argovia program has also contributed to the development of a number of spinout companies such as AG Dubendorf and Concentris GmbH Basel; Re-asserting Basel's influence not only at the cutting edge of basic research, but also as an increasingly important driver of local economic development.

Name › Indiana University Bloomington
Region › Americas
Country › United States
Founded › 1820

www.indiana.edu

Core Research Strengths

With over 100,000 students, spanning 8 different campuses located throughout Indiana state, Indiana University's (IU) size and scale facilitates the incredible diversity one can observe throughout the research enterprise. Increasingly IU has sought to harness this institutional diversity, with a strategic research plan increasingly bringing together schools and disciplines to work on research questions collaboratively; distinguishing core research strengths into increasingly influential clusters.

IU's great strength in IT through institutions such as the IU School of Informatics and Computing have not only laid the foundation for exceptional disciplinary excellence, but have also contributed significantly to the technical and innovative capacity of the institution. IU's I.T. capacity has also underpinned great interdisciplinary collaboration between IU's flagship departments such as between the School of Medicine investigating innovative new techniquesfor integrating IT with healthcare delivery, as well as increasing IU's capacity in cutting edge research areas such as bio-informatics. IU also is an international leader in the increasingly important areas of cyber security and networking technologies.

In the health, life and biological sciences, IU's research portfolio consists of a broad cluster; investigating a myriad of questions from cancer to model systems in biological research. A key IU strategy is to significantly increase the university's profile and reputation in the life sciences over the coming years, thus significant investment and external partnerships will continue in this broad research cluster. The university also has invested significantly in research facilities in recent years, with a goal of enhancing both student experience and IU's research capabilities.

IU's great strength throughout the social sciences facilitates exceptional strength in the environmental sciences with the university both a key player from a policy and understanding perspective; but also an excellent innovator developing new technologies that will assist in our overcoming major environmental challenges associated with phenomena such as climate change. Indeed, IU's School of Public and Environmental Affairs is ranked among the top three schools of its kind in the U.S., while the IU Energy Institute, established in 2010, is at the forefront of such innovative work as investigating new energy generating technologies from wind power to fuel cell technology for energy storage.

Finally, one would not be able to speak about IU without mentioning the Jacobs School of Music, the pre-eminent public music school in the United States; covering the entire gamut of musical instruments and styles; whilst having a hugely positive effect on the social and cultural environment at IU.

Major Discoveries

IU is set to remain at the forefront of IT research having recently agreed purchase of the fastest university super computer in the United States, significantly enhancing the pioneering work being undertaken in areas such as bioinformatics.

Researchers at the IU School of Medicine are pioneering treatments for some of the most prevalent cancers, having received a great deal of attention for their work on testicular cancer and breast cancer in recent years.

Partnerships, Innovation & Translational Research

Collaborative research partnerships are a very natural part of the research enterprise for IU, with the university an experienced associate of countless institutions. IU remains very much open for working in partnership with a broad range of potential partners. Intellectual property policy at IU is particularly attractive for external partners, with leaders throughout the venture capital industry commenting upon it being one of the most progressive and enlightened policy approaches in the United States.

The Indiana University Research and Technology Corporation acts as the interface between IU and its industry partners, as well as continuing to drive the university's improved performance in translational research and technology transfer. IU's two major technology parks in Indianapolis and Bloomington facilitate growing collaboration between enterprise and researchers; as well as continued success as an incubator for spin out companies such as with Angel Learning and Marcadia; sold for US $100 million and US $250 million in recent years respectively.

Teaching, Learning & Student Life

The diversity and choice that IU's size and scale facilitates in the research enterprise very much filters through down to the teaching and learning experience. Students are encouraged to diversify their study choices and work throughout the disciplines with pioneering courses such as the Liberal Arts and Management Program combining arts, languages and the humanities with business and economics; laying an excellent foundation for students to move into business and management upon graduation. IU also is one of the most internationally focused universities in the United States, ranking in the top 10 for both the number of international students attending IU and the number of students who study abroad while at IU.

Despite being a beautiful place to live, Indiana is one of the lesser well-known parts of the United States to the untrained observer, and IU President Michael McRobbie highlights what newcomers can expect through his own experiences:

"I moved here 15.5 years ago and have never regretted the move for even a nanosecond. Bloomington is a beautiful place to live and it's a classic American college town. It's not tiny by any means, but it is relatively small (population about 81,000 people, plus 42,000 students). It's manageable, it's safe and the campus itself is regularly ranked as one of the most beautiful in America."

OSAKA UNIVERSITY

Name › Osaka University
Region › Asia/Pacific
Country › Japan
Founded › 1931

www.osaka-u.ac.jp

Core Research Strengths

Osaka University's history dates back as far as 1838 when Tekijuku, a private school of Western medicine and sciences, was founded by Koan Ogata. Its official establishment in 1931 was the next evolutionary step from the Osaka Prefecture Medical College enshrining the university today in a long tradition of research strength in the medical sciences. Osaka University is a global leader in the study of immunology, ranked 4th internationally in terms of citations related to this vital area of medical sciences research. President Toshio Hirano, an award winning immunologist and a pioneer of interleukin 6, elaborates further on Osaka University's leadership in this area: "Osaka University is a Mecca for international immunology research and has many leading researchers such as Professors Shizuo Akira and Shimon Sakaguchi, only a handful of others in the world compare with our expertise."

President Hirano believes Osaka University's multidisciplinary approach is critical to its research successes: "We have recently established the Institute for Academic Initiatives (IAI) to build on our established interdisciplinary strengths that reflect our comprehensive research prowess covering humanities, social sciences, natural science, engineering, and life sciences. The complexity that surrounds many of today's most critical research challenges makes the interdisciplinary approach fundamental, without it our chances of success would be limited."

Closely intertwined with Osaka University's traditions in the life sciences, is the university's leadership in regenerative medicine, particularly with the use of stem cells, most notably somatic stem cells. Researchers have been some of the first in the world to develop successful treatments with the use of stem cells in a clinical setting. Presently Osaka University is presently leading the way in the treatment of a variety of ailments with the use of stem cells ranging from loss of vision to heart failure.

Japan's global leadership in the study and development of robotics has its origins in pioneering institutions such as Osaka University. Under the directorship of Professor Hiroshi Ishiguro, Osaka University's Intelligent Robotics Laboratory is taking an international role in the research and development of interactive robots. Drawing upon expertise through disciplines such as engineering, robotics and cognitive science, Professor Ishiguro has developed androids to study human – robot interactions.

Major Discoveries

Professor Akira, a multiple award-winning researcher, has made paradigm shift discoveries relating to the concept of "innate immunology". Once considered a primitive concept, Professor Akira's discoveries relating to Toll-like receptors have opened up entire new avenues for research in this area.

Nano-photonics pioneer Professor Satoshi Kawata was entered into the Guinness Book of World Records for producing the smallest ever laser fabricated structure. This was a 3 dimensional shape of a bull, measuring 7μm high and 10μm long; approximately the same size as a red blood cell.

Partnerships, Innovation & Translational Research

Although basic research remains the fundamental mission, President Hirano is developing new strategies as the importance of industry collaboration grows: "Ahead of other universities, Osaka University has started a new approach referred to as the 'Industry on Campus' program. In this program, companies establish independent research organisations within a campus where researchers from both sectors conduct joint research. In this way, Osaka University is aggressively facilitating university-industry collaboration; we are a front-runner in this area."

Collaboration with Osaka University, needless to say, is not limited to industry; particularly given President Hirano's vision for the university to become thoroughly internationalized: "One of the key elements that defines Osaka University's approach to teaching and fostering innovation is aggressively promoting internationalization. Osaka University aims to achieve an environment where Japanese and international students understand each other's cultures and improve themselves by learning from each other – a global campus."

Osaka University's collaborative culture extends as far as its participation in networks such as Global 30, Association of Pacific Rim Universities and Campus Asia.

Teaching, Learning & Student Life

President Hirano's vision for a university that shines forth even into the 22nd century is one with its foundation in the development of people. Osaka University's focus in teaching is to nurture proactive citizens who pursue enquiry driven by curiosity, adhere to fundamental principles regardless of scientific field and act on convictions based upon deep learning.

Currently with approximately 2000 international students, Osaka University aims to significantly increase student exchange both by developing more English language instruction, as well as developing a unique approach to developing Japanese language skills in its most talented international attendees. Starting with a relatively small number of students, but progressively growing year on year, Osaka University has initiated a 6-month program of intensive Japanese instruction for those relatively new to the language that will enable them to study in Japanese following completion of the course. This offers an excellent opportunity for international students to learn one of Asia's most important languages whilst studying for a degree at one of the world's leading universities.

Osaka Prefecture has been found to have the friendliest locals among major East Asian host cities of international students, rendering the environment active and engaging from a social perspective. Still one of the most significant urban areas in Japan, international students in Osaka will find themselves in welcoming surroundings in a manageable, safe and socially invigorating city environment.

Name › University of Utah
Region › Americas
Country › United States
Founded › 1850

www.utah.edu

Core Research Strengths

The University of Utah is a public coeducational space-grant research university in Salt Lake City, Utah. Every year it generates a research budget of around $400 million. The University of Utah Research Foundation guides the university's research efforts, which focus on science, technology, medicine, pharmacy, engineering, natural resources, energy, business and education.

The university's College of Engineering has a long proud history. For example it was one of the original four nodes of ARPANET, the world's first packet-switching computer network and embryo of the current worldwide internet. The school has pioneered work in asynchronous circuits, computer animation, computer art, digital music recording, graphical user interfaces, and stack machine architectures. Nowadays that work is carried out by the Scientific Computing and Imaging Institute, which continues to make advances in visualisation, scientific computing, and image analysis.

In the sciences, the university is strong in chemistry, earth sciences and life sciences. Utah has made unique contributions to the study of genetics due in part to long-term genealogy efforts of the Mormon Church, which has allowed researchers to trace genetic disorders through several generations. The relative homogeneity of Utah's population also makes it an ideal laboratory for studies of population genetics. The University of Utah Center for Clinical and Translational Science builds on the University's strengths in genetics and bioinformatics to translate research into practices that improve human health. The Center also serves as an academic home for clinical and translational research, developing innovative health services for the community and health researchers, and training a new generation of clinical and translational investigators.

Utah is always looking to improve its offering and in 2012 announced plans to create a new academic college, the college of dentistry.

Major Discoveries

Given Utah's leading role in genetics it is fitting that one of its most recent major discoveries came in the field. In 2007, Mario R. Capecchi won the Nobel Prize in Physiology or Medicine for the discovery of principles for introducing specific gene modifications in mice by the use of embryonic stem cells.

Partnerships, Innovation & Translational Research

The University of Utah has an incredible track record creating start-up companies from student and faculty research. It started 18 new companies during fiscal year 2011 and is perennially ranked as a top start-up creator among US universities. This good work is led by the Technology Venture Development unit, known informally as Tech Ventures. The university also uses a dedicated research park to interact with companies such as ARUP Laboratories, Evans & Sutherland, Sarcos, Biofire Diagnostics and Myriad Genetics.

Like many leading international universities Utah is keen to increase the internationalisation of its student body. The main focal point for that effort is the International Center, which serves as the campus contact for international students, scholars, and alumni.

Teaching, Learning & Student Life

The University of Utah is located in Salt Lake City in the foothills of the Wasatch Mountain Range. That means students can have the best of both worlds. More adventurous students can enjoy the rugged mountain bike trails and seven world-class ski resorts that are within an hour's drive from the university. The more urbane students can ride the free light rail train system to downtown Salt Lake City, a pleasant, clean metropolis that offers great restaurants, bars, arts and entertainment. Highlights include the Utah Symphony, Ballet West, Utah Opera, many theatre companies, a professional basketball team (the NBA's Utah Jazz) and a professional soccer team (Real Salt Lake of the MLS). And, perhaps best of all, the city is small enough that all of those attractions are within easy reach. The university

campus also offers a lot to do. Students are free to wander around campus and enter the concerts and museums or join one of the many sports programmes.

With more than 32,000 students, Utah is a large university by American standards. That's reflected in the course menu, with over 90 major subjects at the undergraduate level and more than 100 major fields of study at the graduate level, including law and medicine.

The university places a particular emphasis on encouraging students to engage in the learning process. One way it achieves this is by making students take responsibility for their course structure and learning. That responsibility is rewarded by the opportunity to work closely and cooperatively with professors and classmates. The university also promotes civic engagement and work in the community as an essential part of a student's learning experience. The university has several innovative programmes that encourage students to think about life beyond the campus. For example, many Utah students participate in work placements or internships with private sector firms. These experiences help students realise how their studies relate to the outside world while also proving useful in the post-graduation job search.

Stockholm University

Name › Stockholm University
Region › Europe
Country › Sweden
Founded › 1878

www.su.se

Core Research Strengths

With more than 65,000 students, Stockholm University is one of Sweden's largest. However, former Vice-Chancellor Kåre Bremer believes any description of the university should begin with an understanding of its symbiotic relationship with the neighbouring KTH Royal Institute of Technology and Karolinska Institutet. "All three institutions collaborate very closely and complement each other's strengths because of our close proximity and historical relationships," says Bremer.

"We also have a lot of cooperation together. We have several research institutes, departments and educational programmes that we operate together. In fact we operate the entire physics area together with KTH. We do not see each other as competitors but rather as partners, because we have an overlap in our agendas given the other two are single faculty universities so to speak."

The combination of resources and expertise creates comprehensive research facilities that span a wide number of disciplines. As is now a growing trend with leading international universities, these research capabilities are often organised on a thematic basis. For example, one of Stockholm University's leading areas is climate change – a challenge that uses many separate fields.

"The Swedish government has given Stockholm University substantial amounts of money to establish research centres related to strategic areas, e.g. our Bert Bolin Centre for Climate Research. The University has been awarded several grants for research into climate change and environmental change. We also have a lot of work in environmental science, and have established a research institute for environmental science, especially related to the social sciences. It is called the Stockholm Resilience Centre and the university has received a great deal of international attention for this development."
Other research strengths of Stockholm University include chemistry, biochemistry, organic chemistry, astrophysics and particle physics. Former Vice-Chancellor Bremer also likes to note that while the university is internationally renowned for its achievements in science, it also has significant capabilities in humanities and social sciences.

Major Discoveries

Some of the university's most important breakthroughs have come in the field of environment and climate change. For example, in 1995 Paul Crutzen received the Nobel Prize in chemistry for his research on the formation of the hole in the ozone layer in the atmosphere, and its relation to CFCs.

Partnerships, Innovation & Translational Research

"Stockholm University is currently re-examining its partnerships with the private sector", says Astrid Söderbergh Widding, present Vice-Chancellor. "Cooperation with the industrial sector and international companies has in the past not been very well developed. I would not say that is the strongest area for Stockholm University." Instead, says the Vice-Chancellor, the university has been focusing more on basic research and co-operation with other universities, other research institutes and research organisations.

However, Vice-Chancellor Söderbergh Widding is now looking to remedy that and increase interaction with private-sector partners. One of the most positive steps in this direction is the innovative partnership with clothing retailer H&M. Thanks to generous financial support from the Erling-Persson Family Foundation, the university has established "a new academic discipline" – Fashion Studies. "Fashion is a very prominent feature in society today. It has very large cultural and economical applications so it's as much as an academic study as literature or music," says the Vice-Chancellor. The university has recruited leading researchers in the field and the course has proved a hit with students.

Teaching, Learning & Student Life

As one of Europe's cleanest, least-polluted capital cities, Stockholm creates the perfect environment for peaceful study. Indeed there is no shortage of extra-curricular activities in the Scandinavian city. Stockholm is built on 14 islands connected by 57 bridges. The beautiful buildings, the greenery, the fresh air and the proximity to the water are distinctive traits of the city. Unsurprisingly for such a green city it has the distinction of creating the world's first National City Park. Nature isn't the city's only appeal. With its 750-year history and rich cultural life, Stockholm offers a wide selection of world-class museums and attractions. Most of the city's attractions can be reached on foot, and there's a good chance of experiencing a lot of things in a short time.

Many foreigners are fascinated by Swedish life, culture and politics, says Vice-Chancellor Söderbergh Widding. However, she is also frank about the challenges. "One drawback is the housing situation in Stockholm, which is difficult, and acts as a limitation on this." Another challenge for students from other countries is that Sweden's living costs are higher than average.

However, when it comes to life inside the lecture halls, one thing international students don't have to worry about is speaking Swedish, says Vice-Chancellor Söderbergh Widding. "It is not necessary to learn Swedish to come to Stockholm University, even if you're studying at the graduate level. You'll do perfectly well with English because all of our Master's programmes are in English, and some of our most popular undergraduate programmes in the social sciences, such as political science, operate in both Swedish and in English because there is such a high demand for them."

Name › Moscow State University
Region › Europe
Country › Russia
Founded › 1755

www.msu.ru

Core Research Strengths

Moscow State University is Russia's first, and largest, classical university. Classes began in the spring of 1775, in a building near the Voskresenskiye Gate in Red Square where the State History Museum is situated now. One interesting thing about the university is that it has played a major role in establishing its competitors. Over the years former members of staff from the university have helped to create around 60 higher educational institutions, including the largest in Russia, the Sechenov Moscow Medical Academy.

The university has always been strong in the fields of science and the humanities. Its science focus was intensified in the 1950s when a new university campus was constructed on the Lenin Hills. Because of the then geopolitical situation, it was deemed imperative that the USSR build up expertise in both fundamental and applied science. As a result university researchers went on to make considerable contributions to space exploration, to the study of atomic nucleus structure, to the development of computers and many other branches of science. That tradition of scientific excellence continues today, albeit in a very different geopolitical context.

Recently, 12 new faculties have been established, to address the most promising areas of research. They include Faculties of Materials Science, Bioengineering and Bioinformatics, the Moscow School of Economics and the Faculty of Fine and Performing Arts. MSU continues to lead research innovation in the country. For example, it was the first in Russia to establish a science park with private industry interaction. More expansion is being planned. Indeed to celebrate the university's 250th jubilee, a new Intellectual Centre, Fundamental Library and Medical Centre are being built.

Major Discoveries

One of the university's most recent significant research breakthroughs came in the early part of this century when Alexei A. Abrikosov and Vitaly L. Ginzburg pioneered contributions to the theory of superconductors and superfluids. They were jointly awarded the 2003 Nobel Prize in Physics for their efforts.

Partnerships, Innovation & Translational Research

One of the most innovative tools that MSU employs to interact with commercial partners is its science park. Spread over 11,500 square metres it is home to 40 small innovative businesses and 2,500 personnel, most of who are graduates, undergraduates, graduate students and professors of Moscow State University. Around 60% of the companies are focussed on IT and software production, while the rest cover a range of telecommunication, biotechnology and new materials. The combined turnover of all the companies present is more than $50 million.

The other strand of MSU's interaction with the outside world is its academic partnership strategy. The university has more than 350 with universities in 75 countries. For obvious reasons special attention is being paid to the links with universities in the Commonwealth of Independent States (CIS). In cooperation with them, the Eurasian Universities' Association was set up. To further these partnerships Moscow State University opened its Black Sea branch in Sebastopol, Ukraine, and a Kazakhstan branch in Astana.

The university has also been working to increase the internationalisation of its student body and in recent years, the number of international students at MSU has doubled, totalling 5,000 from 80 countries.

Teaching, Learning & Student Life

Since 1953, most of the university's faculties have been situated on Sparrow Hills (formerly Lenin Hills), in the southwest of Moscow. At the time this was in the outskirts of Moscow, but since then the city has grown around it. Now the campus is located about halfway between the centre of Moscowat the Kremlin and the city's current limits. Moscow, the capital of Russia, has a population of some 9 million people. It is a city rich in cultural, architectural, historical and revolutionary monuments and, at the same time, a rapidly developing modern urban community which reflect Russia's recent resurgence. Students can enjoy long, straight and broad avenues, parks, gardens, stadiums, schools, cinemas, department stores and recreation centres. Though forward-looking, it cherishes the memory of its past, and its old sections lend it a special charm. The historical centre of Moscow is home to The Red Square, the Kremlin, St. Basil's Cathedral and Tverskaya Street, which is the equivalent of Oxford Street in London.

As for the campus, it is like a city within a city. It is a very complex system, with 1000 buildings and structures. Of course with around 50,000 students and staff it needs to be big. Especially as around 12,000 students live on campus. The learning experience is styled by the university's commitment to the "indissoluble connection of fundamental education and fundamental research". Indeed students will work closely with highly qualified specialists and graduate with high levels of expertise. The learning experience is also boosted by MSU's collaboration with the Russian Academy of Sciences. There are a number of joint research and teaching projects, which give students the chance to rub shoulders with the 300 members of the Russian Academy of Sciences and other national academies that work at the university.

ARIZONA STATE UNIVERSITY

Name › Arizona State University
Region › Americas
Country › United States
Founded › 1885

www.asu.edu

Core Research Strengths

Arizona State University's approach to research under the leadership of President Michael Crow is truly ground-breaking. Having been inaugurated in 2002, President Crow has led the research strategy; looking out into the long-term one of differentiation based upon the fusion of academic disciplines in a concerted effort to develop solutions to major global challenges. One could confuse the approach for simply being a standard multidisciplinary approach.

President Crow clarifies ASU's research vision: "Our overall strategy is one of differentiation, ASU has no aspiration to chase anyone else. We are not concerned about the rankings and maintenance of academic disciplines, and instead we pursue a differentiated academic profile, which includes research in areas of critical national interest, research that addresses the so-called "grand challenges." Our theme-based focus is related to what we term "intellectual fusion," which is one of eight design aspirations. Intellectual fusion could also be termed transdisciplinarity. So our research strengths and initiatives assume intellectual fusion and represent opportunities that we believe will advance discovery and innovation. We need fundamental disciplines like physics or chemistry or engineering. But that alone is insufficient so we put our emphasis on differentiation. Our approach is to identify an intellectual trajectory that addresses a range of problems, which may sound like a subtle deviation from standard practice but it is actually quite meaningful. The term "interdisciplinary" is in some ways too general to capture the complexity of what we're trying to accomplish. We have introduced the inter or transdisciplinary approach, the function of which is to take a completely new conceptual approach."

ASU's "intellectual fusion" strategy has resulted in significant increases in research productivity and recognition; with the university attracting increased funding for a wide range of projects from the National Science Foundation, National Institutes of Health and the Department of Energy to name but a few.

Bio-design and Sustainability are two of the areas where intellectual fusion is most advanced, President Crow elaborates: "The transdisciplinary research we conduct in the Biodesign Institute, for example, is representative of this approach. The Biodesign Institute advances biologically inspired design to address global challenges in healthcare, sustainability, and national security. The Global Institute of Sustainability (GIOS) brings together scientists and engineers with government policymakers and industry leaders to develop solutions to critical challenges. Sustainability represents an integrated systems level approach to such issues as rapid urbanization, water quality, habitat transformation, the loss of biodiversity, and the development of new forms of renewable energy. GIOS integrates something like forty disciplinary areas around that theme and the objective is to advance science as well as to position us for breakthrough impacts."

Major Discoveries

Researchers in ASU's Biodesign Institute are pioneering a new approach to virology, investigating the possibility of triggering the human genome's ability to combat viruses without the necessity of vaccines; often costly and time consuming in their development.

Partnerships, Innovation & Translational Research

Global engagement is a critical component of ASU's development towards President Crow's vision of evolving into the New American University. Partnerships as a result are encouraged on a multitude of levels: "We urge our faculty that have the capacity to work in that modality to do so by offering them whatever they need for a partnership to be successful. So we have one partnership with thirty companies working on advanced solar technology, we have another partnership with thirty more companies working on advanced flexible display technologies. These are areas where our scientists and engineers and our students all collaborate."

ASU's approach to technology transfer is to prioritise impact, paying less attention to the traditional revenue generation model: "We've moved away from the notion of money being the objective that we're pursuing from our intellectual property activity. What we're actually after is speed-to-market, and then if something happens as a function of that, then, you know, we're happy to benefit in the long run. So we have no short-run objectives, only long-run objectives. Financially, our only short-run objective is to get the technology to the market."

Teaching, Learning & Student Life

ASU's pioneering approach to research through the intellectual fusion model has very much filtered through to the institution's pedagogical philosophy. Students are encouraged to integrate their studies throughout different disciplines, whilst degree programs are increasingly structured to accommodate the complexity one finds at the cutting edge of research today. ASU has now introduced in excess of 15 transdisciplinary schools such as the School of Earth and Space Exploration where astronomy and geology have been combined with astrophysics, astrobiology and systems engineering setting exploration and collaboration quite clearly as the operative contexts for the course.

ASU has an exceptionally strong entrepreneurial culture, with an almost unprecedented 11,000 students involved in entrepreneurial activities; linking together their education and exposure to research with the university's mission of having a measurable impact on the economy and society through knowledge driven innovation. ASU's range of accelerator and incubator programs such as Furnace and Technopolis only serve to further enhance the opportunities for students and faculty to have a real impact on the outside world through the discoveries made at this pioneering institution.

Technion
Israel Institute of Technology

Name › Technion-Israel Institute of Technology
Region › Asia/Pacific
Country › Israel
Founded › 1924

www1.technion.ac.il

Core Research Strengths

Founded in 1912, Technion started out as an engineering school, and this has remained its core research fields – Material, electrical, computer, mechanical, civil and chemical engineering are very strong research groups. There is also an excellent biomedical engineering department, which is an interface between biology, medicine and engineering whose research productivity grows at the interface between these subject areas. The sciences are well represented in chemistry, physics (principally optics and nanotechnology) biology and medicine.

Technion President Prof. Peretz Lavie believes foresight plays a significant role in the institution's success and research focus. "What distinguishes universities that rank very highly is their ability to predict the future and make changes accordingly. Early in the 21st century, we realized that we must move to an interdisciplinary phase of our research, and we established five virtual research centres. The first one was nanotechnology and nanoscience, comprising more than 100 researchers from 13 faculties. The second one is life sciences and engineering, and here we started to recruit faculty members that feel comfortable in engineering as well as biology and medicine. Third is energy research, and fourth is autonomous systems, which is robotics and beyond robotics. The fifth and newest is computer engineering, particularly hardware architecture and man-machine interfaces."

Major Discoveries

The Technion has made many influential discoveries in the sciences and engineering. There have been three Nobel Laureates in the field of Chemistry. The 2011 Nobel Prize was awarded to Dan Shechtman for the discovery of quasicrystals.

The development of the Lempel-Ziv algorithm for data compression in the 80s paved the way for the modern IT revolution, winning numerous engineering prizes such as the Marconi Prize and the BBD Prize. In fact, every smart-phone contains some portion of this algorithm inside it.

Other Technion alumni to have made landmark discoveries include Dov Moran, who invented the USB flash drive.

Partnerships, Innovation & Translational Research

"I jokingly say that the spirit of high-tech or entrepreneurship replaced the spirit of the Kibbutz from 50 years ago, " says President Lavie. "The reason Israel is a start-up nation is because of Technion graduates. 85% of our engineering students are involved in the high-tech sector in Israel, 42% are involved in starting a new company, one in four has at least one patent after graduating from the Technion. Most of them are in managerial positions, and if you take the number of Israeli companies registered on the NASDAQ, we are second or the third after the US and China. More than two-thirds of these companies were either founded and/or are run by Technion graduates. So, there is something in the education of the Technion that instils in the students the spirit of pioneering, innovation, entrepreneurship and leadership." Technion has a well-established two-part system to aid entrepreneurship, innovation and technology transfer. The Technion Liaison Office promotes research and development opportunities, and deals with the formation of partnerships and business plans. Its four-point structure includes funding grants, connecting companies to relevant Technion resources, R&D development programmes and researcher mobility.

T³ is the commercialization unit of the Technion that is dedicated to transforming discovery and innovation into practical applications. T³ is responsible for the protection and maintenance of IP development, IP licensing, and all business regarding industries and spin-off companies. Bylaws are such that the IP belongs to the Technion, but all profits are shared 50-50 between researchers and the institution. One of its major success stories is the drug Azilect for treating Parkinson's.

The Technion also provides financial support to associated companies and is dedicated to closing the "valley of death": the point between proof of concept and commercial viability where many ideas never get off the ground.

Teaching, Learning & Student Life

Whilst the Technion is demanding of its students intellectually, several projects have been implemented to ease the pressure placed on them. Freshmen benefit from a more individual approach to teaching, with smaller groups and a great emphasis placed on mathematics to provide a solid foundation for the STEM focused education one can expect at the university.

A committee of students and faculty pick the top 10 educators of the year, and award significant prizes to encourage continual improvement and open dialogue between students and their professors.

Internationalisation of the student body has been tackled in numerous ways through the newly formed Technion International School. It covers a range of activities, including (i) summer high school programs for high school kids to nurture the scientists and engineers of tomorrow, (ii) full undergraduate programs in engineering taught in English (BSc Civil and Environmental Engineering) (iii) semester and summer programs for international students and (iv) graduate full-time degrees in English in business, engineering and medicine. Students live in on-campus dormitories and are offered a holistic experience that includes social activities, trips around Israel, and individual counselling.

Technion's international profile was significantly boosted by its landmark partnership with Cornell University, in winning the competition to establish a new applied science campus in New York City.

ARIZONA ®

Name › University of Arizona
Region › Americas
Country › United States
Founded › 1885

www.arizona.edu

Core Research Strengths

Founded in 1885 the University of Arizona actually predates the eponymous state, which was founded in 1912. Nowadays the university is ranked among the top 20 of America's public research universities and commands an annual research budget of $600 million. Its research strengths include environment, optics, astronomy and space sciences, biosciences and Southwest border issues.

Arizona's space sciences programme particularly stands out. It is awarded more NASA grants for space exploration than any other university nationally. For example the UA was awarded over $400 million for its Lunar and Planetary Laboratory (LPL) to lead NASA's 2007–08 mission to Mars to explore the Martian Arctic. The LPL's work in the Cassini spacecraft orbit around Saturn is larger than that of any other university in the world.

Of course working in a cutting edge area like space requires significant investment in research infrastructure. To this end the UA harnesses the collective strength of the Association of Universities for Research in Astronomy, a consortium of institutions pursuing research in astronomy. The association operates observatories and telescopes with one of the most famous examples being the Kitt Peak National Observatory located close to the UA, just outside of Tucson. Looking forward, one of UA's exciting current projects involves building the world's most advanced telescope. Known as the Giant Magellan Telescope, the instrument will produce images 10 times sharper than those from the Earth-orbiting Hubble Telescope. The telescope is set to be completed in 2016 at a cost of US $500 million. Researchers from at least nine other institutions in the association are working to secure the funding for the project.

When the new project is complete it will greatly improve humankind's understanding of the world around it. As such it's a good example of how the university tries to produce research that changes the world.

Major Discoveries

Given the university's expertise in space sciences it is little surprise that some of its most significant discoveries have come in related fields. For example Nicolaas Bloembergen won the 1981 Nobel Prize in Physics for his contribution to the development of laser spectroscopy.

Partnerships, Innovation & Translational Research

The university launched Tech Launch Arizona to facilitate the transfer of discoveries at the UA into intellectual property, inventions and technology. It also supports the UA's robust entrepreneurial approach to company start-ups and investment.

The other important way that Arizona extends its influence in the society around it is through its students. It has created the US BRAVO programme to provide global research experience for talented undergraduate science majors. This program is open to UA undergraduates with at least six months of research experience. It offers the opportunity to travel to a foreign country and work with an expert in the student's field of study. Interested students present a detailed proposal to a faculty committee that selects the scholars. To date, more than 200 students have conducted research at more than 80 institutions in 35 countries.

Teaching, Learning & Student Life

With more than 40,000 students the UA is a large-sized American university. The main campus sits on 380 acres in central Tucson close to the city's downtown. That means there is plenty for students to enjoy when they're not hard at work. As the second-largest city in the state of Arizona, Tucson is full of excellent outdoor activities, shopping, museums, and art galleries. Another great plus is the weather. Boasting an average 350 sunny days a year and warm dry air, Tucson's climate is ideal for year-round outdoor recreation. For example summer's cooler early mornings and late evenings invite outdoor dining and activities like hiking, and horseback riding; early and later tee times are available at seasonally reduced prices. Even winter,

where temperatures average highs of 64-75 °F, is perfect for major events. Some of the most famous are the WGC-Accenture Match Play Golf Championship, La Fiesta de los Vaqueros-Tucson Rodeo and the Tucson Festival of Books.

There is also plenty on offer inside the classroom too as the University of Arizona offers a wide variety of academic programs, many of which are among the nation's best. Students can choose from more than 340 undergraduate and graduate degrees through 20 colleges and 19 schools on three campuses. The university also places great store in research-led teaching. Arizona's researchers teach and students work alongside world-class professors to discover new knowledge and launch their own careers. The university's academic mission stresses the importance of access and quality. And, with the university ranked 19th by the National Science Foundation for its research, students have great access to top quality professors.

**UPPSALA
UNIVERSITET**

Name › Uppsala University
Region › Europe
Country › Sweden
Founded › 1477

www.uu.se

Core Research Strengths

As Sweden's first university, founded in 1477, Uppsala University's (UU) long tradition of academic excellence has had a significant influence on Sweden's socio-cultural, political and economic development in recent centuries. Today UU's broad strength throughout the academic disciplines has culminated in an interdisciplinary research strategy covering three broad interrelated fields – Nature, Environment and Technology, Life and Health; and Individuals and Society. UU's organisational strategy is designed to harness excellence in basic research and disciplinary strength towards overcoming complex challenges for the benefit of society and the economy.

Under the broad umbrella of Life & Health, UU draws upon its great strengths in areas such as cancer research, drug development and discovery, as well as genomics to help overcome today's critical healthcare challenges such as neurological disorders associated with ageing, resistance to antibiotics and the development of more effective diagnostic methods and treatments for a range of cancers. SciLifeLab Uppsala is a particularly exciting development; working to better understand the most basic molecular basis for complex disorders so as to be able to identify things such as genetic risk factors with the hope of earlier diagnosis and more effective treatments.

Under the auspices of Nature, Environment & Technology the broad strategic direction is on global survival through the development of a sustainable environment; perhaps today's most critical issue. Renewable energy and functional materials is of paramount importance within this context, a field that UU is at the cutting edge of throughout a range of technologies from next generation batteries and smart grids, to more efficient solar cells and wind turbines.

Human interactions with cutting edge science and subsequent social change are also of great importance, it is within the broad topic area of Individuals & Society that these sorts of questions are investigated and our understanding improved. By integrating disciplinary strengths in areas such as behavioural science, peace & conflict research, religions and economics UU researchers are furthering our understanding of how conflicts are resolved and how human understandings of major international challenges such as energy security are evolving.

Major Discoveries

Uppsala is mustering its forces to enhance our knowledge of infectious diseases and antibiotics resistance. Humans and animals are largely susceptible to the same pathogenic viruses and bacteria. This is why we need a concerted effort from multiple actors to fight infectious diseases.

Blue and green algae, long thought to be one of the possible solutions to human energy demand are being developed by UU researchers with a goal of developing algae based fuels. These living fuel machines can convert sun and water to energy through photosynthesis.

A new DNA study from UU shows humankind's complex origins in Africa. The Khoe and San peoples in southern Africa are directly descended from the first branching of the genealogical tree of today's humans. The findings play an important role for the understanding of the evolutionary history of humans.

Partnerships, Innovation & Translational Research

Similarly to most leading research universities, UU's approach to collaboration is increasingly taking on an international dimension, as well as a growing emphasis upon working across a diverse array of institutions from philanthropic funding groups to multinational corporations. Whilst the priorities of generating additional funding opportunities and developing new areas of knowledge are of paramount importance; UU will not consider sacrificing basic academic principles such as those of curiosity driven research, and the right to publish in favour of the priorities for collaborative partners.

UU Innovation acts as the interface between the university and external partners in industry. UU Innovation's activities are two-fold, on the one hand developing collaborative research projects, on the other developing intellectual property and patents for commercialisation either through licensing agreements or spin-off companies. Established in 2007, UU Innovation has made major contributions to recent increases in Uppsala's portfolio of spin-off companies.

UU has approximately 500 collaborative and exchange agreements with universities throughout the international community, as well as being a member of prestigious university consortia such as the Coimbra Group, the U4 Network and the Matariki Network.

Teaching, Learning & Student Life

As Sweden's pre-eminent university town, students at UU can expect beautiful surroundings with a diverse portfolio of buildings dating back to the University's founding in 1477. This comes with the added benefit of Uppsala arguably being one of the world's safest international student destinations. A tradition with its origins in the 17th century, the organisation of students into 13 different associations called "nations" is a unique aspect of student life at UU; enabling students to socialise and meet new friends whilst undertaking interesting activities in their respective nations. Facilities at UU campus areas are very modern; students can expect to find ubiquitous wifi networks and the latest equipment to support their studies.

UU's teaching approach has evolved towards collaborative, problem based learning with students often working in groups bouncing ideas off each other with the informal guidance of their professor or course instructor. The learning environment at UU is very laid back with students and faculty often discussing their opinions over a coffee. The problem based learning approach feeds into students being encouraged to think innovatively and make new discoveries, with new ventures into the market place supported by UU Innovation.

UNIVERSITY OF HELSINKI

Name › University of Helsinki
Region › Europe
Country › Finland
Founded › 1640

www.helsinki.fi/university

Core Research Strengths

Over the past few decades Finland has transformed itself from an agricultural economy to a leader in several high tech fields. The success of many of its companies, especially Nokia, has helped plough further revenue into research. Another key cornerstone of its success is the University of Helsinki. The university coordinates 25 of the 41 National Centers of Excellence, selected by the Academy of Finland by international evaluation on the basis of research quality.

The university has a broad research remit, says Chancellor Ilkka Niiniluoto. "The key principles of its research strategy concern the selection of research focus areas, the regular use of research quality assessments, improving research infrastructure and services, recruiting talented scholars, establishing new paths of academic careers, and improving doctoral education in doctoral schools."

With regards to improving research infrastructure the university has established institutes for high-energy physics, information technology, biotechnology, neuroscience, drug discovery, molecular medicine, environmental research, urban studies and European studies.

One of the most exciting new centers is the Institute for Molecular Medicine Finland (FIMM), says Chancellor Niiniluoto. "It is making very advanced use of the bio-banks of the Finnish genomic and disease data. Medical treatments may depend on your genetic background and the aim is to create a personal genetic profile that helps the doctors to develop special treatments for the problems that you may have such as cancer."

Of course creating so many institutes costs a lot of money, but by virtue of being among the ten most successful European universities, the University of Helsinki has received 26 grants from the European Research Council (ERC). In total the university receives €225 million in research funding each year with the majority coming from public sources like the Academy of Finland and the European Union.

Major Discoveries

One of the University's most notable research awards came in 1945 when A.I. Virtanen was awarded the Nobel Prize in Chemistry for his research into agricultural and nutrition chemistry, especially for his fodder preservation method.

Partnerships, Innovation & Translational Research

A modern research university must have intensive international collaboration, says the Chancellor. To that end the University of Helsinki was one of the twelve founding members of the League of European Research Universities (LERU). Today LERU has 21 leading research-intensive universities as its members, selected by criteria of research excellence.

Chancellor Niiniluoto is also keen to improve links with private-sector companies. "Our Bioscience Campus in Viikki hosts a business and science park for start-up companies in the biosciences and biotechnology. The university also participates in several new strategic centers of science, technology and innovation."

The University is also the owner of a technology transfer company Helsinki Innovation Services Ltd and a shareholder of a regional development company Culminatum. The aim of the two companies is to generate IP for the university. The challenge, admits the Chancellor, is striking the right balance in IP negotiations. "We want our ideas to benefit the world, but we also want to receive fair reward for the research."

The university also has close relations with other research institutes. It has well over 100 bilateral agreements with other leading universities, is an active participant in European student exchange programmes and frequently sends scholars to international conferences.

Teaching, Learning & Student Life

Finland has a truly world-class education institution with many high-quality vocational, non-academic options for its young people. As a result university education, which is free, is restricted to the top applicants. This is reflected in the size of the University of Helsinki, which awards close to 6000 degrees per year, of which almost 500 are doctoral degrees. In addition there are another 2000 foreign degree students who participate in English language Masters programmes and doctoral schools.

One of the key elements of a student's learning experience at the university is the multidisciplinary study programme, says the Chancellor. "We try to encourage students to take subjects from other faculties. In many cases each student can create sort of individual study programmes. So for example, we have a program for environmental studies, which is open to students not only from the biosciences but also from the social sciences. So, it combines approaches from several different disciplines."

Outside of the classroom Helsinki has plenty to offer, having consistently been ranked as the one of the best student cities. Although the university dates back to 1640 it moved to Helsinki in 1828 – 16 years after that city became the new capital. As a result it has a prime location in the old centre of the city. The 'centre campus' is in the downtown of Helsinki, while three newer campuses for medicine, natural science and biosciences, have since been built in the suburbs. With a population of 1 million people, if you include the surrounding areas, Helsinki has grown into a vibrant modern capital. Attractions include walking by the sea, taking a boat or visiting the spectacular surrounding countryside.

Universiteit Leiden
The Netherlands

Name › Leiden University
Region › Europe
Country › Netherlands
Founded › 1575

www.leiden.edu

Core Research Strengths

Leiden University is the oldest university in the Netherlands and has a rich academic history. It was the first university in the Netherlands to practise freedom of belief and religion, as reflected in the university's motto, Praesidium Libertatis (Bastion of Liberty). Indeed it was this enlightened atmosphere that provided the right environment for philosophers such as Spinoza and Descartes to develop their ideas.

Of course no university can afford to live on its past and today Leiden has restructured its research capabilities to focus on six themes it believes will have a key role in the future. These research themes are: Fundamentals of Science; Health, Life and Biosciences; Health across the Human Life Cycle; Law, Democracy and Governance; The Asian Challenge; The Global Interaction of Civilizations and Languages.

Needless to say, researching these themes transcends the traditional boundaries between disciplines and faculties. And that calls for a multidisciplinary approach, says Rector of Leiden University, Paul van der Heijden. "For example in life sciences we have all kinds of research, including anything connected to bio life sciences. Really it's a combination of fundamental and natural sciences and biosciences, together with health."

The next important step is great research infrastructure, says the Rector. "When it comes to Health, Life and Biosciences, we have a big academic medical hospital and a bioscience park that has around 7,000 people working there."

Location also plays an important role in the university's research efforts. Leiden has had a leading role in international law for more than 400 years. And having The Hague just ten minutes away by train is a massive advantage, says the Rector. "The Hague is the legal capital of the world. It gives our academics a front row seat on some of the most important events in their fields. It also gives us access to leading figures from around the world when they visit The Hague." Indeed the university has opened up an office in The Hague to make sure it takes full advantage.

Major Discoveries

Over its long history Leiden has won leading research awards across many disciplines. There are too many to mention here but an interesting cross section is the decade starting in 1973. In less than ten years Leiden professors won a Nobel Prize in Medicine in 1973 (Nikolaas Tinbergen), The Sveriges Riksbank Prize in Economic Sciences in 1975 (Tjalling Koopmans) and then the Nobel Prize in Physics in 1981 (Nicolaas Bloembergen).

Partnerships, Innovation & Translational Research

Like many Dutch universities, Leiden is very open and has a wide range of partnerships with other research institutions, non-profit organisations, government authorities and the business sector.

One of the best examples, says Rector van der Heijden, is the Medical Delta. "It is a co-operation between our medical school and the medical school of Rotterdam, Erasmus University and Delft University of Technology."

The university also has strong ties with the private sector, says the Rector. "We are working together with industries in the pharmaceutical area. We have an institute for pharmacology and the development of pharmaceuticals. I would say there is a strong relationship with business in our bioscience park - they are working closely together with our institute for pharmaceutical research."

Leiden, like many of its peers, is following a strong internationalisation policy. For example it wants to increase the proportion of foreign students from 15%, which is already relatively high, to 20%. To achieve that aim the university is using one of its best assets – its proximity to The Hague. "We are starting an international studies programme in the Hague and a three-year undergraduate programme. It is in English and it is attracting great numbers of international students."

Teaching, Learning & Student Life

Being in Leiden for more than 400 years means that the university has 'grown up' with the city. It permeates the local surroundings and university premises are scattered throughout Leiden. For students that means that wandering to class involves walking past the canals, historical buildings and alleyways that have been home to some of modern European culture's finest moments. If students crave a 'big city experience' Amsterdam is only 20 minutes away on the excellent train service. However, they should make sure they are in Leiden on October 3rd when the town's annual festival takes place.

Life inside the classroom is also very appealing. Unlike some competitors, who concentrate on well-funded research and leave educating to junior staff, Leiden closely integrates the two aspects. Indeed one of the key skills taught in Leiden is the ability to carry out independent research and all students are required to carry out a research project to complete the Bachelor's programme.

Rigorous though the Bachelor's is, the university encourages students to take a Master's stage, on the principal that it is the only way to deliver a complete educational programme. The Master's can either consist of a one-year programme or a more challenging two-year research variant. And students certainly won't be short of academic choice. In total Leiden offers over 50 three-year bachelor's programmes and almost a 100 one or two-year master's programmes.

Leiden University
Netherlands

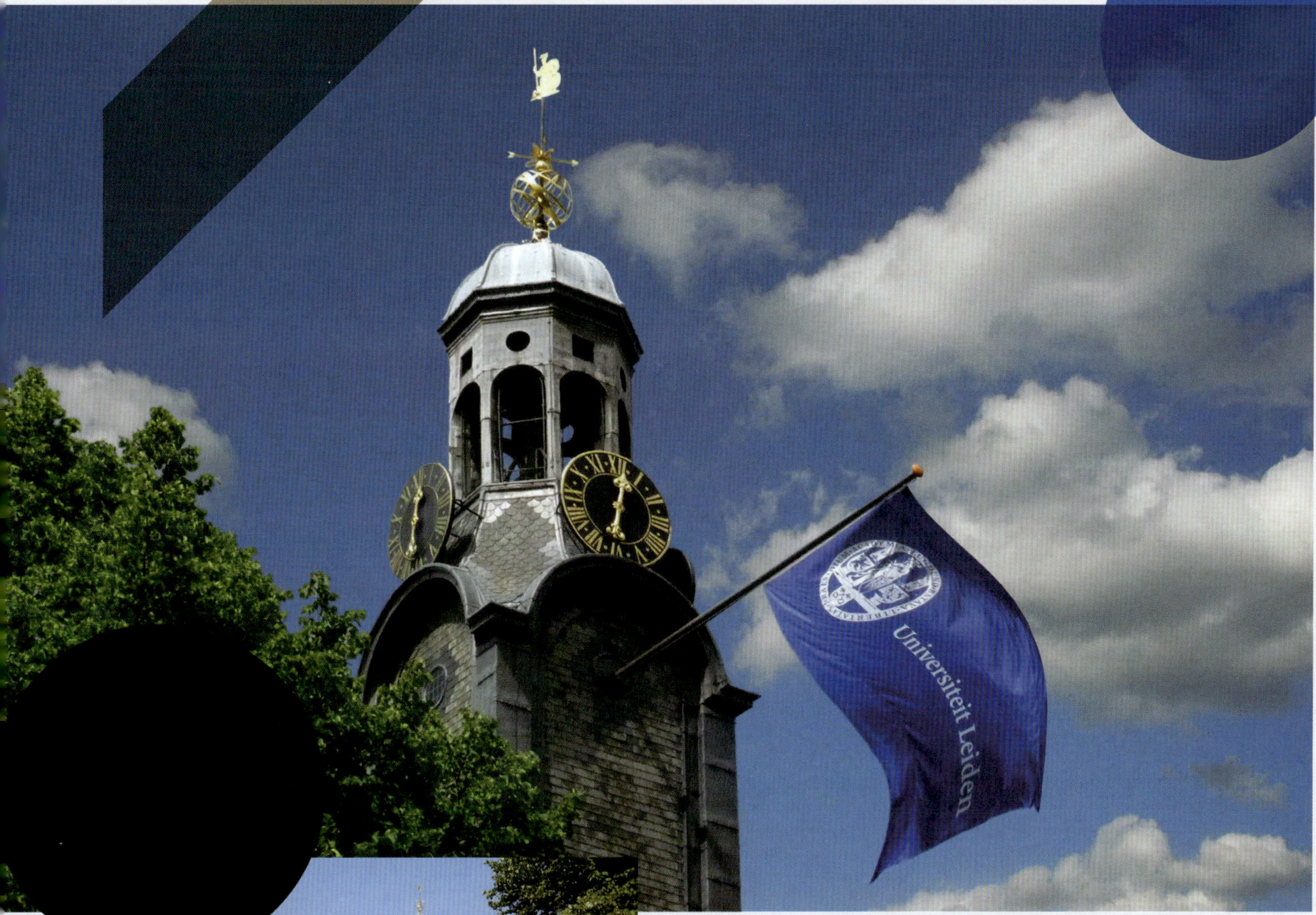

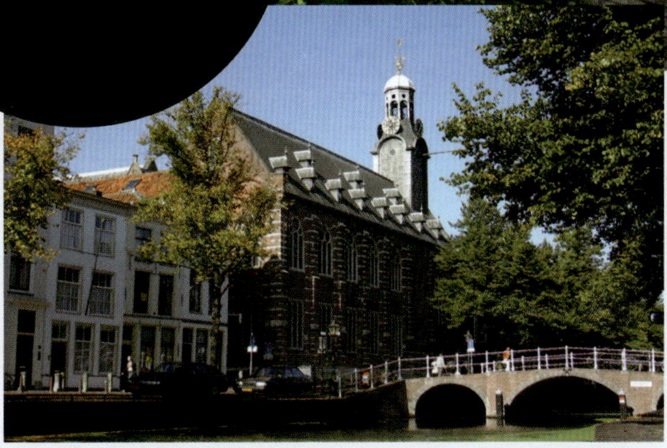

ENS
ÉCOLE NORMALE SUPÉRIEURE

Name › Ecole Normale Superieure – Paris
Region › Europe
Country › France
Founded › 1794

www.ens.fr

Core Research Strengths

Ecole Normale Supérieure (ENS) is a french elite institution that encompasses both science and humanities. It has a strong international reputation in particular for its research and education centers in physics, mathematics, biology, cognitive studies, philosophy and ancient studies.

Teaching and research are organized into fourteen departments, seven in sciences (biology, chemistry, cognitive sciences, computer science, geosciences, mathematics and physics) and seven in humanities (ancient studies, art studies, economy and social sciences, geography, history, literature & languages; and philosophy). These departments are structured into 37 research units. The exposure of students to cutting edge research is central to the educational project at Ecole Normale Supérieure. Shared infrastructure platforms provide strong support for experimental studies. The main library of humanities and social sciences, with about 1.000.000 volumes in providing free access to researchers, is a renowned center for research in Paris.

Interdisciplinary research is strongly encouraged, and can be run efficiently thanks to the relatively small size of the institution. There exist several formal inter-departmental groupings such as a structure at the interface of physics, chemistry and biology, one in environmental & ecological research, as well as actions that span sciences and humanities, in history and philosophy of sciences, and in geophysics, chemistry and archaeology. The department of cognitive sciences is intrinsically interdisciplinary, as it involves researchers ranging from neurobiologists to mathematicians and from physicists to philosophers.

Research policy objectives for the period 2010-2013 include "developing international networks in order to attract more researchers and students, promoting interdisciplinary and pioneering research, and enforcing an overarching research policy that facilitates interactions and innovative themes." Director Marc Mezard believes this approach is strongly beneficial: "Interdisciplinary research is part of the general climate at Ecole Normale; we insist a lot on collaboration between research groups from very different horizons. This in turn helps to shape innovative courses, and I think that students really benefit from it."

Major Discoveries

Ecole Normale Supérieure is unrivalled in its reputation for educating many of France's leading intellectuals, from Sartre to Merleau-Ponty or Foucault. Its alumni include thirteen Nobel Prize Laureates – eight of which were in the field of physics, including the 2012 prize awarded to Serge Haroche, who carries his research in the Ecole's physics department. The Ecole boasts all the ten French holders of the Fields Medal.

Partnerships, Innovation & Translational Research

In recent years Ecole Normale Supérieure has joined a group of 13 similarly strong research-led institutions, known as Paris Science et Lettres (PSL). This allows to tighten its traditional links with partner institutions like College de France and Observatoire de Paris, and also to extend it to new disciplines, like management and artistic creation. At the core of this cluster are the governmental research organisms, CNRS, INSERM and Inria, which are major partners of ENS for research activities. Development and commercialization of findings are handled in partnership with CNRS, inside PSL. Cooperative structures exist with the main Paris universities.

International collaboration exists not only in the European community, but with more than 100 countries around the world, including the US, Canada and parts of Asia to tackle global issues at an international level.

Teaching, Learning & Student Life

Ecole Normale Supérieure can be considered a hybrid of France's two university systems in that it complies to the selective process of Grande Ecoles, but functions as a research university.

Each year about 200 new French students are accepted from the selection system of Grandes Ecoles and about 120 through other channels, around 40 international students, and around 100 exchange students – a relatively small number. Typically the total of 2,500 students is comprised of approximately 700 Phd students. Most of the student body, live and study together, mostly on the historical Rue d'Ulm buildings in Paris' Latin Quarter, benefiting from the close-knit and entirely integrated community, with its intense cultural life.

Ecole Normale Supérieure involves students in its research from their first year at the institution, which is typically their third year of university studies; researchers on an intense one-to-one basis tutor them. Director Marc Mezard believes this is a key pillar of Ecole Normale's success "We are extremely active to have our students embedded as soon as possible in research, and tutored by researchers from the community at Ecole Normale. This is made possible by the fact that we have a relatively small group of very high level students".

Internationalization is a key topic on the institution's agenda, with steps being taken to increase the number of foreign students at all levels depending on departmental focus. In physics and biology, International Masters are taught in English; intensive French lessons are provided so that the students can get the best of the Paris cultural life; there are also specific fellowships for students coming from abroad.

Name › University of Florida
Region › Americas
Country › United States
Founded › 1853

www.ufl.edu

Core Research Strengths

Florida's leading university traces its beginnings to a small seminary in 1853. It opened its doors in Gainesville in 1906 with 102 students. Today, it is one of the most comprehensive and academically diverse universities in the United States, and commands an annual research budget of $619million.

"One of the unique aspects of the University of Florida, when compared with other universities around the world, is that we are so comprehensive", says President Bernie Machen. "We cover almost any kind of research from space, agriculture and animal medicine to human pathogens as well as plant pathogens. Thus, we have huge strength in our ability to bring multidisciplinary teams together to help find solutions to major global issues. This plays out in health, it also plays out in agriculture, as well as in sustainability and ecology as we try to look at problems there. Our core strength is in our ability to bring together different research disciplines and produce excellent results; this very much differentiates us from some of the other universities."

While it is certainly true that UF is a very comprehensive institution – it is one of only six U.S. universities with colleges of medicine, veterinary medicine, law, engineering and agriculture all on one campus – there is also a clear health focus. For example, more than $323 million of the total research budget was spent on health-related issues. The money is split between various dedicated centers, such as the Institute on Aging, the McKnight Brain Institute, the UF Genetics Institute, the UF Shands Cancer Center, and the Emerging Pathogens Institute and the six colleges of the Health Science Center.

Some of the university's research is heavily influenced by its location in Florida, says President Machen. For example it has a heavy focus on citrus fruits and water-related issues, which are both important to the region's famous orange juice industry. "These types of agricultural engineering programmes use our multidisciplinary strength to find solutions to problems." UF also has more distinctive areas of expertise. For example it is one of only

25 universities that have a veterinary medicines programme."

Major Discoveries

The university's most recent Nobel Prize came in 2005 when Robert Grubbs was awarded The Nobel Prize in Chemistry for his work in the field of olefin metathesis. A less cerebral, but much more well-known discovery, came in 1965 when scientists at the university invented Gatorade – named after the college football team – which went on to become the world's most popular sports drink.

Partnerships, Innovation & Translational Research

When it comes to interacting with private-sector companies, it is a big advantage to be based in America, says President Machen. "The commercialisation of research is an area where I think the United States is uniquely ahead on now." One reason for this is public policy, explains the President. "The states and the Federal Government are telling universities that they would prefer us to spend more time developing the results of our research, rather than just doing the research."

That support has translated into funding dollars. For example, the Federal Government provided more than half the funds to build UF's latest incubator, Innovation Hub at UF. It's an approach that appears to work as there are 22 start-up companies in that incubator receiving logistical support and advice in order to help them become commercially sustainable.

Indeed research from the University of Florida has already resulted in several commercially successful products. Aside from Gatorade, there has been many more, including Trusopt, a leading treatment for glaucoma, and the Sentricon Termite Elimination System.

When it comes to research collaborations, UF has teamed up with Scripps Florida, the Burnham Institute for Medical Research and the Moffitt Cancer Center.

Teaching, Learning & Student Life

Aside from Disney World, the main reason people come to Florida – one of the world's most popular tourist destinations – is the weather. Students might be there for different reasons but they still want to enjoy Florida's famous all-year-around sunshine. Fortunately UF's spacious, 2000-acre campus is designed to let them do just that. Many outdoor activities are available for students, with a host of courts and playing fields on campus. There are also picnic spots, a lake and an 81-acre wildlife sanctuary. The campus is also surrounded by Florida countryside, so those who venture out have many recreational lakes and rivers to enjoy.

Another plus for students is the university's commitment to integrating graduate education and research. UF undergrads, through the University Scholars Program, work one-on-one with Florida faculty on selected research projects. Undergraduates also may take advantage of the new Innovation Academy. IA gives students a small-college experience focused on delivering curricular and co-curricular activities centred on innovation, creativity, entrepreneurship, ethics and leadership.

Students also benefit from low student to faculty ratios, with most class sizes capped at 25. As would be expected from such a comprehensive university, there is a wide array of courses for prospective students to choose from. The Graduate School coordinates almost 200 graduate programmes, while the various professional degree programmes include dentistry, law, medicine, pharmacy and veterinary medicine.

71

Name › Boston University
Region › Americas
Country › United States
Founded › 1839

www.bu.edu

Core Research Strengths

A comparatively young university in terms of research, Boston University (BU) has completely reinvented itself in the past 30 years. It has gone from an institution recognised predominantly for its strengths in the social sciences and humanities to a global brand, excelling in medical science, science and engineering as well as its traditional disciplines. The university's relative youth has allowed it to grow research areas considered important today and into the future, with highly streamlined departments that focus on specific areas whilst maintaining a cross-disciplinary approach.

BU's relative youth is a key advantage for President Robert Brown: "Because we are a young university, we did not grow up having to have all our disciplines to have equal strength, and we have been able to focus on places we think are very important to today and for the future. I will give you an example. We have a wonderful college of engineering. They only have three departments and one division. There are a number of the traditional engineering disciplines, including my own – I am a chemical engineer by training, which we do not have because that was not inside of the scope that we wanted to put together. For example, we have a biomedical engineering program that's one of the top ones in the country; that has been a focus or strength for us for the last 20-25 years. We saw very early the importance of bringing engineering research into the medical community."

The university's science department invests in a detailed range of research and technology, from photonics to nano-technology, the output of which is then linked back to biomedical application and nano-medicine. Systems neuroscience is another research area shared among the disciplines, as is their work on emerging infectious diseases

Importantly, alongside the rapid innovation in these research pockets, Boston University has reinforced its credentials in the humanities, business, media and social sciences.

Major Discoveries

Recently awarded the Research Centre of Excellence in Autism by the National Institute of Health – the second of its kind in the US. BU researchers made the front page of Time Magazine with their work showing National Football League (NFL) players exhibiting neurological symptoms similar to Alzheimer's disease. Boston University also has a group of professors at work on the Large Hadron Collider at CERN and in 2012 it became a member of the Association of American Universities (AAU) – an association of the 62 leading research universities in the US and Canada.

Partnerships, Innovation & Translational Research

Boston University is a vocal champion of interdisciplinary research for its ability to generate innovative interaction and ways of thinking. Although it is invested in creating a faculty of leading scholars and researchers, BU does consider Translational Research and Technology Transfer in terms of the economic gain or quantitative output it can generate. Partnerships are taken on area-by-area interest wherein partners are sought for the interests held by the faculty. The photonics laboratory has invested in creative partnerships with companies as well as benefited from government support. Amongst the successes stemming from this approach are ground-breaking research on energy consumption, greenhouse gas emissions and computing environments.

The Office of Technology Development has systems in place that can give potential partners support in proof of concept for products or processes with commercial potential. BU also aids in getting outside start-up capital in ways many universities do not. There are set policies and practices that facilitate the collaboration between faculty and companies, that are able to manage contentious issues such as conflict of interest and intellectual property.

Boston University is also committed to international interactions and collaborations that tackle global problems. For example, influential research into the development impact of public health issues, such as the spread of HIV / AIDS and urban management, is carried out under the Smart Cities project.

Teaching, Learning & Student Life

Beginning as a regional teaching university for students of the Boston area, today's student body is thoroughly international. This global flavour is enriched with a great history of international programmes – there is a large study abroad programme built around BU's own facilities in 23 countries. Each year 2500 students take part in these programmes.

Boston University is an institution where students from around the world can benefit from a low student-to-faculty ratio of around 12 to 1, which allows for excellent interaction opportunities and a very personalised education. Traditional liberal arts as well as sciences are offered, with a full range of undergraduate professional schools. This allows undergraduates to major in one part of the university but participate in, and interact with, a broad range of other subject areas, thus encouraging interdisciplinary innovation.

Boston University is in the sixth year of the "choosing to be great" ten-year plan to commit and generate resources to improve the excellence of the university through recruiting world-leading faculty members, developing new programmes and enhancing the undergraduate experience.

Student life at Boston University benefits from its unique setting in this famous college town, rubbing shoulders with academic neighbours Harvard and MIT, and counting Martin Luther King Jr. as one of its alumni. President Brown strongly believes BU's location significantly enhances the experience: "Boston is probably the best college town in the world density-wise. We are a very unique university because as I sit in my office I can see out of my window Memorial Hall at Harvard and I can see the dome at MIT right now across the river. We stretch as a campus for almost 2 miles down the Charles River on the south side of the river across from Harvard and MIT. We are a very residential university. We house over 80% of all of our students on our campus for all four years. We have 13,000 spaces for students in residences. So, we offer this very unique sort of a residential urban university experience."

University of BRISTOL

Name › University of Bristol
Region › Europe
Country › United Kingdom
Founded › 1876

www.bristol.ac.uk

Core Research Strengths

The University of Bristol is one of the UK's leading research institutions. It received its royal charter in 1909 and now has an annual external research budget of approximately £110million. The significant research focus is reflected in its membership of the Russell Group of British research universities, the European-wide Coimbra group and the Worldwide Universities Group.

As Professor Guy Opren, Pro Vice Chancellor for Research and Enterprise, explains, the university's research remit covers a wide range of disciplines. "We have leading research programs and individuals across our many academic areas, and a culture of research-led education and entrepreneurship. We have world-leading research activity in the arts and humanities and the medical, life, mathematical, physical and social sciences, as well as engineering.

We have recently established two major multidisciplinary University Research Institutes addressing grand societal and intellectual challenges, one in Health, the Elizabeth Blackwell Institute, the other in global risk and hazards, the Cabot Institute. We own and operate the UK's National Composites Centre, which brings together industry and academics to deliver world-class open innovation in the design and rapid manufacture of composite materials."

Indeed its expertise in the composite materials that are replacing steel in many car and aeroplane designs is one reason why European aeroplane manufacturer Airbus has located its wing development center there.

Professor Orpen goes on to explain: "High quality research and innovation are embedded in the culture of the University of Bristol, and across undergraduate and postgraduate curricula. As a world leading institution, we attract and retain the best researchers, who inspire and educate their students with research-led, cutting edge innovative teaching and discovery. Our range of innovation and entrepreneurship activities available to students is highly valued, and has won awards."

Major Discoveries

The university has a proud history of scientific discoveries. Probably the most significant was the work of Sir Nevil Mott. His work on 'solid state physics' led to the development of the transistor, arguably the most influential invention of the 20th century.

Partnerships, Innovation & Translational Research

Bristol is probably one of the most successful examples of translational research. Its National Composites Centre partners with some of the best names in global engineering. From British stalwarts like Rolls Royce to leading international players like Airbus, the centre is one way the university interacts with the private sector.

Another partnership model that the University uses is SETsquared - a collaboration between the universities of Bath, Bristol, Exeter, Southampton and Surrey. The idea is to partner in enterprise activities and collectively support the growth and success of new business opportunities through spin-outs, licensing, incubation and education. Professor Orpen says: "The University has always recognized the value of partnerships and collaboration, both nationally and internationally. We are a member of the Worldwide University Network, one of the premier global networks of research intensive universities. We have an important strategic relationship with Kyoto University, Japan, and with a number of other high quality universities around the globe. Increasingly our doctoral education is done in partnership with others, to maximize the quality of education and research training that our students experience. We are a member of the SETsquared Partnership which has developed leading practice in innovation, technology transfer, business incubation and acceleration, and enterprise education."

While the commercial aspect is important, it's not just about making money, says Professor Orpen: "Our partnerships are always based on excellence and a shared culture and values. They help accelerate the impact of our discoveries and thus benefit society as a whole."

Teaching, Learning & Student Life

A quick glance at the application statistics shows that Bristol is one of the UK's most popular universities. It has an average of 14 applicants for each undergraduate place, with more popular courses, such as Economics and Law, the applicant to place ratio is 40:1. So what is it that draws students to Bristol?

One factor is clearly the learning experience, says Prof Orpen. "As a world leading institution, we attract and retain the best researchers, who inspire and educate their students with research-led, cutting edge, innovative teaching and discovery. Our range of innovation and entrepreneurship activities available to students is highly valued, and has won awards."

"Places at the University of Bristol remain among the most sought after. The University's high popularity is further illustrated by the fact that Bristol was one of the few leading UK universities to modestly increase its undergraduate student numbers this year. At Bristol we expect the best for and from our students and that ethos supports us in partnering with our students to help them unlock their potential during their time at Bristol, and then as they embark on their chosen careers all over the world."

Another factor is the place itself. Situated on the banks of the River Avon, the city provides a bustling, picturesque place for students to unwind. Moreover, its history as a major port – it's a short, navigable journey to the Bristol Channel – has given Bristol a lively, multicultural atmosphere.

UNIVERSITÉ DE GENÈVE

Name › University of Geneva
Region › Europe
Country › Switzerland
Founded › 1559

www.unige.ch

Core Research Strengths

Founded in 1559 by John Calvin, arguably one of the most influential men of the last millennium, the University of Geneva (UNIGE) was initially focussed on theology. As the centuries passed it broadened its horizons, gradually adopting new disciplines as the world around it changed. Remarkably, in 1873 the university founded by a religious figure had become a secular institution. The changes have continued to the present day, but one thing that has remained constant is the university's adherence to humanistic values.

Today it is the second-largest university in Switzerland with 16,000 students from 140 nationalities. The University of Geneva offers more than 280 types of degrees and more than 250 Continuing Education programmes covering an extremely wide variety of fields: exact sciences, medicine and humanities. UNIGE also has a strong focus on international relations, thanks in part to Geneva being home to a vast number of international organisations.

UNIGE's research projects cover one hundred subjects and every year this leads to fruitful results such as 3300 publications in 2012. UNIGE is host and co-host to six National Centres of Competence in Research. It leverages the advantage of being based in the home of the Geneva Convention with a dedicated Academy of Human Rights, which is a joint venture with the Institute of International and Development studies (IHEID).

Major Discoveries

Perhaps the best proof of the university's success at adopting new disciplines is the array of research achievements in different fields. 10 Nobel Prize laureates have studied, researched or taught at the university. In 2010, Stanislav Smirnov is the latest being awarded the 2010 Fields medal for the proof of conformal invariance of percolation and the planar Ising model in statistical physics.

Partnerships, Innovation & Translational Research

The UNIGE has built up an extensive research network, thanks to which its scientists work closely with researchers from the United Nations Environment Programme, the European Organization for Nuclear Research, the European Organisation for Astronomical Research, the European Space Agency and NASA. In addition, UNIGE faculty members cooperate with colleagues from other Swiss universities and colleges in National Centres of Competence, four of which are based at the UNIGE itself.

Over the last few decades UNIGE has built on its existing links with other Swiss universities and developed a comprehensive network of international academic alliances. Thanks to the Erasmus programme and the Student Exchange Network of the Coimbra Group – it has partnerships with more than 100 international institutions for exchange.

UNIGE participates in European research programmes, either under the aegis of a European Union Research Framework Programme or as part of a European or international R&D programmes. It also has numerous partnerships with other institutions around the world. Membership of academic networks like the League of European Research Universities, Coimbra group or G3 give UNIGE researchers ample opportunity to meet their counterparts at partner universities in the course of joint projects.

Teaching, Learning & Student Life

Geneva is probably one of the World's most unique cities. It is, by international standards, a relatively small city but it offers cultural programs and infrastructure that larger rivals would be proud of. There is cuisine and people from all over the world, while nature lovers enjoy the 310 hectares of parks and 40,000 trees in public areas, along the lake shores or surrounding mountains, including Mont-Blanc, the highest peak in the Alps. Even though it is small and green there is still always something going on. Students can enjoy operas, movie festivals, concerts and theatre plays. All these assets stand Geneva out as one of the best international cities for its quality of life. The university has over 16,000 students. More than one-third of all students come from abroad, attracted by the University's quality and location in the heart of an international city, which is home to many international organizations. Like many other leading universities, Geneva has re-written its educational programme over the last decade in the wake of the Bologna Process. As a result it now has three main study cycles: the Bachelor's, the Master's and the Doctorate, with instruction coming through courses given ex-cathedra, seminars and practical works. Credit transfer is thus facilitated.

As appealing as Geneva is, one of the university's other main attractions is that it allows students to broaden their experience in other places. Its mobility policy allows students to continue their Bachelor's, Master's or Doctorate studies at another university in Switzerland or abroad for one or two semesters. The idea behind the programme is to improve their knowledge of a foreign language, and help them approach their studies in their chosen discipline from a different angle, as well as helping their development as true global citizens.

Name › King's College London
Region › Europe
Country › United Kingdom
Founded › 1829

www.kcl.ac.uk

Core Research Strengths

King's College London consists of nine Schools, which offer over 200 undergraduate and more than 230 postgraduate taught programmes as well as an extensive range of research opportunities for postgraduate students and staff. With over 25,000 students and over 6,500 staff it is one of the biggest universities in London. King's is one of the top seven UK universities for research earnings and has an annual overall income of more than £550 million.

King's has a particularly distinguished reputation in the humanities, law, the sciences (including a wide range of health areas such as psychiatry, medicine, nursing and dentistry) and social sciences including international affairs. It has played a major role in many of the advances that have shaped modern life, such as the discovery of the structure of DNA and research that led to the development of radio, television, mobile phones and radar.

Kings is in the top 25 in the world for arts and humanities and in the top 30 for biomedicine. Its Dental Institute is one of the most prestigious dental research institutions in the United Kingdom, while the Dickson Poon School of Law (renamed in 2012 thanks to a £20m donation from Hong Kong business man and philanthropist Dickson Poon) and Department of War Studies are both often ranked highly in the UK.

The Dickson Poon School of Law recently launched the largest ever scholarship programme for Law in the UK and rest of Europe, worth £2million a year, to attract the brightest and best students from around the world.

Research at King's is often based on specialist centers. It has five prestigious Medical Research Council centers and is one of only five Academic Health Sciences Centres in the UK. King's Health Partners is a pioneering global collaboration between the College and three of London's most successful NHS Foundation Trusts - Guy's and St Thomas', King's College Hospital and South London and Maudsley NHS Foundation Trusts.

The College continues to strengthen the connections between its Health Schools on the one hand, and its Arts & Sciences Schools on the other. King's Cultural Institute was established in 2011 to create an effective bridge between King's and the cultural and creative industries, providing leadership across King's College London to extend and enrich its range of collaborative activities with artists, arts professionals, cultural organisations, creative industries and cultural policy makers.

Major Discoveries

There are ten Nobel laureates who were either students or academics at King's and it has regularly made major contributions to the betterment of mankind. Some of the most notable include:

1917 Charles Barkla- Physics-For the discovery of X-ray fluorescence

1929 Sir Frederick Hopkins- Physiology or Medicine- For research on vitamins and beriberi

1951 Max Theiler- Physiology or Medicine- For developing a vaccine for yellow fever

1962 Maurice Wilkins- Physiology or Medicine- For the discovery of the structure of DNA

1988 Sir James Black-Physiology or Medicine- For the development of beta-blocker and anti- ulcer drugs

Partnerships, Innovation & Translational Research

One of the ways that King's interacts with the outside world is by providing higher education services to external organisations. In a typical year its consultancy services can earn revenues of £12m while its Professional & Executive Education service has annual revenues in excess of £18m.

Significant partnerships have been established with important companies such as Pfizer, Glaxo SmithKline and Tate & Lyle. The Intellectual Property (IP) Group has played a large role in supporting spinouts. Eighteen have been launched over the past five years and one is now listed on the Alternative Investment Market (AIM) in London.

Teaching, Learning & Student Life

The university is spread across four Thames-side campuses in central London, with another in South London. The campus environment has benefitted from a £1 billion redevelopment programme, which is transforming its estate.

Obviously one major advantage is London itself. The UK capital is a world centre unlike any other. London is the centre of the government and law in Britain. It is the financial capital of the world, it is one of the world's leading medical, legal, corporate, religious and research centres and it is a world cultural centre. In other words it is the perfect location for an institution with King's research strengths.

Teaching is underpinned by leading edge research, and rapid advances in knowledge inform the content of taught programmes. Students coming to King's will often work with academics that are national or international leaders in their respective fields.

The Students' Union offers membership of over 50 sports clubs and 200 societies and activity groups.

UiO : University of Oslo

Name › University of Oslo
Region › Europe
Country › Norway
Founded › 1811

www.uio.no

Core Research Strengths

Given that Norway is one of Europe's leading oil and gas producers, it is perhaps no surprise that energy is an important research focus area for the University of Oslo. What is remarkable, however, is that researchers are addressing all types of energy, including renewables. The idea, explains Rector Ole Petter Ottersen, is a holistic approach that examines every aspect of the energy problem. "We have just launched a new research and educational program called the Energy Initiative to explore how new forms of energy can be exploited and applied. This involves scientists from four of our eight faculties, i.e the faculties of Law, Social Sciences, Humanities and Mathematics and Natural Sciences."

A multidisciplinary approach is used to address a number of themes, says Rector Ottersen. For example a programme called KULTRANS investigates cultural transformations in the age of globalization, while another looks at emerging challenges in molecular life sciences.

Indeed, as Ottersen proudly points out, the university has a very broad research remit which requires excellence in a variety of fields. "We have research strengths in many fields, not just in the traditional medical and biological sciences, but also in the social sciences and the humanities." This wide-ranging research capability has been a key factor in winning research funding. The European Research Council grants serve as an objective measure of where we excel. The University of Oslo now has 22 ERC grants altogether; within fields as diverse as astrophysics, medicine, geosciences, chemistry, human rights, mathematics, philosophy, economics and social anthropology.

"Furthermore, since the Research Council of Norway began awarding centres of excellence (CoE) in 2003 we have received over 30% of the national total CoE's within the fields of Medicine, Mathematics and Natural Sciences, Social Sciences and the Humanities. So, the University of Oslo clearly has multiple strengths across many different disciplines and we are exploiting this through seven multi-faculty research programs."

Major Discoveries

Many universities claim to be broad-based research-intensive universities, but the University of Oslo has the research awards to prove it. In 1969 Odd Hassel was awarded the Nobel Prize in Chemistry for his work in the structure and transformation of organic molecules, and Ragnar Frisch won the first Nobel Prize in Economics in 1969; while in 1989 Trygve Haavelmo won the Nobel Prize in Economics for his work in econometrics.

Partnerships, Innovation & Translational Research

Securing funding is one of the key challenges for any research-intensive university. For Rector Ottersen, the public-funding model works well. "Most of our budget is based on government funding. The most important funding source aside from the government is the European Union framework programs. At the moment we have more than 100 running European Union-funded projects, whereas funding from industry is modest by comparison."

For readers in the US or UK, where institutions have long sought private partners to fund research programmes, the University of Oslo's public model may seem privileged. Rector Ottersen is aware of its many advantages. "We believe in a university where researchers are free to initiate their own projects." Nevertheless, the university does work with private partners where they share the same goals, says Ottersen, having recently established a TTO-office to encourage relations with external partners.

"Two years ago we founded what now stands as one of the biggest technology transfer companies in the Nordic countries, Inven2, which is jointly owned by the University of Oslo and South-Eastern Norway Regional Health Authority. The establishment of Inven2 was an important achievement that is likely to bring innovation at our university to a new level."

Teaching, Learning & Student Life

By international standards the University of Oslo is a medium-sized institution in a small capital city with 27,000 students, while Oslo itself has a population of 600,000. Yet that is also an advantage. The size and location mean that everything students need is within a short distance of the main campus, in a city surrounded by magnificent scenery from the fjords to the forested hills. Another plus is that Norwegian universities charge no tuition fees even for students from outside of the European Union.

These advantages attract many international students, something Rector Ottersen sees as extremely positive. "We strive to recruit students from all parts of the world, with different cultural backgrounds and a good gender balance. As we see it, the learning environment is reinvigorated by exposure to a multitude of views and perspectives. We are talking about 'internationalization at home'. Students from abroad are prioritized when it comes to housing, and more than 1000 topics are currently being taught in English."

Studies have shown that the academic appeal of the university is another major factor in attracting students. Indeed, high teaching quality is often listed as the number one reason that students choose to come to Oslo, where students also benefit from research opportunities, says Rector Ottersen.

"When we establish new interfaculty research areas, the premise is that these should be coupled to education. Thus, our new interfaculty energy initiative will serve as a platform for a multidisciplinary teaching program."

THE OHIO STATE UNIVERSITY

Name › The Ohio State University
Region › Americas
Country › United States
Founded › 1870

www.osu.edu

Core Research Strengths

With over 6200 academics and in excess of US$832 million in expenditures, Ohio State University's (OSU) research enterprise is an enormous operation spanning a vast spectrum of academic disciplines and interest areas. The scope and scale of the institution's research strength presents a significant challenge in highlighting specific core strengths aside from the university's ability to draw together a diverse array of expertise in multidisciplinary centres investigating complex issues of critical importance to people, environments and ecosystems around the world.

This interdisciplinary approach punctuates an excellent departure point to highlight some of OSU's core strengths. The university's has adopted a series of broad interest areas to define the scope and priorities from a research perspective; namely the broad areas of sustainability, food & agriculture and health & wellness. Under the umbrella of these broad interest areas some truly world-class research strengths stand out.

Led by the Byrd Polar Research Center, climate change research at Ohio State touches all seven continents and chronicles the change in our environment from centuries ago to the present. Research at the Center focuses on the role of cold regions in the Earth's overall climate system and encompasses geological sciences, geochemistry, glaciology, paleoclimatology, meteorology, remote sensing, and ocean dynamics.

Food and food security is another area in which OSU leads through the Food Innovation Center leading on numerous food associated issues such as food for health, nutrition, obesity, food safety, food production, and food strategy and policy.

In the broad area of advanced materials, OSU's Institute for Materials Research coordinates a large network of research facilities investigating cutting edge technologies from semiconductors and polymers to photovoltaics and bio-emergent materials.

Major Discoveries

Researchers at OSU have made advances in clean coal technology called chemical looping paving the way for a much more efficient use of coal, whereby CO_2 captured from the burning of coal is looped back into the process of energy generation reducing wastage and significantly increasing efficiency.

Following 5 years of construction, the Scarlet Laser was first switched on. The laser has the capacity to reach a peak intensity of 400 trillion watts, and has a diverse array of uses from the development of novel new cancer treatments to the prevention of smuggling in and out of US borders.

Doctorate student Jed Johnson discovered Nano Fibre Solutions, a revolutionary technique to grow human cells. Using microscopic fibres no bigger than a human hair, he developed 3D scaffolds of human tissue that mimic the human body's physical structure.

Partnerships, Innovation & Translational Research

Ranking second in the United States for industry-sponsored research, collaboration is very much in the DNA at Ohio State University. The university counts over 760 companies in its portfolio of private sector partners, over half of which are based in Ohio. OSU is an experienced international collaborator working alongside major multinational corporations such as the relationship the university has had with Honda since the 1980's. OSU's Industry Liaison Office (ILO) acts as the conduit between OSU faculty and potential private sector partners.

OSU has in recent years pioneered the "Gateways" strategy whereby opportunities are facilitated between the university to collaborate with public and private sector institutions, as well as universities in some of the world's most exciting emerging regions and cities. OSU has established strong relationships in China and India through the Gateways initiative, and is in the process of building closer links in Brazil beginning through initial collaborations in Sao Paolo.

Teaching, Learning & Student Life

OSU's sheer size and scale with over 65,000 students, 6200 faculty and 14 colleges all conducting research distinguishes the university from many counterpart institutions, with undergraduates and graduates alike presented with enormous variety in their teaching and learning options. Far from creating distance, OSU's culture of collaboration has reengineered the university's size into a massive advantage, with new partnerships and relationships developing throughout colleges and faculty each day.

The "First Year Experience" scheme at OSU facilitates the smooth transition for first year undergraduates into the university environment ensuring long-term success for all at OSU. The Living & Learning Environments program further enhances the university's sense of intimacy, community and collaboration with students sharing accommodation based upon their pre-defined interests and areas of study; a remarkable achievement for an institution of OSU's size and scale.

All OSU students are encouraged to get involved directly with research as soon as possible. The university's considerable industrial research agenda provides a myriad of opportunities for students to work on real world research questions and challenges. The thriving entrepreneurial culture at OSU allows for students to try to translate their research discoveries into the real economy, and out to the benefit of society through the Office of Technology Commercialization.

BROWN

Name › Brown University
Region › Americas
Country › United States
Founded › 1764

www.brown.edu

Core Research Strengths

Established in 1764, Brown is the seventh-oldest university in the United States. Nowadays, it is a research-intensive institution with an annual research budget of approximately US$170 million. It has core research strengths in the humanities, social sciences, life sciences, physical sciences and engineering.

Within those main research areas there are a number of programmes that are particularly prominent, says Vice President for Research, Clyde Briant. "One that we are very much involved with right now is the brain sciences program. We have the Brown Institute for Brain Sciences and one of its great achievements is that by implanting a small electrode in the brain, and then connecting that to a computer, it allows people who have lost the mobility of their arms and legs to control things. Either to control a mouse effectively on a computer screen, open their emails or play computer games."

The work of the Institute is important, says the Vice President, not only because of its amazing results but because it is a hallmark of the university's interdisciplinary approach. "It involves engineering, computer science, neuroscience and some of our affiliated clinical hospitals." Another good example of Brown's multidisciplinary approach is the Joukowsky Institute of Archaeology and the Ancient World. "It is a reasonably new institute that has been formed here at Brown and brings together people from the classics, from anthropology, from different disciplines to really look at a number of problems in archaeology as it relates to the ancient world."

Another interesting research strategy is that employed by the Institute for Computational and Experimental Research on Math (ICERM), which is sponsored by the National Science Foundation. "Instead of having one research topic that everyone is focused on for five years, there are short (three weeks to three months) symposia on different topics. People come from around the world and participate in these, and then they go back to their institutions hopefully with new ideas, having formed new collaborations and really built up a network so that they can work on these mathematical problems together."

Major Discoveries

Brown has a proud tradition in delivery of groundbreaking academic research, including the work of Nobel Prize Laureate Leon Neil Cooper. Professor Cooper, along with John Bardeen and John Robert Schrieffer, developed the BCS theory of superconductivity. He is also the namesake of the Cooper pair and co-developer of the BCM theory of synaptic plasticity.

Partnerships, Innovation & Translational Research

Brown has a number of important partnerships with the private sector, says Vice President Briant. "For over ten years we have run the Collaborative Research Lab with General Motors. It has been a terrific partnership. They wanted to be able to design new materials using computation and they recognised that our computational mechanics and material science programs are really outstanding."

Aside from direct bilateral partnerships like the one with GM, Brown also has a dedicated office to help commercialise its research. "We call it the Technology Ventures Office, and our job is to try to help the faculty get their research to society. We want to have an impact. We do feel that the university has an important role to play in the economy through this contribution."

In addition to the private sector, research is supported by government agencies, such as NASA and the National Science Foundation.

Brown is open to expanding its already well-developed international academic network. "We are always looking for universities to have partnerships with in various ways. We have a number of different types of collaborations with different universities around the world."

Teaching, Learning & Student Life

The university is located in Providence's East Side on picturesque College Hill, surrounded by dozens of historic homes and landmarks. "It's a very residential campus", says Vice President Briant, "a significant fraction of the undergraduates live in dorms and the campus is not too large, which helps to create a positive learning environment."

Close to campus are the vibrant Thayer Street, Wickenden Street and Wayland Square, where students and residents find ample shopping, dining and entertainment. Downtown Providence, with its popular mall, many restaurants, concert venues, train station, hotels, and scenic riverfront, is just a short walk from campus. Providence is known for its varied and high-quality restaurants.

Fortunately for students the choice of educational courses is just as varied as the food. Graduate students are enrolled in a total of 51 doctoral programs and two dozen Master's programs. Undergraduates can pursue bachelor's degrees in more than 70 concentrations, ranging from Egyptology to cognitive neuroscience. Another interesting element of the learning experience at Brown is the university's commitment to undergraduate academic freedom. But students be warned: that freedom works both ways and means students must take responsibility as architects of their courses of study.

More than 500 Brown undergraduate students study outside of the United States each year through numerous international partnerships offered by the Office of International Programs. Students can be found in classrooms, laboratories, libraries and research sites around the globe, participating in academic programs offered by Brown or in courses approved for credit by the university.

Australian
National
University

Name › The Australian National University
Region › Asia/Pacific
Country › Australia
Founded › 1946

www.anu.edu.au

Core Research Strengths

As a comprehensive university ANU is strong in a broad range of academic disciplines. Its scientific research efforts have won acclaim in a number of fields including Medical Sciences, Philosophy, Physical Sciences and Climate Change. The university also has some of the best humanities departments in the world.

One of the subjects that really stands out at ANU is Public Policy. Vice-Chancellor of the university Professor Ian Young AO explains why ANU excels at Public Policy.

"You need to appreciate that ANU is Australia's national university; that it has a special role within the Australian context in terms of its place in Canberra, the national capital. We have a strong relationship with government, and we feel that one of the critically important roles of the university is to play an important role in shaping the nation's future both in terms of the quality of the research we do, but also in terms of how that research is used to then influence government policy and public policy more generally. For a number of years now, building a very strong emphasis on these issues around public policy has been a priority at ANU."

Prof. Young also feels that the University's work in climate change is key both for the university and the world.

"We have the greatest concentration of climate researchers of any university in Australia, and this area is one of the most important of problems that faces humanity today." In particular, Vice-Chancellor Young feels that the ANU interdisciplinary approach is essential to solving the complex challenge of climate change.

"We have a broad sweep of people working in climate, from atmospheric modellers all the way to engineers working on new solar technology, to people in the humanities and social sciences looking at the political impacts, and the social issues that are associated with climate change. We have a very broad multidisciplinary focus."

Major Discoveries

Despite being a relatively young institution – it was established in 1946 – the university has already made significant contributions to academia.

In addition to the numerous Nobel Prize winners with connections to the university, there have been several seminal theories proved there. Professor Harsanyi taught economics at ANU from 1958 to 1961, completing some of his early research on game theory while at the university. More recently, Professor Rolf M. Zinkernagel and Professor Peter Doherty, who went on to complete ground-breaking work in immunology, were colleagues at the university. And in 2011 Prof. Brian P Schmidt AC jointly won the Nobel Prize in Physics for observations on the accelerating universe.

Partnerships, Innovation & Translational Research

ANU welcomes partnerships with academic and corporate organisations and, as Prof. Young explains, the university is taking a fresh approach to these relationships.

"We need to ensure that our institution is accessible to the outside world. Often governments and industries find universities impenetrable for all sorts of reasons; they don't understand who they should talk to or how to approach us. So we're trying to provide a front door for external people, agencies and institutions so that they can approach us relatively easily."

Another way that the university interacts with society is through its technology transfer initiatives. Prof. Young admits that commercialising research isn't easy but says it's a key goal for the university.

"It's a priority. I think like many universities we do not do this as well as we would like. The challenge is trying to get your incentive structures right within the organisation. We have a very open Intellectual Property policy in the sense that the university owns the IP, but essentially we allow our researchers to commercialise or license that IP in ways that they see fit."

Teaching, Learning & Student Life

When it comes to learning experience, any Australian university has a headstart – being located in one of the world's most striking landscapes. Prof. Young is understandably proud of the University's picturesque setting. "Canberra is a relatively small city with about 400,000 people, and students find this quite an idyllic environment in the sense that the ANU campus is a beautiful, spread out campus, which sits inside a very large block of land on the shore of the lake here in Canberra. So physically it's a very attractive environment."

On campus, one of the most striking elements of the ANU student experience is its international culture. Around a quarter of all students are international, while at the postgraduate level that figure is almost 50%. The University's strong Asia-Pacific focus is also reflected in student life, says Vice-Chancellor Young.

"We do have a lot of our students focusing on Asian studies, languages and culture. So providing an international experience for those students is a critical element of what we do, and we work very hard to try and enhance the numbers of our students who have an international experience."

Another distinctive element of the ANU learning experience is that almost half of all students are currently studying double degrees – i.e. not focused on solely one subject but mixed with another. Prof. Young believes this approach helps create more rounded students.

Name › McGill University
Region › Americas
Country › Canada
Founded › 1856

www.mcgill.ca

Core Research Strengths

McGill University was awarded 163 government and industry-sponsored research contracts valued at over C$17.5 million in 2011-12. If you add in the amount that goes to affiliated hospitals the research budget swells to a massive C$510 million.

Principal of the University, Heather Munroe-Blum, believes the money is put to good use. "With a strong focus on interdisciplinary work, we rank among the finest research-intensive universities in the world, and carry on a tradition of excellence that includes Sir Ernest Rutherford, Wilder Penfield, Charles Taylor and many others."

The main focus is health sciences which make up roughly half of the university's enterprise, says Principal Munroe-Blum. "Beyond health sciences, major themes of research at McGill include fundamental questions about humanity, identity and expression – and that's everything from ethics, digital media, intellectual property, languages, literature and culture - and the interaction between what we classically think of as the humanities and new technologies."

Another focus is the improved delivery of care, says Principal Munroe-Blum. "That might sound conventional but it's really not. Somehow the Western world's regressed in the delivery of health care, and in the area of health promotion. So we've really taken that on and are also looking very much at how the basic sciences behind those areas – biology, physiology, new technologies, bioinformatics – can promote the way we think about health care delivery and health outcomes."

In recent years the university has honed its research strategies, says Principal Munroe-Blum. "One of the hallmarks for McGill, I would say for the last ten years, has been planning and developing strategies to make sure that all of our traditional strengths, such as medicine and neurosciences, remain strong and in a lead role, but really looking across the university and across our hospitals, and looking at our obvious partners, and saying 'what are the areas where we could and should be putting an emphasis?', where we have a distinctive advantage to make a real contribution?"

Major Discoveries

1890 James Naismith developed the sport of basketball.

1902 Atomic disintegration and transmutation – Ernest Rutherford (Nobel Prize winner, 1908)

1965 Discovery of carcinogenic embryonic antigen (CEA), which is the leading diagnostic for cancer - Sam Freedman & Phil Gold

Partnerships, Innovation & Translational Research

McGill University is a global research player and, as such, has several international academic partnerships, says the Principal. "Our professors participate in very dense research collaborations. For example, in the neurosciences we've chosen British and European partners. Naturally we already have strong research collaborations with American and Canadian universities." McGill also partners with institutions in India, Japan, Israel and Hong Kong, among others.

The other way that the university interacts with wider society and gains funding is by forming strategic alliances with the private sector. "We make a big investment in it, and we have a good if not perfect performance in the whole area of intellectual property management", says Principal Munroe-Blum.

Her confident assessment is supported by the success of the university's Office of Technology Transfer. 19 licences and options to license were granted to the private sector in 2011-12, creating a cumulative total of 175 active licences. Indeed McGill has one of the largest patent portfolios among Canadian universities. In 2011-12, 38 national and international patents were granted to McGill. The university was also the top Canadian institution for U.S. patents granted in 2010.

Teaching, Learning & Student Life

McGill's main campus is situated in downtown Montreal at the foot of Mount Royal. Most of its buildings are situated in a park-like campus. The Faculty of

Agricultural and Environmental Sciences is located on a second campus, at the Western tip of the island of Montreal. 11 faculties and 11 professional schools offer more than 300 programs to some 38,000 graduate, undergraduate and continuing studies students. With 20% of students coming to McGill from more than 150 countries, the student body is very internationally diverse.

Indeed Principal Munroe-Blum feels the university has its own special charm. "There is something unique about McGill. We have a high emphasis on academic and research standards, but also on creating an experience. When I meet with our alumni, one of the greatest parts of their experience is the other students they met. We have Canada's most international student body, and at the same time we're probably the most Francophone/Anglophone university in the world because of our presence in Quebec."

Students will also benefit from the interdisciplinary approach to learning, says Principal Munroe-Blum. For example, other areas that McGill's strategic research plan will be looking at over the next few years include "public policy and a deeper understanding of social transformations", the "convergence of life sciences, natural sciences and engineering, "technology and its applications in the Digital Age" and "Earth, space and the Universe", each of these themes spanning many disciplines.

UNIVERSITÄT
HEIDELBERG
ZUKUNFT
SEIT 1386

Name › University of Heidelberg
Region › Europe
Country › Germany
Founded › 1386

www.uni-heidelberg.de

Core Research Strengths

Heidelberg University has twelve faculties with a total of more than 30,000 students and a research staff of more than 5,000 scientists, among them almost 440 professors. The university has a very strong emphasis on research, having been associated with 55 Nobel Laureates.

That research capacity is spread among a broad range of subjects, says Professor Dr. Bernhard Eitel, Rector of Heidelberg University. "We are a comprehensive university. So, our strengths are in the humanities, the life sciences, natural sciences and medicine, as well as in the social sciences. We do not offer the engineering disciplines because we are in the middle of a network of technical universities with Karlsruhe located in the south, Kaiserslautern in the west and Darmstadt in the north."

Rector Eitel is adamant that the university's research capacity benefits from being at the centre of a network in the Heidelberg area. "There are the Max Planck Institutes, the German Cancer Research Centre, which is part of the Helmholtz Association, and other extra-university research institutions which form a conglomeration that is much stronger than the university alone or each part alone."

"It's our strength that we do not focus on only a few topics. We are very diversified, that's a real advantage of Heidelberg University. The life sciences, of course, and the medical faculty in particular are one major area of strength, and in chemistry and in physics we are one of the leading universities in Germany. In addition, Heidelberg University has the biggest faculty of astronomy in Germany. We also have an excellent scientific computing department, and are famous for the humanities and social sciences as well as psychology."

Major Discoveries

› The invention of spectroscopy and of the Bunsen burner

› The discovery of the chemical elements Caesium and Rubidium

› The identification of two types of human papillomavirus (HPV) as the cause of cervical cancer which led to the development of a vaccine

Partnerships, Innovation & Translational Research

Internationalism may currently be en vogue among the world's leading universities, but Heidelberg has been doing it for centuries, says Rector Eitel.

"The university was founded as an international university in 1386: The founding rector was a Dutch professor coming from Paris University and the first professors he brought to Heidelberg were coming from Paris and Prague. This tradition continues today; for example, 20% of our scientific staff are international. For Germany, that's a high level. Even though we are not English speaking, we have a lot of courses and programmes in English." Meanwhile interaction with the private sector is growing.

"It's an increasing process, we interact with industry or other companies more and more. We do not do industrial research, we do fundamental research, but we make contributions to the interface of basic research and applications. This produces many spin-offs. Normally, we have several new companies per year from the computational sciences to imaging, for example, or from the medical sciences and pharmaceuticals."

Teaching, Learning & Student Life

One of Heidelberg University's biggest advantages is its location, says Rector Eitel. "We are situated within a conglomeration of about 2.5 million inhabitants. Even Frankfurt airport in the south of Frankfurt is so close by that it's "our" airport. So we have the entire infrastructure for a big global university without any disadvantages of our location in the conurbation, which makes us unique at least in Germany."

Another plus is the proximity of leading firms and institutions. "Heidelberg is a wonderful place because we have so many different organisations within the scope of the city, as well as in the region within a range of about 30 kilometres that can easily be reached by car in half an hour. So, that's the big

advantage of Heidelberg. That makes Heidelberg a city of science, a little bit like Oxford."

When it comes to attracting the best teachers, researchers and professors, Rector Eitel believes it is important to build momentum. "You can offer scholarships to the best students, and we certainly do that. But for attracting the best, you also need the best conditions on campus and then the money will come. For example, in our excellence initiative projects, funded by the German federal and state governments, we have about 40% to 47% of international young researchers up from the PhD level. So, that's good publicity; that's the best incentive for others to come to Heidelberg University.

When scientists and scholars find an attractive environment, where they can use state-of-the-art technology platforms and core facilities; and where they meet other people in the same situation and are supported by senior professors who are not defending ancient territories, but guiding their younger colleagues – that's creating a stimulating atmosphere to do excellent research."

University of Heidelberg
Germany

University of Heidelberg

RUTGERS
THE STATE UNIVERSITY OF NEW JERSEY

Name › Rutgers, University of New Jersey
Region › Americas
Country › United States
Founded › 1766

www.rutgers.edu

Core Research Strengths

Rutgers approximate US$473 million in research expenditures for fiscal year 2011, the most recent year tallied by the National Science Foundation, was distributed throughout the university's diverse array of 245 research centres and institutes. The university's interdisciplinary research strategy harnesses outstanding core strengths in areas such as computer science and mathematics into research institutes addressing some of the world's most pressing challenges and questions.

Expertise from disciplines as diverse as psychology, linguistics, computer science and philosophy have come together in the Rutgers University Center for Cognitive Science (RUCCS); investigating basic questions surrounding the nature of intelligent performance and the inner workings of the human mind.

Scientists at Rutgers' new Center for Integrative Proteomics Research, study structures, functions and interactions of proteins to advance medicine by increasing the ability to concentrate on each patient's unique biological profile. It is led by Stephen K. Burley, an internationally recognized physician and scientist, and an expert in structural biology, drug discovery, clinical medicine and oncology. The center will house sophisticated instruments that determine the structures of molecules and proteins at the atomic level.

Established in 1999, the Rutgers University Cell and DNA Repository (RUCDR), is the world's largest university-based biorepository, working alongside a myriad of academic disciplines and collaborative industry partners to help better understand the genetic drivers behind disease and illness. The RUCDR is one of the most outstanding facilities at the heart of the increasingly exciting research activities being undertaken globally in the spheres of genetics and biotechnology.

Led by internationally renowned neuroscientist, Dr Wise Young, the W.M. Keck Center for Collaborative Neuroscience harnesses expertise from throughout the natural sciences, life sciences and engineering to better understand and develop treatments to brain injuries and neurological disorders such as Alzheimer's and Parkinson's disease. The Spinal Cord Injury Project is the W.M. Keck's flagship program, drawing expertise and support from a diverse arena of stakeholders with a view to developing comprehensive treatments and rehabilitation for spinal cord injury victims.

Major Discoveries

Professor Selman A. Waksman discovered several antibiotics whilst at Rutgers, culminating in his co-discovery of Streptomycin; one of the first cures for tuberculosis, for which Professor Waksman received the Nobel Prize in 1952.

Partnerships, Innovation & Translational Research

Home to the most extensive network of research laboratories and facilities in New Jersey, with over 1100 active patents under management and close to US$500 million in external research funding; Rutgers research infrastructure is a vital resource for the local economy and global community alike.

The Office of Research Alliances (ORA), serves Rutgers and the university's external research partners by identifying collaborative opportunities for synergies, and then building long-term mutually beneficial relationships for both sustained, positive research outcomes and commercial opportunities for Rutgers' student community. Through the ORA companies are able to access Rutgers' equipment, researchers, students and courses to advance the technical abilities of their employees.

The Office of Technology Commercialization (OTC) is responsible for translating some of the countless new discoveries and inventions made at Rutgers from initial disclosures into patents and viable businesses. The OTC negotiates research contracts and patents, protects intellectual property and helps translate marketable technologies into licenses and start up companies. Life sciences related innovations lead patent disclosures from Rutgers University followed by those relating to engineering and agriculture. The OTC has a proven track record in building spin out companies with successes such as Axion International, Connotate and Reva Medical Inc.

Teaching, Learning & Student Life

Undergraduates have over 4000 courses to choose from to combine within the scope of 100 major programs. Interdisciplinary learning is encouraged at all levels, with options available to combine a diverse array of courses based upon ones' individual curiosities and long-term aspirations.

With nearly 60,000 students from over 125 countries and all 50 states of the USA, diversity is one of the hallmarks of the Rutgers experience. Students come from a variety of social backgrounds with approximately 80% of undergraduates receiving financial support. One can expect to work alongside a very talented peer group with over 40% of Rutgers undergraduates ranking in the top 10% of their high school class.

With over 500 student organisations, Rutgers plays host to a vibrant social life and a multitude of extra-curricular activities. Sporting activities are particularly prominent with athletics and American Football attracting the greatest following amongst student supporters and local enthusiasts.

Name › University of Munich
Region › Europe
Country › Germany
Founded › 1472

www.uni-muenchen.de

Core Research Strengths

One of the leading research universities in Europe, Ludwig-Maximilians-Universität (LMU) in Munich has a distinguished history stretching back over 500 years. Some 700 professors and 3,600 academic staff members conduct research and teach in the University's 18 faculties. The spectrum of disciplines ranges from the humanities and cultural studies through law, economics and social studies to medicine and the sciences. The University's stature in research is evidenced by its designation as a "University of Excellence" in the context of the German Excellence Initiative, a nationwide competition to promote top-level university research.

LMU provides a state-of-the-art infrastructure for research, both within individual disciplines and through inter and transdisciplinary collaborations. In this way, the University seeks to make optimal use of the wide range of expertise available, says President Professor Bernd Huber. "We place great emphasis on interdisciplinarity at our university, and promote collaborations between different fields of research. A good example is our Graduate School of Systemic Neurosciences, where doctoral candidates from a wide range of fields such as medicine, biology, philosophy and psychology collaborate."

Many leading universities are now adopting multidisciplinary strategies. What is really interesting about LMU is that its President is also keen to stress that it is equally important to nurture the specific strengths of individual disciplines. "LMU fosters excellence in individual subjects as well, as it is the foundation for all transdisciplinary cooperation. The challenge is to create an environment in which both approaches can flourish."

Major Discoveries

The quality of research at LMU is also reflected by the number of prestigious grants regularly awarded by national and international agencies, such as the European Research Council in disciplines as diverse as medicine and physics, phonetics and sociology. In 2005, Theodor W. Hänsch won the Nobel Prize in Physics for his contribution to the development of laser-based precision spectroscopy.

Partnerships, Innovation & Translational Research

LMU Munich has always devoted much effort to developing relations with other institutions. It is a founding member of the League of European Research Universities (LERU), a network of 21 top institutions. Additionally, the University maintains strategic research collaborations with universities around the globe, such as Harvard Medical School, the University of California at Berkeley and University of Tokyo (Todai).

The University has concluded faculty-based cooperation agreements with well over 400 partner universities worldwide. The accords regulate areas ranging from academic contacts and student exchanges, to the design of joint degree programs. LMU is also very active within the European Union's successful mobility and grant programs.

LMU also works closely with leading German businesses, explains the President. "The greater Munich area is a hub for innovation and entrepreneurial spirit. We maintain contacts to many important manufacturers, such as pharmaceutical companies or e.g. Audi, as well as financial service companies like Munich Re. Collaboration with these firms is vital, as many of our alumni work for them."

Teaching, Learning & Student Life

With degree programs in 150 subjects, the array of courses available is extremely broad. Some 48,000 students, including Master and PhD students, are currently enrolled at the University. Among them are more than 7,000 foreign students, originating from 125 countries.

One distinctive aspect of the study programs is research-oriented teaching, which emphasizes close contact between students and faculty, says the President. "Our students benefit from close interaction with top-level researchers, who often offer tutorials with relatively small groups. This helps to arouse an early interest in research."

LMU Munich's inner city campus is home to the natural sciences, the social sciences and humanities. The University Library and the Bavarian State Library form one of the finest library systems in Germany and are located close to LMU's historic Main Building. In combination with various important museums and archives, this provides an ideal infrastructure for research and study.

The Life Sciences are concentrated at the HighTechCampus in Grosshadern-Martinsried. This greatly facilitates scientific interaction at all levels – from basic research in collaboration with extramural research centres, such as nearby institutes of the Max Planck Society, to the translation of results into practical applications.

The Munich Metropolitan Region is one of the leading European economic areas, with strong growth and high employment. With more than 1.4 million inhabitants, Munich is one of Germany's major cities, and students and researchers alike love its unique atmosphere. Situated on the banks of the River Isar, to the north of the Bavarian Alps, it is set in beautiful surroundings. The city offers a huge range of amenities, from restaurants and theatres to museums and its famous beer-gardens. Munich's location also makes it an ideal base from which to explore the rest of Europe.

The local advantages are manifold, says President Huber. "The city is very vibrant. It is easy to build a network with interesting, inspiring minds, be they future employers, research partners or just friends."

University of Zurich UZH

Name › University of Zurich
Region › Europe
Country › Switzerland
Founded › 1833

www.uzh.ch

Core Research Strengths

The University of Zurich (UZH) has a rich history of innovative research, to which its 12 Nobel Prizes attest. Today, UZH is particularly strong in medicine, immunology, genetics, neuroscience and structural biology as well as in economics. The Faculty of Economics, Business Administration and Information Technology is one of the best in continental Europe, while the Faculty of Medicine and Faculty of Science are ranked in the top ten.

The University underpins its research excellence through a number of strategies, including hiring the best minds for its staff of over 4,100 researchers and instructors. Furthermore, the University of Zurich is leading house at six National Centres of Competence (NCCR), which were established by the Swiss National Science Foundation as an instrument to permanently strengthen cutting-edge research in Switzerland.

UZH is equipped with an excellent research infrastructure, including more than 150 university departments and numerous associated institutes as well as a university hospital and a veterinary hospital. These play a crucial role in translating theoretical research into 'real world' applications.

The University promotes interdisciplinary and integrative research through its thirteen University Research Priority Programmes (URPP), which are designed to provide key impulses and insights in a variety of fields in the natural sciences, arts and social sciences, medicine, and economics. The programmes profit from existing excellent foundations in research and strongly support the academic career development of young researchers.

The University of Zurich enhances its research strengths by teaming up with like-minded institutions. Particularly in the fields of bioscience and finance there is a close-knit collaboration between the University of Zurich and ETH Zurich (Federal Institute of Technology), which is located right next to the University.

Major Discoveries

Over the years, UZH professors and researchers have helped to revolutionise the world of medicine with groundbreaking work. One of the most notable discoveries was made by Rolf M. Zinkernagel, whose research on how the immune system recognizes and destroys virus-infected cells earned the 1996 Nobel Prize in Medicine.

Partnerships, Innovation & Translational Research

The academic excellence of the University of Zurich brings benefits to both the public and the private sectors. Knowledge is shared in a variety of ways: in addition to granting the general public access to its twelve museums and many of its libraries, the University makes findings from cutting-edge research available to the public in accessible and engaging lecture series and panel discussions.

A further sign of UZH's innovation and research excellence is the increasing share of third-party funds awarded to the University. UZH has been successful in winning competitive bids from the country's national research funding institution, the Swiss National Science Foundation, as well as from the European Research Council's Funding Schemes.

UZH promotes the transfer of research-based knowledge to private enterprise, and its spin-off ventures and business partnerships regularly lead to the creation of attractive jobs in innovative fields. Together with the University of Bern and the University of Basel, UZH runs Unitectra, which serves researchers and the management of the three universities as an interface between academia and enterprise. Every year, Unitectra concludes hundreds of contracts and issues dozens of licences for UZH researchers.

Through its membership in the prestigious League of European Research Universities, UZH has numerous academic partnerships which further promote its ability to engage in innovative research and translate academic findings to practical applications.

Teaching, Learning & Student Life

The city of Zurich itself has much to commend it. Situated in the German-speaking part of Switzerland, Zurich – despite its small size – is a thriving metropolis with international flair. Renowned establishments such as the Opernhaus Zurich (opera), the Schauspielhaus Zurich (theatre) contribute to the city's reputation as a major cultural centre. There are also many smaller venues that provide entertainment for all tastes, including unconventional concerts in former factories, dance performances at the river, and art exhibitions in trendy galleries. Another striking feature of the city is its prime location on Lake Zurich, close to the Swiss Alps with their breath-taking ski resorts and well-marked hiking paths. Given this impressive combination of cultural and outdoor activities, it is no wonder that Zurich regularly ranks at the top of charts measuring the quality of life in the world's major cities.

The University of Zurich has three main campuses in the city, which are arranged according to subject area. Should students need to transfer from one campus to another, there is no difficulty at all thanks to Zurich's dense and well-planned public transport system.

With its 26,000 enrolled students, the University of Zurich is Switzerland's largest university. Made up of seven faculties covering some 100 different subject areas, the university offers a wide variety of Bachelor's, Master's and PhD programmes. In addition, UZH's continuing education programmes offer excellent learning opportunities in a wide variety of subjects.

The University of Zurich is committed to providing a stimulating and inspiring learning environment. It supports innovative, high-quality teaching through its multi-media and eLearning services, and has repeatedly won prizes for its eLearning environment. To further promote scholarship, UZH has recently opened its Graduate Campus to support the very best students in PhD programmes.

Imm. Tremillius

Leon. Gmelin.

RUTGERS
THE STATE UNIVERSITY OF NEW JERSEY

Name › Rutgers, University of New Jersey
Region › Americas
Country › United States
Founded › 1766

www.rutgers.edu

Core Research Strengths

Rutgers approximate US$473 million in research expenditures for fiscal year 2011, the most recent year tallied by the National Science Foundation, was distributed throughout the university's diverse array of 245 research centres and institutes. The university's interdisciplinary research strategy harnesses outstanding core strengths in areas such as computer science and mathematics into research institutes addressing some of the world's most pressing challenges and questions.

Expertise from disciplines as diverse as psychology, linguistics, computer science and philosophy have come together in the Rutgers University Center for Cognitive Science (RUCCS); investigating basic questions surrounding the nature of intelligent performance and the inner workings of the human mind.

Scientists at Rutgers' new Center for Integrative Proteomics Research, study structures, functions and interactions of proteins to advance medicine by increasing the ability to concentrate on each patient's unique biological profile. It is led by Stephen K. Burley, an internationally recognized physician and scientist, and an expert in structural biology, drug discovery, clinical medicine and oncology. The center will house sophisticated instruments that determine the structures of molecules and proteins at the atomic level.

Established in 1999, the Rutgers University Cell and DNA Repository (RUCDR), is the world's largest university-based biorepository, working alongside a myriad of academic disciplines and collaborative industry partners to help better understand the genetic drivers behind disease and illness. The RUCDR is one of the most outstanding facilities at the heart of the increasingly exciting research activities being undertaken globally in the spheres of genetics and biotechnology.

Led by internationally renowned neuroscientist, Dr Wise Young, the W.M. Keck Center for Collaborative Neuroscience harnesses expertise from throughout the natural sciences, life sciences and engineering to better understand and develop treatments to brain injuries and neurological

disorders such as Alzheimer's and Parkinson's disease. The Spinal Cord Injury Project is the W.M. Keck's flagship program, drawing expertise and support from a diverse arena of stakeholders with a view to developing comprehensive treatments and rehabilitation for spinal cord injury victims.

Major Discoveries

Professor Selman A. Waksman discovered several antibiotics whilst at Rutgers, culminating in his co-discovery of Streptomycin; one of the first cures for tuberculosis, for which Professor Waksman received the Nobel Prize in 1952.

Partnerships, Innovation & Translational Research

Home to the most extensive network of research laboratories and facilities in New Jersey, with over 1100 active patents under management and close to US$500 million in external research funding; Rutgers research infrastructure is a vital resource for the local economy and global community alike.

The Office of Research Alliances (ORA), serves Rutgers and the university's external research partners by identifying collaborative opportunities for synergies, and then building long-term mutually beneficial relationships for both sustained, positive research outcomes and commercial opportunities for Rutgers' student community. Through the ORA companies are able to access Rutgers' equipment, researchers, students and courses to advance the technical abilities of their employees.

The Office of Technology Commercialization (OTC) is responsible for translating some of the countless new discoveries and inventions made at Rutgers from initial disclosures into patents and viable businesses. The OTC negotiates research contracts and patents, protects intellectual property and helps translate marketable technologies into licenses and start up companies. Life sciences related innovations lead patent disclosures from Rutgers University followed by those relating to engineering and agriculture. The OTC has a proven track record in building spin out companies with

successes such as Axion International, Connotate and Reva Medical Inc.

Teaching, Learning & Student Life

Undergraduates have over 4000 courses to choose from to combine within the scope of 100 major programs. Interdisciplinary learning is encouraged at all levels, with options available to combine a diverse array of courses based upon ones' individual curiosities and long-term aspirations.

With nearly 60,000 students from over 125 countries and all 50 states of the USA, diversity is one of the hallmarks of the Rutgers experience. Students come from a variety of social backgrounds with approximately 80% of undergraduates receiving financial support. One can expect to work alongside a very talented peer group with over 40% of Rutgers undergraduates ranking in the top 10% of their high school class.

With over 500 student organisations, Rutgers plays host to a vibrant social life and a multitude of extra-curricular activities. Sporting activities are particularly prominent with athletics and American Football attracting the greatest following amongst student supporters and local enthusiasts.

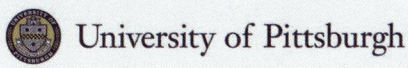

University of Pittsburgh

58

Name › University of Pittsburgh
Region › Americas
Country › United States
Founded › 1787

www.pitt.edu

Core Research Strengths

The University of Pittsburgh is among the United States' oldest and most distinguished comprehensive universities, with a wide variety of high-quality programmes. It has an enormous annual research budget of $899 million and receives the fifth-largest amount of federally sponsored research funding among U.S. universities.

That research is channelled through 16 schools and a network of thriving multidisciplinary centers. Of all these centers some stand out in particular. For example the centers for Aging, Bioengineering, Computer Modelling, Drug Discovery, Energy, the Mascaro Center for Sustainable Innovation, Biochemistry and Organ Transplantation, are all leaders in their fields. The university is very comprehensive but its health sciences, computing, engineering, neuroscience, and philosophy are among its strongest fields.

Indeed Pitt has a very strong position in health sciences; the university is a major center of biomedical research and ranks fifth in the nation in terms of competitive peer-reviewed NIH funding allocations. Another example of this is the 17,000 organ transplants carried out by Pitt surgeons, which have established Pittsburgh as the world's transplantation capital. Their colleagues in the School of Dental Medicine have also made a name for themselves by creating what is believed to be the world's only DNA bank to share data among dentistry colleagues.

The other thing to understand about Pitt's research structure is that it is closely intertwined with the neighbouring institute of Carnegie Mellon University (CMU). In some cases, buildings of the two universities are intermingled. This helps to facilitate a myriad of academic and research collaborations between the two schools. There are many joint projects, with one example being the Pittsburgh Supercomputing Center. The universities also offer multiple dual and joint degree programmes, while some professors hold joint professorships between the two schools, and students at each university can even take classes at the other.

Major Discoveries

Researchers at the University of Pittsburgh have made discoveries that have changed the world. Pitt researchers led by Jonas Salk developed the first polio vaccine, saving millions of lives. Discoveries in organ transplantation at Pitt made this life-saving technique commonplace. More recently Pitt professors Yuan Chang and Patrick Moore isolated the virus that causes epidemic cancer among HIV/AIDS patients and professor Olivera Finn developed a vaccine that triggers immunity to colon cancer.

Partnerships, Innovation & Translational Research

The mission of the University's Clinical and Translational Science Institute is to efficiently move biomedical advances into use by the community. In addition, the University's Office of Technology Management (OTM) and its affiliate Office of Enterprise Development (OED) serve as the hub for transforming Pitt's vast and diverse research endeavours into useful and often life-saving products and processes.

The university is also trying to expand its global reach. To this end it has signed more than 140 international research and exchange agreements, while it teaches in more than 35 different languages. It also encourages its students to take an outward view. The PittMAP programme requires participating students to work on a common topic as they visit three cities on three different continents.

But the university is not resting on its laurels. It has created a policy document 'Global Vision' that aims to boost its internationalisation by 2020. The university claims that this commitment "will influence all aspects of our research, teaching, and service missions and will serve to enhance the University's reputation as a leader in global education. We will pursue research and scholarship that increase global understanding, develop our students into global citizens and leaders, and improve people's lives by studying and solving the world's most critical problems."

Teaching, Learning & Student Life

Pittsburgh is a city made up of a host of unique neighbourhoods. That means students have a wide range of places to explore and get to know. For example Squirrel Hill has an appealing mix of retail outlets and eateries while neighbourhoods like Bloomfield, Friendship, and South Side have their own distinct charm. There are also plenty of outdoors activities. Pittsburgh is home to three rivers, which means students can take part in kayaking, rowing or dragon boating. For the more extreme student there is also the option of white-water rafting on the nearby Youghiogheny River and plenty of rock climbing sites.

The main campus is within a short walking distance of many recreational, cultural, and educational institutions that also populate the Oakland neighbourhood. For example, the campus is directly adjacent to Schenley Park and its world-renowned Phipps Conservatory; the main branch of the Carnegie Public Library; the Carnegie Museums of Natural History and Art, and the Carnegie Music Hall. And with 25,000 undergraduates and 10,000 graduate students you are not likely to be short of new friends.

The university's learning style is also a major attraction. Pitt's outstanding faculty members collaborate with graduate and undergraduate students on research projects. At Pitt, students get to work side by side with internationally recognised leaders in their academic disciplines. Another advantage is that Pitt students have access to the 22nd largest academic library system in North America, as well as to the CMU library system and the Carnegie Library of Pittsburgh.

THE UNIVERSITY OF
MELBOURNE

Name › University of Melbourne
Region › Asia/Pacific
Country › Australia
Founded › 1853

www.unimelb.edu.au

Core Research Strengths

The University of Melbourne has a research budget of $800 million dollars per year. At present about 55% of that comes from the traditional resource of competitive government research grants. The rest is made up of a combination of mission-oriented government, private enterprise, industry and philanthropy.

However, Deputy Vice-Chancellor (Research), Prof. James McCluskey expects the funding mix to change in the future. "I think that in the next five years, those lines will cross, and that it will become more than half from those categories, and less than half from the traditional competitive research grants or sources. We expect that it could develop further to one-third over the next 10 to 15 years."

Although Melbourne is a comprehensive university, which includes a prestigious law school and successful science, economics, engineering, and humanities faculties, in the last 15 years there has been much growth in biomedicine.

One reason for this, says Prof. McCluskey, is the university's location.

"The physical location of the university, just on the northern city fringe, centred around major public hospitals and independent medical research institutes; means we've got a very dense biomedical cluster, there are 10,000 researchers in that cluster; from PhD students to professors, to clinician scientists, to the basic scientists, to the support scientists. Such a model has been replicated on other sites. That clearly is one of our strengths and probably, in some way, the backbone of the university."

Biomedicine at the university also draws strengths from other disciplines. "We have a tremendous School of Engineering," says McCluskey, "and they have always had a very strong bioengineering focus because of the strength of biomedicine in the university. In addition, expertise from the physical, quantitative and life sciences resident in the Faculties of Science and Veterinary Science also complements the biomedicine enterprise."

This collaborative research is one key element of Vision 2025, the university's research strategy. Indeed, as you can see below, it's an approach that's already yielding results.

Major Discoveries

Melbourne developed the initial phases of the Cochlear bionic ear implants in a joint project between the Medical Department of Otolaryngology and the Electrical Engineering Department

The University is now part of a major consortium working on a bionic eye that has led to some very advanced developments, including recent clinical trials of retinal implants using some of the technologies from the bionic ear.

Partnerships, Innovation & Translational Research

The university is very keen to expand new strategic alliances with research partners and fellow universities around the world. Melbourne already has strong links with the UK, France, Japan, the US and Canada; but now it is looking to enlarge its links in four geographic areas - China, India and Europe through Germany, and South America through Brazil.

Another key partnership is with the private sector – especially when it comes to converting great theoretical work to practical, commercial, 'real world' applications. However, as Prof. McCluskey candidly admits, progress there has been slower than in other areas.

"I think most Australian universities still have a lot of work to do in this area and we are no exception. We have some terrific discoveries that have been translated into the community with the help of other partners, and we are very proud of those. But we are not yet as slick as we would like to be when it comes to taking an idea, an invention, and working it through the pipeline, and delivering it into the community in partnership with a commercial agency. We are getting better at it, and we have had as a part of our 2025 vision, a major reflection on how we do this."

Teaching, Learning & Student Life

Students at Melbourne now encounter a completely different experience to those who studied there in past years. That's because the university has completely redesigned its undergraduate programme. Under the leadership of Prof. Glyn Davis the curriculum was remodelled and six 'new generation degrees' were created.

The new degrees will have a profound effect on a student's learning experience says Prof. McCluskey.

"Hardwired into this new generation of degrees are a couple of key features. One is a renewed emphasis on some form of research experience, and research-led teaching, and with that comes critical thinking etc … A second major component is a compulsory requirement for a proportion of all courses to contain breadth. Breadth means that students have to take a subject outside of the primary disciplinary area."

The results, says Prof. McCluskey, have been spectacular. "We found a lot of students sampling business, law, or languages. Some pursue further studies in musical areas in which they have skills, as well, many of the scientists undertake humanities and arts subjects to broaden their thinking, and end up being much better at writing than they would have been if they had just done science. The breadth component has been a really important innovation in the Melbourne curriculum because it has meant the students that emerge are just that little bit broader, and just that little bit more exposed, and no longer narrowly defined by core subjects."

Name › Purdue University – West Lafayette
Region › Americas
Country › United States
Founded › 1869

www.purdue.edu

Core Research Strengths

With US$354 million in external research funding in fiscal year 2011/12 and US$650 million in total research expenditures spread throughout Purdue University's ten colleges and schools, 7000 faculty and some 40,000 students; diversity and scale very much define the research operations of this land, sea and space grant flagship institution. Such size and scope has facilitated Purdue's endeavours in synergising disciplinary strengths in what is a university increasingly defined by its interdisciplinary approach, investigating critical international challenges such as food security, energy security and cyber security.

The Discovery Park development has facilitated interdisciplinary strength at Purdue in accordance with the university's earlier visionaries. Provost Timothy Sands elaborates: "Certainly a hallmark of Purdue is that we have a very interdisciplinary environment. There are institutions within this environment that focus on interdisciplinary research and collaboration; that's always been true to some degree but really became a priority back in about 2000 when Martin Jischke became President. He had a vision to create Discovery Park which I think has become a global leader, not the only one doing this, but one of the handful where the priority became how do we create an environment that will attract researchers who are going to work on the big problems, that would like to work in teams with multiple disciplines. That vision has really shaped our current research priorities."

Counting 23 astronauts as alumni including the first and most recent to land on the moon, space sciences are a long held tradition of strength at Purdue. Working in close collaboration with internationally leading institutions such as NASA, Purdue leverages its scope of expertise to continue to push the boundaries at the frontiers of propulsion technologies and fuel technologies.

Purdue's fundamental strengths in engineering and the computer sciences set an excellent foundation for the university's continued growth in prominence in the fields of cyber infrastructure, information security and defence. Discovery Park serves as an excellent facility for collaborative efforts between Purdue research institutes and private companies in developing technologies at the cutting edge of these increasingly important fields.

Major Discoveries

Professor of Chemistry Phil Low has made some very interesting discoveries relating to cancer that are in the process of being commercialised through the spin out company Endocyte. Professor Low has developed a method for fluorescence-guided cancer surgery, whereby one can actually see the cancer infected cells because the fluorescence that has attached to them.

Purdue's long tradition of work in the development of solar cell technology over the past 40 years is starting to yield considerable returns with the university's expertise in nano-technology and computational sciences combining to develop new technologies such as those using new low cost 3D printing technologies.

Of particular note with relation to Purdue's increasing prominence in the development of energy technologies is Winthrop E. Stone Distinguished Professor of Chemical Engineering, Professor Rakesh Agrawal. One of the most decorated engineers in the United States, Professor Agrawal holds 116 U.S. patents, nearly 500 non-U.S. patents and has authored 93 technical papers. Professor Agrawal recently received the National Medal of Technology & Innovation for his contributions to innovation, and his on going work in developing more sustainable energy sources.

Partnerships, Innovation & Translational Research

Purdue's diverse funding portfolio is derived directly from the university's openness and experience in developing collaborative partnerships. The university's relatively high proportion of industry funded research, currently standing at 21% of total research funding is testament to forward thinking approach.

Provost Sands recognises that the university has to continue building upon this strength moving forwards: "One of the areas that I think will be an emphasis in the future are partnerships with government and industry instead of relying simply on research grants coming from federal agencies. We are now looking at much bigger efforts that require that the state or the federal government or in some cases foundations partner with industry, and with the university and our partnering universities. So, we are thinking down the road that is going to be more and more important. There is a great dialogue going on amongst the state of Indiana right now about that. The next challenge is to figure out how to make those three-way partnerships work well, and we are doing more and more on that. So, I think there is no big barrier in the way; it's just big waves sweeping over that we are going to have to look out for. When we are talking about 10 years or 20 years out, the university is going to be doing well to figure out how to develop those partnerships."

Although Purdue remains in the top 10 nationally for industry funded research, technology transfer operations are considered more of a means of attracting and retaining talent and having a positive social impact as opposed to being revenue generators.

Teaching, Learning & Student Life

Purdue has placed a major emphasis on the philosophy of Active Learning in recent years, with expertise from throughout the institution such as with experts from the Centre for Instructional Excellence and Information Technology at Purdue (ITAP), combining to develop innovative new pedagogical approaches and tools to help stimulate both the best practices in faculty and resultant greatest outcomes amongst students.

Purdue's interdisciplinary traditions in research have begun to filter through to the university's teaching and learning approach, with a healthy culture of collaboration between college deans developing into a significant proportion of the joint and interdisciplinary degree programs.

Purdue's share of approximately 50% of undergraduates directly involved in research is set to grow significantly with the roll out of facilities such as the Innovation Commercialisation Center,

and qualifications such as the Certificate for Entrepreneurship and Innovation helping to develop students' ambitions of developing into the next generation of job creators and entrepreneurs.

Often labelled as simply cornfields and not much else, the Mid West environment, although relatively unknown has a far richer cultural, social and physical environment than most stereotypes would permit. Relatively safe, with a beautifully balanced four season climate; the cost of living in a location such as West Lafayette is exceptionally attractive when compared with better known parts of the United States – Particularly when you consider the university's distance from Indianapolis and Chicago being one and two hours respectively.

Universiteit Utrecht

Name › Utrecht University
Region › Europe
Country › Netherlands
Founded › 1636

www.uu.nl

Core Research Strengths

Founded in 1636, Utrecht University is one of Europe's leading research universities, recognised internationally for its high-quality, innovative approach to both research and teaching. It is a large comprehensive research university with interests ranging from humanities to medical sciences.

Despite its broad-based approach there are four research areas that really standout, says University of Utrecht Rector, Professor Bert Van Der Zwaan.

"The first is in life sciences, where we specialise in stem cell research and regenerative medicine. We also look at the transfer of diseases between animals and humans. The next main research area is sustainability. This area investigates how resource depletion, growing populations and urban areas interlink. The third issue is youth. In particular this examines challenges relating to identity, migration, and all problems dealing with disorder and learning. The fourth is an area, which we call Institutions of Open Society where we bring together all the work done in the area what is the meaning of institutions. This ranges from United Nations to institutions within a village, informal and formal institutions, but specifically what are the characteristics of an open society, and there are economists working together with historians working together with people from humanities and social sciences."

These four research aims are, like research in many top international universities, arranged thematically to meet certain societal challenges head on. However, one area where Utrecht differs is in the organisation of this multidisciplinary research, says Rector Van Der Zwaan.

"In contrast to the United Kingdom we never organise new schools, not even new institutes. We try to leave people in their place, and try to have virtual collaboration as they are almost there. The idea of establishing new institutes or schools is not encouraged here because it takes a lot of effort, a lot of energy and gives to some extent some inflexibility."

Major Discoveries

Utrecht has won many of the world's top academic awards, including various Nobel Prizes. The most recent Nobel Prize came in 1999 when G. 't Hooft won the Nobel Prize in Physics 1999 for elucidating the quantum structure of electroweak interactions.

Partnerships, Innovation & Translational Research

The university has established several centres to act as interfaces with wider society. A number of centres, such as the Utrecht Sustainable Institute, the Utrecht Life Sciences and the Centre for Institutions, which is now being developed, are hubs for transferring knowledge to interested companies or institutions.

When it comes to working directly with private-sector companies, Utrecht's strategy is to target big investors in R&D, says Rector Van Der Zwaan. "Instead of bringing a lot of companies, we try to bring large knowledge institutes and large research labs on to the campus, like the European Lab of Danone, where we have an open innovation environment where people from Danone, the medical centre and people from the science faculty focus on specialised food. So, the idea is to try to bring as many knowledge institutions on the campus as possible."

Teaching, Learning & Student Life

The University is situated in Utrecht, a lively student city located in the heart of the Netherlands and considered the 'gateway to Europe'. Utrecht has a rich history going back almost 2,000 years, and an architectural legacy that includes both ancient and completely contemporary buildings. One of Utrecht's charming features is that it has retained the old inner-city, with its gracious parks and picturesque canals, cafes and concert halls. The impressive Dom tower looms above the city centre. Below the Dom lie international restaurants, cinemas, clubs and boutiques that give Utrecht its unique, stimulating atmosphere.

The two large faculties of Humanities and Law are situated in the inner city of Utrecht. The other five faculties and most of the administrative services are located in De Uithof, a campus area on the outskirts of the city. University College is situated in a former army base.

When it comes to learning students can expect a very intensive course style, says the Rector. "We have very innovative teaching systems ranging from university college where we have a liberal arts and science program, to new teaching methods where we have strict rules about the number of students per group and the number of hours they need to study per week."

Teachers are also subject to lots of attention, says the Rector. "We really invest a lot of money improving our teachers. For example we have an internal college of excellence in teaching. We have made a system where we provide and really carefully monitor the facilities and quality of our teachers. Teachers are not allowed to start teaching before they have really showed that they are able to that."

So far the approach is yielding success and the University of Utrecht has the highest result per year of finalized studies.

האוניברסיטה העברית בירושלים
The Hebrew University of Jerusalem

Name › The Hebrew University of Jerusalem
Region › Asia/Pacific
Country › Israel
Founded › 1925

new.huji.ac.il

Core Research Strengths

The Hebrew University of Jerusalem has the illustrious history that one would expect of Israel's second-oldest research institution. Along with other great minds of the 20th century, the university's founders include Albert Einstein and Sigmund Freud. The university is strong in the social sciences, natural sciences, humanities and biomedicine, and its research strengths are evident in all areas of human endeavour, says its president, Professor Menahem Ben-Sasson.

In the humanities, the university is understandably strong on Jewish studies, while it also excels at archaeology, history and philosophy. Other major research areas include medical sciences and agricultural studies. "We have the only faculty of agriculture in Israel. That's important for us and a necessity for the country, because we are short of water and short of land. As a result we have to be very creative and find novel ways to resolve these natural challenges." Innovations from the faculty of agriculture have had worldwide impact, from cherry tomatoes to drip irrigation.

Recently the university has reorganised its research strengths to take a more multidisciplinary approach, explains President Ben-Sasson. "In the last five years we have changed the way we carry out research to be more interdisciplinary in nature. To put this into practice we built new physical facilities in order to enable different faculties to work together in various research areas."

A good example of this process is the field of medical sciences. "When it comes to medicine, we have a combination of a hospital and research clinics. We have also complemented our basic medical research with a school of pharmacology, and the university just broke ground on a multidisciplinary brain science center that will be the largest in Israel and one of the most ambitious in the world. This commitment to bringing people from diverse fields together creates dialogue between the departments."

This new multidisciplinary approach crosses borders at the Institute for Medical Research-Israel Canada, where top Israeli and Canadian scientists cooperate in biomedical research to find solutions to the world's most serious medical problems. "They talk to each other on a daily basis and look at issues such as cell biology and genetics," says Ben-Sasson.

Major Discoveries

Faculty and alumni of the university have won seven Nobel Prizes and a Fields Medal in the last decade, encompassing fields such as economics, chemistry and physics. Its current faculty includes Nobel Prize winners such as Professor Robert John Aumann, who works at the university's Center for the Study of Rationality and won the 2005 Nobel Memorial Prize for Economics for his work on conflict and cooperation through game theory analysis.

Partnerships, Innovation & Translational Research

The Hebrew University of Jerusalem is very keen to work closely with the private sector, says President Ben-Sasson.

The university has a very impressive record of commercialising research. The Yissum Research Development Company was founded in 1964 to protect and commercialise Hebrew University's IP. Since then it has registered more than 7,000 patents covering more than 2,000 inventions. That's led to 530 technology licenses and 72 spin-off companies. Products based on the university's technologies now generate more than $2 billion in annual sales. Unsurprisingly Yissum is now ranked among the top technology transfer companies.

One area that stands out in particular In this regard is nanotechnology, says President Ben-Sasson. "The State of Israel handed the responsibility for some of its nanotechnology projects to the university and since then we have developed around 25 patents, some of which are already marketed."

Teaching, Learning & Student Life

Jerusalem is one of the world's great historical cities. It is home to sites of immense importance for the Jewish, Christian and Muslim faiths and is an incredible mix of culture. Lovers of history will be amazed by famous areas such as the City of David, the Western Wall and the Armenian Quarter. The city is also home to the world-famous Israel Museum, which attracts one million visitors a year. But it would be misleading to just portray Jerusalem as a city of the past. It has a vibrant scene of contemporary culture, including night clubs, bars, theatres and restaurants. The city also goes out of its way to entertain visitors by holding a number of spectacular festivals every year. For example during the International Ice Festival an ice city is created in Jerusalem, complete with palaces made from ice. There are also any number of concerts, music festivals and cultural programmes running throughout the year in Jerusalem's many cultural hotspots.

One thing that President Ben-Sasson is keen to emphasise to prospective international students is that just because it is called the Hebrew University of Jerusalem, doesn't mean that students have to speak Hebrew. "Being the minority in the world, you have to talk more than one language, so we have courses in English, Arabic and other languages. We want to raise the level of teaching by having students from abroad." Students from 70 countries including Singapore, Australia and the UK are among approximately 2,000 foreign students from studying at the Rothberg International School this year.

Another characteristic of the learning experience at the Hebrew University of Jerusalem is multidisciplinary teaching, says President Ben-Sasson. "Every student has to be exposed to other disciplines of thinking. Some of the faculties deliberately added courses that are involved with entrepreneurship, not only in the business school but also in the faculty of law, in the school of engineering and in the faculty of agriculture. This enables students to be exposed to other methods of thinking."

TUM
Technische Universität München

Name › Technical University Munich
Region › Europe
Country › Germany
Founded › 1868

www.tum.de

Core Research Strengths

First established in 1868, the Technische Universität München (TUM) has been one of Bavaria's most important institutions in the state's transition from an agricultural economy to one of the world's most important hubs of engineering and technology-led economic growth. TUM's motto as "The Entrepreneurial University" is very much indicative of the institution's unique mix of research strengths that distinguish the university amongst counterparts in Germany.

Germany is world renowned for its leadership in engineering, whilst TUM reflects this with exceptional expertise in the engineering sciences; this is also combined with the natural sciences, medicine, life sciences and quite uniquely a world-class business school. The TUM School of Management adds an entrepreneurial flavour to disciplinary expertise in areas such as chemistry, engineering and medicine.

Considered one of the most research-focused universities in Europe, and one of Germany's first Universities of Excellence, TUM is increasingly recognised for its core strength in interdisciplinary research, with many of its innovations coming from collaborations at the interface of traditional disciplines.

President Wolfgang Herrmann cites electromobility as a leading example. "If you focus on electromobility, then clearly you must have an entire set of expertise originating, in our case, from eight different departments out of a total of thirteen. Eight departments share activities in electromobility. We have constructed our own electric car, which has had very strong resonance since its debut appearance at the 2011 international car show in Frankfurt."

Major Discoveries

TUM can claim 13 Nobel Prize winners honoured for discoveries in the fields of chemistry, physics, and physiology or medicine. Such basic research continues to play an important role even as TUM focuses on pressing societal challenges. One recent example cited by Herrmann is a fundamental discovery in neuroscience, revealing distinct stages

in the development of Alzheimer's disease, which might also provide a key to diagnosis and therapy in the future.

TUM researchers have played a central role in an international satellite mission of the European Space Agency. The GOCE (Gravity Field and Steady-State Ocean Circulation Explorer) mission produces the most accurate measurements of Earth's gravitational field and has made it possible, for the first time, to measure ocean currents from space. This is a major contribution to understanding climate change.

Partnerships, Innovation & Translational Research

President Hermann believes that research partnerships throughout the public and private sectors alongside counterpart universities are of critical importance: "Partnerships are really essential; science has become so complex that as an isolated institution you never can make significant advances in these complex scientific challenges. For that reason we exploit our network in the international science community on the one hand, but also in industry, because our understanding of the university's mission includes supporting the economy of our country."

TUM's industry partnerships stretch back to the Linde Company in the 1870's. Today TUM partners with key players in the German automotive industry, including giants such as BMW and Audi, to ensure a transfer of knowledge and technology into the economy. TUM has an alliance with the Munich-based Max Planck Society, an independent think tank funded by the German government, which conducts general research in the public interest. The commitment to societal benefit is also reflected in the recently opened Munich Centre for Technology in Society: an integrative research centre that attempts to combine technological progress with societal requirements and evaluation.

TUM has clear business acumen and an understanding that universities can play a big role in the business community as a place to incubate spin-off companies and consultancies. UnternehmerTUM is the innovation and business creation company of the university, which works alongside the

TUM School of Management and with the support of TUMentrepreneurship. This programme offers advice and financial support to potential innovators and entrepreneurs. In the past 20 years, this has led to the charter of almost 400 companies with a current workforce of 11,000.

Teaching, Learning & Student Life

Munich is a cosmopolitan city with an international outlook. President Herrmann passionately believes there is much more to the city than cars and beer as cultural stereotypes would have one believe. "Munich, first of all, is an educational hub. It is rich in culture, literature, theatre, and music. Also, there are wonderful lakes around Munich, and the mountains of course. You find everything, skiing in the winter, swimming and hiking in the summer. And Bavarians are very open-minded. Bavaria is a very open, international community."

Teaching and the student experience at TUM centre on two main concepts: the entrepreneurial philosophy and the interdisciplinary approach to education and learning. Four professors are dedicated to entrepreneurship issues, and it is a central theme of many courses, research projects, and teaching topics. The TUM Graduate School is a full international graduate school system, which ensures that PhD candidates are not only trained in their traditional disciplines but acquire the relevant skills needed to succeed in the labour market and to understand their place in an increasingly complex and interconnected world.

Technical University Munich
Germany

THE UNIVERSITY *of* EDINBURGH

Name › The University of Edinburgh
Region › Europe
Country › United Kingdom
Founded › 1583

www.ed.ac.uk

Core Research Strengths

After Cambridge, the University of Edinburgh is the most comprehensive research university in the UK. As a result it has a very broad base of research interests and is far larger than the average British university.

One of Edinburgh's great strengths is medical sciences, explains Principal of the University Professor Sir Timothy O'Shea. "The University of Edinburgh has internationally renowned strengths in regenerative medicine and the application of stem cell research; one name that stands out in this regard is Professor Ian Wilmut who cloned Dolly the Sheep. Within this context we are doing a huge amount of fundamental and targeted work looking at conditions such as Parkinson's Disease and Multiple Sclerosis. There is also a great deal of work undertaken on genetic diseases and those diseases that create global challenges such as HIV-Aids."

Sir Timothy is proud of Edinburgh's involvement in 'Dolly the Sheep', which is probably the most famous genetics experiment of its generation. But, as he points out, the university is involved with world famous experiments in other fields too.

"In the sciences, the University of Edinburgh's core strength is in the material sciences, looking at the fundamental nature of matter such as the search for the Higgs Boson particle. The Large Hadron Collider at CERN is the most expensive science experiment ever constructed; the University of Edinburgh is an integral member of the research team involved with this project."

Major Discoveries

In 1996 Professor Ian Wilmut led the research team that first cloned a mammal from an adult somatic cell. The mammal was a Finnish Dorset lamb that became known as Dolly the Sheep.

In 1974 in the field of wave energy technology, the University of Edinburgh's Professor Steven Salter first developed the technology to transfer energy from waves into electricity.

Partnerships, Innovation & Translational Research

Given the university's research prowess it's small surprise that its academics regularly make discoveries with great commercial potential. The challenge for the university, says Sir Timothy, is to find the best way for those discoveries to reach wider society. One of the most obvious avenues, and one that the university has pursued with considerable success, is commercialisation of the technology.

"So far this year the University of Edinburgh has produced 35 spinout companies; last year the number was 42. Although the University of Edinburgh's philosophy is clearly to allow academics and researchers to follow their own interests and curiosities, the university is statistically comparable with MIT or Stanford in terms of releasing intellectual property and the production of spin out companies."

The other way that the university's research can benefit society is when it addresses particular problems. At present, explains Sir Timothy, the university has three agencies that help co-ordinate its international partnerships.

"We engage on the international stage all the time concerning a wide range of major global challenges. In particular, the University of Edinburgh has very strong links investigating treatments and immunology trends for a number of tropical diseases. Furthermore, we have a Global Development Academy headed by Professor Prof van Gardingen, a UNESCO Professor of international development currently leading a £14.8 million research program in partnership with the University of Oxford, Imperial College London and a number of government agencies from South Asia, Africa and Latin America."

The final aspect of Edinburgh's internationalisation strategy is to engage in partnership with other leading universities, says Principal O'Shea. Citing examples such as the University of Delhi and the University of Korea, he concludes that "the University of Edinburgh has a strong portfolio of research partnerships such as these throughout the international community."

Teaching, Learning & Student Life

"A distinctive point of the University is that it has always been very closely integrated into the city and students are very much part of the city", explains Sir Timothy. "Volunteering for example is a very strong aspect of Edinburgh's student culture. Another key distinctive point about the experience at the University of Edinburgh is the four-year undergraduate degree program; the exceptional quality that is derived from the fourth year is extraordinary, and offers real value to those that have graduated from Edinburgh.

I recently attended an exhibition of fourth year geography dissertations, the standard of this work was excellent, and many of them were publishable research papers. On top of this, the University of Edinburgh has a firm commitment to inter-disciplinary learning; a vast range of languages courses for example are open to our undergraduates; you can learn a range from Japanese to Brazilian Portuguese. A final, very distinctive aspect to the Edinburgh experience comes with the Fringe Festival, and the opportunities this gives students who have an interest in the arts, this is a unique asset unrivalled throughout the world's leading universities."

And when it comes to the classroom, students certainly won't be short of options. The University of Edinburgh has over 600 degree combinations making it the most comprehensive teaching university in the UK, after Birmingham.

"There are a very high number of options open to our undergraduates in terms of combined study and multi-disciplinary learning", says O'Shea.

Carnegie Mellon University

Name › Carnegie Mellon University
Region › Americas
Country › United States
Founded › 1900

www.cmu.edu

Core Research Strengths

Carnegie Mellon University (CMU) is a global research university. Home to some of the world's leading experts in a range of fields, including computing, the arts, energy, environment and biotechnology, CMU's award-winning faculty works closely with students with a strong focus on finding practical answers to complex scientific, technological and societal problems.

Multidisciplinary projects define the university's research strategy. For example, CMU researchers are working to land and operate a robot on the moon through Google's Lunar X Mission - a project that involves several disciplines from technology to art. "The idea of teamwork, collaboration, especially across different disciplines is a very important core strength here," said Carnegie Mellon President Jared L. Cohon.

"Computational finance is a great example," he said. "At any other university it is done inside a business school. At Carnegie Mellon it is a collaboration of our department of mathematics in our College of Science, our department of statistics in our College of Humanities and Social Sciences, and our Business School. So three different departments in three different colleges and that's the way we do computational finance."

The successful integration of different academics from different fields is one reason why Carnegie Mellon has been so successful, says President Cohon.

Another good example is energy. "Virtually every research university in America and the world is focused on this, but we put a special Carnegie Mellon spin on it. We work at the intersection of technology and policy – i.e. what's possible and how it can be implemented. Also when we tackle an issue like energy we look at a broad cross-section of games/ multimedia/ human computer interaction. Obviously that's a very broad waterfront with a lot of different meanings. But the key is that it represents a collaboration of people from the arts, from computer science, and from psychology. They are the three key pillars of our research approach."

Major Discoveries

Carnegie Mellon has an extensive 'hall of fame' of researchers who have made ground-breaking discoveries. Two of the most recent include Paul Lauterbur, a Mellon Institute researcher who was awarded jointly the Nobel Prize in Medicine in 2003 for work with magnetic resonance imaging, and Theodor W. Hänsch, who won the Nobel Prize in Physics in 2005 for his contribution to the quantum theory of optical coherence.

Partnerships, Innovation & Translational Research

Throughout its 112-year history, CMU has an enviable track record of bringing good ideas to market and creating successful businesses. These days a key part of that process is the university's Greenlighting Startups initiative, which is dedicated to help faculty and students quickly move research from the lab to the marketplace. In the past 15 years, CMU faculty and students have helped to create more than 300 companies and 9,000 jobs, making CMU a destination of choice for young innovators. Home to 118 research institutes and centres, CMU's entrepreneurial spirit has caught the attention of cutting-edge companies such as Google, Apple, Disney and Intel, who have opened space on or near CMU's Pittsburgh campus.

The other way that Carnegie Mellon interacts with the outside world is through its student body. Aside from its main base in Pittsburgh it has campuses in Qatar and Silicon Valley, and degree-granting programs around the world, including Africa, Asia, Australia, Europe and Latin America. Indeed nearly 35% of CMU's students are from countries outside the US, giving the university one of the ten most international student bodies among four-year U.S. institutions. The internationalisation works both ways and Carnegie Mellon students from all majors can study abroad for a summer, semester or full academic year through the Office of International Education.

Teaching, Learning & Student Life

Oakland is the academic, cultural, and healthcare centre of Pittsburgh and is Pennsylvania's third largest 'downtown', after central Philadelphia and Pittsburgh. As a result the neighbourhood is urban, diverse and home to an abundance of shopping and restaurants.

Including international students Carnegie Mellon has around 92,000 alumni in total but on campus it's a much more intimate feeling with 12,000 students and 5,000 faculty and staff. The compact campus atmosphere offers opportunities to engage in ground-breaking research. And undergraduates, who often work alongside professors that are leaders in their fields, benefit from a student-faculty ratio of 10:1. Of course a world class education is not just about quantity, quality matters too. Carnegie Mellon scores well on this front as 99% of all undergraduate classes are taught by faculty, while around 96% of these faculty members have a Ph.D. or equivalent degree in their field.

The strong interdisciplinary nature of the university's research is also translated to its learning style. The university also offers programs that are specifically designed to cross disciplines. Of course it helps that one of the university's research areas involves "something we call learning science", says President Cohon. "As the name implies, it's bringing together science, in this case of artificial intelligence and cognitive science, to understand how people learn. They use that understanding to create computer platforms to support education. That's why our online learning platforms are considered to be the best available."

Name › Vanderbilt University
Region › Americas
Country › United States
Founded › 1873

www.vanderbilt.edu

Core Research Strengths

With approximately US$575 million in annual research funding and more than 3,500 faculty members, Vanderbilt University's research intensity and productivity are amongst the highest in the world. The university's broad base of expertise throughout academia poses somewhat of a challenge in defining all of the university's research strengths; nevertheless there are some clear areas in which Vanderbilt is widely acknowledged as an international leader.

Areas in which Vanderbilt is at the cutting edge internationally are bioinformatics and personalized medicine. Working across the university's disciplinary strengths in areas such as genetics, genomic science and clinical pharmacology; Vanderbilt researchers have developed one of the world's largest human DNA data banks called BioVU. BioVU is electronically linked to de-identified medical records, allowing for this vast range of data to be translated into research findings. Vanderbilt is also pioneering new personalized medicine treatments based upon patients' individual genetics.

Vanderbilt University is also a powerhouse in the arts, humanities and social sciences – subjects often wrongly considered to be less important than STEM subjects today. Vanderbilt Chancellor Nicholas S. Zeppos underlines the continued value of such subjects: "I think that we should never lose sight of who is doing the most important work in philosophy, literature, ethics and creative fields like poetry, because I think from my vantage point the true seeds of a great university are linked to freedom of enquiry, freedom of thought, and the ability to write history, poetry, theatre and to interpret Shakespeare. We have tremendous strength in Shakespeare studies and Elizabethan religious history. One thing I'm really proud of is we have a really powerhouse university across the humanities and the social sciences, and they are very critical to the great advances made in American universities because they go to the question of: 'What do you think? What are your ideas?'"

Such broad based research strengths enable Vanderbilt researchers to operate across a broad spectrum of disciplines in a multidisciplinary way. One such area where the multidisciplinary approach is a key enabling factor in Vanderbilt's international leadership is in nanotechnology. Approximately 40 faculty members converge from their respective disciplines in areas such as science, engineering and medicine to develop nanoscale innovations in medical care, virology, alternative energy and other applications that will help overcome many of today's critical challenges.

Major Discoveries

On fundamental questions about health and obesity, Professor Roger Cone has discovered a receptor in the brain that regulates metabolism and appetite. This opens the possibility for developing drugs to target this receptor and effectively combat childhood obesity.

Vanderbilt researchers have developed a family of compounds that disrupt mosquitos' sense of smell; potentially paving the way for a method to prevent the transmission and spread of malaria and other insect-borne diseases.

Partnerships, Innovation & Translational Research

Whilst very much open to working in collaborative research partnerships both with private sector companies, governments and counterpart universities; the philosophy at Vanderbilt is very strategic. Quality is preferred over quantity, whereby the university makes a careful assessment of its investments and excellence in relation to the objectives and quality of partners before making a decision on whether to move forward with a partnership agreement. Vanderbilt enjoys rich relationships with a global network of world-class universities based upon this philosophy.

Vanderbilt's research excellence throughout the education sciences has seen the university develop a growing number of collaborative partnerships, predominantly with institutions in China. In partnership with Sun Yat-Sen University and South China Normal University, Vanderbilt recently opened the U.S.-China Center for Education and Culture in Guangzhou, China.

As part of Vanderbilt's new technology transfer and economic development strategy, translational research is of enormous importance. Chancellor Zeppos underscores the university's commitment to this aspect of their mission: "It is one of my greatest priorities. It is very much our mission, and it is very much our strategy to dramatically affect the local, regional, state, national and global environments; and from an economic standpoint Vanderbilt is a huge economic engine, and through discovery and innovation our budget every year is about three and a half to four billion dollars. I think our economic impact just locally would be three times that. When you think of our graduates who start companies and stay in Nashville, the impact is tremendous. Now, what we're focusing even more right now is driving the local economy for innovation, entrepreneurship and discovery."

Teaching, Learning & Student Life

Whilst Vanderbilt pioneers in much of its research operation, the university is still very much committed to the more traditional basic skills in teaching and learning such as critical thinking, analysis and careful writing. All first year students are given meticulous instruction in these core areas, which lay the foundation for their success within a particular discipline and, for many students, for success in a guided research process. The Vanderbilt education is very much characterised by small classes, a lot of writing, a lot of discussion, and the freedom to conduct research, create and be entrepreneurial in one of the USA's most vibrant musical and cultural hubs, Nashville, Tennessee.

Name › Pennsylvania State University
Region › Americas
Country › United States
Founded › 1855

www.psu.edu

Core Research Strengths

Pennsylvania State University is a public state related research university with campuses and facilities spread across Pennsylvania. Founded in 1855, the university has grown to command an annual research budget of more than US$750 million, putting it in the top ten U.S. universities in terms of research income. That huge research budget is mostly focused on defence related research. Indeed the main thrust is even narrower than that, explains Dr Henry Foley, Vice President for Research.

"Within defence we are very much focused on ocean science and engineering. Underwater systems are a core strength of ours as we have been working alongside the US Navy in this area now for more than 70 years. As a result we really understand the physics and the dynamics of ocean systems, we understand the acoustic phenomena; we are even looking at biological phenomenon and the impacts of navy vessels and communications on mammals and other species whose habitats are in the ocean."

It is currently in vogue for universities to talk up their interdisciplinary capabilities to help win research funding. However, Dr Foley believes that PSU is a world leader in this type of research. "Interdisciplinary research is a natural here; I think we do this better than any other university in the United States, and maybe the world. That may sound like hyperbole, but we have really torn down the walls between the disciplines with our top-level institutes such as the institutes of material sciences, social sciences, energy, environment, life sciences and now computational sciences. We co-fund faculty members within disciplines, so in that sense we are able to help disciplines find their way forward to cutting edge areas of research and teaching."

The approach has paid off in various ways. For example PSU was recently selected for the prestigious science award, the CTSA. It's also led to a research funding boom, says Dr Foley. "In the past decade we have grown by 7% per year. We even grew again last year while other institutes were shrinking."

Major Discoveries

Despite PSU's expertise in ocean science and engineering one of its most impressive discoveries came in the field of astrology. In April 1992 Alexander Woltschan discovered two planets orbiting the pulsar - Exoplanet PSR 1257+12, the first detection of true Exoplanets.

Partnerships, Innovation & Translational Research

Dr. Foley says that partnerships are a very high priority for Pennsylvania State University, and the one that he is most proud of is PSU's involvement in one of only three National Department of Energy Hubs in the US. "The Penn State Hub, is in Philadelphia, and it's a partnership that brings together other universities, nongovernmental organizations and corporations. Our goal is to improve energy efficiency, and our work here could have a massive impact on society."

At present IP is one of the most controversial topics involving research institutions. The spectrum of opinions and policies ranges from closely guarding university IP to literally giving it away for free. PSU is more towards the latter camp, with Dr Foley offering an interesting justification for that stance.

"I think that our role as a public university which is receiving enormous amounts of public dollars is not to be selfish in protecting the IP. Actually, it is to facilitate innovation. So we have made the decision that we'd rather have the IP go back to the corporations that have gone into research partnerships with us. The predominant benefits of doing work with industry for us are: bringing new agencies together with daily practices, academic researchers together with practical researchers and developers."

Teaching, Learning & Student Life

The university is split into various campuses that are spread along the state. University Park, the flagship campus, lies within the Borough of State College and College Township. That site was chosen because it lies in the geographic centre of the state.

It is by far the most popular with students and subsequently the most difficult to apply for. The Penn State Dickinson School of Law has facilities located in both Carlisle and State College, and the College of Medicine is located in Hershey. Penn State has another 19 commonwealth campuses and 5 special-mission campuses located across the state. The university also has one of the most extensive and sophisticated online, distance learning course programmes in the United States. In many ways the programme is an extension of the distance learning course that Penn State pioneered as a service to remote farmers in the second half of the 19th century.

For students on campus, 'hands-on' research-led teaching is a key part of the learning experience. The university prides itself on conducting research, creating new knowledge with that research; and then subsequently bringing that knowledge into the classroom as soon as possible. Research staff make up a high proportion of teachers, while the university encourages interaction between undergraduates, postgraduates and professors.

Students should also be aware that the university is constantly updating and upgrading its courses, adapting to the world as it changes, says Dr. Foley. "For example, in material sciences, Pennsylvania State started one of the first engineering colleges in the country."

Name › UT Southwestern – Texas
Region › Americas
Country › United States
Founded › 1943

www.utsouthwestern.edu

Core Research Strengths

The University of Texas Southwestern Medical Centre (UT Southwestern) is one of the leading medical education and biomedical research institutions in the United States and commands an annual research budget of $417 million.

Within biomedical research, core strengths of the institution include metabolism, structural biology, human genetics and chemical biology. There is also a focus on translational research and the basic mechanisms of cancer. Given the natural overlap between different areas of research, the university has long pioneered a multidisciplinary approach to science and medicine, says Dr J Gregory Fitz. "I think one of the strengths of the institution is the interdisciplinary approach taken to solve a given biomedical challenge, which has been here from the very beginning; we're not newcomers to the concept of synergy between different areas and technologies. The departmental walls here are very thin. It is thus very easy to access other investigators and to incorporate new ideas to expand your own; we work actively to foster collaboration on campus."

Dr. David Russell agrees. "The genetics of mice, humans, and fruit flies are tightly intertwined between our clinical and basic science faculties, which allows us to gain unique insight into common diseases. When this genetic expertise is combined with biochemistry, metabolism and clinical medicine, discoveries are made. Many people don't realise it but science and medicine practiced at the high level they are here are more alike than different."

Another of UT Southwestern's strengths is its research facilities, adds Dr. Fitz. "We're committed to developing the technology and infrastructure of research. Our shared facilities often act as platforms for future discoveries. With this in mind, I would say one of the growth areas where we think we'll see progress in the next several years is neuroscience. This field is experiencing a really steep growth curve here and its expansion is immensely satisfying to participate in."

Major Discoveries

Despite being a relatively young, post-war institution, UT Southwestern already has five Nobel Laureates to its name. The university's most recent breakthrough was Bruce A. Beutler's discovery concerning the activation of innate immunity. He was rewarded with the Nobel Prize in Physiology or Medicine 2011.

Partnerships, Innovation & Translational Research

The university is very open to partnerships, says Dr. David Russell. "For example, with one corporation, we have a number of initiatives seeking to develop new methods in mass spectrometry, new technologies for automated analysis of tissues by pathologists, and the development of high-throughput drug screening methods."

Another prominent partnership is with Merck and Company, one of the world's largest pharmaceutical firms. "We are working with Merck scientists to develop small molecules that target hyperlipidemia and cardiovascular diseases like heart attacks and strokes. These types of alliances are usually open research partnerships between individual investigators on campus and a given company. They often involve financial support, and even more important, an open exchange of results and data between the two partners."

In addition to these bilateral partnerships, the university has an active technology transfer office to commercialize exciting research coming out of the institution. The office is staffed with lawyers, licensing agents and patent experts who analyse and develop potential commercial applications of new research.

Teaching, Learning & Student Life

Made famous by the eponymous TV series, Dallas offers UT Southwestern students a great way to relax outside of the classroom. It is one of the 10 largest cities in the U.S., and on any given night you can find a blend of live music performances, professional sports and a world-class arts scene. Dallas also has several scenic spots for out-door activity, including the 1,000-acre

White Rock Lake and its surrounding park. But while life in Dallas may be relaxing, study at the university is anything but, says Dr. Fitz. "There is a special environment here where many learners are really aggressive in their pursuit of discoveries, and I think that medical and graduate education here are very science based. The ability to enter the laboratory to take advantage of clinical observations and recent scientific advances is very important."

Another notable feature of the learning experience is the influence of various disciplines, continues Dr. Fitz. "There's a large degree of trafficking of students across disciplines, so the door is always open to complimentary training with valuable experiences arising from multiple areas of investigation. Consequently, I think the students end up with a higher degree of exposure to wide-ranging disciplines; this exposure creates a very firm foundation for career development."

This trend is reinforced by the physical layout of the campus, says Dr. Russell. "In one building you'll have pulmonologists working next to molecular geneticists and diabetes experts. Everything is interspersed, and all the buildings on a given campus are interconnected. You end up constantly interacting with people in the hall who hail from all walks of research and medicine. These exchanges drive spontaneous collaborations between students and faculty members from different disciplines, and the resulting cross fertilisation has been synergistic at all levels in linking important medical problems with basic research."

UNIVERSITY OF CALIFORNIA

Name › University of California, Davis
Region › Americas
Country › United States
Founded › 1905

www.ucdavis.edu

Core Research Strengths

With a research budget of more than $680 million, the University of California, Davis is a preeminent institution in the fields of biological, veterinary, environmental and agricultural sciences. Areas of research distinction at UC Davis include microbiology in animal and human cells, life sciences and biotechnology.

Sustainability is a core area of interest throughout the university with a focus on environmental science, climate change, energy, transportation, and water. The university is also home to the Agricultural Sustainability Institute. Another considerably distinct area is the Department of Viticulture and Enology, in which UC Davis has been responsible for several advancements in winemaking. Other schools of research include medicine, nursing and engineering; law, education, management; and the College of Letters and Science, which includes the humanities, arts, cultural studies, mathematics, physical sciences, and the social sciences.

Interdisciplinary research has been a key strength since the university's founding in 1908. Chancellor Linda P.B. Katehi believes the university's collaborative culture is especially engaging for researchers at the interface of different disciplines. "We are a unique institution, positioned through our excellence and academic strengths to stay at the forefront of higher education," says Katehi. "Using cutting-edge technology and techniques, and collaboration both internally and externally, we are addressing the century's most pressing issues in such topics as food, water, health, society, energy and the environment."

There are 94 graduate programs set over eight broad fields with each one bolstered by state-of-the-art laboratories and facilities. The university offers the necessary resources and programmatic support to promote faculty collaboration across a range of fields. Not only are the sciences highly collaborative, but new ventures between the arts, humanities and social sciences are uniquely innovative in their interdisciplinary sense as well.

Major Discoveries

UC Davis has made many significant contributions to science, the arts and culture. It has led the way in modernizing agriculture and animal sciences. It is known as the birthplace of the modern plug-in hybrid vehicle.

Recently, Time Magazine named autism research by UC DAVIS MIND INSTITUTE Professor of Psychiatry and Behavioral Sciences Sally Rogers fifth among the Top 10 Medical Breakthroughs of 2012.

Also in 2012, research by UC Davis that developed a process and equipment for "bio-digestion," which converts waste into methane gas was brought to market for commercial usage.

Scientists in the immunology department developed a vaccine for salmonella that is presently undergoing clinical tests.

Partnerships, Innovation & Translational Research

UC Davis is boosting its ability to translate basic sciences into viable programs and services, as well as facilitating big projects with multiple partners through the framework of an established infrastructure, policies and regulations. In particular, the university builds relationships with venture capitalists and secures funding to support innovation.

UC Davis views technology transfer beyond the benefits of short-term returns and through long-term investments in the economy and society.

The Office of Research is divided between three units: (1) Interdisciplinary Research and Strategic Initiatives, (2) Research Administration and Compliance, (3) Technology Management and Corporate Relations. This unit deals with all matters pertaining to research, including establishing relationships with government and industry, and the coordination of patenting and licensing of campus intellectual property. The office can also assist in facilitating access to university services and facilities.

The Child Family Institute of Entrepreneurship and Innovation offers a program in entrepreneurship and training and support to students,

faculty and staff who are looking to start up new companies. Similarly, the College of Engineering advises and provides funding opportunities and connections for new start-ups.

Teaching, Learning & Student Life

UC Davis encourages independent thought with a close and informal relationship between students and faculty members — in particular, debates and challenges are encouraged. The Undergraduate Research Center strives to make research opportunities available to all students before they graduate. As part of this, there are two research symposiums – one for undergraduates and the other primarily for graduate students, but with a level of undergraduate participation. The university believes that innovative skills are best developed through direct involvement in research projects.

Sustainability is also a major aspect of teaching and student life at UC Davis. It is cultivated through environmental issues, food and nutritional education, and throughout the campus itself. This is reflected in the university's sustainable design; focus on using local or self-produced foods, use of landfill, and its extensive bicycling infrastructure. In 2012-13, UC Davis won recognition for its sustainability programs from Sierra magazine by being named the #1 Cool School in the United States.

The largest campus in the University of California system and located advantageously in Northern California, UC Davis is well poised for growth and expansion. Its Vision of Excellence is a strategy to deepen and strengthen UC Davis' status as a world-class university. This strategy takes into consideration the need for internationalization with an increase in study-abroad participation and international students on campus. This reflects the institution's goal to engage its students and scholars with the rest of the world.

University of
Southern California

Name › University of Southern California
Region › Americas
Country › United States
Founded › 1880

www.usc.edu

Core Research Strengths

The University of Southern California is a premier research institution producing a steady stream of new knowledge, art and technology. USC has an annual research budget of more than $600 million and ranks among the top ten private universities in federally supported research activity.

One of the university's main strengths, says Vice President for Research Randy Hall, is information sciences. "Our success in that field is largely down to the institutes we have developed. The Institute of Creative Technologies in particular has laid the foundation for the leading work we do in processing multimedia such as computer graphics, graphics that go into movies and artificial language translations. The University of Southern California leads in these areas of electronic engineering."

Given its location in America's film-making state, it is little surprise that USC has one of the best cinematic art programmes in the USA. "We have internationally renowned training programs for writers and directors interested in cinema production. Many of the creative arts courses have research programs accompanying them with interests in areas such as the expression of the arts, and the creative technologies that underpin the arts. Blending the arts with engineering, information technology and computer science is a great strength at the University of Southern California."

Many thanks for the success must go to George Lucas, creator of the Star Wars franchise, says the Vice President. "George Lucas donated US$175 million to the University of Southern California, enabling us to develop a campus within a campus with world-class facilities for our faculty and student population focused on the cinematic arts. This is as good as anything you will find in the industry"

Another strength is in the biomedical sciences, says Vice President Hall. "However, on a comparative basis, USC does not get as much recognition for this area due to the fact that so many other universities have research strength in this area." Away from these core strengths the university also has professional schools in sociology, law, business, pharmacy, communications and dermatology.

Major Discoveries

While USC is very proud of its successes in information sciences and cinematography, it's a testament to the broad base of its research that many of its other faculties have also made significant international breakthroughs. For example, in 2000 Dr. McFadden was awarded the Nobel Prize in Economic Science for the development of theories and methods for analysing discrete choice.

Partnerships, Innovation & Translational Research

One of the most tangible ways that a university can interact with the wider society around it is through technology transfer. To that end USC's intellectual property policy reflects the university's strong desire to support creative activity and reward inventors and authors. Ultimately the university owns the IP but there are exceptions to allow for the academic tradition of faculty ownership of certain scholarly works. Moreover the university tries to encourage staff to find applications for their research through the Center for Technology Commercialisation.

In addition to these start-ups the university also has a number of agreements with large companies. For example it has a research partnership in India with software companies such as Infosys. It also has corporate partnerships with Korea Airlines and Airbus.

When it comes to academic alliances, USC is very proactive in searching the world for the best possible partners. For example, it recently signed a partnership agreement with the state of Sao Paolo in Brazil jointly funding scientific research and student exchanges.

Teaching, Learning & Student Life

When it comes to university locations few are as glamorous as Los Angeles, home to Hollywood, the world's largest film industry. A truly global city of 4 million people, it is the commercial heartbeat of California, the world's 15th-largest economy. When students aren't hard at work they can be hard at play. The city's beaches are lined with basketball courts and eateries while the Santa Monica Boulevard is full of trendy bars. Or, if you fancy some highbrow culture, Los Angeles has more museums per capita than any other city in the world, including the famous Los Angeles County Museum of Art and the Getty Center. The weather isn't bad either, with Los Angeles's subtropical climate providing plenty of sunshine throughout the year.

And because the USC campus is close to the centre of town, students will get to experience all that LA has to offer. The University Park campus is in the University Park district of Los Angeles, two miles from downtown Los Angeles. That places students within walking distance of Angeles landmarks such as the Shrine Auditorium, Staples Center, and Los Angeles Coliseum.

Life inside the classroom is marked by the close access that students have to participate in research projects and other creative endeavours, and to interact with distinguished faculty members. The university has a strong tradition of integrating professional and liberal education and students rarely stay within the confines of their chosen discipline.

Anyone studying cinematography or a related information science clearly benefits from USC's California location. But those studying its other strength, biomedical science, will also gain. That's because USC operates the Health Sciences Campus, a major center for basic and clinical biomedical research in the fields of cancer, gene therapy, the neurosciences, and transplantation biology.

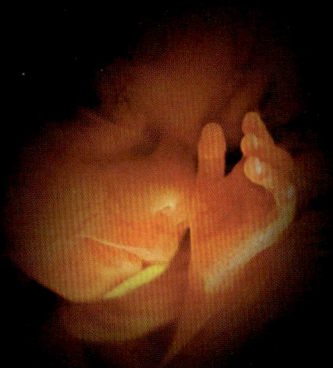

The University of Hong Kong

UC Irvine

Name › University of California, Irvine
Region › Americas
Country › United States
Founded › 1965

.www.uci.edu

Core Research Strengths

Established in 1965, the University of California, Irvine (UC Irvine) has grown rapidly into a formidable research enterprise hosting distinctive academic disciplines, a major teaching hospital and medical centre, and a dozen world-renowned multidisciplinary research centres. With more than 28,000 students, more than 1,000 faculty, and annual research funding topping $320 million, UC Irvine enjoys wide-ranging research expertise and world leadership in many fields.

One example of research excellence is the Sue & Bill Gross Stem Cell Research Center where UC Irvine makes critical advances in understanding the characteristics and clinical applications of stem cells – specifically for spinal cord injury, retinitis pigmentosa, and neurological disorders such as Alzheimer's disease and multiple sclerosis.

The California Institute for Telecommunications and Information Technology is an example of UCI's interdisciplinary centres. It draws together more than 200 research staff in a four-story, 120,000-square-foot laboratory complex. Under its roof, collaborations foster development of beneficial technologies and innovations in transportation, emergency management, healthcare, education, entertainment, the environment and more

At the recently established Steele/Burnand Anza – Borrego Desert Research Center, scientists, scholars and artists collaborate to preserve the delicate habitat. This distinctive institute reflects UCI's general commitment to sustainability in natural and built environments, and its leadership in atmospheric and earth science.

In addition to its strong multidisciplinary research, UC Irvine offers undergraduate and graduate students opportunities for focused study in highly-ranked programs in the arts, humanities, engineering, information and computer science, the natural sciences, social sciences, and education, and in professional graduate schools of law and medicine. The campus constantly develops new

majors at graduate and undergraduate levels, including programs in business, public policy, public health, pharmaceutical sciences and nursing science.

Major Discoveries

The first clinical trials using stem cells to repair spinal cord injuries are employing treatments developed and tested at UC Irvine.

In 1995, UC Irvine rocketed to national prominence when two of its professors were awarded Nobel Prizes in chemistry and physics, becoming the first university to win in different research areas in the same year. In 2004, another Nobel Prize for chemistry was awarded to a UC Irvine professor.

Partnerships, Innovation & Translational Research

The entrepreneurial spirit of UCI faculty members is evident in their application of academic research to real-world practice through collaborations with public and private partners. Such alliances demonstrate UC Irvine's commitment to extending its impact beyond the campus. To facilitate more partnerships, the campus established TechPortal locations on campus and at the UC Irvine Medical Center that offer affordable space, technical assistance, mentoring opportunities and networking prospects to fledgling UCI-based companies. In addition, the Small Business Innovation and Research (SBIR) program increases private-sector commercialisation of federally funded research innovations.

"UC Irvine faculty and students benefit from a number of campus research partnerships with corporations ranging from start-ups to multinationals," says Mark Warner, associate vice chancellor for research. Undergraduate research opportunities and valuable corporate contacts are particular advantages to students.

In one recent success, UC Irvine became the research home to National Center for Rapid Technologies, or RapidTech, the only non-profit in the U.S. dedicated to training community college and university students in the next wave of advanced manufacturing. UC Irvine also opened a $12.5-million research

centre in 2012, funded by chip maker Intel Corp. The Intel Science and Technology Center for Social Computing applies social science and the humanities to the design and analysis of digital information.

Teaching, Learning & Student Life

UC Irvine strongly encourages undergraduate research, as Vice Provost Michael Clark explains: "We have one of the most extensive undergraduate research programs in the University of California. In addition to their coursework, more than 600 students each year work with faculty in our Undergraduate Research Opportunities Program to present papers at an annual symposium, and UROP publishes many of those papers in its own journal. Engaging undergraduates in real research projects at this large scale makes our graduates some of the most innovative, imaginative and creative students graduating from any U.S. university."

Name › University of Copenhagen
Region › Europe
Country › Denmark
Founded › 1479

www.ku.dk

Core Research Strengths

The University of Copenhagen (UCPH) has more than 37,000 students. Together, the six faculties offer more than 200 programmes for study in health and medical sciences, humanities, law, science, social sciences, and theology.

In order to deliver the best research the university has developed a matrix structure, says Pro-rector, Thomas Bjoernholm. "In one dimension we have core disciplines such as health sciences and humanities; we strive to ensure that they remain internationally competitive as disciplines in their own right. In the other dimension we have what we call the cross-disciplinary projects that combine these research strengths."

Of course on its own a structure is not enough to deliver success. The university has focussed on attracting talent. Today one third of the university's 1500 ph.d's are international and so are 1000 of its researchers. Another strategy is the creation of 25 dedicated basic research centres. "For example we just recently hired a former professor of Harvard University, Charles Marcus who is now heading up a new quantum mechanics centre".

Another example is the Centre for Subjectivity Research, says the pro-rector. "It's really an investigation into the concept of the self and the centre is using an interdisciplinary approach, promoting the dialogue between philosophy, psychiatry and psychopathology".

Major Discoveries

Some of the university's most notable discoveries have come in medicine and physics, resulting in 8 Nobel Prizes for results such as the discovery of Vitamin K and a theory of the structure of the atomic nucleus.

Among recent major discoveries are the hormone GLP1, leading to a treatment for diabetes, a new global security paradigm known as the Copenhagen School or the many results on climate change from the Centre of Ice and Climate.

Partnerships, Innovation & Translational Research

Nearly all-leading universities try to establish strong international alliances with other universities. Where they differ is the strategy they employ to build those partnerships. The UCPH's approach is through supranational groups. For example, it is a member of the International Alliance of Research Universities (IARU), which consists of ten leading universities worldwide. On top of the alliance UCPH has another 150 bilateral agreements with universities around the world. A strong bond also exists with China. Recently, the Beijing Genomics Institute chose to place their research centre BGI Europe at UCPH. Also, alongside other Danish universities and Chinese universities, UCPH has established the Sino Danish Centre to strengthen and develop collaboration between Danish and Chinese research and education.

While Pro-rector Bjoernholm is clearly proud of these academic links he also places great stock in the university's tie-ups with private industries.

He notes that the university earns $100 million annually from private-sector research contracts. Moreover, it is a trend that is set to increase, says the Pro-rector. "We are moving steadily in that direction, and we are also integrating joint projects with industry into the masters and PhD level in a systematic way. Another goal we have set for ourselves is that 15% of all master thesis should be done with external partners."

But not all private-sector interaction is revenue driven. He notes that the university has established a new Easy Access IP policy. "Our goal is not to make money but to transfer knowledge."

Teaching, Learning & Student Life

Copenhagen is one of Scandinavia's great cities and was recently described as "an innovation centre" in Fortune Magazine. As a royal city it is filled with impressive architecture. Meanwhile the canals, coast and multiple parks and gardens make it a pleasant place to explore. Copenhagen also has a vibrant youth culture. Christiania is one of the largest hippy communes in northern Europe, while parts of the city's old

industrial centre have been converted to post-modern bars and clubs.

Moreover, students have every chance to explore the city as the university is actually made up of around 100 different institutes, departments, laboratories, centres and museums dotted around the city. Classrooms range from the botanical gardens to high-technology laboratories.

Learning at Copenhagen comes with a strong emphasis on post-university employment. As a result, education at the University covers specific skills and scientific methods as well as other more theoretical skills that will enable graduates to improve their qualifications. Teaching and research are closely integrated in order to achieve this, first and foremost by according them equal importance in the daily work of the academic and scientific staff, and whenever possible using teaching-led research.

The university also has its distinct learning ethos, says the Pro-rector: "We have a strong focus on producing independent students that form their own opinion and establish their own take on a topic." Another key element of the student experience is an external placement programme in the final year of undergraduate or PhD studies where students can chose to work with companies or NGOs.

UPMC
SORBONNE UNIVERSITÉS

Name › Pierre and Marie Curie University
Region › Europe
Country › France
Founded › 1971

www.upmc.fr

Core Research Strengths

Pierre & Marie Curie University (UPMC) is one of Europe's leading scientific and medical universities. An annual research budget of €400 million funds more than 5,000 researchers and professors working in over 120 laboratories across four interdisciplinary divisions: Modelling & Engineering; Energy, Matter & the Universe; Living Earth & Environment; Life & Health. The research ranges from fundamental to applied, with the aim to push the boundaries of knowledge and to explore major issues of sustainable development that preoccupy our society in the twenty-first century.

Modelling and Engineering may seem an odd focus, but it's an area that has become increasingly important in today's society. UPMC plays a predominant role in this virtual world, especially in robotic technologies, the architecture of the future Internet or in reducing noise in transportation systems. The university's multidisciplinary approach means that it combines researchers from pure and applied mathematics, computer science, mechanics, electronics, robotics and medical engineering.

As the name suggests the Energy, Matter and the Universe division has a very broad scope. These laboratories look at a very wide range of scientific challenges, such as understanding the structure of the universe and matter, quantum information technologies, nanosciences and new multifunctional materials and molecular chemistry applied to health and sustainable development.

The Living Earth and Environment division is a collection of multidisciplinary laboratories that examine the physics and chemistry of the solid earth, atmosphere and oceanography to ecology, biodiversity and biology of natural species. The university has excellent research infrastructure to support this, for example it has three marine stations on the coasts of France, which act as ocean observatories.

The final division, Life and Health, combines all facets of genetics and biology, including clinical research in neurosciences, vision, cardio-metabolism, immunology and infectious diseases, cancer, ageing and health engineering.

Major Discoveries

In recent decades the university has been particularly successful in physics. For example, the Kastler Brossel Laboratory's researcher Serge Haroche received the Nobel Prize in Physics in 2012 for ground-breaking experimental methods that enable measuring and manipulation of individual quantum systems.

Partnerships, Innovation & Translational Research

UPMC is very keen to work with private-sector organisations and files around 20 patents each year. In total more than 425 technologies developed in the laboratories of UPMC are patent protected. These technologies now generate annual license fees worth €1 million for the university.

UPMC has done its best to encourage faculty and students to create spin-off companies and has established a complete range of independent structures to facilitate its technology transfer: SATT LUTECH for maturing technology, Agoranov for start-up incubation, and Quadrivium venture capital. It also welcomes entrepreneurs that want to develop a project with the university. This process is managed by the Business and Technology Transfer Office of UPMC.

The university is also keen to work with larger, more established corporations. Research cooperation agreements have been set up with leading industrial groups through the Research and Technology Transfer Department. This department implements science policy at the University, monitoring the activities of research and technology transfer, and supporting University research organizations.

Teaching, Learning & Student Life

Pierre & Marie Curie University is located in the Latin Quarter of Paris. For those unfamiliar with the city that basically means that the university is situated in the heart of one of Europe's great capitals. Students will have the opportunity to explore one of the world's most intellectually vibrant cities, where history and contemporary life are in constant dialogue. Daily contact with French culture and French people will be an essential part of a student's education. The university also offers students the opportunity to study at one of the three marine stations located on France's coasts, and the country's excellent high-speed rail system makes it easy to quickly travel to these locations.

Another advantage of being located in a large city like Paris is that students will have plenty of opportunities to work with leading international firms. Indeed the university's courses are especially designed to increase employment opportunities after graduation. Students are taught to work as part of a team and given valuable practise in project management. These skills are taught right from the start of the programme while, as the course develops, students are expected to understand the practical aspects of research. And because the university is one of the leading scientific and medical centres in France, it is able to offer its 32 000 students a very diverse curriculum. It offers nine Bachelor's diplomas, 10 Master's diplomas and has 19 Doctoral schools.

Students also benefit from the excellent learning infrastructure. For example the university has a comprehensive French library centre. Meanwhile the University's Faculty of Medicine "Pierre and Marie Curie" has two large teaching hospitals, Pitié-Salpêtrière and Saint-Antoine, which give students the opportunity to gain real life experience. The university also has four museum collections, with hundreds of works of art.

Karolinska Institutet

Name › Karolinska Institute
Region › Europe
Country › Sweden
Founded › 1810

www.ki.se

Core Research Strengths

The Karolinska Institutet is one of the world's leading medical universities. It has a central role in the Swedish health care system, accounting for more than 40% of the medical academic research conducted in Sweden and offering the country's broadest range of education in medicine and health sciences. Because of its vaunted position it commands a research budget of SEK4.4 billion including SEK1.6 billion of direct government funding and SEK2.8 billlion of external funding from research councils, county and municipal councils, foundations and the business sector. Another sign of the university's prestige is that since 1901 it has selected the Nobel laureates in Physiology or Medicine.

President of Karolinska Institutet, Anders Hamsten, believes one of the university's main assets is its close interaction with the front line of healthcare delivery. "The core strength is that we are working very well integrated with the healthcare system. So, a lot of the work we are doing is taking research and applying it to patients and clinical situations etc."

Despite its focus on medicine, the President says it's important for Karolinska Institutet to have expertise in other related fields. "Today in order to move science forwards or in order to even move medical science forward, it's not enough to just stay within your own discipline. Rather you need to use inter-disciplinary approaches to find new ways and new openings"

As a result the university has developed skills in new areas, in particular; epidemiology science, population-based science; science based on the bio-bank and databases. Moreover, the university's long tradition and extensive archives means that it is able to test new theories against comprehensive sets of data.

Major Discoveries

Given that it is one of the world's leading medical institutions, it is perhaps little surprise the university has several Nobel Prize laureates to its name. Some of the most notable came from Erik Jorpes in the 1920s and 1930s. First he developed a method

for the production of pure insulin then he followed it up with a method for the production of safe, non-toxic heparin, a substance that prevents the coagulation of blood.

Partnerships, Innovation & Translational Research

One of the university's most important relationships is the local health service, says the President. "As a medical university, it is essential to work in concert with the healthcare services, in particular with the Stockholm County Council (SLL)."

The University also has strong links with the private sector, says President Hamsten. "We have major agreements with quite a few of the larger pharmaceutical companies in the world and also have agreements with computer companies for bio-informatics around some of the analysis we are conducting."

The university's leading research role means that its academics often make discoveries that could have commercial applications. To this end the university has established an innovation system – to help develop concepts – and a technology transfer office. These types of units are now common at leading universities. However, what's interesting about the Karolinska Institutet system is that any academic using its technology transfer office or innovation suite must also allow the institute to publish research results in academic journals. The aim says the President, "is to work out a system where it's clear that we keep academic freedom, regulate the IP rights and then we share the results with industry."

Teaching, Learning & Student Life

Karolinska Institutet is mainly divided into two campuses, one in Solna and one in Huddinge, although a considerable amount of teaching and research is conducted throughout Stockholm through the university's comprehensive collaboration with the local health authorities.

These close links with Stockholm give students a chance to enjoy one of Europe's truly unique capital cities. Stockholm is built on 14 islands connected by 57 bridges. The beautiful

buildings, the greenery, the fresh air and the proximity to the water are distinctive traits of the city. Unsurprisingly for such a green city it has the distinction of creating the world's first National City Park. Nature isn't the city's only appeal. With its 750-year history and rich cultural life, Stockholm offers a wide selection of world-class museums and attractions. Most of the city's attractions can be reached on foot, and there's a good chance of experiencing a lot of things in a short time.

The university also has a lot to offer from a learning perspective. It offers the widest range of medical education under one roof in Sweden. Several of the programmes include clinical training or other training within the healthcare system. The close proximity of the Karolinska University Hospital and other teaching hospitals in the Stockholm area gives students plenty of hands-on experience. Indeed Teachers at Karolinska Institutet often carry out research in parallel with teaching. This ensures that students are involved in the latest advances within the medical field.

UNC
GLOBAL

Name › University of North Carolina
Region › Americas
Country › United States
Founded › 1789

www.unc.edu

Core Research Strengths

Carolina ranks among the top U.S. public universities in research support. It attracted more than $767 million in total research grants and contracts in 2012. UNC-Chapel Hill's federally sponsored research is primarily based in the College of Arts and Sciences, the five health sciences schools (Medicine, Public Health, Pharmacy, Dentistry and Nursing), and professional schools such as the School of Library Science.

"UNC has a very impressive interdisciplinary research programme that builds on all of the schools and expertise that's here", says Barbara Entwisle, Vice Chancellor for Research. "That multidisciplinary approach is one reason our research programmes have been so successful." One good example of that is the Gillings School of Global Public Health. "It collaborates with the entire campus in the area of nutrition and obesity."

Indeed medicine is one of UNC's great strengths, says Prof. Entwisle. "We have a very strong presence in basic and translational medicine, where we have made a $245 million commitment to develop strength in that area. We are trying to increasingly develop the basic and applied science needed to use genomic science in clinical settings."

Another area that stands out is computer science, says Prof. Entwisle. "We have very strong departments in these disciplines, and they are doing really exceptional work in the areas of material science, energy and nanomedicine."

The ability to analyse and present big data is one of the major themes at present. Indeed UNC is using its skills in this area to make breakthroughs in marine science. "We have some very interesting simulation work, which is informed by basic science, but creates accurate hurricane storm surge prediction models."

Major Discoveries

Given the university's current push in the field of genetics, it is fitting that in 2007 Oliver Smithies won the Nobel Prize in Medicine for the discovery of principles for introducing specific gene modifications in mice by the use of embryonic stem cells.

Partnerships, Innovation & Translational Research

Because of the UNC's leading position in several fields it often generates research with considerable translational potential. To that end it has established a technology transfer office that helps with licensing and the filing of patents. It also has a variety of programmes on campus designed to assist the faculty in establishing start-up companies. Indeed there have been more than 50 spin-off companies resulting from UNC discoveries. One notable recent example is Synerca Pharmaceuticals, which is based on work by Scott Singleton in the Eshelman School of Pharmacy, to develop an enzyme inhibitor that makes antibiotics more effective.

The university also has important research alliances with fellow institutions, explains Dr. Ron Strauss. "We launched four years ago the Global Research Institute, which is a world-class think tank for fellows to come together at faculty levels from all over the world for different periods of time to collaborate with our faculty around major issues. The focus of this period now with our campus-wide theme, Water in the World."

Teaching, Learning & Student Life

UNC is located in the beautiful college town of Chapel Hill, and is part of the Raleigh-Durham metropolitan area. With a population of almost 60,000, Chapel Hill is a small, friendly town where life has been shaped by the university since it opened its doors to students in 1795. That impact is visible from the many large murals that have been painted on local buildings by UNC alumnus Michael Brown. It's also noticeable in more subtle ways, such as the proliferation of liberal coffee shops and a thriving arts scene. From the Ackland Art Museum and the Morehead Planetarium and Science Center to the North

Carolina Botanical Garden and Carolina Performing Arts, Carolina offers a vast array of educational and cultural opportunities.
Meanwhile students should make sure they don't miss the annual street fair, Festifall, in October. The fair has a mix of live music, street performers, arts and crafts and general celebratory atmosphere.

The university has a similarly dazzling array of academic choice. Carolina offers 77 bachelor's, 107 master's, 69 doctorate and six professional degree programs through its 14 schools and the College of Arts and Sciences. Students benefit from this array of courses because there is a lot of interaction between schools, says Dr. Strauss. "I would say increasingly our interdisciplinary research approach is reflected in the classroom. We are seeing a great deal of growth in cross-school and cross-department course offerings, as well as interdisciplinary curricular offerings, the university facilitates that by making it easy to do that."

The other striking element of life at UNC, is travel, says Dr. Strauss. "Almost 40% of our undergraduates spend at least a semester studying elsewhere in the world. It's really about learning about culture, and learning about different systems of education and scholarship in the process of the classroom and the laboratory. We built our system of world exchanges around partnerships not around branch campuses."

The University of Manchester

Name › The University of Manchester
Region › Europe
Country › United Kingdom
Founded › 1851

www.manchester.ac.uk

Core Research Strengths

The relatively recent merger between the UMIST and the Victoria University of Manchester has enabled the University of Manchester as a whole to leverage a number of economies of scales in its operations that have contributed to the research capacity. Indeed the university now commands an annual research budget of almost £200 million. Moreover, since the 2004 merger the University has invested approx £600 million in new buildings.

Vice Chancellor Professor Dame Nancy Rothwell says the new university is now a potent research force. "The University of Manchester excels in the fields of nuclear research, cancer research and material sciences. On top of this, the University of Manchester is very strong in a number of medical sciences, life sciences, health policy, public health, physics and chemistry. The University of Manchester also receives a great deal of positive feedback from the private sector in particular with regards to our ability to produce effective inter-disciplinary research teams that are able to group around complex challenges and provide solutions to them."

But the University's interdisciplinary approach is not just harnessed for commercial gain. It is also used to try to help with some of humanity's most pressing issues, says the Vice Chancellor.

"The University of Manchester has major research programs across disciplines covering some of the most significant international challenges such as global poverty and climate change, as well as throughout disciplines such as systems biology. We were recently awarded the national centre that integrates a range of disciplines such as biology, medicine and mathematics".

Major Discoveries

In 2004 Andre Geim and Kostya Novoselov managed to extract single-atom-thick crystallites of graphene from graphite. Both were later awarded Nobel Prizes for what many scientists believe could remain the most important breakthrough of the 21st century.

Partnerships, Innovation & Translational Research

Partnerships are a key way for the university to achieve its goals says Vice Chancellor Rothwell. "The University of Manchester places great emphasis on partnerships, not just with the private sector but also throughout the public, voluntary and third sectors; as well as with charitable foundations and research councils."

She cites the university's partnership with the International Red Cross as a prime example of a non-commercially driven collaboration.

Nevertheless, says Luke Georghiou, Vice Chancellor of Research and Innovation, tie-ups with the private sector are also important. "In terms of technology transfer and economic valorisation, the University of Manchester is usually ranked in the top 3 universities nationally for the number of spin off companies produced at the university. One of the standout companies is called NanoDot now valued at over 100 million pounds. The company produces Nano-dots; these are of vital importance to the future of LED screens resulting in major exports to emerging Asian markets for the company. The University of Manchester has a science park housing over 100 companies, the vast majority of which have their origins at the university."

It's an impressive record, and one that would be the envy of many peers – but what's the reason for the success? One factor, says Pro Vice Chancellor Georghiou, is the innovative incentive programme in place.

"The University of Manchester has a particularly unique approach to technology transfer in that 85 % of the earnings that come from intellectual property successfully taken to the market go directly to the researchers responsible for its invention. As a university we have a very strong commitment to facilitating the development of valuable intellectual property and its transfer into the economy, we have a duty to the economy and to society as a whole in this way. As long as the process of technology transfer pays for itself, we will continue to encourage this as a strategic policy.

Teaching, Learning & Student Life

The main beneficiaries of the university's capital-intensive building programme have been the students themselves. However, the improvements aren't just restricted to nicer lecture halls and amenities. Changes have also been taking place in the classroom, says Vice Chancellor Rothwell.

"At undergraduate level, the university is in the midst of developing the 'University College'. This has been in development for the past 6 years as a broad program, working towards fostering valuable skills such as leadership, entrepreneurialism and volunteering. This has involved a number of inspirational speakers attending the university, such as the head of corporate social responsibility from Barclays. This program has been hugely popular, being stretched to capacity with over 1000 students currently enrolled and all places heavily oversubscribed. This popularity has been the stimulating factor in the development of the University College. The University College will offer a suite of courses such as business entrepreneurialism, global challenges and social entrepreneurialism."

Vice Chancellor Rothwell underlines the importance of the University College, noting that regardless of the discipline studied, there are certain characteristics – "such as communication and leadership" – that all employers will look for.

Name › University of British Columbia
Region › Americas
Country › Canada
Founded › 1908

www.ubc.ca

Core Research Strengths

With C$549 million per year in research funding, the University of British Columbia is one of Canada's leading research universities and is consistently ranked among the top 40 in the world.

One of the main points to stress about UBC is that it is "truly comprehensive", says President Stephen Toope. "It has a very wide spectrum of strengths across a whole range of disciplines. I think historically the university was often seen as particularly strong in basic science research and that continues to be the case."

President Toope notes that a quantum material is one area where UBC is particularly strong. Another is neuroscience. "We are particularly strong in neurodegenerative diseases, it's been a very strong group that's developed particularly in the last decade, decade and a half at UBC. This expansion was built on a base of historical strength at UBC in Parkinson's disease research."

Understandably, given Canada's expansive commodity industries, UBC has expertise in studies of the natural environment, resource-based issues and biodiversity, explains the president. "Because of funding factors and internal decisions we've had, bio diversity has arisen as a very strong area at UBC relating to sustainability issues, such as sustainability of fisheries. So there's been a lot of work in that area", says President Toope.

"Another area of focus for UBC historically, and just because of where we are in the world, is Asian research. So there's a lot of emphasis across many different departments. We have one of the largest programs for teaching Mandarin as an additional language."

Major Discoveries

2011 Julio Montaner – Treatment as Prevention for HIV Transmission. This is the use of anti-retroviral drugs in a cocktail having the secondary impact of actually reducing transmission rates of HIV dramatically.

2003 - Mark Halpern and Gary Hinshaw – The WMAP experiment. WMAP stands for Wilkinson Microwave Anisotropy Probe and this was a study of the microwave background in the universe. Understanding the pattern of microwaves in the universe helps understand the basic structure of the universe.

Partnerships, Innovation & Translational Research

UBC has several important partnerships with the private sector, says President Toope. "We're partnering both with a local company with some experimental technology, and with General Electric through the provision of some of their most advanced engines."

One of the key parts of the university's partnerships strategy is to help link local firms with multinationals, says the President. "We've got partnerships with major global companies like Honeywell developing monitoring systems on campus, and what we're trying to do is serve as a focal point so that small local industry can connect with global industry. So we've got a project with something called Pulse Energy, which is a local company."

Like many universities, UBC is keen to commercialise its best research, says Vice President of Research Dr. John Hepburn. "The whole concept of technology transfer is an on-going challenge for universities, and we continue to evolve the way we do things. What we have learned in the 25 years we've been doing this is that the solution that works for things like drug development is not the solution that works for software engineering. So flexibility is the main thing, that's why discussions about intellectual property ownership rules are sort of irrelevant because the ideal policy for one sector of the economy doesn't work for other sectors."

So far it seems the approach is working as 149 companies have spun off from UBC research.

Teaching, Learning & Student Life

The university is spread over two major campuses. Surrounded by the ocean, the city and 763 hectares of forested park land, the Vancouver campus is UBC's largest campus with twelve faculties. The campus is located 20 minutes from the heart of downtown Vancouver. The other main campus is Kelowna, also in the Okanagan Valley. In addition, UBC has a downtown presence in Vancouver at UBC Robson Square and at the Great Northern Way campus, located south east of downtown Vancouver.

Of the 55,000 students almost 10,000 are from abroad, helping to create an international atmosphere. "We are fundamentally committed to increasing the number of international students", says President Toope. "We're roughly at 12% of our students from our undergraduate body and 27% from our graduate body. The largest single source of students for us not surprisingly is China. The second largest being the United States but then Korea, Japan and other Asian countries are very high on the list."

The president believes this policy helps both incoming students and locals. "We believe that internationalising the campus is a benefit for all of our students especially for those who don't have the opportunity to study outside of Canada."

The teaching style at UBC has a big focus on learning opportunities outside the classroom. This includes informal educational settings and enriched learning opportunities–co-op placements, international service learning, and community service learning.

UNIVERSITY OF MARYLAND

Name › University of Maryland
Region › Americas
Country › United States
Founded › 1856

www.umd.edu

Core Research Strengths

The University of Maryland, College Park is a public research university, the flagship campus of the University System of Maryland and the original 1862 land-grant institution in the state. The university has an annual research budget of more than $518 million. It also recently completed a very successful fundraising campaign called 'Great Expectations,' which raised more than $1 billion in private donations.

The university's core academic disciplines are in physics, astronomy, mathematics, engineering, computer science, business and economics, explains President Wallace Loh. These strengths are combined to research four general themes.

"One of these areas is space science. In particular, we specialize in unmanned planetary explorations, partly because we are so close to NASA Goddard – the agency's unmanned flight center. We are also close to Lockheed Martin, the defence contractor. So, we work together to build satellites that go for unmanned space flights to comets, for example. "The second area is environmental sustainability. Again, location plays a part as we are next door to the National Oceanographic and Atmospheric Administration (NOAA). They've just opened a major research agency right on our campus, which gives us the largest concentration of earth scientists in the United States.

"The third area is National Security, and again you can see the influence of the Federal Government. We work with a range of government bodies, including the Defence Department, the CIA, The National Security Agency and the Department of Homeland Security."

The fourth and final area is food security, says the President. "Around 60% of all our fruits and vegetables, for example, are now imported from abroad. We explore how we can stop them from becoming contaminated by bad growing techniques or bioterrorist attacks. For example, we are training groups of people from China, India and Latin America to conduct sophisticated analysis up to American standards of safety."

Major Discoveries

Given the university's expertise in space, it is little surprise that one of its most recent major discoveries came in a related discipline. In 2006, John C. Mather won the Nobel Prize in Physics for the discovery of the blackbody form and anisotropy of the cosmic microwave background radiation.

Partnerships, Innovation & Translational Research

The breadth and quality of the University of Maryland's research, coupled with its proximity to the nation's capital, has resulted in strong research partnerships with the Federal government. However, President Loh is keen to improve the university's ties with private-sector partners. "College Park alone, without the biomedical sciences, currently creates ten new high-tech start-ups a year, and my goal is to triple that to 30 within the next five years. This is achievable if we work closely with biomedical sciences," he says. One of the key steps in this strategy is the recent establishment of an operation called University of Maryland Ventures, which joins the tech commercialization operations of both the health sciences and the College Park campuses. The university also employs 'site miners' who go into the labs and identify inventions that have market potential.

Perhaps the most innovative element of this strategy is that President Loh is keen to involve students. "We have 3,500 professors, of whom probably no more than 100 are actively involved in tech commercialization. The real way that we are going to have an impact, in terms of creating not only new companies but also whole new industries, is not through our faculty, it's through our students – after all we have 37,000 students." To that end, the university has created an academy for innovation and entrepreneurship. One key initiative of this academy is to expose all students in all disciplines to a meaningful innovation experience.

Teaching, Learning & Student Life

The University of Maryland is very popular with students, says President Loh. One reason is its location near Washington, D.C. "Being close to

Washington presents opportunities. For students there are enormous internship opportunities with companies and the Federal Government. The reality is when you can get from your agency or your federal lab to the campus in 20 or 30 minutes at the most, you just jump in the car and you develop these personal relationships."

On the academic side, there are two main reasons why so many top students want to come to the University of Maryland, says the President. "One reason is the interdisciplinary learning. The second is the coupling of that interdisciplinary learning with what we call living-learning communities. We have, for example, two living-learning communities on innovation and entrepreneurship."

With a total of 26, these "Living and Learning" programs allow students with similar academic interests to live in the same residential community, take specialized courses and perform research in those areas of expertise. For example, the University Honors College, which is geared toward students with exceptional academic talents, welcomes students into a community of faculty and intellectually gifted undergraduates committed to acquiring a broad and balanced education. Beginning fall 2013, the college will offer seven living and learning programs: Digital Cultures & Creativity, Entrepreneurship & Innovation, Honors Humanities, Gemstone, Integrated Life Sciences, University Honors and Advanced Cybersecurity.

UNIVERSITÉ
PARIS
SUD

Comprendre le monde,
construire l'avenir®

Name › University of Paris Sud
Region › Europe
Country › France
Founded › 1971

www.u-psud.fr

Core Research Strengths

Established in 1971, Paris-Sud University may seem a very young institution. However, it was created following the breakup of the University of Paris and as such has academic heritage going back to the middle of the 12th century. The university inherited its predecessor's advanced research facility to the south of the capital, and now commands an annual research budget of €80 million. As a result of the facilities it inherited its core research strengths are fundamental sciences, mathematics, physics, I.T. and software sciences, and biology. However, the university is not a truly comprehensive university, as it doesn't cover the humanities but it is present in law, economics and management.

President Professor Jacques Bittoun is keen to point out that the university also has a very strong health and medical sciences department. "It focuses on cancer research, transplants and biotherapy, the domain of public health and epidemiology, medical pharmacology and medical screening." Other smaller but still important areas of research at the Paris-Sud University include chemistry, economics, law, management, sports science and engineering, among others."

But research at the university is currently undergoing a huge change, through the aegis of the Campus Paris-Saclay Project, says President Bittoun. "This project is to create a new university called 'Université Paris-Saclay' by grouping the University of Paris-Sud with some of the most prestigious Grandes Écoles (like École Polytechnique and École Nationale Superieure) and some leading research institutes (like CNRS, the French National Centre for Scientific Research, and the CEA, the Atomic Energy Commission)."

One of the first examples of the result of this new approach is the Institute of Extreme Light. The physics department set it up with other partners; its main project is to develop an ultra high-density laser.

Major Discoveries

Given the university's strong science focus, it is little surprise that some of its greatest research achievements have come in related fields. In 1991 Pierre-Gilles de Gennes won the Nobel Prize in Physics for discovering that methods developed for studying order phenomena in simple systems can be generalized to more complex forms of matter, in particular to liquid crystals and polymers. That success was followed up by Albert Fert winning the same prize in 2007 for the discovery of giant magneto resistance.

Partnerships, Innovation & Translational Research

Like many French universities the majority – about 75% - of the university's budget comes from public-sector funds. However, Professor Bittoun is keen to change that, and increase private-sector revenues. "We have recently been in discussion with Group PSA, France's leading automobile company. Today in the car industry, electronics and software are increasingly important in order to build the vehicle of the future, especially in the fields of I.T. and energy. We think we can help them. "Indeed the university has already worked on a joint hydrogen battery project. These projects aren't just about obtaining funding, says the President. "Through this partnership, Citroen hopes to develop and train engineers who can become part of the PSA group working on the vehicle of the future. Therefore, Citroen will provide not just financing, but also orientation and training to develop future engineers for their automobile group."

Students are also integral to the university's interaction with the outside world, especially to its internationalisation strategy. At present around 5,000 of the university's 30,000-strong student body, are international students. Yet President Bittoun feels more could be done to accommodate students from abroad. "There are no courses designed specifically for international students, and in order to increase the internationalisation of our university, it will be necessary to develop specialised English-taught programs."

Teaching, Learning & Student Life

Paris-Sud University has the largest campus in France. It has five locations, namely in the towns of Orsay, Sceaux, Châtenay-Malabry, Cachan, and Kremlin-Bicêtre, all in the southern suburbs of Paris. The scientific campus at Orsay particularly stands out. It spreads across more than 200 hectares and is beautifully landscaped with woods and a botanical garden. Moreover, while the university may not be in the centre of the city, its headquarters and institutes are strategically placed along the RER B train line, ensuring direct access to Paris.

When it comes to life inside the classroom students at Paris-Sud can look forward to an interactive approach, which offers plenty of exposure to research, says the President. "We are focused on research-driven teaching, even for undergraduates. All of our lecturers and professors are also researchers; this inspires our teaching methods. In addition, we offer many internships in research laboratories, as well as hands-on experience in real projects and an emphasis on case studies rather than just learning facts."

Students should also benefit from the recently launched Paris-Saclay Entrepreneurial Student Program (PEEPS), which will provide students with increased knowledge of the business world. At undergraduate level, the PEEPS programme gives students an idea of how business works, whilst encouraging entrepreneurialism and the creation of business. For post-graduates, this programme enables the simulation of setting up their own business; thus allowing students at Paris-Sud University to be supported from an early stage right up to the creation of their own business when they leave university.

Duke
UNIVERSITY

Name › Duke University
Region › Americas
Country › United States
Founded › 1838

www.duke.edu

Core Research Strengths

Duke University is a private research university located in Durham, North Carolina, United States. Duke's growth and academic focus have contributed to continuing the university's reputation as an academic and research powerhouse. As a result Duke now commands a research budget of almost $1 billion per year, making it the fifth-largest research university in America.

The university focuses its research efforts on business, engineering, the environment, law, medicine, nursing and public policy. The university's approach to medicine involves integrating patient care at Duke University hospital with the clinical, training and research programmes of the Duke University Health System, Duke University School of Medicine and Duke University School of Nursing. The hospital, which includes two community hospitals and hundreds of ambulatory care clinics, is a way of ensuring that academic theories are borne out of real world experiences.

Of course, like many internationally-leading research universities, Duke has long practised an interdisciplinary approach. For example, in 1994 it opened the Levine Science Research Center. Touted as a "building without walls" to foster collaboration across disciplines, it is one of the largest single-site interdisciplinary research facilities in the U.S. The 341,000 square-foot facility is a multipurpose center housing classrooms, laboratory space and offices shared by various schools and departments.

But the university has not rested on its laurels and ten years later it launched the $97 million Fitzpatrick Center, which brings together faculty in four research initiatives: biology, photonics, materials and integrated sensors. The center also helps the Pratt School of Engineering's partnership with the School of Medicine by providing laboratories for collaborative research in health care, genomics and biotechnology.

Major Discoveries

One of the most telling signs of a successful university is recent recognition of its research. For example Duke's research power was highlighted

in the latest Nobel Awards ceremony when Robert J Lefkowitz won the 2012 Nobel Prize in Chemistry for studies of G-protein-coupled receptors.

Partnerships, Innovation & Translational Research

Given Duke's huge research budget and expertise in several areas, there is significant private-sector demand to work with the university. Initial enquiries are handled by the Office of Corporate and Foundation Relations. From there, depending on the type of relationship being proposed, firms will work with other offices. For example the Duke Career Center provides a variety of options for companies interested in recruiting Duke students. Another important point of liaison is the Duke Clinical Research Institute, which is responsible for patents, technology licenses and new venture developments.

Like most leading universities these days Duke is a very international institution – something that's reflected in the makeup of the student body. More than 8% of fulltime students are international, while – in the other direction – almost half of Duke under-graduates participate in the study abroad scheme. That's the highest rate of any of the top ten private research universities. Another measure of Duke's internationality is that it has more than 300 partnerships with international institutions. Duke has also partnered with the National University of Singapore to open a research-focused medical school in Singapore, and is participating in the development of a new joint venture university in Kunshan, China.

Teaching, Learning & Student Life

One of the first things an undergraduate will notice about Duke is that despite its impressive research pedigree, it places a heavy emphasis on learning. One powerful element of the learning programme is the blend of disciplines. For example even students studying medicine will leave with a liberal arts education and an understanding of how other themes interact with health. Fortunately this is supported with choice, so students can choose which interdisciplinary areas they find most appealing from an extensive menu of majors, minors and

concentrations. Indeed the innovative Program II curriculum allows students to focus their undergraduate studies on what most excites them intellectually. In effect, that means each student has the primary responsibility for his or her program of study and course selection. Students of all levels should also be ready to roll up their sleeves and help senior staff as around half of all undergraduates participate in faculty research.

Outside of the classroom, students will find plenty to help them relax. The campus is set in 8,000 acres of land. Natural attractions include the vast Duke Forest and the equally impressive Sarah P Duke Gardens. Buildings on campus are divided into four main areas: West, East, and Central campuses and the Medical Center, which are all connected via a free bus service. The West Campus stands out in particular and its distinct architecture has earned it the nickname "the Gothic Wonderland" among Duke students.

Outside of the university is the bustling city of Durham. Frequently voted one of the nation's best cities to eat, play and live, it is home to a thriving high-tech community and flourishing art scene. Because the area also has two other leading universities Durham has a very lively, young population. It has also become one of the nation's great technology incubators, with countless small start-ups.

THE UNIVERSITY OF TEXAS AT AUSTIN

Name › The University of Texas at Austin
Region › Americas
Country › United States
Founded › 1883

www.utexas.edu

Core Research Strengths

With annual research expenditures in the region of US$580 million annually, the University of Texas, Austin's portfolio of world-class research runs throughout a diverse array of academic disciplines ranging from expertise in architecture and business studies through to computer science.

Home to Ranger, one of the world's fastest supercomputers housed in the Texas Advanced Computing Center, computer science is the best-known world-class research strength at the University of Texas, Austin. Strengths in hardware development are complemented by strengths in software development and electrical engineering pioneered in the Center for Agile Technology and Microelectronics Research Center respectively.

Excellence in the technical sciences at the University of Texas, Austin are not confined to electrical engineering and computer sciences, with pioneering programs in energy and biomedical engineering also a hallmark of the institution. Founded in 2009, the Energy Institute plays host to cutting edge research programs investigating technologies such as solar, biofuels and battery energy storage; thought to be of vital importance to ensuring energy sustainability and security long into the 21st Century.

Major Discoveries

Astrophysicist Karl Gerbhardt recently discovered the largest black hole in the universe using the world's third largest telescope at UT's McDonald Observatory. The black hole is estimated to weigh 17 billion times more than our sun.

Professor Luis Caffarelli received the 2012 Wolf Prize in Mathematics for his work in nonlinear analysis, partial differential equations and their applications - calculus of variations and optimization.

Partnerships, Innovation & Translational Research

The University of Texas, Austin's Office of Industry Engagement (OIE) leads efforts in bringing together external collaborators from the private sector with UT's researchers and institutes. Whilst clearly focused upon preserving the principles of academic freedom and curiosity driven research, the OIT's team strives to develop long-term research partnerships between industry and the university's researchers; ensuring that breakthroughs and knowledge discovered at the university benefits society and the broader economy as a whole. The approach to intellectual property management is flexible, with OIE staff able to develop specific models that satisfy the interests of the university and its research collaborators on a case-by-case basis.

Having produced over 800 patents, the innovative capability at UT is without doubt. The Office of Technology Commercialisation's mission at the university is to ensure the benefits of each discovery and patent reach their full potential both in the market context, as well as for the broader benefit of society. As well as organizing seminars and events bringing innovators and investors together, the OTC manages processes from disclosure to patent, and ultimate commercialisation. This office is the interface that investors interested in UT research programs from a commercial investment perspective should coordinate with.

Teaching, Learning & Student Life

One could be forgiven for finding themselves a little bit lost amongst the university's more than 170 undergraduate fields of study, 134 master's degrees and 94 doctoral programs; fortunately there is a wealth of support to help students inform their decisions. Interdisciplinary research and study is supported throughout the UT system with an array of dual degrees and combined honours enabling students to creatively combine their various interest areas, so as to meet their career aspirations and interests. Research is strongly encouraged at all levels of UT, combined with

numerous efforts to encourage job and business creation such as the Intellectual Entrepreneurship Program; adding further to the creative and entrepreneurial spirit synonymous with the University of Texas, Austin.

With over 50,000 students on a nearly 350-acre campus in the heart of Austin, students at UT can expect a very lively environment with diversity and creativity at its heart. Approximately 5500 students and 1000 faculty members at UT were born outside of the United States, helping to further enhance the university's cosmopolitan and welcoming atmosphere. Ranking amongst the top five for US universities sending students for international study and research opportunities, UT's international component is far from restricted to the campus in Austin.

The University of Texas, Austin community is a group of open minded, talented and creative individuals coming from the world over. Students in attendance can expect to consistently be challenged by their studies and pleasantly surprised by the creativity and community sprit of their counterparts. With over 1000 student groups and associations, a myriad of activities and leadership opportunities are on offer away from the conventional study program.

Sports are a foundation of the UT culture, with the university alone having won in excess of 120 Olympic medals and the Texas Longhorns being an immutable aspect of student life for athletes and supporters alike.

Name › University of California, Santa Barbara
Region › Americas
Country › United States
Founded › 1909

www.ucsb.edu

Core Research Strengths

The University of California, Santa Barbara is a public research university and one of the ten campuses of the University of California system. UCSB commands an annual research budget of $217 million, with the vast majority of that coming from federal agencies.

That research budget is channelled through academic departments and a network of research centers. Indeed it is worth noting that UCSB houses twelve national research centers, eight of which are supported by the National Science Foundation, including the Kavli Institute for Theoretical Physics, the Center for Nanotechology in Society, the Materials Research Lab, and the National Center for Ecological Synthesis and Analysis. UCSB is also home to Microsoft Station Q, a research group working on topological quantum computing and the Solid State Lighting and Energy Center, focused on new semiconductor based technologies for energy efficient lighting and displays, power electronics, and solar energy conversion. Another standout institute is The Koegel Autism Center, which has been recognised by the National Research Council as one of the top 10 state-of-the-art treatment facilities for autism in the United States.

Most of USCB's research centers are multidisciplinary and achieve their success by bringing together experts in diverse fields. One good example of this is the new interdisciplinary Institute for Energy Efficiency recently established by the College of Engineering. It brings together more than 50 campus researchers with related expertise to develop new energy-saving technologies. The institute's Center for Energy Efficient Materials was awarded a grant of $19 million by the Department of Energy.

But it would be misleading to give the impression that the university is just focussed on science. It is a truly comprehensive institution with strong research capabilities in the humanities. For example it is the editorial headquarters for The Writings of Henry D. Thoreau, a National Endowment for the Humanities (NEH) project that is publishing definitive scholarly editions of the complete works of naturalist and literary artist Henry David Thoreau.

Major Discoveries

Despite the university's broad base of research excellence it has particularly shone in chemistry and physics so far this century. For example in 2000 Herbert Kroemer won the Nobel Prize in Physics for developing semiconductor hetero structures used in high-speed and opto-electronics. Then in 2004 David J. Gross won the Nobel Prize in Physics for the discovery of asymptotic freedom in the theory of the strong interaction. Walter Kohn was awarded the Nobel Prize in Chemistry in 1998 for his development of density-functional theory and Alan Heeger won the 2000 Nobel Prize in Chemistry for the discovery and development of conductive polymers.

Partnerships, Innovation & Translational Research

Perhaps the most telling sign of the university's success at commercialising research is that UCSB faculty and alumni have established more than 80 local companies. This is an ongoing process with an average of five new companies based on UCSB research formed every year. In addition, 66 companies around the world are currently using technologies developed at UCSB.

UCSB launched the Technology Management Program (TMP) in 1998, an interdisciplinary training initiative of the College of Engineering, that teaches the skills required of successful entrepreneurs. Offering courses and mentoring, TMP provides tech-specific education in entrepreneurship and management. Starting in 2014, TMP will offer a one-year Masters in Management - "an MBA for scientists and engineers." By helping to prepare aspiring entrepreneurs to not only interface with investors, but to actually run a business that gets off the ground, TMP is often central to the early success of start-ups.

Teaching, Learning & Student Life

When it comes to on campus attractions USCB has something that very few other universities in the world can offer – its own beach! The campus, bordered on three sides by the Pacific Ocean, has miles of coastline as well as its own lagoon. It also has numerous walking and bicycle paths across campus, around the lagoon and along the beach.

Aside from the natural appeal students will also benefit from the campus upgrade programme that is seeing many of the older campus buildings being replaced with newer, more modern facilities. Another boon for students is the extensive network of UCSB Libraries, consisting of the Davidson Library and the Arts Library. Together they hold more than 3 million bound volumes and millions of microforms, government documents, manuscripts, maps, satellite and aerial images, sound recordings, and other materials.

Prospective students should also take the time to understand UCSB's education style. Like all University of California campuses, UCSB prioritises academic development over vocational learning. Undergraduate teaching is centred on lectures, with larger lecture classes having sections. Sections may be tutorial style, or they may be set up as seminars or discussions.

Students will also gain from working with one of the most impressive faculties in the United States. Indeed among its staff USCB includes five Nobel Prize laureates, one Fields Medallist, 32 members of the National Academy of Sciences, 25 members of the National Academy of Engineering, and 25 members of the American Academy of Arts and Sciences.

University of Colorado
Boulder

Name › University of Colorado Boulder
Region › Americas
Country › United States
Founded › 1876

www.colorado.edu

Core Research Strengths

Similarly to many of the world's leading research universities, the research portfolio at the University of Colorado Boulder encompasses a wide range of academic disciplines and applied areas of expertise. Nevertheless, the University is widely recognised for world leading expertise in some specific areas.

The physics department, particularly in the areas of molecular and quantum physics, is widely acknowledged as being world leading. The university's expertise within the broad area of environmental sciences is also world-renowned with leading research programs ranging from better understanding climate change to Antarctic explorations and the development of cleaner, more sustainable forms of energy. Leadership in developing solutions to today and tomorrow's environmental challenges is underscored at the University of Colorado Boulder by the campus' number one ranking throughout the United States in terms of sustainability.

The university's expertise in mathematics, computer science and engineering has not only laid the foundation for excellence in specific areas of engineering such as aeronautical and information technology, but also facilitated the development of multidisciplinary research programs in areas such as biotechnology and space exploration with Boulder being one of the largest recipients of NASA funding among all U.S. universities.

Major Discoveries

The Bose-Einstein Condensate, a new form of matter, was first discovered at the University of Colorado Boulder.

Distinguished Professor Thomas Cech won the 1989 Nobel Prize in chemistry for his discovery that RNA in living cells is not only a molecule of heredity but also can function as a biocatalyst.

Research by University of Colorado Boulder faculty members has resulted in five Nobel Prize recipients, four in physics and one in chemistry.

Partnerships, Innovation & Translational Research

The University of Colorado Boulder is a very experienced international collaborator working alongside public, private and third sector institutions in developing numerous long-term strategic collaborations addressing key challenges across a myriad of academic disciplines. Increasingly the development of public partnerships in the form of multidisciplinary collaborative centres is at the heart of the university's partnership strategy. Excellent examples of this approach are embodied in the Cooperative Institute for Research in Environmental Sciences, a joint institute of CU-Boulder and the National Oceanic and Atmospheric Administration, and the Center for Membrane and Applied Science Technology, a joint center of CU-Boulder and the New Jersey Institute of Technology funded by the National Science Foundation.

World-leading expertise throughout the environmental sciences is further enhanced with the university's portfolio of research institutes in partnership with federal laboratories such as the Cooperative Institute for Research in Environmental Sciences, and the Renewable and Sustainable Energy Institute in partnership with the National Oceanic and Atmospheric Administration, and the National Renewable Energy Laboratory respectively.

The University of Colorado Boulder's 2030 strategic plan has led to the development of five research initiatives, capitalising on the research expertise at the university toward addressing key global challenges in a diverse collection of fields. The Aerospace Initiative, Biotechnology Initiative, Computational Sciences and Engineering Initiative, Energy Initiative and Geosciences Initiative are the five broad topic areas that the University of Colorado Boulder is working in to help advance solutions to some of the major global challenges facing society today.

Teaching, Learning & Student Life

With approximately 3,500 courses on offer each year in 150 areas of study, the University of Colorado Boulder offers students enormous diversity combined with an almost unparalleled depth of expertise in several disciplines such as molecular and atomic physics. Study abroad opportunities abound with 330 courses on offer in 70 countries for students to choose from.

The opportunity for students to combine their study programs in an interdisciplinary fashion is complemented by a commitment to encouraging undergraduate involvement in research, and the strong entrepreneurial culture that runs throughout the university that encourages student and faculty communities alike to take their ideas as far as they possibly can for the benefit of the economy and society.

Community engagement plays a very important part in the University of Colorado Boulder experience, with the university boasting one of the most active and powerful student governments in the United States. The University of Colorado Student Government oversees a myriad of activities for students at the university, governing budgetary approvals for 120 student groups each year.

One particularly rewarding and beneficial aspect of the student culture at the University of Colorado, Boulder is the commitment to working alongside local communities that helps to develop leadership and communication skills through experiences one would not traditionally associate with university life. Through a variety of programs in coordination with the student government and university, students are able to engage in a variety of activities ranging from long-term projects to internships in the community.

The University of Colorado Boulder campus' distinctive neo-gothic and Tuscan revival architecture is set in a breath-taking backdrop of the Rocky Mountains, facilitating a myriad of interesting leisure activities from skiing and snowboarding in the winter to hiking and mountain climbing in the summer.

Name › Rockefeller University
Region › Americas
Country › United States
Founded › 1901

www.rockefeller.edu

Core Research Strengths

Since being established in 1901, The Rockefeller University has consistently striven for world changing discoveries throughout the medical and life sciences. The University's record of 24 Nobel Prizes in medicine and chemistry is a testament to how seriously this philosophy is taken. With 73 independent laboratories on campus, Rockefeller University's research capacity stretches throughout the spectrum of life and medical sciences. Nevertheless, the university is widely acknowledged as having world-leading programs in numerous specific fields such as immunology, neuroscience, microbiology, structural biology, cell and molecular biology and genetics.

Quite a unique approach, very much the signature of Rockefeller University is to focus recruitment efforts on individuals, not on particular research fields. President Marc Tessier-Lavigne notes how the individual approach to recruitment has led to the evolution of a thriving multi-disciplinary environment: "We recruit the person and not the field. As a result, it's a very interdisciplinary environment where you will have immunologists in laboratories next to neurobiologists who are in laboratories next to cell biologists and so forth. We believe that going for the best people, focusing on the individual as opposed to the specific scientific area, and fostering an intense interdisciplinary environment have been the main sources of our success."

Major Discoveries

Professor Ralph Steinmann won the 2011 Nobel Prize for his work identifying dendritic cells, sentinels of our immune system that detect pathogens.

Professor Roderick Mackinnon won the 2003 Nobel Prize in Chemistry for his work on the structure and operation of ion channels.

Professor Sir Paul Nurse won the 2001 Nobel Prize for the discovery of mechanisms that control of the duplication of cells throughout the cell cycle.

Professor Paul Greengard won the 2000 Nobel Prize for his discoveries concerning signal transduction in the nervous system.

Professor Günter Blobel won the 1999 Nobel Prize for the discovery that proteins have intrinsic signals that govern their transport and localization in the cell.

Partnerships, Innovation & Translational Research

Fundamental academic principles such as being able to publish findings openly are at the core of Rockefeller University's institutional philosophy. Whilst the university remains very open to the prospects of collaborative research partnerships, any agreements that are entered into have these principles at their foundation.

President Tessier-Lavigne addresses the institutional approach to collaborative research efforts at Rockefeller University: "Within the framework of respecting academic principles, we think that there are many, many opportunities, and many virtues in striking up relationships with private sector entities. They can bring tools and technology that aren't readily available to our scientists, which help them to explore the problems that they are interested in, in greater depth. They can bring resources as well.

We have several kinds of interactions. We have interactions where single faculty members have research collaborations with a private sector entity. We also have agreements where we have one entity and multiple researchers. Over the years people have come to recognize the value of these interactions if they are done right, and see that it's not one size fits all but that different types of needs are met by different types of partnerships. We therefore try to be flexible to try to create win-win situations, relationships that are good for the scientist and that are also attractive to the corporate partner."

Teaching, Learning & Student Life

Located in a park-like 14-acre campus on the Upper East Side of Manhattan in the heart of New York City, Rockefeller University's environment is one of tranquillity and peace whilst having the world's foremost global city on its doorstep. The campus itself is like an oasis in the middle of Manhattan. So, when you are on campus, it's like you are in the countryside, but then you can step out on to the streets of Manhattan to recharge your batteries and go to experience the fun of the city.

Rockefeller University's exclusively graduate student population draws upon the greatest talent the world over. Approximately 40% of students are international, and all students have their studies funded by the university. This allows the university to recruit the world's most promising young scientists interested in its research agenda, and it also frees its scholars from financial burdens and makes it possible for them to focus fully on their training.

The university's philosophy is to get students into labs conducting research as quickly as possible. Typically students take a handful of rotations in different subject areas before choosing the lab they want to join, but they are also free to join labs immediately upon entry into the university if their interests are already decided. President Tessier-Lavigne highlights what students can expect at Rockefeller University: "Students will be exposed to awe-inspiring science. They will have huge flexibility to sample many different kinds of biological science and to then choose their path. They will be funded so neither the student nor the laboratory they choose needs to worry about the cost."

Washington
University in St. Louis

Name › Washington University in St. Louis
Region › Americas
Country › United States
Founded › 1853

www.wustl.edu

Core Research Strengths

Receiving over US$600 million each year in external research funding, Washington University in St. Louis has strength in depth throughout a diverse range of research competencies, however is best known for the university's outstanding research portfolio in the life and biomedical sciences.

Washington University in St. Louis is best known for outstanding strengths in bio-medical research with a particular focus on genetics. Since completing the mapping of the largest section of the human genome project, Washington University in St. Louis has emerged as one of the foremost global centres of genetics and genomics. In particular the university excels in understanding the genetic origins of disease, and now is one of the major players in using this kind of information to begin guiding chemotherapeutic approaches to dealing with cancer. Cancer genomics is one of the major areas Washington University in St Louis leads globally in, with the Alvin J. Siteman Cancer Centre at the forefront of these efforts.

In the life and biomedical sciences, Washington University in St. Louis also leads in continuing our understanding of Alzheimer's disease, as well as better understanding the microscopic organisms that live in our intestinal tracts through the Human Microbiome Project.

From an entirely different spectrum of science, Washington University in St Louis also excels in developing technologies to facilitate the robotic exploration of planets such as with Mars Curiosity through the Department of Earth and Planetary Sciences.

Major Discoveries

Researchers at Washington University in St. Louis, undertook the largest section of the sequencing of the human genome.

Researchers at Washington University in St. Louis, developed Positron Emission Tomography, which is a major diagnostic research tool using magnetic resonance imaging technology.

Partnerships, Innovation & Translational Research

Whilst funding sources for research activities are relatively diverse at Washington University in St. Louis, it remains a core strategic objective for the university to continue building new partnerships throughout various sections and sectors of society so as to ensure that the challenges being investigated are as relevant as possible to external needs, but also to ensure that funding sources remain on a stable upward trajectory.

The growing importance of external collaborative partnerships are not lost on Chancellor Mark Wrighton "The diversity of funding sources is something we would like to build and our largest single sponsor is the National Institutes of Health that supports a very large fraction of research at U.S. universities. In the future, by strengthening faculty recruiting we hope to diversify funding sources in the Federal Government. We already have support from the Department of Energy, the National Science Foundation and NASA. As our faculty in engineering expands and grows we would expect more funding from the Department of Energy, more National Science Foundation and more Department of Defense, which is another major sponsor. With our ability, which is strong in terms of building teams of people we feel that increasingly we will be attractive to corporate sponsors who have technology problems that could be addressed with these interdisciplinary approaches which we have."

Increasingly the additional mission of translational research and successful technology transfer is felt at Washington University in St. Louis; Chancellor Wrighton intends to place increasing strategic focus on these areas moving forward, given the responsibility felt by the institution "We feel that with the great investment being made in us, largely by the public through federal sponsorship, we have a responsibility to have what we do to benefit society as rapidly as possible. In some cases this will necessitate our engagement with mature companies that can take advantage of the new knowledge that is created. In other cases, we want to be proactive in

spawning new enterprises that are going to be a commercial success from an advance in science where engineering and medical sciences work combines well. We now have a pro-active effort to strengthen our entrepreneurial culture, developing professionals who can help us in the spawning of new enterprises."

Teaching, Learning & Student Life

Washington University in St. Louis' aforementioned strengths in the sciences are complemented by tremendous strengths throughout the arts, humanities and social sciences providing myriad opportunities for students to develop their studies across a diverse range of disciplines. The St Louis environment, although quite unknown generally; to the learned observer is a vibrant cultural hub, home to well known poets, artists and one of the greatest music scenes in the United States. One of the world's largest urban parks in Forest Park is located directly adjacent to the university campus, home to a museum, zoo and golf course aside from numerous sporting and leisure activities students are able to undertake. All of this at the fraction of the cost of living one can expect from counterpart institutions in some of the United States' better-known urban centres.

NORTHWESTERN
UNIVERSITY

Name › Northwestern University
Region › Americas
Country › United States
Founded › 1851

www.northwestern.edu

Core Research Strengths

Northwestern University is best known internationally for, and most highly ranked for the institution's strengths in Nanotechnology, chemistry and the applied social sciences. Northwestern University's strength in Nanotechnology research has earned the university the nickname Nano-U; after having invested millions of dollars over several decades in this area. Northwestern's enormous Nanotechnology and Nano-medicine centres are world leading, very few other centres or institutions internationally compare with this strength at Northwestern University.

In the applied social sciences, Northwestern is particularly strong in business with the Kellogg School of Management, as well as having excellent departments of economics and journalism. The Medill School of Journalism is typically ranked as having the number one full service journalism program – both undergraduate and graduate – in the world.

In the creative arts, Northwestern excels in theatre and in TV and film production with the internationally renowned School of Communication. Countless Broadway and Hollywood stars from actors and actresses, through to screenwriters, producers and directors have graduated from Northwestern's School of Communication going all the way back to the 1930's.

Major Discoveries

Lyrica, the drug used to treat conditions such as Parkinson's disease and epilepsy was developed at Northwestern University. Initially discovered by Professor Richard Silverman and then licensed to Pfizer, Lyrica has the world record for patent value for a single higher education institution discovery.

Professors Chad Mirkin and Mark Ratner have pioneered nanolithography and microelectronics at Northwestern University.

Researchers at Northwestern University are helping to pioneer the international battle against HIV / AIDS. A low cost, high accuracy, portable testing device was recently developed at the university.

Partnerships, Innovation & Translational Research

From a strategic perspective, one of the distinguishing points about Northwestern University is the institution's diversity in funding sources; a major contributory factor to this level of diversity is the myriad of collaborative research partnerships that the university is engaged with. From being a major contributor to the energy hub at Argonne Laboratories alongside the University of Chicago and University of Illinois, to major research partnerships with international pharmaceutical companies, Northwestern's flexible approach has guaranteed success in the increasingly important area of collaborative research efforts.

Since the discovery and runaway success of Lyrica, the culture of entrepreneurialism and technology transfer at Northwestern University has grown exponentially into what is now regarded as one of the most successful, entrepreneurial faculties in the world. President Morton Schapiro elaborates on this point further: "There is an entrepreneurial culture here at Northwestern. We have a group who actually looks at different things and whether or not we want to invest in them. We are very active in bringing things to the market with our patent office. We are quite good at this, as our revenues demonstrate.

It's funny that people naturally don't think of Northwestern as the place for translational research, but if you look at the money that we generate now, we are leaders in the field. We have quite a number of things that we think are going to pay off that are now in trials. Especially with the nano group and others we have dozens and dozens of spinoff companies. I think, it's 60 companies now, many of them in the science park about 5 miles from where I am sitting right now. The faculty are really entrepreneurial, and the good thing is that it generates royalties. I think that's fabulous, but it also helps bring to market things that improve people's lives. So, we are really excited about that, but I don't feel like we really need to create any added incentive. I think Rick Silverman did that himself."

Teaching, Learning & Student Life

Northwestern's beautiful lakeside location in Evanston, just a short drive from downtown Chicago gives students the best of both worlds in a lovely setting for study and research, combined with doorstep access to one of the world's great cities.

The culture of pioneering, interdisciplinary research at Northwestern University permeates throughout the faculty and into the student population, with undergraduates encouraged to learn across disciplines and get directly involved with research projects at the university. The Midwestern culture of equality and inclusivity makes all newcomers feel very welcome, whilst further fuelling the spirit of research collaboration and entrepreneurialism that makes Northwestern so enjoyable and successful as a university.

UNIVERSITY OF MINNESOTA
Driven to Discover℠

Name › University of Minnesota, Twin Cities
Region › Americas
Country › United States
Founded › 1851

www1.umn.edu/twincities

Core Research Strengths

With the fourth largest student body in the United States, the University of Minnesota is an enormous institution with research strengths across a broad range of disciplines. The University of Minnesota is best known for strengths in the biomedical and life sciences, chemical engineering, food and agriculture, pharmacy, psychology, psychiatry and a number of social sciences and humanities areas such as business, economics, history, political science and English. The University of Minnesota also has an outstanding mathematics department, ranked just outside the top 10 globally. The Schools of Pharmacy and Public Health are widely regarded as in the very top tier throughout the United States.

Interdisciplinary research is also of particular importance at the university, with projects such as the collaboration between the engineering and medical schools resulting in a wave of new innovations that feed into the medical devices industry, of great importance to the regional economy.

In the medical sciences, the University of Minnesota has great strengths in neuroscience with a particular emphasis on Alzheimer's disease, cancer biology, stem cell research and transplants.

Major Discoveries

Earl Bakken invented the pacemaker at the University of Minnesota in the 1950's

University of Minnesota, Twin Cities researchers have pioneered HIV/AIDS treatments developing some of the most important compounds in today's treatments.

Alzheimer's disease research at the University of Minnesota, Twin Cities has reversed the effects of memory loss in laboratory animals, even after neuronal death. This has never been done before.

Partnerships, Innovation & Translational Research

Through the Community of Institutional Cooperation, the University of Minnesota works very closely in collaborative research efforts with counterpart Big 10 Conference universities, developing a model and base of experience that enables the university to partner with institutions at the international level.

The university's expertise in the medical sciences and public health has led to a number of vital international outreach programs and collaborations in developing countries throughout Africa and Asia alongside USAID. Furthermore, strengths throughout the food and agriculture spheres have facilitated the expansion of major research partnerships at the governmental level, such as the Center for Animal Health and Food Safety funded by the Federal Department of Homeland Security.

President Eric Kaler highlights the increasing need for research partnerships: "We have a growing emphasis on collaborative research. It is just too difficult. The problems, as you mentioned, already are too large, too complex, and sometimes cost prohibitive for any single institution. So, our strength is actually in unison as opposed to working independently."

The University of Minnesota excels in working alongside private sector partners, such as in the fields of food and chemicals with Cargill and Dow Chemical respectively. The medical devices and engineering industries are a vital component of the local economy in Minnesota, with major players such as Boston Scientific conducting collaborative research. In IPRIME, the University of Minnesota has developed an innovative model whereby small - and medium-sized engineering companies are able to partner collaboratively through a single organisation that specialises in developing mutually beneficial research operations.

Teaching, Learning & Student Life

One of the standout features for students at the University of Minnesota is the focus upon facilitating research opportunities for students. A significant majority of undergraduate students take advantage of this well structured program, which offers financial support for students to get involved in research projects, and incentives to faculty that take interested young people on-board.

The size and scale of the University of Minnesota presents great benefits, diversity and opportunity in itself through social and cultural clubs, interdisciplinary learning and the strength and breadth that the university displays.

President Kaler elaborates further on the lifestyle and learning opportunities students at the university can expect: "There are a very broad range of opportunities and experiences for students here, a great opportunity for interdisciplinary work among faculty as well as experiences for students. So that's a big positive. Another thing that I think people actually like is that we are a very large university in the middle of a metropolitan area, which I think offers all of the advantages or many of the advantages of much larger metropolitan areas, but in a much more user-friendly package. We have great artistic offerings. We have great entertainment offerings. You are now a part of all sorts of recreational opportunities here around the campus. So, from a student experience point of view, there is just about every kind of experience they can go. for right here on campus or in close proximity. So, that's actually, from a quality of student life perspective, a very, very much-appreciated asset. The university is in a beautiful place. It's just remarkable. It is wooded and pleasant, has many lakes, and the Mississippi River. It's a beautiful place. In wintertime it has a pretty ferocious reputation, but the people enjoy winter sports and are outside in that weather, too. The Twin Cities, as I mentioned earlier, is a culturally magnificent place with world-class museums, theatres, art and spectacular restaurants. It really is a wonderful part of the country."

UNIVERSITY OF TORONTO

27

Name › University of Toronto
Region › Americas
Country › Canada
Founded › 1827

www.utoronto.ca

Core Research Strengths

The University of Toronto (UoT) is one of the most respected and influential institutions of higher education and advanced research in the world. Toronto's ranking amongst the top three universities for total academic publications is perhaps the best indicator of disciplinary strength that ranges across astrophysics, engineering, law, medicine, women's studies and zoology, with much else between. The breadth and depth of the university's research and teaching strength facilitates interdisciplinary collaboration among faculties and with partner institutions, this lays the foundation for a formidable portfolio of discoveries. Examples from two disciplines follow.

Research in the life sciences has long been a strength at UoT, dating back to the discovery of insulin in 1921. In the early 1960s, University of Toronto professors Ernest McCulloch and James Till discovered stem cells, and UoT faculty members have continued to capitalise on this discovery. Today, Toronto has a remarkable research cluster not only in stem cell research, but also in related disciplines such as regenerative medicine and tissue engineering.

Computer science is among Toronto's best known and most internationally competitive research areas. Bill Buxton, principal researcher at Microsoft, and William Reeves, Supervising Technical Director of Pixar, are among the many distinguished alumni of the computer science department. Professor Geoffrey Hinton's pioneering research in back propagation neural networks has most recently yielded ground-breaking speech recognition software now in use at Microsoft, Google and IBM. The university is also a leader in cloud computing, quantum cryptography and quantum information control.

Major Discoveries

The University of Toronto's Centre for Sustainable Energy – a team of researchers, educators, students and partners – are working to improve Canada's energy efficiency and better manage its carbon emissions. Among the group's achievements is the development of colloidal quantum dot films, which pave the way for solar cells that can quickly and cheaply be "painted" onto surfaces to convert the sun's energy into usable electricity.

UoT researchers, led by Professor Stanley Zlotkin, have developed a tasteless and odourless micro-nutrient powder called "Sprinkles" that can be packaged in single-serving sachets and added to almost any food. These dietary supplements, given to children in the developing world, have a significant impact on anemia and Vitamin D deficiency.

Professor Aaron Wheeler of Chemistry and his research group have developed a "lab-on-a-chip" that will permit (for example) faster and less invasive breast cancer screening and newborn genetic testing.

Partnerships, Innovation & Translational Research

UoT's close association with the MaRS Discovery District, its ten affiliated teaching hospitals, and its industry partnerships place it at the hub of one of the most productive centres in North America. With almost 1,000 invention disclosures filed between 2007 and 2010, UoT is far ahead of any Canadian institution and third among public universities in North America. In the same period, 39 companies were established based directly on UoT research, among the highest totals for public universities in North America. Internationally, the university is developing major collaborative consortia with other research universities, including the Structural Genomics Consortium: a partnership with the Karolinska Institute, Oxford University, and the University of Sao Paulo. And through a USD210-million collaboration with IBM, the university is developing analytical models to provide public services – including water, healthcare and energy – in the most efficient ways.

Teaching, Learning & Student Life

The University of Toronto's diverse academic community includes 80,000 students across three distinctive campuses. With over 800 undergraduate programs, 150 graduate programs, and 40 professional programs, UoT attracts students of the highest calibre, from across Canada and from 160 countries around the world.

The university is structured to offer students the advantages of a small college experience within the nation's top research university. Every Arts and Science student, for example, is affiliated with one of seven colleges. President David Naylor explains the strategy: "The collegiate system is hugely important in creating navigable neighbourhoods for young people who attend the University of Toronto. It provides a site for students to share a study space, common rooms, a cafeteria, and a sense of being part of a smaller community within the University." The colleges foster close-knit intellectual and social communities, as do the smaller east and west campuses and the smaller faculties.

Academic programs are structured to capitalize on the breadth and depth of the university and on the teaching strengths of its outstanding faculty. Small-group seminars and tutorials, combined with large lectures and online support, give students the opportunity to develop a spectrum of skills and knowledge. Students are attracted to UoT by the opportunity to work closely with top researchers and to engage in research from early in their academic careers. The university's "Entrepreneurship 101" course is increasingly popular, and the new Banting and Best Centre for Innovation and Entrepreneurship provides a home for student – and faculty-spun companies to commercialize their research.

NEW YORK UNIVERSITY

Name › New York University
Region › Americas
Country › United States
Founded › 1831

www.nyu.edu

Core Research Strengths

New York University (NYU) is particularly renowned for great strength in depth throughout the arts, humanities and social sciences, with a particular emphasis on philosophy, law, economics, finance and theatre. In economics, NYU has long been one of the pioneering institutes investigating the processes by which we make decisions within a market context, with the development of sub-disciplines such as neuroeconomics.

Mathematics is also a particularly strong research discipline at NYU, with the Courant Institute of Mathematical Sciences widely acknowledged to be one of the pre-eminent mathematical institutions globally. Well known for basic research into mathematical concepts such as probability and partial differential equations.

Exceptional professional schools complement NYU's international excellence in mathematics, the humanities and social sciences in business, medicine, dentistry, arts and engineering.

NYU's 18 schools, colleges and institutes are well established in the multi-disciplinary research approach, continuing to develop based upon their foundation of internationally renowned research centres such as the Alexander Hamilton Center for Political Economy.

Major Discoveries

Astronomers at NYU have recently created the largest ever 3D map of massive galaxies and dark matter, helping to provide insight into the mysterious concept of dark matter.

New York University Economics Professor Thomas Sargent was awarded the 2011 Nobel Prize in Economics for his empirical research on cause and effect in the macro economy.

Partnerships, Innovation & Translational Research

A diverse network of partnerships has long been of critical importance to NYU's reach, scope and capacity from a research perspective. The university is an experienced collaborator both with government, industry, charities and counterpart institutions. The Provost

for Research's Office manages NYU's research enterprise and acts as the interface for partnerships.

New York University's Global Institute for Advanced Study is a new initiative focused upon extending collaborative research efforts for NYU students and faculty throughout the international community, enabling long-term partnerships that facilitate wide reaching and in depth research programs.

NYU has one of the strongest records both nationally and internationally in terms of transferring research discoveries into the real economy. Faculty and students have embraced the entrepreneurial spirit that thrives in the university, and work tirelessly to bring their innovations to the broader market place for the benefit of society and the broader economy.

Teaching, Learning & Student Life

With several Nobel Laureates and cutting edge researchers on the NYU faculty, Students can expect to learn directly from those at the very forefront of their respective fields. Lectures are supplemented by seminars and the opportunity for students to debate their opinions so as to construct solid arguments in preparation for examinations and respective paths beyond graduation.

Through facilities such as the Student Resource Center, NYU ensures that students have access to all the resources that they require both within the context of study, and support services beyond that in terms of social events, cultural activities, careers services and such like.

NYU's record of facilitating study abroad is almost unparalleled in the United States, with the university's extensive network of international partners and 14 Global Academic Centers (New York, Florence, London, Prague, Paris, Berlin, Accra, Madrid, Shanghai, Buenos Aires, Tel Aviv, Abu Dhabi, Sydney and Washington DC) providing a wealth of opportunity for students to develop their cultural, social and linguistic skills around the world.

NYU's diversity both in terms of schools and international students lays down

the perfect platform for those attending the university to experience friendships, and social experiences with people from countless walks of life and talents. This diversity very much reflects the host city, with New York perhaps considered the pre-eminent destination of all for international students interested in the USA.

As well as providing an unprecedented backdrop from a cultural and social perspective, New York City also provides an excellent platform for young entrepreneurs to develop their ideas and ambitious young professionals to get a step ahead in their careers with internship and graduate opportunities unparalleled in their availability there.

There are over 450 student clubs and associations on campus, facilitating interests as varied as music, arts, media, sports, political activism, religious interests and entrepreneurial activities.

京都大学
KYOTO UNIVERSITY

Name › Kyoto University
Region › Asia/Pacific
Country › Japan
Founded › 1897

www.kyoto-u.ac.jp

Core Research Strengths

Aside from uncertainty over the exact beginnings of the academic tradition in Kyoto, the city's flagship university, often more affectionately referred to as Kyodai, is very much the embodiment of the Japanese university tradition of making quiet strides into the pinnacle of world-class research. As reform in Japanese higher education continues to orientate its institutions more towards the international community, we can expect to be learning a great deal more about universities such as Kyodai in coming years.

President Hiroshi Matsumoto speaks frankly about the evolving relationship between Japan's academic institutions and the broader international community: "Japan has never been invaded as a country, and has largely grown in isolation from much of the outside world. When you look at Japan's neighbours, we have developed as a society more rapidly during the 20th century; thus have often been overlooked when it comes to our leadership in academia and research. Kyoto University has been a pioneer in reversing this trend, and will continue to show leadership as a Japanese university on the international stage, whilst at the same time remaining true to our principles of diligence and ethics."

Kyoto University's research portfolio is both extensive and world-class; Kyodai is particularly renowned for its excellence in stem cell research, chemistry, physics and mathematics. However, as the boundaries between disciplines continues to become intertwined amongst the global paradigmatic shift towards interdisciplinarity, Kyodai's expertise is increasingly manifested in its interdisciplinary research programs and institutes.

Led by Nobel Prize winner Dr Shinya Yamanaka, the Center for iPS Cell Research and Application (CiRA) is one such institute, at the very cutting edge internationally in furthering our understanding of the most fundamental microbiological processes, and developing applications using innovations such as stem cells based upon that knowledge.

Kyoto University's portfolio of seven institutes receiving funding under the Global Centers of Excellence Program in fields as diverse as frontier medicine, energy science, next generation physics and sustainability / survivability science are indicative of the university's continued expansion into diverse and interesting fields. President Matsumoto is particularly proud of the institution's tradition of thinking outside the box: "Global society is faced by many challenges associated with population growth, the availability of resources and the ways in which human lifestyles are not harmonious with our environment. Kyoto's tradition has always been to use our imaginations and think at the frontiers of science to try and figure out ways of managing these challenges."

Major Discoveries

With 8 Nobel Prize winners, 2 Fields Medals, 1 Gauss Prize, 4 Lasker Awards, 2 Japan Prizes and 3 Kyoto Prizes there is almost an unparalleled tradition of research excellence at Kyoto University.

The latest addition to Kyodai's pantheon of Nobel Prize winners is Dr Shinya Yamanaka (2012 – Physiology or Medicine) for his work discovering that mature cells can become pluripotent; a revolutionary discovery with great implications for stem cell production and regenerative medicine.

Partnerships, Innovation & Translational Research

Under the leadership of President Matsumoto, Kyoto University has built upon its traditions of collaboration, first founded under scientists such as Professor Yukawa, towards more collaboration internationally. The Organization for the Promotion of International Relations (OPIR) is the key interface for potential partners with interests closely aligned to Kyodai's expertise. Most recently, Kyoto University has developed a major strategic partnership with the University of Bristol in the UK, with closer collaboration between researchers and more intensive student exchange the two key pillars of this emerging relationship.

As Japan's leading university in the production of patents, the Japanese proverb "everything new comes from

Kyoto" rings true for the university today. This level of innovation provides excellent opportunities for industry collaboration; nevertheless, President Matsumoto is passionate about the university's fundamental mission and values "Kyoto University's core value is academic freedom. We insist at all levels that our researchers are able to pursue their own curiosities through the research they undertake, and have complete freedom to publish their work. Our role in society is to help develop our fundamental understanding of the environment around us, and provide answers to some of society's most critical challenges, whilst keeping our focus on teaching the next generation of leaders in their field. Collaboration is part of Kyoto's culture, but it will never be more important than our fundamental mission."

Teaching, Learning & Student Life

Kyodai's philosophy of teaching and learning is one that places great value on self-reliance. Students in attendance will rapidly become familiar with the Japanese concept of kokoro – harmony between one's mind, spirit and surroundings as this is instilled in students through the institution's diligent approaches to teaching and research.

The foundation of self-reliant learning, according to President Matsumoto comes from "encouraging the fires of ambition and inspiration in our students." Kyodai's diverse portfolio of world-class research and prize-winning researchers is an inspiration in itself, let alone before one starts to think of the excellent facilities available for students. From sports grounds through to nuclear facilities, Kyoto University has an excellent infrastructure stock to keep students engaged and entertained.

Kyoto University's portfolio of English language programs continues to grow as its international focus and collaborative efforts increase exponentially into the 21st century.

ILLINOIS
UNIVERSITY OF ILLINOIS AT URBANA-CHAMPAIGN

Name › University of Illinois
Region › Americas
Country › United States
Founded › 1867

www.illinois.edu

Core Research Strengths

As a flagship state university with over 40,000 students, the University of Illinois at Urbana Champaign offers a diversified mix of research expertise. The university is ranked highly for its research strength in a number of disciplines. In particular, the University of Illinois at Urbana Champaign is renowned internationally for its strength in science, technology, engineering and maths (STEM) subjects and for its leadership in the agricultural sciences. The College of Agricultural, Consumer, Environmental Sciences (ACES) focuses on major issues such as sustainable agriculture and global food security.

Interdisciplinary research is a natural pre-requisite for an institution of the size, scale and excellence one finds at the University of Illinois at Urbana Champaign. Chancellor Phyllis Wise elaborates further on this pioneering approach taken at the university "In my professional lifetime, I have been at several different universities, and we all talked about how interdisciplinary we were and how wonderful it was that we talked with people who are not in our direct discipline. But I have never been at a university where we walk the walk, so to speak. Interdisciplinary work here is so in our DNA that I am not sure we would know how to do the disciplinary work the way most universities envision it. Obviously, interdisciplinary work depends upon the excellence of the discipline - that is interdisciplinary work is the bridge across the pillars, and if the pillars aren't strong the bridge obviously won't hold up. I can say that the meaning of interdisciplinary work is much more substantial here than ever before, and it is enabled in part by actual physical buildings like the Beckman Institute, which was a gift from Arnold Beckman where faculty come from different disciplines. They come and do their work there but their academic home is within their discipline."

Major Discoveries

Professor John Bardeen, who died in 1991, won a Nobel Prize in physics while at the University of Illinois at Urbana Champaign for his contribution to our theoretical understanding of superconductivity. He had shared in the 1956 Nobel Prize in physics for the invention of the transistor. In 2007, Don Wuebbles, Atul Jain, John Walsh and Michael Schlesinger were among the members of the Intergovernmental Panel on Climate Change, who with Al Gore, were awarded the Nobel Peace Prize.

Materials science Professor John Rogers has recently developed a portable, self-destructing sensor that can be used to sense blood pressure, blood sugar, heart rate or any number of other physiological processes. These sensors have vast potential in medical and health applications.

Partnerships, Innovation & Translational Research

The University of Illinois at Urbana Champaign's track record with external partnerships is exceptional, with the university having an extensive portfolio of major corporations such as BP and Abbott Laboratories working alongside leading faculty and research teams in a mutually beneficial way. The university is working to leverage these novel partnerships to augment research resources from federal grants, philanthropic organizations and private donors.

From a technology transfer perspective, the University of Illinois at Urbana Champaign believes that traditional ways of managing intellectual property, patents and such processes has focused too much on protecting potential revenues – possibly restricting the volumes of new products and innovations that reached the market place. The university is now moving towards a more open access model whereby the process for external collaborators investing in, and developing intellectual property developed at the university will be simpler and more streamlined, thus resulting in the faster diffusion of innovations into society.

Teaching, Learning & Student Life

The University of Illinois at Urbana Champaign has leveraged technical research strengths in order to develop comprehensive online and support services for students, thus increasing flexibility and enabling greater innovation in pedagogical approaches. Chancellor Wise says: "In terms of classroom innovation, I think that we are on the cutting edge of this. We have for a long time used online learning and hybrid mechanisms where part of the course is taught online and part of the course is taught through traditional classroom methodologies."

Entrepreneurialism is also a growing characteristic of the learning experience at the university, with campus units such as the Academy for Entrepreneurial Leadership laying the foundations for tomorrow's innovators and entrepreneurs.

Chancellor Wise's experiences perhaps best reflect the environment students can expect to find at the University of Illinois at Urbana Champaign: "I am still aglow with being a newcomer to this student community and I have to say it is welcoming, it is generous, people reach out, they take time to really get to know you and they actually care. It's not just a 'Hello. How are you?' and they are off to the next thing. There is a sense of commitment and the importance of social equity here that belies the fact that we are a relatively small town."

Imperial College
London

Name › The Imperial College London
Region › Europe
Country › United Kingdom
Founded › 1907

www3.imperial.ac.uk

Core Research Strengths

Imperial College London is the flagship technology university of the United Kingdom, and widely regarded as one of the foremost scientific institutions globally. Imperial focuses exclusively on science, technology, engineering, medicine and business. It is within this context that Imperial's research operation leads internationally in areas such as biotechnology, mathematics, epidemiology, public health, chemical, civil, mechanical, aeronautical and manufacturing engineering.

Imperial has three faculties (Engineering, Medicine, Natural Sciences), as well as the Imperial College Business School. Its research strategy focuses on the four broad themes of healthcare, energy, environment and security in an interdisciplinary manner working towards addressing major global challenges. The College's research institutes address major global challenges, while its centres coordinate interdisciplinary research activities. Underpinning this is Imperial's research excellence in core disciplines.

Major Discoveries

Narinder Kapany and Harold Hopkins discovered in the 1950s that light could bend with the right stimulus, paving the way for the development of fibre optics.

Imperial researcher Dennis Gabor went on to invent the method of producing holograms.

Eric Laithwaite designed the world's first magnetically levitating train at Imperial College London.

Partnerships, Innovation & Translational Research

Imperial has always fostered external research collaborations both with public, private and third sector institutions where there are synergies that all partners, and the wider research agenda will benefit from. Historically, the development of such collaborations has been approached from a bottom up perspective, however increasingly the university is taking a more strategic approach in developing institution to institution agreements as with the Francis Crick Institute, alongside the Medical Research Council, Cancer Research UK, the Wellcome Trust and University College London. The purpose of the partnership is to establish one of the foremost biomedical research laboratories in the world.

Expanding and improving Imperial College London's portfolio of external partners forms a key foundation of the university's 2010 – 2014 strategy, and is a vital component in maintaining the university's research excellence in the face of broader changes in research funding dynamics. It is widely expected that the proportion of industry funding will increase over the medium term with new collaborations such as the US$70 million Qatar Carbonates and Carbon Storage Research Centre in partnership with Royal Dutch Shell, Qatar Petroleum and Qatar Science and Technology Park. Imperial's Corporate Partnerships team provides an overarching coordination role to strengthen the interface between the university's academic community and its portfolio of private sector partners.

From a technology transfer perspective; Imperial Innovations manages commercialisation activities for the university. Since being established in 1986, Imperial innovations have managed over 70 spin out companies from the laboratory to the market place. Imperial Innovations also advised the UK government on the continued development of Britain's knowledge economy and has long-term commercialisation agreements with multinational companies such as BAE Systems.

Teaching, Learning & Student Life

Students attending Imperial College London can expect a substantial array of support mechanisms from the College as part of their teaching and learning experience. These include a personal tutor system, college tutors, a Dean of Students, counsellors, residential wardens, disability advisors, and health and dental services.

Students benefit from a research-led approach to teaching, together with opportunities for the entrepreneurially minded to hone their business skills. An increasing number of international exchange opportunities are also on offer at leading institutions globally such as the National University of Singapore and UC Berkeley in the United States.

Imperial College London's student community is extraordinarily diverse with approximately 50% of the population in attendance at the university from outside of the UK. Imperial's South Kensington campus is situated just a few minutes' stroll from either the London Science Museum, Natural History Museum and Victoria & Albert Museum. London's iconic Hyde Park is also just a few minutes walk from the campus, providing the ideal setting for relaxing and/or reading up before exams in a quiet and relaxed environment.

ETH
Eidgenössische Technische Hochschule Zürich
Swiss Federal Institute of Technology Zurich

Name › ETH Zürich
Region › Europe
Country › Switzerland
Founded › 1855

www.ethz.ch

Core Research Strengths

ETH Zurich is ranked as the best research university in continental Europe and is considered to be one of the world's leading universities of science and technology. It has more than 17,000 students from over 100 countries, 3,700 of whom are doctoral candidates. More than 400 professors teach and conduct research in the areas of engineering, architecture, mathematics, natural sciences, system-oriented sciences, management and social sciences. ETH Zurich particularly focuses on developing applications and innovations that arise from its research. Each year, the university applies for about 80 patents.

21 Nobel laureates are associated with ETH Zurich, the most celebrated being Albert Einstein in 1921 for his services to theoretical physics.

Based on its excellence in core scientific disciplines, ETH Zurich conducts multidisciplinary research on complex issues such as energy supply, risk management, global food security, human health and developing the cities of the future. In such research initiatives the relevant disciplines are brought together in common labs, thereby helping to find long-term solutions to global challenges. This experience in interdisciplinary research flows directly into the curricula. New departments such as Health Science and Technology encompass multiple disciplines in emerging fields of academic endeavour that are evolving in line with technological developments.

Major Discoveries

ETH Zurich researchers have made major contributions to the development of several significant technologies such as Complementary Metal Oxide Semiconductors (CMOS) or control systems for catalytic converters. ETH scientists have also improved the current understanding of diabetes, one of the major global health challenges of the 21st century. Furthermore, ETH Zurich experts have made major contributions to the construction of long transportation tunnels through the Alps, as this work requires the highest accuracy in engineering, surveying and geology.

Partnerships, Innovation & Translational Research

Collaborative research with external partners brings the university closer to the market. It ensures better understanding of industry needs related to upcoming topics and job requirements for future employees. Research collaboration is thus of great importance to ETH Zurich, preferably with companies that are active in Switzerland, be it a Swiss or a multinational company. Nevertheless, ETH Zurich remains focused on basic research with its longer-term perspective, in contrast to industry's emphasis on product development, which should pay back quicker.

ETH President Ralph Eichler explains the institution's philosophy in respect of external partnerships: "Research partnerships are very important. The task of ETH Zurich is to act as a pillar for our society and our economy. We educate the experts who go into industry, doing jobs that require a research-based education. We support innovation and an entrepreneurial spirit amongst faculty and students with translational research and technology transfer as important parts of the university experience."

Every year, ETH researchers set up some two-dozen start-up companies. And these companies are successful: Five years after they have been established, nearly 90% are still in business – a remarkably high number, which reflects the exceptional quality of innovation and entrepreneurial culture at ETH Zurich. One of the best-known trade names is Doodle, a software start-up established by ETH Zurich graduates. An upcoming product is the mouse scanner, invented and developed by the ETH spin-off company Dacuda.

Teaching, Learning & Student Life

ETH Zurich is a very international environment with more than one third of its students and 70% of professors coming from abroad. Thus, students can expect to work alongside highly gifted students and be supervised by world-class scientists from all over the world. This illustrates the attractiveness of the institution – despite the high requirements in education.

At ETH Zurich, first-year tuition focuses on ensuring a strong theoretical base in physics, mathematics and chemistry. The comprehensive examination taken at the end of the first year tests the undergraduates' knowledge in these three core sciences, and determines who is allowed to progress on to the 2nd year. ETH students' workload is high throughout their studies. They are considered to be some of the busiest in Europe with lectures, seminars and coursework amounting to almost double of that of some counterpart institutions. Whilst this could seem daunting, the effort is worthwhile: The graduates at ETH Zurich are an important factor for attracting multinational companies to set up offices in Zurich.

ETH Zurich offers plenty of scope for a rich campus life. Numerous canteens and cafeterias provide lively meeting places, which enhance interaction within the university. The main campus is right in the centre of the beautiful city of Zurich. The second campus on the "Hönggerberg", a hill just outside the city, is a modern complex of laboratories housing most of the university's science departments. There are well over 100 student associations at ETH Zurich with a wide variety of activities from sports and music to entrepreneurship or sustainability.

Leading Research Programs

Research is the main source of innovation in knowledge-based societies and the foundation of an excellent university education. ETH Zurich stands for fundamental research at the highest level. The research activities of its 16 departments are complemented through the creation of thematic focal areas, which allow for cross-departmental, interdisciplinary research collaboration. Currently, ETH Zurich concentrates on five thematic focal areas.

Sustainable worlds

"Sustainable worlds" brings together three research fields of particular scientific actuality and societal relevance: Energy and climate change, future cities, and global food security. Climate change is one of the most complex scientific challenges. Clean, affordable and reliably available energy is of paramount importance for the well-being of modern societies. Therefore, ETH Zurich supports a number of interdisciplinary competence centres in these subject areas. The Future Cities Laboratory at the Singapore-ETH Centre for Global Environmental Sustainability is investigating how cities might be designed, produced, managed, maintained, and inhabited in a way that supports the aims of global sustainability. The World Food System Center is addressing the global challenges at the nexus of global food and nutrition security, food production and processing, as well as environmental, economic and social well-being.

Technology and knowledge for health

In 2012, ETH Zurich set up the Department of Health Science and Technology to explore new areas of research at the interface of health sciences and engineering. The department brings together food and nutrition sciences, human movement sciences, neurosciences and medical technology. It is the main link between ETH Zurich and the strategic initiative "Hochschulmedizin Zürich" – a joint undertaking by ETH Zurich, the University of Zurich and University Hospital Zurich working on the medicine of the future.

Complex systems

Within the thematic focus "complex systems", ETH Zurich is concentrating on computer-assisted modelling and risk research. Modelling and simulation – along with theory and experimentation – are becoming increasingly important as the third pillar of scientific research. The Swiss National Supercomputing Centre is an autonomous ETH unit, which enables world-class scientific research by pioneering, operating and supporting the leading-edge supercomputing technologies needed for that purpose. Risk-related activities of many specialist areas at ETH Zurich have been consolidated in the newly established Risk Center, in order to gain a holistic view of the different types of risk and become one of the leading centres for integrated risk research.

Materials, technologies and industrial processes

New, low-energy materials and processes are essential for using resources sustainably. The Micro and Nano Science Platform at ETH Zurich comprises over forty research groups studying the atomic principles of materials, and developing solutions for high-tech applications. The processes required to manufacture and integrate these materials are also investigated. While new materials can lead to a higher standard of living, they may also bring new risks. This is why ETH Zurich is playing a pioneering role in researching the effects of materials and technology on humans and the environment.

Scientific foundations of the future

ETH Zurich is one of the pioneers in the use of advanced technology combined with the principles of quantum physics, and is leading the National Centre of Competence in Research (NCCR) "Quantum Science and Technology". With the NCCR "Molecular Ultrafast Science and Technology" ETH Zurich investigates the decoding of ultra-fast processes on a molecular scale. This is leading to a deeper understanding of the structural and dynamic behaviour of matter at an atomic level. Systems biology aims for a comprehensive understanding of biological processes and involves researching the interaction between the different elements in an organism. ETH Zurich is responsible for the Swiss initiative to develop systems biology, SystemsX.ch, with the goal of one day making it possible to model living systems.

Technology Transfer

The transfer of knowledge and technology between the university, society and business is a top priority for ETH Zurich. Its "Industrial Relations Program" actively brings together industry and academia to stimulate visionary research activities. Disney Research Zurich is a joint initiative involving the Walt Disney Company and ETH Zurich, conducting research on digitising human faces and their expressions. IBM and ETH Zurich are working together to develop energy-saving and environmentally friendly high-performance computers.

› Every year, ETH Zurich employees or graduates found more than twenty spin-off companies. The following examples show the variety of fields.

› Optotune is a pioneer in adaptive optics, offering a range of tuneable optical devices that help develop products with novel key features.

› Dacuda is a software company developing and marketing low-cost digitisation technology based on real-time image processing and computer vision.

› LEP Consultants provide services and products supported by information technology in the field of urban and transportation development, and the sustainable management of resources.

› Alstom Inspection Robotics is a joint venture between Alstom and ETH Zurich designing autonomous inspection robots for power plants as well as chemical and petrochemical facilities.

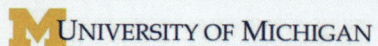
UNIVERSITY OF MICHIGAN

Name › University of Michigan Ann Arbor
Region › Americas
Country › United States
Founded › 1817

www.umich.edu

Core Research Strengths

With annual research expenditures in the region of US$1.2 billion, the University of Michigan, Ann Arbor has one of the most extensive research portfolios of all international research universities. Given the size and scale of the institution, the university increasingly focuses on multi-disciplinary research investigating complex issues and concepts such as efficient transportation systems, energy technologies, advanced manufacturing, Nano-technology, environmental sustainability, bio-medical devices, drug development and health care policy.

Whilst most universities are still working to imbue the interdisciplinary approach throughout their respective faculty and institutions, the University of Michigan, Ann Arbor can claim to have this philosophy running through the institution's DNA as elaborated by President Mary Sue Coleman: "I have been here ten years – and the thing that struck me right away at Michigan was the very low barriers to collaboration across disciplines. It's expected, it's common, there are many joint appointments across departments which means that faculty really have an easy time of contacting colleagues in other departments, becoming active in those departments and doing things jointly."

Aside from the University of Michigan, Ann Arbor's leadership in multidisciplinary research approaches, the university houses world leading research departments in electrical and mechanical engineering, bio-technology as well as in computer science.

Major Discoveries

University of Michigan researchers have launched a major initiative in collaboration with government and industry to develop smart car technology that enables cars to talk to each other, and improve mobility while reducing emissions and crashes by as much as 80%.

U-M played a key role in the team of 3,000 scientists from around the world that recently discovered the Higgs Boson, an elusive sub-atomic particle that is central to our understanding of the basic forces that have shaped the universe since the beginning and will ultimately determine its fate.

The University of Michigan focuses significant research in the area of sustainable freshwater systems, with the goal of improving human access to clean water and developing solutions to increase the resilience of aquatic ecosystems throughout the world. This includes creation in 2012 of a $9 million University of Michigan Great Lakes research and education center to guide efforts to protect and restore the world's largest group of freshwater lakes by reducing toxic contamination, combating invasive species, protecting wildlife habitat and promoting coastal health.

Partnerships, Innovation & Translational Research

Collaborative research efforts and mutually beneficial partnerships are critical to the University of Michigan's strategy, particularly when considering complex questions that span boundaries of culture and academic discipline. President Coleman highlights the importance of partnerships to the university: "I have said for several years now that collaboration is essential to our future as a strong research university. Today's problems are simply too complex to be solved by one person or one institution.

We look for the strongest partners in higher education, in government, and in the private sector. We can draw on each other's strengths and be more powerful overall in addressing global challenges." The University of Michigan Business Engagement Center maintains relationships with more than 1,000 companies, helping industry access the ideas and expertise from the university while keeping the University community informed on the emerging needs of industry.

Technology transfer and translational research operations are facilitated by U-M Tech Transfer, which helps launch businesses, cultivate entrepreneurial talent and manage the transfer of technology to the marketplace. Established in 2008, the Tech Arb student business incubator works exclusively with the University of Michigan's student population, and has nurtured more than 80 new firms since its inception.

Teaching, Learning & Student Life

Established 50 years ago, the University of Michigan's Center for Research on Learning and Teaching pioneers the innovative and creative pedagogical approaches students can expect to find at the university. The center works closely with faculty and graduate student instructors across the university to develop their teaching and learning skills. The model has been replicated at several other universities, and the center now provides training to delegations of administrators and faculty from universities throughout the international community.

Students can expect to find an array of opportunities for interdisciplinary learning, with faculty incentivised to develop innovative means of teaching degree courses throughout multiple disciplines. Research opportunities abound throughout the undergraduate community, with opportunities for entrepreneurialism supported throughout the innovation cycle by the Tech Arb student business incubator. More than 5000 students at the university are now engaged in some kind of entrepreneurial activity.

Despite having over 40,000 students on campus, the University of Michigan has managed to maintain an intimate atmosphere whereby all students' potential and interests are fostered by faculty on a personal level. This approach is not only confined to the classroom with thousands of students being actively engaged in community activities, research projects and entrepreneurial ventures.

Name › University College London
Region › Europe
Country › United Kingdom
Founded › 1826

www.ucl.ac.uk

Core Research Strengths

Widely recognised as Europe's premier university throughout the medical and life sciences, approximately 60% of the University College London's (UCL) research turnover comes from these disciplines. In recent years, UCL's strength in these areas has grown significantly with a series of external mergers and internal investment programs such as with the London School of Pharmacy in 2011 and the development of the Francis Crick Institute, a £650 million development forecast to be Europe's premier biotechnology research institute upon completion.

Specifically within the life and medical sciences, UCL is particularly noted for the contributions made to psychology & psychiatry, immunology, pharmacology & toxicology and clinical medicine. UCL has exceptional strength in the neurosciences, set to be significantly enhanced by the opening of the Sainsbury Wellcome Centre for Neural Circuits & Behaviour in 2013. UCL also has great strength in the field of Opthalmology, with a great deal of work currently underway in curing blindness using stem cells.

From an interdisciplinary perspective, UCL Grand Challenges has been recently launched to bring together world leading expertise from UCL and beyond to address key global challenges such as those associated with sustainable cities, intercultural interaction, global health and human wellbeing.

Major Discoveries

UCL researchers invented the thermionic valve, paving the way for the development of the modern electronics industry. The first antiseptic treatment of wounds was developed at UCL.

UCL researchers first identified hormones and vitamins.

UCL researchers first identified inert gases such as Neon.

Partnerships, Innovation & Translational Research

UCL's portfolio of major partnerships are in the main focused upon philanthropic, funding and public sector organisations such as the Wellcome Trust and a number of leading hospitals in the UK through the UCL Partners program.

UCL Partners is a relatively unique system of collaboration between UCL and partner hospitals such as the Great Ormond Street Hospital aiming to connect academic themes with clinical delivery, working alongside patients in areas such as cancer, cardiology, sight and vision.

Established in 2009, the Yale UCL Collaborative is a major research partnership between UCL, UCL Partners, Yale University, Yale School of Medicine and Yale – New Haven Hospital. This is the most important university research partnership in UCL's history; and has now been extended from its initial foundation in the medical and life sciences to include the humanities and social sciences.

UCL's portfolio of private sector partners is limited, with major pharmaceutical companies such as Pfizer and GlaxoSmithKline comprising the vast majority of industry level funding for the university's research portfolio.

UCL's technology transfer and industry liaison office, UCL Business forms the key element of the university's strategy of raising awareness of UCL's research strengths throughout industry, developing a more open and transparent framework for such partnerships to take place, as well as delivering a greater volume of thriving research partnerships helping to benefit both UCL's research operation, their corporate partners involved and broader society as a whole.

Teaching, Learning & Student Life

UCL runs a series of foundation and transition programs for both first year undergraduates and international students with ambitions to attend a leading UK university to both develop the skills and acquire the required qualifications in order to ensure a fulfilling and rewarding university career.

All UCL students have tutors aligned directly with the courses they are studying, who through weekly meetings and seminars discuss course materials with students, and help to develop important skills such as developing arguments and debating successfully.

All students are encouraged to get involved with research directly throughout their careers at UCL, as a means of developing new knowledge relating to their fields of study or those affiliated to their interests from a multi-disciplinary perspective.

UCL is frequently referred to as London's Global University, taking into account the location in central London, and institution's vast diversity with over 30% of the student population coming from outside the UK. The multi-cultural nature of UCL is a key component of the university experience, providing students the opportunity to meet a diverse array of contacts from around the world centred upon London.

London's diversity also represents an enormous opportunity to UCL's student body, providing a myriad of opportunities in culture, the arts and employment unrivalled in almost any other international study destination.

UCL Student Union's more than 150 social, sporting and cultural clubs provide the ideal centrepiece for the university's social life, enabling students from an array of different cultural, social backgrounds and academic fields to get to know one another in a relaxed and fun environment.

THE UNIVERSITY OF TOKYO
東京大学

Name › The University of Tokyo
Region › Asia/Pacific
Country › Japan
Founded › 1877

www.u-tokyo.ac.jp

Core Research Strengths

The University of Tokyo's research expertise covers a broad spectrum from some of the foremost international institutes conducting basic research in mathematics and the social and physical sciences to leading interdisciplinary institutes in global sustainability and gerontology. The University of Tokyo consistently ranks within the global top three institutions in terms of citation count, and five researchers have earned Nobel Prizes, quantifying clearly the breadth and depth of the university's research excellence.

President Junichi Hamada explains the University of Tokyo's current research strategy: "Historically, we focused on disciplinary excellence alone, but over the past decade we have been promoting interdisciplinary research, which has had a major impact upon our ability to tackle critical issues and complex questions and has stimulated innovation." As a result, distinctive centres of excellence such as the Kavli Institute for the Physics and Mathematics of the Universe address the deepest mysteries of the universe by integrating knowledge at the forefront of mathematics and physics. Additionally, as issues including energy, food security and climate change raise questions about human interactions with our environment, the University of Tokyo has pioneered the IR3S research network, a hub for sustainability research in Japan, connected to global institutions in partnership with the United Nations University.

The University of Tokyo also leads in specific spheres of research of enormous importance to Japan. Japan is one of the most earthquake-prone countries in the world, and the university's Earthquake Research Institute is global leader in earthquake research, disaster mitigation and response. Japan is also one of the world's most rapidly aging societies, and the university has established the Institute of Gerontology to develop a model for the future aged society.

Major Discoveries

Professor Masatoshi Koshiba earned the Nobel Prize in Physics for world-leading research detecting cosmic neutrinos. Today Professor Takaaki Kajita continues that tradition, focusing on neutrino oscillation at the university's Institute for Cosmic Ray Research.

Professor Yoshinori Tokura at the Graduate School of Engineering is a globally recognized leader in condensed matter physics and materials science, including high-temperature superconductors and strongly correlated electron systems.

Project Professor Nobutaka Hirokawa leads a major research group that has discovered and described in incredible detail the kinesin family of motor proteins, employing methodologies from cell and molecular biology to embryology and biophysics. This rich, fundamental research continues to produce startling new discoveries.

Professor Kazunori Kataoka, a researcher in both the Graduate Schools of Medicine and of Engineering, embodies the interdisciplinary strength of the University of Tokyo, having developed nanocapsules capable of identifying and delivering treatment directly to cancerous cells.

Partnerships, Innovation & Translational Research

As Japan's flagship institution the University of Tokyo has strong government support, receiving a large proportion of government research funds. This strong foundation enables the university to tackle major research initiatives that other institutions cannot, but the University of Tokyo assigns high priority to the continued development of collaborative partnerships with industry and the private sector. To President Hamada the benefits are clear: "Not only does collaboration with industry enable us to work on real-world challenges and have a significant impact, it extends the resources we have available to invest in research and promotes innovation." Additionally, the university's Science Entrepreneurship and Enterprise Development Office runs an "entrepreneur dojo" to educate and nurture potential entrepreneurs and promote innovation from within, and supports venture companies exploiting university research.

Teaching, Learning & Student Life

The University of Tokyo's admission requirements are exceedingly demanding, and the excellent student body benefits from access to professors at the very forefront of their fields. But they also benefit from modern Japanese culture, a fusion of many of the best aspects of cultures around the world founded on a unique tradition of excellence that differs from the Western model. President Hamada describes his own experience: "While Japanese law is mostly only applicable in Japan, we have many Chinese students who come to acquire the excellent skills provided by our education, but also because Japanese law is a fusion of the best aspects of legal systems from around the world." This academic and cultural fusion is very much alive at the University of Tokyo.

The University of Tokyo campus and student body are also increasingly internationalized, and there is a strong focus upon attracting international students. Having recently introduced English language undergraduate programs and begun re-aligning the academic calendar with international standards, the University of Tokyo is working overtime to extend diversity. President Hamada outlines his approach: "We are reforming instruction in English, raising awareness about the University of Tokyo as a unique study destination, and deepening the university's integration into the global higher education system."

University of Tokyo alumni occupy leading positions in Japan, Asia and increasingly throughout the world. Employment prospects are excellent, with alumni in great demand from foreign companies in Japan and global Japanese companies.

The University of Tokyo
Japan

Name › University of Wisconsin – Madison
Region › Americas
Country › United States
Founded › 1848

www.wisc.edu

Core Research Strengths

Perhaps the most distinguishing feature of the University of Wisconsin – Madison from a research perspective is the extraordinary breadth the university displays across the entire spectrum of research interests. Collectively as a research institution, there are very few that match the depth in breadth that one finds at the University of Wisconsin – Madison. The standout disciplinary strength of the university is in the bio-medical sciences, however the university's true value comes from the ability to collaborate creatively in a multidisciplinary way.

Provost Paul DeLuca highlights this strategic approach in more detail: "What we want to accomplish, and we have been in that business for a very long time, is to recognize a significant component of discovery. Especially components of discovery that are translational in nature and occur at the boundaries and periphery of disciplines. When material science engineers and physicists in computational sciences overlap in targeted areas your probability of discovery goes up dramatically, especially in the translational sciences.

The University of Wisconsin, Madison does that very successfully; we do that by creating centres that focus on those interdisciplinary aspects. We reduce the hurdles, in fact, we eliminate the hurdles of faculty to move smoothly from one area to another, from one school or college to another. It's very common for a faculty member at our institution to have formal appointments in multiple departments and in several schools. We actively cultivate that."

Major Discoveries

Professor Jamie Thomson discovered human embryonic stem cells at the University of Wisconsin, Madison

Researchers at the University of Wisconsin – Madison, developed radiation-imaging techniques such as digital subtraction angiography and bone densitometry.

Partnerships, Innovation & Translational Research

The University of Wisconsin – Madison takes a pragmatic approach to external partnerships, focusing on real benefits from such partnerships as opposed to simply engaging in partnerships for partnerships' sake. Provost DeLuca elaborates further on this philosophy: "You have to make partnerships occur when there is an advantage in terms of productivity increase, asset increase and range of accomplishment increase. Simply forming partnerships without those kinds of underlying principles doesn't necessarily produce a significant product or an advantage. We actively pursue partnerships, but we try and focus on those areas that really benefit from such partnerships. Private sector partnerships are highly variable depending on the area. For example in drug discovery, major drug companies have certainly not abandoned their research programs. Where the partnership occurs, we have the ability to deeply pursue individual types of therapeutic drugs that a drug company might not be able to dedicate those kinds of resources to. Those are targeted partnerships and relatively straight forward to achieve."

The Wisconsin Idea is the best guide to look towards for an indication of the university's approach to translational research, actively encouraging all stakeholders at the university to bring discoveries to outside communities for the long-term benefit of society as a whole. The Wisconsin Alumni Research Foundation is the greatest institutional embodiment of this philosophy, a stand-alone organization that's wholly affiliated with the university whose only mission in life is to transfer intellectual property produced at the university into society.

Teaching, Learning & Student Life

The University of Wisconsin, Madison's extensive capacity for research throughout a myriad of disciplines translates directly into the teaching and learning experience, with undergraduate research participation a vital component of the student experience. Moreover, this is complemented by students having the option to be creative in learning across disciplines so as to tailor parts of their

degree to their interests and long-term aspirations. The ambition for administrators at the university is to have all undergraduate students getting directly involved with research, focusing on the impacts their discoveries could have on broader society.

Provost DeLuca elaborates upon what graduates from the university can expect to take from their experiences: "When students finish at our institution, walk out the door, they will have been trained for a lifelong commitment to learning experience, to discovery, to understanding critical thinking, to understand how broad and how deep their existing discoveries really are."

Madison, Wisconsin is not the best-known place in the United States despite playing host to one of the most prestigious and high quality research universities in the world. The University of Wisconsin, Madison is located in the south-central area of the state of Wisconsin, within a few hours drive to Chicago, Illinois and Minneapolis, Minnesota. With a student population in excess of 40,000, the university is a major community in itself. Students in attendance can expect to make life long friendships in a close knit community that benefits from the full support and commitment of the people from the state of Wisconsin.

University of California
San Francisco

Name › University of California, San Francisco
Region › Americas
Country › United States
Founded › 1868

www.ucsf.edu

Core Research Strengths

Being the only university in the University of California system fully dedicated to the medical and life sciences, the University of California, San Francisco's (UCSF) core research strengths are in the life and medical sciences, biotechnology and biomedical research. The university currently has 5 Nobel laureates within the faculty and with sponsored research from the National Institute of Health of US$532.8 million in 2011, receives the most health related research funding for any public institution in North America.

The life and medical sciences are particularly broad areas of academic research, and within this umbrella it is important to highlight the areas within which UCSF excels. Research programs in the basic, clinical, social and behavioural, and population sciences are recognized internationally. Preeminent faculty, who are conducting basic science investigations at the genetic, cellular, molecular and systems level, are unmasking the fundamental mechanisms of biology. And acclaimed faculty conducting investigations involving humans are discovering new solutions for preventing and treating a wide array of diseases, including cardiovascular disease, neurological disorders, cancer, diabetes, genetic disorders, immunological and infectious disease, and reproductive and developmental disorders.

Major Discoveries

Nobel Prize winners Michael Bishop and Harold Varmus were the first to discover that cellular genes can be converted into cancer genes in 1989.

Discovery of the techniques of recombinant DNA took place at UCSF, one of the foundations of the biotechnology industry.

HIV as the causative agent of AIDS discovered at UCSF.

Partnerships, Innovation & Translational Research

Founded in 2006, the Clinical and Translational Research Institute is symbolic of UCSF's focus upon expanding the university's network of partners throughout industry and the public sector, as well as managing the complexities of bringing discoveries made in UCSF laboratories to the market place for the benefit of broader society through technology transfer.

UCSF has been exceptionally successful in the sphere of technology transfer, producing more than 600 patents between 2000 and 2009, generating an average annual income of US$64 million; and stimulating the establishment of over 90 start up companies.

Teaching, Learning & Student Life

UCSF is divided into four professional schools focusing on preparing graduate students for professional careers in the medical sciences. The School of Dentistry, School of Medicine, School of Nursing and School of Pharmacy all have exceptional reputations for their teaching and instruction.

As well as an excellent tradition in discovery and research breakthroughs, UCSF also has an excellent tradition of teaching and learning excellence. UCSF prides itself on educating tomorrow's leaders in the life and medical sciences. UCSF faculty are ranked as some of the most productive in the world, focusing student attention on the university's core principles of patient care excellence, healthcare advocacy and inter-disciplinary collaboration throughout the institution's four professional schools.

UCSF has three major campuses throughout the San Francisco area as well as 19 additional sites throughout the city housing specialist centres and care facilities. UCSF's distribution throughout San Francisco is very much symbolic of the university's commitment to the city. In addition to conducting world-class research, UCSF also provides numerous vital services to the local community such as free health care screenings for children and free health care to the homeless and those on low incomes.

As the second largest employer in San Francisco with over 22,000 staff UCSF is very much a core of the local community in the city; however also feels like a global institution with students, faculty and staff coming from over 90 different countries.

JOHNS HOPKINS
UNIVERSITY

Name › The Johns Hopkins University
Region › Americas
Country › United States
Founded › 1876

www.jhu.edu

Core Research Strengths

The United States' first research university, with the largest research budget of any university in the world at approximately US$1.8 billion annually, it goes without saying that Johns Hopkins University has an extremely rich and diverse research tradition. Although it is well regarded across its portfolio there are certain areas within medicine, sciences and engineering for which it has an especially impressive track record.

The first of these is biomedicine, including basic research, clinical research and clinical care. Within biomedicine, neuroscience is one of the university's greatest research strengths, covering the discipline's entire spectrum from molecular neuroscience to computational neuroscience. Another is cognitive science with a particular focus on language and numeracy; related to that is natural language processing through the Whiting School of Engineering. The Centre for Language and Speech Processing runs a summer programme bringing experts from around the world to work on classified projects alongside US intelligence services.

The physics and astronomy department includes two Nobel Prize winners, and the university's Applied Physics Laboratory has designed, developed and launched more than 60 spacecraft. Computational science is an expanding focus through The Institute for Data Intensive Engineering and Science (IDIES), especially under the biomedical programme in an interdisciplinary context.

Johns Hopkins University's research footprint is truly international. With approximately 3500 staff in 90 different countries, one would be hard pressed to find a university doing more work in the area of global health than Johns Hopkins.

Major Discoveries

Johns Hopkins has produced 37 Nobel Laureates, the most recent being in physics. Riccardo Giacconi in 2002 for pioneering contributions to astrophysics, which have led to the discovery of cosmic X-ray sources, and

Adam Riess in 2011 for his contributions to the discovery of the acceleration of the expansion of the universe.

The ground station for the Hubble Space Telescope, The Space Telescope Science Institute (STScI), is located on campus and the university was involved with the MESSENGER spacecraft orbiting Mercury.

In the basic genetics of cancer, 90% of all cancers sequenced have been by Johns Hopkins researchers.

Partnerships, Innovation & Translational Research

According to Vice Provost Scott Zeger, the university was founded "Not just to discover, but to discover and then put into practice. Almost 35% of every dollar we spend at Johns Hopkins is not in teaching, or not in discovery, but putting into practice what we know. It's translating our knowledge."

Johns Hopkins has spent the past decade revolutionising its capacity to translate research discoveries into patents, products and services. The technology transfer office has tripled its business and in the past year made about $16 million dollars in license fees. However they do not see tech transfer simply in terms of profit, it is also about fostering jobs and creating knowledge to benefit the world, which is quite unusual for a private university, but Zeger is quick to point out that there is no one-fit model and Johns Hopkins is always on the look out for the most efficient method.

The Technology Transfer Office handles points of negotiation of intellectual property and patenting. But the university is increasingly involved in material transfer agreements, making university materials available to others for external research. Current focus is on cultivating partnerships with existing organisations, especially in the biomedical sphere.

Teaching, Learning & Student Life

Johns Hopkins has a tradition of learning through discovery. The balance of graduate students to undergraduates is tipped about 3:1, so undergraduates are treated more

like graduate students with a research-focused education. However there are steps being taken to enrich the undergrad experience through engagement in the community, involvement in the arts and humanities, and innovative ways of teaching introductory courses. Graduate students benefit from multidisciplinary learning and research – the motto is "See One, Do One, Teach One".

In recent years, significant efforts have been made to round out the undergraduate program; Vice Provost Zeger believes community engagement is a particularly important aspect of this: "Our students are expected to engage in research or professional practice of some sort because people think that that's how you learn best. I think there's been an effort in the last four or five years since Ron Daniels became our president to round out the undergraduate experience, and they've been putting a lot of other things for the students to engage in, much more engagement in the Baltimore community, there's a lot of opportunities for the students to be out and about in Baltimore and to work on projects in Baltimore, and that's been very attractive to students."

Johns Hopkins has international campuses in Europe and Asia, with faculty and students from around the world. However the commitment to internationalization goes beyond this. The university is focusing campaigns on tackling big challenges of our time – understanding how the planet works through space science, understanding how children learn to improve the quality of education throughout the world and affordable health care provision globally.

Name › University of Washington
Region › Americas
Country › United States
Founded › 1861

www.washington.edu

Core Research Strengths

With research spending standing in the region of US$1.5 billion per annum, the University of Washington has a vast research operation; the second largest of any research university. Although extensive in its breadth, the university has several outstanding strengths that distinguish it internationally. Research relating to stem cells, genetics, DNA and bio-informatics are all recognized as leading internationally.

The University of Washington is also well known for its expertise in the emerging field of big data, whereby enormous data sets are analysed using complex algorithms and super computers to figure out patterns, and be able to make predictions about health and well being globally, and the influence of genetics on peoples' susceptibility to disease.

The University of Washington is also very well known for long held strengths in oceanography and the medical sciences. The university has just laid a 500-kilometre cable on the bed of the Pacific Ocean to take measurements; and has had a long tradition of ground-breaking discoveries in the medical arena such as with kidney dialysis, diabetes and Parkinson's disease.

Relating to more environmental oriented challenges, the University of Washington also has great strength in the development of renewable energies with major programs investigating solar energy and bio-fuels, as well as in species preservation with a particular focus on fisheries. Multi-disciplinary research approaches are of increasing importance with 250 interdisciplinary centres under operation, and that number growing all the time.

Major Discoveries

On-going work mapping the brain is set to significantly expand our understanding of what specifically stimulates the brain, and how the brain develops and grows in its capacity.

Current work on global health metrics is producing the most profound data set relating to global health and the prevalence of disease worldwide.

The cable presently being run under the Pacific Ocean is set to produce more real-time data and information on the ocean than has ever been produced before.

Partnerships, Innovation & Translational Research

Collaborative research partnerships are of enormous importance to the University of Washington. Given the retrenchment of research funding at government level, and the changing dynamics of corporate sector strategy away from basic research, there is huge opportunity for them to complement each other.

President Michael Young elaborates upon the dynamics of this trend, and how the university is adapting to these changes: "I think partnerships are important and getting more important. In part, because I think we are seeing by any reasonable standard a levelling off of government support for research on the side of the universities; but the flip side is you are increasingly seeing companies that used to be known for R&D, now being known largely for D.

In America, for example, four of the five big pharmaceutical firms have largely abandoned research. They do virtually no research anymore; they buy it up. That's not in the long run a sustainable model for them, and the question is can we develop as we have with Boeing and other companies research agendas that don't short change basic research but do satisfy the needs for companies to do the translational and developmental work as well. I think that's very possible. I think we are absolutely going to have to move in that direction."

Teaching, Learning & Student Life

Entrepreneurialism and the opportunities to become involved in business through ideas and innovation at university form an important part of the culture at the University of Washington. The number of entrepreneurial programs has expanded dramatically in recent years with mentoring, cross-disciplinary competitions and business plan development featuring throughout the undergraduate program. Incentive programs for students have been introduced to identify the commercial

potential of discoveries made in the lab, and then to take translational action based upon that. Approximately 6000 undergraduate students are active in research at the University of Washington, enabling the culture of innovation and entrepreneurialism to flourish from the grass roots level.

The University of Washington curriculum is also very flexible, enabling students to combine minors with their major in an inter-disciplinary way so as enabling the pursuit of specific interests in a creative way.

Located in Seattle, the University of Washington attracts a diverse array of students from the vast majority of the world's countries, with a significant contingent from East Asia. Diversity is certainly a strength at the University of Washington, with the student population both contributing to and benefiting from the strong culture of collaboration.

From an innovation perspective, the University of Washington is located in one of the most exciting regions globally. President Young emphasizes this point in more detail "We are situated in one of the most imaginative and interesting business and economic environments in the world right now. We know what's going on with Microsoft and Amazon and in the biotech community. So, really we are at the epicentre of some of the most interesting and dynamic economic developments and changes; that spills over to the university in a really powerful way."

UC San Diego

Name › University of California, San Diego
Region › Americas
Country › United States
Founded › 1903

www.ucsd.edu

Core Research Strengths

Established in 1960, the University of California, San Diego (UC San Diego) has since grown into a globally-ranked university covering all major disciplines apart from Law. UC San Diego's US$1 billion research budget is one of the largest in the world for a university, facilitating inspirational research programs across a multitude of disciplines. The campus' engineering, computer science, life sciences, biotechnology, medicine and oceanography research departments are all considered to be world class.

According to UC San Diego Chancellor Pradeep K. Khosla, the most important distinguishing feature of the university is the ability to collaborate across disciplines: "We are ranked number six in the USA for federal research funding, and a great part of our competitiveness comes from the ability of our researchers to both think and work across disciplines so as to develop innovative new ways to approach complex problems. This is of huge importance to how we approach graduate teaching and learning as well."

The California Institute for Telecommunications and Information Technology (Calit2) is an excellent example of UC San Diego's multidisciplinary approach. By leveraging outstanding disciplinary strength in computer science, researchers have collaborated to extend the application of cutting edge communications technology into diverse fields such as archaeology, where research is helping to improve upon existing archaeological excavation techniques.

Scripps Institution of Oceanography at UC San Diego is widely acknowledged to be one of the world's leading oceanography research centres. Researchers at Scripps Oceanography are now pushing ahead with unique programs in partnership with medical and biological researchers at the university to determine what medicines and pharmaceutical drugs could be developed from raw materials found in the sea. Very few other institutions in the world have the capacity to approach such complex questions in this way. UC San Diego engineers are also working in partnership with researchers at Scripps to develop a means of producing fuel from algae, one of the most exciting areas for the development of alternative fuels.

Major Discoveries

UC San Diego has a history of accomplishments unique to the university, including the following:

Science of Climate Change

Scripps Institution of Oceanography faculty member Charles David Keeling measured concentrations of CO_2 in the atmosphere at Mauna Loa Observatory, Hawaii. These observations have continued without interruption from 1958 through to the present. The Keeling Curve is one of the most recognizable images in modern science and is the foundation for the current science of climate change.

The World's First Outdoor Shake Table

In 2005, the Jacobs School of Engineering's Department of Structural Engineering opened the world's first full-scale outdoor shake table, able to handle structures weighing 2,200 tons and as tall as 100 feet. The shake table, which is able to create realistic simulations of the most devastating earthquakes on record, is being used to verify advances in seismic safety designs for buildings and bridges.

Multidisciplinary, Collaborative Stem Cell Research

Thanks to UC San Diego and partnering research institutions, a new culture of collaboration was born in San Diego and has flourished far more than in any other place in the world. The Sanford Consortium for Regenerative Medicine embodies this collaborative culture. For the first time anywhere, top researchers from UC San Diego, Salk Institute for Biological Studies, Sanford-Burnham Medical Research Institute, La Jolla Institute for Allergy & Immunology, The Scripps Research Institute and other research organizations have teamed up under the same roof, in the same labs and workspaces, to harness the regenerative power of stem cells to diagnose, treat and one day cure degenerative diseases and injuries.

Partnerships, Innovation & Translational Research

With 20 percent of UC San Diego's research portfolio funded by the private sector, collaborative research forms an integral part of the university's overall strategy. The campus has had a significant influence on the broader economy, particularly in San Diego. Chancellor Khosla believes: "It is not a stretch for me to say that the entire development of San Diego's biotechnology industry is based upon research conducted and subsequent spin out companies from UC San Diego."

UC San Diego's excellent track record in translational research is largely down to the culture of the university according to Chancellor Khosla: "The collaborative culture here has fed into the tech transfer process. At the same time, we are trying to continue streamlining processes so as to make it as easy as possible for our researchers to be successful. However, the main point for us is the culture. Our people enjoy collaborating and that makes everything so much easier."

Teaching, Learning & Student Life

UC San Diego is unique among other UC campuses — the university offers undergraduates the "small college" concept. Similar to the model one would find at Oxford in the UK, the campus is organised into six colleges. Each of the undergraduate colleges has its own residence halls, student services, requirements, educational philosophy, traditions, even graduation ceremonies. So, while the undergraduates remain part of one university, they also develop a sense of identity with the smaller family of their chosen college.

UC San Diego's pedagogical philosophy lends itself heavily to interdisciplinary learning; Chancellor Khosla believes that UC San Diego's strength across the disciplines is a tremendous advantage in delivering upon this: "It is vitally important for us to provide a holistic education for tomorrow's leaders, that is left brain and right brain — educated and trained. Our top priority is to be a student centred university; our great strengths throughout the disciplines enable us to do this to a really top-class level."

Through the Moxie Centre in the Jacobs School of Engineering, UC San Diego is going beyond just providing the traditional education one would expect at university—it is also stimulating and extending upon undergraduate students' innovative spirit by providing training programs, funding and consultation to motivate, educate and mentor students to "Dream, Design, Develop" their engineering ideas into commercial products.

Thinking of the broader environment, San Diego has one of the best climates in the United States, if not the world, with sunshine and blue skies expected all year round. Spread throughout UC San Diego's nearly 2200-acre campus is the Stuart Collection, one of the finest collections of site-specific works by leading artists of our time. The university offers countless opportunities for exercise and sporting activities, including surfing — UC San Diego rides a wave of recognition as a top surfing school.

Students can expect changes in line with UC San Diego's strategic plan. Since his first day on campus, Chancellor Khosla has emphasized the importance of defining shared goals and a shared vision for the campus, "This is the right time in our history to evaluate where we are and where we want to be, so we can continue to educate the next generation of leaders and produce meaningful innovation that improves our world and drives our local, national and global economies."

Chancellor Khosla added, "One of the important outcomes of the strategic plan is not just the plan itself, but the process that leads to the plan. It will help us to think about how we can individually and collectively contribute to this university and make it a better place." UC San Diego's strategic planning process is expected to be completed by the end of the 2012-2013 academic year.

UNIVERSITY OF PENNSYLVANIA

Name › University of Pennsylvania
Region › Americas
Country › United States
Founded › 1740

www.upenn.edu

Core Research Strengths

The University of Pennsylvania (UPenn) has one of the largest annual research budgets in the world with expenditure of approximately US$874 million in 2012. UPenn's research enterprise is organized into six broad categories, those of Health, Natural Science, Technology, Social Science, Humanies and Business. UPenn has particularly strong research relationships with government institutes as well as the private sector working collaboratively to answer some of the most complex questions relating to society and industry today.

Medicine is undoubtedly the spine of the university's research enterprise with 57% of UPenn's research budget coming from the US Department of Health. Having established the United States' first medical school and teaching hospital, UPenn has a long and varied tradition in the medical sciences with a particular emphasis on multi-disciplinary collaboration between veterinary sciences and conventional human health under the university's "one health" philosophy.

The multidisciplinary approach to research and education is an engrained part of UPenn's academic tradition and it promotes cross-pollination and integration across its 12 schools, with numerous research centres spanning faculties and disciplines. In 2005, University President Amy Gutmann founded the Penn Integrates Knowledge (PIK) programme. The programme recruits and rewards faculty whose work crosses traditional academic boundaries. A recent outcome of the university's interdisciplinary approach was the 2012 creation of the Centre for the Study of Contemporary China that focuses on the many factors shaping China, and the role the country plays on the international stage.

Major Discoveries

Over the past decade UPenn has produced 9 Nobel Prize laureates. Most recently in 2011, Prof Thomas J. Sargent was awarded for his work in economics for empirical research on cause and effect in the macroeconomy. In 2010 Ei'chi Negishi won the award in Chemistry for advancements inpalladium-catalyzed couplings in organic synthesis.

One of the most important innovations was the development ENIAC, the first general-purpose electronic computer, which began at the Moore School of Electrical Engineering in 1943.

UPenn has been home to some of the most important discoveries in medicine; vaccines for Rubella, commonly known as German measles, and Hepatitis-B were developed at UPenn. A UPenn medical student invented the dialysis machine and the university's work on gene research has led to discoveries in cancer's link with genes.

Partnerships, Innovation & Translational Research

UPenn enjoys a close partnership with the Department of Health and Human Services. Its economic impact throughout Pennsylvania is in the tens of billions of dollars. There is also collaborative engagement throughout the world, especially on global issues such as infectious disease, environmental sustainability and responding to humanitarian disasters.

The Centre for Technology Transfer (CTT) acts as the bridge between the university and industry, managing the various aspects of the commercialisation process including research and development, intellectual property, sponsored research, licensing agreements, marketing and finance. Potential partners are able to search UPenn's extensive portfolio of inventions and technologies online, and through contact with the Technology Licensing Officer. CTT has streamlined its tech transfer policy, emphasizing the importance of good working relationships and a flexible approach to deal-term negotiation.

Connected to CTT is the Fellows Programme, an experiential educational programme in technology transfer for graduate students and Post-Doctoral Fellows; and Upstart, a programme that assists entrepreneurs in company formation and development, dedicated to technology commercialization. It has assisted nearly 100 faculty in launching companies based around new inventions and technology

Teaching, Learning & Student Life

The 12 schools that make up UPenn are all located on one urban campus, creating a well-integrated community of faculty and students both at the undergraduate and graduate level. This is further facilitated through the housing system. Every College House has at least four members of faculty in domestic roles and UPenn students rent much of the residential real estate around campus.

Multidisciplinary learning is fostered from the very beginning of a student's academic career at UPenn with almost a third of undergraduates completing interdisciplinary degree programmes. There is an infrastructure in place, through the Centre for Undergraduate Research & Fellowships (CURF), to ensure undergraduates are involved in research. The CURF Research Directory is a platform where UPenn faculty post projects in which undergraduates can participate and CURF consultations offer support and advice on internships, finding appropriate projects and faculty mentors, as well as on accessing grants and funding.

UPenn has wholly embraced internationalisation, accepting over 5000 international students from around the world and rapidly growing its study-abroad programme. The university currently has 242 academic partnerships around the world that extend as far as Africa, Asia and Latin America. In China alone there are 45 partnerships between UPenn and local universities. The university is currently making great strides towards establishing a global network of alumni poised to tackle global issues.

Cornell University

Name › Cornell University
Region › Americas
Country › United States
Founded › 1865

www.cornell.edu

Core Research Strengths

Cornell University has a very broad base of research strength, however it stands out with exceptional international leadership in specific areas such as the physical and biological sciences, materials science and electrical and mechanical engineering, nanoscale science and nanotechnology, computer and information sciences, and the applied life sciences. Increasingly Cornell's researchers are pooling their disciplinary expertise to work in teams across multiple disciplines, significantly increasing the prospects of making ground-breaking discoveries.

In the areas of biology, ecology and evolution, Cornell scientists are tracking how organisms respond and adapt to their environment, resulting in unprecedented advances in illuminating the connections between an organism's basic functions – its biochemistry, anatomy, physiology, development, and behaviour - and responses to challenges ranging from climate change and diseases in plants to social instability; spanning time scales of milliseconds to millennia.

In computer and information sciences, partnerships between Cornell's computer scientists and colleagues in the life sciences and social sciences are answering long-standing questions about the interactions between humans and their environment ranging from social interactions, human ancestry and genome structure, to human visual perception, and the interpretation of different art forms. This includes work with a variety of robots such as aerial robots, home and office assistant robots, autonomous cars, humanoids, evolutionary robots, legged robots, snake robots and more.

In the field of genome sciences, Cornell life scientists are taking the lead in key discoveries linking genome structure and variation to studies of proteins and metabolites, and functions as diverse as personalized medicine, plant traits important for food production and bioenergy, pathogen biology, and neural circuits that determine behaviour.

Major Discoveries

Consumer economist Professor Brian Wansink's work on mindless eating has identified a number of interesting trends in the 250 or so food decisions that we make each day with huge implications for the challenges of overcoming societal health issues such as obesity, heart disease and diabetes.

Cornell leads international efforts to track and combat the fungal bacteria causing wheat rust. Originally identified in Uganda in 1998, fungus ug99 has the potential to decimate wheat harvests throughout Asia, having severe implications for food security throughout the region. Through a strategy combining basic plant breeding, computer modelling, molecular diagnostic techniques and good outreach to permit seed replication and adoption of the new varieties, Cornell researchers are leading the fight to slow the movement of a serious threat to the global wheat crop.

Partnerships, Innovation & Translational Research

Cornell's diverse network of partners runs through the public, private and university sectors; located in countries as diverse as Ethiopia, Israel, India, China and Italy; as well as of course a comprehensive array of partners in the United States.

President David Skorton elaborates further on the importance of partnerships to the university: "Our experience in countries as diverse as Ethiopia, India and Italy have been long-term, committed partnerships that afford Cornell students and faculty numerous opportunities for research, education and cultural understanding. Most Cornell graduates and our university partners work in the private sector, so inclusion of public-private partnerships is essential if students are to acquire the job skills that employers desire. As the world becomes more connected economically and electronically, the ability to work across cultures is essential to the success of Cornell's students."

Teaching, Learning & Student Life

The words of founder, Ezra Cornell: "I would found an institution where any person can find instruction in any study" very much guide the spirit and philosophy of pedagogy at Cornell given the enormous breadth and depth of expertise one can find at the university. Through undergraduate courses such as "information science" and "environmental engineering", students are able to study throughout numerous departments, as well as having the freedom to combine a myriad of academic disciplines.

Cornell, along with academic partner the Technion–Israel Institute of Technology, has inaugurated a new campus in New York City called Cornell Tech, which will spur economic growth and high-tech entrepreneurship and will cover an 11-acre site on Roosevelt Island in Manhattan by full build-out in 2037. The new graduate-level campus offers a distinctive model of graduate tech education and research that fuses academic excellence with commercial success and societal good. The campus' innovative organization features curriculum and research that spans across multiple disciplines and is directed toward particular sectors of the city's economy. Its entrepreneurial culture leverages the city's spirit and global interconnectedness to inspire and nurture the next generation of technology leaders.

International study and engagement has long been an important component of a Cornell education, ever since the first graduating class of 1872. Among its firsts, Cornell was the first university to teach modern Far Eastern languages. In 2004, the university opened the Weill Cornell Medical College in Qatar, the first American medical school outside of the United States.

The university's diverse student population and extensive international network of partners has provided the ideal platform for Cornell students to study and conduct research on every one of Earth's continents. Student life at Cornell is enormously enriched by the opportunities that the university's 901 associations and clubs present.

Name › University of California, Los Angeles
Region › Americas
Country › United States
Founded › 1919

www.ucla.edu

Core Research Strengths

The University of California,
Los Angeles (UCLA) receives $1 billion
a year in research funding, with
approximately 6,000 funded projects
underway at any given time. UCLA
excels in innovative thinking,
interdisciplinary collaboration and
breadth of excellence across multiple
disciplines: clinical and health
sciences, life and physical sciences,
engineering and technology, social
sciences, arts and humanities.

The university's location – in a major,
forward-thinking city on the Pacific
Rim — enhances its entrepreneurial
spirit and facilitates research
partnerships with other universities
around the world. UCLA's compact
campus fosters collaboration.

"It is in the interface of different
fields that we are making some of our
greatest contributions," said Chancellor
Gene Block. "For example, the California
NanoSystems Institute brings together
scientists from engineering, medicine
and the College of Letters and Science
to work on issues that are deeply
interdisciplinary."

Examples of Interdisciplinary
Collaboration at UCLA:

› Clinical and Translational Science
Institute (partners to translate lab
science to treatments/therapies)

› Eli and Edythe Broad Center of
Regenerative Medicine and Stem
Cell Research Institute of the
Environment and Sustainability

› California NanoSystems Institute

› Institute of American Cultures
(ethnic studies)

› Center for the Everyday Life of
Families (cultural anthropology)

› Luskin Center for Innovation

› Semel Institute/Brain Research
Institute (and other neuroscience)

What UCLA Offers Students, Researchers and Academics

UCLA's combination of basic and
applied research, medical research and
scholarship in the arts and humanities
attracts the best students from
around the globe. The Ronald Reagan
UCLA Medical Center is ranked as one
of the nation's best hospitals and
has been named the best in the
western U.S. for 23 consecutive years.
Located In the heart of the world's
entertainment capital, the UCLA
School of Theater, Film and Television
and the UCLA School of the Arts and
Architecture are among the world's
most renowned.

UCLA is known for cross-disciplinary
research, teaching and collaboration.
It provides access to world-class
scholars who are international
leaders in their fields, many of whom
teach small undergraduate seminars
and supervise both graduate and
undergraduate research.

One of UCLA's greatest assets is its
location in one of the world's premier
urban centers. Los Angeles is the
perfect laboratory, combining a diverse
population, the thriving entertainment
industry, environmental challenges, the
Pacific Rim and a range of businesses
and non-governmental organizations.

Major Discoveries

UCLA researchers have many major
discoveries to their credit, from the
mathematical theory of packet
networks that underpins the Internet
to the first genetically-targeted cancer
treatment. Recent discoveries and
developments include:

› New technique using a DVD burner
to fabricate micro-scale graphene-
based supercapacitors — devices that
can charge and discharge a hundred
to a thousand times faster than
standard batteries

› New energy sources including
converting electricity and CO2 to
liquid fuel, and using proteins as raw
material for biofuels

› A temporary artificial heart
for patients awaiting transplant

› A modified mobile phone that doubles
as a microscope to transmit samples
for medical analysis

› A saliva test that can detect cancer

› A capsule that delivers cancer
drugs to tumors without damaging
surrounding healthy tissue

› Algorithms that help law enforcement
predict where crime is most likely to
occur in Los Angeles

› Innovative smart-grid technologies
that are anticipated to lead to major
breakthroughs for power infrastructure
and reliability

Partnerships, Innovation & Translational Research

As a leading research university, UCLA
collaborates with other institutions
around the globe to help solve some
of the world's greatest problems. "Some
of the largest research issues today
represent global challenges and
require multinational research efforts
to find solutions. External research
partnerships are important and can
take many forms," said Chancellor Block.

A sample of existing
collaborations includes:

› Cross-disciplinary Scholars in Science
and Technology Program, which includes
student and faculty exchanges with
multiple universities

› Joint research institute in science
and engineering with Peking University

› Global Executive MBA for the Americas,
a partnership between the UCLA
Anderson School of Management and
Universidad Adolfo Ibáñez (UAI) in Chile

› California NanoSystems Institute at
UCLA memoranda of understanding with
nanotechnology institutes at Japan's
Kyoto University, England's University
of Bristol, the University of Twente
in the Netherlands, and others to
collaborate on international research
and academic exchanges in nanoscience
and nanotechnology

› David Geffen School of Medicine at UCLA memorandum of understanding with Korea Institute of Science and Technology to promote education, training, research and education in global health

UCLA also works with private companies and community, state and federal agencies. For example, Clean Tech LA, a public/private partnership, seeks to develop more "green" companies in Los Angeles in order to reduce the region's carbon footprint.

To speed the results of research into the marketplace, UCLA recently conducted a national study of best practices to manage intellectual property, enhancing the university's ability to work with external partners. UCLA manages more than 1,800 active inventions, including about 630 U.S. patents. More than 500 UCLA inventions have been licensed to companies, and, in the last five years, almost 100 startup companies have been created based on technology developed at UCLA. The university is creating an entrepreneurial ecosystem on campus to encourage students and faculty members to share the fruits of their research with the broader community both domestically and at the international level.

"We are focused on becoming more company-friendly," Chancellor Block said. "We do not part with our patents, but we work hard to license our technology."

Teaching, Learning & Student Life

UCLA fosters a welcoming, inclusive environment for all students, faculty and staff to ensure that a diverse community can achieve success. Students have access to career and counseling centers, as well as almost 1,000 student organizations. UCLA receives more freshman applications than any other university – more than 80,000 for Fall 2013. UCLA is perhaps the best-known university brand internationally, attracting applicants the world over.

UCLA faculty members regularly receive prestigious awards. Six have been named Nobel laureates; 11 are MacArthur Foundation Fellows; and one has received a Fields Medal.

Los Angeles is the western capital of the Pacific Rim, and its diversity and global worldview are increasingly reflected at UCLA. In addition, the optimistic spirit of California is at the heart of UCLA, and has nurtured such prestigious alumni as Nobel Peace Prize winner Ralph Bunche, former U.S.

Poet Laureate Kay Ryan, astronaut Anna Lee Fisher, baseball legend Jackie Robinson and Olympian Jackie Joyner-Kersee, Oscar-winning film directors Francis Ford Coppola and Alexander Payne, and Elinor Ostrom, the first woman to win a Nobel Prize for economics.

"There are so many great success stories associated with UCLA. Students and faculty have broken barriers in so many ways. In California everything seems possible, with no boundaries to what can be achieved," Chancellor Block said.

Every day, researchers at UCLA create new knowledge that impacts people's lives and serves society. In addition, through basic research, they advance academic disciplines to increase people's understanding of themselves and the universe.

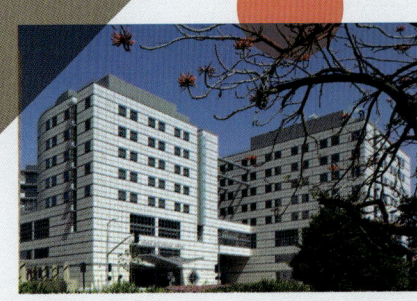

YALE
UNIVERSITY

Name › Yale University
Region › Americas
Country › United States
Founded › 1701

www.yale.edu

Core Research Strengths

Yale University is particularly renowned for the institution's research prowess in the medical sciences, biology, biotechnology, English literature, American history and law.

Yale's strong traditions in the medical and biological sciences are increasingly being leveraged into a series of multidisciplinary research centres and institutes investigating solutions to specific ailments and challenges such as the Center for Interdisciplinary Research on AIDS, Keck Biotechnology Resource Laboratory and the Yale Stem Cell Center.

The Keck Biotechnology Resource Laboratory, a facility for conducting complex tests for researchers working in emerging areas such as bioinformatics and biostatistics is widely regarded as a leading institution of its kind throughout the United States, serving both researchers from Yale and external institutions conducting hundreds of thousands of analyses each year.

Yale also has a very strong tradition in the social sciences, particularly throughout the 20th century in areas such as history whereby Yale's academics in this field were important proponents of the Western style of living, as opposed to anti Western societies such as found in the former Soviet Union.

Major Discoveries

Yale's portfolio of major discoveries are largely dominated by breakthroughs in the medical sciences:

Yale was the first place to treat cancer using chemotherapy, and the site of the first successful treatments using antibiotics in the USA.

Researchers at the University of Yale identified Lyme disease

Yale researchers also discovered the genes responsible for high blood pressure, osteoporosis, dyslexia and Tourette's syndrome

Partnerships, Innovation & Translational Research

Established in 1982, Yale's Office of Cooperative Research (OCR) is responsible for developing both commercial investments in the university's research programs, as well as attracting partners for the commercialisation of research discoveries and patents issued to Yale's faculty and research teams.

The OCR has strived to be the leading office of corporate and commercial engagement since its founding, guided by the principle priorities of stimulating local economic development, enhancing the reputation of the university and generating funds for re-investment in Yale's research operations.

Similarly to all the leading international research universities, Yale University has academic curiosity as the driving spirit behind its research operations. Nevertheless, Yale is well known for the entrepreneurial spirit throughout its faculty and student population, and the university's commitment to creating knowledge that is of benefit to the broader community and economy. These commitments lay the foundation for Yale's commitment to working in partnership with a broad range of partners throughout the public, private and third sectors to collaborate on developing new innovations, ideas and technologies in partnership.

Teaching, Learning & Student Life

Similarly to Oxford and Cambridge, Yale University has a collegiate system organized into 12 residential colleges at which students will find a great deal of teaching and learning support. Specific tutoring and academic support is organised through each college so as to ensure that every Yale attendee is able to keep up with the rigours of their particular academic program.

Yale's colleges also arrange seminars, social events and debates to add further value to the basic student experience of lectures and course programs. A culture of flexibility and accommodation also runs through Yale's faculty with professors and lecturers happy to host impromptu office hours discussion sessions following lectures. Teaching prizes for Yale's lecturers voted for by the student population offer a transparent means for recognising teaching excellence, as well as an incentive structure for academic staff to focus on teaching and fostering creativity, as much as they do on their own research.

Yale's architectural environment is a testament to the neo-gothic style of the early 20th century, and its coastal location in New Haven offers a beautiful environmental setting for students and faculty alike.

Yale students can expect to meet prospective political leaders at the university, with Yale having educated numerous leading US politicians such as Bill Clinton, George W Bush, Hilary Clinton, John Kerry and Gerald Ford.

As well as a myriad of social and sporting clubs for students to engage with, undergraduates are encouraged to develop their leadership skills with a range of social development initiatives working alongside the local New Haven community.

The Yale community are widely regarded as being particularly liberal and progressive with rich diversity in the student population embracing a wide variety of social classes and ethnic origins, distinctive openness to the gay and lesbian community; as well as a number of environmental initiatives to reduce the campus' carbon emissions.

IT IS A GREAT DEAL EASIER TO

IMPACT
THE WORLD

WHEN THE WORLD IS IN
YOUR BACKYARD.

AMONG THE WORLD'S preeminent research universities, only UCLA combines extraordinary academic breadth and depth with a tradition of groundbreaking innovation. Its location in Los Angeles, one of the most diverse and entrepreneurial cities, provides an immense living laboratory for launching world-changing discoveries.

We are proud of UCLA's many partnerships and collaborations with scholars, researchers and industries throughout the world. We are working together to achieve significant advances in knowledge and inventions that enhance quality of life around the globe.

UNIVERSITY OF CALIFORNIA, LOS ANGELES   WWW.UCLA.EDU

Name › University of Oxford
Region › Europe
Country › United Kingdom
Founded › Circa 1096

www.ox.ac.uk

Core Research Strengths

The University of Oxford has over the 900 years of its existence amassed immense strength and depth across a myriad of academic disciplines.

Traditionally Oxford is regarded as one of the world's leading universities in the humanities with ancient collections such as those found in the Bodleian Library. Increasingly, however, the University of Oxford has developed immense strength in the sciences over the course of the past century, with particular strength in certain areas, including global health. Vice Chancellor Andrew Hamilton discusses Oxford's influence: "There is not a university on the face of the Earth that has a more comprehensive and extensive interaction in areas of global health around the world than Oxford University. In historical terms, penicillin was developed at Oxford, both winning the Nobel Prize and having a profound impact upon international healthcare. The University of Oxford's extensive influence in the sphere of global health has now expanded into an international network of collaborative research centres that look at a range of health-related issues. For example, we have a Wellcome Trust-partnered research centre in Thailand examining strains of drug resistant malaria."

Today, the University of Oxford's research portfolio is organised into four clear divisions, these are the medical sciences, humanities, social sciences and mathematical, physical and life sciences. The University of Oxford is pioneering the interdisciplinary approach to research within the context of major global challenges. The Oxford Martin School, for example, issues problem-driven scholarships, so as to enable teams of varied expertise to come together and work on complex research questions associated with issues such as; genetics, ageing societies, climate change, international migration and tropical disease.

Major Discoveries

The University of Oxford has led internationally on the links between smoking and chronic disease, both in the work of Professor Richard Doll and Professor Richard Peto.

The needle free injection was invented at the University of Oxford in 1993

The use of Infrared remote sensing for the study of other planets was pioneered at the University of Oxford in 1970

Partnerships, Innovation & Translational Research

The University of Oxford has a long tradition of working in partnerships throughout the public, private and third sectors. The university is enthusiastic about the prospect of further developing such relationships; however, it is very much focused upon retaining the independence of the university, and academic curiosity as the sole driver of Oxford's research interests.

Vice Chancellor Andrew Hamilton discusses the approach to partnerships in more detail: "The University of Oxford has a long tradition of embracing the world around us. We welcome the opportunity to partner with a diverse range of both private and public sector institutions to ensure our research excellence has the greatest impact possible throughout the international community.

The public sector has traditionally played a dominant role in the funding of research at the University of Oxford. Increasingly, however, sources of research funding at Oxford are evolving to become more diverse. For example, the University of Oxford now receives over 90 million pounds per year from international research funders outside of the UK.

The private sector question is one of enormous importance. Academic freedom and independence is fundamental to the University of Oxford's philosophy and is at the core of how the university operates and is governed. This means there are always protections that need to be in place to ensure that fundamental research is not distorted by partnerships whose goals may diverge away from those of our academics. We ensure that the research at the University of Oxford is curiosity-driven. Having said this, there is a vast range of private sector partnerships that the university is engaged in throughout our world-class schools and divisions. By way of

example, the relationship between Oxford's Department of Engineering Science and Rolls Royce."

Teaching, Learning & Student Life

Undergraduate students at the University of Oxford can expect a unique experience with regards to teaching and learning. Oxford University is arranged into 38 colleges, designed so as to encourage interdisciplinary communities able to teach and learn from each other in a vibrant social environment.

The tutorial system is very much at the heart of the Oxford experience, with students sitting down in weekly meetings with leaders in their field of study having to debate and discuss their ideas; learning how to formulate arguments and construct effective means of answering complex questions. The University of Oxford's environment is a magical transcendence of over 900 years of architecture and ideas. There is a unique atmosphere throughout the university connecting the institution's ancient heritage with the cutting edge ideas and technologies the university is working with today. The university welcomed its first international student in 1190, and since then Oxford has grown into a dynamic community of the world's great young minds.

University of Oxford
United Kingdom

Name › University of Chicago
Region › Americas
Country › United States
Founded › 1891

www.uchicago.edu

Core Research Strengths

Traditionally the University of Chicago's core strengths have been in the social sciences with a particular focus on economics. The University of Chicago's economists had a huge impact upon the development of global economic policy throughout the second half of the 20th Century under the leadership of the legendary Milton Friedman.

As with most other leading international research universities, the University of Chicago's core strength from a research perspective is the institution's ability to leverage strengths across multiple disciplines so as to investigate complex issues in multi-disciplinary centres. The University of Chicago now has 140 multidisciplinary research centres in operation looking at a myriad of issues ranging from Near Eastern and Oriental Studies to Biomedicine and Biomedical Engineering.

The University of Chicago also manages a number of external laboratories such as the Argonne National Laboratory in partnership with the United States Department of Energy investigating a number of key questions linked to sustainable energy production and storage. Both key issues looking forwards into the 21st century.

Major Discoveries

The first self-sustaining nuclear reaction was created at the University of Chicago in 1942.

The existence of Black Holes was first proposed at the University of Chicago.

Theoretical economics was greatly advanced at the University of Chicago under Milton Friedman

Partnerships, Innovation & Translational Research

The University of Chicago Office of Technology and Intellectual Property (UCTech), first established in 2001, is the University of Chicago's one stop shop for managing the university's portfolio of intellectual property, industry partnerships and translational research discoveries that are in the process of raising investment and preparing for entry into the market place.

The University of Chicago can reasonably claim to be one of the most advanced leading research universities with regards to external collaborative partnerships. From a public sector perspective, the university works in close collaboration with the United States Federal Government in a number of major laboratory complexes such as Argonne National Laboratory. Furthermore, the university is an open and experienced industry partner working alongside leading international companies such as Toyota at the Toyota Technological Institute at Chicago.

The University of Chicago's motto: "Let knowledge grow from more to more; and so be human life enriched" is the ideal point to look for an indication as to how the issue of technology transfer is approached at the university. The philosophy is very open to commercialisation and translational research as a responsibility to society, and the public good primarily, as well as a means of generating additional revenues for the university and its faculty members. The approach is market-based, with any decision to commercialise being based upon a cost / benefit analysis within the market context.

Teaching, Learning & Student Life

University of Chicago students are immediately encouraged to take inspiration from the university motto and to work on developing new knowledge, and innovative ideas throughout their time at the institution. It is with this spirit in mind, that undergraduates are encouraged to get directly involved in research, always looking out for entrepreneurial opportunities that could result from engaging in research, as well as debating their opinions and view points on course materials.

Leadership is an important part of any education, and the University of Chicago's commitment to the local community of Chicago through outreach programs and community-volunteering programs are an excellent way for young people attending the university to develop such skills.

The University of Chicago has a well-developed network of international partner universities; study abroad provides an excellent opportunity for students not to just diversify their degree program, but also develop language skills and learn how to do business in a diverse array of international cultures such as in Europe and Asia.

University of Chicago undergraduates live throughout the university's 37 houses in and around the campus. This arrangement is widely acknowledged to have a key influence on how student experiences, friendships and social lives develop whilst at the university.

The more than 15,000 students in attendance at the University of Chicago can expect to have access to world-class facilities at the institution varying from opportunities through the career center, and internship opportunities through to the over 400 clubs and associations serving to enhance student experiences, as well as extend the university's capacity to create, innovate, debate, play sports and have fun.

With Chicago as a host city, those in attendance at the University of Chicago can expect not just world-class facilities on campus, but one of the most interesting, dynamic and multi-cultural cities in the world to develop friends, connections and make visits to some of the world's leading art galleries, shows and museums; as well as begin networking with potential future employers and business partners.

COLUMBIA UNIVERSITY

Name › Columbia University
Region › Americas
Country › United States
Founded › 1754

www.columbia.edu

Core Research Strengths

Columbia University's core research strengths reside in the social sciences, medical sciences and pharmaceutical science; as well as in mathematics and natural sciences.

Traditionally, Columbia University has been one of the most active global institutions in the development of new pharmaceutical products and medical innovations. Columbia faculty are responsible for approximately 175 new such innovations and inventions each year.

Increasingly, similarly to many other leading research universities, Columbia is adopting the strategy of developing multidisciplinary research centres working on major global challenges. Perhaps the best example of this is the Columbia Earth Institute working on critical issues surrounding global climate change, environmental degradation, sustainable use of resources and poverty. Leading international academics such as Jeffrey Sachs work within the Earth Institute to pool a diverse array of expertise helping to better understand some of the most fundamental challenges facing the international community today, and help to devise potential solutions to them.

Major Discoveries

Having been associated with more Nobel Laureates than any other institution in the world, Columbia has a remarkable record of invention and innovation. The university has been responsible for many breakthrough discoveries throughout countless disciplines.

The uranium atom was first split in the Western Hemisphere at Columbia University.

FM Radio and the Laser were both invented at Columbia University.

Columbia has also been responsible for a myriad of leading pharmaceutical breakthrough treatments for diseases such as cancer (Zolinza), arthritis (Remicade) and glaucoma (Xalatan).

Partnerships, Innovation & Translational Research

In accordance with the general trend for leading US research universities, Columbia's openness to collaboration is increasing with a growing number of joint research efforts between Columbia faculty and external partners.

From a revenue perspective, Columbia's record in translational research is, relatively very strong when compared with other institutions both throughout the United States and internationally. Discoveries of major blockbuster pharmaceutical products are in the main the cornerstone of Columbia's patent licensing operation.

Teaching, Learning & Student Life

Students attending Columbia University can expect to work with some of the world's leading academics with almost a dozen incumbent faculty Nobel Prize Laureates such as Joseph Stiglitz (Economics), Richard Axel (Medicine) and Martin Chalfie (Chemistry).

In addition to its two campuses in New York City--the Morningside Heights campus and the Medical Centre campus in Washington Heights--Columbia has embarked on a major campus expansion, a thirty-year building development project in Manhattanville, just north of the main campus, which will further enhance interdisciplinary work with academic centres such as the Mind, Brain, Behaviour Institute.

As a truly global university, Columbia also operates Global Centres located in China, Chile, Jordan, Kenya, France, India and Turkey. Not satellite campuses, the Global Centres promote and facilitate international collabora-tions, research projects, academic programming and study abroad, enhancing the University's historic commitment to global scholarship for both faculty and students.

Columbia greatly encourages undergraduate involvement in research with a particular emphasis on creating new knowledge. Students are encouraged to pursue study abroad opportunities throughout Columbia's international network of partner universities, such as Sciences Po in Paris and Tsinghua University School of Economics and Management in Beijing.

The multi-disciplinary approach to teaching and learning at Columbia has filtered through from the university's approach to major research questions. Students are increasingly able to diversify their curriculum of study across disciplinary boundaries depending upon their interests and aspirations beyond their undergraduate program.

Entrepreneurialism is an increasing part of the culture for undergraduates at Columbia, with a growing emphasis placed upon introducing students to the basics of business through initiatives such as the Columbia University Organisation for Rising Entrepreneurs (CORE). CORE is a student run organisation that aims to foster innovation and entrepreneurialism amongst the Columbia community by organising seminars, courses, competitions and arranging seed capital for the best ideas and business plans.

Columbia University's location on Manhattan Island in New York City is perhaps one of the most highly sought after international locations for students from around the world. The main campus area covers approximately 32 acres, with about 6,000 apartments for faculty, staff and graduate students. There are 18 undergraduate residence halls and 17 brownstones (which house 6 fraternities, 3 sororities, 4 special interest communities and 4 regular housing) located on and around the Morningside campus. This creates a sense of civic society amongst the Columbia community in Manhattan, punctuated by the campus' beautiful architecture centred upon the internationally renowned Butler Library.

The World Leaders Forum, established in 2003 is particularly unique in that it offers Columbia students the opportunity all year round to attend speeches and talks with some of the world's most prominent speakers in religion, politics, business and academia. Since being established in 2003, the Columbia community has hosted a diverse array of leaders from Bill Clinton and Vladimir Putin in politics to the Dalai Lama from a religious perspective.

PRINCETON UNIVERSITY

Name › Princeton University
Region › Americas
Country › United States
Founded › 1746

www.princeton.edu

Core Research Strengths

Princeton's academics thrive in multidisciplinary research environments leveraging the institution's core strengths in economics, engineering, physics, mathematics, energy, super computing and global health to investigate answers to some of the global community's most pressing challenges. In recent years Princeton has established a number of leading interdisciplinary research centers such as the High-Performance Computing Research Center and the Princeton Neuroscience Institute in which some of the most fundamental questions about human consciousness are being worked on such as; what is consciousness, and why do we think and behave the way that we do?

Princeton's strong mix of engineers, scientists and social scientists enables the institution to look into complex global challenges such as those associated with energy security and energy sustainability through centers such as the Andlinger Center for Energy and the Environment. Innovations that are being developed in this center include magnesium ion batteries for large-scale energy storage, renewable production of hydrogen and other fuels, optimization of wind turbine design, and a new type of concrete that can be produced at a lower cost with less carbon dioxide emission and less energy use.

Global Health is another enormously complex issue whereby the collaboration between several disciplines and research approaches are able to develop coherent solutions to the most pertinent global health related questions arising today; thus make dramatic improvements to people's lives around the world. The work led by Professor Ignacio Rodriguez-Iturbe modelling likely hot spots in Haiti for the risk of cholera infection following the 2010 earthquake are an excellent example of this.

Major Discoveries

The 2011 Nobel Prize in Economics was awarded to Professor Christopher Sims for his work developing tools to analyse the effects of monetary policy on the economy.

Biologist Bonnie Bassler continues to push the boundaries on microbiology with her work on understanding quorum sensing, the process by which bacteria communicate with each other.

Computer Scientists David Blei and Michael Freedman were both awarded the Presidential Early Career Award for Scientists and Engineers for their works on high volume computer processing.

Partnerships, Innovation & Translational Research

The collaborative philosophy at Princeton is not exclusive to the university's faculty and academics with a myriad of external partners and collaborative projects managed through the institution's global network. The Dean for Research's office has overall responsibility for managing the university's research operation. 2012 saw 83% of Princeton's sponsored research come from federal government agencies with just 5% of funding coming from industry; offering significant scope for growth in collaboration between Princeton and the private sector.

Princeton's research enterprise is one of the most successful in the United States from a technology transfer perspective, ranking 5th out of all universities in the country for royalty income of US$115 million in 2011; a particularly impressive feat given the relative size of Princeton's research base when compared with larger US institutions. The Office of Technology Licensing issued 31 patents and 27 technology licenses in 2012 for a diverse range of industry sectors such as medical devices, pharmaceuticals, software and computer technologies.

Teaching, Learning & Student Life

As well as opportunities for students at Princeton to develop their own degrees throughout multiple disciplines, the development of leadership skills are also strongly encouraged and well facilitated at the university with numerous opportunities for undergraduates to get involved in societies, run for leadership in the student government apparatus or even establish their own society or association.

Undergraduate teaching and learning combines lectures, more intimate seminars where detailed debates take place, as well as opportunities to conduct research on real world questions alongside faculty and graduate students. Similarly to both Oxford and Cambridge in the UK, Princeton has a unique collegiate system whereby students are organised within six different colleges that form the core of their social and learning experiences whilst at the university.

Princeton's majestic gothic style of architecture conjures up visions of European castles, more than one of the world's leading research universities; nevertheless the environment is one of exceptional calm and convenience for study and research. Whilst at the same time being equidistant from major cities New York and Philadelphia with each city being an hour away in two different directions.

Class governments are an important tradition at Princeton, whereby each year organises itself into a government representing the interests of the students and arranging numerous events of interest to each respective year by a system of voting and discussion. It is widely acknowledged that this means of organisation has only served to enhance the sense of unity and friendship throughout academic year groups at Princeton, and provides an excellent means for young people from different colleges and academic disciplines to get to know and socialise with one another.

Caltech

Name › California Institute of Technology
Region › Americas
Country › United States
Founded › 1891

www.caltech.edu

Core Research Strengths

The California Institute of Technology (Caltech) is very much focused on conducting challenging, fundamental research in core scientific disciplines such as mathematics, engineering, chemistry, biology, geology and physics. Then to leverage the Institute's almost unparalleled core strengths in these areas using an interdisciplinary approach to investigate some of the most exciting and important areas of scientific endeavour today such as energy science, translational medicine, social science, environmental science, materials science, biotechnology, bioengineering, nanotechnology, medical science and space exploration.

Perhaps one of Caltech's most exciting initiatives is the Jet Propulsion Laboratory, managed by the Institute for NASA, which played a significant role in landing the Curiosity Rover on Mars. Nevertheless, one of Caltech's core philosophies is to develop research programs at the cutting edge that will excite and interest people from all around the world given their relevance to major global challenges today.

President Jean-Lou Chameau elaborates further on this philosophy: "If you look historically at Caltech we always try to get involved in exciting science, but also science that has a lot of potential for society. The most important part is to do work that is critical for the future of the country and the world. What excites young people are the areas related to energy, environment, medicine and space. So, we have a team of people at Caltech working on what in simplistic terms is called artificial photosynthesis or the creation of solar fuel that's working.

This gets a tremendous amount of attention from young people, as well as from people who want to come and work here. We are also working to develop what we hope will be a cure to HIV infection in a major laboratory, and again that's what many people really get excited about. In a totally different area, it may surprise you but we have some people working from let's call it bio-inspired engineering or bio-inspired science. We have a professor who looks at how jellyfish behave in nature and from that develop new ways to create sources of energy. So, that's the kind

of exciting research for a lot of people. In addition to that, at Caltech, we are very much involved with space – astronomy, astrophysics and space exploration; another hugely exciting area."

Major Discoveries

The Joint Centre for Artificial Photosynthesis is pioneering a method to create fuel directly from water, carbon dioxide and sunlight.

Chemical engineer Mark Davis has developed unique chemical formulations that attack cancer cells.

David Baltimore is investigating means of using gene therapy to help protect humans from the HIV Virus.

Partnerships, Innovation & Translational Research

Caltech remains extremely open to working in partnerships with a broad range of stakeholders from major government institutions such as NASA and the Department of Energy through to corporations and philanthropic organisations. It is important to note that Caltech's philosophy of research is very much focused on fundamental research looking into basic questions about the world around us. This approach to research is often perceived to be a high-risk pursuit from a funding perspective; however, that risk is offset by the potential of major discoveries, and of opening entirely new fields of research and discovery.

Caltech's approach to intellectual property management is very open and based largely upon discussion with all relevant stakeholders, with a view to finding case by case agreements that work for all partners involved.

Teaching, Learning & Student Life

Caltech is a very small institution when one considers there are approximately 1000 undergraduate students and just over 1200 graduate students in attendance, alongside more than 400 professorial, research, and other faculty. However, this ratio of staff to students leads to an incredibly rich environment for young people to learn from some of the most accomplished researchers and academics in the world in

an environment of innovation and collaboration.

President Chameau best provides an insight into what students can expect at Caltech: "We have many courses and many lectures where the faculty will have five students in a class, and because of the nature of the place we can allow undergraduate and graduate students to be in the same class together. So, essentially all of our students are involved in research and it is not unusual at Caltech for a freshman in his first year on campus to be involved in a research program, and to publish papers. So, small can be beautiful."

A unique aspect of Caltech is the honour code, granting students the freedom to take exams in their own time and space and where they feel comfortable, as opposed to in a standard format. The aim of this approach is to develop a sense of integrity in students, and a sense of respect for their work and for each other. Interestingly the students themselves most enthusiastically uphold the honour code.

UNIVERSITY OF CAMBRIDGE

Name › University of Cambridge
Region › Europe
Country › United Kingdom
Founded › 1318

www.cam.ac.uk

Core Research Strengths

Despite the University of Cambridge's clear strengths across multiple disciplines such as stem cell research, genetics, life sciences, natural sciences, chemistry, physics and mathematics; the university is keen to emphasize the bottom-up nature of the research institution and excellence across a very diverse range of disciplines. Vice-Chancellor Leszek Borysiewicz emphasizes the university's philosophy relating to its research operation as follows:

"The University of Cambridge's approach to research is reflected by the fact that it is not possible to pick out specific core strengths or focuses; our approach as an institution is very much bottom up. Our ambition is to provide an environment whereby those that come to study and research here are able to freely follow their interests; Cambridge does not stipulate the direction of the research that is undertaken here. The University of Cambridge is fortunate to be broad enough to sustain excellence across a very diverse range of disciplines.

One thing that the University of Cambridge does do, however, is analyse the areas of expertise that we have at the fundamental level, and encourage those areas where critical mass is most probable between researchers to approach questions and challenges in a multi-disciplinary manner. So at one end, the University of Cambridge works to foster world-class research from the bottom up, whilst at the same time trying to find aggregate opportunities for leading research teams to work together across several disciplines.

Some examples of areas that this approach is used in are: energy, infection and immunology, public health, neuroscience, linguistics, computing and divinity. The view at the University of Cambridge is that our researchers and academics must have the freedom to define the course of their own interests."

Major Discoveries

The University of Cambridge has made major contributions to the advancement of science from Isaac Newton's work on applied mathematics in the late 17th century, Charles Darwin's work on the theory of evolution and Francis Crick and James D. Watson's work on understanding the structure of DNA in the 20th century.

The first successful test-tube baby, and the pioneering of the IVF technique to enable infertile women to have babies were developed at the University of Cambridge.

World-renowned theoretical physicist Steven Hawking discovered a method for proving that singularities exist in the 1960s.

Partnerships, Innovation & Translational Research

Although open to the development of research partnerships with external partners, the University of Cambridge is very clear on maintaining principles of academic freedom, synergies between partner institutions and ensuring the highest possible quality in potential research partners.

Vice-Chancellor Leszek Borysiewicz elaborates further on the University's philosophy relating to partnerships: "Partners are of great importance to the University of Cambridge, what we very much emphasize though is that any partnerships have to be based upon shared goals and genuine synergies. I believe that such goals and synergies develop from the bottom up and have to be fostered at this level. As a result, the University of Cambridge works at the project level to encourage the greatest frequency of interactions between our academics and external partners.

If we can find interesting synergies at a project level that is the point where we begin to look at further stages of sustainable collaboration, which could ultimately become institutional-level, long-term partnership agreements. It doesn't matter if such partners are private sector companies or other research universities, what matters the most is that there are synergies present, and that our partners are the best in their respective fields. The University of Cambridge will only work with partners who are considered to be the best in their respective field. We will always look at the capacity of our potential partners to engage in the very best levels of research as judged by international standards alone."

Teaching, Learning & Student Life

The University of Cambridge, alongside its Oxbridge counterpart in Oxford, have a very unique organisational set up in the collegiate system that feeds directly into the university's approach to teaching and learning. Students work on a very close level with academic staff within their colleges to discuss and develop the ideas from their respective courses. This gives students the opportunity to learn how to construct arguments, debate points and discuss their areas of study with leading academics in their respective fields.

The University of Cambridge is spread throughout a majestic setting of ancient and modern architecture spanning the 13th up until the 21st century. Attracting many millions of tourists each year, Cambridge's grounds are some of the most beautiful University settings one will find throughout the top 200 ranking.

Student life is characterised by myriad societies and sporting activities where one can expect to meet a diverse array of incredibly gifted young people that have come to Cambridge from over 100 different countries around the world.

University of Cambridge
United Kingdom

Berkeley
UNIVERSITY OF CALIFORNIA

Name › University of California, Berkeley
Region › Americas
Country › United States
Founded › 1868

www.berkeley.edu

Core Research Strengths

The University of California, Berkeley, stands apart from even its prestigious peer institutions for its comprehensive excellence, which spans the physical and biological sciences, mathematics, engineering, social sciences, arts and humanities, and the professions. Its academic depth and breadth make UC Berkeley an exceptionally vital and creative environment for research and teaching. Chancellor Robert Birgeneau elucidates further: "A very deliberate part of our strategy is to have comprehensive excellence. Everybody believes that we're good at everything and, in fact, it is true. However, we work quite hard to make that real."

This strategy has facilitated the university's leadership in developing multidisciplinary centres tackling some of the world's most pertinent and complex challenges, particularly in the areas of health, energy and the environment. These centres include the Renewable and Appropriate Energy Laboratory, the Berkeley Stem Cell Center, the Blum Center for Developing Economies, and the Berkeley APEC Study Center, which investigates ways to foster closer Asia-Pacific Economic Cooperation. Says Chancellor Birgeneau: "At UC Berkeley, we protect traditional disciplines while also trying to stay at the forefront of 21st century challenges, and we aim to change lives through innovation and public service."

Major Discoveries

With faculty and students known for producing challenging ideas that effect positive change in society, UC Berkeley has produced hundreds of important research discoveries. Among them are Vitamin K, the ground-fault circuit interrupter, the reengineering of yeast to produce the lifesaving antimalarial drug artemisinin and robot prototypes that will help the disabled, soldiers, rescue efforts, and the detection of hazardous materials.

UC Berkeley has had 22 Nobel Prize recipients, including professor Saul Perlmutter, who shared a Nobel Prize in Physics in 2011 for his work on dark energy, demonstrating that not only is the universe expanding, but that the rate of its expansion is increasing. Many UC Berkeley professors are also

prolific entrepreneurs whose discoveries and the companies created to manufacture them are spurring the U.S. and Californian economies, and saving lives. Immunologist James Allison, through basic research conducted at UC Berkeley into the fundamental behaviours of cancer cells, developed a promising cancer treatment that has been approved by the U.S. Food and Drug Administration and in Europe for treatment of advanced melanoma.

Partnerships, Innovation & Translational Research

Among UC Berkeley's growing efforts to partner with major research corporations is the partnership it leads with energy company BP and two other academic/research institutions to develop alternatives to the world's dependence on fossil fuels and their alarming contributions to global warming.

The Energy Biosciences Institute is the largest public-private partnership at any U.S. university. It is exploring next-generation, carbon-neutral transportation fuels, with the specific goal of improving technologies for turning plants and plant materials into clean transportation fuels.

Other partnerships include the Center for Information Technology Research in the Interest of Society (CITRIS), which involves four UC campuses and industrial partners from more than 60 corporations, and the California Institute for Bioengineering, Biotechnology and Quantitative Biomedical Research (QB3), where scientists from three UC campuses tackle the fundamental causes of disease.

While UC Berkeley is committed to fundamental research, it aims to become progressively more proficient in translating this research into real world solutions. Its Technology Transfer Office is becoming increasingly important in this work.

Teaching, Learning & Student Life

UC Berkeley's commitment to comprehensive excellence includes the student experience, with priority placed upon facilitating multidisciplinary learning to help its nearly 36,000

students define their academic dreams and do so in a flexible and open environment.

The Center for Teaching and Learning at UC Berkeley serves as a teaching "commons" for faculty and staff who collaborate on new approaches to teaching and learning excellence and innovation. The Center's goal is to ensure that UC Berkeley graduates are well prepared to pursue their interests and aspirations within the context of the 21st century's global market.

Well known for its dynamic research environment, not only graduate students but undergraduates in every department at UC Berkeley are given opportunities for student-initiated research projects. Beyond the classroom, the Undergraduate Research Apprentice Program gives students the chance to advance their skills by assisting professors on faculty-initiated research.

Many international study abroad courses and internship opportunities are available for UC Berkeley students throughout the university's network of partners in key locations around the world.

Set on 1,232 acres on the east shore of San Francisco Bay, the UC Berkeley campus has views of San Francisco and the Golden Gate Bridge. State-of-the-art buildings, mixed with structures in many architectural styles including classical-style, Collegiate Gothic, Mission and Deco, are set in an almost forest-like environment that features rolling hills, creeks and several wooded areas.

UC Berkeley is the national leader for equity and inclusion in higher education and is a champion of a university that is inclusive and representative of California's diverse communities. It also is renowned for helping all admitted students afford an education, including those who are first in their families to attend university, underrepresented minorities, the undocumented, former foster children and military veterans. Chancellor Birgeneau underlines the commitment to equality further: "A critical role for a public university like Berkeley is that we are the conduit into mainstream society for highly talented people from a tremendously varied set of backgrounds. One third of our undergraduate students at Berkeley come from low-income families and are the first in their families to attend university. We view this as a critical responsibility for a public teaching and research university like Berkeley." A spirit of volunteerism and public service has long been part of UC Berkeley. In the history of the Peace Corps, UC Berkeley has enlisted more volunteers (3,000 plus) than any other university.

The campus also is the leading source of new educators in the Teach for America program. The most popular minor field of study at UC Berkeley is Global Poverty and Practice, which gives students the knowledge and experience to use their academic skills to improve life for people in developing countries worldwide.

University of California, Berkeley
United States

MASSACHUSETTS INSTITUTE OF TECHNOLOGY

Name › Massachusetts Institute of Technology
Region › Americas
Country › United States
Founded › 1861

www.mit.edu

Core Research Strengths

The Massachusetts Institute of Technology (MIT) is perhaps the world's most pre-eminent technical university with clear research strengths in areas such as Computer Science, Engineering, Physics, Life Sciences, Mathematics and Natural Sciences. MIT's rich traditions of strength in these areas have for a long time overshadowed the university's strengths in the social sciences with Economics and Business ranked at number 3 and MIT economists having received 5 Nobel Prizes.

Alongside MIT's strengths in well-established disciplines is the university's enthusiasm for interdisciplinary research, focusing upon collaborative research efforts across disciplines and institutions investigating solutions to some of the world's major challenges from sustainable energy solutions through to revolutionary treatments for cancer. MIT boasts over 50 interdisciplinary research centres, bringing together expertise from the world over into a world-class setting.

MIT's global alliances span the world's leading research universities investigating the most pertinent contemporary issues such as biomedicine and biotechnology with the Broad Institute and sustainability related questions at the Alliance for Global Sustainability.

In 2011 MIT disclosed 632 inventions, were issued with 152 patents and earned approximately US$150 million in royalties payments. MIT raised US$661 million in sponsored research from a variety of sources in 2011

Major Discoveries

MIT faculty have made major contributions to some of the most world-renowned research projects from the Human Genome Project to Artificial Intelligence and Robotics. Some of the most important and renowned discoveries made at MIT are the first chemical synthesis of penicillin and vitamin A, developing inertial guidance systems, engineering practical micro-wave radar, building the magnetic core memory that made digital computers possible, inventing a way to duplicate photosynthesis in order to store solar energy and developing a new form of wireless power transmission.

Partnerships, Innovation & Translational Research

MIT is one of the most entrepreneurial universities globally; the total revenues of all the companies founded by MIT alumni in 2011 would aggregate up to the eleventh largest economy in the world. In total, over 26,000 companies have been started by MIT alumni, employing over 3.3 million people with total revenues of US$2 trillion.

The entrepreneurial culture at MIT continues to grow with more and more graduates choosing to opt for innovation and research driven entrepreneurialism as opposed to the more traditional approach for leading university graduates in moving into blue chip graduate schemes.

Working with industry and external partners has been part of MIT's DNA since its establishment as a university. Of the US$661 million invested in research in 2011, US$100 million came from industry partners. Now the university partners with approximately 800 industry partners, the Industrial Liaison Program is the main conduit between MIT and its industry partners.

Teaching, Learning & Student Life

MIT is arranged into 5 schools offering a total of 44 undergraduate programs. All undergraduates are required to complete a core curriculum called the General Institute Requirements running across the Science Department, Humanities and Social Sciences, as well as Communications Department depending upon the major choices of undergraduates.

Pedagogical approaches are diverse including lectures; intimate seminars, coursework, tests and problem based learning sessions. MIT has pioneered the encouragement of undergraduate research involvement with the Undergraduate Research Opportunities Program (UROP) first established at the university in 1969. The majority of students at MIT participate in the UROP with many being published, filing patent applications and establishing start up companies following their experiences in this program.

The culture of entrepreneurialism runs throughout the spirit of the university with undergraduate and graduate students encouraged throughout their experiences at MIT to take their discoveries and innovations to the market with numerous competitions such as the MIT US$100k Accelerate Contest. Entrepreneurialism at MIT continues to accelerate. New students at the university can expect to work at the cutting edge in an institution where new knowledge is created every day; in an environment where the entrepreneurial spirit thrives and opportunities to translate such discoveries into the real economy through start up companies pervades all aspects of the institution.

Varied and unique architecture define much of the MIT campus with the iconic Dome and Building 10 complimented by cutting edge designs such as the Stata Center Houses and Simmons Hall. Undergraduates are guaranteed student housing in one of the university's 12 dormitories, being able to define the community they are interested in living and sharing with through MIT's system of personal preference.

MIT has over 400 student associations varying from campus media organisations to science fiction clubs and entrepreneurship competitions. The campus social life is also complemented by a myriad of legacy traditions and competitions such as Bad Ideas Festival, Educational Studies Program and the MIT IDEAS Global Challenge competition whereby students are encouraged to work in teams and collaborate to develop ideas that will help communities around the world with research and innovation led solutions to major challenges.

STANFORD UNIVERSITY

Name › Stanford University
Region › Americas
Country › United States
Founded › 1885

www.stanford.edu

Core Research Strengths

Stanford's exceptional research portfolio has come to be dominated in the public eye by the university's exemplary strengths in the computer sciences and electrical engineering, and the impact the university has had on the broader economy with companies like Google continuing to strengthen Silicon Valley's leadership of the international software market.

Stanford's world leading strengths in these fields are just one tranche of what is overall a very rich research portfolio in both its depth and breadth. Stanford's research strengths in the social sciences, medicine, natural sciences, mathematics, chemistry, physics, life and agricultural sciences are all ranked in the top 10 globally.

Similarly to many other leading research universities, Stanford's core strength is in the university's openness and capacity to conduct research in a multidisciplinary fashion; bringing together expertise across a myriad of academic and professional disciplines under the auspices of Research Centres looking into major international challenges and the development of new knowledge.

In addition to Stanford's international renown in the STEM disciplines, the university has outstanding strengths in the social sciences and humanities with leading international research centres such as the Hoover Institution on War, Revolution & Peace and the Freeman Spogli Institute for International Relations focusing on governance and international relations respectively.

Major Discoveries

Stanford's prominence in Silicon Valley is significant to the extent that the international software industry's development would have accelerated at a slower rate than it has done up until today without Stanford's influence on the industry's pioneers.

On top of this influence, Stanford has been particularly prominent in the University's contribution to our understanding of the human genome, DNA & RNA interactions and cancer research.

Partnerships, Innovation & Translational Research

Stanford University is one of the international pioneers relating to the increasing trend of universities partnering with a diverse range of research collaborators; thus is often looked upon by research-intensive institutions around the world as a first choice partner.

Responsibility for Stanford's research administration is shared under the management of the Office of the Dean of Research and the Office of Technology Licensing responsible for research administration and technology transfer respectively.

From a translational perspective, Stanford University is one of the best-known universities with one of the best track records in patent approvals and the translation of new discoveries into the real economy. Hewlett Packard, Nike, Google, Cisco Systems, Yahoo and Instagram are all examples of companies established by Stanford alumni.

Teaching, Learning & Student Life

Stanford's pioneering spirit permeates throughout the institution all the way down from the award-winning faculty through to the undergraduate population. Research opportunities abound throughout Stanford for undergraduates to get involved in answering pertinent research questions in real time, and the university's pioneering approach to technology transfer and translational research enables students to learn more about entrepreneurialism with a view to taking discoveries made to the market place; thus contributing to broader goals of economic development and public service.

In Stanford's founding grant document of 1885, founders Jane and Leland Stanford wrote the institution's objectives were to: "To qualify its students for personal success, and direct usefulness in life; And its purposes, to promote the public welfare by exercising an influence on behalf of humanity and civilization, teaching the blessings of liberty regulated by law, and inculcating love and reverence for the great principles of government as derived from the inalienable rights of man to life, liberty, and the pursuit of happiness."

The multi-disciplinary approach to research clearly influences the approach to teaching and learning at Stanford with students able to pick and choose courses from a range of academic disciplines so as to satisfy their individual interests and career aspirations. All Stanford undergraduates are expected to take a foreign language course, as well as two mandatory courses exploring critical thinking and approaches to research.

With a student faculty ratio of 5 to 1, close interactions and consultancy between academics and students forms one of the cornerstones of Stanford's philosophy of pedagogy.

Stanford is very much a campus environment with approximately 90% of undergraduate students living on campus alongside approximately 60% of graduate students creating a unique living and learning environment. The campus has a Tuscan feel with the university's Romanesque architectural style of sandstone arches with the rolling foothills of the Santa Cruz Mountains reaching up into the horizon as the university's backdrop.

Stanford boasts a myriad of student associations and groups with approximately 650 such organisations to get involved with ranging from media groups, hobby related associations and the Stanford Solar Car Project where a solar powered car is designed, constructed and raced every 2 years.

Stanford's heritage has enabled the university to develop a number of unique traditions such as the annual Viennese Ball and Big Game events when the Stanford Cardinal sports team compete with rivals UC Berkeley.

HARVARD
UNIVERSITY

Name › Harvard University
Region › Americas
Country › United States
Founded › 1636

www.harvard.edu

Core Research Strengths

Research expertise at Harvard University is extremely broad with over 100 Research Centres and 13 schools investing over US$750 million each year throughout the university's diverse portfolio. Although Harvard demonstrates an exceptional level of research quality throughout the complete spectrum of disciplines, the university is particularly noted for outstanding departments in the Medical Sciences, Mathematics, Physics, Chemistry, Economics and Stem Cell Research. On top of this expertise, Harvard is one of the best international examples of the increasing trend towards interdisciplinary research whereby diverse teams of experts gather together in research centres with a view to answering some of the world's most complex questions associated with major global challenges such as global warming, food security and the ageing society.

Aside from expertise throughout the science, technology, engineering and mathematics (STEM) subjects, Harvard University also demonstrates incredible depth throughout the arts and social sciences with remarkable departments in areas such as anthropology, archaeology and philosophy complemented by 80 individual libraries containing over 15 million volumes, as well as a number of arts, science and cultural museums within the overall Harvard complex.

Major Discoveries

Although Harvard today is perhaps best known for the initial production of Facebook by one notable undergraduate, the university has made major contributions to our understanding of a myriad of medical conditions from Alzheimer's to cancer, as well as making an enormous contribution to our increasing knowledge relating to the human genome, genetics and the most exciting developments associated with personalised medicine.

Partnerships, Innovation & Translational Research

Harvard University is an experienced international collaborator both with leading universities, government institutions and research driven private sector corporations. Harvard has very clear principles, policies and procedures concerning external partnerships in that the university will not compromise its priorities relating to the free and open pursuit of knowledge for the sake of financial rewards from external organisations. Having said that, the framework is very much open for a diverse array of partners throughout the public, private and university sectors; of which many have resulted in extraordinary discoveries, continued economic development, graduate opportunities and the translation of new discoveries into the real economy.

The "Statement of Policy" most recently amended in 2010 governs intellectual property policy at Harvard University. Effectively, the university, in partnership with researchers has ownership rights over all intellectual property developed at the university, however the key principle of disseminating discoveries, developments and information of perceived public interest remains a priority for the university's approach. The Office of Technology Development has overall responsibility for management and negotiations relating to intellectual property policy at the university.

The Office of Technology Development at Harvard is also responsible for the translation of research discoveries into the real economy through the broad process of technology transfer. Having recently re-structured, the Office of Technology Development is now widely regarded as a leader in this increasingly important sector. The mission of the OTD is to enable the development, transfer and adoption of innovations originating at Harvard for the benefit of society.

Biotechnology is often described as one of, if not the most exciting areas of cutting edge research at the beginning of the 21st century. Harvard has responded to this from a translational perspective with the establishment of the Biomedical Accelerator Fund whose benefits focus upon maximising the chances of potentially life changing technologies reaching fruition for the benefit of the public, society and the economy.

On top of Biotechnology, the Office of Technology Development also leads in developing opportunities relating to other Harvard strengths such as; Chemistry, Nano Technology, Material Science, Energy, Medical Devices and a myriad of related Medical fields.

Teaching, Learning & Student Life

Harvard students have the great privilege of having access to world-renowned faculty and academics throughout their teaching and learning experience. All Harvard undergraduates are required to take a core of 8 courses under the umbrella of general education categories as follows: "Aesthetic and Interpretive Understanding, Culture and Belief, Empirical and Mathematical Reasoning, Ethical Reasoning, Science of Living Systems, Science of the Physical Universe, Societies of the World, and United States in the World"

Interdisciplinary learning is strongly encouraged at Harvard with students being able to pick and choose different subjects across disciplines to satisfy their interests, research curiosities and career aspirations. Undergraduate research is also strongly encouraged and facilitated with undergraduates strongly encouraged to develop entrepreneurial skills and grow into job creators through research-based innovation.

Having featured in numerous feature films such as Good Will Hunting and The Social Network; Harvard's beautiful, red brick university campus will be familiar to many young people around the world.

Having educated a myriad of global leaders such as Theodore Roosevelt, Barack Obama, George W. Bush, Bill Gates and Ban Ki-Moon, as well as 44 Nobel Laureates those considering Harvard as an international study destination should prepare themselves for studying and innovating alongside future world leaders and industry pioneers.